Controversial New Religions

Controversial
New Religions

EDITED BY JAMES R. LEWIS AND
JESPER AAGAARD PETERSEN

OXFORD
UNIVERSITY PRESS

2005

OXFORD
UNIVERSITY PRESS

Oxford   New York
Auckland   Bangkok   Buenos Aires   Cape Town   Chennai
Dar es Salaam   Delhi   Hong Kong   Istanbul   Karachi   Kolkata
Kuala Lumpur   Madrid   Melbourne   Mexico City   Mumbai
Nairobi   São Paulo   Shanghai   Taipei   Tokyo   Toronto

Copyright © 2005 by Oxford University Press, Inc.

Published by Oxford University Press, Inc.
198 Madison Avenue, New York, New York 10016

www.oup.com

Oxford is a registered trademark of Oxford University Press

Library of Congress Cataloging-in-Publication Data
Controversial new religions / edited by James R. Lewis and Jesper Aagaard Petersen.
p.   cm.
Includes bibliographical references and index.
ISBN 0-19-515682-X; 0-19-515683-8 (pbk)
1. Cults.   I. Lewis, James R.   II. Petersen, Jesper Aagaard.
BP603.C66 2004   2005
200'.9'04—dc22
2003024374

9 8 7 6 5 4 3 2 1
Printed in the United States of America
on acid-free paper

Contents

PART III: ESOTERIC AND NEW AGE GROUPS

PART IV: OTHER GROUPS AND MOVEMENTS

Contributors

James A. Beverley is Associate Director of the Institute for the Study of American Religion in Santa Barbara, California, and Professor at Tyndale Seminary in Toronto, Canada. He is the Senior Editor of the forthcoming *HarperCollins' Encyclopedia of Religions in Canada* and the author of the forthcoming *Nelson's Illustrated Guide to Religions*. He also worked as Associate Editor on Melton and Bauman's *Religions of the World* and has written three books on Islam and two books on charismatic Christianity.

James D. Chancellor holds an M.A. from the University of Nebraska, an M.Div. from the Southern Baptist Theological Seminary, and a Ph.D. from Duke University in the History of Religion. He has served since 1992 as W. O. Carver Professor of World Religions at the Southern Baptist Theological Seminary. He is author of *Life in the Family: An Oral History of the Children of God* (Syracuse University Press, 2000).

Dorthe Refslund Christensen holds an M.A. and a Ph.D. in the Science of Religion from the University of Aarhus. She has taught at the Department of the Study of Religion, Aarhus University; the Department for Religion and Philosophy, Southern Danish University, Odense; and the Department of the History of Religions, University of Copenhagen. In 2004 she had a postdoctoral scholarship from the Danish Research Council for the project Religion in Popular Culture and Everyday Life: Religion in Transformation.

George D. Chryssides studied at the University of Glasgow as an undergraduate and gained his doctorate from the University of Oxford. He is currently Head of Religious Studies at the University of Wolverhampton. He has written extensively on new religious movements. His books include *The Advent of Sun Myung Moon* (Macmillan, 1991), *Exploring New Religions* (Cassell, 1999), and *Historical Dictionary of New Religious Movements* (Scarecrow Press, 2001). He has contributed to numerous academic journals and edited collections.

Mattias Gardell is Associate Professor (docent) in the History of Religions, Stockholm University, Sweden. His publications include *In the Name of Elijah Muhammad: Louis Farrakhan and the Nation of Islam* (Duke University Press, 1996), *Rasrisk: Rastister, separatister och amerikanska kulturkonflikter* (Stockholm: Natur & Kultur, 2003 [1998]), and *Gods of the Blood: The Pagan Revival and White Separatism* (Duke University Press, 2003).

Marion S. Goldman is Professor of Sociology and Religious Studies at the University of Oregon. Her books include *Gold Diggers and Silver Miners* (University of Michigan Press, 1982) and *Passionate Journeys: Why Successful Women Joined a Cult* (University of Michigan Press, 1999). Her current research is about Esalen Institute and men's spiritualities.

Gail M. Harley earned her Ph.D. in the History of Religion and Humanities from Florida State University. She currently teaches for the University of South Florida Religious Studies Department. She is the author of *Emma Curtis Hopkins: Forgotten Founder of New Thought* (Syracuse University Press, 2002) and *Hindu and Sikh Faiths in America* (Facts on File, 2003).

Robert Kisala is a fellow at the Nanzan Institute for Religion and Culture and professor of religious studies at Nanzan University, Nagoya, Japan. His publications include *Prophets of Peace: Pacifism and Cultural Identity in Japan's New Religions* (University of Hawaii Press, 1999) and *Religion and Social Crisis in Japan: Understanding Japanese Society through the Aum Affair* (edited with Mark Mullins, Palgrave, 2001).

James R. Lewis is Lecturer in Philosophy at the University of Wisconsin–Milwaukee. His recent publications include *The Oxford Handbook of New Religious Movements* (Oxford, 2004), *The Encyclopedic Sourcebook of UFO Religions* (Prometheus Books, 2003), and *Legitimating New Religions* (Rutgers University Press, 2003).

Rebecca Moore is Associate Professor of Religious Studies at San Diego State University. Her current specialty is New Religious Movements, with a focus on the group People's Temple and its utopian commune Jonestown, which ended in mass murder-suicides in November 1978. She and her husband, Fielding McGehee III, have written and published five books and numerous articles. Dr. Moore maintains a Web site of current resources on People's Temple at http://jonestown.sdsu.edu.

David Ownby is Professor of History and Director of East Asian Studies at the Université de Montréal in Montreal, Canada. He has published extensively on the history of secret societies and popular religions in China and is currently completing a manuscript on the Falun Gong.

Susan Palmer is Adjunct Professor at Concordia University and a tenured Professor at Dawson College, both in Montreal, Quebec. She has written over sixty articles on new religious movements and authored or edited eight books on new religious movements, including *Räel's UFO Religion: Racing and Cloning in the Age of Apocalypse* (Rutgers University Press).

Jesper Aagaard Petersen, M.A., is a teaching assistant at the University of Copenhagen, Department of History of Religions. He is the coeditor with James R. Lewis of *The Encyclopedic Sourcebook of Satanism* (Prometheus Books, forthcoming) and has edited a special issue of *Syzygy* on modern Satanism (2002).

Martin Repp is a Professor at the Graduate School for Pure Land Studies of Ryukoku University (Kyoto) and has been the editor of the journal *Japanese Religions* since 1991. He did extensive research on Aum Shinrikyo and the Aum incident, published in a number of articles and a book. He also teaches Japanese religions and theology at Doshisha and Kyoto Universities.

E. Burke Rochford, Jr. is Professor of Sociology and Religion at Middlebury College in Vermont. He has researched the Hare Krishna movement over the past twenty-eight years. He has written numerous articles on the movement and his second book on ISKCON is in preparation.

James A. Santucci teaches in the Comparative Religion Department at California State University, Fullerton. Professor Santucci is the author of *La società teosofica* (1999), *Hindu Art in South and Southeast Asia* (1987), *An Outline of Vedic Literature* (1976), and coauthor (with Benjamin Hubbard and John Hatfield) of *America's Religions* (1997). He has edited a quarterly journal of research, *Theosophical History*, since 1990, as well as a series of monographs in the series Theosophical History Occasional Papers since 1993.

Diana G. Tumminia studied social psychology and ethnography at UCLA and currently teaches sociology at California State University, Sacramento. She publishes on contemporary and historical new religious movements, among other topics. Her publications in this area range from the social psychology of UFO religions to Native American millenarian movements, as well as new religions like MSIA and ISKCON.

Stuart A. Wright is Assistant Dean of Graduate Studies and Research and Professor of Sociology at Lamar University. He is the author of *Leaving Cults: The Dynamics of Defection* (Society for the Scientific Study of Religion, 1987) and editor of *Armageddon in Waco* (University of Chicago Press, 1995). He has published over thirty articles or book chapters in scholarly venues and has become a widely recognized expert and legal consultant.

PierLuigi Zoccatelli works in Turin as deputy director of CESNUR, the Center for Studies on New Religions. He is the author of several articles and four books on new religious movements and Western esotericism. He has been the associate editor of the monumental *Enciclopedia delle religioni in Italia* (*Encyclopedia of Religions in Italy*, Elledici, 2001).

Controversial New Religions

Introduction

James R. Lewis and Jesper Aagaard Petersen

At the time of the Jonestown suicides in 1978, the field of new religious movements (NRMs) was little more than a specialization within the sociology of religion. There were a few nonsociologists active in the field (such as Gordon Melton, Timothy Miller, and Robert Ellwood), but it took a long time for the academy to accept NRMs as part of religious studies. As I have discussed elsewhere (Lewis 2004), it was not until after a series of high-profile tragedies in the 1990s—the Branch Davidian siege, the Solar Temple murder-suicides, the Aum Shinrikyo incident, and the Heaven's Gate suicides—that the religious studies mainstream truly embraced new religions as a legitimate field of study.

At the time of this writing, the NRM field continues to expand. Some indicators of this growth are the increasing popularity of the sessions of the New Religious Movements Group at the annual meetings of the American Academy of Religion, the growing number of prominent academic presses publishing NRM titles, and the emergence of NRMs as a recognized field of study in graduate programs in a number of European countries, particularly in the United Kingdom. Additionally, an increasing number of NRM academicians are beginning to subspecialize—hence one now encounters self-identified scholars of the New Age, Pagan specialists, historians of Western esotericism, and the like. One advantage of these subspecialties is that they focus on a reasonably well-defined subject matter. The same cannot be said for the NRM field as a whole.

Although the field of new religious movements has achieved the status of a recognized specialty, it is a very odd field of specialization, one that lacks an adequate internal logic for determining which phenomena fall within its purview. Until the development of NRM subspecialities, the core of the field consisted of studies of controversial new religions plus analyses of the "cult" controversy.

In many ways, NRM studies is a residual category. Though the designation "new religions" implies that all kinds of emergent religions are part of this field, in practice NRM scholars have tended to avoid studying movements already claimed by other scholarly specialties. Thus, to cite a few examples, Pentecostalism has been left to church historians and cargo cults to anthropologists (Lewis 2004). This boundary issue is only one of the questions that need to be asked before new religions can become a cohesive field of study rather than an ad hoc grab bag composed of all the groups no other scholarly specialty wants to bother with.

Although NRM studies has been accepted as a legitimate part of the academy, in many ways the field remains segregated from the larger discipline of religious studies, despite the fact that it is easy to make a case for the importance of researching new religions. As Susan Palmer, a contributor to the present collection, noted in a recent interview, "If you're interested in studying religion, . . . NRMs are a great place to start. Their history is really short, they don't have that many members, their leader is usually still alive, and you can see the evolution of their rituals and their doctrines. It's a bit like dissecting amoebas instead of zebras" (cited in Lester 2002). The point here is an obvious one, namely, that the study of current new religions can deepen our understanding of more established religions. On the other hand, the field of religious studies has been deeply interested in the question of the origins of religion. Thus it seems natural to consider whether the formulations growing out of this research might provide insights into the emergence of contemporary new religions, though no one seems to have undertaken this task thus far.

The field of new religious movements has been significantly shaped by the controversies surrounding a set of highly diverse religious organizations. One could reasonably argue that the only common factor uniting them is the fact that they are controversial. Even the relevant controversies, however, are quite diverse. Members of Aum Shinrikyo, for instance, dramatically attacked people outside of the group, precipitating a sharp response from Japanese society. In contrast, the Branch Davidians—who had coexisted quite harmoniously with their neighbors for many years—became embroiled in controversy only after being assaulted by an agency of the U.S. government. And in yet another completely different scenario, Heaven's Gate made international headlines after imploding in a group suicide.

Despite these many differences, the more controversial new religions have been perceived as constituting a common phenomenon, and have been understood in terms of a shared stereotype that has been applied to many such religions. These factors have led to an unusual situation in which, without any sense of stepping beyond the bounds of their expertise, NRM scholars can study a theologically orthodox Christian group like the Family, a Hindu group like the Hare Krishna movement, a neotraditional Chinese group like Falun Gong, and so on—when in other circumstances only academicians with specialized backgrounds in theology, Hinduism, Chinese religion, and so forth would attempt to study these movements.

Another result of the "cult" controversy is that NRM scholarship has tended to cluster around the most controversial groups, particularly the ones that have attracted the attention of the mass media. Thus a comparatively tiny movement like the Family has been the subject of numerous articles and several books. In contrast, a significantly larger but much less controversial new religion like Eckankar has never been the subject of even a single academic journal article. The aim of the present collection is to bring together a series of original studies on the groups that have generated the most academic attention.

The controversy over new religions is a complex social issue that has engendered an emotional and sometimes mean-spirited debate. Decades of social conflict have left their impress on the term "cult," which, to the general public, indicates a religious group that is false, dangerous, or otherwise *bad*. The sharpness of this controversy has tended to polarize observers of such groups into extreme positions, making it difficult to find a middle ground from which to approach the issue. Hence, rather than tackling the problem directly, it might well repay our effort to work our way into the debate indirectly, through the stories of two contrasting religious groups that will serve to highlight some of the dilemmas associated with the controversy.

The story of the Movement for the Restoration of the Ten Commandments of God, the Ugandan group massacred by its own leaders in 2000, will be used to exemplify the concerns "anticultists" bring to the controversy. The Alamo Christian Foundation, an American ministry that has been the target of crippling legal action, will be used to exemplify the concerns of religious libertarians.

When Religion Goes Bad: The Movement for the Restoration of the Ten Commandments

The Movement for the Restoration of the Ten Commandments of God was a doomsday religious sect in Uganda that made headlines in the wake of what was initially thought to be a mass suicide in March 2000. The number of bodies reported by the media increased daily until it exceeded one thousand. About 530 died in a fire that gutted their church in Kanungu, Uganda, on

Friday, March 17, 2000. In the days following the tragedy, police discovered innumerable other bodies at different sites. These others had been murdered prior to the group holocaust, apparently at the behest of the leadership.

The movement was founded by excommunicated Roman Catholic priests, Joseph Kibweteere, Joseph Kasapurari, John Kamagara, and Dominic Kataribabo; two excommunicated Roman Catholic nuns; and Credonia Mwerinde, an ex-prostitute. Most of the group's members were originally Roman Catholic. The group taught that the Catholic Church was badly in need of reform. Their own rules came from the Virgin Mary, as channeled through Mwerinde. The leaders taught that the Ten Commandments needed to be restored to their original importance.

Before the tragedy, Kibweteere allegedly claimed that he overheard a conversation between Jesus Christ and the Virgin Mary. Mary stated that the world would come to an end unless humans started to follow the Ten Commandments closely. The group initially believed that the end of the world would take place on December 31, 1999. During 1999, members sold their possessions in preparation for the end times, when they would be transported to heaven. They slaughtered cattle and had a weeklong feast. When the end did not come, Kibweteere changed the date to December 31, 2000. Later, he taught that the Virgin Mary would appear on March 17 and take the faithful to Heaven. Devastation would then descend upon the world and the remaining six billion people in the world would be exterminated.

The membership appears to have anticipated being taken to Heaven by the Virgin Mary on March 17. They also expected the end of the world to occur at that time. They slaughtered some cattle, and ordered seventy crates of soda for a feast on March 16. They said goodbye to friends and relatives beforehand.

Most of the deaths occurred in Kanungu, a small trading center, about 217 miles southwest of Kampala, the capital of Uganda. Although there may still be some sources that continue to assert that the parishioners committed suicide, the consensus opinion is that the group leader, Joseph Kibweteere, murdered the members by luring them inside the church and then setting it on fire. The church's windows had been boarded up; its doors were nailed shut with the members inside. They sang for a few hours. Some witnesses reported the smell of gasoline at the scene, an explosion that preceded the fire, and some screams from inside the building.

There was one initial report, never confirmed, that members had applied gasoline and paraffin to their skin before the explosion and fire. However, it is difficult to see how the observer could have witnessed these preparations if the windows and doors of the church had been nailed shut. It is now almost certain that the tragedy was a mass murder, not a mass suicide. The fact that the doors of the church were nailed shut seems to indicate that the leadership wanted to confine the full membership within the church in order to murder the entire group. The discovery of additional bodies of members who had been murdered and buried in latrines near the church gives weight to the mass-murder theory. The discoveries of many hundreds of murder victims at other locations also point toward mass murder.

The murders seem to have been precipitated by failed prophecy. When the end of the world did not occur on December 31, 1999, some members of the sect demanded their money and possessions back. This, in turn, may have triggered the mass murders.

The deaths of members of the Movement for the Restoration of the Ten Commandments were part of a series of dramatic incidents that involved members of nontraditional religions. Other incidents include the Jonestown murder-suicides (1978), the ATF/FBI raid on the Branch Davidian community (1993), the Solar Temple murder-suicides (in 1994, 1995, and 1997), the Tokyo subway poison gas attack (1995), and the Heaven's Gate suicides (1997). In the wake of these events, the mass media sought out a variety of "cult experts" in an effort to make sense of seemingly irrational behavior. Most of these experts offered the public an explanation in terms of the notion of cultic mind control, colloquially known as "brainwashing." The seemingly crazy actions of "cult" members were not difficult to explain, this group of experts claimed, as long as one understands that megalomaniacal cult leaders are able to control the thought processes of their followers; under the influence of mind control, members of such groups are capable of anything because they have given up their wills to the leader.

According to spokespeople for "cult watchdog" groups, our society is populated by hundreds—perhaps thousands—of cult groups, many of which are capable of extreme actions. Beyond mind control and the imputation of sinister motives to the leader, standard accusations leveled against minority religions unfortunate enough to be labeled "cults" include deceptive recruiting practices, financial and sexual exploitation, food and sleep deprivation of members, various forms of illegal activities, child abuse, ritual abuse, and so forth. Because of the interest the mass media have taken in this issue, this stereotype has become widely accepted in contemporary society.

Putting aside the problematic notion of "cultic brainwashing" for the moment, there are or have been groups for which some of these accusations are or were appropriate. In particular, children have been abused within a few religious communities. Members of certain organizations have been financially and/or sexually exploited by the leadership. A handful of minority religions have taken the law into their own hands. And at least one group consciously deceived potential recruits by systematically hiding their identity until after workshop attendees had become de facto members.

There are, however, obvious dangers in unreflectively applying the cult stereotype to every religious group that strikes one as strange or unusual. The situation is not unlike that of viewing a race or an ethnicity in terms of a generalization derived from the minority group's least reputable members. The types of problems that can be generated by jumping to the conclusion that unusual religious communities must be guilty of misdeeds simply because extreme accusations are leveled against them are well exemplified in the legal assault on the Alamo Christian Foundation.

When Religion Is Victimized: The Alamo Christian Foundation

The Alamo Christian Foundation, a Pentecostal church with doctrines similar to the Assemblies of God, was opened in 1969 in Hollywood, California, by Tony and Susan Alamo. It drew its early strength from the Jesus movement. In the early 1970s, the Alamo Christian Foundation became controversial and was heavily criticized because of what was viewed as heavy-handed proselytizing. Church members worked the streets of Hollywood, inviting potential converts to evening services. The mostly young recruits were taken by bus to the foundation's rural community in Saugus for an evangelistic meeting and meal. Many of those who converted remained in Saugus to be taught the Bible and become lay ministers.

In 1976, the church moved its headquarters to Alma, Arkansas, where Susan Alamo had grown up. There it developed a community of several hundred members and established printing facilities, a school, and a large tabernacle. As the organization expanded further, churches were opened in other cities. The church developed as an ordered community of people dedicated to evangelism. Converts who wished to receive the church's training and participate in its ministry took a vow of poverty, agreeing to turn over all real property to the church. In return, the church provided the necessities of life. Members were periodically sent out on evangelistic tours around the United States, frequently using the established church centers as bases of operation. Services were held daily at each of the church centers, and free meals were served. In 1981, Music Square Church was incorporated. It superseded the foundation in 1982. Susan Alamo passed away from cancer in the same year.

To support itself and as part of its rehabilitation program, the church developed several businesses in which members, many of whom were former drug addicts, could begin a process of reintegration into society. However, a number of disgruntled former members who later aligned themselves with the anticult movement complained that they should have been paid at least minimum wage for their work while members. These complaints led to a series of lawsuits. In 1985 the Internal Revenue Service stripped the Music Square Church of its tax-exempt status. The church went to court to fight this decision.

In 1988, Tony Alamo was accused of allegedly directing—over the telephone—the beating of an eleven-year-old boy who was at the center of a custody battle between his mother (a member of Alamo's ministry) and his father, who had left the church and aligned himself with anticultists. Charges were filed and Alamo disappeared. For the next three years, Alamo was a fugitive from justice. During this time he moved about the country, frequently making calls to talk shows and even dropping in on public offices for visits. Meanwhile, the church's property in Arkansas was seized to pay off court judgments against the organization. Tony Alamo was arrested in July 1991. The current status of the church, whose membership as of 1988 was approximately four hundred, is problematic.

The concern generated by such activities as the legal assault on the Alamo Christian Foundation has led to the emergence of an alternative school of opinion opposed to the "anticult" perspective. This opposing group comprises a diverse group of religions, religious liberty organizations, and some scholars of minority religions. While not seeking to defend organizations like the Movement for the Restoration of the Ten Commandments, this school of thought asserts that the extreme actions of a few groups should not be taken as representative of all minority religions, any more than that the criminal tendencies of a handful of members of certain racial minorities should be imputed to the race as a whole. Individuals associated with this opposition group see themselves as defending religious liberty.

Because the word "cult" has acquired negative connotations, the people and organizations who defend minority religions do not call themselves the "procult movement," and, further, reject the label "cult apologists" with which anticultists seek to stigmatize them. In fact, this opposition group would reject the use of the term "cult" altogether, instead referring to such organizations as new religious movements (the preferred label among academics), alternative religions, nontraditional religions, or minority religions. Recognizing the term's problematic status, scholars usually avoid the term "cult." It is, nevertheless, still useful to talk about the "cult controversy," and, when appropriate, "cult" can be utilized to discuss the stereotype associated with minority religions more generally.

As with other social conflicts, opponents in the cult controversy have become polarized into extreme positions. Many anticultists have come to adopt an attitude of suspicion toward a broad spectrum of religions, ready to portray almost any unusual group as a potential Heaven's Gate, and almost any charismatic religious leader as a potential David Koresh. Defenders of the rights of minority religions, on the other hand, have tended to downplay all issues except the issue of religious liberty. The result of this polarization is an ongoing and frequently bitter debate that periodically finds expression in books, articles, court cases, and, in recent years, in official reports issued by European governments.

The origins of the contemporary cult controversy can be traced to the early 1970s. In that period, many new religions were arising out of the ashes of the counterculture to become successor movements to the youth movement of the 1960s. Unable to comprehend the appeal of these religions, observers concluded that the founder-leaders of such groups had discovered a special form of social control that enabled them to recruit their followers in nonordinary ways, and, more particularly, to short-circuit their rational, questioning minds by keeping them locked in special trance states. A handful of professionals, mostly psychologists and psychiatrists associated with the anticult movement, attempted to provide scientific grounding for this notion of cultic brainwashing/mind control.

No serious observer would disagree that there are genuine issues of abuse, exploitation, and undue influence associated with at least some minority religions. Serious discussions and analyses of such abuses were, however, overshadowed almost from the very beginning when the debate over new religions came to focus on the notion of cultic mind control. Rather than viewing the social pressures found in minority religions as extensions of garden-variety forms of social influence, anticult professionals argued for the existence of a unique form of influence confined to "cult" subcultures. Viewing this argument as a form of special pleading with potentially grave implications for religious liberty, other professionals—particularly sociologists of religion—focused their scholarly responses to the cult controversy on a critique of cultic mind control. By the mid-seventies, battle lines had been drawn and the debate would rage back and forth over the same ground for the next several decades.

Survey of Contents

Each of the contributors to the present collection provides an overview of each organization or movement. This collection is not, however, simply a series of expanded encyclopedia entries. Rather, each author has crafted an analysis that makes an original contribution to the study of her or his chosen group. Chapters have been grouped into four parts according to the larger religious traditions to which they belong: the Christian tradition, Asian and Asian-inspired, esoteric and New Age, and other kinds of groups and movements.

Part I: Groups in the Christian Tradition

In "A Family for the Twenty-first Century," James D. Chancellor presents an overview of the Children of God (COG), now known as the Family. COG emerged out of the Jesus People Movement as a blend of traditional evangelical Christianity and the 1960s counterculture. COG quickly became the most controversial group on the religious landscape. It is historically important in the history of the anticult movement; the first anticult organization was FREECOG (Free the Children of God), and deprogramming developed in response to COG. Chancellor outlines the history of the movement, its major theological landmarks, and gives particular attention to the substantive changes that have taken place since the death of the founding Prophet.

James A. Beverley's "Spirit Revelation and the Unification Church" focuses on the role of ongoing mediumistic revelations in the life of the Unification Church. The chapter begins with a critical overview of recent events within the church and among members of the founder's family. Beverley also examines Reverend Moon's sense of the importance of his role in history and of the role he plays in the spirit realm. This exalted image of Rev. Moon is reinforced, on the one hand, by the Unification movement's success at attracting world-class religious and political leaders to its conferences and other gatherings. On the other hand, and perhaps more important, a wide variety of different Unificationists have received messages from deceased religious and political leaders, all of whom praise the church's founder as a spiritual virtuoso whose ministry represents a threshold in world history.

In "Reconstructing Reality: Conspiracy Theories about Jonestown," Rebecca Moore examines the conspiracy theories that have arisen to explain the mass murder-suicides of People's Temple members in Jonestown, Guyana, in November 1978. These theories range from those produced by professional conspiracy theorists who see conspiracies everywhere, to theories developed by nonprofessionals that concentrate primarily on Jonestown. Moore explains that conspiracy theories attempt to make sense of what appears ultimately senseless. And such theories are attractive because, despite the threat they represent, they are also comforting since they eliminate uncertainty and moral ambiguity.

Stuart A. Wright's "Explaining Militarization at Waco: The Construction and Convergence of the Warfare Narrative" examines how the Branch Davidians—a small religious group following a peaceful lifestyle in rural Texas—were perceived anew as a dangerously aggressive community that required a major operation to subdue them. The Davidians were brought to the attention of the Bureau of Alcohol, Tobacco, and Firearms through the sustained efforts of apostates and other interest groups; this led to a siege and, later, to a fiery tragedy in which most of the members died. Wright's analysis focuses on the "logic" by which the situation was so dramatically militarized.

Part II: Asian and Asian-Inspired Groups

"Family Development and Change in the Hare Krishna Movement" by E. Burke Rochford, Jr. investigates the role of family life as a source of change within ISKCON. The results of the worldwide Prabhupada Centennial Survey conducted in 1994–1995 are interpreted as indicating a change from collective, traditional, and religious values to private, democratic, and secular values. The organizational foundation has moved from communalism to congregationalist nuclear families, mainly because of alterations in demographics and the controversial actions of the traditional authority structure, which in turn have affected the scope of parents' beliefs and organizational involvement. Thus ISKCON is threatened by a fragmentation of the socioreligious worldview shared by its members.

Marion S. Goldman's "When Leaders Dissolve: Considering Controversy and Stagnation in the Osho Rajneesh Movement" presents an analytic history of the Rajneesh movement, following its various changes and controversies in the United States and India. Despite the many controversies—external and internal—and the death of Osho Rajneesh in 1990, the movement stabilized and continued to exist as a successful (though smaller and lower-profile) organization. On the basis of her analysis, Goldman concludes by observing that an effective strategy for responding to controversy is to "(1) reproach, blame, and ostracize selected individuals for controversy, (2) relocate, (3) rename, (4) reorganize, (5) reemphasize doctrine to support practice rather than allegiance and, finally and possibly most important, redefine success."

In "Soka Gakkai: Searching for the Mainstream," Robert Kisala reviews the conflict-ridden history of the largest new religious movement in Japan, with over eight million members in that country and over one million members abroad. Three sources of discord are covered: Soka Gakkai's aggressive proselytizing activities, its political aspirations, and its pacifist stance, which are connected to the biography of the founder and to the exclusivist interpretation of its heritage from the Buddhist teacher Nichiren. In conflict with both the Japanese government during the Second World War and the larger Nichiren Buddhist tradition, the movement's political power and militaristic missionary work are the most significant contributors to the bad press and popular suspicion the movement has generated.

Martin Repp's "Aum Shinrikyo and the Aum Incident: A Critical Introduction" presents a systematic overview of Aum Shinrikyo, its historical development, and the significant body of scholarship that has been carried out on the movement. Analyses of Aum Shinrikyo—or Aleph as it is now called—must necessarily come to grips with the task of explaining the 1995 poison-gas attack on the Tokyo subway system. This and other criminal acts became known as the Aum incident. Repp's discussion is built around the question, How did a group that began life as a peaceful yoga group transform into an apocalyptic doomsday religion, capable of acts of terrorism?

In "The Falun Gong: A New Religious Movement in Post-Mao China," David Ownby outlines the historical background of, and recent development in, the aggressive repression of Falun Gong by Chinese authorities. Essentially a form of *qi gong*—which is both a nationalistic and materialistic reinterpretation of traditional Chinese healing practices created by the Chinese state in the 1950s and propagated by the establishment into a mass movement in the 1980s and 1990s—Falun Gong nevertheless differs in certain important respects, notably its devotion to the charismatic master and his scriptures, its apocalyptic outlook, and its spiritual aims. Straying from the scientistic and apolitical path outlined by the state, Falun Gong placed itself outside the boundaries of socialist China and thus could not be tolerated.

In "Notes on the Aumist Religion," PierLuigi Zoccatelli describes how Aumism's original Hindu identity was transformed into a universalism that seemed to blend Christianity, Buddhism, Hinduism, Jainism, Islam, and Judaism as a consequence of the founder Gilbert Bourdin's self-identification as the Cosmoplanetary Messiah. This apparent syncretism, however, turns out to be less significant than the role that esoteric, occult traditions play in Aumism, and that constitute a "second pillar" on which Aumism has gradually been constructed as a separate "tradition." Both historically, in terms of Bourdin's background in esoteric study, and sociologically, in terms of the background of a majority of members, Aumism is an esoteric group, which, Zoccatelli argues, is a fundamental type, distinct from religious movements and cult movements.

Part III: Esoteric and New Age Groups

In "Inventing L. Ron Hubbard: On the Construction and Maintenance of the Hagiographic Mythology of Scientology's Founder," Dorthe Refslund Christensen examines how, almost two decades after his death, the work and person of L. Ron Hubbard remain at the very core of the Church of Scientology. The steps that were taken both before and after his passing to make Hubbard the final authority within the church are in part responsible for the ease with which the Scientology organization navigated the potential crisis that could have been initiated by Hubbard's death. Christensen focuses her analysis on the various strategies by which the church has constructed and maintained Hubbard's hagiography, continually affirming him as the sole legitimate source of the Scientology religion.

James A. Santucci's "The Theosophical Society" surveys the history and development of the Theosophical Society and its offshoots. The Theosophical Society was founded in New York City in 1875 by a small group of people with shared interests in spiritualism and occultism. The most important of these individuals were Col. Henry Steel Olcott and Helena Petrovna Blavatsky. Theosophy is not static but is, rather, a living body of teachings that has developed and been reinterpreted over time. The Theosophical tradition has also split into many different streams. Organizations that ultimately derive from the Theosophical Society include the Temple of the People founded by Dr. William H. Dower and Mrs. Francia LaDue, Alice Bailey's Arcane School, Guy Ballard's "I AM" Religious Activity, the Church Universal and Triumphant (formerly the Summit Lighthouse), founded by Mark Prophet, and the Aetherius Society founded by George King.

In "The Solar Temple 'Transits': Beyond the Millennialist Hypothesis," James R. Lewis surveys the Order of the Solar Temple, focusing on Joseph Di Mambro, the founder of the OTS. The founder's idiosyncracies provide keys for understanding the Solar Temple's dramatic final "transit." The focus on Di Mambro then feeds into a broader analysis of the three primary suicide cults examined by contemporary scholars of alternative religions: the People's Temple, the Solar Temple, and Heaven's Gate. Lewis argues that the two factors normally given pride of place in discussions of NRM-related violence, namely millennialism and external provocation, are not as central for understanding suicide groups as previous analysts have suggested. Instead, a leader with failing health along with a combination of certain other characteristics of intensive religious groups are more important factors for predicting which groups are predisposed to suicide.

Gail M. Harley's "From Atlantis to America: JZ Knight Encounters Ramtha" examines the practice of channeling, here exemplified by the Ramtha School of Enlightenment, as a unique opportunity for asserting feminine spirituality. JZ Knight is placed in context of women who utilize charismatic leadership to build bridges to the divine: H. P. Blavatsky, Emma Curtis Hopkins, and Mary Baker Eddy. In addition, Harley considers the eclecticism of the Ramtha school, with its use of gnosticism and quantum physics and its focus on personal transformation, placing it within the modern New Age subculture that itself attempts a gender-equal construction. Finally, the controversy of gender is used to analyze society's validation of women who channel the divine and advocate an immanent God.

Diana G. Tumminia's "Heart and Soul: A Qualitative Look at the Ethos of the Movement of Spiritual Inner Awareness" analyzes the interpretations and practices of the Movement of Spiritual Inner Awareness (MSIA) through frame alignment theory and Weberian sociology in light of normative socialization. The group is a syncretistic organization, described as a "seminar religion" that combines Christianity and Sant Mat practices as well as typical esoteric pursuits found in New Age groups. The controversial side of MSIA lies in its awkward relations with the wider society; as such, the analysis provides an insider's portrait and outsider's assessment of what is unproductively labeled a "cult."

Part IV: Other Groups and Movements

George D. Chryssides's " 'Come On Up, and I Will Show Thee': Heaven's Gate as a Postmodern Group" examines the worldview of the Heaven's Gate in terms of the concept of postmodernity. After the mass suicide of 1997, the group provoked controversy as an example of a "suicide cult" equivalent to the People's Temple, the Branch Davidians, and the Solar Temple. Through a closer look at the radical physicalistic interpretation of the Book of Revelation presented by Marshall Applewhite and Bonnie Nettles, Chryssides demonstrates that the actions undertaken make sense in light of the group's worldview. Additionally, the group's idiosyncratic use of science fiction and Christianity parallels the construction of meaning in a postmodern society.

In "The Raëlian Movement: Concocting Controversy, Seeking Social Legitimacy," Susan Palmer presents the conscious strategy of the Raëlian Movement regarding media attention. By presenting controlled "outrages" with a clear social orientation in publicity campaigns—such as "Operation Condom" in front of Catholic schools and the Baby Eve cloning announcement—they direct the image of the movement in the public space and deflect the more serious charges usually aimed at new religious movements. Thus a mild level of cultural conflict is nurtured to enhance visibility and empower social legitimacy. This strategy has been successful except in French-speaking Europe, where the persecution of new religious movements is vigorous, and could be counterproductive for the survival of a millenarian group with a charismatic leader.

In "White Racist Religions in the United States: From Christian Identity to Wolf Age Pagans," Mattias Gardell provides a historical overview and analysis of the development of racist religions in North America. White religious racism is not a single creed, but rather consists of many different orientations linked by their participation in the white-power subculture. Gardell focuses on three categories: racist (particularly Identity) Christianity, religious national socialism, and racist paganism. Though paganism has been gaining ground among younger racists, the importance of Christianity to traditional American culture means that Identity is unlikely to be completely supplanted by racist paganism.

Jesper Aagaard Petersen's "Modern Satanism: Dark Doctrines and Black Flames" begins with a short historical and sociological sketch of the Satanic subculture (or movement) followed by a discussion of the connecting themes, beliefs, and practices in an attempt to systematize them. Then some common typologies are addressed to establish a general analytical frame of reference, and the various groups and spokespersons are presented to outline the source material available. Finally, some suggestions for future research are put forward.

WORKS CITED

Lester, Toby. "Oh, Gods!" 2002. *Atlantic Monthly* 289.

Lewis, James R. 2003. *Legitimating New Religions*. New Brunswick: Rutgers University Press.

———. 2004. *The Oxford Handbook of New Religious Movements*. New York: Oxford University Press.

Robinson, Bruce A. 2000. "Movement for the Restoration of the Ten Command-
    ments of God." Ontario Consultants for Religious Tolerance. www
    .religioustolerance.org/dc_rest.html.
Ross, Nancy. 2001. "The Tony Alamo Story." Holy Alamo Christian Church. www
    .scvhistory.com/scvhistory/alamo-ross.html.

PART I

Groups in the Christian Tradition

I

A Family for the Twenty-first Century

James D. Chancellor

The Jesus People movement began in the United States as a fusion of an evangelical Christian awakening and the youth counterculture of the 1960s. The Children of God (COG), now known as the Family, was the most controversial group to arise out of this broader religious landscape. The call on young people to a life of radical separation from family and conventional society, the bitter denunciation of American values, and the confrontational style of the movement soon elicited considerable hostility from family members, government, and the media. David Brandt Berg, founding prophet of the Family, left the United States in 1972.[1] He encouraged his followers to flee to more hospitable lands in Europe, Asia, and Latin America, and within a few years, most of the disciples responded to this call. Those who remained went underground; the Children of God virtually disappeared from the American landscape.

Though a few communities always remained in the United States and Canada, in the late 1980s the North American disciples began to return home in large numbers. The Family had meanwhile gone through radical theological, organizational, and lifestyle changes. This small North American countercultural movement had grown into a worldwide religious subculture of some ten thousand people. This chapter will outline the history of the movement and its major theological landmarks, and give particular attention to the substantive changes in the Family since the death of the founding Prophet in 1994.

History of the Family

The Children of God: The Formative Years

The Family began with David Brandt Berg. Born in 1919, by 1944 Berg was in full-time Christian service. He was ordained to the ministry in the Christian and Missionary Alliance and spent twenty years in and out of various religious positions.

In the mid 1960s, Berg began to envision himself as a uniquely called and gifted missionary to the lost and confused youth of America. In 1966 he and his wife and four children took to the road as an itinerant singing and evangelistic team. He acquired several disciples along the way, and in early 1968 Father David and his extended "family" settled down in Huntington Beach, California. He and his children began a strongly youth-oriented evangelistic ministry, and the first shot in the Jesus Revolution had been fired. Father David's revolution was not only for Jesus. It was also against the "System," the corrupt educational, political, economic, and religious structures of contemporary American society that were soon to be consumed by the wrath of God. Those young people who "received Jesus" were further challenged to "forsake all" by rejecting every tie to the evil System, commit full time as disciples, and move in with Father David and his growing "family."

In April 1969, Father David took his band of young charges on the road again. A young woman named Karen Zerby (Maria) joined up. She soon became Father David's secretary, and they began a sexual relationship. The community settled temporarily at a campground in the Laurentian Mountains in Canada. Here Father David announced the founding prophecy for the Children of God: "A Prophecy of God on the Old Church and the New Church."[2] God had rejected the old System church in favor of his New Church, the Children of God. Father David also announced to his inner circle that he was separating from his old wife and taking his young secretary, Maria, as his new wife. She gradually rose in status within the movement, and eventually inherited the mantle of leadership upon Berg's death.

Soon the disciples were on the move again, living off the land. They survived on gifts from their families, funds brought into the community when new disciples joined, and "provisioning" most food and necessities by appeal to the public. By February 1970, they numbered nearly two hundred and had settled on a ranch in west Texas.

During this phase, the basic patterns for COG life were established. The disciples established a routine of Bible memorization, Bible studies developed by Father David, provisioning, jobs to maintain community life, devotional and fellowship meetings, training in witnessing strategies (persuading people to say a prayer inviting Jesus into their lives), and witnessing ventures. The group continued to grow, and soon the members were dispersed. By the end of 1971, sixty-nine colonies were spread out across the United States and Canada, with almost fifteen hundred disciples.

The summer of 1971 marked the beginning of Free the Children of God (FREECOG), the original anticult organization. FREECOG began a propaganda campaign that accused the COG of kidnapping, drug use, and psychological terror by hypnotizing and "brainwashing" innocent young people. These and other attacks only exacerbated a fortress mentality that already laid heavy emphasis on the otherness of the outside world.

In this formative period, Father David received two revelations that would begin a series of "revolutions" within the Family. In December 1970, he had a dream that led him to withdraw from personal contact with the disciples.[3] He began to teach and guide them through his writing; from this point on, he channeled his charisma and authority through his correspondence, known as MO Letters. In the spring of 1972, Father David had a dream of mass destruction in the United States. He urged his North American followers to flee as soon as possible and to begin the missionary task of reaching the world for Jesus. They heard the call, and by the end of 1972 colonies had been established in much of Western Europe and Latin America, Australia, New Zealand, Japan, and India.

With the migration out of North America, the overtly confrontational, antiestablishment component of the COG message began to soften. This change in posture was consistent with an enlarged vision for a worldwide missionary enterprise. The explosive growth, rapid spread, and youth and inexperience of most disciples left the organization with serious leadership problems. In 1973, Father David attempted to slow the growth of the movement and develop more capable leadership. He also introduced a new strategy for getting out the message: the wide distribution of COG literature. This activity was termed "litnessing."[4] Since the literature was exchanged for "a small donation," finances improved dramatically.

Music was always a central aspect of the Family vision. Disciples have written hundreds of songs of protest, praise, and proclamation. By 1974, several COG bands had achieved wide public acceptance and popularity. In addition, numerous "poor boy clubs" that featured dancing, recorded and live music, and dramatic skits were opened around the world.

By the mid-1970s, Berg had come to a new understanding of his own role in human history: he was not only God's unique End Time Prophet, but also King of God's New Nation. Some top-level leadership began to chafe at this new status. In turn, he was concerned about the arrogance and harshness of many leaders, and their lack of concern for the welfare of the ordinary disciples. In the "New Revolution" of early 1975, Father David established a new "chain of cooperation" in an attempt to address these problems.[5] Most of the leadership under the chain of cooperation came from the old guard, and the reform lacked effect. The chain also further distanced Father David from the vast majority of young followers, and life for most of the ordinary disciples grew more difficult.

In the early 1970s, Father David began the most sensational aspect of his "revolution," a complete transformation of sexual ethos. Shortly after taking Maria as a second wife, Berg began having sexual encounters with other female disciples in his inner circle. By the early 1970s, the top level of leadership was also experimenting with multiple partners. These activities were unknown to the vast majority of disciples, whose sexual mores continued to reflect their evangelical Christian roots.

In March 1974 Father David and Maria relocated to the resort of Tenerife in the Canary Islands. He gathered a small group of attractive female disciples to begin an experiment in a new witnessing strategy, which he termed "flirty fishing," later shortened to "Ffing." The female disciples would use the full range of their feminine charms, including sexual intercourse, to witness for Jesus and to make supportive friends for the movement. Few field disciples were aware of the extent of this new strategy. In 1976, MO Letters came out that described the Ffing of Maria and others in graphic detail, set the model for the larger community, and encouraged the disciples to begin this new "ministry."[6] Acceptance was by no means universal. Many disciples had strong reservations, and a significant number left the movement.

Flirty fishing marked some significant changes. The confrontational approach was now gone forever, replaced by a strong emphasis on the love and compassion of Jesus. Additionally, the target audience had shifted almost completely away from "hippies and dropouts." These and other substantive shifts in Family orientation brought serious internal conflicts.

The Family of Love: Degeneration and Regeneration

By the end of 1977, a number of leaders began to question Father David's status as God's End Time Prophet. They also raised doubts regarding some of his teachings, particularly the radical shift in sexual mores. And Father David became more aware that many leaders were abusively authoritarian, and were living in luxury by means of exorbitant "taxes" on field colonies. In January 1978, Father David issued "Re-organization Nationalization Revolution" (RNR), the most significant event in the history of the Children of God.[7] The organization itself was dismantled and some three hundred leaders were dismissed and either ejected or ordered into the streets as ordinary disciples. The movement was renamed "The Family of Love." All those loyal to the king were welcome to remain directly faithful and responsible to the Prophet.

There was considerable loss of membership in 1978, even with the birth of some six hundred children. The Jonestown tragedy brought fears of anticult hysteria, and the disciples were urged to go underground. Many "went mobile," traveling about in campers or caravans as itinerant missionaries, often not identifying themselves as Children of God. Their only direct connection to the movement was the MO Letters. Though the disciples continued to litness and witness, flirty fishing increased dramatically after the RNR. In some areas it became the primary means of witness and financial support.

In the mid-1970s, the sexual ethics of the COG grew increasingly liberal. The practice of multiple sexual partners (sharing) had filtered down from leadership to all of the field colonies. By 1978, Berg was strongly encouraging sexual experimentation, and he freed the disciples from any leadership constraints. Nudity within the homes and sexual liaisons between members became common practice. Father David understood human sexuality as a beautiful, natural creation of God. In exploring how this principle might relate to children, he sent out Letters detailing his early childhood sexual experiences, and directives for adults to allow children the freedom to express their natural sexual inclinations. From 1978 to 1983, he and the entire Family were exploring the outer limits of sexual freedom. Most disciples were aware that sexual contact between adults and children was occurring in the Bergs' household.[8] Some disciples interpreted some of the MO Letters as allowing for sexual interplay of adults with minors. It is not possible to determine the extent or degree of this activity, but it was occurring in Family homes around the globe.

By the end of 1980, the Family of Love was growing again. Dispersed throughout the world in small homes, most disciples were isolated and somewhat adrift. In 1981, Father David ordered the disciples to begin weekly fellowship meetings with others in their area.[9] A new hierarchical structure was established. Large homes, which functioned as national headquarters, were set up in each country.

By the end of 1981, another significant transition overtook the Family. In 1981 there were 719 births. Since birth control was strictly prohibited, from this point on, children constituted the majority of members. The care, discipline, and education of children soon began to require an increasing portion of energy, time, and resources.

The Family: Serving a Sexy God

From 1982 to 1984, the Family reordered itself back into a tightly knit organization. At the same time, many disciples responded to Father David's call to carry the message of Jesus to the Third World. By the end of 1982, 34 percent of the disciples were in Latin America and almost 40 percent in Asia.

By 1982, children began to play greater role in outreach ministries as an increasing amount of attention was given to child rearing. Significantly, the Family began to see the youth as the hope of the future, the disciples who would carry the movement and the message to the End. The recruitment of new disciples continued, but the numbers of these fell considerably. The total number of full-time members reached ten thousand in 1983, and hovered

FIGURE I.I. "Our Heavenly Home," a poster produced by the Family.

around that mark for the next ten years, despite an average of over seven hundred births per year. Many of the new disciples proved to be short-term, and as the first wave of children began to mature, the Family began to lose more people than were joining through evangelism and recruitment.

The Family began to face a new and troubling phenomenon: teenagers. Several "school homes" were established for the education and discipleship of the growing number of teens. In 1983, Father David received disturbing reports of misconduct at one of the teen homes. He responded with strict guidelines for the youth, and high expectations for their personal conduct.[10]

By the early 1980s, flirty fishing was widespread and becoming increasingly central to the life of many communities. Ffing was originally envisioned and theologically justified as a witnessing strategy, but not as a useful tool to recruit new disciples. It did serve another vital purpose, however. Ffing became a primary source of financial support and political protection. Many female disciples established long-term relationships with wealthy or influential men, who often provided resources, help in immigration, and protection against social and political repression. In some areas of Asia, Europe, and Latin America, female disciples went to work for escort services, providing sex for a fixed fee.[11]

The issues of sexuality and distinctive sexual practices were playing an ever increasing role in Family life. In the spring of 1980, Father David sent out a message, "The Devil Hates Sex!—But God Loves It!"[12] In his own "revolutionary" style, he made very clear that the disciples served a "sexy God" and that God loved sex and wanted his Children to enjoy it fully. But as nudity and open sexuality became more and more common, real problems were surfacing.

Sexually transmitted diseases began spreading through the Family. It was common practice to have a considerable amount of sexual sharing at area fellowships, facilitating the spread of disease from home to home. In March 1983, Father David issued the message called "Ban the Bomb!"[13] He halted sexual activities at area fellowships, and limited all sexual relationships to persons residing within the same home—although he exempted himself from this restriction, of course. This is the first point at which the Family began to face the negative spiritual and social consequences of unrestricted sexual freedom. In December 1984 Maria prohibited new members (Babes) from any sexual encounters during their first six months.[14] The pendulum of sexual freedom had reached its apex, and began a slow swing back toward a somewhat more conventional sexual ethos.

Also in 1984, Maria commissioned certain musically talented homes to produce a series of audiocassettes for the general public. The tapes were an immense success and soon became a central focus of outreach. They were also an additional source of financial support.

As the Family was reconfigured toward a more tightly structured organization of large communal homes, other problems developed. In 1985, World Services (the overall leadership structure of the Family) received reports of harsh and oppressive leadership practices in Japan and other areas. They responded with a flood of literature reasserting the hierarchical nature of the leadership structure, but also urging local and area leaders to carry out their duties as servants, dealing with disciples under their care with love and understanding.

The Family was evolving and maturing. Almost all homes included a good number of children and, given their strong communal lifestyle, parents were becoming increasingly wary of inviting total strangers into their communities. Family homes began to require a six months' probationary period for prospective members. The probation period has gone a long way toward stabilizing community life and eliminating short-term disciples. In the late 1980s, quite a few former disciples began to return to the fold. Many were teenagers who were in need of spiritual direction and training. To meet this need, the Family established Teen Training Camps in Mexico, South America, Europe, and Asia.

While in the Teen Training Camps, several teenage girls reported inappropriate and uninvited sexual advances by adult males. When Maria became fully aware of the extent of this problem, she responded. In August 1986, she prohibited sexual contact between adults and minors. However, the Prophet had repeatedly affirmed that sex should be enjoyed as fully as possible. Stepping away from such a total affirmation proved difficult.

The Family continued to place further limits on sexual expression. By the end of the 1980s, sexual activity among children or young teens was increasingly discouraged. Current policy forbids sexual intercourse between children under the age of sixteen. As might be expected, the policy is not uniformly kept, and sanctions are not severe. However, adult sexual contact with a minor is now a most serious breach of Family rules and results in automatic excommunication.

By 1987, flirty fishing was central to the life of most communities, but it had become problematic. Many homes were overly dependent on it, and depended heavily on influential supporters developed through long-term relationships. The AIDS epidemic was the primary reason for halting the practice. In the fall of 1987, a policy memo banned sexual contact with outsiders, except "close and well-known" friends who had long-term relationships with Family women. This policy is in force today, and there are very few women who continue in relationships with their "fish." Beyond these, any sexual contact with outsiders is now an excommunicable offense.

Throughout the late 1980s, the Family continued to evolve. Education emerged as a top priority, with large school homes established in all areas. Teaching the youth became a primary Family concern. By the end of 1989, there were almost one hundred school homes, serving over three thousand children.

As the teens continued to gather in larger numbers, disruptive and destructive conduct increased. The Family responded with "Victor Programs," which were periods of intense discipline, work, and spiritual oversight. In some places these programs were harsh and abusive. Many, if not most, of the first wave of teens rebelled and left. After a few years, Maria found certain aspects of the program far too harsh, and she ended it. She apologized and ordered the key adult leadership to apologize personally to teens they had mistreated.[15]

By the late 1980s, India was the most fruitful mission field, with over two thousand disciples. Most were North Americans or Europeans on tourist visas or in the country illegally. In 1988, the Indian government clamped down, and many were forced to leave. Confident that the End was near and persecution would greatly increase, Father David ordered the disciples in India to go home. By the end of 1989, over eight hundred disciples had returned from the East. The return of these battle-hardened missionaries pointed up again the disparities in the standard of Family life. In an effort to create an End Time Army ready for the final tumult, World Services suspended all homes in North America and Europe until they could be reviewed and recertified as legitimate Family communities.

Many failed the test. A new category of membership was established, Tithing Report Forms Supporter (TSer) (TRF refers to the Tithing Report Forms used by full-time members). These were persons who wished to remain connected to the Family, but were unable or unwilling to maintain the standard of disciple life.[16] In 1989 almost fourteen hundred were "TSed"—essentially kicked out. Regular disciples were prohibited from direct contact with them. They were encouraged to remain loyal to the Family vision, however, and were viewed as partial members if they continued in their financial support. Many were TSed as family units, but there were a number of situations where spouses were separated, and in some cases parents were separated from their children. From 1989 to 1994, the total number of disciples remained at approximately twelve thousand, but the percentage of those on TS status increased from approximately 10 to 25 percent.[17] After 1993, the attitude toward TSers softened considerably. Currently termed "Fellow Members," they enjoy fellowship with disciple homes and take a much more active role in support of Family objectives.

After 1989, the Family began to focus on newly opened mission fields in the former Soviet Union and Africa. Hundreds of disciples, mostly second-generation young people, now work in Eastern Europe and Africa, almost all as underground, unregistered missionaries.

The Family: Persecution and Maturation

At the close of the 1980s, the Prophet was tired, ill, and aging; he essentially retired at the end of 1988. Maria assumed the role of spiritual leader and guide. Peter Amsterdam (an administrator who worked closely with Father David and Maria) took over administrative control of the Family, although this was never formalized or announced. Few disciples were conscious of the change, though all knew that Father David was grooming Maria, allowing her ever greater latitude and authority.

In October 1994, David Brandt Berg passed away. Shortly after his death, Peter and Maria were married. They now lead as a team. However, Father David still speaks regularly and guides the Family from heaven.

Although various internal forces constantly worked to reconfigure the community, forces from the outside fostered a significant shift in the early 1990s. The disciples had always faced strong and often hostile opposition: they have been harassed, kidnapped, and assaulted by religious opponents, and intimidated, arrested, and imprisoned by law enforcement authorities. Virtually all opposition has been interpreted as religious persecution. When persecution came, they suffered, sought the assistance of "friends," and went underground or moved on to more receptive fields. But when their children became the target, attitudes changed quickly.

Beginning at the end of the 1980s, persons within the anticult movement, supported by the testimonies of a number of exmembers, laid charges of child abuse and sexual molestation against the Family in Europe, Australia, and South America. Various attempts to remove children dramatically changed the way the Family related to the outside world. Father David instructed the disciples to stand and fight for their children. Disciples all over the world began active protests against the governments that were attacking their communities. Sometimes the Family took preemptive measures, inviting in law enforcement and social services agencies to conduct investigations of the children. In addition, Family leadership opened their communities to legitimate scholarly inquiry, confident they had nothing to hide.[18]

But the movement had been forever altered by these experiences. The event that most rocked the Family came in 1993, in England. A wealthy widow, whose adult daughter had joined while on a religious quest in Nepal, filed suit in the British High Court, seeking custody of the daughter's infant son. The judge conducted a lengthy inquiry, not only into the actual circumstances of the child in question but also into Family history, ideology, and moral conduct. The anticult establishment became actively involved, and the case lasted almost three years. Throughout the process, Family leadership was required to come to terms with the past; to explain passages in their literature that did condone sexual contact with minors; and to respond to the testimony of numerous former members who had been mistreated and abused. The closet doors were kicked open. And in the midst of the whole painful process, Father David died. In order to close out the case, Peter Amsterdam was required to write an open letter to the judge, which admitted that the policies and practices of the Family had in some instances been harmful. The letter identified Father David as a root cause of some of this destructive behavior. It was a painful but necessary catharsis.[19]

Though that have finally admitted the extent of past abuse, Family disciples have successfully defended themselves against all charges of current sexual misconduct with minors, or any form of child abuse or neglect. Worldwide, over six hundred children have been removed from their homes and examined by court-appointed experts. These experts have detected no abused children. Without question, there are numerous incidents of child sexual abuse in Family history, but the members have attempted to put these things behind them. To date, no adult has been found guilty of misconduct. But attempts will surely continue to bring offending individuals and Family leadership to justice over this sad and bitter aspect of their past.

Though the 1990s were a time of renewed "persecution" and a time of winnowing out the uncommitted, the Family began to mellow. Father David set himself and his followers against the church, "the god damned, hypocritical, idol worshipping, churchianity of the System."[20] But in late 1991, he began to encourage disciples to visit and perhaps even establish fellowship with open-minded congregations. In general, this has not worked well. More significantly, he directed the disciples to send their many converts toward local churches for care and training in the Christian life.[21] This proved to be a temporary strategy, but is clear evidence of an attempt to lower tension with the outside. Attitudes toward members who left were always negative and strained. But by the late 1980s an increasing number of teens were leaving, and many parents wished to maintain a good relationship with these departing children. The Family has made an about-face on this sensitive issue. It is now recognized that only a few of the children will remain committed. Efforts are made to prepare the others for life on the outside, and parents are encouraged to keep the relationships strong and the lines of communication open. This softened attitude has extended to all former members. From 1994 on, the Family has committed to a "ministry of reconciliation."[22] Peter Amsterdam has taken the lead in attempting to reach out to ex-members around the world in an effort to heal old wounds and establish friendly relationships where possible. These attempts have met with some success, though small cadres of former members still remain hostile and aggressively opposed to the Family.

This shift in attitude toward the outside is also evidenced in a transition in the approach to social ministries. Since the beginning, the disciples have been concerned almost completely with the spiritual salvation of potential converts. But in 1992, Father David directed his followers to begin helping the poor and the helpless, "like Jesus did."[23] Almost immediately, disciples started ministries to prisons, street gangs, undocumented aliens, unwed mothers, drug addicts, refugees in Eastern Europe and Southeast Asia, and abused children all over the world. Social ministry has taken root very quickly and is now central to the life and practice of most disciples, particularly the second generation.

The Family: The Post-Prophet Era

After the death of David Berg in the fall of 1994, the transition of authority that had been ongoing for a number of years was completed, and his mantle fell easily on Maria and her consort, Peter Amsterdam. Although the transition went quite smoothly, the Family changed dramatically in 1995. World Services implemented the "Charter of Rights and Responsibilities." The charter contains the movement's basic beliefs and details the fundamental rights and responsibilities of the disciples, as well as the rules and guidelines for communal life. Queen Maria and King Peter retain overall and supreme authority, but day-to-day life is far more democratic than previously. The disciples are strongly encouraged to live "according to their own faith" with a minimum of supervision and direction from a radically altered leadership structure. Smaller home size is mandated and, most significant, disciples have the absolute right of mobility. Recently, the Family has moved toward a "Board vision" in which the various aspects of communal life and ministry will be under the direction of a wide and popularly elected board of directors.[24]

The charter greatly improved the life experience of most disciples and has led to greater contentment. It went some way toward curbing the mass exodus of young people from the movement, but it has not been without its problems. The Family has struggled to find its way under the kinder and gentler approach to leadership. Toward the end of the 1990s, Maria and Peter were becoming increasingly concerned with the lax attitudes and low productivity of many disciples. In a take-off from the Y2K phenomenon (the worldwide celebration of the millennium), they issued S2K—Shakeup Two Thousand.[25] Discipline and community standards were reaffirmed, and those unwilling to conform were strongly encouraged to become Fellow Members, or leave the movement completely. This purge has been ongoing, and some fifteen hundred disciples have been pushed out into the world.[26] The quest has been to create a leaner and more productive Army of the Lord, more prepared to carry out the mission and to face the tumult of the End of Days.

The two most significant changes in the Family since the death of Father David are in the areas of spiritual life and community vision. Interaction and communication with the Spirit world has been a feature of Family life from the beginning of the movement. Disciples were open to the possibility of prophetic experiences and guidance from those who have gone on. But the vast majority of substantive communication came through Father David. Not long after his death, Maria opened up the channels in several significant ways. Father David continued to lead and guide the community from the spirit world by "speaking" prophetically through Peter Amsterdam and several other receptors in the central household. This quickly expanded, so that Jesus, Father David, the apostle Paul, and any number of other persons now regularly communicate directly with the Family. Much of the guiding vision and strategy now comes directly from above, and the substantive portions of the Letters are direct utterances from the spirit world, most often from Jesus and David Berg.

In conjunction with this shift, the disciples themselves are strongly encouraged to develop the prophetic gift within themselves. Most have. Direct revelations and prophecy are now a normal feature of disciple life, both in private experience and community prayer.[27] The vast majority of disciples now look to prophecy to guide decision making in virtually all aspects of their lives. The shift seems to have created a greater sense of ownership in their various ministries, confidence, and a sense of shared vision. The disruptive potential for such openness to prophecy within a tightly structured community is obvious. To minimize this potential, Maria has retained the role of "wine taster," essentially holding the keys to the kingdom. All prophecy that might impact the broader community in any way is subject to her evaluation and validation.[28]

An equally significant shift has occurred in the conceptualization of the purpose of the Family. From the very beginning, witnessing for Jesus and the spiritual salvation of as many souls as possible before the End has been the essential task of Family life. To that end, Family disciples have been highly mobile, and generally not geared toward the spiritual development and care of converts. The development of follow-up literature, the involvement in social ministry, and the encouragement of coverts to make contact with outside churches represent the beginnings of a shift. But at the opening of the twenty-first century, a fundamental reorientation has occurred: an Activated Program has been developed and implemented worldwide.[29] This is not an option, but rather the new Family vision. Considerable resources have been poured into developing quality educational materials for new converts. And Family disciples are strongly encouraged to settle down in one place, focus their evangelistic efforts, work at developing what are essentially congregations that will be directly related to local disciple homes, and look after those disciples as spiritual mentors, guides, and pastors.

Analyzing the motivations for significant shifts in movements like the Family is no easy task. Two factors seem to be at work here, both growing out of an apparent delay of the Second Coming of Jesus. To date, the Family claims to have led more than twenty-three million persons to pray the salvation prayer and receive Jesus as their personal savior. However, that is simply a number on a piece of paper. In the overwhelming majority of cases, the disciples have had little or no contact with these "converts." For most of their history, the Family lived in high expectation of an immediate end to human history as we know it, and the singular task was to get as many people saved as possible. The care of souls was a very low priority. It seems clear that the Activated Program represents the beginning stages of an accommodation to the possibility of a much longer-than-expected mission in this world.

Beyond that, many of the disciples are beginning to age. Given their strong apocalyptic bent, most have made no provision at all for an extended life, but that is changing. Family leadership is quite open in describing the Activated Program as the potential retirement package for faithful disciples.[30]

It remains to be seen how well the "radical revolutionary Children of God" can sustain this shift toward more conventional religious life. There are real challenges, especially in the degree to which outside members can participate in some of the distinctive aspects of the Family ethos. But the Activated Program seems to be catching on, particularly in certain areas of Latin America and Asia, where the disciples have generally been more geographically stable. Though the number of committed, full-time, communal disciples is down somewhat, the overall membership is expanding quickly into the tens of thousands. It seems clear that Queen Maria and King Peter are leading the Family on a journey from "cult" to "sect."

Theology of the Family

Although the Family can be viewed and examined from many perspectives, it is essentially a religious movement grounded in a clearly articulated belief system. The Family boasts an extraordinary range of educational, religious, cultural, ethnic, and national backgrounds, and the disciples are guided and sustained by a common vision and a coherent set of theological commitments.

This theological system has developed and evolved through the years, but is grounded on the twin rocks of biblical authority and the prophetic office of Father David. The Christian Bible was the sole source of religious authority at the beginning of the movement, and disciples remain deeply immersed in the sacred text. Father David adopted a position of "progressive revelation," however, which keeps open the possibility of revision or change, and has placed his writings on an equal footing with the Bible.[31]

An exhaustive analysis of Family doctrine is beyond our scope.[32] I will attempt to explore the core beliefs that are central to the Family experience. These core beliefs center on Jesus and human salvation, Father David as God's prophet, the spirit world, the End Times, the System, and the sexual ethic.

Jesus and Salvation

Human salvation through faith in Jesus Christ as the only Savior is the cornerstone of Family theology. The disciples generally share an understanding of Jesus Christ that is consistent with evangelical Protestant Christianity. Jesus was born of a virgin, lived a sinless life, died on the cross for the sins of the world, rose from the grave, and is returning soon to this earth. All people are "lost" and without hope in this world, but eternal salvation is available to all who will, in faith, simply repeat a short prayer inviting Jesus to come into his or her life as personal Savior. Once an individual repeats this prayer, that person is saved and has secured an eternal home in heaven with Jesus. Witnessing, or the attempt to get as many people as possible to pray this simple prayer, has been the central task of discipleship from the beginning. Paradoxically, Father David taught that in the end, all creation would be reconciled to God. But this universalism has set very lightly on the disciples and never dampened their evangelistic fire.

The Prophet

In the early days, David Berg claimed no special status or office. As the movement developed, however, he came to a radically different self-understanding. By the end of 1970, Father David had emerged as God's Prophet for the End Time. He quickly established his absolute authority over the disciples.

His claims of divine appointment and absolute spiritual authority roughly coincided with his withdrawal from direct contact with the disciples. He channeled that authority through the MO Letters, affirming them as "new scripture" that clarified or superseded the Bible, and was more likely to be of immediate value.

At times, Father David's claims to divine insight and authority seemed almost limitless.[33] And though he consistently emphasized his own humanity

FIGURE 1.2. "The King's Return."

and fallibility, he remained throughout his life (and beyond) the divinely anointed leader and spiritual guide for the Children. He also claimed the title of King of God's New Nation, with all the political authority and homage due the rightful king. After the necessity to win souls for Jesus, Father David's claim as prophet and king is the most consistent theme in Family life and literature. The full acceptance and affirmation of the Prophet's role and status was a central component of the socialization process. Disciples could remain in the Family harboring "doubts and struggles" over some of his more extreme claims, some viewing him as both a prophet and "a weird old man," but no open challenge to his position or authority was possible. Many of the disciples, particularly the females, developed an extraordinary emotional bond as well.

If anything, Father David's status has been enhanced by his death. And though Maria and Peter now rule over the Family as co-regents, Father David now sits at the very right hand of Jesus, in a much stronger position to lead and guide the Children.

The Spirit World

The work of Father David in heaven is consistent with long-established Family theology. Father David's direct encounters with the spirit world began in 1970, when the spirit of Abrahim, a fourteenth-century gypsy Christian, entered his body and began to speak through him. This was a watershed event for the Children of God.[34] The reality and immediacy of angels, spirit helpers, and dark spirits became an ever-increasing dynamic of Family life. Virtually every disciple regularly prays for and receives comfort, assurance, and guidance from God through dreams, visions, or experiences of "prophecy" in a context of personal or communal prayer.

Encounter with the spirit world seems to have escalated in the wake of a terrible tragedy that struck the Family in the summer of 1995. A van full of young people was involved in a serious accident. Five teenage girls were killed. Voices from the spirit world responded. Father David, Jesus, and the apostles Paul and Peter spoke in prophecy through several members of Maria's personal household. Soon, the spirits of the five young women began to communicate from the spirit world to other disciples, offering forgiveness to the driver and expressions of joy and ecstasy at being in heaven with Jesus and Father David. Even before this incident, many disciples recounted moving and profoundly shaping experiences of visions, dreams, and encounters with the spirit world.

The spirit world also has a dark side, however. The Devil and his demons are ever present and actively at work in the world. And the primary target is God's own special End Time People. Opposition and persecution, physical illness, community discord, lack of disciplined behavior in children, and personal failures of all types are primarily conceptualized as the result of Satan's attacks. The disciples are humorous people, with a wonderful capacity to laugh at themselves. But one never hears joking or in any way making light of evil spiritual forces. Father David clearly taught that Satan has no ultimate power over them, however. The disciples are confident that God is with them and that adequate spiritual power is accessible to eventually thwart any attack from the Dark Side.

In keeping with their understanding of spiritual forces, disciples practice a form of spiritual healing common to the Pentecostal wing of Protestant Evangelicalism. Conventional medical care is uniformly supported and disciples who pursue treatment for medical problems are not viewed as spiritually problematic. The fundamental cause of illness or physical affliction is most often understood to be spiritual, however. Thus it is reasonable and prudent to seek a spiritual cure as a first response.

The Children generally conceptualize problems, difficulties, and human weakness in distinctly spiritual terms. A significant number of young adults still carry unresolved resentments related to the treatment of their childhood misbehavior as a spiritual problem. However, most disciples are strengthened and empowered by their access to spiritual resources and power. The disciples interpret life as a profoundly spiritual adventure. This adventure is both personal and cosmic in scope.

The End of Days

Millennial expectation is a central focus of the movement's theology. David Berg taught that human history would climax in a worldwide political, economic, and moral meltdown. The Antichrist will arise to save the world and for three and a half years will establish his reign as a wise and benevolent leader. Then his true nature will be revealed. He will declare his divinity and require the world to worship and obey him, persecuting unto death all those who refuse. Satan, acting through the Antichrist, will have almost total control of the earth. All people will be required to carry the "Mark of the Beast" as a control mechanism. The Great Tribulation will last for three and a half years; then Christ will return for his Church. The Antichrist will be defeated in the Battle of Armageddon, Satan will be bound, and Christ will establish His millennial reign on earth. At the end of a thousand years, Satan will be released for one final confrontation. At Satan's ultimate defeat, the Kingdom of Heaven will be established forever, and God's Children will live with him in the Heavenly City.[35]

This overall construct is generally consistent with beliefs that are held in substantial sections of the Christian church. What distinguishes Family theology is the special role the Children will play in this grand drama, and the intensity of their conviction that the End Time is near.

The disciples do not "believe" the End is near; they know it. And they live out their lives accordingly. Early in the movement there was considerable hope that 1993 would be the time, and there was considerable disappointment as the year passed. Since then, the Family has been reluctant to set specific dates. But the knowledge that each day is lived in the shadow of the End remains a powerful dynamic and informs life at all levels. It continues to serve as the primary motivation and justification for the life of sacrifice and hardship.

Until very recently, Family disciples have been loath to make long-term plans for life in this world. Disciples do not plan for the future. The depth and intensity of the End Time vision clearly sets them apart. There is also a firm conviction that their separation from the world, absolute dependence on God, communal lifestyle, suffering, and hardship will uniquely prepare them both to survive the Great Tribulation and lead other faithful Christians through those very dark years.

The System

Family disciples have a strong sense of special status with God, a status that sets them in full and deadly opposition to the world that is under the control of Satan, the System. The System is evil, dangerous, corrupt to the core, and forms the fundamental "other."[36] And the disciples maintain as much distance from the System as possible. They hold passports, obtain driver's licenses, and get legally married when necessary. But they operate on the fringe, with as little interface with government or any other System institution as possible. They do not participate in civic life at any level. They educate their own children. They intentionally insulate themselves as much as possible. In general, this insulation extends to Christians outside the movement, especially the institutional church. This position has moderated over the last few years, and the disciples are much more open to working in cooperation with Christians outside their community. But they generally do not identify or establish "fellowship" with outsiders, and the basic view of the church as part of the System remains.

Their special status with God carries a high price. The disciples live in an environment of almost continual crisis. To survive and complete the assigned mission requires absolute dedication and a level of unity and discipline that can only be achieved through a structure of authority similar to that of a military establishment. Though authoritarianism has softened and the leadership structure is more open and democratic under the Charter of Rights, participation in God's elite End Time Army still requires total obedience to God, and to the structures of authority God has ordained in Father David and the leadership of that Army.

When questioned about the problems arising from the authority structure, many are quite open. Several themes consistently emerge. The era prior to 1978 is the Dark Age of the abuse of power. The disciples believe that changes in policy and spirit have worked to minimize the potential for mistreatment and abuse. However, the RNR did not alter the basic orientation that requires an authoritarian system of community organization and control.

Generally, the disciples hold a complex and somewhat ambivalent appreciation of the authoritarian nature of their movement. They accept the necessity of discipline and clear lines of authority. They are aware of trials, trauma, and abuse. Yet, even in the face of serious abuse and profound personal loss, disciples consistently attribute these difficulties to the character flaws of individuals. They do not find fault with the nature of the community, and especially not with the vision or leadership of Father David or Maria.

Radical commitment to Jesus, the prophethood of Father David, communion with the spirit world, and the End Time vision inform every facet of Family life. The Children have also retained their early vision of "Revolution for Jesus." And no aspect of their shared experience has been more revolutionary than the total restructuring of the sexual ethic.

Sexual Ethos

The renunciation of the "System," interplay with the spirit world, and authoritarian leadership structure has set the Family off as an unusual and distinctive religious movement. But it is their "revolutionary" theology of human sexuality that has marked them off, in the minds of many observers, as a dangerous cult. It is the single most distinguishing mark of this unusual community. The sexual lifestyle of the Family is grounded on two assumptions that flowed straight from the mind of the Prophet. The first premise is that sex is not only a clean and pure God-given gift, but also a basic human need, essentially no different from the need for sleep, food, or water. Therefore, it is not only acceptable but also a Christian duty to meet the need of a brother or sister.

The second premise flows out of the special nature of the time and the people. Father David taught the disciples that the close of the age required new and innovative understandings of God's purposes and his will. As well, the Children were God's chosen End Time Army, and as such had received a special dispensation, freeing them from some of the legal and ethical constraints that are normative to the less committed Christian community still operating in the System. This is "The Law of Love."[37]

Sexual purity was a key element of the early COG lifestyle. When the revolution came, however, it came swiftly and fully. Many could not make the adjustment and left. Those who stayed made the adjustment, and the new sexual ethos spread rapidly throughout the worldwide community. We have already addressed the three principal components of the revolution: sexual sharing, flirty fishing, and childhood sexuality.

Sexual sharing had a twofold purpose. The first was the straightforward enjoyment of sexual pleasure and fulfillment by as many disciples as possible. The other purpose was to break down old, System loyalties and allegiances, in order to establish primary loyalty to the Family and to the Prophet. By the early 1980s, the Family had reached a level of sexual freedom and experimentation rarely imagined—never mind practiced—by most human beings. Nudity was a common feature of home life. Father David lay open the possibility of lesbian intimacy, though he maintained a strong aversion to male homosexuality. Flirty fishing was ubiquitous, and the vast majority of women were having regular sexual encounters with both strangers and long-term "fish," in order to fulfill the mission and support the home. Sexual sharing with multiple partners became so commonplace that in some areas the home leader would post "sharing schedules" on the bulletin board. Twelve-year-old children were considered "adults" and often sexually initiated into the group. Sexual interplay with even younger children was never officially sanctioned, but did occur from time to time and place to place. But this almost limitless freedom came with a heavy price.

We have already addressed the dangerous and then life-threatening spread of sexually transmitted diseases throughout the movement. Beyond that immediate threat, it is not hard to imagine the strain such activity placed on normal marital and family relationships. And then there are the children. They suffered not only from direct sexual encounter but also from the instability of family life, never being quite sure whom their mother might be sleeping with the next night. It is little wonder that very few of the first wave of children remain in the Family.

In time, Family leadership became cognizant of these issues and began to address them. Flirty fishing was halted and all sexual contact with the outside world was banned.[38] Strictly enforced limitations were placed on the sexual experience of children, and fixed age limits were established for any sexual contact. And the practice of sexual sharing has cooled off considerably since the wild years of the early 1980s. For one thing, the first generation is beginning to gray, and it is hard to imagine them keeping up the pace. And the second generation paid the price for such rampant promiscuity. They are not anxious to head down that road. In general, the younger generation is considerably more conservative than their parents. But the essential theological convictions on which the sexual ethos is grounded remains intact. Though flirty fishing was halted, it was never repudiated. Quite the contrary, it is still viewed as a valid and proper technique for the times. And some women are nostalgic for the old days. The Law of Love, the Family theological position that all activity done in love is of God, remains in force, and sexual sharing is still a significant component of the Family lifestyle and an essential aspect of communal bonding. Maria has actually found it necessary, on several occasions, to admonish the older teens and young adults to be more sexual active, participating more fully in the "sexual fellowship" of the community.[39]

The continued prominent place of sexuality in Family ideology is clearly demonstrated in the most recent sexual innovation, the "Loving Jesus Revolution." Maria and Peter received revelations from Jesus that he was most pleased with their commitment and fulfillment of their mission, but was not fully satisfied with the level of their devotion and the expression of their love for him. Jesus wants it more clearly understood that the Children are his Bride, and he is their Husband.[40] To that end, in 1996 the Family began to incorporate the sex act into their private worship of Jesus. This is done though autostimulation or during sexual intercourse with a partner, imagining that partner as Jesus and expressing one's love for the Lord through the sexual partner. The Loving Jesus Revolution, like many of the innovative practices of the Family, was too much for some disciples, and they moved on. But in general the revolution has been accepted and is now a common feature of the disciples' devotional life. There is a place for "Loving Jesus" within group devotional experiences, but not in the presence of children.

The disciples have experienced any number of undulations in their sexual lifestyle. But there is little doubt that the "revolution" begun by Father David in the early 1970s lives on, and remains integral to Family identity.

The Future of the Family

It seems clear that the golden age of the "radical, revolutionary Children of God" is behind them. The disciples have matured considerably in the expression of the revolutionary components that remain. The Consider the Poor Ministry, the large number of the second generation who have left, and the more recent Activated Program are clearly blurring the once very sharp lines between discipleship and the System. The continual reduction in tension with the outside world is evident in many areas. The disciples still understand themselves to be God's unique End Time Army, however. The Family would like a truce with the greater church, but has no interest in joining the team.

Surely the greatest challenge facing the Family is an internal one. Their unique role in God's mission remains justified and energized by the passionate and unequivocal expectation of the imminent End of Days. Like many movements before them, they will have to come to terms with an extended stay in human history. But if the Family is anything, it is flexible. The have demonstrated a remarkable capacity to survive repression, persecution, monumental leadership failures, and radical theological restructuring. The have survived the death of the Prophet and come to terms with the loss of many of their youth. Given their eccentricities, it is doubtful that the Family will ever become a large movement. But they are a people filled with energy, confidence in their calling and mission, and above all hope. That hope has carried them though many dark nights, and there is no reason to believe that it will not carry them well into the future.

NOTES

1. "The Great Escape!" MO Letter #160. April 1972. Zurich: World Services.
2. "The Old Church and the New Church!" MO Letter #A, August 1969. Zurich: World Services.
3. "I Gotta Split?" MO Letter #28. December 1970. Zurich: World Services.
4. "Shiners?—or Shamers!" MO Letter #241. Zurich: World Services.
5. "The Shake—Up!—or Reorganization—The New Revolution Part 3—The Chain of Cooperation." MO Letter #328C. February 1975. Zurich: World Services.
6. "The Family of Love—Sin or Salvation?" General Publication #502R. Zurich: World Services.
7. "Re-organization Nationalization Revolution." MO Letter #650. January 1978. Zurich: World Services.
8. *The Story of Davidito.* 1982. Zurich: World Services.
9. "Fellowship Revolution." MO Letter #1001. April 1981. Zurich: World Services.
10. "Teen Terrors!" MO Letter #1512. May 1983. Zurich: World Services.
11. "The Seven Fs of Ffing." MO Letter #1083. January 1983. Zurich: World Services.

12. "The Devil Hates Sex!—But God Loves It!" MO Letter #999. May 1980. Zurich: World Services.

13. "Ban the Bomb!" MO Letter #1434. March 1983. Zurich: World Services.

14. "Sex with Babes?" MO Letter #1909. December 1984. Zurich: World Services.

15. "Discipleship Training Revolution." MO Letter #2677. Zurich: World Services.

16. "WS Advisory: "Tightening up Our Family." July 1989. Zurich: World Services.

17. "1994 Family Statistical Report." January 1995. Zurich: World Services.

18. "PEN—Persecution End Time News." October 1993. Zurich: World Services.

19. See "BI Case" in Chancellor 2000, 133–134.

20. "The Old Church and the New Church!" MO Letter #A, August 1969. Zurich: World Services.

21. "Go to the Churches." MO Letter #2867. Zurich: World Services.

22. "The Ministry of Reconciliation." *New Good News*, no. 653, October 1995. Zurich: World Services.

23. "Consider the Poor!—Our New Ministry in the U.S. to the Poor!" MO Letter #2755, March 1992. Zurich: World Services.

24. "The Board Vision." Good News #949 Charter Member/Full Member. August 2001. Zurich: World Services.

25. "The Shakeup 2000—The S2K!" Good News #3257. September 1999. Zurich: World Services.

26. "Coming Persecution: Conviction versus Compromise Part 1." Good News 957 Charter Member/Full Member. September 2001. Zurich: World Services.

27. "Understanding Prophecy!" Good News 876 Charter Member/Full Member. January 2000. Zurich: World Services.

28. "Three Gifts of the Lord's Love!" MO Letter #3005. March 1995. Zurich: World Services.

29. "Heading into 2002!" GN 3382A CM/FM. December 2001. Zurich: World Services.

30. Personal interview with Maria and Peter Amsterdam. October 2002.

31. "The Word, the Word, the Word!" MO Letter #2494. November 1988. Zurich: World Services.

32. See Chancellor 2000, Appendix A, for the complete less "Family Statement of Faith."

33. "A Psalm of David!" MO Letter #152. January 1972. Zurich: World Services. Also see "The Laws of Moses!" MO Letter #155. February 1972. Zurich: World Services.

34. "Abrahim the Gypsy King: The True Story of Our Spirit Guide." MO Letter #296. April 1970. Zurich: World Services.

35. See Chancellor 2000, Appendix A, Section 29, "Eschatological or Prophetic Considerations," 267–70.

36. "A Prophecy against Our Enemies!" MO Letter #188. October 1972. Zurich: World Services.

37. "The Law of Love!" MO Letter #302. March 1974. Zurich: World Services.

38. "The FFing/DFing Revolution—The Book Is the Hook!" MO Letter #2313, March 1987. Zurich: World Services. See also "Moma on the New AIDS Rules—Its Come to That!" MO Letter #2346. September 1987. Zurich: World Services.

39. Personal interview with Maria and Peter Amsterdam. October 2002.

40. "Loving Jesus Revelation!" MO Letters #3024 and #3025. July 1995. Zurich: World Services.

WORKS CITED

Primary Sources

"The Family History." Unpublished.
The Story of Davidito. 1982. Zurich: World Services.
The Book of the Future. 1984. Zurich: World Services.
PEN—Persecution End Time News. 1993. Zurich: World Services.
"The Ministry of Reconciliation." 1995. Zurich: World Services.
The MO Letters; Volumes 1 to 7. Zurich: World Services.

Secondary Sources

Bainbridge, William S. 2002. *The Endtime Family: Children of God.* Albany: State University of New York Press.
Bozman, John. 1998. "Field Notes: The Family/Children of God under the Love Charter." *Nova Religio* 2, no. 1: 126–35.
Bromley, David, and Sydney Newton. 1994. "The Family: History, Organization, and Ideology." In *Sex, Slander, and Salvation: Investigation of the Family/Children of God,* edited by James R. Lewis and J. Gordon Melton, 41–46. Stanford, Cal.: Center for American Publication.
Chancellor, James D. 2000. *Life in the Family: An Oral History of the Children of God.* Syracuse: Syracuse University Press.
Davis, Deborah. 1984. *The Children of God: The Inside Story.* Grand Rapids, Mich.: Zondervan Books.
Davis, Rex, and James T. Richardson. 1976. "The Organization and Functioning of the Children of God." *Sociological Analysis* 37: 321–39.
Lynch, Zelda. 1990. "Inside the 'Heavenly Elite': The Children of God Today." *Christian Research Journal,* summer: 16–21.
McMannus Una, and John Cooper. 1980. *Not for a Million Dollars.* Nashville: Impact Books.
Melton, J. Gordon. 1994. "Sexuality and the Maturation of the Family." In *Sex, Slander, and Salvation: Investigation of the Family/Children of God,* edited by James R. Lewis and J. Gordon Melton, 71–96. Stanford, Cal.: Center for American Publication.
Millikan, David. 1994. "The Children of God, Family of Love, the Family." In *Sex, Slander, and Salvation: Investigation of the Family/Children of God,* edited by James R. Lewis and J. Gordon Melton, 181–252. Stanford, Cal.: Center for American Publication.
Palmer, Susan. 1994. "Heaven's Children: The Children of God's Second Generation." In *Sex, Slander, and Salvation: Investigation of the Family/Children of God,* edited by James R. Lewis and J. Gordon Melton, 1–26. Stanford, Cal.: Center for American Publication.

Richardson, James T., and Rex Davis. 1983. "Experiential Fundamentalism: Revisions of Orthodoxy in Jesus Movement Groups." *Journal of the American Academy of Religion* 51, no. 3: 397–425.

Shepherd, Gary, and Lawrence Lilliston. 1994. "Field Observations of Young People's Experiences and Role in the Family." In *Sex, Slander, and Salvation: Investigation of the Family/Children of God,* edited by James R. Lewis and J. Gordon Melton, 57–70 Stanford, Cal.: Center for American Publication.

Van Zandt, David. 1991. *Living in the Children of God.* Princeton: Princeton University Press.

Vogt, Nancy R. 1998. "Correlates of Adolescent Sexual Activity in the Family, a Religious Group." Ph.D. dissertation, Fuller Theological Seminary, Pasadena, Cal.

Wallis, Roy. 1976. "Observations on the Children of God." *Sociological Review* 24: 807–29.

———. 1981. "Yesterday's Children: Cultural and Structural Change in a New Religious Movement." In *Social Impact of New Religious Movements,* edited by Bryan Wilson, 97–133. New York: Rose of Sharon Press.

———. 1987. "Hostages to Fortune: Thoughts on the Future of Scientology and the Children of God." In *The Future of New Religious Movements,* edited by David Bromley and Phillip E. Hammond, 80–90. Macon, Ga.: Mercer University Press.

Wangerin, Ruth. 1982. "Make-Believe Revolution: A Study of the Children of God." Ph.D. dissertation, City University of New York.

Williams, Miriam. 1998. *Heaven's Harlots: My Fifteen Years in a Sex Cult.* New York: William Morrow.

Wright, Stuart A. 1994. "From 'Children of God' to 'The Family': Movement, Adaptation, and Survival." In *Sex, Slander, and Salvation: Investigation of the Family/Children of God,* edited by James R. Lewis and J. Gordon Melton, 121–28. Stanford, Cal.: Center for American Publication.

2

Spirit Revelation and the Unification Church

James A. Beverley

On February 6, 2003, over eight thousand Unificationists gathered in Korea to witness the second marriage of Sun Myung Moon and his wife Hak Ja Han before God. This is believed by Unificationists to be the fulfillment of the Marriage Supper of the Lamb pictured in the Apocalypse of John. At the same time Unificationists also witnessed the coronation of Moon as king of all humanity. The followers of Sun Myung Moon believe that these events are crowning examples of the constant interplay between the drama of Moon's life and the unfolding events in the spirit realm.

Revelation from God and other spirit beings has always been a central element in Unification doctrine and life. This essay will focus on the changing patterns of revelation in the history of this new religion and pay particular attention to recent and significant developments in the unfolding of revelation to Reverend Moon. These changes have made the nature and style of Unification doctrine and experience more concrete, explicit, and also more problematic.[1]

The Reverend Sun Myung Moon was born in January 6, 1920, in what is now North Korea. Moon's parents converted to the Presbyterian Church when he was ten years old. Unificationists believe that Jesus appeared to Moon on April 17, 1935, and that he was asked to fulfill the mission of Jesus. This began a nine-year period of spiritual searching, in the midst of study in Seoul (1938–1941) and Japan (1941–1943).

Moon was married for the first time in November 1943. His wife gave birth to a son in April 1946, and two months later Moon traveled to North Korea. He did not see his family for six years. He was arrested in 1946, later released, and then taken prisoner by Communist authorities in 1948. United Nations forces freed Moon on October 14, 1950. He then began an arduous trek to the south and eventually reunited with his wife and son in November 1952.[2]

Moon's marriage ended in 1953, a result of the years of separation, his wife's lack of appreciation for Moon's spiritual calling, and the pastor's neglect of his wife. Moon officially launched the Holy Spirit Association for the Unification of World Christianity in 1954, though he had been preaching since 1946 and had gathered a small group of loyal followers.[3]

In 1959 Young Oon Kim, one of the most important Unification theologians, was sent to America.[4] The next year Reverend Moon married again, this time to Hak Ja Han, the young daughter of a devoted follower. Mrs. Moon had been born on January 6, 1943, and has given birth to thirteen children. She is known as True Mother and has exercised increasing influence in the Unification Church.

Moon visited the United States in 1965 and toured various states. The Korean prophet paid particular attention to his encounter with the famous medium Arthur Ford. Ford was able to receive messages from his spirit guide "Fletcher" about Moon's significance, though the medium did not endorse explicit claims about the alleged uniqueness of Moon.

Reverend Moon moved permanently to the United States in December 1971. He chose to support an embattled White House in 1973. The Unification endorsement of Nixon brought the church its first round of media criticism and scrutiny. The church also received notoriety for its giant rallies at Madison Square Garden (September 18, 1974), Yankee Stadium (June 1, 1976), and the Washington Monument (September 18, 1976). Moon became one of the most visible targets of the anticult movement, and his followers were often subject to kidnapping and deprogramming.[5]

The United States government charged Moon with income tax evasion on October 15, 1981. Although powerful religious groups protested Moon's indictment, the Korean leader was found guilty and sentenced to eighteen months in prison. He began his term in a prison in Danbury, Connecticut, in the summer of 1984 and was released from a Brooklyn halfway house on August 20, 1985. Moon viewed his trial and imprisonment with serenity and received significant sympathy during his time in custody.[6]

Moon's followers were elated by Moon's meetings with Mikhail Gorbachev on April 11, 1990, and with North Korean leader Kim Il Sung in November 1991. These strategic meetings were viewed as evidence of Moon's complete supremacy over communism. Moon took credit both for the fall of the Berlin Wall in 1989 and for the victory of the Allied Forces in the Persian Gulf War in 1991.

Since the mid-1990s, Reverend Moon has invested heavily in land purchase and development of Unification projects in South America. New Hope

East Garden is located in western Brazil and provides a vast site for educational and ecological work. The church has also bought thousands of acres of land in Uruguay. Unificationists regularly visit both countries for spiritual exercises, though the South American projects have received less attention in recent years.[7]

In 1998, Nansook Hong, Moon's former daughter-in-law, published a devastating memoir about life inside the church. Titled *In the Shadow of the Moons*, Hong accused her ex-husband, Hyo Jin Moon, of adultery, drug addiction, and physical and emotional abuse. Further, she claimed that Sun Myung Moon had an illegitimate child who was raised by another Unification family.[8]

Unificationists were shocked by the death of Moon's son, Young Jin, on October 27, 1999. Though police ruled his death a suicide, Reverend Moon proclaimed that the death was providential and that he died as a "sacrifice" so that Satan could not make a direct attack on the True Parents.[9] Two years later, there was a minor tempest when Archbishop Emmanuel Milingo wed Unification member Maria Sung. Milingo later renounced the marriage after a private meeting with the pope and accused the Unification Church of brainwashing him.[10]

The Unification movement has survived these recent crises, though Hong's book created considerable internal turmoil. However, criticism against Sun Myung Moon is met by most followers with complete confidence in what they believe that God has revealed through his life. Moon's directions are obeyed as God's commands, even if these instructions reverse long-standing Unification traditions.[11] The key is trust in God's ongoing revelations to Moon and the theology given to him from the eternal realm.

Unification Theology

The Unification movement retains the outline, though not always the substance, of classical Christian doctrine. *Divine Principle*, the famous Unification "Bible," has been the centerpiece in Unification evangelism and in-house teaching, though academics have often overstated its importance. Moon has always made it clear that his ongoing teachings and sermons constitute the most important source of modern revelation.[12]

The Unification Church is committed to monotheism and does not adopt a Trinitarian understanding of God. Though Moon adopts the use of Father, Son, and Holy Spirit in his language about God, his sermons show no interest in a Nicean understanding of God. Further, *Divine Principle* explicitly distances Unification doctrine from a classical understanding of the Son and the Spirit, though Moon constantly emphasizes his relationship with Jesus and his dependence on God's Spirit.[13]

Moon teaches that Satan seduced Eve sexually and then she engaged in sex with Adam before the providential time allowed by God. A ransom motif dominates Moon's interpretation of God's relationship with Satan. Satan has humans in captivity and God has to work within the boundaries of the protocol that exists between God, Satan, and humanity. The sins of the first couple extend to their blood lineage. God has been looking for a Messiah who would be the new Adam who finds a new Eve.[14]

Moon's understanding of salvation involves the redemption of humanity through the restoration of the family. This explains why Moon puts such great emphasis on the marriage ceremony ("the Blessing") as a central component of Unification ritual. Before Unificationists are married (usually in the famous mass weddings) they engage in the Holy Wine ceremony where they partake of wine derived from Moon's wedding ceremony in 1960.[15]

Moon's more esoteric teachings about Jesus build upon explicit views given in *Divine Principle*: first, that Jesus was not sent to die on the Cross; second, that Calvary was a secondary option that resulted largely from the disobedience of John the Baptist; and, third, that the ideal plan for Jesus was to have found a true Eve to restore humanity. Part of the alleged success of Moon is that he has been able to provide a bride for Jesus in the spirit realm.[16]

Unificationists frequently complain that their teaching on Jesus is misrepresented. At an early scholarly conference on Unification theology, Lynn Kim contended: "We never ever say Jesus failed. That's put on us from outside. We don't ever talk of Jesus as a failure."[17] George Chryssides, the British scholar, has defended Unificationists in his important work *The Advent of Sun Myung Moon*: "Unification Church members often find themselves foisted with the belief that Jesus' mission was a failure. *Divine Principle* does not say this at any point, and UC members feel justifiably indignant when their critics persistently ignored their attempts to explain what they really believe about Jesus."[18]

The chief obstacle to this assertion is the explicit teaching of the Unification leader himself. Moon stated in 1974 that he "must go beyond the failure of Adam, the failure of Abraham, the failure of Moses, the failure of Jacob, Moses and John the Baptist, and Jesus."[19] Moon has also objected to the prayer of Jesus in Gethsemane and his lament at Calvary that he felt forsaken by God. "Father does not accept Jesus' Gethsemane prayer, and the prayer of Jesus Christ on the Cross . . . he does not buy that kind of terrible statement."[20] Moon even contends that Jesus had a streak of selfishness in his walk with God, unlike the Korean leader.[21]

The traditional Christian view of the cross is being challenged in the recent call from Moon for churches to take down the cross. This campaign is being carried out through the American Clergy Leadership Conference and focuses on Black church leaders.[22] This action is defended both on the basis of God's original ideal and the desire to remove a major stumbling block to Jews and Muslims. Andrew Wilson, a leading Unification scholar and a Jew, has argued that "by emphasizing the act of rejecting and crucifying Jesus Christ, the cross sets up a high wall between those who accept Jesus and those who do not."[23]

Both the general contours and the specifics of the Unification system noted above are defended by reference to the claim that God has given new revelation through and about Sun Myung Moon. This apologetic is adopted in the very first section of *Divine Principle* and is emphasized repeatedly in Moon's sermons. It also emerges in the alleged spirit revelations that have dominated Unification life in the last two decades.

The Heavenly Ministry of an Ascended Son

Reverend Moon's second son, Heung Jin, sustained severe head injuries as a result of a car accident near Hyde Park, New York, in December 1983. He died in early January 1984. Moon claimed immediately that his son's loss was a providential act allowed by God in order to protect Moon's calling. "If the sacrifice of Heung Jin Nim had not been made, either of two great calamities could have happened. Either the Korean nation could have suffered a catastrophic setback, such as an invasion from North; or I myself could've been assassinated."[24]

Heung Jin was buried in Korea on January 8, 1984. A week later, Reverend Moon proclaimed that his son had a new mission and that he was free to travel between his spirit world and our physical world. Moon also proclaimed that Heung Jin became a leader to Jesus in the spirit realm and that he had assumed the role of "the commander-in-chief" to those who are unmarried in the spirit realm.[25]

On February 28, 1984, Heung Jin was married postmortem to Hoon Sook Pak, the daughter of Colonel Bo Hi Pak, one of Moon's top aides. Colonel Pak stated that his son-in-law's sacrifice "carries far greater importance then the crucifixion of Jesus Christ."[26] According to Moon, his son needed to be married in order to move from prince to king in the spirit realm. Hoon Sook was positive about her unusual marriage. "I will never forget in my whole life and for eternity this greatest honor of being Heung Jin Nim's bride, which I do not deserve."[27]

Shortly after the death of Heung Jin, Unificationists in different parts of the world claimed to be receiving messages from him. Most of the alleged revelations took place in 1984 and 1987 and were published in book form under the title *The Victory of Love*. In one message dated March 29, 1987, Heung Jin Jin said: "If you are afraid of me or if you fear that I will give you a heavy burden you're like a baby crying at the feet of Santa. I have more precious gifts in my bag than Santa could ever have and today I wish to give to each one of you the tools that you need to build the Kingdom of Heaven."[28]

Revelations are also claimed from St. Francis, St. Paul, Kierkegaard, and Jesus. The last speaks both of his submission to Heung Jin and the True Parents. "I will show them that the Lord of lords and the King of kings and the king of glory is our precious Lord Sun Myung Moon and his beloved bride Hak Ja Han. They reign as king and queen of the entire universe. I, Jesus of Nazareth, known as the Christ, bow in humility before them. Any who will follow me must do the same."[29]

If the death of Heung Jin can be seen as a Calvary for Sun Myung Moon, his postmortem ministry amounts to a second Easter. To this day Heung Jin remains the central child in the ongoing life of the Korean Messiah. Heung Jin's messages from the spirit realm have been foundational to the Unification movement in the last two decades, even as these revelations have been transmitted in rather unusual ways.

Another Heung Jin?

In the summer of 1987, Unificationist leaders heard that Heung Jin had returned to earth in the body of a church member from Zimbabwe. The Japanese missionary to Zimbabwe informed Chung Hwan Kwak, one of Moon's top aides, about the ministry of Heung Jin through the physical form of Cleopus Kundiona. In August 1987, Kwak traveled to Africa and met with the black Unificationist. In November, "Black" Hueng Jin came to America and met the Moon family at East Garden.

Takeru Kimiyama, a leading Japanese Unificationist, described the meeting: "Father and Mother were waiting in the reception area. Heung Jin Nim ran over to father and practically jumped into his arms, saying, 'Father! Father!' Then he embraced Mother tightly, crying, 'Mother! Mother!' He sounded like he was weeping."[30] Black Heung Jin led the church in revival meetings in New York, Washington, San Francisco, and other cities. Many Unificationists greeted him openly and wrote glowing testimonies about his positive impact on them. Other members, including some of the True Children, were skeptical of his claim to be the embodiment of Moon's deceased son.

Reverend Kwak suggested a positive attitude about Black Heung Jin: "If you had a relationship with Heung Jin before, don't try to question him about your former experience together. Many small details of our experience on Earth are [not] needed and forgotten when we go to the spirit world. We should have an open, humble, and penitent mind and accept him 100 percent."[31]

In his public meetings, Black Heung Jin urged serious confrontation about sin in the movement, and members were given severe conditions for repentance. In this connection, there were complaints from some members about excessive physical discipline at the hands of the Black Unificationist. There were reports about broken bones and of members being detained against their will. There were also complaints that Black Heung Jin had a legalistic under-standing of sexual issues.

The biggest controversy surrounding Black Heung Jin arose from the beat-ing of Bo Hi Pak, the father of Heung Jin's bride. Black Heung Jin disciplined Pak in a private session at the church's training center in Tarrytown, New York. Unificationists told me that Pak was beaten so badly that he was unrecogniz-able. He required surgery to relieve pressure on his brain. Michael Isikoff of the *Washington Post* reported that Col. Pak was admitted to a Georgetown hos-pital for tests from December 9 to 17.[32]

Reverend Moon allowed Black Heung Jin to continue his ministry at con-ferences through the early part of 1988 and then told him to return to Zim-babwe. Later that same year it was clear that Black Heung Jin had distanced himself from the ideology and practice of the Unification movement. He re-portedly impregnated the wife of the Japanese missionary to his country and taught that he was the Lord of the Second Advent and that Reverend Moon was a precursor to his ministry.

The Unification Church did not publish much material from Black Heung Jin. His counsel to the Apostle Paul was included, along with messages from the ascended Heung Jin in *A Victory of Love*. "Paul had resentment because some people said he failed. He did not fail; it was Peter who failed his mission. I told him, 'Paul, you did not fail.' He grabbed me and exclaimed, 'Is it really true?' And I assured him it was." Black Heung Jin also claimed that he had some direct words for John the Baptist: "you failed, but now you should just go ahead; hold the dispensation of restoration. Don't sleep and don't cry about your head being cut off."[33]

Revelation for Ancestral Liberation

Though the Unification movement has never abandoned belief in the spirit realm, the debacle with Black Heung Jin created some unease about spirit mediums. However, since 1995 church members have been directed by Sun Myung Moon to pay particular attention to two different mediums who are in contact with Heung Jin and others in the spirit world. The first is Mrs. Hyo Nam Kim, who receives messages from both Heung Jin and Dae Mo Nim, the deceased mother of Hak Ja Han (Mrs. Sun Myung Moon).

Dae Mo Nim is actually the honorific title given both to Soon-Ae Hong (Hak Ja Han's mother) and to Mrs. Kim. Reverend Moon's mother-in-law was born on February 22, 1914. She was involved with several of the native Korean churches that had an impact on Sun Myung Moon's theology. She met Moon in 1955, joined his church, and saw her daughter married to him in 1960. She lived with the Moon family in the United States for many years, returned to Korea in 1979, and died in early November 1989.

After her death, she was assigned a mission in the spirit realm by the True Parents. She was told to work with Heung Jin and help liberate the ancestral realm and subjugate Lucifer to God's plans. Mrs. Hyo Nam Kim was given the responsibility to be the earthly partner to Dae Mo Nim. Mrs. Kim was born on March 13, 1952, and was a relatively unknown figure in the church until her public ministry for Dae Mo Nim began in 1995.[34]

Mrs. Kim claims that she was chosen to work with Dae Mo Nim in 1979. After Dae Mo Nim's death, Mrs. Kim passed a series of tests over a period of two years. She was able to find five sacred trees and a sacred body of water that were chosen by Reverend Moon as holy sites. She endured a forty-day prayer vigil without sleep, where she made 10,300 full bows to Dae Mo Nim and she had to plunge in icy cold water in the dead of winter in order to resist Satan. Mrs. Kim adopted a hairstyle to match that of Dae Mo Nim. Angels are said to have changed the color of her eyes to match those of her heavenly mentor.

Mrs. Kim leads renewal and liberation workshops at the Unification retreat center at Chung Pyung Lake in Korea. Reverend Moon has ordered all Unificationists to participate in her ongoing ministry. Moon believes that Mrs. Kim is helping Heung Jin and the heavenly Dae Mo Nim work with his own mother (Choong Mo Nim) to redeem the souls of ancestors and to renew the lives of Unificationists on earth. Church members are urged to liberate their ancestral lineage from demonic influence and from the toll of human iniquity that plagues generations. Details about one workshop said it costs $1,400 to liberate both sides of a family, though this figure involves only the first generation.

Mrs. Kim can be blunt as she engages in spiritual warfare. At one conference in England in 1998, she stated: "The children must be kept quiet! There are many spirits here out of your bodies yelling and screaming at me. When I get spirits out with the help of angels they try and come to plead their case; there are so many now out in front of me yelling and screaming, talking to me. I am talking to you but also to the spirits at the same time. The children are making so much noise; I am having a difficult time talking to you. Those of you with children who make noise: please calm them down or take them out." She also offers very specific guidance about purity. "I see people wearing shirts so short that they are showing their belly buttons and trousers so long that they drag on the floor—our second generation should not do such things—we should look neat and clean. God is clean and pure and God is a beautiful God so we must keep ourselves clean and neat. So boys, young men should not have long hair, Satan likes that a lot. Also no earrings on the ears. You should make yourself look neat and clean so that God can love you."[35]

In a speech to husbands at Chung Pyung Lake, Mrs. Kim warned of the danger of smoking and drinking. "For those who smoke, you must understand that the smell lingers, even years after you quit. It's in your skin, in your body, down to the bone. And you may not believe me, but both drinking and smoking lead to the sexual fall. Smoking creates such a low spiritual atmosphere and invites many low spirits. Smoking and drinking open up many holes in your spirit for satanic spirits to invade."[36]

Mrs. Kim's work gained particular fruition at the mass Unification Blessing held at RFK Stadium in Washington on November 29, 1997. On that day she was able to work with Dae Mo Nim to liberate many ancestors from the spirit realm. The founders of the world's great religions attended the ceremony, including Buddha, Jesus, Muhammad, and Confucius. In early 1999, Mrs. Kim sent 106 missionaries to America from the spirit world, including Aquinas, John Calvin, Martin Luther, Saint Matthew, and even doubting Thomas. The Unification movement recently announced that Mrs. Kim has dispatched angels to leading hospitals in the world to do research that can be used at the retreat center.[37]

Heung Jin and a Scholar's Revelations

The second aspect of Unification spirit mediumship involves Dr. Sang Hun Lee, a famous Unification scholar who died on March 22, 1997. Immediately after his death Young Soon Kim, a Unificationist, claimed to be receiving messages from Heung Jin and from Dr. Lee. The first revelations from 1997 and 1998 were published in the book *Life in the Spirit World and on Earth* and include details about his death and his wishes for his immediate family.

The book also contains passing comments about details of life in the spirit realm, explanations of Unification doctrine, and records of Dr. Lee's meeting with leading religious and political figures. Lee tells Young Soon Kim that the cars used in heaven can move very fast, propelled by thought projection. Unificationists have special privileges, and a prison holds those who have committed grave sins. Spirit beings cannot improve without help from their family members on earth—a notion that fits with the ancestral liberation done by Dae Mo Nim.

According to Lee, Jesus is lonely in the spirit realm and will not advance to Heaven until the True Parents arrive. Mary and Joseph are strangers to one another. Buddha regrets that he did not know about God, Lee states, while Confucius spends a lot of time in meditation in the snow. Muhammad was difficult to visit, Socrates was egotistical and argumentative, and Judas was resistant to talking. Eve admitted to Lee that she found Lucifer irresistible, confirming Unification teaching that Eve had sex with the fallen angel.

Lee also met with the former North Korean leader Kim Il Sung, who said that "North Korea will perish" unless his son learns to follow Reverend Moon. Lee found Karl Marx shouting communist slogans while surrounded by shabby buildings and people "who looked like remnants of a defeated army." Lenin was plotting a revolution in the spirit realm, while Hitler was hanging naked on a tree, being attacked by angry mobs of former victims. *Life in the Spirit World and On Earth* also contains a letter from Jesus that states that he is not worthy of the love of Sun Myung Moon.[38]

The revelations from Dr. Lee have continued. In 1999, Young Soon Kim received a lot of material about and by Lucifer, including letters of repentance that were written to God. In 2000, Lee sent an elaborate set of new confessions from Saint Augustine. This was followed the next winter and spring by statements from four major religious leaders (Buddha, Confucius, Muhammad, and Jesus). In the summer and fall of 2001, Lee passed on messages from 120 Christian leaders that were released under the title "God Is the Parent of Humankind." This ran as an advertising supplement in *The Washington Times*.

Young Soon Kim also received a major report from Lee about a meeting he conducted on Christmas Day, 2001, with the leaders of the five major religions. The fathers of Buddhism, Hinduism, Confucianism, and Islam met with Jesus to proclaim their total alignment with the True Parents. This document was translated from Korean into English and then published in July 2002 in some of the major newspapers of the world as "A Cloud of Witnesses." In 2002, Lee also sent messages from 120 Communist leaders and then 12 journalists to record their endorsement of Moon. In 2003, the Unification movement released Lee's channeled messages from thirty-six deceased presidents of the United States, all testifying to their recognition of the truth and importance of Reverend Moon's life and message.[39]

The general theme of the entire corpus from Lee involves a multifaceted endorsement of Moon, expressed in an unequivocal manner, making it abundantly clear that the Korean prophet is the true Messiah, the Lord of lords, and the ultimate eternal answer to all problems, both on earth and in the spirit world. Though some Unification scholars have tried to argue for an ecumenical reading of these documents, their pleadings seem hollow in light of the dogmatic and exclusivist language of all the messages.

For example, Judas reports that Jesus was deeply distressed at the pain brought to God by his earthly mission and by the work Moon endured "to reorganize that remorseful history." Jesus prayed in great distress, and "some disciples were choked with tears, and others cried stamping their feet or hitting their own bosoms." The Apostle Paul recanted his teaching on predestination in light of Dr. Lee's lectures, as did John Calvin. Thomas Aquinas states that Divine Principle lectures "will develop endlessly here, like clouds gathering at one place in the sky."

Karl Barth, the famous Reformed theologian, has been particularly upset about his failed theology. According to Lee, Moon's teaching "puts Karl Barth to shame and has silenced him." Barth recognizes that he has led "a meaningless life and is an incredibly incapable person." The Swiss professor proclaims: "Theologians of today, raise up your heads! Open your two eyes and pay attention." He ends his declaration: "The Second Coming, Reverend Moon, Savior of humanity, and our True Parent, I thank you. Please save my fellow theologians."

Charles Russell, Mary Baker Eddy, and Joseph Smith each announce that they have turned to Divine Principle as truth. Pope John XXIII pledges his commitment to teach Unification principles, as does Henry VIII, George Whitfield, St. Francis, Karl Rahner, and George Whitfield, among others. Whitfield states: "Even after ransacking every chapter and verse in the Bible from Genesis to Revelation, we couldn't come across any clarification as crystal clear as the Unification Principle." Count Zinzindorf claims that Reverend Moon is "marvelously neat," and Roger Williams states that he will contact all the Baptists in the spirit realm and get them to attend Unification lectures.

The declaration of the five religious leaders from Christmas Day, 2001, is quite explicit about affirmation of Moon's centrality and commitment to serve him. The text reads in part: "We resolve and proclaim that Reverend Sun Myung Moon is the Savior, Messiah, Second Coming and True Parent of all humanity," and "We resolve and proclaim that the Unification Principle is a message of peace for the salvation of humanity and the gospel for the Completed Testament Age." The text ends with these words: "The representatives of the five great religions resolve and proclaim that we will harmonize with one another, unite and move forward, in order to bring about the nation of God and world peace, while attending [the] True Parents."

The revelations from thirty-six former U.S. presidents adopts the same stance toward Sun Myung Moon. From George Washington to Lyndon Johnson, each president gives a testimony about discovering the true ideology in Unificationism. No statement is given from Richard Nixon, though he served as representative and led his colleagues in a cheer for God and Reverend Moon. The presidents included in their declaration the affirmation: "We resolve and proclaim that Reverend Sun Myung Moon is the Lord of the Second Advent, the Messiah, the Savior and the True Parent."[40]

Spirit Revelations and the Mind of a Messiah

How should scholars of new religions respond to the nature of the modern revelations in the Unification movement? Further, what are the larger implications of the stress placed on these revelations during the twilight years of Moon's life? Stanley Johannesen, a Canadian scholar, has made a point about Moon's *Divine Principle* that may have some relevance. He suggested that the text of the movement is ideologically unstable and that it contains a "a vast, and swiftly accumulating, burden of anxious responsibility." He worried that the book's "extraordinary demands on personality" could lead either to "the narcotizing of temperament in self-defense or the radical internalizing of cosmic mission in the form of compulsive, megalomaniacal work obsession with fantasies of superhuman personal significance and authority."[41]

Although Johannesen hoped for maturation in Unification faith, his concerns bear scrutiny in relation to the issue of divine revelation through Moon's son and other mediums. The Korean Messiah reveals in his sermons and in the recent focus on spirit revelations an anxiety that illustrates an extraordinary demand on self, one that has manifested in terms of a "cosmic mission" that is compulsive and narcissistic, with constant assertions of "superhuman personal significance and authority." The revelations from Heung Jin and the other Unification mediums have a compulsive tone to them and share an obsessive emphasis on defending Sun Myung Moon. In his sermons Moon is also too concerned about self-apology. He brags about his grasp of literature, "and even boasts about his head size."[42] Moon claims that he could have won "dozens of different doctorates in different fields."[43] Moon asked this question in one sermon: "What if I did not exist? It would be as if all the world were here but were empty."[44] In 1976, he told his followers: "I really keep the FBI busy trying to keep track of me. After the Washington Monument Rally their biggest question was what in the world I would do next. Even Satan is saying, 'What is Reverend Moon's next move? Where should I take my big guns?' But most important is that even God is asking, 'Where are you going next?' My plan is simple and clear, I am inexorably moving toward the absolute center of the universe."[45]

Scholars of Unificationism have in Moon's sermons a wealth of primary material about his understanding of self, particularly in relation to his belief in God's calling in his life. This self-understanding is mirrored in the spirit revelations from his son and other mediums. The picture of grandiosity that emerges in his sermons synchronizes with the unrelenting focus and apologetic given to Moon in the alleged communications from beyond. This is a pattern that contrasts with both Moon's explicit commands to humility and the sacrificial and humble path chosen by most of his followers.[46]

Appeal of the Unification Church

At the height of what Bromley and Shupe called "the great American cult scare" of the 1970s, the appeal of Sun Myung Moon and his church was often explained on the basis of brainwashing theories.[47] It is still commonly believed that certain religious groups known as "cults" recruit members through brainwashing techniques.[48] But Eileen Barker showed in her magnificent work *The Making of a Moonie* that there is little to support brainwashing as a plausible theory for why people joined the Unification Church or remained in the movement.[49] Better explanations lie in the more mundane realities of religious and social life. First, many of Moon's ideas are rooted to some extent in the religious milieu of Korea during his early years, where there were several groups contending that the messiah prophesied in the New Testament would come from Korea. Second, Moon's first followers would have been drawn to his dynamic and passionate faith, and to himself as a visionary who endured torture and jail for his beliefs. Whatever one may say critically about Moon, he is an amazing survivor.

Converts to the Unification Church have often been introduced to Sun Myung Moon through an extensive series of lectures about the Divine Principle. This apologetic would leave the impression, especially among the uninformed, that the Unification ideology was rooted in careful biblical study and the unfolding of progressive revelation. Moreover, Unificationists have always believed that Moon's life and mission clearly duplicated those of Jesus.

Beyond this, the Unification Church has always excelled at public relations and image. Church publications have constantly documented the fact that many of the world's leading academics have taken part in Unification-sponsored events. Moon has continually attracted famous politicians, clergy, media figures, and even Hollywood stars. *The Unification News* and *Today's World* picture Moon in poses with figures like Jerry Falwell and former President Bush. Ex-Polish leader Lech Walesa attended the Unification-sponsored World Summit on Leadership and Governance in Seoul in February 2003.[50]

Moon has obviously gained credibility through his many educational, media, political, and religious organizations. He achieved significant attention when he founded *The Washington Times* in 1982, as he was facing income tax charges by the United States government. He also owns the *Segye Times* (Korea) and *The Middle East Times* (Cairo) and took over United Press International (UPI). He is the founder of the International Conference on the Unity of the Sciences, the Professors World Peace Academy, the Summit Council for World Peace, and the World Media Conference, among other educational and political enterprises. He also started the Sun Moon University in Korea, and the movement runs Bridgeport University in Connecticut. Moon is credited with initiating the International Highway Project, attempting to unite China, Korea, and Japan. Moon has founded ballet and dance schools (most notably the "Little Angels" program) and is also involved in support of the World Culture and Sports Festival. He also created the Women's Federation for Peace in Asia.

Critics of Moon often refer to the Unification "front groups."[51] Though Unification organizers sometimes hide Moon's connection, the diverse portfolio of the movement is best understood as a genuine attempt to address all aspects of life in terms of a Unification worldview. Unificationists receive strong justification for their faith in light of Moon's wide-ranging vision and also in relation to the endorsements given by the leaders who participate in his multifaceted projects and conferences. The 176-page volume "The Hope of

All Ages" illustrates the apologetic power of Moon's projects. Released on the occasion of Moon's eighty-second birthday, the book contains elaborate commendations of Moon by political, academic, and religious leaders, including E. V. Hill (former pastor of Mt. Zion Baptist Church), Kessai Note (president of the Marshall Islands), Dan Quayle (former U.S. vice president) and Dae Wood (Korean Buddhist priest and poet), among many others. There are several writers who argue that Sun Myung Moon should be nominated for the Nobel Peace Prize. The praise of the many authors is often directed toward Moon's vision as expressed in the conferences, organizations, newspapers, and educational institutions that he finances.[52]

The direct appeal of the Unification Church, of course, lies in the power of a utopian vision fostered by a dedicated and committed following. The movement's exoteric message is one of radical love for God, professed allegiance to Jesus Christ, openness to all religions, and deep commitment to solving the world's problems. In spite of his egocentrism and his heterodox teachings, Moon has inspired a generation of highly moral and loving disciples. Moon's followers are his best advertisement as they work tirelessly to obey their messiah's call to love and to serve.

Both the endorsement of Moon by the world's elite and the persecution of Moon by his detractors are viewed as proof that the spirit world is behind the Korean prophet. The long-standing focus on messages from that world serves as ongoing reinforcement for Moon's claim to be the Second Coming of Jesus Christ. What will be fascinating to witness is how the Unification movement adapts to new or competing revelations when the Korean messiah passes beyond his earthly sojourn.

NOTES

1. Some parts of this essay build on a more limited essay of mine in Ronald Enroth's edited volume on new religions to be published by InterVarsity Press in 2004.

2. For biographical data on Moon's early years, see Michael Breen, *Sun Myung Moon* (West Sussex: Refuge, 1997).

3. On the church, see Massimo Introvigne, *The Unification Church* (Salt Lake: Signature, 2000).

4. The most significant work on the American Unification movement is Michael Inglis, ed., *40 Years in America* (New York: HSA, 2000). The historical material is written by Michael Mickler, a leading Unification scholar.

5. See David Bromley and Anson Shupe, Jr., *"Moonies" in America* (Beverly Hills: Sage, 1979).

6. For a sympathetic portrayal of Moon's tax case, see Carlton Sherwood, *Inquisition* (Washington, D.C.: Regnery Gateway, 1991).

7. See Moon, "New Hope Farm Declaration" (April 3, 1995); this and other Moon articles cited here are available at www.unification.org. For critical perspectives

on Moon's South American ventures, see Tom Gibb, "Brazil Probes Moonie Land Purchases," *BBC News* (February 28, 2002), available at www.bbc.co.uk.

8. Nansook Hong, *In the Shadow of the Moons* (Boston: Beacon, 1998). See also James A. Beverley, "Moon Struck," *Christianity Today*, November 16, 1998. In a conversation I had with Nansook Hong in Toronto she reversed her opinion expressed in an interview with Mike Wallace that Reverend Moon was a con artist. Upon further reflection, she stated that she thought he was totally convinced of his messianic status.

9. James A. Beverley, "Son's Death Shakes Up Unification Church," *Christianity Today*, December 13, 1999.

10. For details on the Milingo affair, see the reports at www.cesnur.org and www.archbishopmalingo.org.

11. One of the most significant changes involved Moon's announcement at the church's fortieth anniversary in 1994 that focus was to turn from the church to the newly founded Family Federation for World Peace and Unification.

12. In 1997 Moon announced the new tradition of Hoon Dok Hae, in which disciples spend 6 a.m. to 7 a.m. every day in the study of the most important of Moon's sermons.

13. Moon's sermons are replete with references to his unparalleled obedience to God, but there are also frequent hints that God is fortunate to have Moon on his side. "I know I am the only person on earth who truly knows God and can comfort him. God has now said I have done enough and He told me to relax because He has been comforted by me, but that is the one command from God that I am defying." See Moon, "The Stony Path of Death," April 27, 1980, p. 5.

14. See Moon, "CAUSA Seminar Speech," August 29, 1985, p. 4.

15. Couples also participate in what is known as the Indemnity Stick ceremony. The custom has roots in Korean shamanism; Moon mandates the couple to beat each other on the posterior. This physical discipline is to teach both the need for human involvement in the salvific process and the pain and humiliation connected with physical abuse. After the Blessing and a period of waiting, married couples follow a special Three-Day ceremony during which specific sexual positions are followed in order to reverse the impact of the distorted sexuality that brought humanity's fall. For analysis, see Ed Mignot, "Married Rituals in Tongil," *Areopagus*, Trinity 1989, pp. 36–37.

16. According to Moon, Jesus is the product of a sexual relationship between Mary and Zechariah, the father of John the Baptist. Joseph never discovered who was the real father of Jesus. Moon even claims that Mary and Joseph purposely left Jesus behind in Jerusalem when he was visiting at Passover at age twelve. Moon states in one sermon that Jesus was actually at the temple "because he was forsaken by his mother and father." Moon adds: "The fact that Jesus could not get married was directly due to the failure of responsibility on Mary's part. How can Mary be a great woman?"

17. Lynn Kim, quoted in Darrol Bryant and Susan Hodges, eds., *Exploring Unification Theology* (New York: Rose of Sharon, 1978), p. 31.

18. George Chryssides, *The Advent of Sun Myung Moon* (New York: St. Martin's, 1991), p. 32. Chryssides's work is usually accurate but contains strained apologetics.

His inadequate attention to esoteric literature is documented in my Ph.D. thesis; see James A. Beverley, "The Religious Teachings of Sun Myung Moon," University of Saint Michael's College, 1994.

19. Moon, "Human Life," December 1, 1974, p. 11.

20. Moon, "Address to the Prayer and Fast Participants," July 29, 1974, p. 6.

21. Moon, "The Way Our Blessed Family Should Go," August 28, 1971, p. 12.

22. See www.aclc.info for Web site data. Some Christian clergy have reported supernatural events connected with the removal of the cross from their churches.

23. Wilson, "Removing the Curse of the Cross," lecture at Unification-sponsored conference in Jerusalem in May 2003. Available at www.tparents.org.

24. Moon, "Let Us Go over the Hill," February 7, 1984, p. 9. Available at www .tparents.org.

25. Moon, "The Necessity for the Day of Victory of Love," January 15, 1984, p. 12. Available at www.tparents.org.

26. *Today's World,* January-February 1984, p. 7.

27. *Blessing Quarterly,* Winter 1984–1985, p. 11.

28. *The Victory of Love* (New York: Holy Spirit Association for the Unification of World Christianity, 1992), p. 42.

29. Ibid., p. 65.

30. See *Today's World,* January 1988, p. 28.

31. "Guidance from Reverend Kwak," *Today's World,* January 1988, pp. 26–27.

32. See the *Washington Post,* March 30, 1988.

33. *The Victory of Love,* p. 259.

34. The most detailed study on Mrs. Kim is found in Chang Skik Yang, "Understanding Dae Mo Nim's Earthly Activity," four-part series at www.tparents.org.

35. Mrs. Kim, "The Chung Pyung Providence," lecture at Cleeve House, December 1998. Available at www.tparents.org.

36. Mrs. Kim, "Living a Life with No Shadows," lecture at Chung Pyung, January 2002. Available at www.tparents.org.

37. For full documentation on data about Mrs. Kim, see the material under "Dae Mo Nim" at www.tparents.org.

38. See Sang Hun Lee, *Life in the Spirit World and on Earth* (New York: Family Federation for World Peace and Unification, 1998).

39. The various documents from Lee can be seen at www.tparents.org.

40. Many of the Lee revelations are available in book form and on the Internet at www.messagesfromspiritworld.info.

41. See Johannesen, in Frank Flinn, ed., *Hermeneutics and Horizons* (New York: Rose of Sharon, 1982), pp. 310–311.

42. Moon, "Today in the Light of Dispensational History," February 23, 1977, p. 13; Moon, "Good Day," July 3, 1977, p. 7, and "Day of All Things," June 13, 1980, p. 7.

43. Moon, "The Blessing," February 20, 1977, p. 13.

44. Moon, "Our Family in Light of the Dispensation," March 1, 1977, p. 15.

45. Moon, "The Final Warning Concerning Good and Evil," December 26, 1976, p. 9. Moon has even argued that God had finally learned the true meaning of love because of him. "God has to be educated. People will say that I am a heretic, but it is

true. God doesn't know about love—He hasn't experienced it before. God has no sexual organs, so until a man becomes one with God, he cannot experience making love to a woman. Through me, God has done this." See Moon, "God's Day Morning Address," January 1, 1990, p. 2.

46. For concerns about spiritual grandiosity, see comments in Dick Anthony, Bruce Ecker, and Ken Wilber, eds., *Spiritual Choices* (New York: Paragon, 1987), pp. 69, 167–168, 190, 341.

47. See David Bromley and Anson Shupe, *Strange Gods* (Boston: Beacon, 1981).

48. For an example of recent scholarly exchange about brainwashing, see Benjamin Zablocki and Thomas Robbins, eds., *Misunderstanding Cults* (Toronto: University of Toronto Press, 2002). Also note Jack Hitt, "The Return of the Brainwashing Defense," *New York Times*, December 15, 2002.

49. Eileen Barker, *The Making of a Moonie* (Oxford: Basil Blackwell, 1984).

50. For information on the program, see the Web site of the Family Federation for World Peace and Unification at www.familyfed.org.

51. For a very helpful and extensive listing of such "front" groups, see the data on the Unification Church at www.freedomofmind.com. The site features the work of Steve Hassan, an ex-Unificationist, and one of the most influential exit counselors dealing with new religions. Other significant ex-member sites are at www.xmoonies .com (Craig Maxim) and www.allentwood.com (Allen Tate Wood).

52. Thomas G. Walsh, Gordon L. Anderson, and Theodore Shimmyo, eds., *Hope of All Ages* (Tarrytown, N.Y.: Interreligious and International Federation for World Peace, 2002).

3

Reconstructing Reality: Conspiracy Theories about Jonestown

Rebecca Moore

As I was describing this chapter to a colleague during a taxicab ride at a conference, I noticed that our driver was listening intently. When we got out of the cab, I asked him what he thought. He said it was "interesting." Coincidentally or not—in the world of conspiracism there are no coincidences—the same driver picked us up later that evening. I asked what he knew about Jonestown; he said that he had been in the Air Force in November 1978, and had been in contact with people who participated in the evacuation of the 913 bodies of Peoples Temple members who died there. The CIA was definitely involved in Jonestown, he said, but things got out of control when the congressman was killed. The discussion then turned to Waco, the Branch Davidians, and the government conspiracy there, and to Timothy McVeigh, who was then awaiting execution for the Oklahoma City bombing. Our conversation with the cabbie revealed what we more or less already knew: that the official accounts of the murders and suicides that occurred in Jonestown, Guyana, have generated belief in a number of conspiracy theories. This chapter discusses what these theories are, and why they have arisen.

On 18 November 1978, residents of the Peoples Temple agricultural project assassinated Congressman Leo Ryan, and killed four others at a remote airstrip in the northwest corner of Guyana. At their settlement a few miles away, Temple leader Jim Jones assembled more than nine hundred followers who then ingested a mixture of potassium cyanide and tranquilizers in a fruit punch, either voluntarily or by force.

Initial accounts were conflicting. It was not clear if weapons had been involved. The reported number of those who died kept increasing as more and more bodies were uncovered. The appearance of the dead—laid out in neat rows—raised questions about how they died. Was it suicide or was it murder? The quantity of psychoactive drugs at the settlement seemed to indicate the possibility of widespread behavioral control or modification. In addition to the sheer magnitude of the numbers, the utter incomprehensibility of parents taking their children's lives generated shock and disbelief. Skepticism thus arose concerning reports on the exact sequence of events.

At the same time, conspiracy theories about Jim Jones, about the assassination of Ryan, and about the nature of the agricultural project itself took root shortly after November 1978. Within weeks, political activist Dick Gregory claimed that CIA-FBI forces killed the people in Jonestown in order to use their bodies to smuggle heroin into the United States (Hall 305). In 1979 an organization sponsored by the Church of Scientology began to circulate reports that a CIA agent had been present in Jonestown at the time of the deaths (Alliance for the Preservation of Religious Liberty). In addition, Joe Holsinger, Congressman Ryan's legislative assistant, testified before the House Foreign Affairs Subcommittee on International Operations in 1980 that the CIA had a covert operation in Guyana. Those comments would later serve in part as the source for a number of conspiracy theories. A report dated 20 July 1980 by Infor-

FIGURE 3.1. Jim Jones.

mation Services Company notes connections between the CIA and Jim Jones, as well as CIA interest in Guyana politics. The document connects the Hughes-Ryan Amendment of 1974, which required prior review of CIA and National Security Council operations, with the death of one of its cosponsors at the Port Kaituma airstrip (Information Services Company).

In the twenty-three years since the deaths in Jonestown, conspiracy theories have blossomed in number and sophistication. Time has not adequately answered the initial questions. Rather it has spawned new questions, with new and surprising answers. These answers constitute what I would call a canon of conspiracy theories.[1] Some are more plausible than others. Some are better researched. All of them attempt to explain the mysteries and ambiguities that available narratives fail to address.

This article focuses on some specific conspiracy theories about Jonestown, after first discussing the nature of conspiracy theories in general. The Jonestown theories fall into three main categories: those produced by professional conspiracists who tend to see conspiracies everywhere; a subgroup of the professionals, which comprises Internet conspiracy sites; and those theories developed by nonprofessionals that concentrate primarily on Jonestown. What these theories demonstrate is that in the absence of a credible narrative—that is, a believable reconstruction of what happened in Jonestown and why—alternative explanations arise. The conspiracy theories attempt to make sense of what appears ultimately senseless: that parents willingly killed their children and their elders, and that they willingly chose a rather painful death. Instead of accepting this possibility, the conspiracy theories provide alternatives that blame conspirators for the deaths. The theories argue for coercion, either through external violence or internal "brainwashing," enforced by a few individuals. Furthermore, they reject the possibility that Jonestown residents made a rational choice in terminating their collective project through what they considered mercy killings and suicide. Indeed, the presupposition of most of the conspiracists is that Jonestown residents did *not* make a choice. This view challenges most popular and scholarly accounts of the events of 18 November 1978.

Conspiracy Theories

The title of this chapter, "Reconstructing Reality," may suggest that I have a clear and accurate picture of what the reality of Jonestown was. I do not. At issue here is not the truth or falsity of these conspiracy theories, but rather their nature and purpose in explicating the Jonestown tragedy. As David Brion Davis notes, "[T]he phenomenon of countersubversion might be studied as a special language or cultural form, apart from any preconceptions of its truth or falsity" (Davis xv). I plan to examine the phenomenon of conspiracism in light of Davis' observation, rather than to refute any theory.

The word "conspiracy" works much the same way the word "cult" does to discredit advocates of a certain view or persuasion. Historians do not use the word "conspiracy" to describe accurate historical reports. On the contrary, they use it to indicate a lack of veracity and objectivity. I am not using the word "conspiracy" in this derogatory sense, but rather in a descriptive way to mark those views that depart from popular or scholarly explanations of what happened in Jonestown.

A number of writers have identified a rise in conspiracism in the twentieth century in general and in the postwar United States in particular. Richard Hofstadter calls it the "paranoid style," which sees a huge sinister conspiracy "as *the motive force* in historical events" (Hofstadter 29, italics in original). In other words, nothing happens randomly or according to chance. All events are connected and stem from a specific cause or causal agent. Dieter Groh notes the problems in attributing causality to agents of history, which include the "underestimation of the complexity and dynamics of historical processes," and "[t]he [faulty] belief that one can ascribe in a linear manner the results of actions to certain intentions" (Groh 11). He sees yet another problem with the argument for causality, which is the inability to demonstrate a "causal nexus" between two or more historical events.

Despite the failure to certify causality, conspiracists are nevertheless able to marshal an incredible number of facts—or "factoids" in the words of Daniel Pipes—to support their assertions (Pipes 41). Hofstadter calls it an "obsessive" accumulation of evidence, and finds the plausibility of conspiracism "in this appearance of the most careful, conscientious, and seemingly coherent application to detail" (Hofstadter 37). Conspiracists pay careful attention to sources; the good ones use footnotes, sometimes extravagantly. There is a genuine type of scholarship in the citing of references, and indeed references are not the problem. It is the conclusions that the conspiracist draws from the sources that are problematic. The conspiracist finds causality here, determines linkages there, and constructs an impregnable edifice out of myriad facts and details.

When I say impregnable edifice, I mean that such theories are difficult to disprove. The good ones are logically consistent, very plausible, and frequently "equipped with everything associated with a scientific paradigm as understood by modern history of science" (Groh 4). But unlike academic hypotheses, particularly in the field of history, conspiracy theories leave no loose ends. Absolutely everything is accounted for, fitting together into a single jigsaw puzzle. The conspiracist begins with the completed puzzle, however, rather than its pieces, or in Timothy Melley's phrase, "the master narrative" (Melley 8). Although Melley says that conspiracies are "hermetically sealed," I would assert that conspiracy theories are also hermetically sealed, due to a worldview that abhors both coincidence and ambiguity.

What is the appeal of these master narratives? Analysts of conspiracy theories offer several explanations. Melley says that the rise in conspiracism in postwar America stems from "agency panic," that is, the "[i]ntense anxiety about an apparent loss of autonomy or self-control—the conviction that one's actions are being controlled by someone else, that one has been 'constructed' by powerful external agents" (Melley 12). Groh sees them as coming from individuals' sense of injustice. "The world is no longer as it was and as it should be," he writes. "It is unhinged, turned upside down" (Groh 7). Because things are not the way they are supposed to be, people search for the guilty: Who is responsible? This view is quite evident in African American culture, according to Patricia A. Turner, who documents the history of conspiracy and contamination motifs in Black American folklore (Turner 6). Arie Kruglanski sees conspiracy theories as a form of scapegoating, related to the search for the guilty party (Kruglanski 219). Frequently the scapegoats are foreigners, aliens in our midst. The presence of the "other" creates "the need to *integrate* one's image of society in one cause," according to Serge Moscovici (Moscovici 157, italics in original).

I would add to these analyses the clarification that it is the marginalized people of society who tend to believe in conspiracy theories. They might be materially marginal, which is to say, poor, and seeking an explanation for their poverty. Or they might be ideologically marginal, which is to say that they believe their (correct) views have been pushed aside by powerful outside forces. This explains how Ross Perot, a billionaire, can believe that political forces tried to disrupt his daughter's wedding, how bankrupt farmers in the Midwest can believe that Jewish bankers are foreclosing on their farms, and how urban African Americans of different socioeconomic classes can believe that government scientists are promoting AIDS in their communities. The marginalized believe that someone is benefiting at their expense. In fact, the question of "who benefits" is key to understanding the popularity of conspiracy theories, and the answer reveals the universe of good guys and bad guys.

Almost by definition, conspiracy theorists exhibit dualistic thinking, the us-versus-them mentality. How could one consider compromising with conspirators? The idea is unthinkable. Those running the conspiracy seek power and fortune at the expense of everyone else. They are inherently evil. "The paranoid spokesman sees the fate of this conspiracy in apocalyptic terms—he traffics in the birth and death of whole worlds, whole political orders, whole systems of human values," says Hofstadter (Hofstadter 29). One's adversary is an enemy, rather than a mere opponent, and thus is capable of almost any depravity (Pruitt).

Professional Conspiracists

Dualistic thinking certainly characterizes the writing of the professional conspiracists, whom I define as those writers who see all events through the hermeneutical lenses of conspiracy. They have developed a reputation among followers of knowing what is really happening. They interpret the daily news in the light of an overarching story in which current events serve as plot developments in an ongoing soap opera. Ultimately the drama depicts a battle between the forces of good and evil. The primary professional conspiracists who analyzed the Jonestown events include Mark Lane, John Judge, Jim Hougan, the Church of Scientology, and Dr. Peter Beter.

Dr. Beter is perhaps best known for the 1973 bestseller *The Conspiracy against the Dollar*. He saw three rival factions vying for world power: the Rockefeller Cartel, the Bolshevik-Zionist Axis, and the new Kremlin rulers (Anonymous).[2] The summary to Dr. Beter's collection of 80 audiotapes concludes admiringly that "[t]he most striking thing about this picture is that countless seemingly unrelated, chaotic-appearing news events turn out not to be chaotic at all. Instead they are all tied together by a limited number of forces at work behind the scenes. Once one knows these forces, one becomes far better able to sort out the true meaning of events" (Anonymous).

Dr. Beter's Audioletter 40 for 30 November 1978 explains that the events in Jonestown were staged to camouflage the United States' destruction of a Soviet missile base located in Guyana (Beter). According to this account, U.S. intelligence agents infiltrated Peoples Temple in the early 1970s. These intelligence forces converted Jim Jones into a "semiconscious agent of death and intrigue." Given the fact that Jones was "born a Jew," it was only natural that he would organize his group along the style of a kibbutz. The U.S. State Department deliberately provoked Congressman Leo Ryan into going to Jonestown in order to hide the true nature of the upcoming military operation. The deaths at the Jonestown kibbutz served as the excuse for a massive influx of U.S. military personnel into Guyana, and concealed the casualties that resulted from the military operation, which involved both U.S. and Israeli forces. In other words, the U.S. government and military benefited from the deaths in Jonestown, because they disguised the real possibility of the upcoming "Nuclear War One."

One might wonder what happened to Jim Jones in this scenario. According to Beter, the body identified as Jones was a double. The real "cult leader" fled to Israel to receive cobalt treatments for the cancer that had infected his head, his left lung, his stomach, and his colon. Told that he would receive additional treatment elsewhere, Jones boarded a small airplane, "shortly after 5:00 P.M. Israeli time," and headed for Turkey. "At about 35 miles east of the town of Jerablus on the Euphrates River, the plane crossed briefly to the Syrian side of the border. At that point the door of the plane was thrown open and three men grabbed Jones. In his weak condition and caught by surprise, he was thrown out of the plane with almost no struggle" (Beter). Dr. Lawrence Schacht, the presiding doctor in Jonestown, had also flown to Israel, arriving in Jerusalem "[a]t approximately 3:00 A.M. Israeli time December 11." Dr. Schacht also had cancer, and like Jones, was thrown from an airplane along the Turkish-Syrian border.

I begin with Dr. Beter's explanation of Jonestown because it is the most seamless of all conspiracy accounts of the tragedy, by which I mean that it fits into an ongoing metanarrative with little interest in, or even consideration of, the particulars of Jonestown. It really doesn't matter what happens in history: Dr. Beter will weave it into his analysis. His depiction is rife with the kind of minute details that characterize celebrity interviews in *Vanity Fair*. The exact times of the flights, the geographical specifics, and other small points all create the impression that Dr. Beter knows what he is talking about. The overarching history is created in the details, which simultaneously defuse skeptics and disarm critics.

Much more convincing accounts by professional conspiracists come from John Judge, Jim Hougan, Mark Lane, and the Church of Scientology. After all, they generously footnote or cite their sources. Although Dr. Beter seems to know a great deal, these others provide independent confirmation: you don't have to take *my* word for it, they suggest, here is the source. For example, John Judge has 291 endnotes for his twenty-five-page essay "The Black Hole of Guyana." Judge looks skeptically at the changing body counts and explains the growing numbers by suggesting that British Black Watch troops who were on "training exercises" with American Green Berets killed seven hundred Jonestown residents who had fled into the jungle. He asserts that they were all murdered after living a terrible existence in a CIA-sponsored program of mind control, known as MK-ULTRA. "The story of Jonestown is that of a gruesome experiment," he says, "not a religious utopian society" (Judge 141). Indeed, Judge argues that Jim Jones had ties to the CIA, that other Temple members had ties to Nazi war criminals, and that still others had ties to the assassination of Dr. Martin Luther King, Jr. (Judge 146). "The ultimate victims of mind control at Jonestown are the American people," he concludes. "The real tragedy of Jonestown is not only that it occurred, but that so few chose to ask themselves why or how, so few sought to find out the facts behind the bizarre tale used to explain away the death of more than 900 people, and that so many will continue to be blind to the grim reality of our intelligence agencies" (Judge 151–152). In other words, Judge puts the tragedy at Jonestown into the context of his larger concern, which is the threat to democracy posed by U.S. intelligence agencies. This is a theme throughout his work, and in this sense the Jonestown piece fits well into his worldview.

Jim Hougan has only sixty-eight footnotes for his eighteen-page article "Jonestown. The Secret Life of Jim Jones: A Parapolitical Fugue." He is indebted to Judge, in part, and yet skillfully points out the problems in Judge's account. Of all the conspiracy theories extant, Hougan's is the best researched and the most convincing. He concentrates on the mysterious character of Jim Jones, tracking down his connections to Dan Mitrione, an American intelligence agent who was ultimately killed by Uruguay's Tupamaros. He traces Jones's movements throughout the Western Hemisphere. Like Judge, Hougan asserts that the people in Jonestown were murdered, albeit for a different reason: "Jones initiated the Jonestown massacre because he feared that Congressman Leo Ryan's investigation would disgrace him. Specifically, Jones feared that Ryan and the press would uncover evidence that the leftist founder of the Peoples Temple was for many years a witting stooge, or agent, of the FBI and the intelligence community, where it was feared that Ryan's investigation would embarrass the CIA by linking Jones to some of the Agency's most volatile programs and operations" (Hougan 2).

In his book *The Strongest Poison*, Mark Lane also argues that people in Jonestown were murdered. Hired by Peoples Temple to explore what the group believed was a government conspiracy against it, Lane accompanied Ryan to Guyana. He remained behind in Jonestown when the congressman left for the airstrip, and fled into the jungle with another Temple attorney, Charles Garry, as the deaths were beginning. He reported hearing automatic weapon fire, and presumes that U.S. forces killed Jonestown survivors. He believes that, given the radical politics and power of Peoples Temple, intelligence agencies regularly monitored the group in the United States and in Guyana. American officials, particularly at the State Department, allowed Congressman Ryan to visit Jonestown knowing that it was a dangerous mission. Lane places blame for the murders of the Jonestown residents on Jim Jones and on armed security guards who forced people to take poison. But he also blames U.S. officials who knew that violence was a real possibility, and who in fact exacerbated the dangers with agents provocateurs. By labeling the deaths suicide rather than murder, both the government and the media covered up evidence of the existing conspiracy to destroy Jonestown as a progressive political organization—much as these same forces had destroyed Martin Luther King.

Like Lane, the Church of Scientology believes that government agents had penetrated Jonestown and Peoples Temple, although—unlike Lane and others—Scientology has been claiming this for years. In a 1997 article, the Scientology magazine *Freedom* depicts Jonestown as a mainstream, progressive organization with wide support, and reports that Ryan was pleased with what he saw in the community (Whittle and Thorpe 8–9). But CIA operatives deliberately targeted Ryan for assassination because of his previous opposition to the agency's activities, including his cosponsorship of the Hughes-Ryan Amendment in Congress. The article mentions a lawsuit filed by the Ryan family which charged that the CIA had infiltrated Jonestown. The lawsuit was dismissed, "for reasons that have to date never been fully disclosed" (Whittle and Thorpe 10). According to Charles Huff, a former Green Beret who was one of the first at the scene, many in Jonestown had been forcibly injected with poison, or had been shot as they ran toward the jungle. United States Air Force Colonel L. Fletcher Prouty suggested that the deaths in Jonestown masked the real victim and target. Paraphrasing Prouty's remarks, the authors write that "Leo Ryan had moved in too close to certain skeletons that could never be safely disturbed. A relentless and uncompromising investigator, nothing could stop Ryan—short of violence. But how could such a high-profile personality be eliminated without bringing down upon the perpetrators an investigation to end all investigations?" (Whittle and Thorpe 11). The solution was to obscure the assassination by making it part of a larger catastrophe.

We see that the theme of the professional conspiracists is that people in Jonestown were murdered by U.S. government agents—either military or intelligence. These agents committed the murders to conceal some other, more damaging information: a military operation against the Soviet Union; the assassination of a member of Congress; the disclosure of the true identity of a radical leader; the revelation that the government was conducting mind-control experiments. What is most striking is the conviction these writers hold that so many lives were deemed expendable for so little. This view reflects either the deepest cynicism, or the deepest fear, one can imagine: nine hundred lives sacrificed to get one individual? or to spare one individual humiliation? But that is the nature of conspiracism: with high stakes, the conspirators take big risks. And since conspirators by nature are depraved and indifferent, we should expect nothing less from them.

Internet Conspiracists

The Internet conspiracists form a subcategory of professional conspiracists, since their meat and potatoes is exploiting rumors, innuendoes, and wild stories.[3] There is frequently a sense of humor and fun in most of the conspiracy sites, best illustrated in the comments of Jonathan Vankin and John Whalen, coauthors of *The Seventy Greatest Conspiracies of All Time*, a major source for the Jonestown Internet conspiracists: "Back in the good ol' days when conspiracy theorists were still considered crackpots, it actually took some kind of evidence to get this kind of frenzy underway. . . . Now anytime some poor sap dies every frat boy with an Internet account races to be the first in his quad to post the conspiracy of the moment" (Vankin and Whalen, quoted by a reviewer on amazon.com). It is not clear, therefore, how deeply committed the Internet conspiracists are to their beliefs in various conspiracies.

A search of the word "Jonestown" on google.com came up with 55,400 hits on 22 January 2002. After eliminating all of the hits for the Jonestown, Texas, Pennsylvania, and Mississippi Chambers of Commerce, and hotel-motel guides; and after eliminating all of the sites devoted to the Brian Jonestown Massacre, a rock band; and after eliminating a number of anticult sites, that is sites devoted to alerting readers to the dangers of cults, and thus forming their own conspiracy category, there are only a few conspiracy sites that continue to pop up under different headings or guises. These comprise a Crime Library article by Fiona Steel (number 12); Vankin and Whalen's frequently reprinted article, "The Jonestown Massacre: CIA Mind Control Run Amok" (appearing as number 14, under www.conspire.com and as number 56 under former United Kingdom Green Party Leader David Icke's "Mind Control Archives," at www.davidicke.net); Scientology's *Freedom* Magazine site, with information noted above (number 25); and Ken McCarthy's brasscheck.com, which is devoted to exposing the "unholy alliance of media, government, and big business" (number 32).

Since Vankin and Whalen pop up across the Internet, it is appropriate to note their argument. They question the idea that Jim Jones was a "lone madman," and challenge the plausibility that nine hundred people willingly took their own lives at his request. They claim that there are hints of human experiments in mind control, even genocide, "and the lurking presence of the CIA." Vankin and Whalen cite sources that include books written within one or two years of the Jonestown deaths, as well as Tim Reiterman and John Jacobs's *Raven*, an extensively researched account of Peoples Temple and Jim Jones, and my own *A Sympathetic History of Jonestown*. Most illuminating, however, is the authors' acknowledgement that "[t]his chapter owes a debt to research assembled by John Judge."

Judge's influence seems evident in "The Jonestown Genocide" by Robert Sterling, as well.[4] This article includes reports of British Black Watch troops and Green Beret involvement in the deaths, in addition to the Jim Jones–Dan Mitrione connection (developed by Jim Hougan, but first introduced by Judge). Sterling also quotes Michael Meiers, author of *Was Jonestown a CIA Medical Experiment? A Review of the Evidence*, who answers his own question affirmatively (Sterling). (Although I discuss Meiers below, it is important to point out here that he bases much of his book on Joe Holsinger's charges.) Like Holsinger and Meiers, Sterling believes that the CIA's secret program was about to be exposed by Leo Ryan, and thus Ryan had to be killed.

The twelfth site listed under Google's hits on "Jonestown" is Fiona Steel's "Jonestown Massacre: A 'Reason' to Die," which appears as part of the Crime Library's "Crime Stories." The blurb that accompanies a glamour shot of Fiona Steel says that the author "is a former marketing and business administrator whose writing talents include writing top-selling marketing and training video scripts for international companies as well as writing training manuals on business skills and computer software." The chapter titled "Sinister Connections?" repeats the theories of CIA involvement, the Jones-Mitrione connection, and the animus the CIA had toward Congressman Ryan because of his support for legislation restricting agency activities.

Ken McCarthy authored "Made in San Francisco. Jonestown and Official San Francisco: The Untold Story," which appears on his brasscheck.com site.

McCarthy emphasizes the ties Jim Jones had with San Francisco's political leaders, such as then-assemblyman Willie Brown; former mayor George Moscone, who was assassinated along with Harvey Milk by ex-supervisor Dan White in November 1978; former county district attorney Joseph Freitas; former governor Jerry Brown; former mayor Art Agnos; and former police chief Charles Gain. McCarthy describes himself as a defender of human rights who is fighting for the underdog. His site seems more focused on discrediting San Francisco's liberal Democratic establishment, however, than on Peoples Temple.

Perhaps the most honest, and entertaining, of the Internet conspiracists is Matthew Farrell, who publishes the "World Domination Update" online. The December 2000 issue featured an article Farrell wrote on "Jonestown: A Skeptic's Perspective."[5] The article asks what happened exactly, and replies that "[t]here are no easy answers, unless you swallow the Brain Police's placebo explanations." Farrell examines the question of whether or not Jim Jones killed himself: "You'd think if Jones killed himself it'd be known anti-Jones propaganda. Likewise, if the whole thing was framed to *look* like a group suicide, why would 'they' be so sloppy about details: just shoot Jones and put the gun in his hand—that's a *no-brainer*. The very *absence* of such important information makes me wonder—and starts my spidey senses *tingling*" (Farrell, italics in original). Farrell considers the CIA to have been involved in some way, although he is not sure how. He finds the fact that the MK-ULTRA program "officially" ended in 1973, the year before Peoples Temple members began to settle in Guyana, significant. He rejects the idea of suicide, saying "[i]t was *not* a 'Masada wet run' or a 'Waco beta test' which *they* want you to think it is." He concludes: "Something *bad* happened in Guyana, and we will probably not find out exactly what it was" (Farrell, italics in original).

The evidence shows that Jonestown conspiracism is alive and well on the Internet. But rather than develop new sources, the Internet conspiracists have relied on print sources, primarily Judge, Hougan, and Scientology.[6] At times these sources are mediated through the reading of Vankin and Whalen; at other times they seem to have been excerpted directly. Like their professional counterparts working in print, the Internet conspiracists discount the suicide explanation as implausible and unlikely, preferring to see the deaths as murders conducted to protect CIA or other government interests. Compared with the professional conspiracists, however, the Internet conspiracists seem to write more in a sense of play. The game is to be outrageous, and the Internet writers appear to take the deaths less seriously. It's not the deaths that are important, but rather the idea of conspiracy. The deaths merely incidentally prove the existence of the conspiracy.

Nonprofessional Conspiracists

In some respects, the nonprofessional conspiracists argue a bit more believably than the professionals because they concentrate on Jonestown rather than on external forces or ongoing narratives. Nevertheless, most come to the same conclusion, namely, that residents of Jonestown were murdered. Some believe that Jonestown was a mind-control experiment. Others have focused on the conspiracy *against* Jonestown, which persuaded people it was better to die than to live. In general, however, the nonprofessionals, with one exception, argue that people in Jonestown were murdered. Even if they killed themselves, it was still murder because the victims had been brainwashed, tortured, or coerced in some fashion.

The title of Michael Meiers's book, for example, says it all: *Was Jonestown a CIA Medical Experiment? A Review of the Evidence.* Relying on interviews he conducted with Ryan's legislative aide Joe Holsinger, the author concludes that it was part of such an experiment, that is, the CIA's MK-ULTRA program, which tested mind-control drugs on unsuspecting victims. Meiers argues that the quantity of psychoactive drugs, together with the meticulous medical records and the layout of the bodies, indicates an attention to detail and evidence that the experimenters wanted to follow. "As the cause of death was noted on the medical records of each Test Person," writes Meiers, "the corpses were dragged to one side and placed in neat, orderly piles" (Meiers 413). The cause would be suicide or murder, since not all victims went willingly. Of course, part of the experiment was to test not the children but rather the willingness of mothers to kill their children (Meiers 445). A convenient side benefit was the CIA's assassination of Ryan. Another benefit was the discrediting of Mark Lane, who had been targeted for assassination. It was more advantageous to destroy his career than his life, since he was within days of proving the conspiracy against Martin Luther King, and his death might have led others to continue his investigation.

I should add that Meiers says that "[i]t is entirely possible that Rebecca Moore was a communications conduit between the experiment and the faction of the federal government that sponsored it" (Meiers 509). Just for the record, I am not and never was a communications conduit for any government agency.[7] Despite this warning, Meiers highly recommends my book, *A Sympathetic History of Jonestown*, as long as readers understand that it is a defense of my family's connection to Jim Jones and the CIA.[8]

Meiers provides a universal conspiracy theory that ties Jones and Jonestown to Nazis, AIDS, the assassinations of George Moscone and Harvey Milk, the Symbionese Liberation Army, the Bay of Pigs, Richard Nixon, and the NAACP, to name just a few. Dan White allegedly murdered Moscone and Milk—after all, we only have his confession—because they had learned of Jim

Jones's connection to the CIA. Most interesting in this regard: "There is absolutely no record of Jim Jones or his Peoples Temple ever having anything to do with Dan White, which is somewhat suspicious in itself, considering the major influence Jones exerted in San Francisco politics" (Meiers 326). Like Matthew Farrell, noted above, Meiers sees the absence of evidence as evidence itself.

Another nonprofessional conspiracist, Nathan Landau, looks at Jonestown from the opposite perspective in *Heavenly Deceptor*. Far from Jonestown being a CIA operation, it was an un-American and anti-American concentration camp that Jones established so that he could take over Guyana in preparation for launching an assault against the United States. More effective than his Nazi antecedents, Jones used drugs to control "poor black pseudo-slaves who were totally exploited by their new masters on the Jonestown plantation" (Landau 101). Jonestown's "final solution" focused on homosexuals, blacks, and drug users, who were murdered. Meanwhile, many in the white leadership group, including Jim Jones, planned to escape with millions of dollars. "A man planning to die doesn't deposit *hundreds of millions* of dollars into foreign bank accounts" (Landau 14, italics in original). Leo Ryan interrupted the group's plans, however, and had to be eliminated in order for Jones to get away with the money.

Landau is also sympathetic to Joe Holsinger, and admits that Jonestown's successful behavior modification program might suggest the involvement of the CIA. But this view "discredits the very highly skilled and motivated upper echelon members of Jonestown who really engineered the commune" (Landau 164). Jonestown was essentially a prototype for small fascist groups that are targeting certain races and religions for elimination.

One of the most distinctive conspiracy theories concerning the deaths in Jonestown comes from Laurie Efrein Kahalas, a former member and Temple loyalist. She writes that a government conspiracy followed Peoples Temple from San Francisco to Guyana and ultimately caused the deaths of the Jonestown residents by framing them for the murder of Leo Ryan. Her book *Snake Dance: Unraveling the Mysteries of Jonestown*, provides documents supporting her belief—and that of Temple members—that different government agencies were spying and harassing the organization.[9] Kahalas claims that an elite core of Army sharpshooters, not Jonestown residents, shot Ryan. As part of her evidence, she cites the audiotape made on the final day on which Jim Jones says, "I didn't order the shooting. . . . I don't know who shot the congressman" (Kahalas 321). Kahalas believes that government assassins killed Ryan because of his support for congressional oversight of the CIA. His assassination set the stage for the deaths in Jonestown because the community would have to take the blame for it. She again cites the death tape: "Now there is no choice. Either *we* do it or *they* do it. . . . When they're shooting out of the air, they'll shoot some of our innocent babies. . . . They'll torture our people. We cannot have this" (Kahalas 323, italics in original). In this way, government forces eliminated two thorny problems: Leo Ryan and the Jonestown community.

An interesting footnote to all of this is Jeff Brailey's description of his visits to Jonestown in the week after the deaths. Brailey came as part of the 193rd Infantry Brigade from Panama to evacuate the bodies from Jonestown. He writes that as he was leaving Jonestown by helicopter, an American government official hopped on board, carrying a large crate of documents he had retrieved from the community. The man told Brailey to shoot anyone who attempted to take the crate away. Brailey said he wouldn't, but he assumed the man was "a spook," that is, a CIA agent, who was removing incriminating evidence (Brailey 104–105).

With the exception of Kahalas, the conspiracy theories developed by non-professional conspiracists tend to locate the evil at the very heart of Jonestown: it was either a mind-control experiment or a concentration camp. Either way, people did not actually "choose" to die in any meaningful sense of the word. In this respect, the nonprofessional conspiracists are similar to the professionals and to the Internet conspiracists, who all believe that the residents were murdered. In other words, no one finds the option of mass suicide credible.

Conclusions

There are definite gaps and problems in the official story, which the Jonestown conspiracy theories address with varying degrees of success. Much information remains classified, and the suspicion that it demonstrates the culpability, in one way or another, of the U.S. government in the deaths also fuels the conspiracy fires. The elements of the story are titillating, as well: drugs, sex, race relations, communism, and violence make a much more interesting story than do farming, furniture-making, or playing basketball, all part of the daily life of the Jonestown community. Finally, professional conspiracists will find conspiracies everywhere, a tendency that discredits them to all but their true believers. Even if they were right this time, we would never know.

Moreover, the question of suicide feeds the conspiracy theorists. I would agree that the deaths of the children and the seniors were acts of murder, since they had no choice in the matter. It is the deaths of the able-bodied adults—the perpetrators, if you will—that are at issue. Eyewitness accounts are conflicting. Evidence from audiotapes indicates that the community had rehearsed suicide on several occasions. Was the group merely completing a ritualized behavior? Or was external coercion involved? The conspiracy theorists either ignore the suicide rehearsals or they explain them as part of a mind-control experiment.

The fact that almost all of the theories reject the suicide explanation is significant for several reasons. First, they imply that people in their right minds do not commit suicide. Similarly, sane people do not kill either their children or their parents. If they do commit suicide, infanticide, or parricide, it follows that they must be insane, or certainly not of sound mind. Therefore, if the people of Jonestown did commit "suicide," it was certainly not voluntary. That means that they were drugged or tortured. The most likely scenario, according to the theorists, is that the people were sane, and hence had to have been murdered.

By rejecting the suicide explanation, the conspiracists attempt to seek justice for the victims. In their dualistic worldview, which pits the evil forces of government conspirators such as the CIA or the Green Berets against the forces of good embodied in individual American citizens, calling the deaths "suicide" allows the conspirators to get away with murder. They read Jonestown as a political rather than a religious event. They see it as a battle between great secular forces of good and evil, with evil embodied in the CIA, Nazis, racists, or megalomaniacs. The religious aspects of the group fade away in the face of this explanation.

Conspiracy theories, for all their inherent secrecy and implicit danger, are nonetheless comforting because they eliminate uncertainty and moral ambiguity. It is far more troubling to think that people had practiced suicide and then went through with it, believing that they were doing something noble and right, than it is to think that malign powers did away with them for nefarious purposes. It is far more disturbing to imagine that sane and even idealistic people more or less willingly killed their children than to imagine that some suprapersonal power of darkness killed them. Thus conspiracy theories reassure us that what appears wrong or out-of-kilter in the world has a cause outside of individual or collective human weakness and vulnerability. In other words, the moral order, though jeopardized by conspirators, remains in effect.

If we believe that ordinary decent people did extraordinary acts of "evil," then the moral order is demolished. It seems preferable to believe in evil in the guise of conspirators than in evil in the guise of our neighbors. Given the profound questions raised by the events themselves, conspiracy theories about Jonestown will undoubtedly continue to proliferate, because they attempt to restore morality and order to a chaotic and immoral world.

NOTES

1. Rebecca Moore, "Is the Canon on Jonestown Closed?" *Nova Religio* 4.1 (October 2000): 7–27.

2. Though the Web site containing "A Bird's-Eye View of the Dr. Beter AUDIO LETTER (R)," is maintained by Michael Christol, a Ufologist from Owensboro, Kentucky, Christol does not appear to be the author of the "Bird's-Eye" digest.

3. I would like to thank Amanda B. Hensley, a student at Oakland University in Rochester, Michigan, for pointing me in the right direction for some Internet conspiracy sites.

4. I last accessed "The Jonestown Genocide" on 6 May 2001 at www.parascope .com/articles0997/jonestown.html, but the site was no longer online as of 22 January 2002. An announcement said that the Web site was moving to a new server in 2002. Sterling continues to maintain links to Jonestown conspiracy sources, however, at www.konformist.com/vault/jnstwn.htm (accessed 22 January 2002).

5. Farrell's article, available May 2001 at http://members.aol.com/stshade/ wdu46.html#jones, was no longer online on 22 January 2002.

6. Another article relying on these sources is "Jonestown, the CIA, and Mind Control," at www.totse.com/en/conspiracy/mind_control/jjones.html (accessed 24 January 2002).

7. In the world of conspiracism, of course, my denial merely proves the truth of Meiers's assertion.

8. The irony of all this is that we provided Meiers with much of the material for his book, and recommended the Edwin Mellen Press after the volume had been rejected by other publishers.

9. For more information on U.S. government harassment of Peoples Temple, see Rebecca Moore, "American as Cherry Pie: Peoples Temple and Violence in America," in *Millennialism, Persecution, and Violence: Historical Cases*, edited by Catherine Wessinger (Syracuse: Syracuse University Press, 2000), 121–137. I argue there that U.S. government agencies were in fact monitoring the activities of Peoples Temple, and were threatening the group's survival in a number of ways.

WORKS CITED

Alliance for the Preservation for Religious Liberty, (APRL), "Unanswered Questions Involving Jonestown and the CIA," 31 March, 1980, contained in the "Moore Family Papers," North Baker Research Library of the California Historical Society, San Francisco.

Brailey, Jeffrey. *The Ghosts of November: Memoirs of an Outsider Who Witnessed the Carnage at Jonestown, Guyana.* San Antonio: J & J Publishers, 1998.

Davis, David Brion. *The Fear of Conspiracy: Images of Un-American Subversion from the Revolution to the Presence.* Ithaca: Cornell University Press, 1971.

Groh, Dieter. "The Temptation of Conspiracy Theory, or: Why Do Bad Things Happen to Good People? Part I: Preliminary Draft of a Theory of Conspiracy Theories." In *Changing Conceptions of Conspiracy.* edited Carl F. Graumann and Serge Moscovici. New York: Springer-Verlag, 1987, 1–13.

Hall, John R. *Gone from the Promised Land: Jonestown in American Cultural History.* New Brunswick, N.J.: Transaction, 1987.

Hofstadter, Richard. "The Paranoid Style in American Politics." In *The Paranoid Style in American Politics and Other Essays.* edited by Richard Hofstadter. New York: Knopf, 1965, 3–40.

Hougan, Jim. "Jonestown. The Secret Life of Jim Jones: A Parapolitical Fugue." *Lobster* 37 (Summer 1999): 2–20.

Information Services Company. "People's Temple, Ryan Assassination Investigation," 20 July 1980, contained in the "Moore Family Papers," North Baker Research Library of the California Historical Society, San Francisco.

Judge, John. "The Black Hole of Guyana: The Untold Story of the Jonestown Massacre." In *Secret and Suppressed: Banned Ideas and Hidden History,* edited by Jim Keith. Portland, Or: Feral House, 1993, 127–165.

Kahalas, Laurie Efrein. *Snake Dance: Unravelling the Mysteries of Jonestown.* New York: Red Robin Press, 1998.

Kruglanski, Arie W. "Blame-Placing Schemata and Attributional Research." In *Changing Conceptions of Conspiracy,* edited by Carl F. Graumann and Serge Moscovici. New York: Springer-Verlag, 1987, 219–229.

Landau, Nathan. *Heavenly Deceptor.* Brooklyn: Sound of Music Publishing, 1992.

Lane, Mark. *The Strongest Poison.* New York: Hawthorn Books, 1980.

Meiers, Michael. *Was Jonestown a CIA Medical Experiment? A Review of the Evidence.* Lewiston, N.Y.: Edwin Mellen Press, 1988.

Melley, Timothy. *Empire of Conspiracy: The Culture of Paranoia in Postwar America.* Ithaca: Cornell University Press, 2000.

Moore, Rebecca. *A Sympathetic History of Jonestown.* Lewiston, N.Y.: Edwin Mellen Press, 1985.

Moscovici, Serge. "The Conspiracy Mentality." Translated by Kathy Stuart. In *Changing Conceptions of Conspiracy.* edited by Carl F. Graumann and Serge Moscovici. New York: Springer-Verlag, 1987, 151–169.

Pipes, Daniel. *Conspiracy: How the Paranoid Style Flourishes and Where It Comes From.* New York: The Free Press, 1997.

Pruitt, Dean G. "Conspiracy Theory in Conflict Escalation." In *Changing Conceptions of Conspiracy,* edited by Carl F. Graumann and Serge Moscovici. New York: Springer-Verlag, 1987, 191–202.

Reiterman, Tim, with John Jacobs. *Raven: The Untold Story of the Rev. Jim Jones and His People.* New York: E. P. Dutton, 1982.

Turner, Patricia A. *I Heard It Through The Grapevine: Rumor in African-American Culture.* Berkeley: University of California Press, 1993.

Vankin, Jonathan, and John Whalen. *The Seventy Greatest Conspiracies of All Time: History's Biggest Mysteries, Coverups, and Cabals.* New York: Citadel, 1998.

Whittle, Thomas G., and Jan Thorpe. "Revisiting the Jonestown Tragedy." *Freedom* (1997): 4–11.

INTERNET SOURCES

Anonymous. "A Bird's-Eye View of the Dr. Beter AUDIO LETTER (R)," excerpted from the Dr. Beter AUDIO LETTER(R) REFERENCE DIGEST, c. Audio Books, Inc., 1983. www.virtuallystrange.net/ufo/updates/1999/jul/m28-005.shtml (accessed 22 January 2002).

Beter, Peter. "Audioletter 40." www.etext.org/Politics/Beter.Audio.Letter/dbal40,30 November 1978 (accessed 22 January 2002).

Farrell, Matthew. "Jonestown: A Skeptic's Perspective." http://members.aol.com/stshade/wdu46.html#jones (last accessed 19 December 2000, no longer online 22 January 2002).

McCarthy, Ken. "Made in San Francisco. Jonestown and Official San Francisco: The Untold Story." www.brasscheck.com/jonestown (accessed 22 January 2002).

Steel, Fiona. "Jonestown Massacre: A 'Reason' to Die." www.crimelibrary.com/
    serial4/jonestown (accessed 22 January 2002).

Sterling, Robert. "The Jonestown Genocide." www.parascope.com/articles0997/
    jonestown.htm (last accessed 6 May 2001, no longer online 22 January 2002).

Vankin, Jonathan, and John Whalen. "The Jonestown Massacre: CIA Mind Control
    Run Amok?" In David Icke E-Magazine, "Mind Control Archives." www
    .davidicke.net/mindcontrol/research/re020600a.html, and at www.conspire
    .com/jones.html (both accessed 22 January 2002).

4

Explaining Militarization at Waco: The Construction and Convergence of the Warfare Narrative

Stuart A. Wright

The Branch Davidians offer a legacy unique in modern American religious history. As a small religious sect that carved out a separatist lifestyle and community in the rural farmlands of central Texas, it gained the attention of federal authorities in the early 1990s, largely through the dogged actions of disgruntled apostates and allied interest groups, and eventually became the target of a disastrous federal siege that destroyed all but a remnant of the group. Significant historical, legal, and social science research has been devoted to analyzing the events surrounding the Waco tragedy (for example, Hall, 2002; Hall and Schuyler, 1998; Kopel and Blackman, 1997; Reavis, 1995; Tabor and Gallagher, 1995; Wright, 1995a, 1999, 2001, 2002a, 2002b). But one feature of this tragedy has yet to be fully explored or explained. I refer here to the martial logic by which the Branch Davidians came to be seen as such a perilous threat by the state that a massive paramilitary raid was required. Paramilitary raids by "special operations" units such as the one deployed at Mt. Carmel are usually reserved for terrorist groups or drug traffickers. The Davidians were neither. Yet the actions taken by federal law enforcement were tantamount to a counterterrorism strike, transforming Mt. Carmel Center into a battleground, a theater of war. In the aftermath of the initial raid by the Bureau of Alcohol, Tobacco, and Firearms (ATF), the incident was allowed to escalate into a final reckoning leading to the deaths of seventy-six men, women, and children. The FBI determined after fifty-one days that negotiations had failed and launched a CS gas attack, breaching the Mt. Carmel complex with combat engineering vehicles and firing ferret rounds into the structure to force the barricaded sect members out. Six hours later, the building erupted into a fiery inferno that killed most of the residents.

One of the most confounding questions surrounding the Mt. Carmel incident is why a relatively small, benign religious sect would evoke such an aggressive and sustained military-like response from authorities. Investigations would later show that the ATF developed a grossly exaggerated perception of the Branch Davidians as an ominous threat to society and to themselves. As a result of this distorted perception, federal agents eschewed safer and less violent means of enforcement and chose to conduct a dangerous, high-risk "dynamic entry." In the formal review of the ATF's actions at Mt. Carmel by the U.S. Treasury Department months after the ill-fated raid, officials expressed dismay at decisions that put both agents and citizens in harm's way. The Treasury report notes that the ATF failed to consider fully its options and describes the planning of the operation as "steps taken along what seemed at the time to be a preordained road" (1993: 174). The report's characterization of this flawed planning process is telling, but the reasons for the agency's actions are left unexplained.

What is clear, however, is the degree to which the ATF perceived and overreacted to the alleged threat. The ATF paramilitary raid on the Branch Davidians constitutes the largest enforcement action ever taken by this storied agency. The dynamic entry by the ATF's Special Response Team was planned with military assistance by the U.S. Army Special Forces Rapid Support Unit at Ft. Hood in three days of training in close quarters combat exercises. The raid plan, given the code name "Operation Trojan Horse," involved eighty federal agents outfitted in camouflage and full combat gear, including Kevlar helmets and flak jackets; they wielded MP–5 submachine guns, semiautomatic AR–15s, Sig Sauer 9MM semiautomatic pistols, .308–caliber high-power sniper rifles, shotguns, and concussion grenades. The objective of the raid was to execute search and arrest warrants for Vernon Wayne Howell, the sect's leader who had changed his name to David Koresh, for firearms violations and possession of a destructive device. The Mt. Carmel complex housed approximately 130 people, about 70 percent of whom were women, children, and elderly persons. The failure by ATF to consider the reckless endangerment of residents who were not named in the warrants was an egregious miscalculation. As investigators later learned, the Davidians were tipped off about the raid by a Waco news cameraman who was trying to get to Mt. Carmel to cover the story. ATF undercover agent Robert Rodriguez was inside Mt. Carmel on the morning of February 28 when sect member David Jones arrived and informed Koresh about the impending raid. Rodriguez promptly departed the building, went immediately across the road to the surveillance house, told his superiors that the element of surprise had been lost and advised that the raid be called off. ATF commanders Philip Chojnacki and Chuck Sarabyn ignored the agent's warning and proceeded with the raid. Accounts differ about who fired first, but a shootout ensued and six Branch Davidians and four federal agents were mortally wounded.

Subsequent investigations by congressional committees, scholars, and news organizations revealed that the initial ATF raid was imprudent and unnecessary. For example, one of the justifications for the raid given by ATF was predicated on the claim that David Koresh never left Mt. Carmel and thus could not be apprehended alone and away from the property. That claim proved to be false. In fact, Koresh left Mt. Carmel on a number of occasions during the two-month undercover and surveillance operation conducted by the Bureau, even jogging down Double E Ranch Road directly in front of the two undercover houses. The failure to apprehend Koresh was cited as a critical flaw in the final report by the Committee on Government Reform and Oversight and the Committee on the Judiciary which held hearings on the Waco incident in the summer of 1995: "David Koresh could have been arrested outside the Davidian compound. The ATF chose not to arrest Koresh outside the Davidian residence and instead was determined to use a dynamic entry approach. In making this decision, ATF agents exercised extremely poor judgement, made erroneous assumptions, and ignored the foreseeable perils or their course of action" (*Investigation*, 1996: 4).

The report went on to castigate the ATF for a "grossly incompetent" investigation, citing "an incredible number of false statements" in the affidavit accompanying the warrants, and for misrepresenting to Defense Department officials "that the Branch Davidians were involved in illegal drug manufacturing" in order to obtain military training and support (p. 4) The congressional report also made the damning observation that "The decision to pursue a military style raid was made more than 2 months *before surveillance, undercover, and infiltration efforts were begun*" (p. 4, emphasis added). This statement corroborates the Treasury Department report's observation that criticized the ATF raid plan as proceeding on a "preordained road." It appears that ATF officials were determined to conduct a raid irrespective of intelligence operations that showed Koresh could be apprehended away from Mt. Carmel or that the element of surprise had been lost only minutes before the incursion.

There is some evidence that the ATF insisted on a dynamic entry because it would create favorable news coverage just prior to budget and appropriations hearings in Washington. ATF Public Relations Officer Sharon Wheeler contacted media organizations in Waco and Dallas two days before the raid to inform them that "something big" was going to take place in Waco over the weekend. Wheeler had gathered a staff of public relations personnel in Waco prepared to send faxes and issue press releases in anticipation of a successful raid. This self-serving effort backfired, however, as one local news crew inadvertently tipped off the Davidians about the operation and ironically captured the only film footage of the bungled siege. The news crew also filmed the flight of National Guard helicopters circling Mt. Carmel just minutes before the raid party on the ground arrived, a fact that the ATF initially denied (because it could be asserted that the helicopters inadvertently alerted sect members to the impending raid). One of the most peculiar features of "Operation Trojan Horse" was the failure to ensure adequate emergency medical service or fire department backup, an essential component for a high-risk raid (McMains and Mullins, 1996: 325–326). Though ATF apparently had asked an EMS company to be on standby, raid officials had no means of contacting the unit once the operation disintegrated. The extraordinary care taken to provide news media with preraid information, contact persons and phone numbers, and presumably post-raid press releases and video coverage of the arrests, while failing to ensure lifesaving arrangements with the emergency medical service and the fire department, have led some to conclude that the ATF was seeking publicity through the raid. On March 10, 1993, while the outcome of the standoff was still in doubt and the revelations concerning the ATF's misdeeds were yet unknown to the public, ATF director Stephen Higgins told the House Appropriations Subcommittee, "the agency needs tighter laws and a national willpower against violent criminals who have arsenals and supplies of explosive" ("Tougher Rules Urged on Explosives, Guns," *Houston Chronicle*, March 11, 1993). Higgins also reminded the subcommittee that 60 percent of the bureau's work was enforcement of firearms laws.

Although publicity seeking may have contributed in part to the rationale for a raid, it does not fully provide an explanation for what was certainly a more complex process of decision making and planning. Research suggests that in the course of the investigation, the ATF garnered an exaggerated image of threat posed by the Davidians and became convinced that this inflated danger was real. The Branch Davidians were cast as a violent, apocalyptic "cult" that was preparing for a war with the government. The unprecedented size and scope of the ATF operation supports this contention. The affidavit accompanying the search and arrest warrants, though replete with factual errors, misstatements of law, and inflammatory information unrelated to the ATF's jurisdiction, methodically argues that the Davidians were amassing a stockpile of weapons and possibly bomb-making materials in preparation for Armageddon. David Thibodeau, a Branch Davidian survivor, later explained that the group was buying legal AR–15 semiautomatic rifles and devices used to turn them into automatic M–16s for a licensed gun dealer in the Waco area, Henry McMahon (Thibodeau and Whiteson, 1999: 128–129). McMahon intended to sell the popular automatic weapons for a significant profit before the guns became banned, and the Davidians saw this as an income-producing venture. However, McMahon "got nervous" after a compliance check by the ATF sometime in the summer of 1992, according to Thibodeau, and "canceled the contract, leaving us with an inventory of unlicensed guns" (1999: 129). Technically, it was incumbent on the Davidians to apply for a federal license to purchase or convert automatic firearms, which they did not. But the Treasury report omits an important fact about the ATF compliance visit. Gun dealer Henry McMahon phoned Koresh during the compliance check and informed him of the ATF investigation, prompting Koresh to invite the agents to Mt. Carmel to inspect his firearms. McMahon testified under oath in the 1995 congressional hearings on Waco that he offered the phone to the ATF agents so that the federal inspectors could examine Mr. Koresh's guns. Curiously, the agents refused to speak to Koresh and never attempted to inspect the weapons prior to the February 28 raid. Koresh's attempt to cooperate with federal law enforcement was rebuffed. ATF officials later defended their actions, indicating that accepting such invitations violated normal investigative techniques. But the final congressional report on Waco rejected this explanation and concluded that the ATF had erred in their refusal to accept the invitation by Koresh. "It is unclear why the ATF did not accept the offer to conduct a compliance inspection of Koresh's firearms. What is clear is that the agents' refusal of Koresh's invitation was the first of a series of instances in which the ATF rejected opportunities to proceed in a non-confrontational manner. The agents' decision to decline Koresh's offer was a serious mistake" (*Investigation*, 1996: 13).

In order to understand fully the narrow and unyielding course of action taken by the ATF, it is necessary to examine how the Davidians came to be defined publically, in a carefully constructed narrative, as a violent cult bent on war. This public narrative was repeated time and again by federal officials and appropriated by the press and the larger public. The task of this study is to explore how this narrative developed and explain why it attained legitimacy. Building on earlier studies, I argue that a potent script emerged from a convergence of narratives among the cultural opponents of Koresh allied with public agencies that served to consolidate the mutual interests of both law enforcement and Davidian antagonists. In the emergent play of cultural meanings, an overarching "warfare" narrative was constructed that depicted the Davidians as an armed apocalyptic group preparing for a final battle with the Antichrist government forces. The convergence of narratives, in which the theme of "warfare" was central, helps explain the mentality of federal officials that led to excessive force demonstrated at Mt. Carmel. As such, it was not solely the weapons violations that moved federal officials to a full-blown paramilitary plan of assault to execute the warrants but also the imputed link of a "warfare" narrative to the firearms infractions that fueled an inflated sense of threat. Federal agents became convinced that the Davidians would not cooperate in an investigation, hated the federal government, were controlled by a fanatical cult leader, and would launch a "holy war" if challenged. This is readily apparent in the affidavit accompanying the warrants. What shapes and frames the "warrior cult" motif in the affidavit are the accounts by ex-members and detractors who provided ATF agent Davy Aguilera with embellished descriptions of life at Mt. Carmel. Here one finds stories of armed sentries, paramilitary maneuvers and training, weapons stockpiles, "shoot-to-kill" orders regarding intruders, discussions of an imminent war, contingency plans for mass suicide, the group's purported hatred of the government and their contempt for gun laws, and Koresh's messianic claims (not to mention polygamy and the sect leader's conjugal unions with underage women). Without these lurid and dramatic tropes to magnify the alleged threat posed by the Davidians, it is questionable that the ATF would have taken such extreme measures. The most crucial mistake the agency made was to base part of its investigation on unreliable information generously supplied by adversaries and opponents of David Koresh who were engaged in a moral campaign to repudiate the sect leader and his movement. As I hope to show, disgruntled apostates teamed with anticult leaders and selected media to cast the Davidians as an evil and dangerous cult requiring a military-like intervention by authorities.

It may be argued, with good reason, that ATF officials were predisposed to believe these exaggerated claims because to do so served their own interests. The new Clinton administration, which took office in January 1993, was determined to push through tighter gun controls, making the ATF the greatest beneficiary of the new policies. Officials in the bureau were certainly aware of the changing political climate in Washington. Previous presidents Ronald Reagan and George H. W. Bush were both card-carrying members of the National Rifle Association, a strong and vocal critic of the ATF. Neither president supported more restrictive gun legislation. The Clinton administration, on the other hand, subsequently lobbied Congress to pass the Brady Bill, which imposed a six-day minimum waiting period to purchase handguns, and the 1994 Federal Crime Bill, which outlawed seventeen types of assault weapons. Moreover, Bill Clinton had been the governor of Arkansas during the infamous federal siege of the violent Christian Identity group, the Covenant, Sword and Arm of the Lord in his state in 1985 (Coulson and Shannon, 1999; Noble, 1998). It is possible that Clinton may have been seen by ATF officials as more sympathetic to a similar enforcement action eight years later in Waco as the new president took office. The affinity between the ATF's mission and the new administration's preference for reducing violent crime through heightened gun controls was clear. Given the timing of the raid, ATF director Higgins's statements to the House Appropriations Committee, the "grossly incompetent" investigation, the "incredible number of false statements" in the affidavit accompanying the warrants, the inordinate attention given to public relations while neglecting arrangements for emergency medical service backup prior to the raid, the decision to "pursue a military-style raid . . . more than 2 months before surveillance, undercover, and infiltration efforts were begun," and the ATF commanders' decision to proceed with the raid on the morning of February 28 even after the element of surprise was lost, one can make a compelling case against the agency.

Equally important, however, was the emergent "warfare mentality" (Wagner-Pacifici, 1994) of law enforcement in the years leading up to the siege of Mt. Carmel. Numerous studies have documented the increased reliance of law enforcement on a "war model" of crime control (Dunn, 1996; Kraska, 1994, 1996, 2001a; Kraska and Kappeler, 1997; Skolnick and Fife, 1993; Walker, 1994). Alternatively referred to as a "military model" of crime control (Skolnick and Fife, 1993), this trend is rooted in the conceptualization of policing as a "war on crime." What these studies have shown is that the metaphor of war for crime fighting has been more than just a harmless construct; it has become a means by which official policies and practices have crystallized. For example, during the early years of the Reagan administration, in an effort to combat drug trafficking, Congress passed the Defense Authorization Act permitting military assistance in the "drug war." This law relaxed the historical separation between civilian police and the military, enacted in the Posse Comitatus Act after the Civil War. A series of laws were passed over the next decade that further eroded the line between domestic police and the military, all under the banner of the "war on crime and drugs." According to scholars, the effect of increased integration of police and military forces (joint task forces, coordinated assistance, interagency cooperation, weapons and technology transfer) has produced a "militarization of law enforcement" (Kraska and Kappeler, 1997). Within police culture, the attraction of military weaponry and training, the adoption of camouflage and military issue, close-order drill and military courtesy, the routinization of combat exercises (strike force operations, dynamic entries, reconnaissance, PSYOPS, urban warfare, close quarters combat) and the use of militarylike designations to replace traditional terms for police units (platoons, divisions, squads, details, chain-of-command) all point to such a transformation. The emergence of the war model of crime control also produced the inevitable "casualties of war," as evidenced particularly at Waco and Ruby Ridge (Dunn, 2001; Kraska and Kappeler, 1997), but also documented in various other, less public, incidents (Duke and Gross, 1993; Dunn, 1996; Kraska, 2001b; Miller, 1996; Wagner-Pacifici 1994). The deadly outcomes at Ruby Ridge and Waco—which were separated by only a few months and involved some of the same federal personnel—were a culmination of more than a decade of police militarization. By the time of the federal siege of Mt. Carmel, the warfare mentality was encoded so thoroughly into the culture of law enforcement that the planning, tactics, weaponry, and attitudes of the ATF Special Response Team and the FBI Hostage Rescue Team bore unmistakable marks of militarism.

Warfare as Narrative Construction

Following the lead of John Hall, the following analysis relies on the study of "intrinsic narratives," defined as "the diverse stories that various social actors tell within emergent situations to which they are mutually oriented, but in different ways" (1995: 206). According to Hall, this approach can help to explain how "cultural meanings become nuanced, shaded, interpreted, challenged, and otherwise reworked by participants, and how such meaning shifts affect the course of unfolding events" (p. 206). Using this approach allows us to ascertain the importance of cultural narratives when affinities of meaning develop between groups. In a seminal study of the Waco tragedy, Hall analyzed how the narrative of mass suicide—appropriated from the 1978 Jonestown incident—was invoked and reworked in ways that shaped the escalating trajectory of conflict at Mt. Carmel. Even before the ATF raid or the fatal CS gas attack by the FBI, Hall observed, Waco was becoming "another Jonestown." Hall makes a persuasive argument that the cultural meanings about mass suicide were interwoven into narratives about Waco, creating a self-fulfilling prophecy (see Hall, 1995, 2002). For the purposes of this study, Hall offers an important conceptual framework for analyzing how narrative convergence can produce a kind of rhetorical hegemony that pushes out competing explanations or understandings of events: "(N)arratives are particularly important when the meaningful content shifts, when the narrative moves from one source to another, when affinities develop between the narratives of two individuals or groups, and when the incorporation of a received narrative rearranges other meanings for an individual or group. When such narratives are freighted with cultural meanings, they may exercise influence on a course of events in ways that exceed or do not depend upon merely factual, legal, or professional considerations" (Hall 1995: 210). Indeed, when affinities develop between the narratives of groups, a common meaning and purpose may be found, alliances may be formed, and a dominant "cultural script" may be forged. I hope to show that one narrative promulgated by the cultural opponents of Koresh found particular resonance and legitimation among federal law enforcement agents, engendering a unified, refashioned single "warfare" narrative or script that served the interests of all parties and shaped the direction of the ATF investigation, the siege, and the standoff.

Elsewhere I have analyzed the social construction of a "cult" threat aimed at the Davidians and carried out in the form of a moral crusade by an alliance of disgruntled apostates, anticultists, and selected media (Wright, 1995b). The previous analysis focused largely on exaggerated threats constructed from cult stereotypes by allied detractors who emphasized "brainwashing," inflated claims of control or manipulation, and a litany of moral and sexual offenses. But further analysis suggests a distinct theme of warfare in the stories and claims of allied opponents made to authorities. This theme deserves a closer look. I believe this is a critically important cultural script in the greater interplay of rhetorical meanings forged with the ATF investigators in the months and weeks before the raid.

Warfare Narrative of Cultural Opponents

The early construction of a warfare narrative is apparent in the communication and claims-making activities of one key ex-member, Marc Breault. Breault's efforts are recorded in a scurrilous paperback entitled *Inside the Cult*, coauthored with a reporter for the tabloidlike TV program, "A Current Affair" (Breault and King, 1993). The blurbs appearing on the book cover trumpet claims of rape, beatings, "torturous rules of behavior," the threat of Koresh's "Mighty Men," training in military tactics and weaponry, and members' expectation of "the ultimate battle with the outside world." These are only exceeded by the sensational tropes contained within the book. Marc Breault is a principal figure in the construction of a warfare narrative and in the mobilization of an organized opposition against Koresh that fueled the fears of authorities. Though he had departed Mt. Carmel four years prior to the federal siege, Breault engaged in a flurry of claims-making activities—lobbying officials, networking with other ex-members, hiring a private investigator to collect damaging information about the sect, teaming with reporters in Australia and in Waco to scandalize Koresh—and eventually he became a primary source for the ATF and other federal agencies. Breault provides a record of these contacts prior to the raid, and boasts of almost daily phone calls from "senior officials of the United States Government, which included the ATF, the FBI, Congress, the State Department, and the Texas Rangers" (p. 295).

Breault claims that as early as 1988 the group began to post guards or sentries around the perimeter of Mt. Carmel and conduct "military training" (Breault and King, 1993: 178). The guards, he asserts, had shoot-to-kill orders regarding any suspicious intruders (p. 172). These claims are significant because they became part of the evidence record in support of the federal warrants. Indeed, Breault is named as the source for both the "shoot-to-kill" orders and the twenty-four-hour armed sentries cited by Special Agent Davy Aguilera in the ATF affidavit accompanying the warrants (U.S. District Court, 1993: 12). The details of the alleged military training and armed sentries at Mt. Carmel are vague, however, and Breault's story is conveyed through the eyes of a moral crusader, reconstructed from memories that appear to be heavily edited and generously sprinkled with aspersions. This problem is compounded by the fact that it is not clear which parts of the book are Breault's own account of events and which are King's recasting or retelling of the story. This muddled commingling of first-person and third-person voices leaves the reader confused and makes the so-called eyewitness account even more ambiguous. In any case, the imaginative gest is replete with warfare and military themes that are significant in the eventual formation of the warrior cult image.

In one portion of the book, Breault describes an incident in which a Davidian, Wally Kennett, was standing guard at the entrance of Mt. Carmel and almost shot a newspaper delivery man, mistaking him for an uninvited intruder. According to Breault, "Suddenly there was a loud shout from the guard house, which was only about 20 yards from the bus in which I was sleeping" (p. 171). Breault claims the guard screamed "halt" and fired two shots into the air. "I could make out the shadow of the guard leveling his Ruger .223 rifle at a man," he writes (p. 172). The time of the incident was "5 A.M., still dark and dead quiet." Breault alleges that Kennett was acting on Koresh's shoot-to-kill orders. The story is continued with commentary, apparently by coauthor King, who writes, "You'd think gunshots at 5 A.M. would have everyone rushing from all directions. Incredibly, Marc Breault was the only person who investigated the disturbance" (p. 172). King chides "other cult members" for sleeping through this near tragedy and opines that everyone must have become "used to the sound of gun-fire at any hour of the day or night" (p. 173).

The account of this event, which is told to buttress the claims of round-the-clock armed guards and shoot-to-kill orders, has several critical flaws. First, the conditions under which Mr. Breault allegedly saw the incident occurred at 5 A.M., while it was "still dark." From an estimated distance of twenty yards, even those with good eyesight presumably would have had trouble making out "the shadow of the guard leveling his .223 Ruger rifle at a man." Marc Breault does not have average eyesight, however; he is legally blind. The Davidians I interviewed have been quick to point out that Mr. Breault could not read without holding printed materials up to his face; that he could not recognize people or objects even from a short distance away; and that many of the things he claimed to have seen were questionable because of his poor eyesight. Curiously, Breault and King avoid any discussion in the book of how Breault's blindness may have affected his credibility as a firsthand observer. More disturbingly, there is no mention of this fact by Special Agent Aguilera in the affidavit filed to obtain the search and arrest warrants. One might assume that a primary source for the ATF criminal investigation, leading to the securement of the warrants and authorization for the raid, would be thoroughly checked out with regard to his credibility. And in fact, it appears that Aguilera was aware of Mr. Breault's disability. Breault claims that he was flown to California on January 7, 1993, at ATF expense, and met face-to-face with Aguilera (pp. 303–304). At the meeting, Breault answered detailed questions about Koresh and the Davidians in discussions that lasted into the night of the seventh and continued the following day. The text of these discussions and descriptions of their conversations are reproduced in Breault's book (pp. 303–313). If Breault's account of this meeting is correct, it would be virtually impossible for the agent not to recognize the disability. Mr. Breault's impairment is evident even to the most casual observer.

Another problem with this account is that the sect member in question, Wally Kennett, disputes Breault's story. In a 1993 interview, Kennett told me that Marc Breault was his roommate during part of his stay at Mt. Carmel and that he came to know the young Australian man pretty well. Kennett suggested that Marc Breault had "a tendency to tell tall tales," and gave several examples of embellished stories told him by Mr. Breault. In one unsolicited remark, Kennett stated, "The guy also claimed he had seen me level a Ruger mini fourteen at the paperboy's head at four o'clock in the morning when it was pitch dark" (Wright 1993a). Packaging these "tall tales" together, Kennett said of Breault, "this guy is full of crap" (ibid.). Kennett indicated that the members tolerated Breault's tendency to exaggerate because he was "a nice guy."

One prominent theme of warfare in the book is Breault's multiple references to the "Mighty Men," which he suggests was an elite security cadre designed to protect Koresh. Breault's disparaging characterization of the Mighty Men as "hand-picked goons who enforced Koresh's discipline" (p. 10), however, differs dramatically from the accounts of others who were at Mt. Carmel during this time. Davidian survivors generally have described the Mighty Men as a reference to spiritual qualifications, not martial qualities. The notion of Mighty Men stems from the biblical story of the guards of King Solomon's bed (Bromley and Silver, 1995: 62). David Thibodeau, who escaped the April 19 conflagration and later wrote his own biographical account, described the terminology in this way: "The term 'Mighty Men' came from King David's psalms. It was not a term for some inner core of armed guards protecting David, as some people later claimed. Actually, it could be applied to anyone who was given strength by faith, including women" (Thibodeau and Whiteson, 1999: 125). But Breault portrays the Mighty Men as Koresh's "most intimidating weapon" (p. 10) and suggests in another part of the book that he feared that when his disloyalty was discovered he might "be beaten to a pulp" by these guardians (p. 203) The latter statement is preceded by the observation that "the Branch Davidian cult was run like the Gestapo" (p. 202).

Breault also describes how David Koresh told his followers, "You've gotta be ready for war" after forcing them to watch a "marathon of violent Vietnam War movies" (p. 184) Breault infers that the "violent Vietnam War movies" served as de facto training videos. The movies to which he refers include such controversial films as *Hamburger Hill*, *Platoon*, and *Full Metal Jacket*. Breault's aversion to the dark side of the Vietnam war experience, however, may reveal more about his outsiderness as an Australian than anything else. The movies identified were essentially a genre of anti-war films that exposed the ugliness of violence and war; they did not celebrate war or glorify the feats of American soldiers in Southeast Asia. Nonetheless, he contends that the videos were part of a larger program of psychological conditioning for war, which "began at dawn and continued all day until late at night." In this subversive atmosphere, he intones, "mind-control reached such a pitch that his subjects were putty in [Koresh's] hands" (p. 184). A few pages later, Breault remarks that "Mount Carmel was like an army base now" (p. 186). This image is reiterated in a remark about Koresh's "100-man army" (p. 250).

The theme of warfare is expanded to include the allegation of "terrorism" in latter segments of the book. Following the comment that Breault received almost daily phone calls from senior officials in the U.S. government, coauthor King remarks that "guns and terrorism were endemic" at Mt. Carmel (p. 295). Breault gives further support for the terrorism theme after learning from the ATF that they plan to conduct a raid. "Once they obtained warrants to conduct the raids, how were they to proceed? The Branch Davidians were not an ordinary group of criminals. They were religious zealots who would think nothing of dying for their leader. In many respects, they were like terrorists" (p. 297).

As the ATF intensified its operation, Breault was asked to provide "psychological profiles" of sect members, including "how much military training they had" (p. 298). Breault enthusiastically became an ATF operative and supplied federal agents with information about "the military history of cult members." Undaunted by the paltry number of veterans found ("several") among the 130 residents at Mt. Carmel, Breault cautioned that "David Jones, Vernon's brother-in-law and chief Mighty Man, is the biggest danger. He's a real crack shot and has taught others a lot" (pp. 300–301).

Breault's book is instructive in chronicling the organization and mobilization of apostates, families of members, journalists, anticultists, and government officials. These facts are corroborated by other sources. Davidian survivor David Thibodeau describes Breault's pivotal role in spearheading an organized campaign against Koresh in his autobiographical account (see Thibodeau and Whiteson, 1999: 54, 119–122). Other Davidian survivors I have interviewed (Catherine Matteson, Rita Riddle, Sheila Martin, Clive Doyle, Wally Kennett) have provided similar observations. These sentiments might be summarized in the words of long-time Davidian Catherine Matteson: "Well, that man [Breault] started it all. He started all our problems. He started them about three years before we had any contact with the government in any way. . . . And I personally hold him totally responsible, because without him then we never would have had any problems" (Wright 1993b).

The Treasury Department report documents Agent Aguilera's contacts with Breault "which continued until the ATF raid on February 28" (1993: 29). The allegations of armed guards and "shoot-to-kill" orders are attributed to Breault, as are claims that "many cult members carried firearms, including AK–47s" and the episode of Kennett's alleged shooting at the newspaper delivery man (p. 29). The report also links Breault to reporter Mark England of the *Waco Tribune-Herald*, the paper that ran a sordid six-part series about Koresh entitled "The Sinful Messiah" just prior to the raid. Accounts by other ex-members who joined with Breault are also mentioned prominently in the report (Robyn Bunds, Janine Bunds, Debbie Bunds, Lisa and Bruce Gent). The report also makes reference to deprogrammed ex-member David Block, whom Breault tracked down at the behest of ATF (Breault and King, 1993: 310), and Block's deprogrammer, Rick Ross (U.S. Department of Treasury, 1993: 32, 1443–1444), an outspoken anticult activist. As stated earlier, the ATF affidavit cites Breault as a source (p. 12), and records interviews with ex-members Robyn Bunds, Debbie Bunds, Janine Bunds, David Block, and others. The *Waco Tribune-Herald's* investigative series cites interviews with the same organized opponents, and Breault is the primary source. These interconnections among disgruntled apostates, anticult organizations, and media have been documented in greater detail in a previous work (see Wright, 1995b).

The Warfare Narrative of Federal Law Enforcement

The ATF developed an exaggerated martial image of the Davidians as a violent cult bent on war with the government. But this image did not develop in a vacuum. It appears that the atrocity tales of apostates, taken largely at face value by investigators in the course of the interviews, helped give substance and shape to a refashioned warfare narrative. This narrative features prominent aspects of the "received" narrative of Koresh's opponents and incorporates the "warfare mentality" of law enforcement that developed within police culture during the previous decade. Indeed, the receptiveness of the ATF to the warfare narrative of Koresh's opponents was probably due to its strong affinity with the "war" model of crime control. As such, ATF investigators framed the information they received to fit the narrative of warfare, causing them to overlook or ignore contradictory, conflicting, or ambivalent evidence. This explains the puzzling decisions by ATF officials who failed to consider less lethal options or opportunities as they arose in what the Treasury report referred to as "steps taken along what seemed at the time to be a preordained road."

One example of how reliance on the received narrative of Koresh's opponents was used by the ATF to shunt the law and justify the raid can be seen the following case. According to the final congressional report, the ATF lacked evidence for probable cause to obtain a warrant in December 1992 (p. 11). In order to gain more evidence, director Stephen Higgins directed the ATF to initiate the undercover and surveillance operation (U.S. Department of Treasury, 1993: 27–28). The congressional report notes that "no additional evidence of criminal activity" was produced in the undercover and surveillance operation, but it records that "Former Davidians were interviewed in December 1992 and January 1993" (p. 11), implying that additional evidence came from the interview material with ex-members. During this same period, interviews were also obtained from oppositional allies. The problem here is that much of the material appearing in the affidavit is specious, inflammatory, and fails to consider the reliability of the sources. For example, the affidavit cites an interview with Joyce Sparks, a social worker with the Texas Department of Human Services, who "received a complaint from outside the State of Texas that David Koresh was operating a commune type compound and that he was sexually abusing young girls" (p. 7). The source of this complaint "outside Texas" was Marc Breault, as records later show. Agent Aguilera proceeds to describe an interview with Ms. Sparks, who interviewed "a young boy about 7 or 8 years old" (p. 8). The boy reportedly said he was in a hurry to grow up so he could "get a 'long gun' just like all the other men there" (p. 8). The boy also volunteered that "all the adults had guns and they were always practicing with them."

The inclusion of this material in the affidavit is problematic for several reasons. First, the affidavit makes no mention of the fact that the Texas Department of Human Services investigated the allegations of sexual abuse and eventually dismissed the case for lack of evidence. Second, the material alleging sexual abuse does not belong in the affidavit in the first place because the ATF has no legal jurisdiction over sex abuse; it is a state matter. The material is inflammatory and irrelevant and is clearly intended to inflate the putative threat posed by Koresh. Third, no consideration is given to the fact that the boy telling this story is seven or eight years old and may have had a healthy imagination, or at least exaggerated parts of his story; or that Spark's interpretation of the boy's story lacks detail and context. Ex-Davidian David Thibodeau, in his autobiographical account, has indicated that although everyone at Mt. Carmel was expected to be able to handle a gun, many of the members had an aversion for them: "For most of us," he states, "weapons were something we stayed away from as much as possible" (1999: 126). Finally, what is the criminal violation alleged by the agent in the telling of this story? There is no technical violation of firearms law cited, only the implication that Mt. Carmel is an armed "compound," with the tropes of the apostates to bridge the logical leap in the construction of the warfare narrative.

Agent Aguilera offers as further evidence in the affidavit—not of criminal activity but of the warfare narrative—the presence of "clandestine magazines" at Mt. Carmel such as *Shotgun News*; this was according to deprogrammed ex-member David Block (p. 14). No other "related clandestine magazines" mentioned in the affidavit are identified by title, though Block alleges that he "heard extensive talk of the existence of the 'Anarchist Cook Book' " (p. 14). Once again, this material is problematic. The characterization of *Shotgun News* as "clandestine" is misleading and disingenuous. The magazine has a circulation of about 165,000, and its readership is largely recreational hunters and gun collectors. Yet there is a clear intent to communicate the warfare image through the manipulation of language, as illustrated in the use of the word "clandestine." *Webster's New Universal Unabridged Dictionary* (2nd ed.) defines clandestine as "secret, hidden, withdrawn from public view; generally implying craft, deception or illicit purpose." Further manipulation of language to convey warfare, or what Wagner-Pacifici calls a "discourse of war," can be found in the repeated references to Mt. Carmel Center as a "compound." ATF's request to the military for assistance in serving the federal search warrant refers to the Davidians as "a dangerous, extremist organization" (*Investigation*, 1996: 46n), a term often applied to terrorists. The affidavit also contains the references supplied by Marc Breault's interview to "armed guards," "military training," and "shoot-to-kill orders" (military rules of engagement) cited previously. Packaged together with the equivocal description of "talk" about the "existence" of a book (*Anarchist Cookbook*), which deprogrammed ex-member Block never actually saw, the federal agents effectively convey the "message" they want to send.

Elsewhere in the affidavit, agent Aguilera describes an interview with one female ex-member, Deborah Bunds, who surmised that gunfire she heard while at Mt. Carmel was machine-gunfire. "She is sure the firearm was a machinegun because of the rapid rate of fire," the agent states (p. 10). Yet no information is provided by the agent to explain why this young woman is qualified to make such a judgment. A "rapid rate of fire" does not necessarily indicate that a firearm is a machine gun. Some semiautomatic weapons, as the Treasury Report later noted, may be equipped with a legal "hell-fire trigger" that enables "a semiautomatic weapon to be fired more quickly," a device of which Koresh was aware (1993: 35n) Another female ex-member, Janine Bunds, claimed to have identified an AR–15 from a photograph shown to her, but the same criticism applies—the qualifications of this witness to make such an assessment are unknown. The congressional report recognized the problem in using these witnesses to corroborate a technical issue of weapons violations, stating that "the affidavit included misleading . . . statements, . . . and failed to properly qualify witnesses' testimony when obviously called for based on their backgrounds" (p. 12).

Moreover, both of these women had been away from Mt. Carmel Center for an extended period of time. This raises another critical point. The congressional report chides the ATF on a point of law—that the events described by former members occurred more than a year earlier, making the evidence "so stale as to be of little of no value" (p. 11). Indeed, Marc Breault had departed four years earlier and the women had left in 1991. It is reasonable to assume that federal officials in ATF were aware, or should have been aware, of the legal principle of stale evidence. Constitutional law scholar Edward Gaffney has expressed unease with the ATF search warrant because "information submitted to a magistrate must be based on recent information that supports the conclusion that the item sought in a search warrant is probably still in the place to be searched" (Gaffney, 1995: 337). Did the ATF consider the staleness and, hence, unreliability of the evidence it offered in support of the warrants? This was the basis of a criticism made by the Treasury report, which faulted the ATF for relying on information supplied by deprogrammed ex-member David Block because it was stale: "Nor did the planners pay appropriate attention to the fact that Block had left the Compound over six months earlier" (p. 144). Block had given the ATF raid planners faulty information about where the weapons were stored.

The most blatant example of ATF's predisposition to a warfare mentality is found in the false claim of a drug nexus that allowed the Bureau to secure military training and assistance in the raid. The ATF alleged to the Department of Defense for the purposes of obtaining military assistance that it had evidence of an "active methamphetamine lab" on the Mt. Carmel property. According to the McClennan County Sheriff's Department, Koresh found methamphetamine lab equipment upon taking possession of Mt. Carmel in 1988 and reported it to authorities. An associate of the previous occupant, George Roden, was responsible for the drug lab equipment. The Sheriff's Department investigated the incident and removed the equipment. But at the behest of ATF, Marc Breault sent a fax to Special Agent Aguilera implying that the lab might still be operational, stating ambiguously that one person present at Mt. Carmel during the sheriff's visit "did not personally observe" removal of the drug lab equipment. The evidence for a drug nexus claimed by ATF was based largely on this deceptive and fabricated tip. The final congressional report concluded that "ATF agents misrepresented to Defense Department officials that the Branch Davidians were involved in illegal drug manufacturing" (p. 3) and exposed the deception in some detail (see pp. 45–46). Indeed, there was never any evidence of drug manufacturing or trafficking by the Davidians, and the building in which the lab equipment was found in 1988 burned to the ground in 1990, three years before the ATF raid.

The allegation of a drug nexus by ATF was imperative in order to obtain military assistance legally and without reimbursement. In the War on Drugs, Congress has created provisions for military assistance in drug interdiction on the basis that drug trafficking constitutes a national security threat. These provisions allow for an integration of civilian police and military forces. That the ATF knowingly fabricated a drug nexus to secure military training and assistance in the planning and execution of the raid on Mt. Carmel supports the contention of a predisposition to a warfare mentality. According to the congressional report, Marc Breault's fax to agent Aguilera included information that would have dispelled the drug lab claim (p. 45). But the ATF omitted this information and did not communicate contravening evidence to the military. On the contrary, ATF became engaged in an ongoing program of misrepresentation, requiring a series of fraudulent claims to Department of Defense officials and the Texas National Guard. In this regard, the agency's actions indicate an independent decision and preference to pursue a military-like response. This independent course of action is suggestive of an emergent law-enforcement culture that views police as "soldiers" in a war against crime and drugs, and contributes to what Skolnick and Fife (1993: 16) call a "siege mentality" engendering such incidents of lethal and excessive force. ATF vigorously sought counterdrug military assistance through Operation Alliance, which acts as the clearinghouse for requests in drug interdiction along the Southwest border. The ATF's proclivity toward militarization is most evident in the frequency with which it makes counterdrug military assistance requests. Through fiscal year 1989, the ATF had initiated 232 requests to Operation Alliance for military assistance (*Investigation*, 1996: 35). As stated earlier, the trend of police militarization is well documented, as is its vital connection to the drug war, where law enforcement has been given the greatest latitude in acquiring military support (Kraska, 1994). The linkage of the Waco tragedy to a militarized police culture was not lost on the congressional investigators, who concluded that "the ATF was *predisposed* to using aggressive military tactics in an attempt to serve the arrest and search warrant. . . . The bias toward the use of force," they asserted, "may in large part be explained by a culture within ATF" (p. 17).

Conclusion

The problems associated with the fabricated drug nexus, stale evidence, inflammatory and irrelevant material, and reliance on apostates and allied opponents of Koresh in the ATF investigation and planning of the raid highlight what the congressional report bluntly labels a "grossly incompetent" operation that "lacked the minimum professionalism expected of a major Federal law enforcement agency" (p. 4). Yet these baffling miscues can be explained by our model. The reliance on the warfare narrative of Koresh's opponents produced an exaggerated but convergent image that led to an overreaction by ATF. It did not seem critical to ATF investigators that the information supplied by former members was stale or irrelevant, nor did they raise questions about the objectivity or reliability of their sources. The investigators were inclined to believe the claims were true because they had resonant meaning. To disinterested observers, the ATF investigation leading to the raid plan had an irrational configuration. It was irrational because it was predicated on an inflated narrative image that resulted in egregious errors, misstatements of law, and unprofessional conduct. Yet this is precisely what the model predicts: "When such narratives are freighted with cultural meanings, they may exercise influence on a course of events in ways that exceed or do not depend upon merely factual, legal, of professional considerations" (Hall, 1995: 210).

WORKS CITED

Breault, Marc, and Martin King. 1993. *Inside the Cult: A Chilling, Exclusive Account of Madness and Depravity in David Koresh's Compound*. New York: Signet.

Bromley, David G., and Edward D. Silver. 1995. "The Davidian Tradition: From Patronal Clan to Prophetic Movement." Pp. 43–74 in Stuart A. Wright, ed., *Armageddon in Waco: Critical Perspectives on the Branch Davidian Conflict*. Chicago: University of Chicago.

Coulson, Danny O., and Elaine Shannon. 1999. *No Heroes: Inside the FBI's Secret Counter-terrorism Force*. New York: Pocket Books.

Duke, Stephen B., and Albert C. Gross. 1993. *America's Longest War: Rethinking Our Tragic Crusade against Drugs*. New York: Tarcher/Putnam.

Dunn, Timothy J. 1996. *The Militarization of the U.S.-Mexico Border, 1978–1992*. Austin: Center for Mexican-American Studies and the University of Texas Press.

———. 2002. "Waging War on Immigrants at the U.S.-Mexico Border," Pp. 65–81 in Peter B. Kraska, ed., *Militarizing the American Criminal Justice System*. Boston: Northeastern University Press.

Gaffney, Jr., Edward McGlynn. 1995. "The Waco Tragedy: Constitutional Concerns and Policy Perspectives." Pp. 323–58 in Stuart A. Wright, ed., *Armageddon in Waco: Critical Perspectives on the Branch Davidian Conflict*. Chicago: University of Chicago Press.

Hall, John R. 1995. "Public Narratives and the Apocalyptic Sect: From Jonestown to Mt. Carmel." Pp. 205–35 in Stuart A. Wright, ed., *Armageddon in Waco: Critical Perspectives on the Branch Davidian Conflict*. Chicago: University of Chicago Press.

———. 2002. "Mass Suicide and the Branch Davidians." Pp. 149–69 in David G. Bromley and J. Gordon Melton, eds., *Cults, Religion and Violence*. New York: Cambridge University Press.

Hall, John R., and Phillip Schuyler. 1998. "Apostasy, Apocalypse, and Religious Violence: An Exploratory Comparison of People's Temple, the Branch Davidians and the Solar Temple." Pp. 141–70 in David G. Bromley, ed., *The Politics of Religious Apostasy*. Westport, Conn.: Praeger.

Investigation into the Activities of Federal Law Enforcement Agencies toward the Branch Davidians. Thirteenth Report by the Committee on Government Reform and Oversight Prepared in Conjunction with the Committee on the Judiciary, August 2, 1996. Washington, D.C.: U.S. Government Printing Office.

Kopel, David B., and Paul H. Blackman. 1997. *No More Wacos: What's Wrong with Federal Law Enforcement and How to Fix It*. Amherst, N.Y.: Prometheus.

Kraska, Peter B. 1994. "The Police and Military in the Post-Cold War Era: Streamlining the State's Use of Force Entities in the Drug War." *Police Forum* 4: 1–8.

———. 1996. "Enjoying Militarism: Political/Personal Dilemmas in Studying U.S. Police Paramilitary Units." *Justice Quarterly* 13: 405–29.

———, ed. 2001a. *Militarizing the American Criminal Justice System: The Changing Roles of the Armed Forces and the Police*. Boston: Northeastern University Press.

———. 2001b. "Playing War: Masculinity, Militarism and Their Real World Consequences." Pp. 141–62 in Peter B. Kraska, ed., *Militarizing the American Criminal Justice System*. Boston: Northeastern University Press.

Kraska, Peter B., and Victor Kappeler. 1997. "Militarizing American Police: The Rise and Normalization of Paramilitary Units." *Social Problems* 44 (1): 1–18.

Lewis, James R. 1994. *From the Ashes: Making Sense of Waco*. Lanham, Md.:: Rowman and Littlefield.

McMains, David, and Wayne J. Mullins. 1996. *Crisis Negotiations*. Cincinnati: Anderson.

Miller, Richard Lawrence. 1996. *Drug Warriors and Their Prey: From Police Power to Police State*. Westport, Conn.: Praeger.

Noble, Kerry. 1998. *The Tabernacle of Hate: Why They Bombed Oklahoma City*. Prescott, Ontario: Voyageur.

Reavis, Dick J. 1995. *The Ashes of Waco: An Investigation*. New York: Simon and Schuster.

Skolnick, Jerome H. and James J. Fife. 1993. *Above the Law: Police and the Excessive Use of Force*. New York: Free Press.

Tabor, James D., and Eugene H. Gallagher. 1995. *Why Waco: Cults and the Battle for Religious Freedom in America*. Berkeley: University of California Press.

Thibodeau, David, and Leon Whiteson. 1999. *A Place Called Waco: A Survivor's Story*. New York: Public Affairs.

Wagner-Pacifici, Robin. 1994. *Discourse and Destruction: The City of Philadelphia versus MOVE*. Chicago: University of Chicago Press.

Walker, Sammuel. 1994. *Sense and Nonsense about Crime and Drugs*. Delmont, Calif.: Wadsworth.

Wright, Stuart A. 1993a. Interview with Wally Kennett, December 23. On file with author.

———. 1993b. Interview with Catherine Matteson, September 10. On file with author.

———, ed. 1995a. *Armageddon in Waco: Critical Perspectives on the Branch Davidian Conflict*. Chicago: University of Chicago Press.

———. 1995b. "Construction and Escalation of a Cult Threat: Dissecting Moral Panic and Official Reaction to the Branch Davidians." Pp. 75–94 in Stuart A. Wright, ed., *Armageddon in Waco*. Chicago: University of Chicago Press.

———. 1999. "Anatomy of a Government Massacre: Abuses of Hostage-Barricade Protocols during the Waco Standoff." *Terrorism and Political Violence* 11 (2): 39–68.

———. 2001. "Justice Denied: The Waco Civil Trial." *Nova Religio* 5 (1): 143–51.

———. 2002a. A Critical Analysis of Evidentiary and Procedural Rulings in the Branch Davidian Civil Trial." Pp. 100–113 in Derek H. Davis and Barry Hankins, eds., *New Religious Movements and Religious Liberty in America*. Waco: J. M. Dawson Institute of Church-State Studies and Baylor University Press.

———. 2002b. "Public Agency Involvement in Government-Religious Movement Confrontations." Pp. 181–99 in David G. Bromley and J. Gordon Melton, eds., *Cults, Religion and Violence*. New York: Cambridge University Press.

U.S. Department of Treasury. Report of the Department of Treasury on the Bureau of Alcohol, Tobacco, and Firearms Investigation of Vernon Wayne Howell, also known as David Koresh, September, 1993. Washington, D.C.: U. S. Government Printing Office.

U.S. District Court, Western District of Texas. Application and Affidavit for Search Warrant, W93–15M, filed February 26, 1993, Waco, Texas.

PART II

Asian and Asian-Inspired Groups

5

Family Development and Change in the Hare Krishna Movement

E. Burke Rochford, Jr.

Marriage and family life have played a central role in the development of religious communities and institutions (Berger 1969: 133; Foster 1991; Kanter 1972: 86–92). Dobbelaere underscores this fact when he argues that "the family allows us to now analyze empirically the *ongoing* processes of secularization and desecularization" (1987: 116, his emphasis). This chapter considers family development and change within the International Society for Krishna Consciousness (ISKCON), more popularly known as the Hare Krishna movement. I focus specifically on the demise of communalism in ISKCON's North American communities and the emergence of the nuclear family as the foundation of ISKCON's socioreligious world. As ISKCON became a householders' movement, collective forms of involvement gave way to growing privatization. At the same time, ISKCON parents challenged traditional sources of religious authority in favor of more democratic and bureaucratic structures. By the onset of the 1990s, ISKCON's previous sectarian structure and lifestyle had become secularized in North America.

Before turning to family development and movement change, I begin by describing briefly ISKCON's origins and beliefs as well as its American development.

Origins, Beliefs, and American Development

On September 19, 1965, the steamship *Jaladuta* sailed into New York harbor from Calcutta and docked at a Brooklyn pier at Seventeenth Street. Sixty-nine-year-old A. C. Bhaktivedanta Swami emerged from the ship to fulfill the instructions of his spiritual master to teach the Chaitanya cult in the West. No one could have imagined that this elderly Vaishnava sadhu from India would build a worldwide movement in just twelve years.

Bhaktivedanta Swami's Hare Krishna movement can be traced to sixteenth-century Bengal. Aligned with Hinduism, the Krishna Consciousness taught by Bhaktivedanta traced its roots to the Krishna *bhakti* (devotional) movement founded by Sri Chaitanya Mahaprabhu (1486–1533). Chaitanya preached that all people, regardless of their caste, could reach spiritual realization through service to Krishna (God). Central to this process is the chanting of the Hare Krishna mantra: Hare Krishna, Hare Krishna, Krishna Krishna, Hare Hare, Hare Rama, Hare Rama, Rama Rama, Hare Hare. Those taking initiation from Bhaktivedanta Swami agreed to commit themselves to chant sixteen rounds of this mantra daily on a string of prayer beads, and to abstain from eating meat, illicit sex (sex other than for procreation), taking intoxicants (such as cigarettes, alcohol, and drugs), and gambling. They also committed themselves to distributing their guru's translations and commentaries of various sacred Vedic texts in airports and other public locations. The latter financially supported ISKCON's American and worldwide expansion during the 1970s (Rochford 1985: 171–189).

Within a short period after his arrival in the United States, Bhaktivedanta turned his efforts to the young people living on the Bowery on the Lower East Side of New York City. After the Swami was observed chanting in Tompkins Square Park, word about him spread among the musicians and bohemian crowd of the area. Soon afterward several of those interested in the Swami and his teachings helped establish a small temple on Second Avenue. During his first year in New York, Bhaktivedanta, by now called Prabhupada by his young followers, initiated nineteen disciples. In 1966, Bhaktivedanta formally incorporated his nascent movement as the International Society for Krishna Consciousness (Goswami 1993).

ISKCON underwent major changes in the beginning of 1967, when Prabhupada traveled to the emerging hippie community in the Haight-Ashbury section of San Francisco. Thousands of young hippies were migrating to the neighborhood where one of Prabhupada's disciples had rented a storefront. During the first two years in the Haight-Ashbury, ISKCON recruited an estimated 150 to 200 converts (Johnson 1976: 33). To hold the countercultural youth being attracted, ISKCON developed a communal structure (Rochford 1982, 1985). From San Francisco, Prabhupada sent disciples to Los Angeles, Montreal, and England to establish ISKCON communities in the late 1960s. Thereafter, ISKCON communities emerged in major cities worldwide. In 1975, there were thirty-six ISKCON communities and preaching centers in North America, and forty more worldwide. By 1983, the total number spanning the globe had grown to nearly two hundred and, in 2003, ISKCON had over three hundred communities and preaching centers. Before his death in 1977, Prabhupada initiated approximately five thousand disciples into his movement worldwide. A large majority of these later disciples defected from ISKCON in the years after Prabhupada's death.

Following Prabhupada's death, ISKCON faced ongoing succession problems. Questions arose almost immediately about whether Prabhupada's successors actually had been appointed by him to serve as gurus in his absence (Rochford 1985: 221–255; 1989, 1998b). Within a decade, the majority of Prabhupada's eleven guru successors were forced from the movement because of moral transgressions and/or illegal behavior. After a number of reforms were implemented to limit the volatility of the guru institution (see Rochford 1998b), ISKCON now has approximately one hundred gurus initiating disciples throughout the world. Despite these changes, however, controversy persists about the role and authority of ISKCON's gurus and the guru institution as a whole (see, for example, D. G. Dasa 2002; Das and Das, 2001; *The Final Order* 1996; Rochford 1998a: 16–21, 1998b). ISKCON's worldwide Governing Body Commission (GBC) also received widespread criticism because it supported what many believed was a corrupt guru system (Rochford 1998b). As one ISKCON guru and GBC member stated:

> And now the GBC has become very, very weak. The principal reason for this has been the fall-down of spiritual masters [gurus] and the decay of spiritual authority in general. This applies to *sannyasis*, gurus, and the GBC. There has been a big overlap of these three categories and they are all in disrepute. The renounced order of life has come to be called the denounced order of life—we hear this all the time. People are very dubious about gurus—everyone is wondering when the next one is going to fall. And the GBC seems to be floundering and cannot do anything about it. There is a feeling that we do not know where our vision is going to come from (R. S. Dasa 2000: 38)

As this statement makes clear, ISKCON's structures of authority were weak and under attack in the years following Prabhupada's death. This resulted in ongoing organizational conflict and the rise of an insurgent movement within ISKCON that sought to redefine the guru institution and replace the existing members of the GBC (Rochford 1998b).

Over the past two decades, ISKCON has experienced a shift in the demographic profile of its membership. In North America, and in some other locations in Europe (such as Britain), ISKCON has become increasingly dependent upon its Indian congregation (Carey 1987; Nye 1997; Rochford 1995a; Zaidman 2000). In fact, ISKCON's temples have become places of worship for many thousands of Indian immigrants in North America, although few have become initiated disciples of any of ISKCON's gurus. Most limit their involvement to the Sunday program at their local ISKCON community, where they worship and socialize with other Indian people. A number of ISKCON communities in America rely heavily on the financial contributions of their Indian congregations in order to support the temple. In a few locations (such as Houston, Detroit, Chicago, and Vancouver) Indian people have taken on positions of leadership as temple presidents. It is likely that the ongoing Indianization of ISKCON will continue in the future, with the possibility that some ISKCON temples in America will become ethnic churches (Rochford 1995a). Of the approximately fifty thousand ISKCON members in North America today, a slight majority are Indian immigrants (Rochford forthcoming).[1]

The growth of marriage and family life has also changed the membership profile of ISKCON in North America. During ISKCON's beginning years in the late 1960s and early 1970s, there were few married members, and fewer still who had families. Even in 1980, there were about equal numbers of single renunciates and married people residing within ISKCON's communities. Only about one in four had children at that time. By the early 1990s, however, ISKCON had become a householders' movement, with the substantial majority of its membership married and having children (Rochford 1995c: 156; 1997; 1998a).[2]

Householder Life and Organizational Change in ISKCON

Up until the early 1980s, ISKCON retained considerable control over marriage and family life (Rochford 1995c, 1997). Indeed, virtually all ISKCON members were subject to the control of the movement and its largely renunciate leadership. As Ravindra Svarupa Dasa (2000: 37) has argued, this was because ISKCON members were financially dependent on the movement. Yet marriage and family life were subject to still further control by leaders who preached that marriage was suitable only for those unable to live a strict Krishna conscious lifestyle (R. S. Dasa 1994; Rochford 1997, 1998c). Marriage was thus devalued and involved a loss of status for men (Rochford 1997).

ISKCON's economic fortunes changed dramatically after 1976, as book distribution declined significantly. By 1980, book distribution had declined to less than one-quarter of its North American peak (Rochford 1985: 175). With far fewer financial resources at its disposal, ISKCON was no longer able to support a communal way of life. The nuclear family emerged as the foundation of ISKCON's social organization (Rochford 1995c, 1997). Associated with this were a number of related changes: Most parents were forced into the outside labor market to seek employment; children previously educated and cared for in ashram-based *gurukulas* (boarding schools) were returned to their parents; and householders increasingly lived independently of ISKCON, forming enclave communities near an ISKCON temple (Rochford 1995c, 1997). These changes only intensified the crisis surrounding ISKCON's leadership (Rochford 1995c: 168–71; 2002). Householders, struggling to establish themselves and their families in the outside culture, saw the renunciate leadership as simultaneously hostile and indifferent to their plight. As one long-time ISKCON member and householder recounts, "They [leaders] forced us out to find jobs and live on our own; to raise our families with little money and after being separated from our children for so long. After so much service. Now they [the leaders] turn around and criticize us because we did what they told us to do. That somehow we are materialistic because we [now] live outside. How can I have respect for them?" (Rochford 1995b: 171).

Tragically, the disinterest displayed by the leadership toward family life played a direct role in the abuse of children in ISKCON's boarding schools during the 1970s and 1980s (Rochford 1998c). As a stigmatized and politically marginal group, householders were left powerless to assert their parental authority over the lives of their children. In the past decade, child abuse has played an influential role in the ongoing politics surrounding the authority and legitimacy of ISKCON's leadership. For many devotees, both inside and outside of the movement, child abuse stands as a powerful symbol of the failure of ISKCON's traditionalist, communal, and hierarchical form of organization. The betrayal of trust represented by child abuse has challenged, if not undermined, the ISKCON commitment of many first- and second-generation members alike (Rochford 1998c). As institutional trust gave way to anger and doubt, householders became less willing to commit their lives to ISKCON than they had been in the past (Rochford 1995c, 1997, 2002). Many devotee parents abandoned ISKCON. Others joined forces with a growing congregation of independent householders and their families residing on the margins of ISKCON's North American communities (Rochford 1998c).[3]

By the 1990s, ISKCON in North America had become a very different movement from that of its early years. Congregationalism displaced ISKCON's previous sectarian structure and way of life as householders took up independent living situations. Traditional structures of religious authority were also under attack by devotees in and outside of ISKCON. It is these latter issues and their implications that frame the remainder of the chapter.

Findings and Discussion

Kanter's (1972: 86–92) investigation of nineteenth-century American communes demonstrated that successful utopian communities, both religious and secular, controlled or otherwise regulated two-person intimacy and family relationships. Only by renouncing couples and family relations could intimacy become a collective good serving the interests of the community as a whole. With the demise of communalism in the early and mid-1980s, ISKCON effec-

tively lost its ability to control marriage and family life. Devotee families became self-supporting and increasingly independent of ISKCON and its control
mechanisms.

Building on my previous research (Rochford 1995c, 1997, 2000, 2002), I
consider here how the ascendancy of the nuclear family influenced householder's commitments and patterns of involvement. To do this, I compare
parent and nonparent ISKCON members in North America.[4]

The findings in Table 5.1 report mean scores for a number of summary
measures of commitment to and involvement in ISKCON and Krishna Consciousness (see the appendix for specific measures used in the summary
scales). The findings reported compare parents and nonparents who are either
full-time or congregational members. The findings allow for comparisons
within and between membership categories. As one might readily expect, full-
time members with and without children are more committed and involved
in ISKCON and Krishna Consciousness than are congregational members.
Although these relatively higher rates of commitment and involvement exemplify their full-time status, they also speak to ISKCON's greater ability to
exert institutional control over full-time devotees than among its congregational members.

Full-time Member Comparisons

As indicated in Table 5.1, parent and nonparent full-time members share similar commitments to ISKCON and to their Krishna-conscious beliefs. This includes commitments to preaching Krishna Consciousness. Noteworthy differences revealed in Table 1 relate to questions of organizational involvement,
religious practice, and to the authority accorded ISKCON's leadership.

Full-time members without children are far more involved in the collective
religious life of the movement. They are also somewhat more likely to engage
in volunteer work in their local ISKCON community, and when they do, they
commit considerably more hours per week. These findings strongly suggest
that family life limits the availability of full-time devotees to take a more active
role in their ISKCON community. With children to get off to school and one
or more adult getting ready for work, parents find it difficult, or impossible, to
attend the morning temple programs and to commit longer periods of time to
performing community service. This is made even more difficult by the fact
that full-time parents often live farther from the temple and are more likely to
be employed in the outside labor market than those without children.

Although there are differences with respect to collective forms of participation in ISKCON, full-time members with children are just as likely as their
childless counterparts to involve themselves in the movement's private religious practices, such as chanting their daily *japa* (repeated mantra) and reading

TABLE 5.1. Mean Differences for Full-Time and Congregational Members with and without Children

Involvement and Commitment Dimensions	Full-Time Members Children		Congregational Members Children	
	No	Yes	No	Yes
I. Commitment dimensions				
A. Commitment to Krishna	20.31	19.97	16.29	17.45@
Consciousness	(131)	(117)	(49)	(89)
B. Commitment to ISKCON	17.07	17.21	15.08	15.15
	(131)	(117)	(49)	(89)
C. Commitment to preaching	9.32	9.16	7.31	7.62
	(131)	(117)	(49)	(89)
II. Collective involvement/participation				
A. Collective religious practices	24.04	20.72***	12.04	13.07
	(131)	(117)	(49)	(89)
B. Service/volunteer work in ISKCON community				
(a) Percentage who volunteer	88%	82%	43%	53%
	(105)	(91)	(20)	(45)
(b) Mean number of hours per week	33.27	16.88***	6.28	4.07
	(92)	(85)	(16)	(36)
(c) Medan number of hours per week	30.00	10.00***	4.00	3.50
	(92)	(85)	(16)	(36)
III. Individual involvement/participation				
A. Private/household religious practices	22.16	22.87	17.51	19.85*
	(131)	(117)	(49)	(89)
B. Follow regulative principles	39.36	38.97@	36.14	36.70
	(131)	(117)	(49)	(89)
IV. Leadership management, governance structures				
A. Authority of the gurus/guru institution	23.28	21.29**	20.49	19.90
	(96)	(106)	(12)	(34)
B. bureaucratic control of gurus required	9.18	9.58@	8.85	9.71
	(96)	(106)	(12)	(34)
C. Authority of the GBC	18.97	17.03***	16.35	15.89
	(131)	(117)	(49)	(89)
D. need for democratic govern structures	14.57	15.40**	15.19	15.72
	(131)	(117)	(49)	(89)

@p < .10 *p < .05 **p < .01 ***p < .001

the books of ISKCON's founder, Srila Prabhupada. Although they are less likely to attend morning temple programs, householders make up for this by holding morning worship services in their homes. They are, however, somewhat less strict in following the movement's regulative principles than nonparent full-time members.

A significant difference exists between parent and nonparent full-time members with respect to the authority attributed to ISKCON's leadership. Householders express far less support for ISKCON's gurus and the guru institution, as well as for the movement's governing authority, the GBC. Given this lower level of support, householders favor the expansion of democratic forms of governance within ISKCON and placing greater bureaucratic controls on the gurus.

The similarities in commitment, combined with significant differences in organizational involvement and collective religious practice, raise the distinction between *force* and *scope* (Chaves 1994; Yamane 1997). The concept of force indicates how strongly individuals hold to their religious beliefs. Scope, by contrast, refers to "the breadth of the applicability of those beliefs," both within and beyond the religious sphere (Yamane 1997: 116). Force therefore speaks to the question of commitment, whereas scope highlights the degree to which religious beliefs inform action. Although these concepts normally refer to religious beliefs and their application, in a more limited way they can also be used to understand organizational commitment and involvement. As we have seen, full-time parents and nonparents share in the force of their religious beliefs and organizational commitments, yet they differ sharply in their application or scope. Family life in ISKCON's case has acted to reduce the scope of parents' religious beliefs and organizational involvement. As we have seen, full-time parents are far less involved in collective forms of religious practice and contribute considerably less time doing ISKCON-related volunteer work. Moreover, because of long-standing opposition to marriage and family life by ISKCON's leadership, householders express far less support for the authority of the gurus and the GBC.

Congregational Member Comparisons

Table 5.1 reveals two statistically significant differences between congregational members with and without children. Householders have a somewhat greater commitment to Krishna Consciousness than do devotees without children. They also have considerably higher levels of private religious practice. Although it is not statistically significant, it is worth noting that householders are also more involved in ISKCON's collective religious practices and are more likely to volunteer in their local temple community. They do, however, contribute somewhat fewer hours of community service than those without family responsibilities.

As we compare full-time and congregational members, we find that congregational members with children express the least support for the leadership among the four comparison groups. They have the lowest mean scores for the authority of both the gurus and the GBC. Moreover, they more strongly favor placing greater bureaucratic controls on the guru institution and expanding democratic forms of governance within ISKCON. These findings are consistent with the fact that congregational members with families were most likely to have been directly affected by the collapse of communalism in the 1980s.

The findings presented demonstrate clearly that family life had a greater impact on full-time members than for ISKCON's congregation. For adherents who commit their lives full time to the group and its objectives, marriage and family demand various types of compromise. For congregational members, however, whose commitments are more segmental and less intense, the added responsibility of family has much less impact on their organizational and religious activities.

Conclusion

As ISKCON's communal structure disintegrated in North America in the 1980s, and independent nuclear families became the foundation of the movement's social organization, new patterns of individual religiosity emerged. The private dimensions of Krishna Consciousness gained prominence over collective religious practice and ISKCON involvement for both full-time and congregational parents. In part, this shift toward privatization can be attributed to reduced availability, as householders simply had less time to contribute toward group activities. Yet there are other factors at work.

According to Bryan Wilson, religion necessarily functions within the context of community. Secularization represents the decline of community (Wilson 1976: 265–266). When community no longer serves as a meaningful basis of social organization, religion succumbs to privatization, its more public and collective elements fading into the background, thus leaving the residual, individual religiosity as the essence of religious life. This is largely because group ritual and participation lose meaning and relevance in the absence of a functioning community of believers (Wilson 1982: 160).

The demise of community and the ascendancy of the nuclear family within ISKCON was also related to the decline of religious authority. As ISKCON's communities lost their previous "sacred" quality, traditional structures of authority simultaneously lost their ability to exert control over the actions of individual believers. Although it is true that ISKCON's elite faced significant challenges to their authority following Prabhupada's death, conflict only deepened when families were forced out of the movement's North American communities to establish independent households. Traditional structures of authority, the GBC and the guru institution, therefore lost the ability to exert control over the actions of householders. The result was growing privatization and secularization. As Chaves has argued, "[s]ecularization at the individual level may be understood as the decrease in the extent to which individual actions are subject to religious control" (1994: 757).

The developments discussed here suggest that the home has become the center of Krishna-conscious social and religious life; congregational religious life is inevitably centered around family life. Even among orthodox believers of other faiths who do not live communally, the household serves as the central location where religion finds practical relevance and meaning. As a Hasidic Jewish woman from the Crown Heights section of New York remarked, "A lot of what we do is done in private [within the household], but in our lives 'private' does not mean 'inferior.' Despite what everyone believes, the synagogue is not the center of Jewish life. The home is . . . the place where all the really practical bridges to a religious life are built" (quoted in Harris 1985: 125–126).

Although Krishna Consciousness in North America will continue to be practiced largely in the context of family life, there are dangers ahead. As Peter Berger states in his classic text, *The Sacred Canopy*, the family is a "tenuous construction" for religious meaning. Religion within the subworld of the family challenges the very possibility of sustaining an "integrated set of definitions of reality that . . . serve as a common universe of meaning" (1969: 134–135). A religious system increasingly practiced within the nuclear family risks fragmentation, as individuals craft their own religious worlds relatively unencumbered by religious authority. This trend may be countered by religious authorities who can exert control over householder life. Yet, as we have seen, this authority is presently under siege within ISKCON. Over the past two decades ISKCON has witnessed a "decay of spiritual authority in general" (R. S. Dasa 2000: 38). Without the embodiment of religious authority within the GBC and guru institutions, Krishna Consciousness as a "lived religion" is likely to move along a variety of paths, thus potentially compromising the vitality of the tradition.

APPENDIX: SUMMARY DIMENSIONS AND MEASURES

I. *Commitment to Krishna Consciousness and ISKCON*

A. COMMITMENT TO KRISHNA CONSCIOUSNESS

My religious faith is (Check one). (1) Only of minor importance for my life; (2) Important, but no more important than certain other aspects of my life; (3) Of central importance, and comes before all other aspects of my life.

At this point in my life I am most committed to: (a) Advancing in Krishna Consciousness; (b) Improving my *sadhana* [religious practice]; (c) Following the four regulative principles; (o) Not at all committed ... (3) Moderately committed ... (5) Strongly committed.

How would you characterize the strength of your commitment to: (a) The practice of Krishna consciousness. (o) Not at all committed ... (3) Moderately committed ... (5) Strongly committed.

B. ISKCON COMMITMENT

How would you characterize the strength of your commitment to: (a) ISKCON leadership and present structure; (b) ISKCON's purposes and goals. (o) Not at all committed ... (3) Moderately committed ... (5) Strongly committed.

I have a sense of pride about being a member of ISKCON. (4) Agree strongly, (3) Agree, (2) Disagree, (1) Disagree strongly.

Whatever ISKCON's past or present faults, it still represents Prabhupada and on that basis I will forever be connected to ISKCON. (4) Agree strongly, (3) Agree, (2) Disagree, (1) Disagree strongly.

My identity as a person is defined largely by my ISKCON involvement. (4) Agree strongly, (3) Agree, (2) Disagree, (1) Disagree strongly.

C. PREACHING COMMITMENT

I have little desire to go out in public and distribute books and preach. (1) Agree strongly, (2) Agree, (3) Disagree, (4) Disagree strongly.

I actively preach to non-devotees at work and/or as part of my daily routine. (4) Agree strongly, (3) Agree, (2) Disagree, (1) Disagree strongly.

At this point in my life I am most committed to: (a) Preaching Krishna Consciousness. (o) Not at all committed ... (3) Moderately committed ... (5) Strongly committed.

II. Collective Commitment and Involvement

A. INVOLVEMENT IN COLLECTIVE RELIGIOUS PRACTICES

How often do you: (a) Attend *Mangala arti* [morning service]; (b) Attend *Guru Puja*; (c) Attend *Bhagavatam* class. (6) Daily, (5) 5–6 days, (4) 3–4 days, (3) 1–2 days, (2) Less than once a week, (1) Rarely or never.

B. SERVICE/VOLUNTEER WORK

Do you spend time doing regular *unpaid* duties in your local ISKCON Temple community? (1) No (2) Yes.

If yes: On *average* how many hours *a week* do you spend performing unpaid duties? # Hours a week. (Range: .5 hrs. to over 90 hrs/week)

III. Individual Involvement and Participation

A. PRIVATE/HOUSEHOLD RELIGIOUS PRACTICES

How often do you: (a) Chant *japa*; (b) Offer your food; (c) Read Prabhupada's books; (d) Listen to tapes of Prabhupada; (e) Hold morning
program at home. (6) Daily, (5) 5–6 days, (4) 3–4 days, (3) 1–2 days, (2)
Less than once a week, (1) Rarely or never.

B. FOLLOW REGULATIVE PRINCIPLES

Do you engage in: (a) meat eating; (b) eating eggs; (c) eating meat products; (d) consuming alcohol; (e) smoking marijuana; (f) taking LSD,
cocaine or other drugs; (g) using tobacco; (h) consuming caffeinated
coffee or tea; (i) gambling; (j) illicit sex—in or outside of marriage. (4)
No, (3) Rarely, (2) Sometimes, (1) Often.

IV. Leadership, Management, Governance Structures

A. AUTHORITY OF THE GURUS/GURU INSTITUTION

To what degree have the following positively influenced your willingness
to be connected to and/or involved in ISKCON? Spiritual potency of
ISKCON's present gurus. (0) No influence . . . (3) Some influence . . .
(5) Major influence.

To what degree have the following limited your ability or desire to remain actively involved in ISKCON? (a) Lack of respect for ISKCON's
current gurus. (5) No influence . . . (3) Some influence . . . (0) Major
influence.

The "reform movement" of the mid-1980s basically resolved the guru
controversies within ISKCON. (4) Agree strongly, (3) Agree, (2) Disagree, (1) Disagree strongly.

The atmosphere of controversy surrounding the new gurus following
Prabhupada's disappearance had a profound negative influence on my
commitment to ISKCON. (1) Agree strongly, (2) Agree, (3) Disagree,
(4) Disagree strongly.

To my understanding, Prabhupada appointed the 11 first gurus as *ritviks*
[ceremonial priests who initiated devotees] with the idea that they
would become regular initiating gurus [on his behalf] after his departure. (4) Agree strongly, (3) Agree, (2) Disagree, (1) Disagree strongly.

I respect the spiritual potency and authority of ISKCON's current gurus.
(4) Agree strongly, (3) Agree, (2) Disagree, (1) Disagree strongly.

The grand-disciples of Srila Prabhupada are fully connected to the *parampara* [tradition]. (4) Agree strongly, (3) Agree, (2) Disagree, (1) Disagree strongly.

B. BUREAUCRATIC CONTROL OF GURUS REQUIRED

There should be enforced standards limiting an ISKCON guru's material lifestyle. (4) Agree strongly, (3) Agree, (2) Disagree, (1) Disagree strongly.

Aspiring ISKCON gurus should be required to pass the Bhaktivedanta degree. (4) Agree strongly, (3) Agree, (2) Disagree, (1) Disagree strongly.

ISKCON's initiating gurus should be subject to regular reviews by the GBC. (4) Agree strongly, (3) Agree, (2) Disagree, (1) Disagree strongly.

C. AUTHORITY OF THE GBC

To what degree have the following limited your ability or desire to remain actively involved in ISKCON? (a) Lack of trust in the GBC. (5) No influence . . . (3) Some influence . . . (0) Major influence.

When you have important decisions to make in your life, how often do you seek guidance from: (a) the local GBC representative. (1) Never, (2) Rarely, (3) Sometimes, (4) Often, (5) Always.

The GBC represents my interests and concerns as a devotee. (4) Agree strongly, (3) Agree, (2) Disagree, (1) Disagree strongly.

I accept the GBC as the legitimate governing authority within ISKCON. (4) Agree strongly, (3) Agree, (2) Disagree, (1) Disagree strongly.

The GBC is a closed and elitist group. (1) Agree strongly, (2) Agree, (3) Disagree, (4) Disagree strongly.

GBC decisions have little or no relevance to my life as a devotee. (1) Agree strongly, (2) Agree, (3) Disagree, (4) Disagree strongly.

D. NEED FOR DEMOCRATIC GOVERNING STRUCTURES

Members of the GBC should be elected to office rather than appointed to the GBC. (4) Agree strongly, (3) Agree, (2) Disagree, (1) Disagree strongly.

The GBC should be structured to ensure representation for a greater variety of devotee viewpoints. (4) Agree strongly, (3) Agree, (2) Disagree, (1) Disagree strongly.

ISKCON needs to have a well-functioning and impartial system of justice to deal with problems and abuses that take place. (4) Agree strongly, (3) Agree, (2) Disagree, (1) Disagree strongly.

Devotees should have the right to congregate freely and discuss any and
all issues of mutual concern, no matter how controversial. (4) Agree
strongly, (3) Agree, (2) Disagree, (1) Disagree strongly.

Local temple management should be the responsibility of an elected
Board of Directors. (4) Agree strongly, (3) Agree, (2) Disagree, (1) Disagree strongly.

NOTES

1. For a more detailed discussion of ISKCON's development in North America,
see Daner 1976; Goswami 1993; Judah 1974; Rochford 1985, 1995a; and Shinn 1987.
For a history of ISKCON's growth in Britain, see Knott 1986, 2000; in India, see
Brooks 1989; and in Western and Eastern Europe, see Rochford 1995b, 2000.

2. These findings about marriage and children should be considered reasonable
estimates rather than precise figures. Neither the 1980 nor the 1991–1992 surveys
were based on probability samples and thus cannot be considered representative samples.

3. On June 12, 2000, a federal lawsuit was filed in Dallas, Texas, on behalf of
forty-four young men and women who alleged that they were subjected to "sexual,
emotional, mental, and physical abuse and exploitation" while minors in ISKCON's
gurukulas during the 1970s and 1980s (Children of ISKCON, et al. v. The International
Society for Krishna Consciousness et al 2000). The plaintiffs in the case sought a total
of $400 million—$200 million in actual damages and $200 million in punitive dam-
ages. Defendants in the case were also charged with violations of the Racketeer Influenced and Corrupt Organizations Act (RICO). The lawsuit was dismissed by the federal court when the judge ruled that RICO violations were not involved in the alleged
abuse (ISKCON Communications 2001). In October 2001, the lawsuit was refiled in
state court in Dallas, with the number of plaintiffs increasing to over ninety.
Thereafter, ISKCON attorneys filed for Chapter 11 bankruptcy protection for those
ISKCON communities named in the complaint (Cooperman 2002). On February 27,
2004, ISKCON's Chapter 11 Reorganization Plan was filed in the U.S. Bankruptcy
Court. Compensation will be offered to over five hundred young people who attended
ISKCON's gurukulas, rather than to only the initial plaintiffs in the lawsuit. The tort
fund to compensate claimants will hold as much as $15 million. The Plan allocates $2
million from the fund for a nonprofit youth development and support organization,
which will provide continuing assistance to former and present students of ISKCON's
schools. It is anticipated that the Reorganization Plan will be finalized by the end of
2004 (das, Gupta 2004).

4. Findings presented are based on data from the Prabhupada Centennial Survey. This worldwide survey was conducted in 1994–1995 with approximately two
thousand respondents from fifty-three different countries (see Rochford 1998a,
1999). The findings reported here include full-time and congregational ISKCON
members residing in the United States (N=285) and Canada (N=111). The appendix
details the commitment and involvement dimensions, variables, and specific mea-

sures used in the present investigation. A discussion of the procedures used in scale construction can be found in Rochford 1998a.

WORKS CITED

Berger, Peter. 1969. *The Sacred Canopy: Elements of a Sociological Theory of Religion.* Garden City, N.Y.: Doubleday.

Brooks, Charles. 1989. *The Hare Krishnas in India.* Princeton: Princeton University Press.

Carey, S. 1987. "The Indianization of the Hare Krishna Movement in Britain." In R. Burghart, ed., *Hinduism in Great Britain.* London, Tavistock.

Chaves, Mark. 1994. "Secularization as Declining Religious Authority." *Social Forces* 72(3): 749–774.

Children of ISKCON et al. v The International Society for Krishna Consciousness et al. 2000. Dallas, TX. (author's files).

Cooperman, Alan. 2002. "Krishna Temples Plan Bankruptcy Filing over Abuse Suit." *Washington Post,* February 9.

Daner, Francine. 1976. *The American Children of Krsna.* New York: Holt, Rinehart and Winston.

Das, Adridharan, and Madhu Pandit Das. 2001. "The False Dawn of Guru Reform." Unpublished manuscript.

das, Gupta (Joseph Federowsky). 2004. "ISKCON Chapter 11 Reorganization Plan Filed." Chakra Web site (www.oldchakra.com accessed March 3).

Dasa, Dhira Govinda. 2002. *Srila Prabhupada: The Prominent Link.* Alachua, Fla. : Satvatove.

Dasa, Ravindra Svarupa. 1994. "Cleaning House and Cleaning Hearts: Reform and Renewal in ISKCON." *ISKCON Communications Journal* (two-part essay). 2(1): 43–52; 2(2): 25–33.

———. 2000. "Restoring the Authority of the GBC." *ISKCON Communications Journal* (8)1: 37–43.

Dobbelaere, Karel. 1987. "Some Trends in European Sociology of Religion: The Secularization Debate." *Sociological Analysis* 48: 107–137.

The Final Order. 1996. No author specified. Paper presented to a select committee of the Governing Body Commission, October.

Foster, Lawrence. 1991. *Women, Family, and Utopia.* Syracuse, NY: Syracuse University Press.

Goswami, Satsvarupa Dasa. 1993. *Srila Prabhupada Lilamrta.* Los Angeles: Bhaktivedanta Book Trust.

Harris, Lis. 1985. *Holy Days: The World of a Hasidic Family.* New York: Collier Books.

ISKCON Communications Press Release. 2001. "$400 Million Suit against Hare Krishna Dismissed." Chakra Web site (www.oldchakra.com/articles/2001/10/03/lawsuit.dismissed/index.htm; accessed October 3).

Johnson, Gregory. 1976. "The Hare Krishna in San Francisco." Pp. 31–51C. in Glock and R. Bellah, eds., *The New Religious Consciousness.* Berkeley: University of California Press.

Judah, Stillson. 1974. *Hare Krishna and the Counterculture.* New York: John Wiley & Sons.

Kanter, Rosabeth Moss. 1972. *Commitment and Community.* Cambridge: Harvard University Press.

Knott, Kim. 1986. *My Sweet Lord: The Hare Krishna Movement.* Wellingborough, U.K.: Aquarian Press.

———. 2000. "In Every Town and Village: Adaptive Strategies in the Communication of Krishna Consciousness in the UK, the First Thirty Years." *Social Compass* 47(2): 153–167.

Nye, Malory. 1997. "ISKCON and Hindus in Britain: Some Thoughts on a Developing Relationship." *ISKCON Communications Journal* 5(2): 5–13.

Rochford, E. Burke, Jr.. 1982. "Recruitment Strategies, Ideology and Organization in the Hare Krishna Movement." *Social Problems* 29(4): 399–410.

———. 1985. *Hare Krishna in America.* New Brunswick: Rutgers University Press.

———. 1989. "Factionalism, Group Defection, and Schism in the Hare Krishna Movement." *Journal for the Scientific Study of Religion* 28(2): 162–179.

———. 1995a. "Hare Krishna in America: Growth, Decline, and Accommodation." In T. Miller ed., *America's Alternative Religions.* Albany: State University of New York Press.

———. 1995b. "Crescita, Espansione e mutamento nel movimento degli Hare Krishna." *Religioni e Sette nel monde* 1(1): 153–180.

———. 1995c. "Family Structure, Commitment, and Involvement in the Hare Krishna Movement." *Sociology of Religion* 56(2): 153–75.

———. 1997. "Family Formation, Culture, and Change in the Hare Krishna Movement." *ISKCON Communications Journal,* 5(2): 61–82.

———. 1998a. "Prabhupada Centennial Survey: Final Report." Submitted to the Governing Body Community, November, 1998.

———. 1998b. "Reactions of Hare Krishna Devotees to Scandals of Leaders' Misconduct." Pp. 101–117 in A. Shupe, ed., *Wolves within the Fold.* New Brunswick: Rutgers University Press.

———. 1998c. "Child Abuse in the Hare Krishna Movement: 1971–1986." *ISKCON Communications Journal* 6(1): 43–69.

———. 1999. "Prabhupada Centennial Survey: A Summary of the Final Report." *ISKCON Communications Journal* 7(1): 11–26.

———. 2000. "Demons, Karmies and Non-devotees: Culture, Group Boundaries, and the Development of the Hare Krishna in North America and Europe." *Social Compass* 47(2): 169–186.

———. 2001. "The Changing Face of ISKCON: Family, Congregationalism and Privatization." *ISKCON Communications Journal* 9(1): 1–11.

———. 2002. "Family, Religious Authority and Change in the Hare Krishna." Paper presented at the meetings of the Center for Studies on New Religions, Salt Lake, Utah, June.

———. Forthcoming. "Hare Krishna." *New York Encyclopedia.* Syracuse: Syracuse University Press.

Schachter-Shalomi, Zalman. Forthcoming. "Interview with Rabbi Zalman Schachter-Shalomi." In Harold Kasimow, John Keenan, and Linda Keenan, eds., *Beside*

Still Waters: Jews Christians, and the Way of the Buddha. Boston: Wisdom Publications.

Shinn, Larry. 1987. *The Dark Lord: Cult Images and the Hare Krishnas in America.* Philadelphia: Westminster.

Wilson, Bryan. 1976. "Aspects of Secularization in the West." *Japanese Journal of Religious Studies* 4: 259–76.

———. 1982. *Religion in Sociological Perspective.* Oxford: Oxford University Press.

Yamane, David. 1997. "Secularization on Trail: In Defense of a Neosecularization Paradigm." *Journal for the Scientific Study of Religion* 36(1): 109–122.

Zaidman, Nurit. 2000. "The Integration of Indian Immigrants to Temples Run by North Americans." *Social Compass* 47(2): 205–219.

6

When Leaders Dissolve: Considering Controversy and Stagnation in the Osho Rajneesh Movement

Marion S. Goldman

Contemporary religious movements and also established faiths must remain flexible in terms of organizational structures, stewardship, and doctrines, in order to sustain membership and maintain a favorable position within their host societies (Stark 1996a). If a group deviates too fundamentally from its original leader's visions, however, it may fail by becoming something entirely different through fundamental change or merger with a different faith (Wilson 1985). The path to success involves flexibility around a central core of history, doctrine, and organizational leadership.

Every major faith in the United States has experienced transitions that reflect shifting demographics, changing social environments, and also internal organizational struggles and constraints (B. Johnson 1992, and Finke and Stark 1992). This general process of internal change is particularly visible among controversial new religious movements that are attempting to sustain their unique identities without antagonizing the wider society surrounding them. Some groups, such as the Family (Children of God), Scientology, or the Rajneesh movement, have been lightning rods for controversy, almost perishing in the wake of conflict with the wider society (Bainbridge 2000; Hall et al. 2000).

The Rajneesh movement experienced two tumultuous periods of internal power struggles coupled with external attacks. The first major controversy developed in India, and it paved the way for a second conflict in the United States, which many outsiders believed would destroy the movement (Goldman 1999). Over the past decade, especially after Osho Rajneesh's death, the movement has been involved in a delicate rebalancing, which has facilitated worldwide retention and recruitment of about six to eight thousand committed followers (known as sannyasins) and fellow travelers, as well as a far larger group of circulating affiliates and clients, whose allegiances are to Osho as well as to different, complementary spiritual paths.

After almost two decades of controversy and a subsequent decade of accommodation, the movement has positioned itself within the vital marketplace of novel religions. Most movement insiders and younger spiritual seekers no longer perceive the Friends of Osho as spiritual lightning rods. Devotees have redefined their leader's contributions and reframed the movement's central doctrines to make them less controversial to outsiders. In addition to movement shifts, the host societies in the United States, Western Europe, and India have become more accommodating to American-influenced yoga, meditation, and diverse spiritual texts (Dinan 2002). Just as the Osho movement has changed, the grounding context has risen up to meet them and a host of similar religious movements.

Leaders in the Pune headquarters and regional centers downplay the Oregon experience of the 1980s, which is still considered as a defining moment by many scholars and by Americans who remember the media blitz concerning criminal activities at the short-lived communal city, Rajneeshpuram. The movement continues, and much of the remaining controversy involves historical memory rather than present experience.

This chapter will consider the history and philosophy of the Rajneesh movement beginning in India in the 1970s through the current phase. This serves as background for examining the ways in which the movement stabilized after Osho changed his name from Bhagwan Shree Rajneesh, retreated into the background, and finally left his body (died) in 1990. In his last years, Osho encouraged an Inner Circle of twenty-one rotating members to spread his ideas and develop a governance structure. After his death in 1990, there were splits and divisions within the movement, but Osho's reframed teachings drew people together, the World Wide Web permitted communication to continue, and the flagship center in Pune attracted thousands of clients who have helped fund the movement.

Currently, some younger sannyasins advocate depersonalizing the movement and allowing Osho's teachings to overshadow his old charismatic identity. They question the viability of the Osho movement leadership in Koregaon Park, and suggest a more general movement that supports human freedom (Sannyas' News November 9, 2002). Others, most often longtime members, resist. This latest challenge dramatically illustrates how leaders in the Osho Rajneesh movement generated survival tactics and encouraged the formation of local,

FIGURE 6.1. Bhagwan Shree Rajneesh.

semiautonomous groups, allowing them to overcome lingering high levels of tension with host societies, the death of their founder, and current internal challenges to the Osho movement itself.

During each phase of its development, the Osho movement redefined itself, moving from an initial period of inclusivity to exclusivity in the mid-1970s and 1980s, and back to inclusivity in the twenty-first century. Prior to 1970, followers were permitted, if not encouraged, to explore and sustain spiritual allegiances to other spiritual traditions along with Osho, in an inclusive movement. However, as Rajneesh assumed the role of enlightened spiritual master, sannyasins were increasingly required to renounce other paths and personal ties. After his death, the movement grew more inclusive, suggesting Osho's meditative discipline could be amplified by connections with other faiths.

The movement's most controversial years were those when exclusive commitment was required. Official narrative now downplays the events in Oregon, which almost destroyed the group. In addition, there is increasing emphasis on Osho's statements about creating noninstitutionalized spirituality: "Those who have been in communion with me will have learned one thing absolutely, categorically: that life cannot be confined into institutions" (Osho [1982] 2001: 236).

Osho Rajneesh and His Movement(s)

Many of Osho's sannyasins characterized him as a mercurial mixture of mad-man, savior, charlatan, and saint (Franklin 1992). His various biographies and autobiographical assertions can support any of these characterizations, yet there is surprisingly widespread agreement about the basic outlines of Osho's own story.

He was born to a Jain family in Kuchawada, India, in 1931 and named Mohan Chandra Rajneesh. Jainism is an independent Indian faith closely re-lated to Buddhism. Thus, Rajneesh was raised outside the dominant Hindu paradigm, in a tradition that synthesized different philosophies much as his own would, three decades later.

Rajneesh received an M.A. in philosophy from Saugar University and im-mediately took a job at Raipur Sanskrit College (Sanskrit Mahavidyalaya). His lectures created so much controversy that Rajneesh transferred to another uni-versity the next year, and then received a promotion to professor in 1960. When college was not in session, he traveled around India lecturing about politics, sexuality, and also spirituality.

He was a perceptive, captivating lecturer who soon gained a loyal following that included a number of wealthy merchants and businessmen. These clients gave Rajneesh donations for individual consultations about their spiritual de-velopment and daily life. These were commonplace, for throughout India peo-ple seek guidance from learned or holy individuals in the same way as Amer-icans might consult a psychologist or pastoral counselor, and Rajneesh's private practice was not unusual in itself (Mehta 1979). The rapid growth of his cli-entele, however, was somewhat out of the ordinary, suggesting that he was an unusually talented spiritual therapist.

By 1964, a group of wealthy backers had set up an educational trust to support Rajneesh and the occasional rural meditation retreats he led. Like many professionals whose client base grows quickly, Rajneesh acquired a busi-ness manager around this time. She was Laxmi, an upper-class, politically well-connected woman, who became his first personal secretary and organizational chief.

Rajneesh's early career reflected his individual charismatic attributes of intelligence, emotional appeal, and ability to communicate directly to individ-uals, even when they were part of a large audience (Weber [1922] 1968). He was highly energetic, with an alluring emotional volatility that attracted both seekers in India and a small but growing number of Europeans and North Americans (B. Johnson 1992).

At the request of university officials, Rajneesh resigned his post at the University of Jabalpur in 1966 and started to use the name Acharya Rajneesh,

denoting his primary role as a spiritual teacher. He supported himself by lecturing, offering meditation camps, and individually counseling affluent Indian
clients. Rajneesh critiqued established politics and religions, and advocated
more open, liberated sexuality. Building from the work of the Western philosopher Gurdjieff, he also developed active meditation exercises that facilitated
individuals' ability to observe their own physical, mental, and emotional processes.

Word of mouth and occasional published references to his gifts brought
Westerners to the Mt. Abu meditation camps that Acharya Rajneesh directed
in the late 1960s and early 1970s. In 1971, *I Am the Gate* was the first of
Rajneesh's many books to be published in English. Visitors from the West
sought out Rajneesh in the airy Bombay apartment he acquired late in 1969.
He sent a number of these first guests back home to start an international
network of meditation centers.

In 1971, as his following grew and diversified, Rajneesh exchanged the title
of Acharya, which means teacher, for the more expansive, Bhagwan, signifying
enlightened or awakened one. For the first time, Rajneesh acknowledged that
he had experienced the profound nothingness of true satori constituting enlightenment almost twenty years earlier, on March 21, 1953.

As the movement grew in the early 1970s, an official organizational structure emerged (Carter 1990: 70). Devotees received new names, often those of
revered Hindu gods and goddesses, signifying their psychological and spiritual
rebirth through taking sannyas (vow of renunciation), opening themselves to
Bhagwan, and renouncing their pasts. Around this time in Bombay, Bhagwan
also asked all of his followers to wear saffron orange clothing, a traditional
color of holy men in India. The names and clothes that signified instant holiness, coupled with Rajneesh's free-wheeling political and sexual philosophy,
deeply offended the local population while enchanting Westerners, who began
to outnumber the Indians visiting Rajneesh. The tension with Indian host
society grew as Rajneesh began to cultivate a formal movement. His reputation
as a radical academic, his philosophy, and the privileged Westerners flaunting
Indian conventions all combined to generate tension with the surrounding
culture. That tension, however, functioned to help define the movement for its
members and to generate internal solidarity (Erikson 1966).

In 1974, Bhagwan relocated his headquarters to Pune (previously known
as Poona), one hundred miles southeast of Bombay. With considerable Western
backing and additional financial support from long-time Indian devotees,
Bhagwan moved to a six-acre enclave and acquired adjoining real estate in
Koregaon Park, an elite Pune suburb. Over the next five years, the Shree Rajneesh Ashram grew to include a meditation hall where Bhagwan could lecture
to several thousand people, a smaller auditorium, facilities for a multitude of
human potential therapy groups, a medical clinic, cottage industries, restau-

rants, shops, classrooms, and housing for sannyasins who lived year round at the ashram. The movement was clearly stratified, with affluent and talented sannyasins receiving the most access to Bhagwan.

At this point, Rajneesh enhanced his charisma by adopting the long, flowing beard associated with Indian holy men. His clothing was white, differentiating him from all others in the ashram (B. Johnson 1992). As the movement grew, he could no longer have regular daily contact with most sannyasins, but he became present everywhere in the ashram through ubiquitous photographs and rumors of occasional, almost random, encounters with rank-and-file sannyasins. In addition, his evening darshans (audiences), at which Rajneesh answered sannyasins' written questions, provided a symbolic closeness, as did his habit of presenting important visitors and departing sannyasins with gifts of small wooden boxes or clothing that symbolized his continuing presence in their lives (Goldman 1999).

Well-known Western presses such as Harper and Row translated and published some of Bhagwan's discourses. At the movement's peak around 1976, close to thirty thousand Westerners visited the Shree Rajneesh Ashram yearly, and the worldwide movement included more than twenty-five thousand sannyasins (Milne 1987: 23; Carter 1990: 59–60). After 1976 or 1977, however, recruitment stagnated and many sannyasins left the movement. There was greater competition in the American spiritual and self-actualization marketplaces, Western economies were constricting, and some influential figures in the human potential movement, like Richard Price of Esalen Institute, publicly denounced violence in the Rajneesh therapy groups (Anderson 1983: 299–302).

There were also political difficulties in India that stemmed from Bhagwan's public lectures against the powerful Janata party. Bhagwan talked to his devotees about the Buddhafield, a spiritual community built around him and his teachings, but none of the regional governments in India was willing to permit the commune. In Pune, sannyasins spread rumors of death threats to Bhagwan by members of various Indian sects, accompanied by terrifying descriptions of his growing emotional stress and his declining health. There were also reports of violent incidents between sannyasins and Indian opponents of the Shree Rajneesh Ashram.

The Indian government investigated allegations of Rajneesh-sanctioned prostitution, international drug trafficking, gold smuggling, money laundering, and tax evasion. Sannyasins have always denied most of these charges, but the criminal investigations created many difficulties for the movement and its leaders. The first period of extreme controversy, 1976 to 1980, created an impetus for Rajneesh to relocate to the United States. In June of 1981, the founder and his inner circle flew to New Jersey. The Shree Rajneesh Ashram began to shut down, except for a small remaining crew of resident caretakers.

The flight from India represented an attempt to deal with increasing ex-

ternal pressures, as the host society confronted Rajneesh's hostility to traditional rules and values. This confrontation with convention reflected the tensions that are commonly associated with spontaneous, innovative charismatic
leadership (Wilson 1987). Rajneesh could have minimized friction and risked
losing some of his charismatic appeal. Or he could have held his ground in
India and faced painful sanctions against him and his sannyasins. Instead he
fled in order to rebuild his movement in North America, where large numbers
of sannyasins resided.

On July 10, 1981, Bhagwan's representatives purchased the 64,229-acre
Big Muddy Ranch in central Oregon for $5.9 million, and they started building
the Buddhafield at Rajneeshpuram. Rumor had it that the decision to move to
Oregon reflected the relatively inexpensive price of the ranch and his new
personal secretary's misplaced assumption that all of Oregon was peopled by
tolerant liberals who smoked marijuana and left their neighbors alone. Wasco
County proved to be far less laid-back than she had expected. During the next
four years, the ranch became the site of considerable accomplishment and also
considerable intrigue and crime. Debates still rage within and outside the
movement about who did what to whom and why. One of the central questions
is whether or not Bhagwan knew about a whole array of plots and criminal
activities on the part of his personal secretary, Ma Anand Sheela, at Rancho
Rajneesh.

The Big Muddy had been zoned as restricted farmland, and until the com-
munity disbanded, there were public charges made by environmental groups
such as 1,000 Friends of Oregon, as well as civil lawsuits, government investigations, and fines levied for land use and building code violations. The
Oregon attorney general, David Frohnmayer, challenged the incorporation of
Rajneeshpuram itself as an unconstitutional merger of church and state. In
December 1985, after Rancho Rajneesh was already up for sale, the Federal
District Court enjoined Rajneeshpuram (the City of Rajneesh) from exercising
governmental power because there was no effective church-state separation.

Along with land use and legal questions, there were also disputes about
who was using the land. The federal Immigration and Naturalization Service
(INS) closely investigated Rajneesh's immigration status from the very beginning. Rajneesh's formal visa application stated his intention to seek American
medical treatment, requiring a stay of less than a year. He later requested
extensions of his visa because of his work as a religious teacher. After legal
disputes with Rajneesh attorneys, INS rescinded its earlier deportation order
(Carter 1990: 161–165). Nevertheless, federal agencies continued to investigate
sannyasins who were foreign nationals and had recently married U.S. citizens
(Carter 1990: 150–152).

State and local elections also generated tension with outsiders. Shortly after
sannyasins purchased the Big Muddy, they began buying real estate in the tiny
hamlet of Antelope, the town closest to Rajneeshpuram. By the spring of 1982,

the forty or so longtime residents feared that they would be overrun by san-nyasins unless they voted to disincorporate. The disincorporation election failed because of new Rajneesh voters, whose representatives soon controlled both Antelope's city council and its school board. The townspeople's varied battles against the newcomers, who eventually changed Antelope to City of Rajneesh, drew widespread public attention and generated a number of law-suits.

More national attention turned toward central Oregon in the autumn of 1984, when Rajneesh's personal secretary, Sheela Silverman, and her inner circle developed a plan to bus in several thousand homeless individuals, mostly men, recruited in cities across the United States. They were to be rehabilitated in the Buddhafield and, not coincidentally, they could also vote in the Novem-ber election in which sannyasins were candidates for seats on the Wasco County Commission. Massive negative publicity, state monitoring of voter reg-istration, and legal opposition doomed the plan. At the last minute Sheela instructed everyone at Rajneeshpuram to boycott the polls.

By the end of 1984, almost all of the homeless visitors had left. Before the election, however, information about the conflict and impending debacle spurred Bhagwan to abandon his vow of silence and begin speaking to a small group, the Chosen Few. Although control of Rajneeshpuram shifted, state and federal officials continued investigations of Sheela, her entourage, other san-nyasins, and Rajneesh himsef.

The following year, a handful of influential sannyasins who had been there since the Pune days defected and began to talk with authorities. On September 14, 1985, Ma Anand Sheela and members of her inner circle fled Rajneesh-puram for Europe. Rajneesh accused them of a wide variety of crimes against sannyasins, the public, and the state of Oregon. The crimes included mass salmonella poisoning of 750 individuals in almost a dozen restaurant salad bars located in the county seat of the Dalles. This was the largest known in-cident of germ warfare in the United States, and Sheela had designed it as a test run for a more massive effort that could temporarily incapacitate large numbers of anti-Rajneesh voters on the upcoming election day (Carter 1990: 224–226). This was the apex of the second wave of tension, which continues to characterize the movement for many outsiders.

Rajneesh accused his former personal secretary and her circle with drug-ging sannyasins, wiretapping, arson, and embezzlement of Rajneesh move-ment funds. In the wake of FBI investigations of these allegations, dozens of sannyasins received subpoenas to testify before the county grand jury, and Rajneesh himself was served on October 6, 1985. There were also rumors that warrants were being prepared for his arrest.

Less than two weeks later, federal agents in Charlotte, North Carolina, captured Rajneesh, when two Lear jets carrying him and a handful of sanny-asins stopped to refuel in route to Bermuda. He was taken from North Carolina to Oklahoma and back to Oregon, where his attorneys posted bond so he could return to Rajneeshpuram. Rajneesh left the United States less than two weeks later, after filing no contest pleas to two counts of immigration fraud and paying fines and prosecution costs of $400,000 (McCormack 1985: 116). This marked the most negative moment of Rajneesh's career within his movement. It could have led to the disintegration of the movement or the displacement of Rajneesh as its leader. Instead, most sannyasins blamed Rajneesh's former personal secretary for the misguided and exploitative policies that doomed Rajneesh-puram, and threatened Rajneesh and his movement's existence.

Bhagwan and his new staff traveled all over the world seeking asylum, and met rejection from a number of countries. Eventually, his representatives bar-gained with the Indian government and resettled in Pune. A number of long-time sannyasins began to return to the Shree Rajneesh Ashram, renamed Osho Commune International, and now recently renamed Osho Meditation Resort. They quietly refurbished each building and cultivated the magnificent Zen gardens. Pune was once again Bhagwan's home, and it was a destination resort for spiritual therapy, meditation, and personal growth.

In 1989, Rajneesh decided that Bhagwan was no longer an appropriate title for him because too many people understood it to mean God. He tried out the name Buddha, and met with resounding negative feedback from out-siders. Then he changed to Shree Rajneesh. He finally settled on Osho, a name that varied sources have explained differently.

The Friends of Osho trace the derivation to William James's word *oceanic*, which implies dissolving into the whole of human existence—in other words, being at one with everything there is. They note that Osho also carries the meaning of "The Blessed One on Whom the Sky Showers Flowers" (Osho Commune International Press Release 1991). Others write that Osho comes from the Japanese language, implying great gratitude and respect for one who expands consciousness (Palmer and Sharma 1993: 53–54). Like almost every-thing else about Osho Rajneesh, his name itself created initial controversy. It could be interpreted broadly to mean a revered teacher of meditation (Palmer and Sharma 1993: 54).

The movement continued after Osho died on January 19, 1990, as san-nyasins heeded his message that his spirit was with them, and he had merely left his body. A dozen years later the ashram/commune/resort in Koregaon Park still throbs with music, new meditations, a mystery school, and personal growth groups. Although the Indian government has renamed Poona as Pune in order to delegitimate colonial history, the city is much as it was twenty years ago, when the ashram was at its peak and Bhagwan lectured daily.

Osho left twenty-one members of his Inner Circle in charge of the orga-nization, and several of them have emerged as leaders. The small, international movement keeps attracting affluent seekers from the Americas, Europe, Japan, Australia, and, most recently, Israel. Some are drawn to the Pune Ashram, while others affiliate through local centers in a number of locations, including Sedona, Arizona, and Byron Bay, Australia.

Sannyasins keep in touch by means of their sophisticated electronic network of group and individual home pages on the World Wide Web. Through their visits to Pune, personal contacts, and small active Osho centers, and a number of spin-off groups and personal growth institutes, sannyasins, old and recent, continue the work of transforming themselves and creating a new consciousness that synthesizes spirituality and material pleasure.

Osho Rajneesh and His Philosophies

Since 1974 in Pune, almost every word Osho uttered had been faithfully recorded and published or filmed. He was fond of asserting that there were 108 beads on the malas (necklaces) that his devotees wore to suspend their lockets with his photograph, and there were likewise 108 paths to travel toward enlightenment. In almost five hundred books, which were transcriptions of his lectures, initiation talks, and pithy sayings, almost every major religious and philosophical tradition received Osho's attention. He lectured about Buddhism, Christianity, Hasidism, Sufism, the Upanishads, Yoga, and Zen, as well as Marx, Freud, and Henry Ford.

These traditions were not always well understood by sannyasins or seekers, but they melded together in an interesting, palatable spiritual stew dominated by Zen Buddhism. Bhagwan asserted that the many internal contradictions and paradoxes in his philosophy were essential to an individual's spiritual development. People could choose to accept or reject any part of his philosophical discourses. In the 1970s and 1980s it was up to individuals, so long as they remained connected to Bhagwan and accepted him as the ultimate master. Currently, there is greater emphasis on consistent meditation and less on an explicit master/disciple relationship. Despite changes, elaborations, and advocacy of individual choice, the two most important themes in Osho's philosophy remain surprisingly clear and consistent. They are first, surrender of individual ego and second, integration of the individual's material and spiritual selves.

A recent Web site displayed Osho's ten commandments, which he wrote when he was Archayra Rajneesh in 1970 (www.otoons.com/osho/10.htm). He noted that writing this was difficult because he objected to commandments of any sort. Nevertheless, he wrote:

1. Never obey anyone's command unless it is coming from within you also.
2. There is no God other than life itself.
3. Truth is within you, do not search for it elsewhere.

4. Love is prayer.
5. To become a nothingness is the door to truth. Nothingness itself is the means, the goal and attainment.
6. Life is now and here.
7. Live wakefully.
8. Do not swim—float.
9. Die each moment so that you can be new each moment.
10. Do not search. That which is, is. Stop and see.

Numbers 3, 7, 9, and 10 were underlined by Osho in his original letter.

These Commandments are a constant doctrine that has grounded the Osho movement for more than thirty years. Free choice was the essence of Osho's philosophy, but the ultimate freedom of enlightenment was disappearance of ego through surrender to his teachings, and after 1990, to his meditations. As with almost everything else in the movement, there has always been considerable latitude for individuals to construct their own meanings of surrender.

During the exclusive phases of the movement from the early 1970s through 1990, much emphasis was placed on the individual's relationship to Rajneesh, but that changed after he died. Being a sannyasin made it possible to become a new person and achieve enlightenment someday. Throughout his life, Osho asserted that every sannyasin had to follow a slightly different spiritual path, but all of their personal quests absolutely required an invisible line reaching directly from his teachings to each devotee's heart.

Osho returned again and again to his vision of a new man who synthesized the worldly and the godly. His ideal was Zorba the Buddha, a consummate being who combined the spiritual focus of the Indian mystic with the life-embracing traits of the materialistic Westerner. Zen, Tantra tradition, and Reverend Ike's message came together in Rajneesh's vision. Bhagwan obviously relished this ideal, which may have been his personal goal, as well. He stated: "A new human being is needed on earth, a new human being who accepts both, who is scientific and mystic. Who is all for matter and all for spirit. Only then will we be able to create a humanity which is rich on both sides. I teach you the richness of body, richness of soul, richness of this world and that world. To me that is true religiousness" (Rajneesh 1983: 14).

Rajneesh's enthusiastic embrace of materialism generated American media feeding frenzies, and most outsiders still remember his collection of more than ninety Rolls Royces before any other characteristic of Rajneeshpuram. The extravagant cars symbolized both Rajneesh's embrace of the corporeal world and his tweaking of Americans' automobile worship. He owned his first Rolls in India, where there was a tradition of the car's association with royalty that dated back to the British Raj. His collection, however, only reached epic proportions after he settled in the United States. Sannyasins appreciated the humor behind the swarm of Rolls Royces. They also rejoiced in their teacher's luxurious appointments in the same way that devout members of many other groups appreciate their leaders' splendor.

Osho also called for transcendence of traditional gender roles. Women and men alike were encouraged to merge their own female and male sides and to strive for flexibility in every aspect of their lives (Goldman 1999). The ideal human being was neither overtly male nor stereotypically female, but Rajneesh placed highest value on traditionally feminine traits like intuition, expressiveness, emotionalism, self-awareness, and sensitivity. Men were admonished to nurture their own feminine traits and women were lauded when they acted assertively. Individuals were exhorted to move toward androgyny, without forsaking their gender identity (Goldman 1999).

Osho Rajneesh's flexible, postmodernist spiritual philosophy made becoming a sannyasin relatively easy. Currently, official sannyas is not essential, although some individuals still become formal devotees through local centers or the headquarters in Pune. In the 1970s some people became sannyasins in Pune and then lived at the Shree Rajneesh Ashram for several years. Others joined the movement somewhat precipitously, on short visits to Pune, during stays at Rajneeshpuram, or in brief ceremonies at one of the urban Rajneesh centers that flourished until 1982. In the late 1970s, many sannyasins simply sent a card to the central office in Pune, requested sannyas, and received new names and a mala, with a locket holding Rajneesh's picture.

From the early 1970s through 1990, prospective devotees checked a box on their application forms to note whether they wanted to keep their old first name, which would now be prefaced with Ma or Swami followed by a brief name such as Anand (Love), or whether they wished to receive an entirely different, Hindu-style name inspired, if not actually bestowed, by Rajneesh. After taking sannyas, in the 1970s and 1980s, devotees were supposed to meditate at least once daily, don sunrise colors (which included a whole spectrum of red-based shades), wear a mala with the locket housing Bhagwan's likeness, and become vegetarian. Along with these practices, sannyasins had to acknowledge their heart-to-heart connection to Bhagwan. These rules became increasingly flexible after Osho's death. Even when the movement had explicit, exclusive boundaries, however, those simple policies were flexible, because free choice was such a crucial element in Rajneesh's philosophy.

Since 1990, the movement has redefined itself a number of times, moving in the direction of greater inclusiveness. The ashram in Pune became known as the Osho Commune International until it was recently renamed Osho Meditation Resort. Some changes resulted from differences between different international centers and the governing council in Pune, but the most pronounced current debates involve the continued centrality of Osho as a spiritual teacher. Recent devotees ask, To what extent does Osho himself continue to be necessary to his teachings?

Diaspora and Decentralization

After Rajneeshpuram collapsed in 1985, American sannyasins gravitated to places with good weather, active alternative cultures, and spiritual diversity, unusually on the West Coast or in the Southwest. They sought out tolerant and beautiful places, where their professional skills and countercultural experiences are appreciated. Large concentrations of American sannyasins, both old and recent, currently live near the Osho Academy in Sedona, Arizona, and the Viha Meditation Center in Marin County, California, and devotees from other places in the United States visit and correspond with them. Wherever they are, devotees often gather together to visit and meditate. Some travel to the Pune headquarters, when they have the time and money, although their trips are less frequent than they were a decade ago.

During the diaspora from the communal city, Rajneeshpuram, some people renounced Rajneesh and embarked on new spiritual paths. Most, however, at least temporarily sustained their still unwavering faith that their spiritual master would guide their futures in some way. The most affluent sannyasins left without need to worry about the years they had devoted to building the ill-fated Buddhafield. Other sannyasins who remained faithful left under less fortunate circumstances. Those without professional credentials or specific skills had to fill huge four- and five-year holes in their résumés (Gordon 1987: 211–212). But devotees with businesses or academic jobs often helped out less fortunate sannyasins like these, offering them references or sometimes employment. One Northwest millionaire recommended dozens of sannyasins on the basis of excellent work in his household or businesses. Most of their work was indeed excellent, but they had carried it out at Rajneeshpuram.

Looking back over more than a decade, many sannyasins have found that their years at Rajneeshpuram provided them with unexpected occupational possibilities. Even in the twenty-first century, however, they seldom share their Rajneeshpuram histories with their business acquaintances, though these sannyasins have built solid professional reputations on skills they honed at the communal city. Their creative problem-solving approaches and their concerns with process as well as outcomes enhance their abilities to function in business or the professions. Their recent occupational successes are embedded in the focus, skills, and intense work ethic that they had developed at Rajneeshpuram. None of these individuals has grown rich, but they survive comfortably within the middle class.

Many sannyasins made the most of the twists and turns of their lives, redefining their parents' and sometimes their own ideas of occupational success. For example, an attorney had supervised one of the Ranch's large communal kitchens, because he lacked credentials to practice law in Oregon. When he left the Ranch, he had no career direction at all, except the desire never to practice law again. After house cleaning, waiting on tables, and wandering, he started a restaurant, employing other sannyasins and outsiders as well. Explaining his current entrepreneurial success, he said, "Need makes you smart. We had to come up with an answer to life."

Coming up with an answer to life after the Ranch meant deciding about work and resettlement. Spiritual issues had already been resolved. Most Rajneeshpuram residents continued to believe that they had found the answer to their fundamental questions about life when they took sannyas. Even those who renounced Bhagwan usually continued to see him as an essential and meaningful part of their histories, somewhat like a former spouse. By sustaining their faith, sannyasins resembled others who are active members of communal new religions for at least two years. Those years fundamentally alter devotees' goals and ways of looking at the world. Long-term members seldom renounce the spiritual priorities acquired as part of an intense collective religion. Even if they disengage or if their groups collapse, they usually remain faithful to the alternative spiritual stances they have adopted (Goldman 1995; Jacobs 1989; Wright 1987). They may move closer to the mainstream, but they retain the overall frameworks that they have acquired through their earlier commitment.

The current Osho movement builds on the experience and dedication of individuals who have retained their commitment for decades. Those who lived at Rajneeshpuram command the same deference once accorded the individuals who had met with Rajneesh in his tiny Bombay apartment in the 1970s. New sannyasins have been recruited from the children of older sannyasins, and from individuals in the twenty-one to fifty-year-old range in affluent, industrial nations where there is resonance for Osho's message of personal exploration and fusion of the material and spiritual.

The Pune headquarters, now Osho Meditation Resort, continues at the center of the movement, governed by the twenty-one members of the Inner Circle, many of whom were called to govern by Osho himself. The movement around Osho, however, grows increasingly decentralized, with direct challenges to the Inner Circle's authority by both recent Indian sannyasins and a group of British sannyasins who have been dissidents for many years. Challengers to a Pune-centered movement suggest that Osho's work and general spirit are more important than the outmoded leadership at the Osho Meditation Resort. It is undeniable that Osho's influence has spread well beyond the confines of a specific organization, but the center at Pune still holds together disparate groups. There are centers in Japan, Germany, Italy, and the United States, which directly acknowledge leadership in Pune and continue to underscore Osho's role as each sannyasin's personal spiritual teacher. Farther from this centralized model, there is a handful of thriving Osho residential centers with unique perspectives differing somewhat from Pune, which nevertheless remain connected to the Meditation Resort. For example, the Osho Academy in Sedona, Arizona, acknowledges one of their own, Kaveesha, who died in 1998, as an enlightened teacher whose words and example provide a bridge to Osho and his teachings.

Some longtime sannyasins also lead independent personal growth centers with have no formal affiliation with Pune or other Osho organizations. The New England Center for Transforming Consciousnes uses Osho's teachings in promoting Consciousness to the highest degree. Another personal growth business, the Hawaii Institute for Wellness, offers workshops and counseling to already self-actualized individuals.

Some former sannyasins who have created organizations of their own separated from Osho and his organization, but still incorporate his teachings in their spiritual work. They acknowledge Osho as a spiritual master without deferring to the Pune Meditation Resort or to any center directly connected to Pune. Although not nominally affiliated, these teachers continue to spread Osho's doctrines. Among the best known are Dolano, Paul Lowe, Mikaire, Nadeen, Tony Parsons, and Matreya.

There are also customers, a few of whom once may have been closer to the formal Osho centers. These thousands of unaffiliated seekers create a market that supports both formally recognized and also unofficial organizations connected to Osho. Retreats, meditations, therapies, and consultations are easily available in regions where there are Osho centers. Major international chain bookstores, Borders, and Barnes and Noble, carry books, videos, tea sets, and tarot cards with Osho's imprint.

A recent Web site, www.rebelliousspirit.com, lists over five hundred Osho-related celebrations, trainings, events, and therapy groups, available from November 2002 through January 2003, in twenty-three countries. The Osho movement continues, surviving both extreme controversy in India and Oregon and after growing internal dissent when the controversies with the outside diminished.

Reconstructing History, Surviving Controversy

The first section of this chapter considered the question of whether Osho and his movement could be considered successful. They were not successful in terms of membership growth, resource accumulation, and social influence after the late 1970s (Stark 1996a). However, the movement continues with the core at the Pune headquarters and Meditation Resort, and widening circles of affiliated centers, personal growth businesses with movement ties, Osho-influenced spiritual teachers, and unaffiliated clients in the spiritual marketplace.

In the early 1980s leaders in the Rajneesh movement defined success as the creation of a huge utopian community with one hundred thousand residents within two decades (Carter 1990). But with Osho's death and the subsequent decentralization of movement authority, the group has generally construed success as broad global cultural influence. This revision allows the movement to claim success on its own terms (Wilson 1985; Dawson 1998). The current vision is legitimated by emphasis on the discourses in which Osho asserted that he never wanted to found or even be part of an organized religion: "I am so inconsistent, that it is impossible to create a dead institution around me, because a dead institution will need the infrastructure of a dead philosophy. I will leave you open" (Osho [1982] 2001: 232).

Benton Johnson (1992) noted that many founders were not particularly concerned with their spiritual movement's organizational survival after their own deaths. He suggested that some leaders like Maharishi Mahesh Yogi (who founded Transcendental Meditation) and Osho Rajneesh had elaborated the traditional Indian form of the private guru to a psychological and religious counselor. Thus a legacy of influence might be all that could be expected from both Osho's primary doctrine and leadership style. The goal of living in the moment—a central tenet of Osho's doctrine—does not encourage the development of a bounded movement destined to last over many generations (just as, in other movements, neither does a Christian emphasis on impending endtimes that makes long-term planning futile). The movement has survived because Osho's Inner Circle saw a future in which the Pune Ashram/Commune/Meditation Resort served as an inclusive hub for worldwide centers and individual clients with varying degrees of commitment.

It is possible to discern progression in the Osho movement and its continued survival, albeit with diluted central authority and amorphous cultural influence. First, Rajneesh ostracized Sheela and attributed all crimes and difficulties to her and her lieutenants. Second, the movement vacated the site of most extreme controversy, dispersed its members to other centers, and reclaimed its original headquarters far from the abandoned communal city in central Oregon. Third, Rajneesh renamed himself, the movement, and its headquarters. Fourth, he established a central council to carry on organizational duties. Fifth, he and the Inner Circle who governed after his death redefined the movement as one of meditation and personal growth informed by Osho's philosophy. Finally, after Osho's death, the movement reemphasized and underscored his focus on organizational diffusion and inclusive spirituality. Success was about truth and influence rather than organization and growth. Thus his legacy became: "Never born. Never died. Only visited this Planet Earth between December 11, 1931 and January 19, 1990" (Osho 1996, 282).

We may chart a more general model, applicable to groups like Children of God/the Family, the movement around George Gurdjieff, or even the hardy, intense groups who still identify with People's Temple, as well as devotees of Rajneesh. An effective movement strategy for overcoming controversy: (1) reproach, blame and ostracize selected individuals for controversy, (2) relocate, (3) rename, (4) reorganize, (5) reemphasize doctrine to support practice rather than allegiance, and finally, and possibly most important, redefine success.

The Friends of Osho continue because they recruit and hold affluent, talented devotees from a number of different nations. Since they are privileged individuals, sannyasins are influential in their societies. They are taken seriously without suffering extreme political repression, and they can remain engaged on an international scale (Stark 1996b, 29–47). Although there are now probably fewer than eight thousand active sannyasins and committed fellow travelers worldwide, they continue to have more influence than their numbers suggest because they are linked by sophisticated computer networks, they provide spiritual goods to a wide market of esoteric consumers, and they come together regularly in small groups. They follow Osho's promise of continuity after his death: "There will be no need to make any special nook and corner for me: I will be dissolved in my people. Just as you can taste the sea and it is salty, you will be able to taste any of my sannyasins and you will find the same taste: the taste of Bhagwan [Osho], the taste of the Blessed One" (Osho [1982] 2001: 239–240).

WORKS CITED

Anderson, Walter Truett. 1983. *The Upstart Spring: Esalen and the American Awakening.* Reading, Mass: Addison Wesley.

Bainbridge, William Sims. 1997. *The Sociology of Religious Movements.* New York: Routledge.

———. 2000. *The Endtime Family: Children of God.* Albany: State University of New York Press.

Carter, Lewis F. 1990. *Charisma and Control in Rajneeshpuram.* New York: Cambridge University Press.

Dawson, Lorne L. 1998. *Comprehending Cults: The Sociology of New Religious Movements.* New York: Oxford University Press.

Dinan, Steven. 2002. *Radical Spirit: Spiritual Writings from the Voices of Tomorrow.* Novato, Calif.: New World Library.

Erikson, Kai T. 1966. *Wayward Puritans: A Study in the Sociology of Deviance.* New York: John Wiley.

Finke, Roger and Rodney Stark. 1992. *The Churching of America 1776 to 1990.* New Brunswick: Rutgers University Press.

Franklin, Satya Bharti. 1992. *The Promise of Paradise: A Woman's Intimate Story of the Perils of Life with Rajneesh.* New York: Station Hill Press.

Galanter, Mark. 1989. *Cults: Faith, Healing, and Coercion.* New York: Oxford University Press.

Goldman, Marion S. 1995. "Continuity in Collapse: Departures from Shiloh." *Journal for the Scientific Study of Religion* 34: 342–353.

———. 1999. *Passionate Journeys: Why Successful Women Joined a Cult.* Ann Arbor: University of Michigan Press.

Gordon, James S. 1987. *The Golden Guru*. Lexington, Mass: Stephen Grenne Press.

Hall, John R., with Philip Schuyler and Sylvaine Trinh. 2000. *Apocalypse Observed: Religious Movements in North America, Europe, and Japan*. London: Routledge.

Jacobs, Janet Liebman. 1989. *Divine Disenchantment*. Bloomington: University of Indiana Press

Jina, Anand. 1993. "The Work of Osho Rajneesh: A Thematic Overview." Pp. 47–56 in *The Rajneesh Papers*, edited by Palmer and Sharma. Delhi: Motilal Banardidass.

Johnson, Benton. 1992. "On Founders and Followers: Some Factors in the Development of New Religious Movements." *Sociological Analysis* 53 (supplement): S1–S13.

Johnson, Miriam M. 1975. "Fathers, Mothers, and Sex-Typing." *Sociological Inquiry* 45: 319–334.

———. 1991. *Strong Mothers, Weak Wives*. Berkeley: University of California Press.

Kilbourne, Brock, and James T. Richardson. 1984. "Psychotherapy and New Religions in a Pluralistic Society." *American Psychologist* 39: 237–251.

McCormack, Win. 1985. *The Rajneesh Files: 1981–1986*. Portland: New Oregon Publishers.

Mehta, Gita. 1979. *Karma Kola: Marketing the Mystic East*. New York: Simon and Schuster.

Melton, J. Gordon, and Robert L. Moore. 1982. *The Cult Experience: Responding to New Religions*. New York: Pilgrim.

Meredith, George. 1988. *Bhagwan: The Most Godless Yet the Most Godly Man*. Poona: Rebel Publishing House.

Milne, Hugh. 1987. *Bhagwan: The God That Failed*. New York: Saint Martin's.

Osho (Bhagwan Shree Rajneesh). [1982] 2001. *The Goose Is Out*. Mumbai: Osho International Foundation.

———. 1993. *The Everyday Meditator: A Practical Guide*. Boston: Charles E. Tuttle.

———. 1996. *Meditation: The First and Last Freedom*. New York: St. Martin's.

Palmer, Susan, and Sharma, Arvind, eds. 1993. *The Rajneesh Papers: Studies in a New Religious Movement*. Delhi: Motitlal Banarsidass.

Rajneesh, Bhagwan Shree. 1983. *Rajneeshism: An Introduction to Bhagwan Shree Rajneesh and His Religion*, edited by Academy of Rajneeshism. Rajneeshpuram, Oregon: Ma Anand Sheela, Rajneesh Foundation International.

Sannyas' News. http://www.sannyasnews.com/index.html.

Stark, Rodney. 1996a. "Why Religious Movements Succeed or Fail: A Revised General Model." *Journal of Contemporary Religion*. 11: 133–146.

———. 1996b. *The Rise of Christianity: A Sociologist Reconsiders History*. Princeton: Princeton University Press.

Stark, Rodney, and William Bainbridge. 1985. *The Future of Religion*. Berkeley: University of California Press.

Strelley, Kate, with Robert D. San Souci. 1987. *The Ultimate Game: The Rise and Fall of Bhagwan Shree Rajneesh*. New York: Harper and Row.

Wallis, Roy. 1979. *Salvation and Protest*. London: Francis Pinter.

Weber, Max. [1922] 1968. *Economy and Society: An Outline of Interpretive Sociology*. Vol. 3. New York: Bedminster.

Wilson, Bryan R. 1985. "Factors in the Failure of New Religious Movements." Pp. 30–45 in *The Future of New Religious Movements,* edited by David Bromley and Phillip Hammond. Macon, Ga: Mercer University Press.

Wright, Stuart A. 1987. *Leaving Cults: The Dynamics of Defection.* Washington D.C.: Society for the Scientific Study of Religion.

7

Soka Gakkai: Searching for the Mainstream

Robert Kisala

Soka Gakkai is a religious group within the Nichiren Buddhist tradition. Until its excommunication in November 1991, it was officially a lay movement within the Nichiren Shoshu sect, and since that time it continues to function as a lay Buddhist movement.[1] With as many as eight million members in Japan, it is the largest of the new religious movements in that country, and a prime example of the mass lay Buddhist movements that began to attract attention in the early postwar period. Furthermore, through its international branch, Soka Gakkai International, it has members in more than 120 countries and territories worldwide, and claims over a million members outside of Japan.

Soka Gakkai and its leader, Ikeda Daisaku, a former president of the organization who now holds the titles of Honorary President of Soka Gakkai and President of Soka Gakkai International, have been controversial throughout the postwar period, initially as a result of the group's aggressive proselytization, and later because of its political involvement. Its involvement in politics, culminating in the formation of its own political party, now nominally independent of Soka Gakkai, is indicative of an active involvement in society that characterizes much of the Nichiren Buddhist tradition in Japan.

The group claims to be a pacifist sect, and it has been prominent in promoting peace activities. In this it reflects another common trait of new religious movements in postwar Japan, and indeed of Japanese religious groups in general. The meaning attached to its pacifism, however, is open to question—yet another source of controversy surrounding the group. In what follows I will outline the history and development of the group, paying special attention to these points of contention: its proselytizing activities, its political activities, and its peace commitment.

Early History

Soka Gakkai was founded by Makiguchi Tsunesaburo (1871–1944), an educator who stressed the role of creativity and personal experience in his educational philosophy.[2] Its original name, Soka Kyoiku Gakkai, or Academic Society for Value-Creating Education, indicates that in its origins the group was primarily composed of educators interested in Makiguchi's philosophy. Indeed, Soka Gakkai traces its foundation to the publishing of the first volume of Makiguchi's opus, *Soka kyoikugaku taikei* (Outline of value-creating education), on 18 November 1930, where the Academic Society for Value-Creating Education is listed as the publisher. It was only in 1937, however, that an inaugural meeting of the society was held, and at that time the group had already taken on a decidedly religious character.

Makiguchi was born in a fishing village in Niigata Prefecture, on the Japan Sea coast. His father left the family when he was three years old, and the resulting financial problems necessitated his adoption into a relative's family. At the age of fourteen he left to live with yet another relative, an uncle in Otaru on the northern island of Hokkaido. Since the financial situation of his uncle did not allow him to continue in school, he soon got a job with the police department, where his hard work and seriousness caught the eye of the station chief. For that reason, he moved to Sapporo at the age of eighteen when the chief was transferred there, and two years later Makiguchi was accepted into the Hokkaido Normal School. After graduation he was employed at the elementary school affiliated with that institution.

Makiguchi is described as a hardheaded rebel in official Soka Gakkai biographical accounts as well as in outside scholarship.[3] Clearly his educational philosophy, which emphasizes creative thought and personal experience, did not conform to educational practice in Japan, where repetitious practice and the rote memorization of facts continue to be valued. For this reason, it seems that Makiguchi's career was one of continuous clashes with his immediate superiors and the educational system in general. In 1901, a dispute over discipline led to the termination of his employment in Sapporo, and he moved to Tokyo with his wife and two children.

In Tokyo, Makiguchi initially tried to support himself as a scholar, publishing his first book, *Jinsei chirigaku* (Life geography), in 1903. This book, which draws connections between geography and everyday life and advocates the study of geography through field trips and other hands-on experiences, seems to have been well received, and through its publication he became acquainted with other scholars such as Nitobe Inazo, the author of *Bushido*, and Yanagita Kunio, the founder of Japanese folklore studies. Makiguchi took on editing work to support his family, and even started his own correspondence school, but when that enterprise failed in 1909 he was forced to find employment once again as an elementary school teacher in the Tokyo school system. Periodic clashes with authorities characterized a twenty-year career there, until finally he was made principal of a school already slated for closure, leading to his early retirement.

It was about the time of his retirement that Makiguchi became involved in the Nichiren Shoshu faith through an acquaintance at the school where he was principal. Nichiren Shoshu is an early offshoot of the Nichiren movement, founded by a disciple of Nichiren, Nikko, who moved from the Nichiren establishment at Mt. Minobu to Taisekiji at the foot of Mt. Fuji in 1289. Nichiren Buddhism in general enjoyed an upsurge in popularity during the late nineteenth and early twentieth centuries, largely due to the popularization of nationalist ideas associated with the sect by Tanaka Chigaku and others. Nichiren Shoshu is perhaps the most militantly exclusivist of the Nichiren sects, its very name proclaiming its belief that it is the True Religion.

There are several reasons that might explain Makiguchi's turn to religion at this time. By the time that he reentered the teaching profession in Tokyo he had fathered five children, but four of them had been lost to disease before he became a Nichiren Shoshu believer, giving us reason to believe that personal misfortune might have been one motivation for his religious faith. Furthermore, he was having no obvious success in promoting his ideas of transforming society through education, and may have felt that religion could be a more effective vehicle to accomplish his aims. Finally, with his own highly principled—some might say stubborn—personality he might have felt at home in the militant atmosphere of this particular religious group. There was a gradual shift to an increasingly religious concern in Makiguchi's writing and activities in the 1930s, which might indicate that although personal misfortune first brought him to religion, it was only later that he came to see religion as important for fulfilling his broader social aims. At any rate, it is clear that by 1936 educational and religious "revolution" had become fused in his thought, for in that year the small group of educators that had gathered around Makiguchi started regular meetings with the title Kyoiku shukyo kakumei shoho kenkyukai, or Study Group for True Law Educational and Religious Revolution. The following year Makiguchi published a pamphlet entitled *Soka kyoikuho no kagakuteki choshukyoteki jikken shomei* (Practical experimentation in value-creating education methods through science and supreme religion), further indicating the increasing emphasis placed on religion as a means of social reform.

In 1937 Makiguchi's followers were organized into the Soka Kyoiku Gakkai with an inaugural meeting held at a Tokyo restaurant. Sixty people were in attendance at this meeting, a number that had risen more than fivefold by the time a second meeting was held three years later. From the time of the first meeting it seems that the main activity of this group was missionary work for Nichiren Shoshu. A primary method of this activity was the *zadankai*, literally a forum or roundtable discussion, held in the believers' homes. These were largely testimonial gatherings, where the believers shared their experiences of the concrete benefits obtained by faith and thus sought to attract newcomers to the religion.[4] This emphasis on personal experience is a characteristic of many of the Japanese new religions, especially those that emerged around this time, as well as a reflection of Makiguchi's educational theories. Testimonials were also prominent in a periodical begun by the group in 1941, *Kachi sozo* (Value creation).

It seems that Makiguchi and his activities began to attract the attention of the authorities shortly after the first publication of *Kachi sozo*, for the magazine was closed down after only nine issues by order of the government. The group claimed more than three thousand members nationwide at that time, a significant movement within the relatively small Nichiren Shoshu sect, and their refusal to bend to the wartime government policy on religious groups was no doubt causing some irritation among the authorities. The official policy of the government since the passing of a Religious Organizations Law in 1939 had been to consolidate religious groups, in order to enhance government control over the groups and enlist their help in the war movement. As part of this policy, the various Nichiren sects were coerced into forming one body, which in fact would have entailed the absorption of Nichiren Shoshu by the much larger Nichiren Shu. Reportedly, some of the Nichiren Shoshu priests were themselves in favor of the merger, a move opposed by Makiguchi as compromising the true faith held by that group alone. The merger was rejected at a meeting of lay and clerical Nichiren Shoshu believers in April 1943, and the group was subsequently able to receive government approval to remain independent.

One other issue included in the government's religious policy proved to be Makiguchi's downfall, however. Since the launching of Japan's drive to become a modern nation-state in the mid-nineteenth century, State Shinto had been created as a complex of beliefs and rituals centering on the emperor in order to serve as a kind of civil religion, integrating and mobilizing the people to carry out the policies of the state. By the 1890s, State Shinto had been defined as a matter of national custom and patriotism, the duty of every loyal citizen that transcended religious belief or practice—a duty that was increasingly emphasized as the country went to war. As a concrete expression of this loyalty, every family was required to accept into their homes a talisman from the central Shinto shrine at Ise, a requirement that once again the priests at Taisekiji were willing to accept but at which Makiguchi balked. His refusal led to his arrest on charges of lèse majesté and violation of the Peace Preservation Law on 6 July 1943, along with twenty other leaders of the Soka Kyoiku Gakkai.

Makiguchi was already seventy-one at the time of his arrest, and he died from malnutrition in prison on 18 November of the following year.

Soka Gakkai as a Mass Movement

Toda Josei (1900–1958) had been an associate and disciple of Makiguchi since 1920, when he joined the staff at Nishimachi Elementary School, where Makiguchi was principal. Toda was born on 11 February 1900, the eleventh son of a fisherman in Ishikawa Prefecture, also on the Japan Sea coast. At the age of four his family moved to Hokkaido, where he eventually found employment as a youth in Sapporo, studying part time in order to qualify as a substitute primary school teacher at the age of seventeen. The following year he was employed at a school in a remote mining town, where he remained until he moved to Tokyo in 1920 and was hired by Makiguchi.

Toda left the school system three years later and started his own college preparation course, where he is supposed to have attempted to implement Makiguchi's educational philosophy. The school apparently had little success, for Dayle Bethel reports that throughout much of the 1920s he was in dire poverty, and his financial state might have contributed to the death of his infant daughter, the loss of his wife to tuberculosis, and his own contraction of that disease. The next decade saw a dramatic turn in his fortunes, however, as a mathematics text published by Toda in 1930 became a runaway bestseller and served as the foundation of a business empire that extended to seventeen companies and a personal fortune of over one million dollars at the time of his arrest with Makiguchi in 1943.[5]

Toda survived his experience in jail, and even claims to have had an intense religious experience while there, as a result of reading the Lotus Sutra and incessantly chanting the *daimoku*, the phrase *namu myoho rengekyo* in praise of the Lotus Sutra. Toda says that after agonizing for a long time over the meaning of the sutra, finally one day he had a vision of the word *seimei*, or Life-Force, flashing in his mind, as well as a mystical experience of seeing himself in attendance in the assembly of the Buddha. This experience was apparently the foundation of Toda's unique contribution to the development of Soka Gakkai doctrine, the theory of Life-Force.[6] This Life-Force is thought to permeate the universe, and it is through connection with the great Life-Force that we can ensure health, prosperity, good relationships with others, and happiness. In Soka Gakkai practice, these benefits are obtained through faith in Nichiren as the greatest and final manifestation of the Buddha, worship of the *gohonzon*, or mandala inscribed by Nichiren, and the chanting of the *daimoku*. Such practice should lead to benefits in this life, and even greater happiness in an unending series of future lives in this world. In this way, Toda laid out a very practical faith of immediate benefits, a classical example of what has been called the "vitalistic" conception of salvation frequently encountered in Japanese new religious movements.[7]

Toda spent the first years after the war trying to rebuild his business empire as well as the organization destroyed by Makiguchi's arrest. At a memorial service held on the first anniversary of Makiguchi's death only some twenty people were in attendance, but the following year Toda started offering courses on the Lotus Sutra out of his office in Tokyo. At the end of the first set of courses on 28 March 1946, Toda changed the name of the organization to Soka Gakkai, dropping the last vestige of the group's roots as an organization of educators. Toda's business went bankrupt in 1950, a turning point in his life that led him to devote himself exclusively to the religious organization, and on 3 May of the following year he took over formally as the second president of Soka Gakkai. In his inaugural speech he announced the "great march of *shakubuku*," with the concrete goal of winning 750,000 families to Soka Gakkai before his death.

Shakubuku is one of two methods of proselytization found in Buddhist canonical sources, the other being *shoju. Shoju*, meaning to "embrace and accept" is a mild method of leading others gradually to the truth without criticizing their previous position. *Shakubuku*, on the other hand, means to "break and subdue," and it involves the use of a rather fierce polemic in order to get the subject to reject his or her previous beliefs. In his writings, Nichiren allows that both methods have their appropriate time and place, but insists that *shakubuku* is to be used in the Japan of his own time in order to rebuke the enemies of true Buddhism and bring the country to faith. Throughout its history there have been arguments within the Nichiren sect as to which method is proper for the contemporary situation, with Soka Kyoiku Gakkai and Nichiren Shoshu advocating the use of *shakubuku* in the prewar period.[8] Indeed, it was the employment of this method that led to the charges against Makiguchi and his lieutenants for violating the Peace Preservation Law.

The drive for membership, carried out under the banner of *shakubuku*, was marked by aggressive, confrontational tactics and, occasionally, military rhetoric. The *Shakubuku kyoten* (Manual of *shakubuku*) was published in 1951 and, in addition to laying out the essentials of Soka Gakkai teaching on the Lotus Sutra and the writings of Nichiren, it also provided sample arguments to be used against the objections of prospective converts. Soka Gakkai youth divisions were organized in the early 1950s to spearhead the proselytization drive, and Murata reports that overtly military language was employed (Murata 1969, p. 99). For example, the young members were organized into *butai* (corps), complete with *butaicho* (corps commanders) and *butaiki* (corps flags), and the central organization was called the *sanboshitsu* (general staff office). At a rally on 31 October 1954, Toda even mounted a white horse as he addressed the assembled columns with the following words: "In our attempt at *kosen rufu* [propagation of Buddhism], we are without an ally. We must consider all religions our enemies, and we must destroy them. Ladies and gentlemen, it is obvious that the road ahead is full of obstacles. Therefore, you must worship the *gohonzon*, take the Soka Gakkai spirit to your heart, and cultivate the strength of youth. I expect you to rise to the occasion to meet the many challenges that lie ahead."[9]

As Jacqueline Stone points out, this policy was changed in the 1970s to one of at least implicit tolerance, and although the word *shakubuku* is still used within the group, it seems to have become synonymous with general proselytization, at least on the official level.[10] Although the militant, even militaristic, stance naturally attracted a considerable amount of bad press and was decisive in forming public opinion about Soka Gakkai that endures in many quarters of Japanese society until the present, it was also effective in laying the foundations for the phenomenal growth of the organization, making it the premier example of a postwar new religion as a mass movement. Toda's goal of 750,000 families was apparently reached in 1957, before his own death on 2 April 1958.

Soka Gakkai and Politics

One more legacy of Toda's leadership is Soka Gakkai's active participation in Japanese politics. Soka Gakkai is not unique among religious groups, in Japan or elsewhere, in seeking to advance its goals—normally seen as religious by their members—through political means. This activity has taken several different forms in postwar Japan. A Tenrikyo official, for example, was a candidate for a seat in the Lower House of parliament in 1946, and Rissho Koseikai lent its support to a conservative candidate in the 1947 Tokyo gubernatorial elections. Seicho no Ie has been much more active in conservative politics, forming a Political Policy Committee in 1953 to coordinate its activities, joining right-wing members of the ruling Liberal Democratic Party in organizing a National Self-Defense Conference in 1958, and reorganizing its political organization into the Seicho no Ie Political Alliance in 1964. What sets Soka Gakkai apart from these other groups, however, is the formation of its own political party, Komeito (often referred to as the Clean Government Party in Western publications), in 1964.

Soka Gakkai's political activities began in 1955, when the group sponsored more than fifty of its own candidates in local elections, resulting in the election of forty-seven Soka Gakkai members to two prefectural assemblies and more than twenty city councils around the country. In national elections held for the Upper House of parliament the following year, three of six candidates sponsored by Soka Gakkai were successful in their bids, garnering more than one million votes nationwide. In 1959, a further six candidates were elected, followed by the reelection of the original three members plus an additional six in 1962, making the Soka Gakkai councilors the third largest group in the Upper

House. On the basis of this success, a decision was made in 1964 to sponsor candidates for the more powerful Lower House, and at the same time Komeito was formed. In the general election in 1967, the first held after the establishment of Komeito, the party won twenty-five seats in the Lower House, attracting almost two and one-half million votes. Two years later these totals were almost doubled to forty-seven seats and over five million votes. However, an attempt in that same year to stop the publication of a book critical of Soka Gakkai and its political activities caused a controversy focusing on freedom of the press, and led Soka Gakkai to disassociate itself officially from Komeito in May of 1970. What this means in practice is that parliamentary members of Komeito will resign from any official posts in Soka Gakkai, but Soka Gakkai's activities in support of Komeito, as well as its influence over Komeito policy, are no secret.

On one level, Soka Gakkai's political activity could be attributed to the legacy of its founder, Makiguchi Tsunesaburo, who apparently saw his religious activity as a means to effect social reform. There is also a doctrinal foundation within Nichiren Buddhism for such activity. Nichiren himself was convinced that the salvation of the nation depended on its conversion to the true faith of Buddhism, and for that reason he was especially critical of other religions, in particular the Pure Land sects, as dangerous to the survival of the nation. The fusion of true religion and politics that would result from this conversion is called *obutsumyogo*, and it was to be represented in the establishment of a *Kokuritsu kaidan*, or National Hall of Worship, to be built at the foot of Mt. Fuji. Throughout the 1950s this was presented as the final aim of Soka Gakkai's proselytization, called *kosen rufu* in Nichiren terminology. Critics of Soka Gakkai's political activity maintain that *obutsumyogo* and the related concept of the establishment of the *Kokuritsu kaidan* call for the establishment of a state religion, explicitly prohibited by the postwar constitution. Perhaps in an effort to defuse these critics, the completion of a massive worship hall at the Nichiren Shoshu headquarters in Taisekiji in 1972 was identified by Soka Gakkai as the establishment of the *Kokuritsu kaidan*, indicating that *obutsumyogo* in fact signifies a broader influence of Buddhist principles in society and that it does not necessarily rely on the conversion of the whole nation and the adopting of Nichiren Shoshu as an official religion.[11]

Although Komeito seats in the Lower House fell to twenty-nine in elections held after this controversy, in subsequent elections the party has consistently polled more than five million votes and its seat count has generally remained in the mid-fifties. This representation made it the third largest party in Parliament, following the Liberal Democratic Party (LDP) and the socialist group, now called the Social Democratic Party of Japan. Following a splintering in the LDP and their loss in elections held in 1993, Komeito joined with all non-LDP parties save the Communist Party of Japan in forming a coalition government—the first time the LDP had to relinquish power in the thirty-eight years of its existence. Since that loss the political situation in Japan has remained fluid, and the controversy surrounding Komeito as a political party with obvious connections to Soka Gakkai has helped considerably to muddy the waters.[12] The situation is even more complex now that the Komeito has joined the LDP to form a ruling coalition, a move that has forced it to abandon some of its overtly pacifist principles.

Although Komeito did not formally join a government until formation of the coalition that ended the postwar conservative monopoly in 1993, it had often been the power broker in the national parliament, reflecting its role as the third largest national party and the fact that it has staked out for itself a centrist position, with the conservative Liberal Democrats and liberal socialists on its flanks. Indeed, from its foundation it has taken as its aim the establishment of world peace based on a "global nationalism" and "human socialism," offered as a way to resolve the conflict between capitalism and socialism, a fusion of opposites that aptly reflects its centrism. As part of its attempt to serve as a centrist power broker, however, Komeito has adopted positions that clearly are not pacifist. Since the 1980s Komeito has been on record as supporting Japan's military alliance with the United States, and after a defeat of the ruling conservative party in Upper House parliamentary elections in 1989, Komeito formed an unofficial coalition with the conservatives, offering their support on key measures. It was in this context that Komeito's support of the Peacekeeping Operations Law, which allowed for the overseas deployment of Self-Defense Forces in UN-sponsored activities, became crucial for the enactment of this controversial law. In response to these developments, Soka Gakkai members are wont to point out that as an independent political party Komeito does not necessarily reflect the position of Soka Gakkai, and, indeed, at least one observer has pointed out that "some Soka Gakkai members were outraged" by the decision of Komeito to support the Peacekeeping Operations Law (Métraux 1996, p. 388).

Since joining the LDP in a coalition government in 1999, Komeito has furthered compromised its centrist position, as seen, for example, in its support of legislation mandating the use of the prewar national anthem and flag, a long-standing conservative issue. In elections held the following year, the party was able to elect only thirty-one of its candidates, but it has remained in the coalition and lent its support to efforts to further expand the role of Japanese Self Defense Forces abroad.

Soka Gakkai's Peace Activities

To say that Soka Gakkai is not pacifist is not to deny that it is very active in trying to establish the basis for world peace. As in the case of its political activity, Soka Gakkai's peace activities can also be traced back to Toda Josei, the second president of the group. At an athletic meeting held in Yokohama in September 1957, Toda called for a complete ban on nuclear weapons, adding his voice to the popular movement in Japan to ban such weapons, especially in the wake of the accident at Bikini Atoll three years previously.[13] Petition drives against these weapons organized by the Soka Gakkai youth group garnered more than ten million signatures and were handed over to the United Nations in 1975. In 1973, the youth division further adopted a resolution for the "preservation of the right to life," and in response to that resolution undertook to raise money for Vietnamese refugees and the starving in Africa, as well as the publication of antiwar books. These books, representing an activity later also adopted by the women's division of Soka Gakkai, amount to more than one hundred volumes at present, and are collections of accounts of survivors of the Second World War. They are meant to educate the postwar generations on the horrors of war, as recounted by those who have lived through the experience.

Such a contribution to peace education is perhaps especially appropriate to a group whose roots lie in an association of educators, and indeed peace education is one of the characteristics of Soka Gakkai's participation in this field. In addition to the antiwar book series, Soka Gakkai International has been active in organizing peace exhibits, beginning with "Nuclear Arms: Threat to Our World," which made the rounds of sixteen countries between 1982 and 1988. A second exhibit, "War and Peace: From a Century of War to a Century of Hope," was opened in the lobby of the United Nations Headquarters in New York in 1989, followed by an exhibit on environmental issues and peace opened to coincide with the United Nations Conference on Environment and Development held in Rio de Janeiro in 1992. Indeed, cooperation with United Nations projects is another characteristic of Soka Gakkai's peace activities. Soka Gakkai has been registered as a non-governmental organization (NGO) with the United Nations' High Commissioner for Refugees since 1981, and two years later the Soka Gakkai International was recognized as an NGO with consultative status in the United Nations Economic and Social Council.

Ikeda Daisaku (1928–), Toda's successor as the third president of Soka Gakkai, was himself a recipient of the United Nations Peace Prize in 1983. Ikeda was born in Tokyo on 2 January 1928, the fifth son in a large family of nine children. His father processed and sold dried seaweed, a job with which he was barely able to support the family. Ikeda was apparently sickly from an early age, and while attending high school during the war years he was also stricken with tuberculosis and pleurisy. After the war he found a job working in a factory, and around the age of nineteen he began to attend Soka Gakkai *zadankai* at the invitation of a childhood friend. He soon joined the group, quickly became a protégé of Toda, and, in 1952, was appointed as leader of Soka Gakkai's youth division. Ikeda's formal education ended in 1949, when he briefly attended night classes at a junior college. After that he is said to have been tutored in various subjects by Toda.

Despite this lack of formal higher education, Ikeda has been prominent in international peace forums, addressing the United Nations General Assembly and keeping a high profile in his frequent exchanges with prominent statesmen and academics. In his numerous proposals on peace and disarmament, Ikeda makes continued reference to the ideal of universal disarmament and resolution of conflict through negotiation.

Ikeda has been a controversial figure in Japan, however. As the leader of the youth division under Toda, he was apparently involved in an attack on an elderly Nichiren Shoshu monk who had been accused of complicity in the wartime arrest of Makiguchi and Toda. His critics accuse him of far-reaching political ambitions, and the tabloid press has played up unsubstantiated reports of sexual and financial scandals. Prefiguring the split with Nichiren Shoshu in 1991, Ikeda resigned as president of Soka Gakkai in 1979, in an attempt to repair the already strained relationship with the Shoshu monks over his power and the personality cult built around him. His continuing paramount role within the group, as well as the cult surrounding his figure, is evident, however, in the treatment afforded him by the *Seikyo Shinbun*, Soka Gakkai's daily newspaper, where the front page is commonly devoted to reports on his activities.

Soka Gakkai Today

Soka Gakkai remains in a period of transition almost ten years after its separation from Nichiren Shoshu. Although Soka Gakkai has been able to retain its membership and financial resources, it has lost some of the religious authority that affiliation with the monks provided. New members can no longer obtain personal copies of the *daihonzon* inscribed by the monks, they are unable to worship in front of the *daihonzon* at Taisekiji, and they cannot call on the monks to perform the funeral and memorial rites so important to Japanese religiosity. Although attempts to address these problems through doctrinal reinterpretation and ritual and symbolic substitution seem to be progressing, the separation from Nichiren Shoshu is not taken as completely negative. For example, some within the group have also attributed its newfound religious tolerance to the fact that they are now free of the monks' control and thus able to abandon an outdated exclusivism.[14] Perhaps in keeping with this more open self-identity—or perhaps in an attempt to substitute for any perceived loss in religious authority—the group has also increased its contact with academics, opening a research institute in Boston and cooperating in my research on its peace activities in Japan (Kisala 1999) as well as studies of its membership in

England (Wilson and Dobbelaere 1994) and the United States (Hammond and Machacek 1999).

The group remains controversial, however, somehow unable to project a more tolerant image effectively, while it still remains very active politically. In recent years it has attracted the attention of the media abroad as well, perhaps most clearly in a documentary, "The Chanting Millions," aired by the BBC in 1995, which unfairly tries to draw parallels between the group and Aum Shinrikyo. In conclusion I think we would have to say that although the group has made considerable efforts to become more mainstream, as long as it is perceived to be more concerned with political power and prestige than with the spiritual quest it will continue to be the object of popular suspicion.

NOTES

1. See Astley 1992, Métraux 1992, and Van Bragt 1993 concerning the split with Nichiren Shoshu. Stone 1994 suggests that at least part of the reason for the split might have been the adoption of an attitude more tolerant of other religions by Soka Gakkai.

2. Much of the history of Soka Gakkai found in this article is taken from chapter 3 of my book on the peace activities of some of the Japanese new religions (Kisala 1999).

3. Soka Gakkai's official account can be found in the fortieth-anniversary history of the group (Soka Gakkai Yonjunenshi Hensan Iinkai 1970). For outside sources on Makiguchi, see Bethel 1973 and Shimazono 1992.

4. Reflecting the pragmatic emphasis of Soka Kyoiku Gakkai, these meetings were called *taizen seikatsu jikken shomei zadankai*, or "forums on practical experimentation for abundant life."

5. This figure is taken from Bethel 1973, p. 99, as representative of Toda's worth at prewar exchange rates.

6. For an explanation of this development, see Shimazono 1999.

7. The vitalistic conception of the salvation is an optimistic view of the universe as giving abundant life, manifested in immediate benefits, to all those who seek to maintain their natural connection with this source of life. See Tsushima et al. 1979 for a more complete description of this concept.

8. See Stone 1994 for a discussion of the use of *shakubuku* throughout the history of the Nichiren sects.

9. Quote taken from Murata 1969, p. 100.

10. Stone 1994. The policy of religious tolerance was made explicit in the charter adopted at the twentieth general assembly of Soka Gakkai International in October 1995. That charter states that "SGI shall, based on the Buddhist spirit of tolerance, respect other religions, engage in dialogue and work together with them toward the resolution of fundamental issues concerning humanity."

11. This particular interpretation of *obutsumyogo* and the establishment of the *Kokuritsu kaidan* led to a split in Nichiren Shoshu, as Métraux points out (1980, pp. 59–60). As a matter of interest, I might mention that as one result of the split with Soka

Gakkai, the worship hall at Taisekiji has been torn down, apparently because the maintenance costs have become prohibitive now that the numbers of worshipers at the temple have fallen dramatically. Billed as the largest religious structure built in the twentieth century, construction of the worship hall cost almost one hundred million dollars, and its demolition is estimated to have cost over forty million dollars.

12. See my article on the 1995 revision of the Religious Corporations Law (Kisala 1997) for a discussion of some of these political developments.

13. The crew of a Japanese tuna boat, the *Dai go fukuryu maru* or Lucky Dragon No. 5, was exposed to radiation from the test of a hydrogen bomb on Bikini Atoll conducted on 1 March 1954, resulting in the death of one of the crew members.

14. This assertion was made in the course of a symposium conducted at the Nanzan Institute for Religion and Culture in 1995. The proceedings of the symposium are available in Japanese (Nanzan Shukyo Bunka Kenkyujo 1996).

WORKS CITED

Astley, Trevor. 1992. "A Matter of Principles: A Note on the Recent Conflict between Nichiren Shoshu and Soka Gakkai." *Japanese Religions* 17: 167–175.

Bethel, Dayle M. 1973. *Makiguchi the Value Creator: Revolutionary Japanese Educator and founder of Soka Gakkai.* New York, Weatherhill.

Hammond, Phillip, and David Machacek. 1999. *Soka Gakkai in America.* Oxford: Oxford University Press.

Kisala, Robert. 1997. "Reactions to Aum: The Revision of the Religious Corporations Law." *Japanese Religions* 22: 60–74.

———. 1999. *Prophets of Peace: Pacifism and Cultural Identity in Japan's New Religions.* Honolulu: University of Hawaii Press.

Métraux, Daniel. 1980. "Why Did Ikeda Quit?" *Japanese Journal of Religious Studies* 7: 55–61.

———. 1992. "The Dispute between the Soka Gakkai and the Nichiren Shoshu Priesthood: A Lay Revolution against a Conservative Clergy." *Japanese Journal of Religious Studies* 19: 325–336.

———. 1996. "The Soka Gakkai: Buddhism and the Creating of a Harmonious and Peaceful Society." In *Engaged Buddhism: Buddhist Liberation Movements in Asia,* edited by Christopher S. Queen and Sallie B. King. Albany: State University of New York Press.

Murata, Kiyoaki. 1969. *Japan's New Buddhism: An Objective Account of Soka Gakkai.* New York: Weatherhill.

Nanzan Shukyo Bunka Kenkyujo, ed. 1996. *Katorikku to Soka Gakkai.* Tokyo: Saisan Bunmeisha.

Shimazono Susumu. 1992. "Seikatsu to kindai shukyo undo: Makiguchi Tsunesaburo no kyoiku shiso to shinko." In *Shukyo to shakai kagaku,* edited by Kawai Hayao et al. Tokyo: Iwanami Shoten.

———. 1999. "Soka Gakkai and the Modern Reformation of Buddhism." In *Buddhist Spirituality: Later China, Korea, Japan, and the Modern World,* vol. 9 of *World Spirituality: An Encyclopedic History of the Religious Quest,* edited by Evert Cousins. New York: Crossroad.

Soka Gakkai Yonjunenshi Hensan Iinkai, ed. 1970. *Soka gakkai Yonjunenshi*. Tokyo: Soka Gakkai.

Stone, Jacqueline. 1994. "Rebuking the Enemies of the Lotus: Nichirenist Exclusivism in Historical Perspective." *Japanese Journal of Religious Studies* 21: 231–259.

Tsushima Michihito et al. 1979. "The Vitalistic Conception of Salvation in Japanese New Religions." *Japanese Journal of Religious Studies* 6: 139–161.

Van Bragt, Jan. 1993. "An Uneven Battle: Soka Gakkai vs. Nichiren Shoshu." *Bulletin of the Nanzan Institute for Religion and Culture* 17: 15–31.

Wilson, Bryan, and Karel Dobbeleare. 1994. *A Time to Chant: The Soka Gakkai Buddhists in Britain*. Oxford: Clarendon Press.

8

Aum Shinrikyo and the Aum Incident: A Critical Introduction

Martin Repp

During the second half of the 1980s, a small group of yoga practioners in the Tokyo area began to gather around a young man whose name was Asahara Shoko.[1] Pictures in publications of this time depict the leader and his disciples peacefully meditating in natural environs such as riverbeds or mountain slopes. The membership of the group, now called Aum Shinrikyo, began to grow. Five years later, however, visual depictions had changed drastically to imagery of catastrophies and doomsday. In 1995, police finally raided their compounds, and apprehended the leaders and a number of followers, who were put on trial for committing not only murder but also the first terrorist nerve gas attack in history. These acts of crime and terror became known as the Aum incident. What had taken place in the meantime? How can these drastic changes and the terrible outcomes be "explained"? Those are the questions any treatise on Aum Shinrikyo faces. The following introduction to Aum (as the group will be called henceforth) and the Aum incident will follow historical order, starting with the beginnings.

Aum Shinrikyo as a Religion

The Founder

Aum Shinrikyo was founded by Asahara Shoko, who was born in 1955 as Matsumoto Chizuo in Kumamoto prefecture in Kyushu. He grew up in a family of modest circumstances. Since he was blind in one eye and had limited vision in the other, he was sent to a government-run boarding school for blind students. After graduation, he became an acupuncturist—a profession traditionally held by people with visual disabilities. In 1977, he moved to Tokyo, and in the following year he married Ishii Tomoko, who subsequently gave birth to six children (*AEN* May 16, 1995). During this time he turned to traditional Asian medicine and developed an interest in fortunetelling, divination, and Daoism. His practice of acupuncture and Asian medicine in Funabashi, Chiba Prefecture (near Tokyo), seems to have been quite successful. Between 1981 and 1984, he was a member of the new religious group Agon-shu.[2] Here, he became acquainted with yoga teaching and practice, and with the early Buddhist Agama Sutras.[3] It is likely that Asahara also became familiar with esoteric Buddhism (*mikkyo*) through books of Agon-shu's founder, Kiriyama Seiyu, who claimed to have caused the *"mikkyo* boom" in Japan during the 1980s (Reader 1988: 248).

During that time, yoga and esoteric Buddhism, especially the idea of acquiring "supernatural powers," became attractive for young Japanese, who were interested in religion while remaining outside the established Buddhist schools.[4] In 1985, the New Age magazine *Twilight Zone* published a picture of Asahara "levitating" during yoga practice on the cover page and included a report about him (cf. Asahara 1991b). This publication caused some young people interested in yoga and "supernatural powers" to gather around Asahara. They became the nucleus of a group called Aum shinsen-no-kai or "Aum group of mountain ascetics," which was formed in April 1986.[5] In the following

FIGURE 8.1. Master Asahara.
Courtesy of Aleph (Aum Shinrikyo).

summer, Asahara traveled to India together with his close disciple Ishii Hisako in order to pursue religious practice under the guidance of a yoga master. He became disappointed with the guru's greediness, however, and continued to practice on his own. At the end of his two-month stay, in July 1986, he claimed to have attained enlightenment, the "state of absolute freedom, happiness and joy where one's suffering is extinguished and [the cycle of] life and death [is] transcended."[6] From the fall of 1986 on, members of the group began to "leave their house" (*shukke*) and become nuns or monks.[7] They started to form a community of celebates, called *samgha*, in order to dedicate their life to religious practice.

Asahara Shoko, born Matsumoto Chizuo, assumed his new name in 1987 because it is written with Chinese characters that are believed to cause good luck.[8] In the same year, Asahara also changed the name of his group to Aum Shinrikyo or "Aum Teaching of Absolute Truth" (*Vajrayana Sacca* No. 9: 36). The group thereby assumed a clearly religious character. The change from "mountain asceticism" (*shinsen*) to "absolute [religious] truth" (*shinri*) and the replacement of the neutral term *kai* (group, association) by *kyo* (religious teaching or school) mark the shift toward a religious organization. Some members did not agree with this change and left the group, because *kyo* sounded "too old fashioned" or "too religious" (Asahara 1992c: 79), in other words, it resembled established religion. In line with the development toward an institutionalization of the young group, Aum applied to the Tokyo metropolitan government in 1987 for recognition as a legal religious body. Concerning the group's name, Asahara (1992e: vi) explained the term "truth" by reasoning that Sakyamuni Buddha had not called his teaching "Buddhism," but rather "truth." Besides yoga, emphasis was now placed on the theory and practice of Buddhism, as, for example, the frequent use of terms such as "suffering" and "enlightenment" demonstrates. In August 1987, the first edition of Aum Shinrikyo's journal *Mahayana* was published, where Asahara wrote: "I tried all kinds of practices such as Taoism, Yoga, Buddhism, incorporating their essence into my training. My goal was supreme spiritual realization and enlightenment. . . . Finally, I reached my goal in the holy vibration of the Himalayas; I attained supreme realization and enlightenment. . . . But my soul . . . was not satisfied. I could not bear the fact that only I was happy and the other people were still in the world of suffering. I began to think: 'I will save other people at the sacrifice of my own self' " (Asahara 1992b: 13).

This statement indicates the shift from a circle of yoga practitioners who aimed at individual self-perfection to a Mahayana Buddhist group that intended to liberate other people. This development can also be perceived as Aum becoming a Buddhist renewal movement, as a statement by the Dalai Lama is reported to have suggested to Asahara when the latter visited Dharamsala in February 1987: "Dear friend, look at the Buddhism of Japan today. It has degenerated into ceremonialism and has lost the essential truth of the teachings.

As the situation continues, Buddhism will vanish from Japan. Something needs to be done, and you should spread real Buddhism there. You can do that well. If you do so, I shall be very pleased and it will help me with my mission" (Asahara 1988: 10).

Asahara used this statement to legitimize his activities (1988: 11). For this reason, he also visited several Tibetan leaders, such as Kalu Rinpoche in 1988 and Khamtul Rinpoche in 1991. During a journey to Sri Lanka in 1991, Asahara is said to have been praised as "the only man who can save the world" (1992f: 154). On this occasion the prime minister presented him with "a piece of Buddha Sakyamuni's relics," an important symbol of religious power and authority.[9] Such attempts at religious authorization resulted in Aum statements such as, "The Buddha in our times is Master Shoko Asahara."[10] Asahara also claimed to be an incarnation of the Hindu god Shiva, the "Lord of Yoga."[11] Such an elevation is reflected in his titles; whereas in early Aum publications Asahara is called *sensei* (teacher) or guru, his appellation then changes to Revered Master (*sonshi*), to which since 1992 the title His Holiness (*saisho*) is added (*Shinri* No. 19)—an expression usually reserved for figures such as the Dalai Lama or the pope.

From early on, it seems, Asahara not only aimed at reaching religious ends but also, as head of a growing movement, he pursued political goals. The combination of religious and political ambitions is not uncommon among Japanese religions. After some difficulties, Aum Shinrikyo gained the legal status of a religious organization (*shukyo hojin*) in August 1989. In late 1989, Aum Shinri-kyo founded the Shinri-to or "Truth Party." Subsequently, Asahara and his disciples campaigned for the Lower House elections scheduled to take place in February 1990.[12] In one of the campaign pamphlets, Asahara wrote: "It takes political action to do what a religion cannot do. Therefore, I am taking a political approach to my activities" (*DY* May 17, 1995). During the campaign, Aum called, for instance, for the abolition of the consumer tax that had been introduced to Japan not long before. It is not clear what Asahara's real goals in this campaign were.[13] The "Truth Party" did not win a single seat in the election for the Lower House. This failure was perceived by Aum as a rejection by society, which in turn became one of the causes for its subsequent antisociety stance.

The Followers

In spite of Asahara's political failure, he was able to attract thousands of mostly young followers. What kind of people were they? What did they find so attractive about his teachings? As many of the followers' testimonies state, they felt that society and established religions were unable to provide answers for which they were searching: finding the meaning of life, filling an inner void, gaining personal understanding and acceptance, and healing psychological wounds and physical frailties. Most of the Aum followers were disappointed with a materialistically oriented world and were searching for spiritual ways of life. It should be recalled that during the 1980s Japan had reached the height of the "bubble economy." Some examples of followers' testimonies illustrate their concerns.

First, the problem of finding her own identity in modern society is expressed by a young woman: "Before joining Aum I was always afraid of showing my real self to other people and was always conscious of other people's eyes. I was always hiding myself because I wanted other people to have a better image of me, or not dislike me. . . . I was never free from worries. . . . The teaching of Aum Shinrikyo was very easy to understand and I found answers to many questions I had, including the meaning of life for which I had been searching for a long time. . . . [The m]aster understands me better than I do myself and always gives me the right advice" (Asahara 1993a: 164 f.). Asahara spoke a religious language that many of his peers could easily understand.[14] Moreover, he also conveyed the feeling of personal acceptance. Aum not only provided answers to personal problems, however, but also offered a kind of alternative society, as the statement of another woman suggests: Aum members "were always cheerful and never said bad things about others, which was quite unlike ordinary society. . . . I could actually see that it was brighter than the other places outside" (ibid.: 166).

Next, the problem of inner void felt in a society ruled by work and achievement is addressed by another follower: "I was feeling stagnant in everything and had lost interest in the worldly way of life. I felt I needed something that would give me strong mental satisfaction, and realized that this thirst could not be healed by devoting myself to work or by enjoying myself" (ibid.: 161).

Third, the related theme of personal growth is addressed by a young man who was impressed by Asahara's charisma: "I was able to meet with the supreme guru, Master Shoko Asahara in this life. His great power has given me peace of mind and many wonderful mystical experiences" (ibid.: 207). He concluded: "An ordinary man was I, but thanks to the Great Guru I was able to grow mentally and spiritually" (ibid.: 208). Young people's concern for personal change or growth, and even for development from the ordinary to the extraordinary, is expressed by a follower who had resigned from a good position in a large company: "I had enough of the materialistic world of business. . . . I couldn't figure out what I should do or why I was there." Then he tried Aum's meditation techniques and summarized his new experiences as follows: "I felt this bursting sensation from inside. It was amazing." Such extraordinary experiences certainly were attractive for young people who ventured to hitherto unknown dimensions of life. In addition, this man felt attracted by Asahara himself; as he says, "I admire the supreme master . . . because he tells us things nobody else could explain so clearly and logically" (JT June 1, 1995). One attraction of Aum was certainly its postulation that "Buddhism is science" (see below). It thus attempted to clear the image of religion from "superstition" or "irrationality." The same tendency to bridge the gap can also be observed in other new religions such as Sukyo Mahikari, Agon-shu, and Kofuku no Kagaku.[15]

These new experiences in Aum also provided the missionary zeal that is characteristic of new religious movements. For example, Joyu Fumihiro, head of the Russian Aum branch and for some time after March 1995 Aum's talented spokesman, wrote: "I would like to do my best to lead others to practice who are vexed with ego like myself. . . . I would like to do my best in cooperating with the salvation activities the master is planning in order to avoid a war" (Asahara 1988: 158).

Thus we see that the followers' experiences centered around the charisma of the group's founder. For example, Hayakawa Kiyohide, one of Aum Shinrikyo's leading figures, stated about his first encounter with Asahara: "While feeling some strain as I listened to his words, I was completely under the spell of the gentle and mild atmosphere of the master I met for the first time" (ibid.: 208).

This leads to an examination of the peculiar nature of the relationship and interaction between Asahara and his followers. Young people, searching for an authentic religious way, met a master whose "personal magnetism" (Asahara 1993a: 256), charisma, and teaching provided answers to their problems. The guru also rendered himself indispensable to his followers by claiming, for instance: "Be aware that you cannot get Dharma without asking it of me" (Asahara 1991c: 85). Elsewhere he stated: "So those of you who are aiming to attain enlightenment must come to me and receive an initiation from me" (Asahara 1992c: 82; cf. 1989b: 26). In such a way, the followers became dependent on the leader. The authority that Asahara claimed for himself eventually extended to the demand that the followers replace their own will with his own (Asahara 1992d: 69). Even the Buddhist precepts could, as far as his believers were concerned, be replaced with Asahara's directives (Asahara 1988: 84).

The admiration by his followers certainly helped to increase Asahara's enormous self-esteem. After police raids of the Aum facilities in March 1995 had begun, in a last message Asahara called upon his followers to act as his hands, feet, and head, and thereby to bring about his "salvation-plan."[16] A former follower who had helped to abduct her father in order to have his estate transferred to Aum, later claimed in court that Asahara "was willing to use any means to serve the interest of the cult. . . . I was his puppet and slave" (JT January 2, 1995). After experiencing such abuse of power, the believers turned from enthusiasm to disappointment. As the dignity of the individual was not respected within the group, so Aum treated people outside similarly, as shown by its record of crimes (to be examined further here).

The Teaching

The teaching and practice of Aum developed gradually through combining astrology, Hinduism (yoga), various forms of Buddhism, and Occidental apocalyptic ideas. These elements, taken from very different religious traditions, times, and geographical regions, coexisted until they were rejected by Aum owing to internal developments. Such a broad variety of religious elements reflects the contemporary religious situation in Japan. For understanding Aum, one has to take into account the spiritual landscape of the 1970s and 1980s. One early important influence on Aum's development was Agon-shu, with its yoga practice and emphasis on early Buddhism, Tibetan Buddhism, and esoteric Buddhism. Additionally, popular and academic authors excerted a formidable influence among many young Japanese, including Aum members. Nakamura Hajime's *Genshi butten* (Original Buddhist scriptures) (cf. Asahara 1991b: 34), Nakazawa Shinichi's book on Tibetan esoteric Buddhism *Niji no kaitei* (Guide of the rainbow), and Sahoda Tsuruji's Japanese translation of the yoga Sutra and his books on Yoga were widely read at the time. With respect to apocalyptic ideas, Goto Ben's numerous books on Nostradamus and his prophecies published since 1973 became very popular. Once the Japanese economic success had satisfied the material needs of people, interest in the "spiritual world" (*seishin sekai*) started to flourish in Japan during the 1980s. These developments also have to be understood in the context of the New Age movement worldwide, and Aum Shinrikyo has to be seen in such an environment.

As mentioned, Asahara started his professional career with traditional Chinese medicine. He also developed an interest in various forms of East Asian astrology and divination (*sensei-jutsu, unmei-gaku*; Asahara 1991b: 24, cf. 28f.). He said, however, that astrology disappointed him because it did not help him to find true happiness (Asahara 1995a: 32). It could inform about future destiny, but not change it (Asahara 1991b: 27). Then he turned to Daoism (*shinsen*), from which the first name of his group was derived. Daoist practice, he expected, would provide eternal youth, immortality, and supernatural powers. It was here that the practice of *ki* (bioenergy) enabled him to "awaken Kundalini." By the controlled flow of *ki* through the body, the chakras were activated and resulted in the awakening of Kundalini. Soon, he turned to yoga, because it was for him a faster method of reaching the same goal (Asahara 1993a: 33–35). Asahara explains how the two religious traditions of Daoism and Yoga relate to each other: "It is an interesting thing that each practice, with its different starting point and different contents, follows the same path, which I believe has its own significance. This is the reason I incorporate other kinds of practices into my yoga" (ibid.: 38). Asahara was aware of the problem of syncretism. Through practical experiments and pecular ways of reasoning he tried to achieve a homogenous system that incorporated elements of Hinduism,

"Hinayana" and Mahayana Buddhism, Tantra-Vajrayana, science, and astrology. We shall discuss each of these strands in turn.

Aum began as a group of yoga practitioners. In his early publication *Seishi o koeru* (1986), Asahara explains the process of yoga practice as follows: First, a human being experiences suffering in this world; thereby, the religious seeker is led to trust the guru or the god Shiva and take refuge in him. Then this person practices yoga in order to "awaken Kundalini," that is, "spiritual energy which raises the human spirit to higher dimensions" (Asahara 1993a: 26). As the practice is continued, the practitioner passes through consecutive phases of ecstasy, joy, calmness, and lightness, finally to reach *samadhi*, the state in which the ultimate liberation from suffering, the state "beyond life and death," is achieved. Later, Asahara modified this process and claimed that the practice of yoga leads only as far as to ecstasy.[17] He stated that he had found the later phases through his own experience and then also in Tibetan Buddhism (ibid.: 37–40).

Aum's central "object" of veneration is Shiva. Asahara himself claimed to have his enlightenment certified by this deity. After that, Shiva played a decisive role in his career, as Asahara says; "I myself have no guru in this life. I taught myself depending on the memory of my past lives. When I came to a deadlock which I could not manage to break, Lord Shiva gave me a suggestion" (Asahara 1988: 98). According to Asahara the name "Aum Shinrikyo" also derives from such a revelation (Asahara 1992c: 81).

In the Hindu pantheon, Shiva often represents the element of chaos and dynamics that leads through destruction to new beginnings. After the Aum incident, the media focused only on the deity's destructive character in order to "explain" the possible metaphysical background of Aum's violent developments.[18] It should be maintained, however, that the deity has also a positive aspect because as the Lord of Yoga Shiva destroys the spiritual hindrances of yoga practitioners and guides them through the perils of practice to the ultimate religious goal.

In his search for attaining "ultimate happiness," Asahara proceeded from yoga to "Hinayana" Buddhism, the oldest Buddhist tradition.[19] The "original Buddhism" (*genshi bukkyo*), Sakyamuni's direct teachings, he claims, changed his life (Asahara 1991b: 34–38). True happiness, he realized, could be found in attaining awakening (*satori*) or liberation (*gedatsu*). Asahara considered the teaching of the Agama Sutras and that of Yoga compatible, since both focus on attainment of *satori* (Asahara 1990: 12). Hence, Aum followers continued to practice yoga, and analogies were drawn between these two religious paths in order to maintain consistency (cf. Asahara 1988: 63). Asahara claims that Sakyamuni's oldest, most authentic teaching and practice are contained in the Agama Sutras, and for this reason they enable a practitioner to surely attain liberation (Asahara 1991b: 36; 1995a: 25). He criticizes the Mahayana Buddhist schools in Japan for having departed from "Buddha's original teaching." For this reason, its followers were not able to attain true awakening and liberation. In contrast, the original Buddhist sutras and the teachings of Aum conform with each other completely (Asahara 1990: 156). New religions, like Aum, try to acquire authorization by basing themselves on "old" and "authentic" scriptures that predate those on which established Buddhist schools rely.

Aum's shift from "Hinayana" to Mahayana Buddhism is marked by the publication of the magazine *Mahayana*, beginning in August 1987. Asahara declared in 1989: "Right now, Aum is Mahayana, the middle vehicle" (Asahara 1992c: 34). The "Four Noble Truths" and the "Eightfold Holy Path" were now declared to form the "essence of Aum's doctrine" (Asahara 1992b: 51). Concepts like karma and suffering moved further into the center of the teaching. Asahara tried to provide "evidence for the law of karma" by drawing a direct connection between certain actions of well-known Japanese personalities and their subsequent fate. A famous baseball player, for example, had to give up his career early because he had appeared in a commercial for insect spray, thus violating the Buddhist precept prohibiting killing. Or a TV personality died of tongue cancer, according to Asahara (1993b: 64; cf. 86f., 138), because of the karma of speech. Bad karma results in suffering; however, suffering is also eradicated by further suffering. Addressing his disciples, Asahara writes: "The suffering you are experiencing now is the suffering of the three miserable realms [of hell, hungry spirits, and animals] which you would have to suffer in your next lives. Therefore, you should suffer a lot and practice a lot to overcome the suffering, and attain true freedom, happiness and joy" (Asahara 1992d: 122).

Karma has "to be washed off" by suffering (Asahara 1993b: 74). In addition to this cleansing function of suffering for one's own liberation, suffering for others also plays a role. Aum believers should proceed from the first form of suffering to the second (Asahara 1992c: 29). Whereas, according to Asahara, "Hinayana" aims at "supreme enlightenment or emancipation of oneself," Mahayana aims at "ultimate freedom and happiness of others" (Asahara 1993a: xi). Aum publications frequently mention the Mahayana Vow to save all sentient beings. The followers' "Affirmation of Suffering Vow" reads as follows: "I make my suffering my joy; I make other's suffering my own suffering" (Asahara 1992b: 93). This concept of suffering stems from the bodhisattva ideal of Mahayana Buddhism. A bodhisattva aims at attaining perfect awakening by taking on the suffering of other living beings and thereby helping them to attain awakening.

According to Asahara, salvation occurs in "Four Stages of Entering the Stream" in order to cross the ocean of birth and death. At the first stage, there are three forms of practice; "the first thing you should do is to consider the Great Lord Shiva, Buddhas, and the Guru as one, as the embodiment of the truth, and to take refuge in them. To take refuge means to learn their teachings, practice offering and to do service for them." Second, one "should take refuge in the teaching, or the absolute truth" (*shinri*); and third, one "should take refuge in the people who are practicing the teaching" (Asahara 1992d: 50). Asahara thus starts with the traditional Three Treasures (*sanbo*) of buddha, dharma (teaching), and samgha (community of monks and nuns), and identifies them with his own person and organization. The second stage consists in learning "the teaching over and over," in listening "to the tapes of my lectures five, ten, or fifteen times, to read [Aum's journal] Mahayana five, ten, or fifteen times." The third stage, then, lies in shattering "our erroneous notions with the information we have taken in the second stage." The fourth stage, finally, is "to put what you have thought into practice" (ibid.). Here, Asahara identifies Buddhist teaching and practice immediately with that of Aum.

Aum's shift toward Mahayana Buddhism with the bodhisattva ideal of universal salvation in 1987–88 indicates its simultaneous opening toward society. The development of Asahara's religious teachings can be understood in the context of Aum's relationship and interaction with society at large. We recall Aum's legal and public recognition as a religious organization and its participation in the Lower House elections in 1989–90. However, after it failed to succeed in the election and owing to other events, Aum leadership became disappointed with Japanese society. The next step of Aum's religious development has to be seen in this context.

One of Asahara's main concerns was the fast growth of Aum's membership. In order to achieve this goal, in his view, the spiritual progress of his followers had to be accelerated. For this reason, in the spring of 1990 he introduced the "Tantra-Vajrayana System of Practice," a form of esoteric Buddhism. For Asahara, this was the "fastest path to attain enlightenment and higher realization" (Asahara 1992c: 114). In March 1990, Asahara declared: "Aum Shinrikyo . . . has passed through Hinayana and Mahayana and is now entering the realm of Tantra-Vajrayana" (Asahara 1991c: 78). Considering the chronological context for this stage of development, this change took place just at the time when Aum Shinrikyo experienced its first harsh criticism by society. In the fall of 1989, the weekly *Sunday Mainichi* published a series of articles criticizing Aum members' practice of "leaving the house" (*shukke*). Electoral defeat occurred in February 1990. In August 1990 there were troubles with neighbors and alleged infractions of the law for constructing buildings in Namino-son (Kyushu), where Aum Shinrikyo had begun to build the "Lotus Village" complex. Asahara perceived this criticism as "persecution" (*honan*), and he suspected that his electoral defeat was the result of manipulation by the government.[20]

During the process of doctrinal changes, Asahara attempted to clarify the consistency of his teaching by identifying the triad of "Hinayana," Mahayana, and Tantra-Vajrayana with Raja Yoga, Kundalini Yoga, and Mahamudra Yoga (Asahara 1991c: 71). This latest change was also reflected in the publication of the journal *Vajrayana Sacca* in the beginning of fall 1994. For him, this shift was not so much a break with earlier teachings as a different emphasis while maintaining continuity. Asahara explained the meaning of Tantric teaching as follows: "Parents accumulate bad deeds because of their children. They work hard; they even lie for their children. . . . However, when the children attain enlightenment and start to save other beings, the bad deeds instantly change into good deeds. This is a Tantric way of thinking. The parents go to a higher world because their children could not live if they had not committed bad deeds" (ibid.: 65). The comparison with the parents' "white lie" derives from the Lotus Sutra, which proposes the application of skillful means (*hoben*) in order to save sentient beings. This concept certainly was not designed for abuse, but during the history of Buddhism it occasionally became a justification for abuse. According to Asahara, Tantric Buddhism allows the principle that "the end justifies the means" (cf. *AEN* April 26, 1996). Asahara proceeds to reverse the generally acknowledged value system by stating:

> If a guru has a crystal clear mind; if a being can see through everything, there will be no lies for him; lies won't mean anything to him. We've been carrying a lot of ideas with us ever since we were born. "Good" is one of these ideas and "bad" is also one of these ideas. Before World War II in Japan, it was considered good to die for the country; it was good to die for the emperor. But after World War II under the Peace Constitution and the compulsory educational system, people have come to think it is nonsense to die for the country or for the emperor. Why? What I want to tell you is that ideas are not substantial; they change according to their conditions. Good and bad also changes according to its conditions. Let's say someone has lied to make someone else practice the teachings of truth. The fact that he has lied will certainly incur him bad karma; but the fact that he has guided someone to truth earns him merit. . . . From a Tantric point of view, it is considered good because you benefit others at your own sacrifice. (Asahara 1992b: 95)

In reversing established value systems, Asahara goes so far as to justify murder for religious purpose. As early as January 1987, he reportedly taught that "the teachings of esoteric Buddhism of Tibet were pretty savage. For instance, when a guru ordered a disciple to kill a thief, the disciple went ahead and did it as an act of virtue. . . . When your guru orders you to take someone's life, it's an indication that the person's time is already up. In other words, you are killing that person at exactly the right time and thereby letting that person have his poa" (*AEN* April 26, 1996).

In Tibetan Buddhism, *poa* designates a ritual performed by a lama in order to lead the soul of a deceased person to a higher spiritual dimension. In the beginning of, and publicly throughout, Aum's development, this term was used in the conventional meaning.[21] Eventually, however, among senior Aum leaders *poa* became a euphemism for murder sanctioned on religious grounds. In a later speech, Asahara allegedly stated the following: "The end justifies the means. Let's say there's a man whose vices are so many that he is certain to go to hell when he dies. If an enlightened individual determines that it's best to put an end to his life sooner and actually goes ahead and kills him, this act would be seen as plain murder by society in general. But in the light of our doctrine, the killing amounts to letting the man have his poa. As such, any enlightened person will see at once that both the killer and the person to be killed are going to benefit from the act" (*AEN* April 26, 1996). Apart from the inversion of values, the crucial problem is that there is no check on Asahara's decisions, because he assumed absolute authority.[22]

The Japanese media frequently noted with surprise the "scientific" character of Aum as a religious group. Many young scientists belonged to the group. With scientific instruments they measured the impact of meditation practices on practitioners. This aspect, however, was not always characteristic for Aum. In the beginning, Asahara still believed the popular notion of antagonism between religion (or "supranatural power") and science (Asahara 1991b). According to information from a member who belonged to the early group of monks and nuns, it was the gifted young scientist Murai Hideo who, after joining the group, launched the scientific and technological twist in Aum's development. The initial yoga practice, performed naturally with the body, was increasingly supplemented by technical devices such as the electrical headgear called PSI (Perfect Salvation Initiation), or later by chemical drugs. The effects of religious practices on the practitioner's body, for example during the underground and underwater *samadhis*, were measured by scientific instruments. Aum thus tried to combine religion and science in various ways. In this respect, Aum is no exception; other Japanese new religions also try to prove scientifically the effectiveness of their practice and the truth of their teaching.

The publication of a series of articles treating the theme of religion and science began in Aum's journal *Mahayana* in November 1987 (No. 4: 70 f.) the series was entitled "Treat the Truth Scientifically: Process of the Creation of the Universe" (*Shinri o kagakka suru: Uchu sosei no purosesu*). The articles of the series were written by an Aum member with the pen name Oumu-shutain, and were published until November 1988. Oumu-shutain is the Japanese pronounciation of "Aum" and "stein," derived from the combination of Aum and Einstein. The author was, in fact, Murai Hideo (cf. Aum Press 1995: 188–255), who is said to have had a very high IQ.[23] In the first article the author claims that with its "yoga theory" Aum can actually prove the astrophysical "Big Bang" theory (*Mahayana* No. 4: 70). The author sees similarities between yoga and the scientific models of the universe, and draws the conclusion that they are identical (*Mahayana* No. 4: 71); in other words, science proves the truth of religion.

Another series of articles entitled "Through Academic Verification: True Religion is Science!" was published in *Vajrayana Sacca* (No. 1 [August 1994]– No. 12 [July 1995]). The author Otaki Toshinari claims that the methods of Aum Shinrikyo and those applied in science conform with each other. He sees the characteristics of science in first, its logical character of analyzing cause, condition, and result of a phenomenon; second, its objectivity; and third, its providing proofs, or the model of theory, test, and verification. These three characteristics, he says, are shared by Aum's methodology (*Vajrayana Sacca* No. 1: 123–125). Because of the common methodology, he calls a union between religion and science "true religion" (*Vajrayana Sacca* No. 3: 155). Asahara once called the envisaged identity of science and religion "spiritual science" (*seishin kagaku*) (Asahara 1995b: 35).

Joyu Fumihiro, who had left a promising career at the National Space Development Agency in order to become a monk in Aum, underwent, with others, an "underground *samadhi*" in a buried airtight container in November 1991 (*Shinri* Nos. 4 and 5). The data of the impact on the practitioners were recorded by medico-technical instruments in order to "prove" the supernatural powers of these religious practices. Thereby Aum intended to provide scientific proof for *gedatsu*, the ultimate liberation from the cycle of birth and death. These tests provided "proof for the truth," and this meant that "Aum is the Truth" (*Shinri* No. 5: 30–32). According to Asahara, this scientific verification of extraordinary religious experiences served the missionary purpose of persuading nonbelievers of Aum's truth (*Monthly Truth* No. 15: 29). Thus, science served as legitimation for Aum's truth, and it was used as proselytization tool.

Murai, head of Aum's so-called "Science and Technology Ministry," which was later blamed for producing stimulant drugs and poison gas, was not only attracted by the miraculous world of religion but also had a strong inclination toward science fiction, the miraculous world of sciences.[24] He once expressed his desire to build a "time machine" and an "almightily creative machine."[25] At this critical borderline between science and science fiction, Asahara (1995d: 266) once remarked, "science fiction becomes science fact."

As we have said, Asahara initially studied and practiced Chinese divination and astrology. He was primarily concerned with his own fate, but he also used his skills for others. Already in the early phase of Aum Shinrikyo, Asahara had asked Murai Hideo and another member acquainted with astrology to develop a computer program for fast calculations of star constellations in order to secure 100 percent correct predictions (Asahara 1991a: 131 and personal information). In 1988, a horoscope series under the title "Grand Universe Astrology" (*Dai-uchu sensei-gaku*) began to appear in *Mahayana* (No. 8). Later, the series was taken up again in the magazines *Enjoy Happiness* (No. 1, 1992) and *Vajrayana Sacca* (No. 1, 1994).

Asahara's concern with his own fate and that of his followers eventually extended to that of humankind (Asahara 1991a: 120). His interest in astrology and his claim to possess supernatural abilities led him to announce prophecies of his own. In his early book *Cho-noryoku himitsu no kaihatsu-ho* (1991b), he claims that in 1986 he had predicted events such as the eruption of Vesuvius, the crash of a Japanese airplane, and the earthquake in Mexico, each two to four weeks in advance.[26] Such ability, he explains, resulted from meditation practice during which he went on so-called astral trips. Trips in the synchronous astral world would enable him to see future events of the phenomenal world (Asahara 1991b: 275). Asahara continued with his predictions throughout the following years. The last in the series was the Kobe earthquake of January 1995 (Asahara 1995c: 80f.). In his book *Supreme Initiation*, Asahara predicted in 1987 a nuclear war if certain conditions were not met:

> This is my prediction. Japan will gradually suffer from economic difficulty after economic friction with the United States and European Countries. It will be triggered off in 1990. However, if AUM has at least one or two branches in each country of the world by 1993, the prophecy I will make from now will not come true. Conversely, if true Bodhisattvas . . . do not gather and AUM does not have two branches or more in each country by 1993, what do you think will happen? Japan will rearm herself in 1993. Then a nuclear war is sure to break out from 1999 to 2003. I Asahara have mentioned the outbreak of a nuclear war for the first time. (Asahara 1988: 87f.)

Asahara proceeds by arguing: "If a country has many believers in the teachings of the truth, it won't have any internal conflicts, and will avoid waging a war against foreign countries. As such countries increase, the earth will be more peaceful and secure. . . . If [Aum] spreads all over the world, we can avoid World War 3 certainly" (ibid.: 92).

Asahara viewed the situation as very serious, but there was still hope for survival if the conditions he set were met. In 1988, he had begun to study the Apocalypse of John and subsequently published the book *Metsubo no hi* (Doomsday) in 1989. According to his interpretation, practitioners with supernatural powers will be able to survive doomsday. They will be led by a king from Japan, but this will not be the Japanese emperor.[27]

Also in 1989, Asahara had begun to study Nostradamus's *Les Centuries* (Asahara, 1992f: 153f.). The first articles on "Nostradamus's great prophecies" appeared in the March and April issues of *Mahayana* (Nos. 20 and 21), in which they were declared to be the "last truth." They are explained as a warning that left only a little time to escape from the pending disaster. In April 1989, publication of the *manga* (comic) *Metsubo no hi* with the subtitle *Harmagedon* (*sic*) followed, an illustration of the "Great Prophecies of the [Book of] Apocalypse."

Because the text of Nostradamus's *Les Centuries* varies according to the edition, Asahara even traveled with some disciples to France in search of the authentic text. The interest of the Aum group focused particularly on the authenticity of the prophecy Ch. X no.72, which reads as follows:

> In the year 1999 and seven months,
> From the skies shall come an alarmingly powerful king,
> To raise again the Great King of the Jacquerie,
> Before and after, Mars shall reign at will. (Roberts [1982] 1994: 336)

This verse was frequently interpreted as a prediction of a major catastrophe such as Armageddon in 1999. However, Asahara maintained that he did not think that in 1999 humankind would be destroyed but that there would be a situation close to such a catastrophe, in the midst of which a "new humankind" would be born; in other words, such a cataclysm would give birth to the "suprahumankind" that would create a peaceful world (Asahara 1991a: 132, 108). Asahara claims to share with Nostradamus a mastery of astrology, meditation (thereby entering a synchronous dimension), and "mystical powers" enabling him to see the future (ibid.: 41, 44, 46). Therefore, it is only Asahara who can decipher Nostradamus's revelations correctly.[28]

The above verse was the focus of the "Nostradamus boom" in Japan (cf. Asahara 1991a: 103f.), which was triggered by the science fiction writer Goto Ben, who had published a series of books on the "Great Prophecies of Nostradamus" since 1973.[29] The subtitles promise a catastrophic event for humankind in 1999. The subtitle of the first volume also mentions the "month seven" or "seven months" of 1999 of the verse of *Les Centuries* quoted above. Before Aum, Agon-shu and Kofuku no kagaku had already taken up this subject.[30] They also focused on the Nostradamus prediction quoted above (cf. Kisala 1998). The popularity of Nostradamus seems to be connected with the sense of crisis currently prevalent among Japanese.[31]

Asahara first employed doomsday predictions in order to warn humankind and to encourage them to take refuge in Aum. His visions, however, became more pessimistic when he felt repeatedly rejected by society. In 1990 Asahara stated: "we are heading for Armageddon. It becomes very clear if you analyze the situation in the Middle East. Also the coming of Haley's comet, the frequent appearances of UFO's, the Soviet Union's democratization . . . and so forth . . . all these incidents . . . are telling us that the world is getting ready for Armageddon. . . . This is why I always say we must think of the way to protect ourselves. . . . I have decided to build a facility for 1,500 to 2,000 people. . . . Nuclear war, bacteriological weapons, chemical weapons, no matter what kind of weapons should attack us, we must protect ourselves and preserve a place for our practice" (Asahara 1992b: 103 f.).

Hope for renewal of the world by converting humankind was given up. Disappointment with society spread, as well as hopelessness (cf. *Shinri* No. 26: 4–16). The only escape from the impending catastrophe was to practice more rigorously and to build shelters for protection (Asahara 1992b: 105f.). This eschatological mood is also expressed in the architecture of Aum facilities. In contrast to the luxurious, impressive buildings of other new Japanese religions, those of Aum looked like factories and were purely functional. Here believers lived, worked, meditated, and protected themselves by filter devices against possible gas attacks. At this point, Aum seems to have returned to the intro-verted practice from which the movement had started. Mahayana Buddhism and the opening up toward society seemed to have been an unnecessary detour (cf. Asahara 1992b: 105).

The most comprehensive Aum publication on the impending disaster and Asahara's predictions is *Hiizure kuni, wazawai chikashi*, published a few days before the Tokyo gas attack in March 1995 (Asahara 1995c). On the back cover of the English version, *Disaster Approaches the Land of the Rising Sun* (1995d), the reader is exhorted to "Survive Armageddon!"—the Third World War. We further read in this introduction:

> This is the prophesied final war which shall surpass all others tech-nologically and in sheer scale of destruction. The book presents a detailed picture of future political and economic events, natural dis-asters, as well as the goals of the worldwide Freemasons conspiracy. With his divine insight, Master Asahara deciphers astrological charts and interprets the prophecies of Nostradamus, the Bible, and others. It includes an explanation of state-of-the-art weapons, some secretly developed by the superpowers that are more dangerous than nuclear weapons. Learn protective measures against them. . . . Master Asa-hara and his followers are preparing for Armageddon by combining the wisdom of spiritual practice with science, and pave the way for a new era of peace. (ibid.: back cover copy)

The book starts in the preface with "The War Has Already Begun," sug-gesting that the Kobe earthquake in January 1995 was caused by an "earthquake weapon" (ibid.: vii; cf. 60). It refers to Nicola Tesla's attempt to create artificial earthquakes.[32] It also quotes a *Yomiuri Shinbun* article of May 4, 1991, accord-ing to which "Russian earthquake weapons" were "in the last stage of devel-opment" (ibid.: vii–x, cf. 58–62). Thus an attack on Japan will become the beginning of World War III; the real attacker, however, will be the United States.[33] In waging such a war, the United States will try to overcome its eco-nomic crisis. Nuclear weapons will be employed or, alternatively, the spread of a false religion (ibid.: 73–81). However, Japan will not be defeated. According to Asahara, "Nostradamus predicted that Japan will be the leader in the coming century" (ibid.: 293; cf. 290). According to this scenario, however, only those Japanese people will survive who are Aum members, because of its unique combination of religion, science, and technology. Besides conventional protec-tive measures such as shelters, meditation techniques will help to prevent panic and to reduce consumption of oxygen in these small shelters (ibid.: 124, 131). Also, protection against electronic warfare, biological and chemical weapons, laser and microwave weapons are discussed (ibid.: 157–169; cf. 108ff.). "The last resort to surviving an attack," we read, "is to do the correct practice" (ibid.: 182).

The core of the final war is, according to Asahara, not political or military but religious. It is a religious war between East and West, between Buddhism and Christianity. As Asahara says: "Religious wars are breaking out throughout the world. Christianity is controlling the world, and there is no doubt that it is persecuting other religions. . . . Everything happens according to the law of the karma. Those who persecute must be persecuted, and those who oppress must be oppressed. I am sure that the final religious war on earth will be a confrontation between Buddhism and Christianity" (ibid.: 268).

Asahara further clarifies the nature of such a confrontation: "The expression *conflict between Christianity and Buddhism* is a metaphor. Actually, the conflict is between Buddhism and the people ruled by materialistic desires, believing in Christianity. This is not Buddhism in the ordinary sense, but a group with the view that the human realm is maya, an illusion. . . . The conflict will take place between this group and the group possessed by materialistic desires" (ibid.: 306).

The predominant tone of this Aum publication is not directed toward actively initiating Armageddon, but toward one's own survival and self-protection. Asahara foresees that Eastern wisdom will not only help people to survive Armageddon but will also become the basis of the new civilization (ibid.: 187, 20). Japan will become a "country that makes true religion its ideology" and "will rule the world" (ibid.: 82). Thus, Asahara sees the ultimate victory of Buddhism to come, and consequently Christianity will vanish, and the "Christian era will end" (ibid.: 100, 291). The "entire world will change into Buddhist countries," and at this time "Aum Shinrikyo will be the center of the world" (ibid.: 131, 297). Here we encounter a Buddhist kind of fundamentalism that is a reaction against Westernization and globalization. Other new religions in Japan express similar resentments and ideas (cf. Agon-shu 1989: 7f.; Davis 1980: 47–50) Asahara perceived himself as the savior of the world at the end of the second millennium. What will the situation be after Armageddon? According to Asahara, "After the Third World War, I imagine that this world will be filled with love. Every person will overcome his or her own suffering and work for the good of others" (Asahara 1995d: 133).

Concerning a definite date for the final war, Asahara's predictions remained vague. Expectation of Armageddon served to strengthen the Aum members' consciousness of being the chosen people to survive (cf. Asahara 1991a: 123). This again contributed to widening the gap between the group and the surrounding society.

The diversity of Aum's teachings and practice, ranging from ancient Buddhist texts to science fiction, or from Mahayana Buddhism to Nostradamus, has led scholars of religious studies to use terms like "syncretic" or "eclectic" to characterize the movement. This kind of labeling, however, tends to be judgmental, and does not contribute to a better understanding of Aum's characteristics. Most, if not all, religions established by a founder are syncretic or eclectic. It might be more fruitful to ask instead whether there is a common thread that binds all the diverse, heterogenuous elements together.

Reviewing Asahara's and Aum Shinrikyo's development between 1986 and 1995, we encounter the following major elements: astrology; Daoism; Hinduism, especially yoga; Buddhism in the forms of "Hinayana," Mahayana, and tantric or esoteric Buddhism; Judeo-Christian apocalyptical traditions; and science, science fiction, and technology. Among these diverse elements, in my view, the common denominator is Aum's peculiar combination of knowledge and power. Aum leaders used knowledge to gain power, and exercised and increased power through constantly acquiring new knowledge.

Application of this hypothesis on the various elements of Aum bears the following results. First, astrology promises knowledge of personal and global fate, gives advice to act accordingly, and as such becomes a means to master fate. Second, Daoism requires much knowledge in its search for immortality, and, once acquired, knowledge provides powers over aging and death. Third, Yoga teaching and practice provide the mastery of body and mind, but also of time and space. It also enables travel in the dimension of the "astral world," where one can gain knowledge about future events. Fourth, in Buddhism, the idea of karma requires certain understanding of the past in order to master one's present and future religious fate. Its main focus is to gain practical insight into liberation from the cycle of birth and death, in other words, to master one's suffering and transitoriness. Whereas Yoga and "Hinayana" provide knowledge and power for one's own individual liberation, Mahayana transmits wisdom and power for the liberation of humankind. Tantric Buddhism is especially known for its transmission of esoteric knowledge and powers. Asahara always stressed the acquisition of supranatural powers (Skt. *siddhi*, J. *chonoryoku*) in Yoga or the divine powers (*shintsuriki*) in Daoism and Buddhism. Asahara (1991b: 3) once pointed out that he had extracted the supernatural powers from Daoism, Buddhism, esoteric Buddhism, and Yoga, and then had combined them. Fifth, proper understanding of the Apocalypse of St. John and Nostradamus's prophecies reveal future catastrophic events of worldwide scope. This knowledge, again, is instrumental in finding ways to survive impending disasters. The one who is able to gain knowledge about past, present, and future has powers over his followers and others, as well. Finally, science and technology represent the modern skills first to acquire knowledge and then to put it powerfully into reality. In other words, the intention is to use knowledge and power to rule the world.

Seen from inside the system, Asahara's religion is in a certain sense coherent. Religious practices, prophecies, science, and technology all "prove" the
truth of his theories and practices. Together they provided the credibility, authority, and "truth" for the Aum followers. Aum's combination of these different elements centered around the core of superknowledge and superpower.
Further, by hiding this core and calling it "secret power" and "secret knowledge" or "wisdom," Asahara's authority remained unchallenged within the
group.

In a sense, Aum Shinrikyo is a very modern religion. Through its attempt
to combine religion and science, it tried to become a "scientific religion." In
the end, however, the whole system boiled down to primitive human instincts.
Since knowledge was used only as a tool for gaining more power, Asahara's
religion came to be centered on power. Aum is, as Asahara once stated, a
"supernatural-power religion" (chonoryoku shukyo) (Asahara 1991a: 83). According to his writings, this may be called "Asahara's Aum Shinrikyo." This
characteristic, however, has to be distinguished from the individual believer's
perception. Most followers were more concerned with gaining peace of mind
or attaining liberation from suffering (gedatsu) and satori.[34] Most of the Aum
members with whom I spoke stressed Buddhist teaching and practice, especially liberation from suffering and from the cycle of birth and death. When
talking about the acclaimed levitation, the initial source for Asahara's claim of
supernatural powers, some only smiled and said this could be explained naturally.

Organizational Developments and Criminal Activities

When writing of Aum Shinrikyo, mass media and academic studies normally
begin with its crimes.[35] By using such a description, right from its beginning
the group is characterized as heavily corrupt and evil, leaving no room for more
nuanced perceptions of the subject. Thus Aum is portrayed as a violent group
which—"from its earliest days" and with "intrinsic" necessity (Reader 2000:
161, 42)—led to crime and terror. It is clear, however, that such an anachronistic
or ahistorical approach does not do justice to the subject.[36]

In contrast to such approaches, the present study first portrays Aum's
development and its religious system, and then provides an outline of the
criminal side. I hereby distinguish between three different layers, namely,
Aum's religious system (teaching and practice), its social organization, and its
criminal activities. In the first section I introduced Aum as a religious entity,
and in this section I treat its social organization as well as its criminal activities.
I argue that it was its social conflicts with the rest of society that led to radicalization and violence of Aum. It was not Aum's teaching per se or other

internal factors alone that led to this development, as police, prosecution, and some scholars suggest.

The following account treats the crimes in the context of Aum's organizational development. Criminal developments within Aum Shinriko began in February 1989, when senior members strangled Taguchi Shuji to death. Taguchi wanted to leave the group because he had witnessed the death of another member caused by rigorous religious training in September 1988 (*JT* April 25, 1996). The leaders feared that he would leak this information to the press or police and thereby create obstacles for the official recognition of Aum as a religious corporation (*shukyo hojin*). Aum had attempted to apply for this legal status with the Tokyo Metropolitan Government in 1988; however, because (according to court hearings) authorities already knew about the troubles between celibate Aum believers and their parents, they had delayed proceedings. Before accepting the formal application in March 1989, they visited Aum facilities in January and February 1989 in order to clarify the problems.[37] Aum received formal recognition only in August 1989. Hence, the first murder in Aum served to remove what the society perceived as a possible obstacle for its legal recognition as religious organization.

Soon after Aum's official recognition, the weekly magazine *Sunday Mainichi* published the first critical media reports of it in a series between October 15 and 29, 1989, entitled *Oumu shinrikyo no kyoki* (The madness of Aum Shin-

FIGURE 8.2. Aum hysteria. Printed with kind permission by Yamanoi Norio.

rikyo). The articles were based on testimonies by relatives of Aum members and targeted not only strange religious practices such as drinking Asahara's blood, but also practices related to Aum's introduction of celibacy (*shukke*), such as individuals donating large amounts of money to Aum or taking their own children into the new community. These articles put Aum under the spotlight of public scrutiny for the first time. Henceforth, criticism focused mainly on Aum's system of requiring members to leave house and family in order to dedicate their lives and possessions to religion. Meanwhile, Aum members perceived these critical reports as "Aum bashing" and "persecution" (Asahara 1992f: 153).

The first murder target outside Aum became lawyer Sakamoto Tsutsumi, his wife, and their baby, in late 1989.[38] Sakamoto had been representing families of Aum members in order to sue the group at court. He also had given an interview to Tokyo Broadcasting System (TBS), which was critical of Aum. TBS gave in to demands of senior Aum members to provide a preview of the interview. After talks failed to convince the lawyer to stop his criticism, in November 1989 a group of senior Aum members killed the family in their apartment and buried them in remote places in the mountains. The Kanagawa Prefectural Police in charge of this case did almost nothing to investigate the case because the lawyer's office had represented a member of the Communist Party at court, whose telephone had been illegally wiretapped by the same police some years before. Later, the head of the National Police Agency, Kunimatsu Takaji, admitted that if the police had acted promptly, "the nerve gas attacks in Matsumoto and on the [Tokyo] subway would not have taken place" (*JT* September 9, 1995). Meanwhile, TBS hid its involvement in this tragic case for over six years until it gave in to public pressure in 1995 and admitted that it had struck a deal with Aum at that time: In exchange for not airing the Sakamoto interview, TBS received a special interview with Asahara. If we analyze the first murders inside and outside the group, we have to conclude that they served the single purpose of protecting Aum as a religious organization from public interference.

In the winter of 1989–90, Asahara and senior followers participated in the elections for the Lower House without any success. This failure caused one of the decisive turning points in the development of Aum. Thereafter, Asahara's teaching turned toward Tantra-Vajrayana and doomsday prophecies, and the gap between Aum and the rest of society deepened further. In May 1990, Aum bought land in Namino-son in Kyushu to set up housing and workshops in order to create the Lotus Village. Because of the provocative behavior of the mostly young followers, conflicts with the people of the village of Namino-son arose. Subsequently, village authorities did not permit Aum members to register as local citizens because they feared a "foreign takeover" of the village.[39] Although this reaction is understandable, the refusal of registration was illegal. In October 1990, the police searched twelve Aum facilities on grounds of alleged infractions of building regulations in Namino-son and arrested several leading members.[40] Aum representatives perceived this as the beginning of "illegal suppression by the state" and as "persecution."[41] The investigation led to a court trial. In the end, the conflict was resolved by Aum leaving the place and the village paying compensation.[42]

By 1991, Aum Shinrikyo had established eighteen centers in Japan, and one center each in New York and Bonn (Asahara 1991c: 126). From this time on, Aum expanded its international activities. In 1991, Asahara traveled widely in the company of many followers. He visited holy places in India, and was said to have been invited as a guest of state in Laos; he reportedly was praised in Sri Lanka as "the only one who can save the world" and received a Buddhist relic from the prime minister.[43] Also in 1991, the first important meeting took place between Aum representatives and Oleg Lobov, the secretary of the Russian Security Council, opening the way for its subsequent activities in Russia. In 1992, Aum began to broadcast its own radio program in Russia (Asahara 1992c: 121, 125), and financially support the newly established Russia-Japan University, which, however, never functioned as an institution for teaching and research (*AEN* May 16, 1995). Also in 1992, Asahara traveled to Moscow, accompanied by three hundred followers, and was received by government officials. In June 1992, the Russian Justice Ministry recognized Aum as an official religious organization, thereby granting it tax exemption and permission to proselytize. The first branch office in Moscow was opened in September (ibid.). It is estimated that in subsequent years Aum gained about thirty thousand followers in Russia.[44]

In 1993, Aum purchased a sheep farm in Australia, probably for providing a safe haven as well as for the purpose of digging uranium.[45] In the same year, Aum founded business enterprises in Japan such as Hasegawa Chemicals, which made it possible to acquire chemicals in large amounts. It also established the company Mahaposha (Mahaposya) for international trade and computer production. Computer parts were imported from Taiwan and assembled by the cheap labor of Aum members. The computers were sold cheaply in Aum's computer stores in Tokyo and Osaka, and the profits contributed considerably to Aum's income. In its New York branch, Aum was not able to gather many followers, but from here it purchased sophisticated computer hardware and software for its scientific activities (Nunn Report 1995: 75–86).

These were Aum's main organizational developments inside and outside Japan when, in June 1994, suddenly a poison-gas attack occurred in Matsumoto (Nagano Prefecture), injuring 147 people and killing 7 (*JT* April 25, 1996). Among the victims were judges involved in court proceedings concerning a building claimed by Aum. This attack shook the sense of public security in Japan. The man who first reported the incident was treated by the prefectural police as the main suspect; his wife was badly injured by the gas and is still in a coma today. A year later, police and mass media had to apologize to him for wrongly accusing him of this crime.

On January 17, 1995, the great Hanshin earthquake in the Osaka-Kobe area occurred, leaving over 5,000 persons dead, more than 26,000 injured, and over 250,000 homeless. Again, the citizens' trust in public safety was tested, and their reliance on government and administration was disappointed (cf. Repp 1995b). It is in this context of a general mood of anxiety that in the morning of March 20, 1995, during rush hour, a gas attack was carried out on five lines of Tokyo Metropolitan Subway, all of them close to government offices and police headquarters in Kasumigaseki.[46] The gas was released from sealed plastic bags that were opened with the sharpened tip of an umbrella. Approximately 4,000 people were injured, many of them seriously and with long-lasting effects; twelve persons died.[47] One victim, representative of all, described his suffering as follows: "I was in hospital for twelve days: vicious headaches the whole time. No pain-killer worked. I was in agony. The head-aches would come in waves all day, receding then getting stronger. I also ran a high fever for two days; as high as 40°C. I had cramps in my legs and trouble breathing for the first three or four days. It was like there was something stuck in my throat. Excruciating. My eyes were so bad I'd look outside and see no light at all. Everything was a blur" (Murakami 2001: 60).

Two days after the Tokyo gas attack, approximately 2,500 armed police, equipped with helmets, gas masks, and crowbars, searched the Aum facilities in Kamikuishiki (Yamanashi Prefecture) and at twenty-four other locations. The event was broadcast live and nationwide by cameramen who had been waiting for the police at the Aum facilities, since they had been informed by police well in advance. The search warrants were issued in connection with an abduction. On February 26, 1995, Aum members had abducted the notary public Kariya Kiyoshi because he had hidden his sister, an Aum follower, when Aum pressed her to donate real estate (*JT* April 23, 1995 and April 25, 1996). Kariya's abduction became the official reason for the massive police search of the Aum facilities. Police later found that he had been killed in Aum facilities by an overdose of drugs. Right from the beginning, however, the investigation concentrated on the stockpiles of chemicals, an alleged poison-gas laboratory, an alleged weapons factory, and other suspicious objects. The investigations lasted for months.

During the subsequent period, further incidents occurred that the media quickly connected with Aum Shinrikyo, rightly or wrongly.[48] On March 30, for example, Kunimatsu Takaji, the head of the National Police Agency, was shot several times when he left his apartment, although he survived. First an Aum member who was a police officer was suspected (*DY* October 29 and 31, 1996), but this story turned out to be a hoax. Even today the Japanese police have not brought to light the truth about the attempt on the life of Japan's top police chief. Apparently, forces more powerful than Aum or the national police were at work here. Another striking example of these turbulent times concerns the murder of Murai Hideo, head of Aum's science and technology department, on April 23. A young Korean hired by Yakuza (Japanese gangsters) stabbed Murai to death as he was about to enter the Aum center in Minami Aoyama, Tokyo. As it happened, the television network TBS had moved its camera team at the right time to the right place and filmed the murder live; the camera was positioned right behind the murderer. Before the actual murder occurred, TBS had already filmed the future perpetrator waiting for the victim, also zooming in on his suitcase (containing his knife) with one lock opened. After the stabbing, the murderer waited for the police to detain him while his two accomplices escaped unnoticed. Although the Korean was sentenced, the Yakuza boss who had given the orders and paid for it went free. This adds another strange story to the incidents involving Aum Shinrikyo, media, and police.

The arrest of Asahara himself occurred rather late, on May 16. Again, a veritable host of journalists and camera teams descended upon Kamikuishiki.[49] After several hours of search, police found Asahara hiding in a low-ceilinged secret chamber in Satian No.6 in Kamikuishiki, the building where he had once lived with his family, and arrested him. The event became a major media spectacle.

Later police revealed that Aum members had previously also attacked a number of individual opponents with VX poison gas between May 1994 and January 1995 (JT April 25, 1996). Further, the police found that between October 1988 and February 1995 thirty-three Aum members had perished through accident, suicide, or murder. Besides these, twenty-one followers were still missing (JT March 3, 1995).

The government treated Aum as organization in the following ways.[50] In October 1995, the Tokyo District Court revoked the religious corporation (shukyo hojin) status of Aum Shinrikyo because of its production of nerve gas (AEN/JT/MDN October 31, 1995). In December 1995, the Koan (Public Security Investigation Agency), the Justice Ministry, and the government announced a plan to apply the Antisubversive Activities Law (habo-ho) to Aum, the first time this law (originally designed for the Communist peril) would ever be used. However, on January 31, 1997, the Public Security Examination Commission, which has to approve such a decision, refused to grant approval to outlaw Aum under the habo-ho, because it considered the group as not dangerous after the arrest of most of its leaders. (JT February 1, 1997). In another attempt, the government drafted a Law for Regulating Groups (dantai kisei-ho) in October 1999, specially designed for Aum, as well as another one aimed at confiscating its assets for redress of its victims.[51] The first law allows the Koan to regularly supervise and restrict Aum activities for three years, and it requires Aum to submit to the Koan detailed reports of names and addresses of members, locations of facilities, amount of assets, and its activities.[52] The Lower and Upper House adopted the two bills in November and December 1999 (*JT* November 18 and December 3, 1999), and finally the Public Security Examination Commission permitted the application of the new law to Aum on January 31, 2000. In contrast to its previous decision, this time the commission recognized the Koan's claim that the gas attacks in Matsumoto and Tokyo had political reasons: to create a "nation under the sovereignty" of Asahara and that the "cult followers still constitute a threat and could commit another indiscriminate mass murder in the future" (*JT* February 2, 2000). In an attempt to survive legal measures, in January 2000 Aum changed its name to Aleph (J. Arephu) (*JT* January 17, 2000).

With regard to court rulings for individual Aum members, four of the five followers who dispersed the poison gas in the subways received the death penalty, and their drivers and the fifth, Dr. Hayashi Ikuo, were sentenced to life in prison. Another five members received the death penalty for other murders or production of poison gas. Most of the sentences are under appeal. (*JT* April 25, 2003). In April 2003, prosecutors demanded the death penalty for Asahara. On February 27, 2004, the court sentenced Asahara to death. Lawyers will appeal this decision.

In the meantime, towns and villages organized anti-Aum movements in order to get Aum members out of their residences.[53] Furthermore, two of Asahara's children were refused acceptance in public school (*JT* June 29, 1999, cf. *DY* April 10, 1999). In several cases Aum members and children of Asahara were not permitted residency in towns (*JT* December 22, 1998, and June 29, 1999). The criminal and terrorist attacks became an excuse for violating basic human rights.

Literature on the Aum Incident

The Japanese literature on the Aum incident is so immense that it requires separate treatment elsewhere. Articles and books in Western languages are numerous, as well, but only the most important ones will be introduced here briefly. The first scholarly articles appearing in 1995 were those of Hardacre (1995), Shimazono (1995), Young (1995), and Repp (1995a); the first scholarly book to be published was Reader's (1996).[54] Being aware that categorizations are generalizations, the following characterizations should be understood as descriptions of major tendencies. First, I treat studies by religious scholars, then studies from other backgrounds, such as those of journalists. The religious studies may be divided roughly among, first, those that tend to portray and explain the Aum incident mainly through Aum internal factors (such as its teachings); second, those that tend to treat it more in terms of external factors (or its context, such as the contemporary Japanese society); and third, those that shift the focus from the Aum incident itself to its consequences, its impact, and the responses it earned.

To begin with the first group of religious studies, Shimazono Susumu's thorough article of 1995 has to be mentioned first, not only because of its early and repeated publication but also because of its influence on subsequent studies. Shimazono states in the beginning "that an understanding of [Asahara's] universe of belief is vital if one is to understand the sect's subsequent actions" (382). In the first English book publication on Aum, Ian Reader (1996) does not pay much attention to this issue; however, in his second, larger book on this subject he acknowledges Shimazono's lead by stating "that the seeds of Aum's violence were more deeply rooted in its basic doctrines, in the movement's image of itself, in its self-proclaimed mission and the personality of its founder" (2000: 4). [55] As Shimazono had already traced the subsequent phases of Aum's teachings from Yoga to Tantra-Vajrayana, Reader pays attention especially to the latter. He analyzes parts of a textbook on Vajrayana, consisting of sermons Asahara gave between August 1988 and April 1994, which were restricted to advanced Aum followers. Reader relates the developments of this teaching to parallel developments of Aum toward violence and terror, and thereby covers the crucial later period of Aum's developments. Reader's second study, though, suffers from an artificial alternative he states in the beginning: "My concern is not so much what happened as *why* it did" (2000: 2). Consequently, interpretations, assumptions, and speculations overshadow the factual side of his study.[56] In stressing that the Vajrayana teachings were the main cause for Aum's violent developments, particularly the legitimation of murder by the term *poa*, Reader and Shimazono are arguing in the same line as the public prosecutor in the Asahara court case.[57] Still, both authors also admit to a limited degree the involvement of social factors in the developments leading to the Aum incident, such as the attacks by mass media and anti-Aum movements. Shimazono concludes his study by broadly blaming the influence of too much "freedom" in Japan's postwar society (1995: 411–414). What he means, is not freedom but libertinism. Both authors, however, put the emphasis clearly on internal factors.

Those authors who focus on Asahara's teaching and personality as main factors for the Aum incident tend to neglect two other internal factors, probably because they are activated only through interlinkage with external factors. These two factors are celibacy and the young age of most leading Aum members. First, Aum's system of *shukke* (celibacy) clearly challenged established society as well as Buddhism in Japan, which has neglected this practice since the Meiji Restoration. From early on, Richard Young pointed out this factor of celibacy when he wrote: "Wherever the world and its ways have been rejected and a separate community of renunciates has been established, Buddhism— or whatever goes by that name—has been denounced as economically unproductive and the Buddhist monks who have been sexually unreproductive have been traduced as unfilial. Productivity and reproductivity are the essential ingredients of the pervasive *musubi* (growth) mentality one finds in Japan. Aum was obviously a threat to both" (1995: 239f.).

A second, equally neglected factor for the growing conflict between Aum and the rest of society was the simple fact that most of its leadership consisted of young people, who were acting according to their specific mind sets. This factor again has two aspects; one is the behavioral pattern of this age group, the other is the worldview (or worldviews) characteristic of young people in contemporary Japan. An important factor leading to the Aum incident is that most Aum members were young people who lacked the experience of what Japanese call *shakai-jin* (person of society), that is someone who had grown out of the "easy life" of young people and learned to behave according to the rules of established society.[58] The resulting inability to solve conflicts in a mature way contributed significantly to the emergence and aggravation of conflicts with families, neighbors, and civil authorities.[59] This problem can also be described as the inability to communicate understandably or to take the other's concerns into account for one's own actions (Repp 2003: 60–62).

The other aspect is the worldview of young people in contemporary Japan. One approach interpreted the Aum incident from the context of Japanese contemporary pop or youth culture. Besides attempting to understand the Aum incident from the perspective of scholars (that is, what they think about Aum), an approach from the point of view of peers of Aum members, the so-called Aum generation, sheds new light on the case (cf. Repp 1997c). In respect to *manga* (comics) and popular literature, Miyai Rika (1997) and Maeda Daisuke (1997) demonstrated that there exists a certain rationale underlying the behavior and acts of Aum members, and that they are not as unintelligible as generally portrayed. Stimulated by their approach, I have further pursued studies of *manga* as expressions of, and factors for, the patterns of thinking and acting of young people in contemporary Japan (Repp 1997b and [revised and abridged] 2000). Viewed in such context, the Aum incident loses some of its seemingly strange and enigmatic aspects, and instead begins to make some sense.[60]

Besides the studies emphasizing internal factors are those that tend to focus on external factors. My own studies (Repp 1995, 1996, 1997a and b, 2001, 2003) belong to this category. Although I do not deny the significance of internal factors in the Aum incident, I also take into account external ones such as contemporary Japanese society, media, police, other religions, and pop culture. For this reason I attempt to apply more complex, interactive models, treating Aum as a challenge and response to contemporary society and religions. Viewed in the broader context of Japanese society and religions, where violence and murder occur frequently, the Aum incident does not appear to be unique, as it is generally portrayed, but represents rather the visible tip of an

iceberg. It was only the two poison-gas attacks that transformed the Aum incident from a criminal affair to a terrorist threat.

Among the external social factors leading to the Aum incident, the shortcomings of the media were treated by Hardacre (1995), Repp (1997a), and
Gardner (1999, 2002a). Hardacre focuses on the Japanese mass media's sensationalistic and one-sided reporting of the Aum incident, their over-reliance
on police sources (thereby becoming a mouthpiece of the police), lack of investigative journalism, and violation of the principle that the "accused are innocent until proven guilty." Two significant (though much-neglected) attempts
to counter the one-sided and sensationalistic mass media reporting on Aum
were the films by director Mori Tatsuya; his films *A* and *A 2* are discussed by
Richard Gardner (1999 and 2002a).[61] In contrast to ordinary media, which
view Aum from outside in, Mori turns the camera's view from inside Aum to
the outside, showing the human side of its spokesman and the intimidation
by camera crews of mainline media as well as the law-breaking tactics and
mean behavior of Koan officers trying to arrest Aum members by illegal
means. Another grave problem concerns the TBS scandal (cf. Repp 1997a: 68–
77), and TBS's involvement in the murder of Murai, as discussed above. An
analysis of these cases suggest that media conspired in, and contributed to,
the Aum incident.

Another exterior social factor contributing to the Aum incident is the neg-
ligence by police and other civil authorities, especially in the cases of the murder of the Sakamoto family and the gas attack in Matsumoto. Analyses of these
failures were conducted by Repp (1997a: 77–79) and Hughes (2001).

An innovative study of the Aum incident is Gardner's investigation
(2002b) of Japanese comic or satiric short poems (*senryu*) by ordinary people
published in main newspapers between March and May 1995. In these poems,
Japanese critically portray the Aum incident with irony and common sense in
the context of history[62] and aspects of contemporary Japanese society,[63] such
as police,[64] politics,[65] and media.[66] In contrast to the stereotypes produced by
mass media, these poems, with engagement and detachment at the same time,
provide an alternative approach to come to grips with the Aum incident, or, in
a way, to make sense of its senseless.[67] It further illustrates the impact of the
Aum incident on the daily life of ordinary citizens, including the most banal
issues.[68] One *senryu* summarizes the enigma and contradictions of the Aum
incident: "Massive search of and reporting on Aum: it seems like I understand
but I don't" (Gardner 2002b: 46).

Finally, in connection with the external factors leading to the Aum incident, Aum's activities abroad also have to be mentioned. This became one
important topic of Aum research. Aum in Russia was treated first by Yulia
Mikhailova (1996), and then featured in *Japanese Religions* by Alexander Kabanoff (2001) and Galina Krylova (2001). Aum's involvement in Australia is
treated in my own study (2003), in which I paid special attention to the peculiar

behavioral patterns of Aum members. Behavior in a foreign country becomes amplified and therefore more easily recognizable. Thus, some strange scenes in Australia, India, and Sri Lanka reveal the comic aspect of Aum. In this connection it must be mentioned that Gardner's (2002) humorous approach is the first of its kind. This is important because most studies treat the tragic side of the Aum incident. However, a humorous approach may contribute considerably to attempts to "making sense of all the nonsense." Thus, cartoons, comics, and poems *(senryu)* pose significant material for research of the Aum incident.[69]

Apart from these studies treating the Aum incident itself are those that focus on the consequences of and reactions to the Aum incident. Robert Kisala (1995) collected responses to the Aum incident by religious organizations in Japan. The incident triggered massive public criticism of religion in general. Another consequence was the "anticult" movement, which became established in Japan through American influence; Watanabe Manabu (1997) documented this development.

The legal implications of the Aum incident are featured in an issue of *Japanese Religions*. Here, John LoBreglio (1997) translated the revised Law for Religious Corporations *(shukyo hojin-ho)*, and compared it with the original law of 1951. Yuki Hideo (1997) analyzed the new law, and Kisala (1997, cf. 1995) presented the reactions of religious bodies to these revisions. In a different publication, Mark Mullins (1997) also wrote about the political and legal responses to the Aum incident. Later legal developments, such as the Law for Regulating Groups *(dantai kisei-ho)* designed for Aum, as well as the court trials of leading Aum members, were treated in an article of mine (Repp 2001).

Kisala and Mullins (2001) recently published a collection of articles under the title *Religion and Social Crisis in Japan—Understanding Japanese Society through the Aum Affair*. Most of the contributions had been previously published, and, as the title suggests, rather than explaining the Aum incident itself most articles focus on its impact on Japanese society.

To conclude this section on religious studies of Aum, the roles of religious scholars themselves have to be mentioned. First, there is the problem of value judgments continually creeping into scholarly treatises. Michael Pye (1996: 261) was the first to take up this problem when he stated, "Aum Shinrikyo looks set to become a textbook case for considering the relationship between a descriptive approach to the study of religion and the need for critical awareness and evaluation." It is also striking that Japan's liberal religious scholars are not well represented in Japanese or (subsequently) in foreign publications. We have observed that mainstream Japanese and consequently foreign scholarship tends to focus either on internal factors or on (secondary) consequences. Conspicuous in both approaches is the neglect of external factors behind the Aum incident. One reason is the silence of liberal scholarship in the Aum case. Its representatives, such as Ikeda Akira, for example, had voiced their critical opinion in previous conflicts between Aum and society. After March 1995, however, mass media forced them to be silent. Therefore, Japanese religious research on Aum was not balanced, and consequently it was not well represented in English publications. Hence, important issues such as human rights violations against Aum members are not mentioned in mainstream publications. James Lewis (1999) shed light on this problem by publishing essays of Japanese human rights advocates.

This leads us from religious scholarship to "secular" treatises. The first attempt to draw a comprehensive picture of the Aum incident from a political perspective by focusing on the proliferation of weapons of mass destruction was the so-called Nunn Report, compiled for a hearing at the U.S. Senate Permanent Subcommittee on Investigations, on October 31 and November 1, 1995. This report covers the development of Aum and its beliefs, its membership and social structure, its financial operations, its production of chemical and biological weapons as well as of drugs, its crimes, and its activities overseas. Given the relatively short and early time of compilation, this report provides a comprehensive account of the Aum incident.

In contrast, the account by D. W. Brackett (1996) portrays Aum in a one-sided manner. The same must be said of the book by the journalists David Kaplan and Andrew Marshall (1996), even though they provide a lot of detailed information on the Aum incident in Japan and worldwide. Because these books are written in sensationalist style and do not provide sources, they are of not much use for scholarly purposes. They also violate the principle that the "accused are innocent until proven guilty," before courts hand down their verdicts.[70]

A similar one-sided approach is that of the psychiatrist Robert Lifton, who tries to come to grips with the Aum incident through his brainwashing theory. Relying heavily on other researchers, resource persons, and translators, he tries to make sense through his psychological approach. Considering the insufficiency of his brainwashing theory, at least in our context, his interpretative framework remains questionable.[71] The lack of reference to sources and the continuous value judgments make it equally difficult to use for scholarly research.

Finally, in contrast to these sensationalist and one-sided books, the novelist Murakami Haruki (1997) published interviews with victims and survivors of the gas attack in Tokyo, which later appeared as an English translation (in hardcover in 2000) together with interviews with some Aum members. This sober-minded and sobering account of the victims' side represents another innovative approach in dealing with the Aum incident. The victims' voices have been much neglected in studies of the Aum incident. Moreover, Murakami's courage in adding statements by Aum members in the English edition, thereby juxtaposing the conflicting sides, creates a unique book.

Factors Leading to the Aum Incident

In conclusion, a summary of the findings above suggests lines for future research. In the analysis of the Aum incident, we observed internal factors as well as external ones. The internal factors consist of Asahara's personality and his charisma, his teachings, and his followers, who formed the religious group Aum Shinrikyo, which supported him and depended on him and his teachings. The dynamic interaction between guru and disciples consisted in mutual dependency on the one hand, and on the other hand in mutual enforcement, though in different form and to different extents on both sides. Asahara's teachings changed according to changing circumstances; they served as (secondary) legitimation (for example, for murder), but then they also gave impulses for new actions. Thus, the Aum teachings have to be considered as both a reactive, secondary factor and as an active, primary factor.

The social structure of the group consisted of a strict authoritarian hierarchy, with Asahara on the top and the leading members directly below him. Information had to flow freely from the bottom to the top, but was strictly controlled in its flow from top to bottom. Horizontal communication of information among individual followers or working units was discouraged or prohibited. Individual members, especially those of the leading group such as Murai or Hayakawa, contributed considerably to the direction and functioning of the group. Last, but not least, the inability to communicate with society outside the group also contributed to escalation of the conflict.

Next we have to consider the external factors. It is no accident that a group like Aum originated and flourished in Japan during the bubble economy and postbubble periods, characterized by material wealth and spiritual emptiness, dissolution of families and loneliness, an education system that tolerated bullying (*ijime*), and did not foster independently thinking persons. Pop culture such as *anime* (animated films) and *manga* (comics) formed the mindsets of young people in brutal as well as in idealized forms. Established religions were not able to attract young people and speak their language. Those were all direct or indirect factors that played a role in the forming of Aum itself. There were also a number of contributing factors for the Aum incident. Media attacked Aum from early on in an aggressive and sensationalistic way that provoked corresponding reactions. The anti-Aum movements, certainly an indispensable group for a democratic society, involuntarily contributed to the escalation in certain ways. Religious groups in Japan were also, at least indirectly, involved through their demand for maintaining privileges without fulfilling social responsibilities accordingly. In this respect, Aum fits in perfectly with most of the other religious groups. Moreover, the reluctance of police to investigate Aum at the proper time was caused, it is said, by fear that other religious

organizations would protest against an alleged interference in religious freedom. Also, the political orientation of the police prevented necessary actions,
as the case of the Sakamoto family demonstrates. There were many other cases
in which police did not take action in time, beginning with the first disappearance of members[72] up the Matsumoto gas attack. Thus, incompetence of
the police certainly was a contributing factor for Aum's continuation and escalation of violence and murder. There were a number of other failures by civil
authorities, such as the fire department's failure to check the Aum facilities in
Kamikuishiki, which was full of chemicals at the time, or the government's
lack of control of the large chemical trade in Japan, a point raised in the Nunn
Report. Also the Yakuza cooperated by selling drugs imported or produced by
Aum. Further, the Aum incident also could have not happened without various
forms of international cooperation. Prominent political and religious figures
recognized Asahara and Aum, thereby enhancing his authority and supporting
his organization. Related issues are the political background and the economic
side of the Aum incident, both nationally and internationally, which were fully
exposed by neither police nor the court.

The Aum incident certainly occurred because Asahara and his followers
were its major agents; however, it could occur only because of a broad variety
of cooperating, contributing factors. The Aum incident is too complex to be
grasped sufficiently by monocausal explanations. It is precisely the complex
interaction of various factors that made it happen as it did. Future research on
Aum, therefore, has to elaborate more precisely the specific interaction of internal and external factors that in combination led to the Aum incident.

Abbreviations

AEN	Asahi Evening News
DY	Daily Yomiuri
JT	Japan Times
MDN	Mainichi Daily News

NOTES

The author is coordinator of the Interreligious Studies in Japan Program at the NCC
Center for the Study of Japanese Religions (Kyoto). He would like to thank Dr. Mon-
ika Schrimpf (Tokyo) and Prof. John Dougil (Kyoto) for helping to edit the manuscript
and correct the English.

1. According to Japanese custom, the first name follows the family name.
2. *Mainichi Shinbun* (May 16, 1995, evening ed.); cf. *Asahi Shinbun* (May 16,
1995, evening ed.); Kiriyama 1995b, 9–24; Asahara 1991b: 36–43.
3. Books on yoga by Sahoda Tsuruji also exerted some influence (Asahara 1991b:

44f.). Motoyama Hiroshi and Oki Masahiro contributed to the popularity of yoga in Japan in the 1980s. At this time Rajneesh's movement was also active in Japan. Asahara's long hair and the Indian-style clothes (*kurta*) of Aum monks and nuns illustrate the Indian influence.

4. Cf. Asahara 1991b: 22ff. Kiriyama's (1973) book *Nenriki* was influential for the popularity of the term "supernatural power."

5. Asahara understands hermits to be "people who are spiritually evolved and have supernatural power" (Asahara 1992c: 79). The word *aum* (also written om) is used as a mantra. According to Miller (1996: 37), "AUM is the primordial sound. . . . It expresses ultimate reality—in the cosmos, in the Lord of Yoga [Shiva], and in the individual."

6. Asahara 1993a: ix; cf. 32; Asahara 1992f: 151, *Vajrayana Sacca* No. 9: 36.

7. Personal information by a member of this time.

8. *JT* May 17, 1995. This custom is based on *seimei handan* (judging one's fate according to one's name); the number of strokes in the Chinese characters is supposed to reveal and determine one's fate.

9. Asahara 1992f: 154. Agon-shu also claims to have received a Buddhist relic from Sri Lanka's President Jayewardene, which has been venerated since 1986 (Reader 1988: 242).

10. Asahara 1991c: preface. According to him, a Buddha is one who is able to solve problems such as "How should we live this life? Is there life after death? What is real happiness?" (ibid.).

11. Asahara 1993b: 105. Identifications with Buddha, Shiva, and later also with Christ (Asahara 1992f) seem offensive to Westerners. In Asia, the idea of an avatar, a person embodying a deity, is more common. A recent example in Japan is Okawa Ryuho, the founder of Kofuku-no-kagaku (Science of Happiness), who claims to be a living buddha and an incarnation of other deities.

12. For reports on the unconventional election campaign, see *Mahayana* No. 27: 145–154, and Young 1995: 232f.

13. In the fall of 1989, he reportedly declared himself to have "become a spiritual dictator, a dictator of the world" (*JT* April 12, 1995).

14. Aum delivered its message in contemporary forms. Like other new religions in Japan, it employed modern media for propagation, such as animated films (*anime*) and comic books (*manga*) that appealed to young people (cf. Asahara 1992a).

15. These statements concerning the motives for joining Aum and its attraction are confirmed by a questionnaire conducted by Aum Shinrikyo among six hundred members after the Aum incident in March 1995 (*Vajrayana Sacca* No. 12: 21ff.). Its results are as follows. 1. Reasons to join Aum: 273 respondents had read Aum books (46 percent); 171 were introduced by friends or relatives. 2. At the time of entering Aum, 341 persons had been in distress (58 percent); 245 did not feel afflicted (41 percent). 3. When entering Aum, 223 persons hoped to gain inner stability, greater spirituality, and reform of themselves (38 percent); 111 desired liberation or enlightenment; 91 expected to attain "supernatural power." 4. Concerning the reason for having faith as lay members, 194 persons agreed with the teaching (33 percent); for 144 experience due to religious practice was important; for 117 the reason was Asahara, and for 97 other disciples were significant.

16. *MDN* March 17, 1995. This text is also printed on a sheet of paper that was put as a "message" for his followers in an envelope and attached to the last page of the January 15, 1995, edition of Asahara's *Seishi o koeru.*

17. According to the Yoga Sutra, this practice leads to *samadhi* (cf. Feuerstein 1989, and Miller 1996, 60). In Buddhism, *samadhi* denotes the mental state of a unity between subject and object experienced in intensive meditation practice, as well as meditation techniques leading to this state.

18. See for example Brackett 1996: 118.

19. Asahara gave lectures about the Agama Sutras and other sutras that were published in *Genshi butten kogi.* In the preface (December 1989), Asahara (1990: 1, cf. 10–12) states that "Hinayana" forms the basis of Aum, and that Mahayana, Vajrayana, and Tantric Buddhism derive from it. Contemporary academic studies do not use the term Hinayana (small vehicle) because of its negative connotation; instead, they use the self-denotation Theravada. Aum normally uses the term "Hinayana," and I write it here with quotation marks.

20. Asahara 1990: 1; 1992f: 153; 1995d: 14, 247; *DY* May 17, 1995. Cf. *Vajrayana Sacca* No. 9: 26, 105ff.

21. See, for example, *Mahayana* No. 1: 103ff. and No. 35: frontispiece; Asahara 1995a: 72; also personal information from Aum members.

22. In the history of Buddhism, murder for religious reasons was frequently justified. During the Meiji period, for example, the prominent Zen priest Shaku Soen wrote: "Even though the Buddha teaches not to take another's life, he also teaches that all sentient beings through the exercise of infinite compassion will be united and thereby obtain final and ultimate peace. As means toward the harmonizing of the incompatible, killing and war are necessary" (Ketelaar 1990: 171).

23. Cf. the articles on Murai in *JT Weekly*, April 29, 1995, and May 27, 1995.

24. See Thomas Caldwell, "Foundation and AUM-pire" in *JT Weekly*, May 27, 1995. Cf. Asahara 1995d: 20, 71, 136, 188, 280f.; Asahara 1995e: 262f.

25. Aum Press 1995: 185f. One of Murai's favorite books was Richard Bach's *Jonathan Livingston Seagull*, which treats the idea of overcoming the limits of space and time.

26. Asahara 1991b: 111f. For other prophesies, see Asahara 1992f: 151; *Mahayana* No. 4: 64–69, and No. 16: 10–16.

27. Asahara 1989a: 18, 179f. A similar nationalistic vision can be found in Sukyo Mahikari, which expects its members to become the "top class" of a renewed civilization arising out of a global disaster. The new society will unite religion and government; it will become a "glorious theocratic society of the future." And "Japan will finally be recognized as the spiritual center of the world, the Japanese as the dominant, chosen race" (quoted in Davis 1980: 49, 50).

28. Asahara 1991a: 55, 146. It may seem strange that a Buddhist group took over millennial or apocalyptic ideas from the Judeo-Christian tradition, because similar ideas exist in Buddhism ("end of the dharma" [*mappo*], belief in the future Buddha Maitreya). For young Japanese, however, the Buddhist concepts sound old-fashioned.

29. See Goto [1973] 1994, [1979] 1984, [1981] 1991, and his numerous subsequent publications.

30. For Agon-shu, see Kiriyama (1981, 1995a) and Irokawa (1990); for Kofuku no kagaku, see Okawa (1988, 1991).

31. Yamashita (1998: 140) writes: "According to newspaper statistics, in the early 1990s, approximately 70–80% of business men reported that they wanted the end of the world to come."

32. For this topic see *JT Weekly*, July 1, 1995.

33. In order to understand the how such a scenario was drawn, one has to consider the lingering resentment of Japanese people against America caused by defeat during World War II and, more recently, by the effects of globalization. America represents the "West" in general (cf. Asahara 1995d: 36). This resentment is also expressed in the form of anti-Christian sentiments, because Christianity is seen as the basis of Western civilization.

34. According to an internal questionnaire, the motive of acquiring supernatural powers ranked only in third place among Aum members (*Vajrayana Sacca* No. 12: 23).

35. Cf. Brackett 1996, Kaplan and Marshall 1995, Reader 1996 and 2000.

36. A related perception is that internal factors, such as Asahara's personality and teachings, are considered to have been the main cause for the violent developments. For more detailed discussion see the sections on "Literature on the Aum Incident" and "Factors Leading to the Aum Incident" below.

37. Mainichi Shinbun-sha Shakai-bu 1997: 101–104. According to *MDN* (March 28, 1997), Aum attempted in 1987 to apply for this legal status. Because Reader's account (2000: 143, 146, 161) provides inaccurate dates, he underestimates the pressure on Aum during this time and reaches wrong conclusions concerning the murder of Taguchi.

38. For early accounts of the family's disappearance by an acquaintance of Sakamoto, see Egawa 1995a: 8–24, and 1995b: 25–113.

39. For a detailed account of the events in Namino-son by local media, see Kumamoto Nichinichi Shinbunsha 1995.

40. This was the first and only police search of Aum before March 1995.

41. Asahara 1992f: 153; cf. *Vajrayana Sacca* No. 9: 36–39. Many authors dismiss this claim as persecution complex, paranoia, and so on. Reader (2000: 247, cf. 190, and 1996: 9), for example, declares that Aum's talk of "persecution and conspiracy were perceptions rather than realities." But even states of mind have to be taken seriously as certain forms of (inner) realities which, in turn, may subsequently create outer realities—for which Aum is a striking example.

42. *AEN* May 16, 1995; *DY* and *JT* May 17, 1995. The incident of Namino-son set the basic pattern of subsequent interactions between Aum and society until today. In their attempts to acquire or rent property, Aum representatives frequently provide wrong data (names) for fear of refusal. Once Aum members move into a new facility, they often behave inconsiderately toward neighbors and community, thereby causing negative reactions. Neighbors and/or communities then organize movements to drive Aum members out of these facilities, and/or municipal authorities do not accept applications for residency. Both types of action are illegal and violate human rights.

43. Asahara 1992f: 154; *Shinri* No. 20: 28–35. Cf. Repp 2003: 63.

44. The Aum-Russia connection poses crucial questions such as: Who intro-

duced Aum to the top politicians in the Kremlin? and what was the real purpose and function of the Russia-Japan University? Hayakawa Kiyohide's activities in Russia consisted of weapons trade and transfer of military technology. However, neither the Russian nor the Japanese authorities ever revealed the true nature of Aum's involvement in Russia. For Aum in Russia, see the Nunn Report 1995: 58–68; Kabanoff 2001; Krylova 2001.

45. For Aum's involvement in Australia, see Repp 2003.

46. Most journalists and scholars uncritically accept the claim by police that the gas was sarin. This was never confirmed independently, however. The claim is problematic for the following reasons: sarin is heavier than air (therefore it should not be released from the ground, as it was), does not have the odor that the victims reported, is not persistent (as it was), and causes symptoms different from those that the victims suffered. Cf. John Parker, "*Tabun*, It's Tabun" (*JT Weekly* April 1, 1995); Yoichi Clark Shimatsu, "The Rashomon Riddle" (*JT Weekly*, April 1, 1995); and "Zettai Tabun" (*JT Weekly*, May 27, 1995).

47. See the description of events according to the state prosecutor's indictment in Mainichi Shinbun Shakai-bu 1996: 53–75, and Kyodo Tsushin-sha Shakai-bu 1997: 239–253. For summarized English translations see *JT* April 25, 1996, and *AEN* April 26, 1996. Cf. Hayashi 1998: 373–452.

48. Mass media sensationalistic reporting played an important role in creating the Aum hysteria. For a critical account of the media in this connection, see Asano 1996: 17–32, and 1997.

49. As usual, TBS topped the list with 660 newspeople deployed, while NTV had 400 engaged, and NHK 300 (*JT* May 18, 1995).

50. For this and the following paragraph, see Repp 2001a for more details and analyses of the legal aspects of the Aum incident until about 2000.

51. The proper name of the first law is *Musabetsu dairyo satsujin koi o okonatto dantai no kisei ni kan-suru horitsu* (Law for regulating groups which committed indiscriminate mass murder). It is also inofficially known as *Oumu tokubetsu rippo* (Special law for Aum) and *Oumu shinpo* (New law for Aum).

52. JT October 30, 1999. Critical voices were also heard. The head of the National Public Safety Commission, Hori Kosuke, stated: "Compared with the Public Security Investigation Agency, police are far greater in their number and will serve to investigate more effectively." Sakamoto's mother-in-law commented: "Had police done their job properly, current laws could have prevented the tragedies. So I can't approve of the bill" (*JT* January 3, 1999).

53. *JT* December 22, 1998; February 3, June 19, and July 10, 1999; cf. note 42 above.

54. To my knowledge, no scholarly studies on Aum in English appeared before the Aum incident in 1995.

55. The title and subtitle of Reader's second book, *Religious Violence in Contemporary Japan—The Case of Aum Shinrikyo* (2000), resemble to a remarkable degree those of my article "Religion und Gewalt im gegenwartigen Japan—Der Fall Aum Shinrikyo" (1996).

56. To present only one example: Reader (2000: 39) attempts to explain Asahara's assumed name by the practice of Buddhist monks, who receive new names in

ordination. However, Asahara himself never had a Buddhist name. Rather, he did so on the grounds of *seimei handan* (see note 8).

57. Cf. Kyodo Tsushin-sha Shakai-bu 1997: 233; Mainichi Shinbun Shakai-bu 1996: 47f. In other words, this is not a very trustworthy analysis, considering the fact that Japanese police and public prosecution provided only very sparse and selective information on the Aum incident to the public. Shimazono is a professor at Tokyo University, an institution whose main task is considered by a number of Japanese scholars not to pursue, first of all, academic research and education per se, but to provide the government with information and young civil servants.

58. An Aum member who had the experience of a *shakai-jin* called my attention to this point. I have elaborated this issue in a recent publication (Repp 2003: 56–58, 62–64).

59. The statement "compromise is crime" (*JT* June 29, 1999) by young people in an unrelated conflict with adults illustrates the basic attitude.

60. Daniel Metraux's (1999) book on Aum and Japanese youth relies heavily on previous studies and lacks original research; contains many mistakes in quotations (26, 70, 82) and in spelling of basic technical terms (75, 76); neglects references (79 [cf. Repp 1997b: 22], 82); tends to conceal its reliance on previous research (24–26, cf. Repp 1995: 233–235); and confuses quotations from primary sources with those from secondary texts (70, cf. Repp 1997b: 21).

61. Even though Gardner's studies belong to the next category below, I include them here because they treat the media.

62. "Aum is imitating the Imperial Japanese Army in waging bacteriological warfare"; "There was a time when all one hundred million Japanese were brainwashed" (Gardner 2002b: 40, 51).

63. "As a result of the love of money and material things, we have a society where Aum lives"; "Even without headgear, I am controlled by my wife"; "Home everyday now as a householder, I am hated by my wife"; "I relax when they don't praise my child for being an excellent student" (Gardner 2002b: 50, 55, 52, 54).

64. "I am worried about where the police are storing all the dangerous substances seized from Aum"; "Television talks too much, police are too silent" (revised according to original); "They could not find a reason to arrest my husband too" (Gardner 2002b: 49, 54, 50).

65. "A government that can handle neither natural disasters nor man-made disasters"; "Aum got enough religious donations to make even a politician jealous" (Gardner 2002b: 44, 53).

66. "Brainwashed by Aum specials with high ratings"; "All the television channels have been abducted to Kamikuisiki"; "Television has put headgear on us" (Gardner 2002b: 41, 45, 50).

67. "With their headgear removed, they return to being the children of humans" (Gardner 2002b: 45).

68. "Ever since that day, I never get sleepy on the train"; "Noticing some newspapers on the overhead rack, I change my seat"; "With no one leaving the newspaper on the train anymore, my daily expenses have gone up" (Gardner 2002b: 47, 43, 45).

69. See the cartoons by Yamai Norio in Repp (1997a), which comment on the incident better than any learned treatise.

70. Useful publications by investigative journalists can be found in *Japan Times Weekly* in 1955.

71. See note 66 and Repp 1995a: 242f.

72. Egawa (1995a: 8) writes that parents searching for their children approached her, a journalist, and the lawyer Sakamoto because the police did not assist them.

WORKS CITED

Aum Publications

Asahara Shoko (Shoko Asahara)
1986   *Seishi o koeru* [Overcoming (the cycle of) birth and death]. Tokyo: Oumu Shuppan.
1988   *Supreme Initiation. An Empirical Spiritual Science for the Supreme Truth.* Translated by Jaya Prasad Nepal and Yoshitaka Aoki. Edited by Fumihiro Joyu. New York: AUM USA.
1989a   *Metsubo no hi* [Day of destruction]. Tokyo: Oumu shuppan.
1989b   *Inishieshon* [Initiation]. Tokyo: Oumu shuppan.
1990   *Genshi butten kogi 1.* [Lectures on the sutras of original Buddhism, vol. 1]. Tokyo: Aum shuppan.
1991a   *Nosutoradamusu: Himitsu no dai-yogen—1999-nen no nazo* [Nostradamus: The great prophecy of secrets—The enigma of the year 1999]. Tokyo: Oumu shuppan.
1991b   *Cho-noryoku himitsu no kaihatsu-ho* [Methods to develop the secrets of supra-natural power]. Tokyo: Oumu shuppan. 1st ed. 1986.
1991c   *The Teachings of the Truth. A Collection of Lectures.* Translated and edited by Aum Translation Committee. Fujinomiya: Aum Publishing.
1992a   (ed.) *Supiritto jampu 1 (Spirit jump 1). Aum Comics.* Tokyo: Oumu shuppan.
1992b   *The Teachings of the Truth Vol. 2.* Translated and edited by Aum Translation Committee. Fujinomiya: Aum Publishing.
1992c   *The Teachings of the Truth Vol. 3. The Preconditions of the True Religion.* Translated and edited by Aum Translation Committee. Fujinomiya: Aum Publishing.
1992d   *The Teachings of the Truth Vol. 4. The Path to Absolute Happiness.* Translated and edited by Aum Translation Committee. Fujinomiya: Aum Publishing.
1992e   *Tathagata Abhidamma. The Ever-Winning Law of the True Victors.* Book 2. Fujinomiya: Aum Publishing.
1992f   *Declaring Myself the Christ. Disclosing the True Meanings of Jesus Christ's Gospel.* Translated and edited by Aum Translation Committee. Fujinomiya: Aum Publishing.
1993a   *Beyond Life and Death.* Translated and edited by Aum Translation Committee. Fujinomiya: Aum Publishing.
1993b   *The Teachings of the Truth Vol. 5. The Law of the Karma.* Translated and edited by Aum Translation Committee. Fujinomiya: Aum Publishing.
1995a   *Seishi o koeru* [Overcoming (the cycle of) birth and death]. 3rd revised ed. Tokyo: Oumu shuppan.
1995b   *Jiko o koete kami to nare!* [Overcoming one's self, become *kami!*]. Tokyo: Oumu shuppan.
1995c   *Hiizuru kuni, wazawai chikashi* [Land of the rising sun: The catastrophe is near]. Tokyo: Oumu shuppan.

1995d *Disaster Approaches the Land of the Rising Sun.* Fujinomiya: Aum Publishing.
1995e *Bokoku Nihon no kanashimi* [The sorrow of Japan's ruin]. Tokyo: Oumu
       shuppan.
Aum Press, ed. 1995. *Kyosei yuki* [A great saint passes away]. Tokyo: Oumu shuppan.

Aum Journals

Aum Shinrikyo, ed./publ.
   Enjoy Happiness No. 1 (1992)
   Monthly Truth No. 15 (1994) [English]
Oumu shuppan/ Aum Press, ed./publ.
   Mahayana No. 1–41 (1987–91)
   Shinri Nos. 1–29 (1991–93)
   Vajrayana Sacca No.1–12 (1994–95)

Other Publications

Agon-shu, ed. 1989. *The Agon-shu. The Original Teachings of the Buddha.* Tokyo: Agon-
    shu.
Asano Kenichi. 1996. *Masukomi hodo no hanzai.* [Crimes of reporting by mass com-
    munication]. Tokyo: Kodansha bunko.
———. 1997. *Oumu 'habo-ho' to masumedia* [The 'Law for anti-subversive activities'
    (applied to) Aum and the mass media]. Tokyo: Daisan shokan.
Brackett, D. W. 1996. *Holy Terror. Armageddon in Tokyo.* New York: Weatherhill.
Davis, Winston. 1980. *Dojo. Magic and Exorcism in Modern Japan.* Stanford: Stanford
    University Press.
Egawa Shoko. 1995a. *Kyusei-shu no yabo* [Ambitions of the savior]. Tokyo: Kyoiku
    shiryo shuppan-kai.
———. 1995b. *'Oumu Shinrikyo' Tsuiseki 2200 nichi* [Aum Shirikyo—2200 days in
    pursuit]. Tokyo: Bungei shunka.
Feuerstein, Georg. 1989. *The Yoga-Sutra of Patanjali.* Rochester, Vt.: Inner Traditions
    International.
Gardner, Richard T. 1999. Lost in the Cosmos and the Need to Know. *Monumenta
    Nipponica* 54 (2): 217–246.
———. 2002a. A Revisited. *Monumenta Nipponica* 57 (2): 339–348.
———. 2002b. " 'The Blessing of Living in a Country Where There Are *Senryu!*'—
    Humor in the Response to Aum Shinrikyo." *Asian Folklore Studies* 61 (1): 35–75.
Goto Ben. [1973] 1994. *Nosutoradamusu no dai-yogen* [Grand prophecies of Nostrada-
    mus]. [Vol. 1] First Japanese printing. Tokyo: Shodensha.
———. [1979] 1984. *Nosutoradamusu no dai-yogen II* [Grand prophecies of Nostrada-
    mus.] [Vol. 2]. First Japanese printing. Tokyo: Shodensha.
———. [1981] 1991. *Nosutoradamusu no dai-yogen III.* [Grand prophecies of Nostrada-
    mus.]]Vol. 3] First Japanese printing. Tokyo: Shodensha.
Hardacre, Helen. 1995. "Aum Shinriko and the Japanese Media: The Red Piper Meets
    the Lamb of God." New York: East Asian Institute, Columbia University.
Hayashi Ikuo. 1998. *Oumu to watakushi* (Aum and me). Tokyo: Bungei shunju.
Hughes, Christopher W. 2001. "The Reactions of the Police and Security Authorities

to Aum Shinrikyo." In *Religion and Social Crisis in Japan: Understanding Japanese Society through the Aum Affair,* edited by Robert J. Kisala and Mark Mullins. New York: Palgrave, pp. 53–69. [First published 1998.]

Inoue Mitsusada and Osone Shosuke, eds. 1974. *Ojo-den. Hokke genki.* [Stories of birth into the Pure Land. Miraculous records of the Lotus Sutra]. Nihon shiso taikei 7. Tokyo: Iwanami Shoten.

Irokawa Chihiro. 1990. *Meshia shutsugen* [The appearance of the messiah]. Tokyo: Hirakawa shuppansha.

Kabanoff, Alexander. 2001. "Aum Shinrikyo in Russia." *Japanese Religions* 26 (2): 149–170

Kaplan, David E., and Andrew Marshall. 1995. *The Cult and the End of the World: The Incredible Story of Aum.* London: Arrow Books.

Ketelaar, James Edward. 1990. *Of Heretics and Martyrs in Meiji Japan. Buddhism and Its Persecution.* Princeton: Princeton University Press.

Kiriyama Seiyu. 1973. *Nenriki. Chonoryoku o mi ni tsukeru kokonotsu no hoho* [Mental power. Nine methods to aquire supernatural powers]. Tokyo: Tokuma shoten.

———. 1981. *1999 nen. Karuma to reisho kara dasshutsu* [The year 1999. Escape from karma and spiritual hindrance]. Tokyo: Hirakawa shuppansha.

———. 1995a. *1999 nen 7 no tsuki ga kuru* [The 7th month of the year 1999 comes]. Tokyo: Hirakawa shuppansha.

———. 1995b. *Oumu Shinrikyo to Agon-shu* [Aum Shinrikyo and Agon-shu]. Tokyo: Hirakawa shuppansha.

Kisala, Robert. 1995. "Aum Alone in Japan—Religious Responses to the 'Aum Affair.' " *Bulletin of the Nanzan Institute for Religion and Culture* 19: 6–34.

———. 1997. "Reactions to Aum: The Revisions of the Religious Corporations Law." *Japanese Religions* 22 (1): 60–74.

———. 1998. "1999 and Beyond: The Use of Nostradamus' Prophecies by Japanese Religions." *Japanese Religions* 23 (1–2): 143–157.

Kisala, Robert J., and Mark R. Mullins, eds. 2001. *Religion and Social Crisis in Japan. Understanding Japanese Society through the Aum Affair.* New York: Palgave.

Krylova, Galina A. 2001. "Psychiatry Treats Heterodoxy: The 1995 Aum Trial in Russia from a Lawyer's Perspective." *Japanese Religions* 26 (2): 171–189.

Kumamoto Nichinichi Shinbunsha, ed. 1995. *Oumu Shinrikyo to mura no ronri* (Aum Shinrikyo and the logic of a village). Tokyo: Asahi Shinbunsha.

Kyodo Tsushin-sha Shakai-bu, ed. 1997. *Sabakareru kyoso* [The founder on trial]. Tokyo: Kyodo tsushinsha.

Lewis, James, ed. 1999. *Aum Shinrikyo and Human Rights.* Special issue of *Syzygi: Journal of Alternative Religion and Culture.* 8.

Lifton, Robert Jay. 1999. *Destroying the World to Save It. Aum Shinrikyo, Apocalyptic Violence, and the New Global Terrorism.* New York: Metropolitan Books.

LoBreglio, John. 1997. "The Revisions to the Religious Corporations Law: An Introduction and Annotated Translation." *Japanese Religions* 22 (1): 38–59.

Maeda Daisuke. 1997. "The Revenge of the Children." *Japanese Religions* 22 (1): 87–91.

Maekawa Michiko. 2001. "When Prophecy Falls: The Response of Aum Members to the Crisis." In *Religion and Social Crisis in Japan: Understanding the Japanese Society through the Aum Affair*, edited by Robert J. Kisala and Mark Mullins. New York: Palgrave, pp. 179–210.

Mainichi Shinbun Shakai-bu, ed. 1996. *Sabakareru 'Oumu no yabo'* [Aum's ambitions on trial]. Tokyo: Mainichi Shinbun-sha.

———. 1997. *Oumu 'kyoso' hotei zen-kiroku 2. Watashi Wa Muzai da!!* [Complete court records of the Aum "founder." Vol. 2. I am not guilty!! Tokyo: Gendai shokan.

Matsuda Yukio. "Back to Invented Tradition: A Nativist Response to National Crisis." In *Religion and Social Crisis in Japan: Understanding Japanese Society through the Aum Affair*, edited by Robert J. Kisala and Mark Mullins. New York: Palgrave, pp. 163–177.

Metraux, Daniel A. 1999. *Aum Shinrikyo and the Japanese Youth.* New York: University Press of America.

Mikhailova, Yulia. 1996. "The Aum Supreme Truth Sect in Russia." *Bulletin of the Japanese Studies Association of Australia* 16 (2–3): 15–34.

Miller, Barbara Stoler. 1996. *Discipline of Freedom.* Berkeley: University of California Press.

Miyai Rika. 1997. A Voice from the "Aum Generation." *Japanese Religions* 22 (1): 91–96.

Mullins, Mark R. 1997. "The Political and Legal Response to the Aum-Related Violence in Japan." *Japan Christian Quarterly* 63: 37–46.

Murakami Haruki. 1997. *Andaguraundo* [Underground]. Tokyo: Kodansha.

———. 2001. *Underground. The Tokyo Gas Attack and the Japanese Psyche.* London: Harvill Press. (First published in hardcover in 2000.)

Nunn Report. 1995. United States Senate. Permanent Subcommittee on Investigations. Committee on Governmental Affairs. Global Proliferation of Weapons of Mass Destruction. Hearings on October 31 and November 1, 1995.

Okawa Ryuho. 1988. *Nosutoradamusu no shin-yogen* [New prophecies of Nostradamus]. Tokyo: Tsuchiya shoten.

———. 1991. *Nosutoradamusu senritsu no keiji* [Nostradamus' revelation of frightfulness]. Tokyo: Kofuku no kagaku shuppan.

Pye, Michael. 1996. "Aum Shinrikyo—Can Religious Studies Cope?" *Religion* 26: 261–70.

Reader, Ian. 1988. "The "New" New Religions of Japan—An Analysis of the Rise of Agonshu." *Japanese Journal of Religious Studies* 15 (4): 235–261.

———. 1996. *A Poisonous Cocktail? Aum Shinriko's Path to Violence.* NIAS Special Report. Copenhagen: NIAS Books.

———. 2000. *Religious Violence in Contemporary Japan—The Case of Aum Shinrikyo.* Richmond, Surrey: Curzon.

Repp, Martin. 1995a. "Who's the First to Cast the Stone?—Aum Shinrikyo, Religions and Society in Japan." *Japan Mission Journal* 49: 225–255.

———. 1995b. "The Earthquake in the Kobe-Osaka Area January 17th 1995. Its Impact on Religions and Their Responses." *Japanese Religions* 20: 207–229.

———. 1996. "Religion und Gewalt im gegenwartigen Japan. Der Fall Aum Shinrikyo." *Dialog der Religionen* 6: 190–202.

———. 1997a. *Aum Shinrikyo. Ein Kapitel krimineller Religionsgeschichte*. Marburg: Diagonal-Verlag.

———. 1997b. "Youth and New-New Religions—Challenges for the Churches in Present-day Japan." *Japan Christian Review* 63: 5–29.

———. 1997c. "The Religious Situation of the 'Aum Generation'—Two NCC Seminars." *Japanese Religions* 22: 87, 97–98.

———. 2000. "Popular Culture and Religion in Contemporary Japan." *Japanese Religions* 25: 105–119.

———. 2001a. "The 'Trial of the Century'?—Legal and Illegal Treatments of Aum after the Aum Incident." *Religion—Staat—Gesellschaft* 2: 289–313.

———. 2001b. "Introduction to 'Aum in Russia.'" *Japanese Religions* 26 (2): 147–148.

———. 2003. "'The Last Continent'—The Involvements of Aum Shinrikyo in Australia." *Japan Mission Journal* 57: 55–66.

Roberts, Henry C., trans. [1982] 1994. *The Complete Prophecies of Nostradamus*. London: Thorsons.

Shimazono Susumu. 1995. "In the Wake of Aum: The Formation and Transformation of a Universe of Belief." *Japanese Journal of Religious Studies* 22 (3–4): 381–415.

Watanabe Manabu. 1997. "Reactions to the Aum Affair. The Rise of the 'Anti-Cult' Movement in Japan." *Nanzan Bulletin* 21: 32–48.

Yamashita Akiko. 1998. "The 'Eschatology' of Japanese New and New New Religions: From Tenri-kyo to Kofuku no Kagaku." *Japanese Religions* 23 (1–2): 143–157.

Young, Richard. 1995. "Lethal Achievements: Fragments of a Response to the Aum Shinrikyo Affair." *Japanese Religions* 20 (2): 230–245.

Yuki Hideo. 1997. "Problems with the Revisions to the Religious Corporations Law." *Japanese Religions* 22 (1): 75–86.

9

The Falun Gong: A New Religious Movement in Post-Mao China

David Ownby

Falun Gong is without doubt controversial. Created in 1992 by Li Hongzhi, an obscure former clerk and trumpet player from northeast China, Falun Gong was part of the *"qigong* boom," a larger mass movement that attracted perhaps two hundred million followers throughout China in the 1980s and 1990s. As part of this movement, Falun Gong grew rapidly, claiming to have drawn tens of millions of practitioners within a relatively short time.

In late April 1999, some ten thousand Falun Gong followers surrounded the headquarters of the Chinese Communist Party at Zhongnanhai, in Beijing, in a stunning nonviolent protest—the largest since the student democracy movement in Tian'anmen Square in 1989. The protest was prompted by what Falun Gong practitioners believed to be repeated media misrepresentation of the nature of the movement. The Chinese government responded with a campaign of severe repression in which the movement has been outlawed and tens of thousands of followers imprisoned, thousands tortured, hundreds put to death.[1] As of this writing (August 2003), the movement has at best an underground status within China, although it remains very active outside of China, chiefly among members of the Chinese diaspora in North America, but also in Taiwan, Australia, and Europe.

Falun Gong practitioners insist that their "cultivation system" is neither a religion nor a "new religious movement."[2] Chinese authorities agree that Falun Gong is not a religion, but condemn it as a dangerous "heterodox sect."[3] Media debates in the West over the proper understanding of the Falun Gong have been extremely polarized, and many journalists have had considerable difficulty in sifting through the competing representations put forward by the Chinese government and by Falun Gong spokespersons.[4] Although a scholarly literature on Falun Gong has slowly begun to emerge, much of it is written by Sinologists better schooled in the nuances of Chinese culture than in the arts of reaching a broader public.[5] The interested layman or even the well-read but non-Sinologist academic specialist hoping to inform himself on the history, beliefs, and organization of Falun Gong might be forgiven a certain frustration.

This essay—written by a Sinologist with some exposure to research in new religious movements—seeks to demystify Falun Gong by placing it in a Chinese context, something that has been largely absent in journalistic accounts. In essence, Falun Gong is a form of *qigong*, the general name for a set of physical and mental disciplines based loosely on traditional Chinese medical and spiritual discourses and organized around a charismatic master who teaches his followers specific techniques as well as general moral precepts, with the goal of realizing a physical and moral transformation of practitioners.[6] Both *qigong* and Falun Gong can be understood to some degree as cultural revitalization movements: *qigong* was created in the 1950s by the Chinese state (through the Chinese medical establishment) as an effort to preserve certain elements of traditional Chinese healing practices in the face of the rapid Westernization of Chinese medicine in the immediate postrevolutionary period. *Qigong* became a mass movement in the 1980s and 1990s in the wake of the failure of Mao Zedong's prolonged attempt to create a new communist Chinese identity through political and cultural revolution, and government and Party authorities allowed the mass movement to take wing in part because *qigong*'s celebration of the glories of traditional Chinese medical-therapeutic culture dovetailed with the Party's celebration of Chinese nationalism (indeed, many high Party and government officials were enthusiastic *qigong* supporters and practitioners). It was the revocation of state support, brought about once again by Falun Gong's encirclement of Communist Party headquarters, that made first Falun Gong and later the entire *qigong* movement controversial, again underscoring the importance of the Chinese state in the creation, propagation, and suppression of Falun Gong and *qigong*.

In addition to the importance of understanding the Falun Gong as the most important contemporary example of a Chinese "new religious movement," and one that has succeeded in establishing an important base outside of China, I would argue that there is also a heuristic value in studying the case of China, where neither "religion," "new religious movements," nor the relations between church and state are understood in the same manner as in the West. In the following essay, I devote as much time to explaining the various contexts that gave rise to Falun Gong as to Falun Gong itself. It is this context that has been sorely lacking from journalistic accounts and that has made understanding Falun Gong quite difficult.

Falun Gong in a Historical Context

Falun Gong and the *qigong* movement as a whole are arguably the contemporary heirs of a particular strain of traditional Chinese popular religion—much modified, I hardly need add—known in Western scholarly circles as White Lotus Folk Buddhism, which, in organized form, goes back to the fourteenth century. Explanation of White Lotus Folk Buddhism requires considerable unpacking.

Buddhism itself entered China from India via the commercial routes linking China with Eurasia in the first century CE, and subsequently became an important Chinese religion in the interregnum between two of China's great dynasties—the Han (206 BCE–220 CE) and the Tang (618–907).[7] Folk Buddhism—a very general term for a wide variety of beliefs and practices—was the product of the mingling of Buddhism with indigenous Chinese elements (a process that transformed mainstream, ecclesiastical Buddhism as well, if in different ways) and of the relative decline of the Buddhist church vis-à-vis the Chinese state from the Song Dynasty (960–1279) onward, a decline that reduced the power of the orthodox Buddhist establishment to intervene forcefully at local levels so as to impose a uniform definition of Buddhist beliefs and practices.[8] "White Lotus" was originally the designation given to a lay Buddhist sect whose origins can be traced to the late Song Dynasty period, one of many groups that sought piety and salvation outside the Buddhist monastic structure. Followers of this White Lotus sect would have seen themselves as thoroughly orthodox and would not have appreciated the pejorative designation "folk."

Over the course of the Ming Dynasty (1368–1644), however, the term White Lotus came to refer to something quite different: a popular religious tradition (or set of traditions, to be more accurate) grounded in Buddhism but incorporating elements drawn from Daoism, popular medicine, folk beliefs, and folklore.[9] The central elements of these traditions were: a goddess, known as the Eternal Venerable Mother, who had created the world and now waited in her paradise for her believers to return from worldly exile; the Maitreya, or Future Buddha, whose messianic arrival on earth would signal a moment of world renewal and the salvation of believers; scriptures (often called "precious scrolls") written by charismatic group leaders and handed down through the generations; a mixture of practices drawn from popular religion, folklore, and Chinese medicine that involved meditation, breathing practices, chanting of mantras, use of talismans, and vegetarian diets. The basic goals of these practices were improved health and protection from disease and disaster. These traditions trace their roots to the villages of north China, where networks of practitioners were held together by charismatic masters, many of whom traveled from village to village to preach the gospel and to celebrate with the local faithful. Before long, however, variants of this White Lotus came to be found throughout most parts of China.

As already noted, the original Song Dynasty White Lotus was lay, but orthodox. These later White Lotus groups, appearing in the Ming and Qing dynasties, had a more distant and more problematic relationship both with the Buddhist establishment and with the Chinese state. The history is complex, in part because the Chinese state came to employ the term "White Lotus" as a label for popular religious groups it feared and hoped to suppress; White Lotus thus came to be the rough equivalent, in late imperial Chinese discourse, of "sect" or "cult" as often used in uncritical contemporary Western writing on new religious movements, in the sense that both are employed as a pejorative label to condemn the group in question. In fairness to the Chinese state, one reason for its apparent paranoia was the believed involvement of groups linked to the White Lotus in the rebellions that had precipitated the fall of the Mongol Dynasty and the return of Chinese dynastic rule in the fourteenth century. Consequently, White Lotus, in the eyes of the Chinese, came to mean violent, rebellious groups, willing to sacrifice themselves to hasten the arrival of the apocalypse, an apocalypse that would wash away the reigning corrupt secular order, which perforce included the political order as well. And indeed, there were numerous rebellions over the course of the later imperial era in which White Lotus discourse and organization played indisputable roles. At the same time, scholarly research into many religious groups identified by the Chinese state as White Lotus seems to suggest that they were peace-loving lay organizations dedicated to salvation, piety, and good works. Generalizations about these traditions are thus difficult, not least because most of our information about the groups in question comes from the archives of the Chinese state and are written by scholar-officials already biased against the groups they are investigating. Peace-loving groups who avoided the Chinese state (and most such groups realized that it was wise to do so) left fewer records.

In any case, the White Lotus came to be an important part of popular religious culture in China from the fifteenth or sixteenth century forward. There is no way to estimate the number of groups or of believers, or to measure the influence such groups had, but practitioners were found in city and village, in north and south China, among the poor and the better off. The groups remained dispersed and largely unaware of one another's existence—except during rebellions, when hitherto unconnected networks could be mobilized by the urgings of a charismatic preacher, by the fear of a coming apocalypse, or by the fear of arrest and torture at the hands of the Chinese state.

Such groups continued, and even multiplied, after the fall of the last imperial dynasty in 1911. Indeed, the Republican period (1912–1949) saw an explosion of popular religious activity in general, including the activities of groups that were either faithful to or who elaborated on the White Lotus folk Buddhist tradition. One scholar of this period refers to these groups as "redemptive societies" because of their pretensions to universal salvation, and adds that they "clearly emerged out of the Chinese historical tradition of sectarianism and syncretism. While some of these societies were closely associated with the sectarian tradition including the worship of Buddhist and folk deities like the Eternal Mother, they also represented the late imperial syncretic tradition . . . which combined the three religions of Confucianism, Buddhism and Daoism in a single universal faith." The groups "ranged from the 'morality cultivating' charitable societies to the occasionally violent, secret-society-like entities," a description that conforms to the traditions I have been describing for the earlier period under the name White Lotus.[10] Many of the groups, in their universal redemptive mission, continued to sound traditional Chinese apocalyptic themes—even as they engaged in modern charitable and philanthropic work.

Taken together, these groups were represented throughout the entire country—as were White Lotus groups in the imperial period—and membership numbered in the millions if not tens of millions; many of these groups appealed to members of the elite as well as nonelite; certain groups, often for reasons of expediency, collaborated with the Japanese invaders, or with the Nationalist armies against the Communists, thus strengthening the Chinese state's tendency to view such groups as political in orientation.

All of these groups were suppressed in the immediate aftermath of the establishment of the People's Republic in 1949, in a series of campaigns that scholars had generally assumed to have been conclusive—particularly since they were carried out by an avowedly atheistic state that had established a stronger presence than any government in Chinese history.[11] Faced with the task of arresting and reeducating millions of people who had been involved in one way or another with these groups, however, the Communist state did what the imperial state had done: arrested and executed the worst of the offenders, imprisoned some others—but simply spoke harshly to the majority and sent them home. This meant that the roots of the traditions remained.

The Invention of *Qigong*

Neither *qigong* nor Falun Gong claims kinship with the White Lotus or with the "redemptive societies." Indeed, the negative stereotype of the White Lotus created by the Chinese state has been largely accepted by the Chinese population at large, which tends to associate the White Lotus with dangerous, "heterodox" groups that are out to overthrow the government. It remains nonetheless true that the White Lotus also served as an important repository of magico-medical knowledge, and a vehicle for the spread of such knowledge, which was more often than not presented in the language of popular Buddhism and in the persons of Buddhist and other gods. Groups linked to the White Lotus tradition were also mysterious if not secret, and groups were rarely conscious of other groups connected to the tradition.

Qigong was created in the 1950s as a conscious effort to preserve traditional Chinese medicine—more particularly Chinese medical practices involving regular physical exercises (not to be confused with calisthenics; *qigong* does not target the cardiovascular system) and mental disciplines aimed at achieving physical and mental health.[12] One of the major objectives of those involved with the creation of *qigong* was to purify these traditional practices, that is, to remove the superstitious and religious packaging that surrounded such practices in imperial times and to incorporate them into a modern, scientific discourse.

The invention of *qigong*, associated with the promotion of Chinese traditional medicine in general, was motivated by both practical and ideological considerations. From a practical point of view, Chinese medicine and *qigong* represented important cost savings over Western medicine, as there were far more medical practitioners with training in Chinese medicine than in Western medicine in the China of the 1950s, and the practice of Chinese medicine, both in terms of diagnosis and treatment, is less expensive than the practice of Western medicine. From an ideological point of view, Chinese medicine was seen to be part of the glorious cultural history of the motherland, a national treasure to be protected from the inroads already made by Western medicine. China's communist revolution was fueled as much by nationalism as by faith in scientific socialism, and both Chinese medicine in general and *qigong* in particular benefited from China's continued efforts to carve out a specifically Chinese model of socialism, distinct from that of the Soviet Union, in the 1950s and 1960s.

In any case, those who created *qigong* in the 1950s sought out traditional healing methods as practiced by charismatic masters, generally in the rural areas, and transplanted them to modern hospitals and sanatoria. In the process of transplantation, the religious, superstitious, and "feudal" language employed by traditional practitioners to describe and explain their art was transformed into a new, more neutral language, and practices directly linked to religion—prayers to specific deities, mantras invoking the names of particular spiritual figures—were dropped in favor of meditation and the development of mental discipline. Those who invented *qigong* believed in the power of such practices, but rejected the traditional discourses surrounding them, and sought to isolate the practices from the discourses, at the same time preserving the miraculous healing power of *qigong* therapy.

Between the early 1950s and the onset of the Cultural Revolution in 1965, *qigong* became relatively popular among the Chinese governing elite, who sought cures for what ailed them in sanatoria that often combined the functions of spa and resort. At the same time, and capitalizing on this elite support, *qigong* slowly carved out a niche for itself within the Chinese medical establishment. *Qigong* research groups carried out experiments and published their results; *qigong* classes were added to the curriculum of certain programs of traditional Chinese medicine. There was, however, no "*qigong* boom" in Mao's China. *Qigong* was created by cadres loyal to the Communist state, and *qigong* therapy was embraced by high-level officials whose ideological commitment to the new regime was beyond question. All aspects of *qigong*, from the training of practitioners through the publication of articles and books on *qigong* and the actual administration of *qigong* therapy, remained firmly under the control of the Chinese medical establishment.

The *Qigong* Boom

Qigong became something quite different in post-Mao China.[13] The *qigong* institutions and networks established prior to the Cultural Revolution (1966–76) had been attacked—and largely destroyed—by the revolutionary iconoclasts who supported the Cultural Revolution, on the grounds that *qigong* was nothing more than feudal superstition. Although these institutions and networks would probably eventually have been revived along pre-Cultural Revolution lines, the emergence of charismatic *qigong* masters in the late 1970s and early 1980s, together with the simultaneous scientific discovery of the material existence of *qi*, forever changed the character of *qigong*, transforming it into a mass movement.

The emergence of charismatic *qigong* masters was an indirect result of the suppression of officially sanctioned *qigong* activities during the Cultural Revolution, as those who remained committed to *qigong* were forced to take their enthusiasm directly to the public. The first such master was a woman named Guo Lin (b. 1909), who began teaching *qigong* in public parks in Beijing in the early 1970s.[14] Guo had been diagnosed with uterine cancer in 1949, and despite removal of her uterus, the cancer returned ten years later. She decided to cure herself through *qigong*, which she finally did, although the cure required yet another decade. Her passion for *qigong* thus grew out of her personal triumph over tragedy. Her public instruction was criticized both by her work unit and by the police; she was banned from more than one park, and her assistants and students were harassed, as well, but she persisted and eventually managed to attach herself to a university, which became her base of operations.

Guo Lin had not been trained in the modern *qigong* institutions created in the 1950s. Her grandfather had been a Daoist master, from whom she learned certain healing techniques that she adapted to the needs of her diseased body. Other masters, emerging at roughly the same time, resembled Guo Lin in that they came to *qigong* from outside the elitist *qigong* world of the 1950s, having learned their craft from a variety of sources, most of which were related to traditional religious or spiritual discourses. In fact, such masters would quite likely not have been allowed to come to prominence had it not been for the simultaneous scientific "discovery" of the material existence of *qi*, a discovery that gave an immense boost to the burgeoning world of *qigong* masters and practitioners.

In the late 1970s, credible scientists, attached to prestigious universities and research institutions, conducted experiments which, so the scientists claimed, illustrated that the *qi* emitted by *qigong* masters could be measured by scientific instruments.[15] The first experiments of this sort were performed by Gu Hansen, a researcher at the Shanghai Institute of Atomic Research, in March 1978, and the publication of his results created a sensation. If *qi* was a scientifically proven substance, then the goal of the pioneer *qigong* workers of the 1950s was attained, in the sense that *qigong* no longer belonged to the world of religion and magic but rather to the world of science. Many proponents of *qigong*, including other prominent scientists, were quick to point out the importance of this discovery, and the newly emerging *qigong* masters were quick to embrace the "scientific" value of *qi* and *qigong*, even if they had had no previous scientific training.

"Science" has a particular status and significance in modern China.[16] The rise of the West to world dominance in the nineteenth century and the consequent Chinese decline from great-power status in East Asia have both been interpreted by the Chinese as the result of Western mastery of science and technology. Reformers and revolutionaries in China have thus tended to view science as a magic formula, the key to a brighter tomorrow, and there is little doubt that Marxist claims to scientific truth were a key element in the conversion of Chinese intellectuals to the cause of scientific socialism. As a result, the scientific discovery of the material existence of *qi*, and hence of the scientific status of *qigong*, was an electrifying event: overnight, *qigong* became a validation of China's past (given that the basis of *qigong* is in traditional medical/spiritual practices), a proof of the value of Chinese socialism (which had had the wisdom to encourage the creation of *qigong*), and an element in the construction of a future China that could be both modern and loyal to its traditional cultural heritage.

Over the course of the late 1970s and early 1980s, a "*qigong* world" came into being as a result of these scientific claims.[17] This world was made up of numerous groups: the scientists and researchers who continued to conduct experiments on *qi* and *qigong*; journalists and other media figures who embraced *qigong* and spread the gospel of *qigong* to the larger public; *qigong* masters, whose numbers increased rapidly with the rising general enthusiasm for *qigong*; and—most important—Party and government officials who endorsed *qigong* as a uniquely powerful "Chinese science" as well as a practical and economical means to achieve a healthier population (and thus a less expensive health care system). This official support for *qigong* was the sine qua non of the formation of the *qigong* world, and took a variety of forms, including private patronage on the part of powerful individual members of the ruling elite and of particular masters and scientists, as well as broader organizational efforts, such as the establishment of the Chinese *Qigong* Scientific Research Association in April 1986.

The formation of the "*qigong* world" quickly gave rise to the "*qigong* boom" from the early 1980s onward, an extraordinary phenomenon in which the Chinese state gave its support to a varied cast of characters pursuing a diversity of ends. Paranormal phenomena, for example, came rapidly to be linked to *qigong*, and journalists tripped over one another to report on youngsters who were able to "read via their ears"—a strange feat whereby someone would write Chinese characters on a piece of paper and the talented youth would read these by wadding up the paper and placing it in his ear. The link between *qigong* and the paranormal was the idea that, through *qigong* cultivation, man could achieve far greater potential than in the past (nor was this idea confined to human potential: it was believed that seeds "enriched" by the *qi* of a potent *qigong* master could radically increase yields). The *qigong* craze swept college campuses and students emerged from their classrooms, literally embracing trees and other flora in the hopes of absorbing the natural *qi* contained therein (until they decided that it was not nice to the trees to rob them of their *qi*).

The most visible and durable symbol of the *qigong* boom, however, was the phenomenon of large, often nationwide *qigong* organizations, led by a single charismatic *qigong* master, many of whom became veritable pop idols.[18] Yan Xin, a hitherto obscure Chinese medical practitioner, was the first to achieve this status, but was only one among many.[19] These masters carried out nationwide lecture tours in which tens of thousands of *qigong* enthusiasts bought tickets for such events, joining others in the local stadium, arena, or gymnasium for what might be hours of *qigong* therapy. Indeed, many of the *qigong* masters of the *qigong* boom promised to "emit *qi*" in the course of their "lectures," a telling indication of the difference between the *qigong* of the 1950s and that of the 1980s: *qigong* in the 1950s had been a therapeutic discipline practiced by the ailing patient under the guidance of a trained professional; *qigong* of the 1980s was a magical power possessed by charismatic heroes whose therapy consisted largely of miracle cures—or at least these miracle cures were the most spectacular manifestation of the efficacy of *qigong* power. At the same time, many *qigong* masters took advantage of the newly liberated Chinese economy to produce *qigong* books, audio- and videocassettes, and a wide variety of paraphernalia, all of which was sold to an eager public. Journalists helped to feed the craze by, among other things, becoming the biographers of *qigong* masters. These biographies became "must" reading, in addition to the how-to manuals and the audio- and videocassettes.

During the height of the *qigong* boom, as many as two hundred million people are estimated to have participated in the movement—almost one-fifth of China's vast population. Many of these people were followers of particular *qigong* masters who built nationwide followings and organizations, but others simply moved from group to group, seeking cures for their ailments or vehicles to achieve their personal ambitions. Most of the activities took place in public parks throughout urban China (although *qigong* was of course known in rural areas, as well), parks being one of the few open spaces available in this over-crowded, overcontrolled country of 1.2 billion.

Li Hongzhi and Falun Gong

Li Hongzhi and Falun Gong appear much less eccentric, indeed much less "controversial," if understood within the context of the larger *qigong* boom. Falun Gong was received as a variety of *qigong* when Li Hongzhi began to publicize his teachings in 1992.[20] True, Li denounced many other *qigong* masters, and other *qigong* schools have since sought to distance themselves from Falun Gong by pointing out Li's statements to the effect that Falun Gong had gone beyond *qigong*, but at the same time, had there been no *qigong* boom, there would have been no Falun Gong, and many of those who rushed to embrace Falun Gong had already tested many other varieties of *qigong*. More-over, Falun Gong was welcomed into the Scientific *Qigong* Research Associa-tion, which sponsored and helped to organize many of Li's activities between 1992 and 1994. Notable among those activities were fifty-four large-scale lec-tures given throughout China to an audience of some twenty thousand. Like other charismatic masters, Li published books of his teachings (actually, tran-scriptions of his lectures), which achieved such success that he was soon able to offer his lectures free of charge—a significant difference from many other schools of *qigong*.

Still, if Li Hongzhi and Falun Gong owed their initial success to their kinship to other *qigong* masters and *qigong* schools, there was, as already men-tioned, something different about Li Hongzhi. Li condemned other *qigong* schools for their materialism, accusing them of charlatanism and/or fraud. More fundamentally, he argued that the *qigong* world as a whole had become unduly obsessed with healing and supernormal powers, neglecting more im-portant spiritual concerns. In a nutshell, Li argued that Falun Gong was *qigong* taken to a higher plane; Falun Gong *could* heal illness and confer supernormal powers, but the more important objective was to arrive at a fundamental trans-formation of one's understanding of the composition of the universe and one's role therein, as well as a physical transformation of one's body.[21]

These transformations were to be effected in part through Falun Gong practice which, like that of other *qigong* schools, included a number of physical exercises.[22] At the same time, Li accorded far more importance to scripture (that is, his writings) than did most other *qigong* masters. The writings of most *qigong* masters either illustrated proper *qigong* technique or offered explanations of the efficacy of their practice. Li's writings were treated as holy writ; even after they became available via the internet, practitioners were forbidden to write on the pages they had themselves printed out on their home computers. It was the reading, rereading, and eventual absorption of Li's teachings through his written materials that constituted the core of Falun Gong practice. Falun Gong also stressed the miraculous, godlike powers of Li Hongzhi (that is, the ability to assure the health and welfare of all of his followers at all times) in a way that other *qigong* schools rarely did in their writings—although those masters who performed miracle cures through the "laying on of the *qi*" in their public lectures were not far from suggesting (if perhaps not claiming outright) godlike powers.

Turning to the contents of Li Hongzhi's teachings, we find an eclectic mixture of Buddhism, Daoism, popular religion, and "scientism." Li's main theological/religious inspiration is Buddhism (or, more precisely, folk Buddhism), and he calls on followers to put an end to all "attachments," be they to meat, alcohol, medicines, material possessions, or other human beings (practitioners are to be compassionate to all, but such compassion should not engender attachments that detract from salvation). Throughout his writings, Li evokes the traditional Buddhist notion of karma, the idea, linked to that of reincarnation, that one's merits and demerits in a present life will be reflected in one's status when reborn in a future life.

Reflecting the "scientistic" cast of Li Hongzhi's message, karma in Falun Gong theology has a material basis: it is a black substance present in the body that can be transformed by suffering and/or by virtuous practice into a white substance (which is "virtue"). The transformation, according to Li, occurs at the molecular level (in other words, it is more than a symbolic transformation), which accounts logically for the improved health claimed by many Falun Gong practitioners. Indeed, the promise of improved health has been the chief attraction of Falun Gong to many practitioners, who consider illness a form of karma to be eliminated through suffering and cultivation. Most Falun Gong practitioners eschew doctors, hospitals, and medication. Many Falun Gong practitioners also claim to have obtained supernormal powers through their practice, but Li Hongzhi insists that such powers will evaporate if used to any end other than that of benevolent morality.

Li argues furthermore that truth, benevolence, and forbearance, the three cardinal principles of Falun Gong practice, are in fact the forces that make up the physical universe; Falun Gong practitioners achieve oneness with cosmic reality in cultivating truth, benevolence, and forbearance in their personal lives. Matter and spirit are thus one. Li himself claims to have transcended science and thus to understand all of reality from another, higher level; at various points in his writings he presents himself as a god or a buddha, possessed of a more complete understanding of our "multileveled" universe than that of ordinary mortals. Still, his writings are full of scientific (or parascientific) references (his reflections on the proper understanding of gravity, for example), which his followers take as seriously as the rest of his writings. Indeed, many North American Chinese followers of Falun Gong have advanced degrees in the hard sciences, such as physics, and have assured me repeatedly that recent developments in theoretical physics have *followed from* Li Hongzhi's insights.

Another aspect of Li's teachings concerns world destruction and renewal; he preaches that the world had been destroyed and created eighty-one times, and claims that certain signs lead him to believe that another cycle of world destruction and renewal is imminent. Li drew these ideas from traditional strains of Chinese apocalyptic thinking, found especially in popularized versions of Daoism and Buddhism, and in the scriptures of the White Lotus groups of the late imperial period; the ideas are thus widely known—if not necessarily fervently believed—throughout China, in the same way that the teachings of the Book of Revelations are generally known in the West. In my reading of Li's writings, he did not stress apocalyptic themes in the period prior to the Chinese government's suppression of Falun Gong, although he certainly makes reference to such themes.

Falun Gong practice is simple, if time-consuming. The exercises, described in the book *China Falun Gong*, are to be performed on a daily basis if possible, alone or with other practitioners. My sense nonetheless is that the exercises are more or less pro forma, for the most important aspect of Falun Gong practice is once again the reading and rereading of Li Hongzhi's most important work, *Zhuanfalun*. This work is held to be the source of all truth; many practitioners report having read it in a single sitting and having experienced an immediate revelation (a revelation often accompanied by physical manifestations—vomiting, diarrhea, an initial purging of the body of noxious elements). For reasons to be explored below, Li left China in 1996 and emigrated to the United States. Since then, and especially since the suppression of the movement in China beginning in the summer of 1999, Li has made his views known to his followers largely via the movement's Web sites. These new "scriptures," many of which are once again transcripts of talks he has given to followers throughout the world, by now constitute an important addition to *Zhuanfalun*, which remains, nonetheless, the Bible of the movement.

Like many other *qigong* masters, Li set up a nationwide Falun Gong organization of "practice centers" in China that came to enrol between two and sixty million practitioners, depending on whose estimates one believes. Li's own lecture tours from 1992 to 1994 provided the initial impetus for the creation of the organization, which one might characterize either as centralized or as decentralized. On the one hand, Li sought to limit the power of local Falun Gong leaders by forbidding them from preaching "the gospel." Local leaders are allowed to do little more than facilitate others' cultivation, providing literature, leading exercise sessions, organizing group activities; Li insists that the genuine spiritual connection be between individual practitioners and the master, a connection unmediated by any "pastoral interference." From this perspective, Falun Gong appears to be dangerously centralized. On the other hand, my impression is that Li Hongzhi never succeeded in building the sort of organization that would enable him actually to impose his will on local groups of practitioners. At least since 1996, when Li left China, and perhaps before, he appears to have been more interested in articulating his vision of truth than in perfecting the organizational mechanisms of his movement. And certainly since the beginning of the campaign of suppression in 1999, he has limited himself to relatively infrequent appearances (the Chinese state essentially put a price on his head) and to fairly opaque statements issued through the Falun Gong Web pages. The result seems to have been that individual Falun Gong groups have been largely left to their own devices, a state of affairs that has encouraged individual responsibility and initiative in all but doctrinal matters.

Chinese authorities have accused the Falun Gong of brainwashing and of placing undue pressure on group members—not to visit the doctor when ill, for example. In my fieldwork in Canada and the United States, I have in general not found that groups exercise this sort of control over their members, which does not of course necessarily mean that Falun Gong groups in China did not do so. Groups in North America do not solicit information about practitioners, do not "register" members, do not maintain membership lists, and do not demand contributions. A spirit of cheery good will characterizes most of the Falun Gong events that I have observed (tainted, of course, in recent years by sadness verging on desperation, given that many groups have tried with some success to mobilize Western governments against the policies of the Chinese state). I have never felt that those present were constrained to be there, nor do most practitioners seek to cut off ties with nonpractitioners, although this can happen; much depends on the personality of the practitioner in question. In general, however, Li Hongzhi enjoins practitioners to remain within the world so as to spread the way and to work off their own karma through the suffering that the world imposes. In sum, my fieldwork does not suggest that the Falun Gong tends to establish strong us-them distinctions or to encourage separation from the unclean world of the nonpractitioners. In other words, I personally have found little evidence of "brainwashing" or "mind control" among Falun Gong practitioners in North America.

The "Controversial" Falun Gong

In most ways, Falun Gong was like other schools of *qigong* and thus was not particularly controversial at the outset, although I should hasten to add that the *qigong* movement as a whole represented an implicit threat to Communist authority by virtue of the fact that it was a mass movement that had little to do with Chinese Communism and that was only marginally controlled by Chinese Communist authorities. Sooner or later, the *qigong* boom would have run afoul of the Chinese state, and it may well be that Li Hongzhi and Falun Gong were simply the unlucky first victims. Retrospectively, however, it is possible to identify certain peculiarities that perhaps help to explain the eventual conflict between Falun Gong and the Chinese state.

First, Li Hongzhi was in some ways less careful than other *qigong* masters to cast his teachings in terms that Party and government authorities would find unobjectionable. Let me be clear here: in his pre-1999 writings, Li Hongzhi appears to be nationalistic, patriotic, and thoroughly apolitical. At the same time, whereas other *qigong* leaders took care to express themselves in such a way as to avoid conflict with the authorities, Li seems to have worried little about the response his writings might evoke, and *Zhuanfalun*, for example, teems with references to spirit possession, world destruction and recreation, alien interference in the affairs of mankind—in short a host of references unlikely to please Communist authorities who were pleased to back *qigong* as long as it appeared scientific. Like other *qigong* masters, Li Hongzhi had the back-stage support of important high officials, in Li's case in the Bureau of Public Security. Whether Li felt that his contacts were important enough to protect him, or whether he was simply naive, or perhaps arrogant, is unclear, but his writings are relatively free of the ritual nods to Communist authorities that other masters were careful to make on a regular basis.

Another particularity about Falun Gong was its propensity to react quickly and vigorously to perceived slights in media representations of Falun Gong, a practice that rapidly became "political," since many media in China are little more than mouthpieces for the regime. Sources hostile to the Falun Gong report more than three hundred such instances, beginning in the summer of 1996, none of which were violent and all of which essentially demanded that "erroneous" information about Falun Gong be corrected.[23] Falun Gong practitioners now liken their protests to those of Gandhi or Martin Luther King, but China has little tradition of civil rights demonstrations, and an action like that of surrounding the state-owned and -run Beijing television station, which Falun Gong practitioners did in May of 1998, was perceived as audacious if not seditious in the Chinese setting. Such reactions are not unique to Li Hongzhi and Falun Gong; China has in general become a much more openly contentious society in the post-Mao period—peasants, workers, and other disgruntled citizens having become increasingly willing to take their complaints to the barricades or to the courts. Still, as the charismatic leader of a mass movement commanding millions of followers, Li Hongzhi seems to have been either naïve in assuming that Falun Gong protests would not ruffle unofficial feathers, or arrogant in assuming that his personal power or the weight of his movement was enough to stay the hand of Chinese authorities.

In any case, the Falun Gong's relationship with the Chinese authorities became troubled fairly early. The Falun Gong parted company with the Chinese Qigong Scientific Research Association in the fall of 1994, although this organization had initially accepted and sponsored the Falun Gong. It is unclear whether the Falun Gong abandoned the Research Association or if the Research Association revoked support for the Falun Gong, but the rupture signaled that all was not well, and indeed that Li Hongzhi had serious detractors as well as supporters in high places. Li's exodus to the United States in 1996 was yet another indication of the deterioration of relations between his movement and Chinese authorities. Indeed, if the movement seemed to continue to thrive despite Li's absence from China, there were repeated if fitful attempts within the leadership to investigate and perhaps close down the Falun Gong, attempts that were, more often than not, stymied by Falun Gong supporters among other high officials. The incidents of media "slander" that so angered Falun Gong practitioners were in large measure part of this semiofficial campaign to undermine the Falun Gong, and the encirclement of Communist Party headquarters in April 1999 by Falun Gong cultivators was the movement's response to such tactics.

The Falun Gong encirclement of Communist Party headquarters was a turning point in the history of Falun Gong and, indeed, of the *qigong* boom; by the summer of 2001, there would no longer be an organized *qigong* movement, and all masters were either in exile or in jail. Stunned and embarrassed, Chinese authorities moved into crisis mode over the course of the spring and summer of 1999, outlawing Falun Gong (as a "heterodox sect") in laws put in place in the summer and fall, and orchestrating a vast propaganda campaign against the movement reminiscent of the vitriol of the Cultural Revolution. Falun Gong books, cassettes, and other paraphernalia were confiscated and destroyed (on occasion by bulldozer, in scenes played and replayed on national television). Falun Gong leaders were arrested, and a price was put on the head of Li Hongzhi after American authorities and Interpol refused extradition. Academics and journalists were called upon to denounce the Falun Gong, superstition, and "sects" in general, and to reaffirm support for science and modernization. Books and magazine articles outlined Falun Gong's crimes: Li Hongzhi's supposed material exploitation of his followers, the numbers of deaths caused by Falun Gong's insistence that practitioners need not seek medical assistance when ill, the numbers of practitioners rendered insane by Falun Gong practice. Authorities assumed that Falun Gong followers would, in the face of such a campaign, renounce their practice, and some surely did. Many did not, however, and their refusal to do so surprised and angered Chinese authorities and broadened considerably the role of public security forces in the anti-Falun Gong campaign.

Many Falun Gong practitioners could not believe what they read about their cultivation practice in official Chinese government publications and refused to accept the outlawing of the movement. Most believed that Chinese authorities were simply uninformed, and they set out to educate them. They sought out local officials first, and on learning that local officials were simply following orders from above, then set their sights on the capital. Over the course of the fall of 1999 and throughout 2000, small groups of Falun Gong practitioners arrived in Beijing hoping to make an "appeal" to higher authorities, a right granted by China's constitution. When such "appeals" fell on deaf ears, practitioners developed other approaches, including peaceful demonstrations in Tian'anmen Square, individually or in groups, seeking in part to convince the public of the righteousness of their cause, but also welcoming arrest as the police were seen as part of the power structure they were hoping to reach.

To put an end to such tactics, the Chinese state tightened security around the all too visible Tian'anmen Square, but also—to the extent possible— around train and bus stations throughout China. Moreover, once arrested, Falun Gong demonstrators were sent back to where they lived, where they were dealt with by local police authorities. Under pressure from above, local authorities became increasingly vigilant and brutal; central authorities were embarrassed at the loss of face suffered both domestically and internationally. International human rights groups began to report increased use of torture and imprisonment from the summer and fall of 1999 onward. Rapidly, the numbers of those arrested mounted to the thousands and tens of thousands.

To the intense dismay of Chinese authorities, Falun Gong practitioners living outside of China began to bring pressure on the governments of the countries where they were now resident to protest China's campaign against Falun Gong. Most of these "foreign" Falun Gong practitioners were in fact Chinese who had left China, often as students, in the 1980s and 1990s. As a result, they were well educated and reasonably well off. In North America, particularly, Falun Gong practitioners succeeded in creating considerable sympathy for the plight of their fellow practitioners in China, playing both on the anti-Communist sentiment that continues to resonate in some parts of the continent, as well as on the claim that freedom of speech and freedom of religion are universal values that should be respected universally. The American and Canadian political establishments called repeatedly on China to moderate its anti-Falun Gong campaign, all the while hoping that such criticisms would not harm commercial relations.

Li Hongzhi himself largely disappeared from view in the months following the encirclement of Party headquarters and the onset of the anti-Falun Gong campaign. Li himself had been in Beijing—en route to Australia—the day before the encirclement, but insisted that this was a mere coincidence and that his ten thousand followers had gathered spontaneously at Party headquarters. In any case, between the spring of 1999 and the fall of 2000, Li gave his followers relatively little public guidance, making only a few cryptic remarks through Falun Gong Web sites. In the fall of 2000, however, Li reemerged and began to make appearances at Falun Gong experience-sharing conferences, which had been his practice prior to April 1999. The tone of his speeches had changed considerably in the interim. Li clearly felt compelled to explain the disaster that had befallen him and his followers, and did so by highlighting the apocalyptic messages which, prior to April 1999, had been a relatively minor part of his discourse; the Communist Party's campaign against Falun Gong was now presented as part of a final "test" leading up to the destruction and renewal of the world. Those practitioners who passed the test—by remaining steadfast in their resolve—would remain part of the elite destined to survive the apocalypse, while those who crumbled in the face of pressure would not. Those who suffered or died for their beliefs, moreover, were offered the promise of instant "consummation" (or enlightenment). Li's speeches during this period are rather dense, and lend themselves to different interpretations, but it seems clear that he encouraged those Falun Gong practitioners who chose martyrdom over prudence. If Chinese authorities clearly lit the fire, Li Hongzhi just as clearly fanned the flames.

Such "flames" became all too literal in early 2001, when a number of Falun Gong practitioners apparently set themselves on fire in Tian'anmen on January 23, resulting in five deaths. This incident remains highly disputed, Falun Gong practitioners and spokesman insisting that the event was staged by Chinese officials (who refused, for example, to allow Western journalists to interview those who survived the attempted self-immolation, although it would seem that such interviews would surely confirm Chinese authorities' contention that Falun Gong was an evil cult). Whatever the truth about the incident, it clearly marked an important public relations victory for the Chinese state within China, as many Chinese who had remained neutral to that point came to share the authorities' view that the Falun Gong was indeed a dangerous heterodox sect. Falun Gong practitioners within China did not of course immediately cease their efforts to propagate their cause, but my impression is that the fight became an increasingly uphill battle from this point forward. Nonetheless, as the wave of Chinese martyrs diminished, practitioners from abroad—both Chinese and foreign—began to make their way to Tian'anmen, taking advantage of the protection afforded them as residents of foreign countries, and of their greater "journalistic value," to try to keep their cause in the headlines.

Concluding Remarks

Both *qigong* and Falun Gong reflect the search for spiritual meaning that has gripped China since the death of Mao and his revolution, a search that has taken many forms, including that of religion, both Chinese and foreign. Ironically, *qigong* and Falun Gong were able to expand as they did precisely because they were not seen as religions but as "scientific cultivation systems." Religion has a very precise meaning in China: according to China's constitution, only the "five great religions"—Buddhism, Daoism, Islam, Protestantism, and Catholicism—are recognized as such, and these are controlled by nationwide organizations whose chief role is to ensure that religion remain firmly under the control of the Chinese state. Other groups who claim to be "religions" are dismissed as "feudal superstitions"; the idea of "new religious movements" makes no sense in China, since the very definition of religion implies a long history, a well-developed hierarchy, and a well-established corpus of scripture. During the heyday of the *qigong* boom, Chinese authorities allowed their enthusiasm for the claims of *qigong* masters to cloud their judgment. That they could ignore the spiritual or "religious" aspects of *qigong* and Falun Gong constituted an act of willful blindness, for, as we have seen, many schools of *qigong* promised miracle cures, supernatural powers, and moral and physical transformation.

Falun Gong was, at the outset, one *qigong* group among many, although it had its particularities (as did other *qigong* schools). It too promised health, happiness, and moral and physical transformation through faith in master Li Hongzhi and embrace of his scriptural truth. Followers were not asked to sacrifice their money or their possessions, or to cut themselves off from non-followers (although some surely did). Followers were expected to manifest a devotion to Li Hongzhi, a devotion that might have taken extreme form if Li were in frequent and close proximity with his followers—but Li has chosen to remain aloof and to establish contact through the Internet and through infrequent addresses given at large Falun Gong gatherings. As a result, practitioners have in general been left with the responsibility of taking charge of themselves—which, at least in the context of my fieldwork in North America, they seem to have done fairly well. Consequently, official Chinese claims that Li Hongzhi bilked his followers, deluded them, drove them to distraction and suicide, strike me as exaggerated, although I hasten to add that I do not endorse Falun Gong's claims to cure illness any more than I endorse the similar claims of other *qigong* groups, or of Christian Scientists, for that matter.

Li Hongzhi seems to be an eccentric personality and, judging by his writings, an untrained thinker. Falun Gong beliefs and practices appear "eccentric" from a Western point of view, but Christian practices look strange to the Chinese. In the final analysis, Falun Gong came to be controversial because of the extraordinary growth of *qigong*, and because of the eventual negative reaction of the Chinese state. Otherwise, Falun Gong is largely consistent with certain traditional popular religious practices well known in pre-Communist China. Given the speed with which *qigong* rose to national prominence, and the existence of Falun Gong networks outside of China, it is difficult to believe that we have heard the last word on *qigong*/Falun Gong, even if the Chinese state has battled the Falun Gong to a stalemate at the moment.

NOTES

1. Falun Gong Web sites keep a running tally of the number of practitioners imprisoned and killed. See particularly www.faluninfo.net. Independent human rights organizations such as Amnesty International and Human Rights Watch in general endorse Falun Gong claims in this regard.

2. Again, Falun Gong Web sites elaborate their position. See www.falundafa.org and www.clearwisdom.net.

3. A shortcut to the voluminous publications of the Chinese government is the rubric "Outlawing Falun Gong Cult" on the site of the Chinese Embassy in Washington, D.C., found at www.china-embassy.org.

4. The Center for Studies on New Religions maintains a good sample of the journalistic record on Falun Gong on its Web site, at www.cesnur.org/2003/falun_gong .htm. Some of the best reporting on Falun Gong was done by Ian Johnson of the *Wall Street Journal*, who won a Pulitzer Prize for international reporting for his work in 2001.

5. Barend J. ter Haar, sinologist at Leiden University in the Netherlands, maintains an up-to-date bibliography of work on the Falun Gong on his Web site. See www .let.leidenuniv.nl/bth/falun.htm.

6. The best treatment of qigong is David Palmer, " '*La fièvre du qigong*': Guérison, religion et politique en Chine contemporaire," Ph.D. dissertation completed at the École Pratique des Hautes Études in 2002. Palmer is translating his work for English publication by Columbia University Press. See also see Zhu Xiaoyang and Benjamin Penny, eds., "The Qigong Boom," *Chinese Sociology and Anthropology* 27. 1 (Fall 1994): 1–94; Nancy Chen, "Urban Spaces and Experiences of Qigong," in Deborah S. Davis, ed., *Urban Spaces in Contemporary China* (Washington, D.C.: Woodrow Wilson Center Press, 1995), 347–61; Miura Kunio, "The Revival of Qi: Qigong in Contemporary China," in Livia Kohn, ed., *Taoist Meditation and Longevity Techniques* (Ann Arbor: University of Michigan Press, 1989), pp. 331–58; and Xu Jian, "Body, Discourse, and the Cultural Politics of Contemporary Chinese Qigong," *Journal of Asian Studies* 58. 4 (1999): 961–91.

7. Among the basic sources on the introduction of Buddhism into China are Erik Zürcher, *The Buddhist Conquest of China: The Spread and Adaptation of Buddhism in Early Medieval China* (Leiden: E. J. Brill, 1959); Kenneth Ch'en, *Buddhism in China: A Historical Survey* (Princeton: Princeton University Press, 1972); Zenryu Tsukamoto, *A History of Early Chinese Buddhism: From Its Introduction to the Death of Hui-yuan* (Tokyo: Kodansha International, 1985); and Arthur F. Wright, *Buddhism in Chinese History* (Stanford: Stanford University Press, 1971).

8. See Patricia B. Ebrey and Peter N. Gregory, "The Religious and Historical

Landscape," in Ebrey and Gregory, eds., *Religion and Society in T'ang and Sung China* (Honolulu: University of Hawai'i Press, 1993), pp. 1–44.

9. Basic English-language treatments of the White Lotus include Susan Naquin, *Millenarian Rebellion in China: The Eight Trigrams Uprising of 1813* (New Haven: Yale University Press, 1976); Naquin, "The Transmission of White Lotus Sectarianism in Late Imperial China," in David Johnson, Andrew Nathan, and Evelyn Rawski, *Popular Culture in Late Imperial China* pp. 255–91 (Berkeley: University of California Press, 1985); Daniel L. Overmyer, *Folk Buddhist Religion: Dissenting Sects in Late Traditional China* (Cambridge: Harvard University Press, 1976); Overmyer, "Values in Chinese Sectarian Literature: Ming and Ch'ing Pao-chuan," in Johnson, Nathan, and Rawski, *Popular Culture in Late Imperial China*, pp. 219–54; Overmyer, *Precious Volumes: An Introduction to Chinese Sectarian Scriptures from the Sixteenth and Seventeenth Centuries* (Cambridge: Harvard University Press, 1999); and Barend J. ter Haar, *The White Lotus Teachings in Chinese Religious History* (Leiden: E. J. Brill, 1992).

10. Prasenjit Duara, "Pan-Asianism and the Discourse of Civilization," *Journal of World History* 12. 1 (2001): 99–130.

11. On these little-studied campaigns, see Holmes Welch, *Buddhism under Mao* (Cambridge: Harvard University Press, 1972); and David Ownby, "Imperial Fantasies: Chinese Communists and Peasant Rebellions," *Comparative Studies in Society and History* 43. 1 (January 2001): 65–91.

12. On the invention of *qigong*, see Palmer, "*La fièvre du qigong*," part 1, ch. 1.

13. On the *qigong* boom, see Zhu and Penny, "The Qigong Boom," and Palmer, "*La fièvre du qigong*," part 2, chs. 2–7.

14. Guo Lin is discussed in Palmer, "*La fièvre du gigong*," part 2, ch. 2.

15. These experiments are discussed ibid.

16. See Danny W. Y. Kwok, *Scientism in Chinese Thought, 1900–1950* (New Haven: Yale University Press, 1965).

17. See Palmer, "*La fièvre du qigong*," part 2, ch. 4.

18. See ibid., ch. 3.

19. Like Li Hongzhi, Yan Xin spends most of his time in the United States, and has set up a similar network of practice centers and Web sites. See www.yanxinqigong.net.

20. On Li's emergence, see Benjamin Penny, "The Life and Times of Li Hongzhi: Falun Gong and Religious Biography," *The China Quarterly* 175 (2003): 643–61.

21. My remarks are based on my reading of Li's works, available via internet at www.falundafa.org.

22. See Li's *China Falun Gong*, which illustrates the exercises. The first Chinese-language version of *China Falun Gong* was published in Beijing in April 1993 by the Military Affairs Friendship and Culture Publishing Company. A revised Chinese-language edition was published in December 1993 by the same press. An English-language translation was published in 1998 in Hong Kong by the Falun Fofa Publishing Company. Both the revised Chinese-language version and the 1998 English-language translation are available on the web at www.falundafa.org.

23. See Tan Songqiu, Qin Baoqi, and Kong Xiangtao, *Falungong yu minjian mimi jieshe: xiejiao Falungong neimu de da jiemi* [Falungong and popular secret societies: Exposing the inner secrets of the Falungong cult] (Fuzhou: Fujian renmin chubanshe, 1999), p. 93.

10

Notes on the Aumist Religion

PierLuigi Zoccatelli

It has been said that "the Aumist religion is an ideal, living laboratory for examining a number of classic and contemporary theories
on religion: the exceptionality of the leader, the routinization of charisma, the institutionalization of belief, the issue of the tomb, the
function of the holy city" (Perocco, 2001: 86). It is thus no coincidence that a detailed ethnological study of Aumism has been conducted in France, and that the publication of its results constitutes
not only an example of valid investigation but also a clear example
of the difficulties—not strictly methodological but rather sociopoliti-
cal and cultural—that the scholar (particularly in France) may encounter (Duval, 2002).

Biography of the Founder: Gilbert Bourdin

Gilbert Bourdin (1923–1998), better known to his disciples as His
Holiness the Lord Hamsah Manarah, was born on June 25, 1923, to
a Catholic family in Martinique, and left the island in 1956. He
chose to hide his autobiography under a veil of inaccessibility—for
example, by placing the following sentence in the frontispiece of one
of his books: "High tradition demands that one not 'speak of a holy
man's past' " (Hamsah Manarah, 1995: 9). Nevertheless, he did include a few autobiographical hints in his works, from which one
may deduce, first, that his childhood and early youth were spent in a
particularly hostile family environment (Hamsah Manarah, 1993a:
401–403), seeming to constitute a dramatic existential preface that

could provide interesting guidelines in a psychological context. After leaving his family, he studied law, philosophy, economics, and medicine, and "after a period of virulent atheism, the youth, by now well-integrated in society, became interested in mystical studies. . . . As often occurs to great missionaries, destiny ordained that an event at the age of 28 would reawaken the spiritual flame that burned in him. . . . A battle raged in him between his desire to climb the social ladder and his desire to search for the Supreme Divinity" (Hamsah Manarah, 1993a: 405–406).

This turning point in Gilbert Bourdin's life seems to be connected to his lively interest and involvement in various esoteric and occult environments. He was a member of the Theosophical Society and the Masonic Grand Lodge of France; he actively participated in Rosicrucian, Martinist, cabbalist, and alchemist societies, and also took part in organizations interested in the Knights of the Holy Grail. Thus, "through assiduous participation in esoteric groups to which I pay homage, I became aware that there existed a strange world, occult, invisible, populated by afflicted souls, demons, angels, bizarre divinities. . . . I began to study all the occult sciences to become more aware of those forces which cannot be seen, but which—secretly—make and unmake the world" (Hamsah Manarah, 1993b: 323–324). But Gilbert Bourdin's spiritual search did not end with these esoteric and occult experiences. In the early 1960s, he traveled to Rishikesh, in the Himalayas, and encountered one of the most important Indian gurus to have influenced the West: Swami Sivananda Sarasvati (1887–1963, born Kuppuswani Iyer), the founder of the Divine Life Society, as well as author of about three hundred publications with which he popularized yoga techniques throughout the world. On February 13, 1961, at the Swami's ashram (founded in 1934 at a place now called Shivanandanagar, three kilometers from Rishikesh), Gilbert Bourdin was initiated as a sannyasin (that is, Renouncer devoted to God) and received the name Hamsananda Sarasvati from Swami Sivananda. Although Gilbert Bourdin's spiritual journey was far from over, it may be said that Sivananda's influence on the founder of Aumism was fundamental. After being initiated as a sannyasin, Hamsananda Sarasvati returned to France where, during the winter of 1962–1963, he withdrew to an isolated cave in Vaucluse, and thereafter began to gather disciples to whom he taught yoga. In the years that followed, he began popularizing yoga by publishing eight highly successful books (the first of which he dedicated to the memory of Swami Sivananda), subsequently translated into Spanish, Dutch, and Italian (Hamsananda Sarasvati, 1976).

In the 1960s, Hamsananda Sarasvati received other honorific titles and initiations loosely associated with the Hindu teachings of Swami Sivananda Sarasvati, ranging from esoteric Shingon Buddhism to Indian Sufism, from Jainism to Tibetan Buddhism, and to some African religious currents, as well. In 1967, he founded the Association of the Knights of the Golden Lotus (replaced in 1995 by the current Association of the Triumphant Vajra), and in

1969 the ashram (holy city) of Mandarom (near the current holy city of Mandarom Shambasalem, in Castellane in the Provencal Alps), which consolidated and replaced the first three French centers: Centrom (in Vaucluse), Celestom (150 kilometers from Paris), and Anandom (30 kilometers from Marseilles).

The founding of the Mandarom ashram eventually led to the birth of the Aumist religion, which gradually took place in the 1970s and 1980s. In this period of time, as briefly mentioned above, Hamsananda Sarasvati (not yet considered Lord Hamsah Manarah by his disciples) had already conducted an extensive series of spiritual studies, which led him: to participate in esoteric and occult environments; to be initiated as a sannyasin; to experience the austerities of asceticism; to receive his first pupils in meditative yoga, thereby planting the first seeds of his future movement; to proceed in the collation of further religious and spiritual affiliations (mainly of oriental extraction); and finally to create his own ashram. Thus, one step at a time, emerged what came to be perceived as his mission, aimed at producing a "spiritual revolution" and establishing the "Universal Religion of the Unity of the Faces of God."

On this premise, we may begin to trace the progression from, on the one hand, Gilbert Bourdin as yoga instructor and acknowledged spiritual teacher (guru) of a Hindu-derived school, known as, Hamsananda Sarasvati; and on the other, his eventual designation as "His Holiness Lord Hamsah Manarah . . . the Cosmoplanetary Messiah, the Avatar of Synthesis, merging in Himself all Energies and all Religions. He is Maitreya, the Buddha of Synthesis, who opens the doors to the Diamond Age. He is the Imam Mahdi Manarah, the Unity of the Faces of God. He is the Total Avatar Kalki, Master of the Maha Kundalini. He is Melkitsedeq, who erased all Curses and granted the Great Pardon to the people of the earth. He is the Cosmic Christ, who destroyed the Roots of Evil and of original sin. He is the Adi Bouddha Mirchoan, the Synthesis of all God's Lights. . . . He is the Hierokarantine, Master of the Selection of Souls . . . , the Great Pontiff of the Cosmic Diamond Order" (www .aumisme.org/gb/titre.htm).

What happened in the interval between these two points in time? This is precisely one of the interpretive difficulties with Aumism as we now know it: Gilbert Bourdin gradually began to interconnect "various prophesies regarding the avatar of synthesis" (Hamsananda, 1990: 19) until he linked them to himself. Thus, during a lavish ceremony on August 22, 1990—and in a certain sense at the end of an osmotic process shared, supported, and strengthened by his followers—Gilbert Bourdin revealed and crowned himself "Cosmoplanetary Messiah."

A kaleidoscope of initiatic titles, heterogeneous religious references, forceful proclamations on the founder's spiritual nature—all seem to confuse anyone who approaches Gilbert Bourdin's spiritual biography. It would be useful at this point, therefore, to provide some background information on how the movement broke loose from its original context, and to ask, above all, whether these affirmations of Bourdin's cosmic attributes have been placed in a context of continuity and tradition.

For such a purpose, given that Gilbert Bourdin's link to Swami Sivananda Sarasvati's Hindu lineage is crucial, it must be considered that in the Hindu religion the quality of divine incarnation (avatar) is often acknowledged among the spiritual attributes of a guru. In Aumism, the fundamental difference with regard to the attributes acknowledged in Hamsah Manarah is the insufficiently polysemous quality of the term "Cosmoplanetary Messiah," to the extent that the term is linked to a conceptual universe of Judeo-Christian origin, in which avatar and messiah are different concepts.

Moreover, apart from the difference between avatar and messiah, however, I believe that there is—at least conceptually—a thread of continuity between Gilbert Bourdin's experience and the path of Sivananda, and that it is worth examining. In truth, where Hamsah Manarah reveals himself as "Avatar of Synthesis," and to the extent that the Aumist religion presents itself as a "Religion of Synthesis," the essential message of which is a "Message of Synthesis," there seems to be a strong echo of the eclectic approach of Sivananda, who, not coincidentally, presented his system of yoga as a "yoga of synthesis" (Sivananda, n.d.).

The Aumist Doctrine of Synthesis

Gilbert Bourdin's spiritual itinerary thus presents a transition from the Hindu substratum to universalism, which the founder defined as a "spiritual revolution." Let us now examine a few of the main doctrines professed by the Aumist religion, according to the twenty-two volumes left by Hamsah Manarah; it was apparently based on a dualistic theology and a cosmology that includes a cyclical theory of time and a relation with other planets and solar systems.

Aumism is presented as the universal religion of the new era (the Golden Age), an active and dynamic philosophy: the "Universal Religion of the Unity of the Faces of God." The foundations of the Aumist doctrine are summed up in "five truths": first, the truth on death, which is nothing but a change of state; second, the truth on suffering, suffering arising from the fear of moving forward; third, the truth on pain, which makes one take giant steps toward God; fourth, the truth on evolution, based on a law according to which every being that is born must have, as its purpose, the attainment of a higher level; and fifth the truth on the ultimate goal to be reached (Hamsah Manarah, 1991: 43–44).

The essential message of the Aumist religion is eclectic, one of synthesis contained in the sound AUM, which Hamsah Manarah's disciples consider to be the source of creation, the primordial sound, the sound that gave birth to all other sounds, the first and highest vibration, also called *pranava* (from *prana*, vital energy, and *va*, vehicle), that is, the driver of energy. In this sense, the three letters of AUM correspond to three principles: the primordial A of the world before the creation (physical level); the U of the creation (mental level); the M of the expansion of creation (spiritual level). Thus, AUM corresponds to the past, the present, and the future, and as such propels toward the absolute, destroying ignorance and evil, uniting Heaven and Earth; it is both liberating and liberator, the name of God, symbol of the supreme reality. According to Aumist doctrine, the sound AUM acts differently depending on how it is pronounced: when enunciated aloud it purifies the environment, crystallizes good vibrations, and eliminates evil; when voiced quietly it calms the mind, prepares for concentration, and promotes healing; when spoken mentally, it helps concentration and meditation.

The concept of reincarnation, linked to the first of the "five truths" (the truth about death), plays an essential role in Aumist doctrine, and Hamsah Manarah dealt with the subject of visible and invisible worlds (including transmigration of souls) by stating that "there are billions of inhabited worlds in intersidereal space, but at different stages of evolution" (Hamsah Manarah, 1991: 13). After death, the soul passes through all levels of the evolutionary scale, from the mineral kingdom to plant, animal, and human, finally reaching the divine (its real nature). In 1985, Hamsah Manarah declared that he had created the Column of Light, an instrument aimed at receiving souls that have left the body, which currently houses about 620 billion evolving souls. The Column of Light is composed of six arms, each with twenty-one levels of consciousness. Considered an "enormous post mortem university," it serves to direct the souls and stimulate them in their evolution toward God, integrating the astral world, the celestial planes, the hells and heavens of the various religions, thus promoting the crystallization and perpetuity of the Golden Age on earth.

To understand this concept, it must be remembered that for Aumists, all worlds are governed by the Law of Cycles. They are born in a Golden Age, but—due to the rebellious nature of the spiritual bodies that inhabit them—soon decline, thus causing the Golden Age to be followed by a Silver Age. In this age, gurus and buddhas prefer to rest in artificial paradises rather than act to protect the world. Their refusal to act constitutes one of the ways in which karma is accumulated. Such decline is even greater in the Bronze Age that follows: corrupt science dominates and conquers the lazy hyperborean Silver Age civilization. In this age of science, a tremendous battle breaks out between Lemuria and Atlantis. Atlantis, which is also the hyperboreans' means of revenge, destroys Lemuria, but in turn is destroyed by a revolt by Nature itself, which is no longer willing to be tyrannized by science. The destruction of Atlantis leads to the fourth age, the Iron Age, dominated by the law of karma, by division, by conflict, and by religion that has transformed itself into superstition. God becomes incarnate in all ages, and in ours he presents himself on earth in the person of Lord Hamsah Manarah, who eliminates corruption and superstition from all religions in order to put an end to karma and to the Iron Age, and to hasten the coming of the Golden Age. Since Lord Hamsah Manarah revealed himself as messiah, the law of karma was abolished whereby all souls can be purified and take their place in the Golden Age (or be destroyed if they refuse to purify themselves). It is absolutely certain that the Golden Age will arrive on earth, because the consequences of the Law of Cycles are inevitable. Nevertheless, accepting or refusing Lord Hamsah Manarah as messiah is important for determining whether the Golden Age will arrive soon or must still be awaited.

A Few Notes on Symbolism

Aumist teachings emerge not only from the doctrine described briefly above; they refer to a complex symbolism as well. From this point of view, the entire holy city of Mandarom Shambasalem constitutes an effective compendium of the Aumist religion. Mandarom follows a peculiar holy geography dotted with monuments that relate to Aumist doctrine. This holy space contains:

- The Lotus Temple (built in 1977, eleven meters high), symbolizing the restored Order of the Cosmic Lotus, and which was the founder's home during his lifetime.
- The statue of the Buddha Maitreya (built in 1981, twenty-two meters high), considered the synthesis of Eastern spiritual energies.
- The statue of the Cosmic Christ (built in 1987, twenty-one meters high), reuniting Western mystical energies.
- The temple of the Golden Age Trimurti (1988), receptacle of the holy energies of Para Trimurti.
- The statue of the Cosmic Maria (1989), symbolizing the Primordial Divine Mother.
- The statues of the four archangels of Aumism (1989), assigned to protect the messiah's mission.
- The mosque of the Imam Mahdi (1989), symbol of the regeneration of Islam.
- The temple of the Column of Fire of the avatar Kalki (1989), the presence of purified Hinduism.
- The Golden Temple of the Lord Melkitsedeq (1989), representing illuminated Judaism.

The return to the unity of the creator word is represented by the Hexamid, the true symbol of the Aumist religion: a multisided pyramid with the colors of the rainbow representing the various religions (natural religions, Hinduism,

Buddhism, Islam, Christianity, Judaism, Jainism) that merge at the top in the sound OM, a white light of synthesis.

The presence of these buildings has generated bitter debate and controversy within France, especially with regard to the statue of the Cosmoplanetary Messiah and the as yet unbuilt Pyramid Temple of the Unity of the Faces of God. Aumists assert that the Pyramid Temple of Unity (the construction of which has never begun, although the first stone was laid on August 22, 1992) was on the earth well before the Great Flood, and aspire to erect it because— it being the most perfect symbol of the unity of man and God—it would allow the reconciliation of humanity.

The iconography and architecture of the Pyramid Temple of Unity, but more generally of the entire Aumist symbolic system—from the existence of Mandarom itself to the Hexamid, from the statues to the temples, and so on— are vitally important to the movement's doctrine. In sociological terms, one could say that an increase in power of the symbolic element produces an increase in the power of the generalization, with dynamics applicable, among other things, to the formation of the neosyncretist school.

Although construction of the Pyramid Temple of Unity is the object of considerable dispute, the matter—tragically concluded—of the statue of the Cosmoplanetary Messiah, one of the fundamental symbols of Aumism, was a much greater harbinger of bitter conflict. Consecrated on August 22, 1990, this thirty-three-meter-high monument erected in the holy city of Mandarom Shambasalem was considered by Aumists to be the receptacle of the energies of the return of God into matter. Erected with a complex symbolism, the statue represented the Cosmoplanetary Messiah on whose heart gleams a lotus with 1008 golden petals, at the center of which beams the Diamond of the Sublime Patriarch. Erection of the statue quickly set off a violent dispute (Introvigne, 1999), whereby anticultists and ecologists (the latter joining forces against the "cult" based on the idea that the mountain had been "raped" by the ugly statues) organized campaigns and instigated criminal actions against the Aumists for zoning violations. The campaign culminated with the destruction of the main statue by the French police on September 6, 2001.

On the other hand, Aumism is well accustomed to controversies—including the refusal by different municipalities to entomb Gilbert Bourdin at Mandarom after his death on March 19, 1998. Much of the controversy arises because it is considered by anticult activists (especially in France) and by an important part of the French media to represent the epitome of "cult." On the whole, in the late 1990s there was a climate of growing tension: "a typical case of exaggerated social reaction," according to Italian sociologist Luigi Berzano (1996: 318). It was a peculiar case, however, especially if one considers that the Aumist religion is not a large movement and is nonetheless often described as the quintessence of the "danger of cults." There was also a lawsuit brought against Gilbert Bourdin by a former member (whose mother still remains a faithful Aumist), who claimed that she was raped by Hamsah Manarah in the early 1980s. The suit led to Gilbert Bourdin's arrest on June 12, 1995 (the very day on which the French State Council was to rule on whether permission should be granted for the construction of the Pyramid Temple of Unity), and to his successive prosecution, which ended before reaching the trial stage because of Bourdin's death.

A Religious or Esoteric Movement?

On the social level, Aumism simultaneously presents itself as a churchlike structure and as an esoteric order. At the exoteric level, the Aumist Church—composed of bishops (about one hundred worldwide), priests and priestesses (about three hundred worldwide)—is the structure set up to serve Aumists from among those who have received Aumist baptism. Aumism performs five sacraments: baptism, confirmation, renewal of vows and promises, matrimony, and transition (death) (Hamsah Manarah, 1994).

At the esoteric level, Aumism has its Association of the Knights of the Triumphant Vajra (formerly the Association of the Knights of the Golden Lotus). Aumism cannot be understood unless one emphasizes that it is essentially an esoteric order much more than a religious order. And such an assertion forces us to change our perception of what has been said up to now with regard to Aumist doctrines, cosmology, and symbolism. But, in perfect "Aumist style," the reality is even more complex; in fact, the Association of the Knights of the Triumphant Vajra is nothing but "the moral initiatic base . . . , the exotericism of the Association of the Diamond" (Hamsah Manarah, 1993b: 45). The alliance between the Association of the Knights of the Triumphant Vajra and the Association of the Diamond involves a system divided into twenty-two initiatic steps. To sum up, the Association of the Knights of the Triumphant Vajra is the esoterism of Aumism, and the Association of the Cosmic Diamond is the esoterism of the Association of the Knights of the Triumphant Vajra.

In Nonconclusion

As we have noted from this overview of the founder's spiritual experience, description of doctrines, and complex symbolism, Aumism's original Hindu-based identity was followed by a transition to universalism, in which Christianity and Buddhism, Hinduism and Jainism, Islam and Judaism blend as a result of the identification of the Cosmoplanetary Messiah, Gilbert Bourdin. This "new recomposition of sense . . . , of rationality and irrationality, of consciousness, possessed by all new forms of religiosity" (Berzano, 1996: 319) would apparently confirm Aumism's definition of itself as a religious movement. At first glance, this analysis would seem to indicate that Aumism is a new form of syncretism, if to this term we attribute the habitual meaning given it by scholars of religion, that is, the need to conciliate and synthesize differing positions, "processes of symbiosis and fusion among different religious traditions, characterized by the fact that the components in question have been independent for a great length of time and/or are still recognizable and, in all cases, by the fact that their union is not theoretical, but rather the result of a meeting of vital religious forces, able to generate formations destined to endure" (Filoramo, 1993: 703).

It seems, however, that the results emerging from a study of Aumism can be fully comprehended only when one understands the importance that esoteric, initiatic, and occult traditions play in it, for these constitute the "second pillar" on which Aumism has gradually been built as a separate "tradition" emerging from a preexisting substrate. Esoteric study constituted Gilbert Bourdin's original spiritual experience, and there are references to esoterism in the context of doctrine, as well, such references seeming to lead to a post-theosophical approach. Moreover, if such observation is true in a historical and doctrinal context, it is no less so when related to a sociographic study of Aumism. From among the approximately four hundred current followers (there have been two thousand initiates from the late 1960s to today; in the early 1990s, there were almost twice the number of members as today; in 2001, there were eleven resident monks at Mandarom, twenty-three in the late 1990s, and about forty in the early 1990s), "56% of members say that they experienced an attraction or performed an esoteric activity . . . before discovering Aumism" (Duval, 2002: 155).

The study and observation of Aumism in the above-described context brings us with increasing awareness to the observation that such a movement seems to elicit from the context what elsewhere I have proposed to call the "esoteric paradigm" (Zoccatelli, 2000). I therefore refer the reader to such a study, specifying that it be placed in the context of a methodological approach aimed at satisfying the need to overcome the current distinction between religious movements and cult movements, because the call to elaborate a criterion of approach of fundamental types of approach to the sacred has often been expressed. If, on the one hand, the religious approach does not apparently exhaust relational potentials with transcendent aspects, neither, on the other hand, does the initiatic approach seem to be conclusive. Rather, it seems the species of a genus: the "esoteric paradigm" as a true alternative (as "fundamental type") to religious reality, especially with regard to a movement such as Aumism, at the center of dispute and controversy for many years, perhaps because "its sin is just that it is too visible" (Introvigne, 1998: 104). With its gigantic statues and temples, the very existence of the Mandarom challenges official French anticult policy.

WORKS CITED

Berzano, L. 1996. "La déviance supposée du 'phénomène sectaire': L'exemple de la religion aumiste." In M. Introvigne and J. G., Melton, eds., *Pour en finir avec les sectes. Le débat sur le rapport de la commission parlamentaire*. Paris: Dervy, 315–320.

Duval, M. 2002. *Un ethnologue au Mandarom. Enquête à l'intérieur d'une "secte"*. Paris: Presses Universitaires de France.

Filoramo, G. 1993. "Sincretismo". In Filoramo, ed., *Dizionario delle religioni*. Turin: Einaudi, 702–703.

Hamsah Manarah, S. 1991. *L'aumisme. La doctrine de l'age d'or*. Castellane: Le Mandarom.

———. 1993a. *La révolution du monde des vivants et des Morts. La justice divine*. Castellane: Le Mandarom.

———. 1993b. *Le flambeau d'unité. "Vous pouvez tous être sauvées."* Castellane: Le Mandarom.

———. 1994. *Le livre des sacrements de l'aumisme*. Castellane: Le Mandarom.

———. 1995. *Périple d'un yogi et initié d'occident*. Castellane: Le Mandarom.

Hamsananda, S. M. 1990. *Je suis le messie attendu, l'avatar de synthèse. Voici les preuves*. Castellane: Le Mandarom.

Hamsananda Sarasvati, S. M. 1976. *Naturopathie et yoga. Santé—guérison—bonheur*. Paris: Albin Michel.

Introvigne, M. 1998. "Religion et politique de la nature. La religion aumiste en France." In B. Ouellet, and R. Bergeron, eds., *Croyances et sociétés*. Montreal: Fides, 103–110.

———. 1999. "Holy Mountains and Anti-Cult Ecology: The Campaign against the Aumist Religion in France." *Social Justice Research* 12/4: 365–375.

Perocco, F. 2001. "Il New Age tra dislocazione sociale e ricomposizione del legame sociale. Il caso dell'Aumismo." *La Critica Sociologica* 137: 82–99.

Sivananda, S. S. n.d. *Yoga of Synthesis*. http://www.sivanandadlshq.org/teachings/yogasynt.htm.

Zoccatelli, P. L. 2000. "Il paradigma esoterico e un modello di applicazione. Note sul movimento gnostico di Samael Aun Weor." *La Critica Sociologica*, 135: 33–49.

———. 2003. "Ossimori e palindromi euristici: L'aumismo, fra religione ed esoterismo." *Religione Società. Rivista di scienze sociali della religione*. Firenze University Press, 17/47, 101–111.

———. 2004. "L'aumisme: Religion de l'unité des visages de Dieu ou nouveau syncrétisme." In R. Kranenborg and J.-F. Mayer, eds., *La naissance des nouvelles religions*. Geneva: Georg Éditeur, 183–212.

PART III

Esoteric and New Age Groups

11

Inventing L. Ron Hubbard: On the Construction and Maintenance of the Hagiographic Mythology of Scientology's Founder

Dorthe Refslund Christensen

L. Ron Hubbard, founder and originator of Dianetics and Scientology, died on January 24, 1986.[1] At the time of his death, he was in absolute control of the organization he had established and continuously altered since the late 1940s—despite the fact that he had been taking precautions, for a number of years, to secure the organization's future after his death. He was still the originator of all new issues brought up within Scientology as well as the only religious inspiration of the church and its followers.

He still is. In Scientology today, Hubbard remains the religious leader and, in many ways, the organizational head even though initiatives have been taken by others to continue the practical work of the organization. The crisis to which religions are often exposed after the death of the founder and/or prophet seems to have been avoided by Scientology. In fact, more than a decade after his death, Hubbard's power seems undiminished. This is no coincidence. When it comes to keeping Hubbard at the head of the religion, the initiatives taken by the church and its different suborganizations are immense. He is not a figurehead with no significance; he is the only ultimate source and legitimizing resource of the religious and therapeutic claims of the church. L. Ron Hubbard and Scientology have always been and will, most probably, always be inseparable.

FIGURE 11.1. L. Ron Hubbard. Courtesy of the L. Ron Hubbard Library.

In this essay I focus on Hubbard's significance in Scientology by analyzing the different initiatives taken by the church to construct and maintain L. Ron Hubbard as the only religious and legitimizing source of Scientology. The most important of these initiatives—and the one that has caused the most controversy, besides the esoteric character of the religion—is the hagiographic production, which constitutes the most significant attempt by the church to continually renew interest in Hubbard, and thereby his religion, by pointing to him as the ultimate source and legitimizing resource. Part of such a hagiographic account will be analyzed after a brief introduction to the religious significance of Hubbard in Scientology. The analysis of the hagiography will be placed in perspective by introducing other church initiatives to promote and protect Hubbard and Scientology and will include introductions to basic Scientological ideas, practices, and important parts of the church's literature. In the bibliography, I include all basic and central Scientology literature and other publications such as videos and booklets besides, of course, all major research contributions on the subject.

The Concept of Charisma: An Analytical Framework

An analysis of the construction and maintenance of the claim to superhuman authority by a religious prophet and his organization is hardly possible without reference to the concept of charisma, which was developed by sociologist Max Weber in the beginning of the twentieth century and applied, interpreted, and discussed ever since by scholars in the field of sociology of religion and elsewhere.[2] Although it is not a goal of this essay to discuss Weber's concept or to contribute to its ongoing development, the concept will be used as a background, or framework, for an analysis of Scientology's perpetual construction and staging of L. Ron Hubbard and his claim to special agency.

According to Weber, the term charisma is "a certain quality of an individual personality by virtue of which he is set apart from ordinary men and treated as endowed with supernatural, superhuman, or at least specifically exceptional powers or qualities. These are such as are not accessible to the ordinary person, but are regarded as of divine origin or as exemplary, and on the basis of them the individual concerned is treated as a leader. . . . What is alone important is how the individual is actually regarded by those subject to charismatic authority, by his 'followers' or 'disciples.' "[3]

Bryan R. Wilson has interpreted Weber as follows: "Weber's concept, *charisma*, denotes a quality not of the individual, but of a relationship between believers (or followers) and the man in whom they believed. His claim, or theirs on his behalf, was that he had authority because of his supernatural competences. Charisma is not a personality attribute, but a succesful claim to power by virtue of supernatural ordination" (Wilson 1975: 7). Thus, charisma is access to the supernatural and/or superhuman qualities claimed by, or ascribed to a person, and the acceptance of these claims by a group of followers. Charisma, as such, is a complex set of social relations.[4]

As noticed by Weber, within different kinds of power relations that share the characteristic of the charismatic, an institutionalization will have to take place—routinization of the charismatic—if the power relations are to be maintained and stabilized (see, for instance, Weber 1968: 485ff. and 1976: 142ff.; 661ff.). No matter how inspiring, revolutionary, and challenging to the existing order the charismatic leader may appear to his followers, his authority and position within the social group are unstable and fragile. Two interrelated aspects of this fragility are relevant in establishing a framework for understanding L. Ron Hubbard, his significance in Scientology, and the steps taken by the church throughout the years, especially after his death, to maintain his charismatic authority. First, on an organizational level an institutionalization must take place in order to transform personal charisma into organizational stability and practicality. If this does not happen the ideas will disappear with its originator when he or she dies. Second, on a religious level the continued success of the charismatic leader is highly dependent on success. His teachings and original practices must constantly be considered effective and relevant by his followers.

In Scientology, the initiatives to emphasize Hubbard's charisma are inseparable from initiatives to routinize it. Although the mythologization of Hubbard seems to have expanded since his death in 1986, another process seems to have been continous since the birth of Scientological ideas and practices in the early 1950s, namely, the textualization of Hubbard. Textualization refers to the process of transforming Hubbard from a historical person to a mythological character identified with a set of religious ideas and practices.

L. Ron Hubbard as Text: Standard Technology

The institutionalization of Hubbard and his teachings has been ongoing since the very early days of Dianetics, Hubbard's self-improvement therapy that aims at transforming traumatic (engrammic) memories to ordinary experience and thereby helping the individual to lead a healthy life based on rational decisions and awareness. The practice of Dianetics in its original form, found in the book *Dianetics: The Modern Science of Mental Health* (Hubbard 1950/1989; hereafter DMSMH), was presented in a somewhat anarchistic manner: "Any person who is intelligent and possessed of average persistency and who is willing to read this book [*DMSMH*] thoroughly should be able to become a Dianetic auditor" (ibid.: 197). As early as July 1950 Hubbard began to talk about Standard Operating Procedure, the therapeutic (and later the religious) practices he prescribed (TB 1991, vol. 1: 69).

No later than 1951, a year after publishing *Dianetics: The Modern Science of Mental Health*, Hubbard was working hard to develop fundamental Dianetics ideas from a "do-it-yourself-therapy" into the religion Scientology.[5] One of the problems that existed during the days of early Dianetics, according to Roy Wallis (Wallis 1976: 77ff.), was that organizational structures were loose, and since the fundamental message of Dianetics was somewhat anarchistic, it turned out to be difficult to maintain control over its development. Furthermore, Hubbard lost the rights to *DMSMH* to the publisher Don Purcell, who bought the rights when Hubbard was troubled by bankruptcy (ibid.).

From the beginning, Hubbard toured the United States giving lectures on Dianetics and demonstrating the very simple therapeutic techniques of "auditing."[6] To comply with the demands of these techniques, it soon became necessary to train auditors. This constitutes the first infringement of the anarchy. As part of the institutionalization, the training of auditors became a pivotal point in the development of Scientology. In terms of organization, Hubbard was able to keep control over his project, since it was he who developed the religious and therapeutic systems as well as the rules for training within these systems. In this way it became possible to proclaim some people heretics and to control access to the management of the newest techniques by monopolizing the education of religious and ritual specialists. Whereas the fundamental claim of Dianetics was that everybody could successfully apply the techniques if they had read and understood *Dianetics* (Hubbard 1950/1989: 197), and that "any case, no matter how serious, no matter how unskilled the auditor, is better opened than left closed" (ibid.: 190), it was now claimed that an auditor could do irreparable damage to his or her "preclear" (someone in Dianetics training who has not yet reached the stage of "clear") if the auditor was not trained in the latest techniques (Hubbard 1951b/1989: 6f.).

When Scientology came into existence in the beginning of the 1950s, the production of different periodicals, technical bulletins, and policy letters became an important part of it from the very beginning.[7] In these publications, Hubbard continued to introduce new steps as soon as the previous ones had been taken. Despite the fact that it remained important for him to travel from one organizational unit to another in various parts of the world, giving lectures and demonstrations, the textualization and institutionalization of Hubbard had begun, in that more and more followers did not meet him in person. However, Hubbard's signature on the material used for auditing was the practitioners' guarantee that the material was "standard."[8]

FIGURE 11.2. Dianetics counseling, one of the core techniques of Scientology, uses an E-meter as part of the procedure of "auditing." Courtesy of the Church of Scientology International.

In Scientology today, the term *Standard Technology* denotes Hubbard's directions for auditing ritual tools applied in the correct manner. At the L. Ron Hubbard Birthday Celebration Event in 1997, the chairman of the board of the Religious Technology Center (*RTC*), David Miscavige, argued that Standard Technology was, and still is, important because "not everybody could be audited by Ron—time alone forbids it—and that is why auditing by standard technology is Ron's substitute" (video, *Birthday Event 1997*).[9] The *Dianetics and Scientology Technical Dictionary* states that "standard tech is not a process or a series of processes. It is following the rules of processing" (TD: 403). It has been claimed that through his findings, extraordinary knowledge, and recognition, Hubbard solved man's mental and spiritual problems by making Standard Tech available. Hubbard's soteriological path and the direct application of the spiritual tools he provided were thereby claimed to be the only way to salvation. Hubbard *is* Standard Tech. Hubbard, in the form of Standard Tech, is the only way to freedom for man. Furthermore, in this framework it becomes crucial for the church to keep followers alert to Hubbard and his life and efforts. Only by the constant presence of Hubbard in the minds of the followers is the Standard Technology legitimized. If the followers do not accept Hubbard's charismatic claims, then they might as well seek their ultimate salvation elsewhere. This, basically, is how important Hubbard is in Scientology and, according to the self-understanding of Scientology, to mankind.[10]

The Hagiography of L. Ron Hubbard:
Some Preliminary Remarks

Scientology's accounts of the life of founder and originator L. Ron Hubbard is one of the fields that have brought on the most controversy in the more apologetic and polemic works on Hubbard and Scientology (see, for instance, Atack 1992: 45–102; Gardner 1990: 263–80; Grønborg 1982: 1off.; Haack 1982: 17–33; Moos 1989: 7–82). The crux of the matter seems to be whether or not Hubbard really did have the theoretical and practical educational background and experiences that he and the church claim. The critics have maintained that the church's accounts of these matters leave much to be desired.

In scholarly analyses on Scientology (until recently primarily carried out by sociologists of religion), there has not been an explicit focus on the Hubbard biography.[11] When his personal history is taken into consideration, however, we discover that the accounts of the church are unreliable.[12] The divergence between the Scientological accounts of L. Ron Hubbard's life and efforts and those produced by non-Scientologists is taken as proof that the Scientological material is without value as a source of the actual life of Hubbard.[13] It is, however, a useful source when trying to grasp the meaning of such accounts for the church, as I shall demonstrate below. After some preliminary characterizations of the genre of hagiography, the presentation of selected aspects of Scientology's accounts of Hubbard's life will aim at demonstrating the legitimizing potential of the material and how the material is actually used by the Church of Scientology in representing its religion, concepts, and practices.

Hagiography: Some Preliminary Characteristics of the Genre

Hagiographic accounts of holy men and women are known in many religions. Islam has its hadith literature on the prophet Mohammad, just as Buddhism has its narratives on Siddharta Gautama's path to spiritual knowledge, and Christianity has its mythological accounts on the life and work of Jesus. The accounts, and their place and importance in their respective traditions, might vary but they are considered essential as sources of knowledge about these persons.

However divergent hagiographic accounts might seem in relation to certain points, they bear a remarkable resemblance to one another, and the information communicated about the holy person follows a recognizable pattern—that is, certain narrative structures seem paradigmatic to the genre. Hagiographies are not "objective" historical accounts put forward in a narrative style meant to reproduce all the highlights of the person's life. On the contrary, hagiographies are social and textual constructions produced with the particular aim of informing the recipient about specific paradigmatic events and actions connected to the founder or originator of a religion, for example.

In the *Encyclopedia of Religion*, William R. LaFleur characterizes *sacred biography* as follows:

> the subjects of a sacred biography will tend to be treated as persons whose life stories need to be told as discrete and continuous lives. The subject of a sacred biography will tend to be treated as someone whose life story can be told from birth to death and, to that degree at least, as it should be treated in a secular biography. The difference from the latter, however, lies in the degree to which such a subject will be represented as carrying out a divinely planned mission, being the possessor of a "call" or visions authenticating such a mission, and having either infallible knowledge or supernatural powers. (LaFleur 1987: 220)

Another of the outstanding differences between secular and sacred biography, or hagiography, is that hagiography emphasizes continuity. A (pre-)

determination of events in the subject's life is stressed so that even the most diverse occurences are tied together in a chain of events thus eliminating co-incidence and stressing continuity. These events are seen as part of a "master plan" that makes them religiously meaningful.

Hagiographies are used to present a certain intention, such as to legitimize a religious tradition and/or the genuineness of a religious revelation by stress-ing the originator's genuine qualities as a human philosopher, enlightened one, and/or as communicator of a divine or spiritual dimension (and in Hub-bard's case as also a scientist, as will be shown below).

In the *New Catholic Encyclopedia*, T. F. Mathews defines "practical hagi-ography" as accounts "that are the spontaneous product of circumstances or have been called into being by religious needs of one kind or another" (Ma-thews 1979). This characterization attaches importance to the use of the hag-iographic account. Hagiographic material and its production are a social con-struction as well as a process aimed at responding to social and religious needs among the recipients, be they the society at large or individual participants of a given religion. Thus the social situation is the point of departure of the hagiography and its production.

The Scientological account of L. Ron Hubbard's life and efforts can be productively approached as a hagiography deeply inscribed into the Scien-tological tradition. The hagiography is closely related to Scientology's own iden-tity, as it represents an integration of the precision of Western science with an anthropology and cosmology inspired by Eastern (Indian) philosophy. By au-thenticating Hubbard's knowledge according to these fields of thought and practice, the church legitimizes Scientology as the kind of religion that it claims to be, a synthesis of scientific and spiritual truth, a religion that appeals to all human beings all over the planet precisely because the origin of the religion lies everywhere.

By focusing on hagiography (as opposed to biography), this essay focuses not on the "historic truth value" but rather on the "utility value" of the accounts of Hubbard's life. It becomes evident in these accounts that the impetus behind every assertion is the need to interpret coincidental events in Hubbard's life as meaningful in the Scientological context and perspective, so that Hubbard appears to be a person who constantly worked toward one goal (coincidence is eliminated and transformed into historical neccessity) and/or to explain how Hubbard's unique knowledge and wisdom, and thereby Dianetics and Scien-tology, contribute to the world (a legitimizing factor). In relation to this, it is obvious that the hagiography accentuates considerations of concepts like *cha-risma* and the *routinization of charisma*, since the church's transformation of Hubbard from person to text, from man to religious institution, seems to have happened so successfully that Scientology as a religious institution seems stronger than ever in relation to its participants.

The Hagiographic Material on L. Ron Hubbard

The analysis of the legendary life of L. Ron Hubbard in this essay is based primarily on the book *What is Scientology?* (WiS 1992: 83–129) published by the Church of Scientology International in 1992. The hagiographic account in this book is a summary account in the sense that it communicates most of the fundamental assertions about the man and his efforts, while the more detailed accounts are found elsewhere.[14] In recent years, initiatives have been taken by the church to produce new and far more detailed accounts of Hubbard's life. The most far-reaching publication series is the *Ron Series*, which consists of magazines dealing with separate parts of Hubbard's areas of experience. At the Birthday Event of L. Ron Hubbard in 1997 at FLAG Landbase (one of the most important Scientology centers today, situated in Clearwater, Florida, and the center of more advanced auditing services), which I attended, a new "biography" was announced to be published during 1999 (this is still "in press"). The biographer is Dan Shermann, a Scientologist who is also the man behind the *Ron Series*.[15] Judging by his work in these magazines, one may expect a collection of an impressive amount of information already partly provided by the magazines. A third vital effort of the Church to supply information about Hubbard's legendary life is the "L. Ron Hubbard Life Exhibition" located on Hollywood Boulevard, Los Angeles. This location holds a large collection of items connected to different aspects of Hubbard's achievements, such as Boy Scouting, expeditions, his production as a science fiction and fantasy writer, and so forth.

In most of the books on Dianetics and Scientology by L. Ron Hubbard, information and assertions about his life can be found. The originator of both these systems, he developed them gradually, and the information and assertions presented in each book seem to have been arranged according to the theme of the book or its group of recipients. The instrumental aspect that exists in relation to hagiographies in general is clearly present in the priorities of the Church of Scientology. In the book *What is Scientology?* a large amount of hagiographic information and assertions are edited and made into a consistent account of Hubbard's life from his birth until the publication of *DMSMH* on May 9, 1950.[16]It is an account that primarily wants to communicate that L. Ron Hubbard led an unusual life since his earliest childhood; that he worked for humanity throughout his life; and that Dianetics and Scientology are based on the unique knowledge and wisdom of this person who has dedicated his entire life to the communication of this knowledge to his fellow man.

Childhood

Lafayette Ron Hubbard was born in Tilden, Nebraska, on March 13, 1911, the son of naval officer Harry Ross Hubbard and his wife Ledora May Hubbard. It is established that Hubbard's mother was atypical for her time, in that she was educated as a teacher prior to her marriage, which made her "aptly suited to tutor her young son" who "was reading and writing at an early age, and soon satisfying his insatiable curiosity about life with the works of Shakespeare, the Greek philosophers, and other classics" (WiS 1992: 87).

Hubbard is presented as the child of parents with a certain social standing in the community. It is characteristic that emphasis is placed on his mother's education, which made her special in her time (when not many women held formal education) since in hagiographies the special character of the subject of the hagiography is often extended to the family in some way, such as the sanctification of Mary, mother of Jesus, and in some traditions, of her mother as well. Not only is it claimed that Hubbard could read and write at an early age and that his insatiable curiosity drew him toward literary classics, it is also claimed that his mother was "aptly suited" to stimulate his early needs *because* she was an educated teacher. Giving this priority of information, her work is subordinate to his needs, and the idea that she was in some way chosen as his mother because she was the most suitable is close at hand. The line of explanation is not that the boy was interested in the classics because she motivated an interest in him but rather that she could meet his demands for stimulation because she was chosen to do so.

The stress on the boy's early reading and writing skills, his curiosity about life and that he sought to meet this curiosity by studying the classics is, in a hagiography, an early indication of how special this person is. That he always possessed exactly the orientation and the personal characteristics necessary to one day discover and communicate a special knowledge to others—this is a kind of rationalization after the fact in the sense that certain qualities possessed by the object in his or her adult state are asserted as belonging to the person as a child, so that these qualities and characteristics are authenticated. The person's knowledge and qualities are thereby stressed as genuine. Scientology as a religion stresses repeatedly that the cognition of the world was discovered and communicated by one man, L. Ron Hubbard, classicly cultured, although critical of the imperfections and shortcomings of classical wisdom. Therefore it it crucial that these qualities appear as early in this person's life as possible. The same goes for Hubbard's general education. According to the Church, it began when he was a very young child, as did his curiousity for life and, as will be demonstrated below, his never-failing contact with ordinary life and people.[17]

When young Hubbard was two years old, he moved with his family to a ranch outside of Kalispell, Montana, and later to the state's capital, Helena. According to the Scientological tradition, "Not only could he ride horses at the age of three and a half, but was soon able to rope and break broncos with the best of them" (WiS 1992: 89). This was another indication that he had skills that are not ordinarily noticed in such a young child, and emphasized his courage and love of adventure. In these surroundings, young Hubbard "first encountered another culture, that of the Blackfoot Indians," and "[h]is particular friend was an elderly medicine man, commonly known as 'Old Tom.' " Through this friendship with the normally taciturn Indian, Ron was soon initiated into the various secrets of the tribe, their legends, customs, and methods of survival in a harsh environment. At the age of six, he became a blood brother of the Blackfeet, an honor bestowed on few white men (ibid.).

These narratives of his first encounters with another culture are, in a broader Scientological perspective, the first accounts of the cross-cultural contacts that developed into rhetorical cornerstones in the understanding of Hubbard's development of Scientology; his adventurous travels and extended knowledge of all kinds of people, societies, and cultures, and his skills to see through their insufficiency constitute one platform for Scientology. His American education and his clash with the establishment of Western science constitute, as will be shown below, another platform.

In 1923, at the age of twelve, Hubbard moved with his parents to Seattle, because his father was stationed at a local naval base. "He joined the Boy Scouts and that year proudly achieved the rank of Boy Scout First Class. The next year he became the youngest Eagle Scout ever, an early indication that he did not plan to live an ordinary life" (WiS 1992: 90). Besides stressing once again his outstanding qualities, this passage claims that it is indicated by his earliest achivments in life that he did not *plan* to live an ordinary life. Behind this lies the idea that L. Ron Hubbard from early childhood worked toward the mission he was to undertake later in life, to lead his fellow human beings toward the safe route to ultimate awareness and spiritual freedom. The hagiography does not claim that there were early indicators that he was not to live an ordinary life but that there were early indications that he did not *plan* to live an ordinary life. The point here is that we are not dealing with a selection by, for instance, a transcendent power manifesting itself in him and providing him with spiritual awareness and knowledge for him to administer and communicate to other people. The motif here is self-reflexive selection, "to be chosen by oneself."

As will be demonstrated below, another aspect of this motif is the confidence offered to him by the people he meets on his way. The Scientological idea behind this is that of the "actual cycle of action," according to which an individual is an active subject in control of his or her existence. This cycle of action is opposed to the "apparent cycle of action," according to which the individual is stuck in a sequence of unfortunate story lines because he or she confuses cause and effect (Hubbard 1956a/1989: 18–25). An understanding of the hagiography demands, on this and on several other points, that we make a parallel analysis of the religious philosophy of Scientology. One of the goals of the Scientological soteriology is to help an individual to regain an understanding of his or her confusion of the two cycles.[18] By subscribing to the premisses of the actual cycle, the individual can move toward the state of fully capable spiritual being without being dependent on the body and the physical universe, and thus move toward the state of OT or Operating Thetan. The claim of the hagiography that Hubbard planned his extraordinary life is information that he had the understanding all the time and that all of his actions happened according to this cognition. The point here in relation to the selection motif is that Hubbard chose himself. From his childhood he sensed and took an interest in human problems and since he knew all along that something was very wrong, all his personal, practical, and theoretical efforts in life were aimed at solving these problems so that human misery could be stopped.

In 1923, Hubbard met Commander Joseph C. Thompson of the U.S. Navy Medical Corps on a journey in the Panama Canal. His hagiographer writes, "Commandor Thompson was the first officer sent by the US Navy to study under Sigmund Freud, and took it upon himself to pass on the essentials of Freudian theory to his young friend. Although keenly interested in the Commandor's lessons, Ron was also left with many unanswered questions." (WiS 1992: 90). Here two points of vital importance for the Scientological self-identity are stressed. First, it is said that Thompson was a student of Freud's and he was even supposed to have been among the first in the U.S. Navy to take upon himself such studies. Considering that Dianetics as a therapeutic self-help system is based on a division of the human mind and mental functions very much inspired by Freudian theory, obviously young Hubbard's tutoring by Thompson is an authentification of his skills in Freudian theory.[19] Second, we are told that he was left with many unanswered questions, which is another emphasis on his reflexive maturity and capability of unique cognition of the world. In relation to the continued Scientological emphasis on how Hubbard in his research and cognition saw through and turned down most of both Western and Eastern science and religion because these fields had not solved man's problems, this hagiographic element is an important authentification. Even this adult and former student of Freud's could not fulfill the boy's intellectual needs.

The hagiographic accounts of L. Ron Hubbard's childhood bear several resemblances to accounts on the childhood and youth of Jesus in the Apocrypha and in the writings of the evangelists—in particular, the emphasis on the clever child having different skills and qualities from those of boys of the same age. To some extent the passage on Thompson's insufficiency as a teacher resembles that of the twelve-year-old Jesus lecturing the scribes during the Easter festival in Jerusalem (Luke 2: 46–47).

Scientology's account of Hubbard, the child, is the part of the hagiography that bears most resemblance to hagiographic accounts in Western religious tradition. This may be considered an overall attempt to legitimize Scientology as a religion.

Youth: The Disappointment with Eastern Wisdom

In 1927, at the age of sixteen, Hubbard set out for the first of several voyages across the Pacific to Asia where "he took advantage of this unique opportunity to study Far Eastern Culture" (WiS 1992: 93). He befriended, among others, an old Chinese magician, Old Mayo, who according to Scientology "represented the last [magician] of the line of Chinese magicians from the court of Kublai Khan. . . . Old Mayo was also well versed in China's ancient wisdom that had been handed down from generation to generation. Ron passed many evenings in the company of such wise men, eagerly absorbing their words" (ibid.). Hubbard was also allowed access to the Buddhist lama temples, where he watched "monks meditate for weeks on end, contemplating higher truths. [And o]nce again then, he spent much of his time investigating and questioning, seeking answers to the human dilemma" (ibid.: 95). At the age of nineteen, "long before the advent of commercial airplane or jet transportation" he had traveled more than a quarter of a million miles, not only to China, but to Japan, Guam, the Philippines and other areas in the Orient. "In a very real sense, the world itself was his classroom, and he studied in it voraciously, recording what he saw and learned in his ever-present diaries, which he carefully preserved for future reference" (ibid.: 98).

This last quote, once again, emphasizes Hubbard's unlimited field of studying: It is the world at large and the human existence in its widest and most profound perspective that is being researched. Furthermore, it is once again stressed that Hubbard was aware that these travels had a goal, a mission, and therefore he kept his diaries for later use. He wasn't traveling as a tourist. As in the earlier passage on Hubbard's contact to the Blackfoot Indians, what is being claimed here is that doors, often kept closed to strangers, were being held wide open for Hubbard. This is another aspect of the selection motif mentioned above. Hubbard very early in life chose himself to solve the problems of humanity, and this decision was met by the confidence of others, and thereby he obtained access to knowledge. The message of the hagiography is that Hubbard was received everywhere because he was special. It is furthermore a very important point that these confident strangers do not impart knowledge to him because they themselves hold special applicable knowledge, but rather in spite of the fact that they do not have it. Hubbard, on the other hand, used his knowledge of their knowledge and his experiences of human misery all over the world to throw away these people's "ancient wisdom" as insufficient: "Why? Why so much human suffering and misery? Why was man, with all his ancient wisdom and knowledge accumulated in learned texts and temples, unable to solve such basic problems as war, insanity and unhappiness?" (ibid.: 96).

Wherever Hubbard traveled, he took the time to teach and help others. For instance, it is told how he "proved to the terrified natives [on a remote Pacific island] that the groans of a ghost in a supposedly haunted cave were nothing more than the rushing of underground water" (ibid.: 98), and how he investigated ancient burial grounds "though his native friends were fearful for him . . . his initiative drawn from the ever-present desire to know more. . . . Yet for all the wonders of these lands and all his respect for those whom he encountered . . . he came to the inescapable conclusion that despite the wisdom of its ancient texts, the East did not have the answers to the miseries of the human condition. It remained evident in the degradation and sorrows of its people" (ibid.: 101, 102).

Hubbard's and Scientology's relations to "Eastern wisdom" as they are represented in different parts of the Scientological material will be put in perspective in a later section. First, however, Hubbard's relationship to Western science will be examined, looking at how this was formed through his attempts to get a formal education.

Adult Life: Disappointment with Western Science

In 1929, now eighteen years old, Hubbbard returned to the United States to resume his formal education; he attended Swawely Prep School in Manassas, Virginia, and finally graduated from the Woodward School for Boys in Washington, D.C.[20] He enrolled at George Washington University, where "fate and his father placed him, fortunately, in mathematics and engineering," even though his subject, it is said, should probably have been ethnology "since he was already an expert in many different cultures," but "[w]ith his knowledge of many different cultures and his growing awareness of the human condition, his background in engineering and mathematics would serve him well in undertaking a scientific approach to solving the riddles of existence and Man's spiritual potential" (WiS 1992: 104).

In this statement, the special coupling appears between all kinds of knowledge and ways of gaining this knowledge that Hubbard impersonates in the Scientological identity. The information that it was fate and his father that decided his subject for him is interesting, since Hubbard's parents do not play important roles in the hagiography (in fact, they are hardly mentioned except in the beginning, where the mother's education and the father's naval position are emphasized). That the father is supposed to have determined Hubbard's choice of subject seems out of step with the rest of the hagiographic account, which indeed emphasizes repeatedly Hubbard's independence and early recognition of human problems—unless, of course, this claim is included to couple the father to Hubbard's Scientological project. A more probable interpretation would be that this element is, in fact, an emphasis on Hubbard's independence: Even though the fatherly authority seems to ruin the promising humanitarian career of his son, this never became possible since the son is capable of combining all his skills and different facets of knowledge in an exemplary way. It might just be that the father's insistance on a mathematical education can be interpreted as an expression of the factors outside Hubbard himself that continuously attempted to ruin his mission. One of the cornerstones of Hubbard's self-understanding and a building block of Scientology as a religion, not to mention an important aspect for many individual Scientologists, is that Hubbard was, from the very beginning, rejected and misunderstood by his surroundings. In several of Hubbard's books and in all other kinds of Scientological material a profound controversy is carried on against psychologists, psychiatrists, doctors, and others said to have been opposed to Hubbard and the Scientological project from day one. Today an important part of Scientology's identity and understanding of interactions with the larger society still bears this frame of mind. Scientology's number one enemy is still the psychiatric establishment and practitioners, as these are considered to constitute a fundamental suppression of the individual and his or her possible development. In a broader perspective, suppressive individuals or groups are interpreted not only as enemies of Scientology but also of humanity, since Scientology is working for the best of mankind. If the information on the father's decision about his son's subject of study is interpreted in this context, the point is that neither his father nor later enemies who did not understand the importance of Hubbard's task were powerful enough to succeed in destroying Hubbard and Scientology.

Hubbard pursued his task of solving the riddles of existence by theorizing that extended knowledge about subatomic particles might be a key to human thought processes; thus he enrolled in one of the first courses in the United States on nuclear physics. He was concerned for the world's safety in relation to the way man handles the atom, and he realized that if the atom was to benefit everyone, man would first have to learn how to handle himself: "His aim, then, was to synthesize and test all knowledge for what was observable, workable, and could truly help solve man's problems. And to that end, he set out to determine precisely how the mind functioned" (WiS 1992: 104).

To understand Hubbard's role as the discoverer of Dianetics and Scientology and the legitimation of the two, as well as Hubbard's importance to Scientologists all over the world, it is crucial to understand that even though Dianetics and Scientology were presented *to* laymen this was not done *by* a layman, according to the Scientological self-understanding. It was presented by a man with an impressive amount of various theoretical as well as practical personal competences and educational qualifications.

One of Hubbard's first pioneering experiments was the examination of how a sound-wave-measuring device called a Koenig Photometer identified speech as poetry regardless of the language spoken. The device's wavelengths were the same for haiku poetry read in Japanese and English, and this made Hubbard conclude that there "was scientific evidence that people were not so different as he had been led to believe, that there was indeed a meeting ground, and that all minds did in fact respond identically to the same stimuli" (ibid.: 107).

This experiment and not least the conclusion are a perfect illustration of the understanding of science that flows through Hubbard's thoughts and production. Canadian historian of religion Irving Hexham has argued that many new religious groups, as well as the New Age movement (and American society at large) promote a *belief* in science rather than a true understanding of scientific thinking and premises (Hexham 1993). It makes sense to interpret Hubbard's scientific ideals in this perspective. On the one hand, Western science at large is being rejected because it is considered too conservative and too isolated from the society that it is supposed to be an active part of and because its premises regarding man are false. On the other hand, Hubbard aims at a sort of scientific discourse and rhetoric. Throughout Hubbard's production it is emphasized that Scientology is not only a religion but the perfection of religion, "A religion of religions."[21] At the same time, Hubbard's "scientific" methodology is emphasized repeatedly in expressions such as "clinical tests prove these statements to be scientific facts" and "at this state of research" (see, for instance, Hubbard 1950/1989: 47). In this way, Scientology is seen as the synthesis of all wisdom, and due to Hubbard, the path to ultimate salvation and freedom for mankind has been made available through this synthesis (see, for instance, Hubbard 1968: 1ff.). The scientific characteristic is considered a guarantee that the Scientological practices always work. Scientology's repeated claim of being a true science, representing scientific precision in its methods and goals, is one of the factors that gives Scientology its very secular character.[22] At the same time this might be considered a sanctification of science. "Reasoning that questions arising from his experiments would best be answered by those who were paid to know about the mind, Ron took [his] discoveries to the psychology department. Rather than answers, however, he found that the . . . psychologists had no comprehension or understanding of the results—but more importantly—they weren't even interested in such things" (WiS 1992: 109). Hubbard was stunned to realize that nobody knew how the mind works and that nobody within psychology or psychiatry had decided to solve the problem: "Not only were there no answers in the East, there were none to be found in any Western center of culture" (ibid.).

The account of how psychologists refused to discuss the photometer experiments with Hubbard is almost etiologic in nature, since it prefigures the very tense relationship between Hubbard (and Scientology) and the psychological and psychiatric professions that later occurred. These professions are claimed to have turned their back on him and, even worse, they turned their back on mankind because mankind was in need of Hubbard's ideas and these professions refused to help. " 'To be very blunt,' he put it, 'it was very obvious that I was dealing with and living in a culture which knew less about the mind than the lowest primitive tribe I had ever come in contact with. Knowing also that people in the East were not able to reach as deeply and predictably into the riddles of the mind as I had been led to expect, I knew I would have to do a lot of research.' . . . Deciding that formal study had nothing more to offer, L. Ron Hubbard left college . . . , again taking his quest to learn about life out into the world . . . to see if [he] could find a common denominator of existence which would be workable" (ibid.: 111).

The Overall Legitimizing Project of the Hagiography

In *What is Scientology?* Hubbard is introduced as follows: "[The] chapter will cover the key incidents that shaped L. Ron Hubbard's life, and the important milestones on the road to his discoveries. By any measure, it was an immensely full and interesting life but the true value of it lies in the legacy that he left mankind" (WiS 1992: 83). Of interest here is the claim that even though Hubbard's life was indeed interesting its real value was that of serving mankind. This may indicate that priority is given to information in the hagiography that illuminates and puts into perspective the philosophy and practice that Hubbard found and shared. It is not his life as such, however interesting it might be, that is important; what is important is his role and activities that deal with Dianetics and Scientology. By putting his knowledge into this kind of perspective, the young developing tradition is given weight.

"Scientology was discovered, developed and organized by L. Ron Hubbard" (see for example, Hubbard 1968b: first unnumbered page). This sentence, often printed in the publications of Scientology, expresses very precisely Hubbard's significance to Scientology. It reflects the idea that the teachings of Scientology present in any culture at any time are a potential knowledge, a latent gnosis. But it was not until Hubbard that anyone possessed the qualities necessary to recognize this knowledge, develop and systematize it, thereby making it available for everyone. The term *discovered* should be understood as opposed to *invented*. Hubbard is not thought to have invented the elements taught and practiced in Dianetics and Scientology. Being the unique person he was, only he could make the necessary connections that made it possible for all the wisdom of the world to be applied by ordinary people. Hubbard himself said, "[In Asia] you could sit on a mountain top for a thousand years and it was perfectly alright with everybody in the whole neighborhood. In the west, they pick you up for vagrancy. So, we combine the collective wisdom of all those ages with a sufficient impatience and urgency, a sufficiency of scientific methodology. I think, by the way, that Gautama Sakyamuni probably had a better command of scientific methodology than any of your Chairs of Science in Western universities" (Hubbard 1968b: 11).

Hubbard emphasized what he considered to be the ignorance in Western science of man's true nature. This kind of science, according to Hubbard, is guilty of a denial of the truths about man's origin that have been known since the Vedas, which are themselves described as the earliest source of Scientology (Hubbard 1968b: 12). In the hagiography, Hubbard is disowned by science, since science will not discuss his experiments and his discoveries although these are founded on ancient truths. Hubbard's description of Buddha as a scientist (ibid.: 19) is identical to the hagiographical description of Hubbard, a man who was capable of seeing through and bringing together various kinds of truthful and useful information in the world. Hubbard is thereby legitimated as a mediator and bearer of truth in a direct line from highly esteemed Eastern religious traditions.

At the same time, and with a legitimizing point of its own, Hubbard is the person who made these traditions accessible, since only he had the true attitude to scientific work that the East, despite Buddha, is not used to. He is practical: "all we want is something with a high degree of workability, that's all any scientist needs" (Hubbard 1955a/1989: 18). This lies behind the idea that Scientology is "the religion of religions." Hubbard is seen as the ultimate cross-cultural saviour; he is thought to be able to release man from his miserable condition because he had the necessary background, and especially the right attitude. These ideas are the basis of the frequently stated Scientology message: "People all over the world consider they have no truer friend."

Keeping Scientology Working: Routinization of Charisma on a Formal Level

The purpose of analyzing important aspects of the hagiographic narrative on L. Ron Hubbard's life in What Is Scientology? was to demonstrate how central elements in the narrative, related to Scientological ideas, establish the narrative of a life, the events of which, like beads on a string, support central aspects of Scientological ideas and self-identity. Analyzing the legitimizing potential in different statements of the hagiography, Hubbard's significance to Scientology as a religion was demonstrated. The overall aim was to exemplify the mythologization of Hubbard in the hagiographic process and production and to point to its religious significance and perspectives, thereby adding an important perspective to the ongoing discussion and controversy on the nature of Scientology's teachings on the founder.

Broadening the perspective of mythologization, the following will point to some of the initiatives taken by the church to carry out the legitimizing potential on an organizational level. These initiatives have consequences on both an organizational and a religious level.[23]

The institutionalization and routinization of Hubbard has been an ongoing process since the early days of Scientology, and the idea of Standard Technology was the cornerstone of Scientological practice even in Hubbard's lifetime. In the last years of his life, Hubbard worked with trusted staff members to develop an organizational structure that would protect his legacy, Standard Tech and Scientology, after his death. In 1982, four years prior to his death, he initiated the ultimate formal routinization of charisma. He transformed himself into the ultimate legitimizing source: a registered trademark handed over to the control of the Religious Technology Center (RTC).[24] This was an organization formed that same year to "preserve, maintain and protect the Scientology religion" (RTC 1993: 4). RTC is not a part of the church organizational hierarchy and is not involved with its daily activities. RTC's work is organized in seven different divisions, all handling different parts of the overall purposes.[25] "All of RTC's activities focus on one purpose: TO KEEP SCIENTOLOGY WORKING BY SAFEGUARDING THE PROPER USE OF THE TRADEMARKS, PROTECTING THE PUBLIC, AND MAKING SURE THAT THE POWERFUL TECHNOLOGY REMAINS IN GOOD HANDS AND IS PROPERLY USED" (ibid.). The "Valuable Final Products"[26] of RTC are:

1. Having the correct technology.
2. Knowing the technology.
3. Knowing it is correct.
4. Teaching correctly the correct technology.
5. Applying the technology.
6. Seeing that the technology is correctly applied.
7. Hammering out of existence incorrect technology.
8. Knocking out incorrect applications.
9. Closing the door on any possibility of incorrect technology.
10. Closing the door on incorrect application. (Ibid.: 28)

These products were formulated by Hubbard in the 1960s, and he defended them and their seriousness by saying, "We're not playing some minor game in Scientology. It isn't cute or something to do for lack of something better. The whole agonized future of this planet, every man, woman and child on it, and your own destiny for the next endless trillions of years depend on what you do here and now with and in Scientology" (ibid.).

Since 1955, Hubbard and his organization have registered certain words and symbols of the religion as trademarks and service marks in countries all over the world. In 1986 there were more than 3,300 registered trademarks and servicemarks in more than 140 countries.[27] Registration of trademarks is usually one of the first activities when Scientology starts a dissemination program in a new country. When Hubbard began to register these marks, "[h]e wanted to make the pure application of one-hundred percent standard technology available to all, and knew that maintenance of the trademarks would help guarantee it" (ibid.: 6). When RTC was formed in 1982, Hubbard donated all the trademarks to the control of RTC, including the trademarks "L. Ron Hubbard," "LRH," "Ron," the "LRH sea symbol" and the "L. Ron Hubbard signature."[28] RTC has given the mother church, Church of Scientology International, the right to use the trademarks as well as to license all other churches to use the marks. The trademarks are a formal cornerstone in the dissemination and practice of the Scientology religion. Without the marks there can be no authority claimed on behalf of any kind of material. Just as Standard Tech is Hubbard's substitute on a practical ritual level, the formal institutionalization of himself as a trademark seems to be a very effective way of keeping Hubbard formally present.

As in other religions, ritual success in Scientology depends on the correct application of ritual tools. A ritual is only considered workable if it is performed in the correct manner. Unlike most other religions, Scientology, being a child of modern Western capitalism and management technology, applies the tools and icons in these cultural settings to protect the religion. No new Hubbard books, films, tapes, course packages, compilations of LRH writings or recordings are released without being thoroughly examined and approved by RTC. No dissemination campaigns or promotional items can be carried out by the church without RTC having approved them "to make sure they are free from alteration or interpretation and are one-hundred percent on-Source" (ibid.: 19). RTC is the institution to contact if one becomes aware that materials are "off-Source" or if individuals are altering or interpreting the material. Besides the trademarks, RTC owns the rights to all "Advanced materials," that is, the Standard Tech used by Scientologists to move up the uppermost levels of the Bridge, Scientology's very detailed path of salvation. RTC is physically present in all "Advanced Orgs" (the larger centers that are able to offer advanced training) to ensure that the technology of these levels and the individuals who apply them are protected from false data.

It is evident that RTC, with its primary assignments of authorization, verification, and correction all aimed at the goal of keeping "Dianetics and Scientology technology safeguarded, in good hands and properly used" (ibid.: 8), is the single most powerful unit within, and yet not quite within, the church's organizational structure. In this context, the interesting part of RTC's control is the control of the trademarks, in particular the Hubbard-names trademarks. On the one hand, as pointed out by the church, RTC is the ultimate protector of Hubbard. On the other hand, it is possible to imagine that the legitimating potential and power of Hubbard's name in its different forms can, if a crisis in the religion occurs, be maneuvered in different directions. In fact, one might ask if it would be possible to publish material, if the situation calls for it, with Hubbard's signature as legitimating source but without the material actually being Hubbard's. It would be in variance with the foundations and formulated valuable final products in RTC but would it, in a crisis, be possible to argue that this would be an initiative taken "to keep Scientology working?" This remains to be seen.

The chairman of the board of RTC is David Miscavige. His position might be considered to be the most important and most powerful in Scientology. Miscavige himself was a "messenger" (see below) to Hubbard when he was a child, and he seems to have proven his commitment to the church since his earliest years. He has held his position in RTC since it was formed in 1982. It should be made absolutely clear that Miscavige's position is not in any way comparable to that of Hubbard's. Hubbard was source and originator. Miscavige is the protector to guarantee this source, and as such he is highly respected by Scientologists. Like other top leaders of Scientology such as the president of the Church of Scientology International, Heber C. Jentzch, and the executive director, Guillaume Lésevre, Miscavige is not, in principle, considered more important than other dedicated staff members.

He has proven, on different occasions, that he is capable of handling crises in the organization. In the 1980s disagreement on how to administer Hubbard's religious legacy led to the exclusion of a number of highly positioned Scientologists. Miscavige was the man to carry the organization through that crisis. In 1995 he took the initiative to develop a new concept of how to train auditors in Scientology, the so called *Golden Age of Tech* program.[29] He has proven himself a loyal and invaluable chairman in the most powerful organizational unit.

Keeping Hubbard Interesting

Whereas RTC is formally the most powerful unit when it comes to organizational efforts to keep Hubbard in control of the organization, another organizational unit supplements it on a practical level. A kind of mediator between the control of Hubbard as formal Source and the realization and confirmation of his qualities by the individuals in Scientology is the Commodore's Messengers' Org (*CMO*), formed in 1969.[30] (Scientology started branches of the organization that operated out of their own ships. These branches took on naval titles like "commodore.") In 1967, when Hubbard formed the Sea Organization, he was sailing around the world carrying out his research on board the vessel Apollo. Hubbard was the commodore of that ship. On board with him was a group of children and teenagers who served as messengers. They were his representation when, for instance, messages where to be passed on from Hubbard to passengers and personnel on board. Being the commodore's messengers they could expect the same respect that Hubbard enjoyed. The CMO was reorganized during the 1970s, especially after Hubbard went ashore in Clearwater, Florida, to form FLAG Landbase in 1975, and CMO's role as providing the messengers for Hubbard was reinterpreted after Hubbard's death in 1986. After the commodore died, his messengers were now to bring messages from the source to the outside world. CMO's "valuable final products" are:

1. Successfully exploited LRH properties of all types to correct publics.
2. Demand for LRH.
3. Demand for LRH products.
4. Increased consumption of LRH products.
5. Confidence in LRH products.
6. Security for LRH by increased repute.
7. Faith in LRH tech and material.
8. Successful defenses of LRH.
9. Broadened knowledge of and respect for LRH.

CMO's role can be divided into two areas: whereas RTC keeps the tech clean by closely examing all new materials and promoting Hubbard on an organizational level, CMO, through the hosts present at all major orgs (organizations), is present as a unit to protect LRH on a daily basis. They are present "on behalf of Ron." In this context, the institutionalization and mythologization of Hubbard, another aspect of CMO's activities, is vital. One may say that while RTC sees to it that individuals who want to apply the tech can be sure that it is "on Source" and promotes Hubbard on a large-scale level through campaigns and, not the least, through annual events such as the Birthday Game and Event, CMO's prime task is to promote Hubbard on a daily basis, in all the smaller formal and informal activities that go on in the orgs, so that Hubbard is constantly kept interesting and attractive. One result of this is the publication and promotion of the Ron Series. More than twenty magazines have been published in this series during more than a decade, all focusing on particular areas of Hubbard's work. One booklet on the series reads: "With each issue of the RON Series, you come to know Ron better and as a result live life closer to the source" (CSI 1998a). As one of my informants put it: "Ron was the first, you are the next." It seems that over time, yet more aspects of Hubbard's character and interests will be published in a narrative form. Just as it is a strategy of the Church to cover as many parts of life as possible, to make as many entrances into Dianetics and Scientology as possible, it seems to be a strategy to make Hubbard as multifaceted as possible so that his appeal attracts the most diverse people. Publishing narratives on Hubbard is a dissemination tool. At the same time it seems to be a form of spiritual inspiration. This is also reflected in another CMO activity, the promotion of Hubbard on a daily basis ensuring that Hubbard is always mentioned in a positive way when spoken of by individuals, for instance, at the Birthday Event, at Friday Graduations, in meetings held at Scientology Orgs where individuals share their success stories, and the like.

Summary

In this essay different Scientology initiatives have been analyzed, especially the hagiographic production and its religious and organizational contexts and consequences. The analyses have been carried out in the framework of concepts such as charisma, routinization of charisma, and legitimation. In connection with this, focus has been placed on L. Ron Hubbard's significance as ultimate religious source and legitimizing resource to the claims of the church.

To sum up briefly, it is reasonable to point to two juxtaposed tendencies in the material: textualization and personification. However opposed these two tendencies may seem to be, in Scientology both of them designate all of the initiatives in one way or another. Another way to say this would be to stress that Hubbard is, at one and the the same time, an ordinary human being and a superhuman being with special, nonordinary qualities.[31] Hubbard is textualized and dehumanized in being considered an agent with special qualities and the only source of true salvation. Standard Technology is Hubbard's ideas and Hubbard's spirit abstracted into a set of principles and ritual tools by means of which ultimate salvation is within ordinary individuals' reach. This part of Hubbard—or the construction of him in abstract form—finds its most profound consequence in the transformation of his name, initials, and signature into trademarks.

At the same time it is repeatedly stressed that Hubbard is an ordinary person with a contact to all kinds of people and all kinds of lives, and with a lot of different interests and skills.[32] Whereas the textualization process shows what can be achieved by following Standard Tech, the Ron Series, for instance, aims at identification with Hubbard. The more different sides he had, the more people are able to identify with him.

Abbreviations

CSI 1965   *The Classification, Gradation and Awareness Chart of Levels and Certificates.* Video of lecture by L. Ron Hubbard on September 9, 1965, at Saint Hill Special Briefing Course.

CSI 1993a   *L. Ron Hubbard. A Chronicle of Research*. Los Angeles: New Era Publications.

CSI 1993b   *The Bridge of Knowledge. Books Containing Ron's Legacy of the Tech*. Los Angeles: New Era Publications.

CSI 1993a   *Ron. Portraits of His Life*. Los Angeles: New Era Publications.

CSI 1998b   *LRH Birthday Game 1998/99. Rules and Tips*. Los Angeles: Bridge Publications.

DMSMH   L. Ron Hubbard. *Dianetics: The Modern Science of Mental Health*. Copenhagen: New Era Publications, 1950/1989.

RTC 1993   *Religious Technology Center*. Los Angeles: New Era Publications.

TB 1976   *The Technical Bulletins of Dianetics and Scientology*. Copenhagen: AOSH DK Publications Department.

TB 1991   *The Technical Bulletins of Dianetics and Scientology*. Copenhagen: New Era Publications.

TD   *Dianetics and Scientology Technical Dictionary*. Copenhagen: New Era Publications.

WiS 1992   *What Is Scientology?* Copenhagen: New Era Publications.

NOTES

1. In Scientology, Hubbard's death is often expressed in ways such as "On 24 January 1986, having completed all he set out to do, Ron departs his body" (CSI 1993a: 15).

2. I define religion as follows: "a largely shared set of concepts and ritual acts including the postulation of agents with special qualities." An agent with special qualities is understood, within a cognitive framework, as, for example, a god, ancestor, extraterrestrial, immortal life-force, animal, or other kind of agent attributed with qualities that transcends the qualities ordinarily attributed to this kind of agent. According to my analyses, Hubbard constitutes one of several such agents in Scientology (see Christensen, 1999/in press).

3. Max Weber, *Theory of Social and Economic Organization*, translated by A. R. Henderson and Talcott Parsons (Edinburgh: Hodge, 1947), p. 329.

4. In her essay "Charismatization: The Social Production of 'an Ethos Propitious to the Mobilisation of Sentiments,' " sociologist of religion Eileen Barker has reflected on the social and processual character of charisma in the group formerly known as Unification Church (Barker 1993).

5. For a thorough analysis of this process, see Christensen 1999/in press.

6. Originally auditing was the therapeutic practice of one person sitting down and listening to another person's engrammic experience in order to work this person back to the earliest engram, called "basic-basic." In Scientology, the term *auditing* refers to the ritual practice in which the "auditor," by means of the E-Meter, helps the

"preclear" to address all the karmic experience on his or her "timetrack" in order to bring about ultimate spiritual awareness and freedom. (The E-Meter is an electronic device that detects changes in one's emotional state.) Standard Technology was thereby transformed to a set of religious precepts ensuring ritual and soteriological success.

7. *The Technical Bulletins of Dianetics and Scientology* (TB 1991) is a compilation of bulletins, policy letters, and other manuscripts from 1950 to 1991 consisting of thirteen chronological volumes, four subject volumes, and one index volume. The volumes are invaluable sources to the development of Dianetics and Scientology. For an analysis, see Christensen, 1999/in press.

8. Even though Hubbard's signature was transformed into a trademark, to Scientologists Hubbard's signature still assures that a publication was originated by him—even though, as I have argued elsewhere, it is evident on certain points that not all material claimed to be his were written by him (ibid.).

9. For an extended presentation of RTC and its work, see below.

10. Scientology's ultimate goal is to "clear the planet," that is, to bring mankind to a certain level of rationality and spiritual well-being and cognition. By this claim the individual's salvational path is placed in a broader soteriological perspective.

11. Except in work carried out by Christensen. This analysis is based on the accounts presented in Christensen 1997a: 35–45 and Christensen 1997b: 15–27.

12. Among other sociological analyses, Roy Wallis has tried to demonstrate that some of the Scientological accounts of Hubbard's life should be modified (Wallis 1976: 21). Whitehead refers to the accounts as marked by "embellishments or omissions" (Whitehead 1987: 46). Bainbridge, in his article, sets out to prove that Scientology's accounts of Hubbard's popularity as a science fiction writer are false (Bainbridge 1987: 67). Lee mentions several assertions put forward by the Church that do not seem to be correct (Lee 1970: 57).

13. In a Hubbard Communications Office Bulletin from December 1955, Hubbard wrote that although it is usually considered to be bad taste to put out data on oneself, he seriously considered doing it since a lot of biased material existed. While there is "plenty of authenticating and documenting material if one cares to look for it," he wrote (TB 1991, vol. 3: 242) it would take a good job of coordination to track down informations from libraries, for example, and get it confirmed. In May 1956, in the introduction of the translated versions of *Scientology. The Fundamentals of Thought* (Hubbard 1956a/1989) Hubbard was presented as a man with "many degrees [and] very skilled by reason of study" (ibid.: 364) and trained in nuclear physics. He was referred to as Doctor Hubbard (at that time there was a title of doctor in Scientology), and it was stressed that he was assisted by the organizations of Dianetics and Scientology, "one of the most numerous organizations in the field of the mind on Earth today" (ibid: 365).

14. For a selection of hagiographic accounts on Hubbard, see the bibliography, the sections *The Ron Series* and *Other Magazines on L. Ron Hubbard*.

15. Sherman's biography on Hubbard has not yet been published. However, in recent years, it has become tradition that Sherman present his latest research on Hubbard at the annual Birthday Event on March 13.

16. I have chosen to limit my analysis to the years from Hubbard's birth until he left university, since the point is not to reproduce the Scientological account in full

but to point to certain elements and structures. The part of the hagiography left out of my analysis includes one point of interest in the hagiographic perspective: the account of how, after service in World War II, Hubbard suffered from lameness and blindness but was declared cured in 1949 (WiS 1992: 119). The point here is that he had cured himself. This perspective is obviously interesting, since it communicates that Dianetics, originally a self-healing system, worked before Hubbard developed it in full. In a broader perspective, this kind of information legitimizes both Hubbard's skills and Dianetics and Scientology.

17. A dominant point in Hubbard's and Scientology's ongoing polemic against psychologists, for example, is that Hubbard, as opposed to psychologists did not sit in an "ivory tower" but lived with ordinary people and knew of their problems.

18. "Regain" as opposed to "gain" because it is held that the individual as a spiritual being, in his or her original state, knew of his or her mental and spiritual capacities. For different reasons, in a remote past and because of the reactivity of the engrams influencing the individual's life in different ways, most individuals no longer have this knowledge. By working through the different stages of auditing on the Bridge, it can be regained. This line of thought is found, for example, in *The Factors* (Hubbard 1952a/1989: 3–8).

19. For the most detailed account of the human mind by Hubbard, see Hubbard 1950/1989.

20. There seems to be a lack of consistency in the chronology here when it comes to Hubbard's age; compare the account of how long he had traveled by the age of nineteen.

21. This expression is found, for example, in an interview with L. Ron Hubbard; see the video *Scientology*.

22. Sociologist Bryan R. Wilson has analyzed Scientology's secular character in relation to the difficulties Scientology has had to gain religious recognition throughout the world (Wilson 1990; see also Wallis 1976).

23. The Keeping Scientology Working Series was originated in 1965. For a full account, see TB 1991, Subject Vol. 2: 3–90.

24. The information that Hubbard's name in its different forms was trademarked in 1982 was provided by an informant of the juridical department of the Church of Scientology International in Los Angeles. It should be mentioned that, according to RTC (RTC 1993), Hubbard began to trademark words and symbols in 1955. In a Professional Auditor's Bulletin from July 1953, however, Hubbard made the following statement: "it is rather amusing that my name is not Hubbard and the fame, if it ever came, would go only to a legal trademark, a thing without body or spirit" (TB 1991, vol. 2: 155). Whether this means that his name was trademarked earlier or Hubbard just foresaw future developments is not to say.

25. Like the rest of Scientology's organizations, RTC is organized in accordance with Hubbard's management technology.

26. "Valuable Final Products" is the expression of the ideal of accomplishment within a branch of Scientology.

27. A record of the development regarding trademarks is found in the video recording of the Birthday Event 1986.

28. Ron and LRH are the names that Scientologists use.

29. "Golden Age of Tech" was presented at the annual celebration of *DMSMH* on May 9, 1995, and denotes a new and allegedly revolutionary way of training auditors. The system, as Scientologists comprehends it, was based on very effective and closely repeated training drills based on Hubbard's writings and taped lectures and includes, in the drilling, a "Hubbard E-Meter Drills Simulator" for the auditor to be absolutely familiar with the different E-Meter readings. For a presentation of this initiative, see *Scientology News Magazine*, issue 2, 1996.

30. My informants on CMO are a staff member in CMO, Clearwater, Florida; and Mr. Carl Helt, juridical department of the Church of Scientology International, Los Angeles.

31. A curiosity is worth mentioning here: in 1954 Hubbard pointed out that a part of basic theory that should be taught to the student of Scientology was that "L. Ron Hubbard is a human being" (TB 1991, vol. 2: 362).

32. Eileen Barker has pointed to the same qualities in the Unification Church's representation of Sun Myung Moon (1993: 195).

BIBLIOGRAPHY: SOURCE MATERIAL, DIANETICS AND SCIENTOLOGY

Books by L. Ron Hubbard

The books are sequenced according to the year of the first copy printed. The year placed after the publisher is the year of the copy used in the analyses represented in this essay.

1950   *Dianetics: The Modern Science of Mental Health*. Copenhagen: New Era Publications International, 1989.

1951a   *The Dynamics of Life*. Copenhagen: New Era Publications International, 1989.

1951b   *Science of Survival. Prediction of Human Behaviour*. Copenhagen: New Era Publications International, 1989.

1951c   *Selfanalysis*. Copenhagen: New Era Publications International, 1989.

1951d   *Advanced Procedures and Axioms*. Copenhagen: New Era Publications International, 1989.

1951e   *Handbook for Preclears*. Copenhagen: New Era Publications International, 1989.

1951f   *Child Dianetics*. Copenhagen: New Era Publications International, 1989. Compilation based on Hubbard's writing on the issue.

1952a   *Scientology 8–8008*. Copenhagen: New Era Publications International, 1989.

1952b   *Scientology. A History of Man*. Copenhagen: New Era Publications International, 1989.

1952c   *Scientology 8–80. The Discovery and Increase of Life Energy in the Genus Homo Sapiens*. Copenhagen: Scientology Publications Organization, 1979.

1953   *How to Live though an Executive*. Copenhagen: New Era Publications International, 1989.

1955a   *Dianetics. The Evolution of a Science*. Copenhagen: New Era Publications International, 1989.

1955b   *Dianetics 55! A Guide to Effective Communication*. Copenhagen: New Era Publications International, 1989.

1955c   *The Creation of Human Ability*. Copenhagen: New Era Publications International, 1989.
1955d   *Notes on the Lectures*. Copenhagen: New Era Publications International, 1989.
1956a   *Scientology. The Fundamentals of Thought*. Copenhagen: New Era Publications International, 1989.
1956b   *The Problems at Work*. Copenhagen: New Era Publications International, 1989.
1957   *All about Radiation*. Copenhagen: New Era Publications International, 1989.
1960   *Have You Lived before this Life?* Copenhagen: New Era Publications International, 1989.
1961   *E-Meter Essentials*. Copenhagen: New Era Publications International, 1988.
1965a   *A New Slant on Life*. Copenhagen: New Era Publications International, 1989.
1965b   *The Book of E-Meter Drills*. Copenhagen: New Era Publications International, 1997. Compilation based on Hubbard's writings on the issue.
1966   *Introducing the E-Meter*. Copenhagen: New Era Publications International, 1988. Compilation based on Hubbard's writing on the issue.
1968a   *Introduction to Scientology Ethics*. Copenhagen: New Era Publications International, 1989.
1968b   *The Phoenix Lectures*. Los Angeles: Publications Organization Worldwide.
1970a   *Scientology 0–8. The Book of Basics*. Copenhagen: New Era Publications International, 1989.
1970b   *The Background and Ceremonies of the Church of Scientology Worldwide*. Los Angeles: Church of Scientology Worldwide.
1971a   *The Basic Dianetics Picture Book*. Copenhagen: New Era Publications International, 1991.
1971b   *The Basic Scientology Picture Book*. Copenhagen: New Era Publications International, 1997.
1982   *Understanding the E-Meter*. Copenhagen: New Era Publications International, 1988. Compilation based on Hubbard's writings on the issue.
1984   *Purification. An Illustrated Answer to Drugs*. Copenhagen: New Era Publications International.
1990   *Clear Body, Clear Mind. The Effective Purification Program*. Copenhagen: New Era Publications International. Compilation based on Hubbard's writings on the issue.
Dianetics and Scientology Technical Dictionary. 1983. Copenhagen: New Era Publications International.
Knowingness. Quotations From the Works of L. Ron Hubbard. 1991. Los Angeles: Vol. 1. Bridge Publications.
Knowingness: The Universal Solvent. Quotations from the Works of L. Ron Hubbard. 1991. Vol. 1. Los Angeles: Bridge Publications.
Modern Management Technology Defined. Hubbard Dictionary of Administration and Management. 1991. Copenhagen: New Era Publications International.
The Technical Bulletins of Dianetics and Scientology. 1976. 12 vols. Copenhagen: AOSH DK Publications Department. Old edition of the *Technical Bulletins*.
The Technical Bulletins of Dianetics and Scientology. 1991. 18 vols. Copenhagen: New Era Publications International. New edition of the *Technical Bulletins*.

Additional Scientology Material

BOOKS

Images of a Lifetime. A Photographic Biography, 1996. Copenhagen: New Era Publications International.

The Scientology Handbook. 1994. Copenhagen: New Era Publications International. Compiled by LRH Book Compilations staff of the Church of Scientology International.

What Is Scientology? 1992, Copenhagen: New Era Publications International. Compiled by LRH Book Compilations staff of the Church of Scientology International.

THE RON SERIES

All magazines in this series were published in Los Angeles by the L. Ron Hubbard Library.

L. Ron Hubbard. A Profile. All magazines in his series were published in Los Angeles by the L. Ron Hubbard Library. 1995.

Ron. The Adventurer/Explorer. Daring Deeds and Unknown Realms. 1996.

Ron. The Artist. Art & Philosophy. 1998.

Ron. The Auditor. From Research to Application. 1991.

Ron. The Humanitarian. Rehabilitation of a Drugged Society. 1996.

Ron. The Humanitarian. The Educator. 1996.

Ron. The Humanitarian. Freedom Fighter. Articles and Essays. 1997.

Ron. The Humanitarian. The Road to Self-Respect. 1995.

Ron. Letters and Journals. The Dianetic Letters. 1997.

Ron. Letters and Journals. Early Years of Adventure. 1997.

Ron. Letters and Journals. Literary Correspondence. 1997.

Ron. The Master Mariner. Issue I: Sea Captain. 1991.

Ron. The Master Mariner. Issue II: Yachtsman. 1994.

Ron. The Music Maker. 1995.

Ron. The Philosopher. Rediscovery of the Human Soul. 1996.

Ron. The Philosopher. Issue I: The Quest for Truth. 1991.

Ron. The Philosopher. Issue II: The Spirit of Man. 1991.

Ron. The Poet/Lyricist. 1996.

Ron. The Writer. The Shaping of Popular Fiction. 1997.

Ron. The Writer. Issue I: The Legend Begins. 1989.

Ron. The Writer. Issue II: Changing a Genre. 1992.

VIDEOS

'*L. Ron Hubbard Birthday Event.*' Los Angeles: Golden Era Productions. The years 1986–.

May 9th Event. Los Angeles: Golden Era Productions. The years 1986–.

Scientology. Interview with L. Ron Hubbard. Los Angeles: L. Ron Hubbard Library, 1990.

The Classification, Gradation and Awareness Chart of Levels and Certificates. Lecture by L. Ron Hubbard on September 9, 1965 at Saint Hill Special Briefing Course.

OTHER MAGAZINES ON L. RON HUBBARD

The Bridge of Knowledge. Books Containing Ron's Legacy of the Tech. 1993. Los Angeles: New Era Publications International.
LRH Birthday Game 1998/99. Rules and Tips. 1998 Los Angeles: Bridge Publications, Int.
L. Ron Hubbard. A Chronicle of Research. 1993. Los Angeles: New Era Publications International.
Religious Technology Center. 1993. Los Angeles: New Era Publications International.
Ron. Portraits of His Life. 1998. Los Angeles: New Era Publications International.
Scientology News Magazine, Issue 2. 1996. Los Angeles: Bridge Publications.

WEB SITES

www.scientology.org
www.lronhubbard.org
www.dianetics.org

Scholarly Analyses of Scientology

Bainbridge, William Sims. 1987. "Science and Religion: The Case of Scientology." In David G. Bromley and Philip E. Hammond, eds., *The Future of New Religious Movements.* Maron, Ga.: Mercer University Press, pp. 59–79.
Beckford, James A. 1985. "Scientology." In Beckford, *Cult Controversies. The Social Response to New Religious Movements.* London: Tavistock, pp. 51–60.
Christensen, Dorthe Refslund. 1994. *Fra Terapi til Religion. En religionshistorisk analyse af centrale begreber i henholdsvis Dianetics og Scientology med særligt henblik på forskellene i diskurs og mål.* Aarhus University: Department for the Study of Religion.
———. 1997a. *Scientology. Fra Terapi til Religion.* Copenhagen: Gyldendal.
———. 1997b. *Scientology. En ny religion.* Copenhagen: Forlaget Munksgaard.
———. 1999/in press. "Rethinking Scientology. Cognition and Representation in Religion, Therapy and Soteriology." Ph.D. dissertation, Department for the Study of Religion, Aarhus University, Denmark.
Kent, Stephen A. 1996. "Scientology's Relationship with Eastern Religious Traditions." *Journal of Contemporary Religion* 11.1: 21–36.
Lee, John A. 1970. "Dianetics and Scientology." In Lee, *Sectarian Healers and Hypnotherapy.* Toronto: Queen's Printer, pp. 57–88.
Lewis, J. 2003. *Legitimating New Religions.* New Brunswick: Rutgers University Press.
Melton, J. Gordon. 2000. *The Church of Scientology.* Studies in Contemporary Religion. Salt Lake City, UT: Signature Books.
Schönbeck, Oluf. 1994. "Scientology og indisk religion." *CHAOS. Dansk-norsk tidsskrift for religionshistoriske studier* (Copenhagen) 21: 171–189.
Stark, Rodney, and William Sims Bainbridge. 1985. *The Future of Religion. Seculariza-

tion, Revival and Cult Formation. Berkeley: University of California Press. Chapter 12, "Scientology: To Be Perfectly Clear."

Sundby Sørensen, Merethe. 1990. *Scientology som identitet og institution: Kernemedlemmer 1986–87.* Datamaterial, DDA–1494, Danish Data Archive, Odense.

———. 1991 "Scientologi." In Tim Jensen, ed., *Minoritetsreligioner—religionssociologisk set.* Copenhagen: Columbus, pp. 179–204.

———. 1998. "Danish Members, Perseptions of the Founder of the Church of Scientology." In Eileen Barker and Margit Warburg, eds., *New Religions and New Religiousity.* Aarhus: Aarhus University Press, 1998, pp. 165–71.

Wallis, Roy. 1975. "Societal Reaction to Scientology; A Study in the Sociology of Deviant Religion." In Wallis, *Sectarianism. Analyses of Religious and Non-Religious Sects.* London: Peter Owen.

———.1976 *The Road to Total Freedom. A Sociological Analysis.* London: Heinemann Educational Books.

Whitehead, Harriet. 1974. "Reasonably Fantastic: Some Perspectives on Scientology, Science Fiction and Occultism." In Irving I. Zaretsky and Mark P. Leone, *Religious Movements in Contemporary America.* Princeton: Princeton University Press, pp. 547–587.

———. 1987. *Renunciation and Reformulation. A Study of Conversion in an American Sect.* Ithaca: Cornell University Press.

Wilson, Bryan R. 1990. "Scientology: A Secularized Religion." in Wilson, *The Social Dimensions of Sectarianism.* New York: Oxford University Press, pp. 267–288

Polemical Works on Scientology—A Limited Selection

Atack, Jon. 1992. *A Piece of Blue Sky.* New York: Carol Publishing Group.

Gardner, Martin. 1990. *Fads and Fallacies in the Name of Science.* New York: Dover, pp. 263f., 309, 346f.

Grønborg, Jan. 1982. *Scientology.* Aarhus: Kirketjenesten i Danmark.

Haack, Friedrich-Wilhelm. 1982. *Scientology—Magie des 20. Jahrhunderts.* Munich: Claudius Verlag.

Moos, Kaj. 1985. *Scientology—fandens eget vÆrk.* Silkeborg: Havmaagen.

———. 1989. *Scientology—videnskab eller svindel.* Silkeborg: Havmaagen.

Perspectives and Background on Charisma and Hagiography

Barker, Eileen. 1993. "Charismatization: The Social Production of an Ethos Propitious to the Mobilization of Sentiments." In Eileen Barker, James A. Beckford and Karel Dobbelaere, eds., *Secularization, Rationalism and Sectarianism.* Oxford: Clarendon, pp. 181–201.

LaFleur, William R. 1987. "Biography." In Mircea Eliade, ed., *The Encyclopedia of Religion.* New York: Macmillan, 1: 220–224.

Mathews, T. F. 1979. "Hagiography." In *New Catholic Encyclopedia*, Washington, D.C., 6: 894.

Robbins, Thomas. 1988. *Cults, Converts and Charisma.* London: Sage.

Wallis, Roy. 1986. "The Social Construction of Charisma." In Roy Wallis, and Steve

Bruce, *Sociological Theory, Religion and Collective Action*. Belfast: Queens University Press, pp. 129–54.

Weber, Max. 1968. *Gesammelte Aufsätze zur Wissenschaftslehre*. Tübingen: J.C.B Mohr.

———. 1976. *Wirtschaft und Gesellschaft. Grundriss der verstehenden Soziologie*. Tübingen: J.C.B. Mohr.

Wilson, Bryan R. 1975. *The Noble Savages: The Primitive Origins of Charisma*. Berkeley: University of California Press.

Assorted Literature

Gilhus, Ingvild S., and Lisbeth Mikaelsson. 1998. *Kulturens Refortrylling. Nyreligiøsitet i Moderne Samfunn*, Oslo: Oslo University Press.

Hexham, Irving. 1993. "Evolution: The Central Mythology of the New Age Movement." Paper read in Marburg, June 28.

Mikaelsson, Lisbeth, ed. 1996. *Myte i møte med det moderne*. Norges Forskningsråd. KULTs skriftserie nr. 63. Olso, Norway.

12

The Theosophical Society

James A. Santucci

The Theosophical Society was founded in New York City in 1875 by sixteen individuals who had shared interests in spiritualism and occultism. Among these sixteen who responded to the call by Col. Henry Steel Olcott (1832–1907) to those "who would agree to found and belong to a Society such as had been mentioned," the most prominent, in terms of their contributions to the incipient society, were Helena Petrovna Blavatsky (1831–1891), Henry Steel Olcott, William Quan Judge (1851–1896), Charles Sotheran (1847–1902), George H. Felt (1831–1906), Henry J. Newton (1823–1895), John Storer Cobb (?–?), and Dr. Seth Pancoast (1823–1889).[1] The objects of the society, according to its bylaws, were to "collect and diffuse a knowledge of the laws which govern the universe." The designation of the society as the Theosophical Society reflects this understanding in general terms, but in all likelihood the term "theosophical" was unfamiliar or strange to some of the participants. As a result, the society should not be interpreted according to the semantic understanding of the term theosophy, but rather according to the understanding that the society has given to the term. Furthermore, Theosophy as understood in the Theosophical Society and in many of the societies that derived from it should not be considered static in its definition and content; rather, it should be understood as an organic body of teachings that has undergone reinterpretation and development over time. Nonetheless, most Theosophical organizations— those that have derived from the parent Theosophical Society founded in New York—understand Theosophy through the teachings of Helena P. Blavatsky, who is regarded as the ultimate and, for some, an infallible source of Theosophical learning.

The mention of organizations that derive from the original society is important to keep in mind, since the history of the Theosophical movement includes not just the original society but also such organizations as the Theosophical Society (Pasadena), the United Lodge of Theosophists, and the Temple of the People, all of which are still in existence. Other organizations derive from the Theosophical teachings of Blavatsky, among which are the Temple of the People (near Oceano, California), founded by Dr. William H. Dower (1866–1937) and Mrs. Francia LaDue (1849–1922), the Arcane School of Alice Bailey (1880–1949), the "I AM" Religious Activity of Guy Ballard (1878–1939), and the Church Universal and Triumphant, founded by Mark Prophet (1918–1973). We will look briefly at all of these.

The Origin and Purpose of the Theosophical Society

The formation of the Theosophical Society took place over a period of seventy days, from September 7 to November 17, 1875. The main contributors to its formation were H. P. Blavatsky, who was primarily responsible for attracting a number of prominent individuals to her soirées and for creating interest in esoteric and occult topics; H. S. Olcott, who first suggested the idea of a society and who contributed to its organization and purpose; and G. H. Felt, who presented the lecture that incited Olcott to suggest forming a society. Its success depended upon an American milieu receptive to the teachings and practices with which the Theosophical Society was identified: an understanding of the universe beyond the purviews of both scientific inquiry and spiritualist phenomena (the belief that the spiritual realm was scientifically verifiable and that its inhabitants—spirits—were in communication with the physical realm). The society reflected for the most part the Western esoteric tradition, defined by the scholar Antoine Faivre as "an ensemble of spiritual currents in modern and contemporary Western history which share a certain *air de famille*, as well as the form of thought which is its common denominator."[2] This tradition is reflected in such early currents and notions as Hermetism, astrology, alchemy, and magic, and in later permutations and manifestations such as Rosicrucianism, Christian cabbala, Paracelsism, and Christian theosophy.

The immediate impetus for founding a society to investigate this topic occurred on September 7, 1875, in H. P. Blavatsky's apartment on 46 Irving Place (New York City). For some months prior to this meeting, Blavatsky had attracted a number of individuals who had more than a passing knowledge in occult or esoteric teachings to listen to her views on "ancient Magic."[3] On the night of September 7, however, George Henry Felt, who was first introduced to Blavatsky by a member of the editorial staff of the New York *Observer*, Henry

M. Stevens, probably because of Felt's research in the cabbala, was scheduled to give a presentation titled either "The Lost Canon of Proportion of the Egyptians" or "The Cabala."[4] The subject on which Felt lectured was nothing new to him, as he had spoken on the topic as early as 1872 to positive reviews in the press and in the Masonic circles with which he was connected.[5]

Rev. James Henry Wiggin's account of the lecture in the *Liberal Christian* is perhaps the more understandable and accurate accounting of Felt's remarks (the other account is given in Olcott's *Old Diary Leaves*):

> First, he explained the diagram that unlocks the Cabala. It consists of a circle with a square within and without, containing a common triangle, two Egyptian triangles, and pentagon, forming the STAR OF PERFECTION.
>
> This diagram he applies to the Pictures, Statues, Doors, Hieroglyphics, Pyramids, Plains, Tombs, and Buildings of ancient Egypt, and shows that they agree so perfectly with its proportions that they must have been made by its rule.
>
> This same canon of proportion he then applies to GREEK ART to show how its masterpieces of sculpture were carved without models by this rule, and how imperfect is living nature itself in the comparison of proportions.[6]

According to the prospectus announcing the publication of Felt's research that was issued some time between late 1874 and 1876 by J. W. Bouton, the occult publisher, Felt claimed to have discovered the "true geometrical system of the Egyptians, the long-lost and eagerly sought-after key wherewith Egypt unlocked the mysteries of Nature and Art."[7] The cabbala, according to Bouton, was the collected wisdom of Egypt, encompassing "a geometrically and at the same time mystically arranged mathematical construction, a key to early Art, and not only to the sculptured but the written religious records of Egypt" as well as the "works of Nature, both animate and inanimate."[8] Likewise, the Greeks knew the Egyptian secret but could not duplicate the proportionality in their art to the same degree as the Egyptians. The combination of geometry and architecture, which might be considered an interest for Masons, was a means of capturing the wisdom of the ages. "Kaballa" was considered by Felt (in Bouton's prospectus) to reflect the wisdom that was transmitted down through the ages from teacher to disciple. Thus it is associated with the *prisca theologia* (First Theology) of Christian cabbala, which emphasizes the transmission of this wisdom located in all esoteric religious and philosophical traditions through a long line of descent from the divine philosopher Hermes Trismegistos to Asclepius, Orpheus, Pythagoras, Plato, the Neo-Platonists, and the Platonist philosophers of the Renaissance, Marsilio Ficino and Pico della Mirandolo, among others. The prospectus defines "Kaballa" in the following manner:

The word was an abstract term, and meant *Reception, a doctrine received by oral transmission,* and was applied to instruction received orally from inspired teachers and hierophants. It included the entire "Literature of Wisdom," attributed to the earliest ages of antiquity, the esoteric religious sciences, the Mysteries, the Oracles, the occult signs, characters and words employed to express them, and a knowledge of the mystical meaning attached to the common signs, and included all secret and abstruse knowledge, especially mystical or relating to the sources of being. It existed at the earliest traditional ages, and in it the secrets of Nature and the mysteries of religion, and the meaning of the divine revelations, were expressed in the signs before referred to, and it was believed that the Kabbala included and comprehended all knowledge.

The lecture was followed by an animated discussion that ended in Olcott proposing, with the attendees in agreement, the formation of a society to study such claims.[9]

This was, however, not the only topic discussed by Felt. Perhaps even more important to Olcott was his claim, in a letter written to the *Spiritualist* on June 19, 1878, to have discovered the Egyptian priests' ability to evoke "the spirits of the elements, and had left the formularies on record."[10] The relevant passage in this letter follows:

That these so-called elementals or intermediates, or elementary or original spirits were creatures that actually existed, I was convinced through my investigations in Egyptian archæology. . . . I then began to understand and appreciate many things in my Egyptian researches that had been incomprehensible before. As a result I have become satisfied that these zodiacal and other drawings are representations of types in this invisible creation delineated in a more or less precise manner. . . . I discovered that these appearances were intelligences. . . .

I was led to believe that they formed a series of creatures in a system of evolution running from inanimate nature through the animal kingdom to man, its highest development; that there were intelligences capable of being more or less perfectly controlled, as able to impress them as being higher or lower in the scale of creation. . . . Recent researches showing that plants possess senses in greater or less perfection, having convinced me that this system can be still further extended.

I satisfied myself that the Egyptians had used these appearances in their initiations. . . . My original idea was to introduce into the Masonic fraternity a form of initations such as prevailed among the ancient Egyptians. . . . I found that when these appearances, or elementals could not be kept in perfect control, they grew malicious, and despising men whom their cunning taught them must be debased, they became dangerous.

"Elementals" play a significant role in many currents of Western esotericism. They are usually associated with Paracelsus (Theophrastus Bobastus von Hohenheim: 1493–1541), who refers to the four groupings living within the elements of earth, water, air, and fire as gnomes, undines, sylphs, and salamanders. The elements also play an important role in magic, as mentioned by Henry Cornelius Agrippa in his *De occulta philosophia* and much later in Éliphas Lévi's *Dogme et rituel de la haute magie*, and also in cabbalistic literature (as noted by Lévi).[11] This connection of elementals with magic and cabbala help explain the seeming disparity between the Egyptian Canon of Proportion and the accidental discovery of evoking elementals. This ability had impressed Olcott so much that in his Inaugural Address (November 17, 1875) he specifically mentioned the "elementary spirits, whom they [the Neo-Platonists] evoked and controlled—a point of especial interest to us."[12]

> Without claiming to be a theurgist, a mesmerist, or a spiritualist, our Vice-President [Felt] promises, by simple chemical appliances, to exhibit to us, as he has to others before, the races of beings which, invisible to our eyes, people the elements. . . .
>
> The day of reckoning is close at hand, and the name of the Theosophical Society will, if Mr. Felt's experiments result favorable, hold its place in history as that of the body which first exhibited the "Elementary Spirits" in this nineteenth century of conceit and infidelity, even if it be never mentioned for any other reason.[13]

The proof that was to be offered by Felt of the "races of beings which, invisible to our eyes, people the elements," clearly established the validity of the esoteric tradition—a tradition that was under siege by both science and orthodox religion—which Olcott identified as the Neo-Platonists, the theurgists, the Jewish cabbala, and "elements of theosophy and philosophy according to the primitive doctrines of the oriental prophets, in combination with poetical Platonism and the positivism of Aristotle in the form of Grecian dialectics," including "the Oriental doctrine of emanation; the Pythagorean Number of Harmony; Plato's ideas of the creation and the separation from the world of sense."[14] It would appear that Olcott's understanding of Felt's research was based upon Ennemoser's *History of Magic*, which served as an important source for those interested in the esoteric tradition.[15] Herein, the author provides more than enough information about the Magi or Wise Ones (Zoroaster, Ostanes, the Brahmins of India, the Chaldean sages, and the Egyptian priests), magic, the sources of the ancient traditions (India, Persia, Chaldea, Egypt), and the earliest records (the Jewish cabbala, the Hindu laws of Manu, the Zoroastrian *Zend-Avesta*).

Considering the interests displayed by the founders of the society, it is a wonder why it was named the Theosophical Society. Olcott mentioned that other names were suggested—Egyptological, Hermetic, Rosicrucian—but it was Charles Sotheran who most likely introduced the term "theosophy" and its adjectival form "theosophical." The term, as defined in the 1875 *The American Dictionary of the English Language*, seemed to fit the purpose of the society: "Supposed intercourse with God and superior spirits, and consequent attainment of superhuman knowledge by physical processes, as by the theurgic operations of some ancient Platonists, or by the chemical processes of the German fire philosophers [Paracelsians]; also, a direct, as distinguished from a revealed, knowledge of God, supposed to be attained by extraordinary illumination; especially, a direct insight into the processes of the divine mind, and the interior relations of the divine nature." This definition, or at least part of it, seemed to echo the demonstration that Felt had promised; accordingly, it was paraphrased in the preamble of the Theosophical Society.[16]

Four days following the society's inauguration, the person who introduced the term describing its purpose and function, Charles Sotheran, presented a lecture, "Ancient Theosophy: or Spiritism in the Past," before the Society of Progressive Spiritualists in New York, wherein he defined theosophy in the following manner:

> Ancient Theosophy—to many it will be an unmeaning term. What is Theosophy? What does it represent? It is the culture derived from illumination, the veil of Isis lifted for the adepts, the pure and learned, who therein receive the esoteric interpretation of divine truth and the sublime mysteries of the hidden secrets of Nature, including a perfect knowledge of the various degrees of spirits in the "Unseen Universe"—spirits waiting to inhabit mortal bodies and spirits metempsychosised from human tenements into the spheres or circles—their invocation, the use for material purposes of hidden truths—Esotericism or the secret philosophy of Spiritology, of Essenism, of Mysticism, of Theurgy, of Rosicrucianism, of Theosophy.[17]

This definition emphasizes the knowledge that it imparts of the "Unseen Universe," its inhabitants, and its specific manifestations.

The Theosophical Society, as understood by the founders, and articulated mainly by Olcott, its president, was to provide a theoretical explanation of phenomena that was described by Felt in his lecture and the phenomena described in spiritualist circles. This theoretical foundation appears in the theosophies of schools, movements, and adepts ranging from ancient to early modern times both in the occident and orient. It is clear that the early society investigated such phenomena such as the testing of spiritualistic mediums and experimentation in psychometry, thought reading, and mesmerism. But of even greater importance was the ability to activate occult powers and therefore share in these powers. There is abundant evidence that Blavatsky, Judge, and even Olcott were capable of what was considered the greatest occult accomplishment, astral projection.[18] The promise of developing latent powers, a practical occultism, which was the impetus leading to the foundation of the society, was eventually replaced by speculative or theoretical occultism by the early 1880s.[19] There were, however, sporadic outbursts of practical occultism, especially during the presidency of Annie Besant (1907–1933) when "second generation" Theosophy was at its height, and a humanistically oriented ethical activism was very much in evidence, especially in the areas of the politics of independence (for India) and antiwar activism.

During the time when the leadership of the Theosophical Society was in New York, three significant events occurred: the publication of the first great opus by the society's corresponding secretary, H. P. Blavatsky, *Isis Unveiled*;[20] the conversion of the Theosophical Society from a public to a secret society; and its association with the Arya Samaj.

The introduction of the two-volume *Isis Unveiled* to the public on September 29, 1877, was conceived as "a plea for the recognition of the Hermetic philosophy, the anciently universal Wisdom Religion, as the only possible key to the Absolute in science and theology."[21] The work covered the entire gamut of divine wisdom, including elements of the wisdom of India, Tibet, Egypt, Central and South America, and the teachings of Hinduism and Buddhism, the "Kabala," Christianity, and Zoroastrianism, all of which derive from a "primitive 'wisdom-religion.' "[22]

Isis Unveiled provided readers with speculative teachings shortly after the society became a secret organization (1876), precisely because of its practical experiments with magic.[23] As a secret organization, the society resembled the Masonic fraternities, with a hierarchical structure of three sections and three degrees within each section.[24] This was not to last, however. By 1885 the rules of the society no longer mentioned the initiation ceremony and secret membership.[25]

Toward the end of Olcott's and Blavatsky's residence in New York, the society took an even more drastic turn. The council of the Theosophical Society decided to unite with the fundamentalist Arya Samaj of India, the brain-child of Swami Dayanand Sarasvati (1824–1883), whose agent, Hurrychund Chintamon, the president of the Bombay Arya Samaj, supplied Olcott and the society with enough information to convince the leaders of the Theosophical Society that the two organizations had identical principles; Swami Dayanand was perceived by Blavatsky to be "an adept of the Himalayan Brotherhood inhabiting the Swami's body." After assenting to the amalgam of the two societies, the Theosophical Society Council changed the society's name to "The Theosophical Society of the Arya Samaj."[26]

Passage to India

In 1878, the decision was made by both Olcott and Blavatsky to leave New York for India, which was considered one of the primary founts of spiritual wisdom. The two leaders left in December of that year, but not until Olcott requested one of the society's prominent members, General Abner Doubleday (1819–1893), to be acting president. After a stopover in Britain, they left aboard the ship *Speke Hall* for India, and arrived at Bombay Harbor on February 16, 1879.

Shortly after their arrival, an event received with much interest by the populace and the British government, they received a letter from the editor of the *Pioneer* (Allahabad), A. P. Sinnett (1840–1921), who wished to make their acquaintance. Sinnett was to be of invaluable service to the Theosophical leaders, since his paper would soon publicize their activities and spread their views.[27] It was the *Pioneer* that first announced plans of the leaders to establish a journal to be known as *The Theosophist*, the first volume of which was published in October 1879, and which is still published at the society's international headquarters in Adyar (Chennai).[28] The magazine contained many valuable articles on Theosophy, including two defining articles by Blavatsky, "What Is Theosophy?" and "What Are the Theosophists?"[29]

Sinnett was soon to take on an important role in Theosophical teaching by engaging in an extended correspondence (1880–1885) with two of Blavatsky's alleged occult teachers or Masters (of Wisdom)—also referred to as Mahatmas, adepts, arhants, Brothers, Initiates, Occultists—named Koot Hoomi and Morya. The masters were not the creation of Theosophical writers; there are certainly connections to the Mahayana interpretation of *bodhisattva* (a being who practices compassion for the purpose of saving all sentient beings from suffering), to the angels and archangels, to yogis and swamis and, perhaps more directly, to the adepts in novelist Bulwer-Lytton's *Zanoni* (1842) and *The Coming Race* (1871). The concept of a master was thus familiar to those knowledgeable of Western esotericism and Eastern (South Asian) philosophy. They were and are "the adepts of occult knowledge," the custodians of the wisdom upon which all great religions base their philosophy, who themselves "constitute a Brotherhood, or Secret Association, which ramifies all over the East," especially in Tibet, and who attain such knowledge only through "prolonged and weary probation, and anxious ordeals of really terrible severity."[30] As perfected men, the Mahatmas have "power over space, time, mind, and matter" and have developed all those human powers that to ordinary humans appear godlike.[31] In brief, what are merely potential abilities in ordinary humans are activated in the Mahatmas.[32]

Sinnett was to be the chief recipient of well over one hundred letters from the Mahatmas over a period of about five years. During this period he completed a summary of the teachings contained in the letters and published them in *Esoteric Buddhism* in 1883.[33] His previous work, *The Occult World*, primarily discussed the phenomena produced by Blavatsky, so both books contributed to the notoriety of both the Theosophical Society and Blavatsky.

Great Britain and India

The first branch of the Theosophical Society was established in Great Britain on June 27, 1878, by its treasurer, John Storer Cobb. The British Theosophical Society was to have a significant impact upon the society and its founders during the early 1880s.

Olcott and Blavatsky, after their arrival in India in 1879, learned more of the conditions of the population of India and its ancient philosophy. The result was that Olcott became more involved in helping the native populations of India and Ceylon revive and retain their religions against the onslaught of Christian missionaries and the actions of the colonial British government, and Blavatsky most likely became more acquainted with Hinduism and Buddhism from the pandits and bhikkhus of their respective religions.

The public inception of activism on behalf of the Buddhists was in May 1880, when the two founders went on their first tour to Ceylon with six members of the society. While there, both formally accepted the Five Precepts (*pansil*) and presumably the Triple Gem (taking refuge in the Buddha, Dharma, and Sangha), thus becoming Buddhists.[34] The tour was successful because of the leaders' empathy with the populace and because they became Buddhists.[35] This served as the initiation of Olcott's effort to bring about a Buddhist revival through a movement that had been begun by Gunananda Mohottivatte, an activist monk who organized the Society for the Propagation of Buddhism and who was an effective debater in opposition to the Christian missionaries. Olcott's efforts on behalf of the Buddhist cause would continue well into the 1890s.

The early association with the Arya Samaj, Olcott's and Blavatsky's move to India, and Olcott's involvement with the Buddhist revival in Sri Lanka, among other factors, helped to create the perception that the Theosophical Society was becoming more entwined in Eastern occultism at the expense of Western occultism or esotericism. Olcott and Blavatsky did incorporate more Hindu and Buddhist teachings in their writings, but they never lost sight of Western esoteric writers and teachings. The perception that they were more involved in Eastern occultism persisted, however, especially in response to Blavatsky's anticlericalism and frequent assertions about Christianity's dogmatic shortcomings and the evangelizing zeal of its missionaries in the India and other parts of the colonized world.

The outcome of this antagonism was an early attempt on the part of the president of the British Theosophical Society, George Wyld (1821–1906) to create an independent society more aligned with Christian teachings than with the Hindu and Buddhist teachings foisted on its members by its leaders. Wyld was to resign from the Theosophical Society in 1882 after his attempt to realign the society proved futile, but soon thereafter, an even more talented and charismatic leader, Mrs. Anna Bonus Kingsford (1846–1888) and her close colleague, Edward Maitland (1824–1897), were to succeed where Wyld had failed. Kingsford's purpose early on was to initiate a "new Esoteric Church" rather than perpetuate current Christian dogma and practice.[36] The outcome of this work was the publication of *The Perfect Way, or, the Finding of Christ*, which focused on Catholic theosophy rather than the Hindu and Buddhist Theosophy of Blavatsky.[37] Following their enrollment in the Theosophical Society on January 3, 1883, Kingsford and Maitland were elected president and vice-president, respectively, during the Annual General Meeting of the Theosophical Society of Great Britain just four days later.

When A. P. Sinnett arrived in London in April 1883, tensions arose between him and Kingsford; his impending publication (June 1883) *Esoteric Buddhism* attracted attention away from Kingsford's recent publication, *The Perfect Way*. Fellows of the London Lodge of the Theosophical Society (the new name of the Theosophical Society of Great Britain as of June 1883) were attracted to the new teachings contained in Sinnett's book. Kingsford, however, would rather have theosophy perceived in terms broader than the theosophy of the Masters or Mahatmas that Sinnett represented. The tensions between the two positions resulted in reorganizing the London Lodge into two branches: one branch to study Eastern theosophy, and the other to study Christian or Hermetic theosophy. The latter, known as the "Hermetic Lodge, Theosophical Society," was organized on April 7, 1884, and for a short while members of the London Lodge could belong to both branches. When Olcott disallowed dual membership, Kingsford and Maitland formed a new and independent "Hermetic Society." Thus was inaugurated on May 9, 1884, becoming the first independent offshoot from the Theosophical Society. Its stated purpose was to concentrate on the study of the Hermetic teachings (named after Hermes, the initiator of the Sacred Mysteries) and the schools that were based upon these teachings—the Pythagorean, Platonic, and Alexandrian—and the Greek Mysteries. Although the new society was initiated because of Olcott's order that dual membership was not possible, the president of the Theosophical Society did not harbor negative thoughts toward the Hermetic Society and, in fact, offered "good wishes and sympathy for the new society."[38] Also, Kingsford and Maitland, while resigning from the London Lodge, did remain members-at-large of the Theosophical Society.

The Coulomb Affair and the Society for Psychical Research

The Theosophical Society retained its novelty status mainly because of the continued interest in all matters occult, especially those that originated in the mystic East, and the ability of Madame Blavatsky to articulate and to demonstrate the powers derived therefrom. It was, therefore, natural to expect some other organization to come into existence to investigate phenomena, "commonly known as Psychical, Mesmeric, or Spiritualistic." In 1882, just such an organization, the Society for Psychical Research (S.P.R.), was established.[39] In a telling statement, the society states quite clearly that "Membership of the Society does not imply the acceptance of any particular explanation of the phenomena investigated, nor any belief as to the operation, in the physical world, of forces other than those recognised by Physical Science."[40] Although the founders of the Theosophical Society thought of themselves as investigators of the occult, the S.P.R. statement indicated that the new organization was to conduct its investigations in a much more scientific and positivistic setting.

On May 2, 1884, the governing council of the S.P.R. appointed an investigative committee to conduct an examination of phenomena associated with the Theosophical Society, including appearances of apparitions (including the two Mahatmas, Koot Hoomi and Morya) and evidence of astral projection by its members, the letters from the Mahatmas that were produced either by the "precipitation" of writing on blank paper by no known means or the transportation of these letters through solid matter, and the "evocation of sound without physical means."[41] Olcott, Blavatsky, Sinnett, and other members of the Theosophical Society were questioned. The preliminary report of the committee was issued in December 1884 and it concluded: "On the whole (though with some serious reserves), it seems undeniable that there is a *prima facie* case, for some part, at least, of the claim made, which, at the point which the investigations of the Society for Psychical Research have now reached, cannot, with consistency, be ignored. And it seems plain that an actual residence for some months in India of some trusted observer—his actual intercourse with the persons concerned, Hindu and European, so far as may be permitted to him— is an almost necessary pre-requisite of any definite judgment."

As the investigation was proceeding, a shocking revelation was published in the September 1884 issue of the *Madras Christian College Magazine*. It was an exposé (under the title "The Collapse of Koot Hoomi") containing fifteen letters purportedly written by Blavatsky to Emma Coulomb, instructing the Coulombs to devise the means for producing false phenomena. Why this piece was published demands some explanation of the character of Emma Coulomb. Born Emma Cutting, she was, at the time of her expulsion from the society on May 14, 1884, the housekeeper at the Theosophical Society headquarters in Adyar, and her husband, Alexis Coulomb, served as its handyman. Blavatsky, however, knew Cutting from 1871, when both were residing in Cairo. Cutting, who married Coulomb in the early 1870s, eventually arrived at the Bombay Theosophical Society headquarters on March 28, 1880, in considerable financial distress. Blavatsky invited them to stay, and just a few days later (April 3), both joined the society and assumed the household duties of the headquarters, at Blavatsky's invitation. The Coulombs remained in that position after the transfer of headquarters to Adyar in 1882. They were not, however, content with their situation there. Mrs. Coulomb spoke ill of Blavatsky, claiming she lent money to her that was never repaid, expressing her hostility toward the society, and claiming that trap doors and other devices were being constructed by her husband, Alexis, to produce trick manifestations. Because of these actions, the Board of Control voted to expel her and her husband from the society for slandering it.[42]

The most serious charge that was raised by the Coulombs concerned the legitimacy of the Theosophical Society, which was established by the Masters, so Blavatsky claimed, and Blavatsky's contention that she was a disciple and messenger of the Masters. Letters from the Mahatmas would appear from no conventional source, or writing would manifest on paper through precipitation. One method was their appearance in a wooden cabinet known as "the Shrine," situated in the "occult room," a room adjacent to Blavatsky's bedroom at headquarters in Adyar. One account by William T. Brown, a Scotsman interested in Theosophy who visited the headquarters in September 1883, describes his experience about "the Shrine":

> One evening, shortly after my arrival at Adyar, some letters were being sent by Chelas [disciples] to their Masters, and I was permitted to enter the "Occult Room" and see the process going on. The letters were put into an almirah, in a richly ornamented recess called by some "the Shrine." There were some seven of us then present, four of whom were Chelas. These gentlemen, after placing their letters as aforesaid, offered up incense and prostrated themselves according to the Hindu manner of evincing devotion and respect. In about two minutes Madame [Blavatsky], who was standing by my side in an attentive attitude, received a psychic telegram, and indicated that the answers had come to hand. The almirah was accordingly opened, and, in place of the letters "posted," others were there, enclosed in Tibetan envelopes and written on Tibetan paper. D[amodar] K. M[avalankar] (a Chela of the Master Koot Hoomi) discovered something more than was expected, and exclaimed, "Here is a letter from my Master to Mr. Brown." I then received from his hands a memorandum, written with blue pencil.[43]

Mr. Coulomb claimed to have prepared sliding panels in the Shrine as well as other construction work that would allegedly allow someone to insert letters in the Shrine from the hollow space between the occult room and the bedroom of Madame Blavatsky.

The Coulombs' publication of letters by Blavatsky admitting fraudulent activity and trickery in their September 1884 exposé was already embarrassing to Blavatsky. The visit in November of the investigator for the S.P.R., Richard Hodgson (1855–1905), to conduct further investigation of the phenomena claimed by the Theosophists, and the *Report of the Committee Appointed to Investigate Phenomena Connected with the Theosophical Society* issued by the S.P.R. on June 24, 1885, would prove devastating to the both Blavatsky and the society. This report, known as the Hodgson Report, concluded that a fraud was perpetrated by Blavatsky: that the letters supposedly written by the Mahatmas Koot Hoomi Lal Sing and Morya were written either by Blavatsky or her Theosophical assistant and chela (disciple) Damodar K. Mavalankar, thus indicating that the Masters were fictional characters; that the Coulombs assisted her in producing fraudulent phenomena; and that many of the witnesses made knowingly false statements about the existence of the Masters. As for her motive, Hodgson concluded that it was neither due to the "aloe-blossom of a woman's monomania" nor due to her desire for monetary gain. Rather, it was his suspicion that she was a "Russian spy" and that the Theosophical Society was actually a political organization. This suspicion was nothing new. It dated back to the time of Blavatsky's and Olcott's passage to India in 1878–1879 and to the British Indian government's surveillance during her first year in India. Hodgson, therefore, concurred with the government's suspicions, namely, that "her real object has been the furtherance of Russian interests."[44]

The Secret Doctrine and Blavatsky's Final Years

Although the Hodgson Report seriously damaged Blavatsky's credibility, the society continued as a viable organization, and a few years later Blavatsky completed her magnum opus, *The Secret Doctrine*.[45] This work, which took up much of Blavatsky's time and effort from the time of her departure from India in 1885 until its publication in 1888, represented a summary of the ancient wisdom as Blavatsky understood it. It was divided into two volumes with a total of 1,474 pages. The first volume, *Cosmogenesis*, discusses cosmic evolution and so expands upon the contents of *Isis Unveiled*, whereas the second volume, *Anthropogenesis*, discusses the evolution of humanity through a succession of "root races," five of which have already appeared on this planet. Based on stanzas translated from *The Book of Dzyan* (seven in volume 1 and twelve in volume 2), a work unknown to modern scholarship, composed by an unattested people and in a language unknown to philosophy,

The Secret Doctrine contains the following ideas: one, there exists a single, supreme, eternal, immutable, unknown and unknowable, infinite principle or reality (1: 14); two, there is a fundamental unity to all existence (1: 120, 276); three, the eternal, manifested universe and everything within it is subject to the "law of periodicity, of flux and reflux, ebb and flow" (1: 17); four, the evolution of nature—material and spiritual—reflects progressive development and not merely repetitive action (1: 43, 277–78; 2: 653); five, the evolution of the individual is not limited to one life but continues through innumerable lifetimes made possible by the process of reincarnation, that is, the entrance of Self—the trinity of Spirit, Soul, and Mind—into another (human) body (2: 302–306); six, this evolution is brought about by the law of cause and effect, or karma—good actions leading to good consequences, bad actions to bad consequences—thus assigning full responsibility to the individual who performs the actions (1: 639, 642–47); seven, the structural framework of the universe, humanity included, is by nature septenary in composition (2: 605–41); eight, the cyclic, evolving universe is hierarchical in constitution, each component—for instance, the planets and the sun in our solar system—consisting of seven constituents, thus illustrating the correspondence between the microcosm of the human being and the macrocosm of the universe (2: 68f., 434f.); nine, human evolution on this planet is progressing through seven distinct stages known as root races, each root race divided further into seven subraces—in our present state of evolution, for instance, we belong to the fifth subrace (the Anglo-Saxon) of the fifth root race (1: 610; 2:lf., 86f., 300f., 434f., 688f.); ten, the individual is a microcosm, a "miniature copy of the macrocosm" (1: 274); and eleven, the universe is guided and animated by a cosmic hierarchy of sentient beings, each having a specific mission (1: 274–77).

In this book and in other activities of this period, Blavatsky established and defined those teachings that would become synonymous with the Theosophical Society. Prior to the publication of *The Secret Doctrine*, she settled in London in May 1887, established the Blavatsky Lodge on May 19, founded the magazine *Lucifer* in order to provide "some sort of public propaganda" for *The Secret Doctrine*, and established the Esoteric Section of the Theosophical Society which, under the leadership of Blavatsky as Outer Head (the Inner Heads were the Masters) for the expressed purpose of instructing a small number of select students on esoteric matters.[46] Because the Esoteric Section was independent of the administration of the Theosophical Society, it could be argued that in all intents and purposes it was a society within a society.

Two significant publications appeared from Blavatsky's pen. While at Fontainebleau in July 1889, Blavatsky wrote or "translated" portions of an alleged work, "The Book of the Golden Precepts," known as "The Voice of the Silence," which was presumed to be part of the same series of texts as that from which the stanzas of the *Book of Dzyan* (appearing in *The Secret Doctrine*) had been derived. This short work was Blavatsky's attempt to delve into the mystical.

During the same month came the publication of *The Key to Theosophy*, a popular work that served as a type of catechism for those interested in the society or for those seeking basic information about Theosophy.

Shortly after these publications, Blavatsky died on May 8, 1891, leaving a void that was filled by a recent recruit into the society who happened to be a well-known advocate in labor activism and Fabian socialism, Annie Besant (1847–1933). Besant soon became the leading propagandist for the society and Outer Head of the Eastern School of Theosophy (the new name for the Esoteric Section), a position she shared with one of the founders of the Theosophical Society, William Q. Judge. Most important, she was to play a major role in the division of the Theosophical Society in the mid-1890s and in introducing, together with her colleague, Charles Webster Leadbeater (1854–1934), a millenarian element in the early decades of the twentieth century in the person of Jiddu Krishnamurti (1896–1986). Even more troubling for some Theosophists was her complicity in what they perceived as a major shift from or alteration of Blavatsky's Theosophical teaching, especially as is explained in *The Secret Doctrine*. This version of Theosophy has been disparagingly called "Neo-Theosophy" by its opponents.

The Division of the Theosophical Society

The partition of the Theosophical Society cannot be blamed solely on doctrinal disagreements but was also due to personal ambitions and visions regarding the direction in which the society would take. This problem was obvious in the circumstances surrounding the formation of the Hermetic Society under Kingsford and Maitland in 1884 and the issue of the place of Christian theosophy within the Theosophical movement. We find a similar situation in France, where another prominent Theosophist, Lady Caithness (née María Mariátegui, 1830–1895), also had an affinity for Christian theosophy, especially in her books *The Perfect Way* and *Théosophie universelle* (the first part of which was titled *La Théosophie chrétienne*).[47] Unlike Kingsford, Lady Caithness never rejected Sinnett's and Blavatsky's Eastern Theosophy and so remained in the Theosophical orbit until her death in 1895. In the same year, a split in the Theosophical Society did occur, brought about by events that have never been completely understood by commentators. A superficial explanation revolves around the two Outer Heads of the Eastern School of Theosophy, Judge and Besant, with a third party, the president of the Theosophical Society, Col. Olcott, also involved. The immediate circumstances surrounding the split involved Judge's "alleged misuse of the Mahatmas' names and handwriting."[48] This charge, brought to Olcott by Besant on February 6, 1894, led to Olcott's suggestion of forming a Judicial Committee to investigate the accusation. The committee met in London in June 1894 to consider "certain charges of misconduct, preferred by Mrs. Besant against the Vice-President of the Society [Judge], and dated March 24th, 1894."[49] Judge submitted a number of protests to prevent the Committee from ruling on the charges. The one protest that had carried weight was the following:

> The reason is not that an investigation is avoided. Such an investigation will not be avoided. But on constitutional and executive principle I shall object from beginning to end to any committee of the Theosophical Society considering any charge against any person which involves an inquiry and decision as to the existence, names, powers, functions, or methods of the "Mahatmas or Masters." I shall do this for the protection of the Theosophical Society now and hereafter, regardless of the result to myself. The Society has no dogma as to the existence of such Masters; but the deliberations of an official committee of the Society on such a question, and that is the first inquiry and decision necessarily beginning such a deliberation, would mean that the Theosophical Society after over nineteen years of unsectarian work is determined to settle this dogma and affix it to the Constitution of the Society.[50]

The committee decided that the issue was out of its jurisdiction, so Mrs. Besant then suggested a Jury of Honor to consider the charges.[51] Judge declined on legal grounds, so the solution that was accepted were the submission of two statements before the European Sectional Convention, one each by Judge and Besant.

Although the European Sectional Convention declared the whole issue settled, the affair did not end there. Disgruntlement continued among some within the society. One member, Walter Old, the treasurer and recording secretary at Adyar who was suspended from the Eastern School of Theosophy for breaking the code of occult secrecy in August 1893, found himself for all intents and purposes identified by Besant in her convention address as a Judge hater, an implication to which he objected to Olcott.[52] His pique led him to turn documents over to a journalist for the *Westminster Gazette*, Edmund Garrett, who then published a series of articles beginning in October 1894 entitled "Isis Very Much Unveiled: the Story of the Great Mahatma Hoax."[53] Following this publication, Judge issued a statement on November 3, *By Master's Direction*, claiming he was the founder of the Eastern Section, that Mrs. Besant came under the influence of certain forces, Black Magicians, who influenced certain Brahmins in India in order to gain control of the Theosophical Society and to nullify Blavatsky's work by accusing her of fraud and forgery.[54] One of the agents singled out was a close associate and guide of Mrs. Besant, Professor Gyanendra N. Chakravarti. The detail of the plot was to have Olcott resign from the presidency of the Theosophical Society, cut off Judge, and to make Mrs. Besant president. It was Judge's contention that the work of the Theosophical

Society was to reflect Western esoteric learning, rather than the learning in India.[55] Finally, at the end of this document was inserted an Eastern School of Theosophy Order declaring Judge to be the sole head of the Eastern School and ending Mrs. Besant's headship of the same.[56]

A month later (April 1895), at the Theosophical Society Convention, Olcott made it very clear that he was upset with the allegations of Judge against Chakravarti and Besant. He also realized that at this juncture the American Theosophical Society would certainly declare its autonomy from the leadership (Olcott) of the Adyar Theosophical Society should Judge be forced to resign. Mrs. Besant then addressed the convention in December 1894 and again reviewed the case, ending with the proposal that he resign the office of vice president of the Theosophical Society.[57] It was clear that positions were taken for and against Judge: that the American section was behind him but many members outside of the United States were resigning or becoming increasingly dissatisfied with the whole affair.

The situation remained unstable in early 1895, until its culmination in the American Section declaring its autonomy and appointing Judge as its president for life at its convention held on April 28–29, 1895.[58] Rather than declaring itself as seceding from the Adyar Theosophical Society, the new society viewed its action at the convention as a declaration of its autonomy from the headquarters in Adyar and reaffirmed its direct relationship with the 1878 society that Blavatsky and Olcott left when they sailed for India. Thus ended the American Section of the Theosophical Society. In its place was the Theosophical Society in America.[59]

The Theosophical Society (Pasadena) and Its Offshoots

The Theosophical Society in America continues to this day under its current title, The Theosophical Society, with headquarters currently in Pasadena and Altadena, California. Following Judge's death on March 21, 1896, the presidency briefly passed to Ernest Temple Hargrove (d. 1939). The Eastern School of Theosophy under Judge's leadership as Outer Head remained within the new society. The new Outer Head, following Judge's death was revealed to be Katherine Tingley (1847–1929), who in 1897 became the head of the Theosophical Society following the resignation of Hargrove. Hargrove in disgust formed his own Theosophical Society in 1898 with two hundred members of Tingley's Theosophical Society in America. His New York-based reformed Theosophical Society in America, later renaming itself the Theosophical Society in 1908, elected A. H. Spencer to be acting president.[60] It remained a viable organization for many years until it, and possibly its Esoteric School of Theosophy, entered a period of "indrawal" from active work.[61]

Tingley pursued a more activist role as leader of the society, emphasizing social and educational reforms in conformity with Theosophical teachings. She moved the headquarters from New York City to the unlikely locale of Point Loma, San Diego, California, laying the cornerstone of the new Theosophical community in February 1897. As the "Leader and Official Head" of an organization that emphasized applied Theosophy, Tingley accordingly renamed the society the Universal Brotherhood and Theosophical Society. One important contribution to applied Theosophy was the establishment in 1900 of an educational system known as Raja Yoga, which was to provide education from the beginning grades up to the university level.

With the closing of the lodges in 1903, most of the committed and talented members moved to Point Loma, engaging not only in the educational experiment but also in related activities such as agriculture and horticulture, writing, researching, publishing, and participating in dramatic and musical productions.

Following Mrs. Tingley's death in 1929, the direction of the Universal Brotherhood and Theosophical Society reflected a more intellectual and passive character under its intellectual and scholarly leader, Gottfried de Purucker (1874–1942). Once again, the society, now renamed the Theosophical Society, moved in the direction of teaching and studying the core Theosophical works. Toward the close of Dr. de Purucker's tenure in 1942, the Point Loma property was sold, partly due to financial concerns, and the headquarters subsequently moved to Covina, a small community east of Los Angeles. In that same year de Purucker died, leaving the society under the leadership of a cabinet for the next three years until a new leader, Col. Arthur Conger (1872–1951), was elected in 1945.[62] Conger's election was not greeted as enthusiastically as Theosophists had hoped, however. For one thing, he suffered from Parkinson's disease, but this was not the reason why "dismissals" of prominent individuals in the cabinet took place in 1946. According to certain documents, dissatisfaction with Conger's leadership arose with his assertion that he was a "Teacher," thereby claiming the same status as H. P. Blavatsky. The opposition to Col. Conger's claimed esoteric status on the part of a number of prominent members, that is, to his claim that he was the Outer Head of the Esoteric Section, the "Messenger of the Masters," and the Teacher of esoteric truths, led to a number of members being relieved of their positions at headquarters. Some of those thereafter chose to leave the headquarters.[63] One of Conger's last acts was to move the headquarters in Covina to Pasadena and Altadena in 1950 and 1951. Conger continued as leader until his death in February 1951, which led to another controversial episode in the Theosophical Society's history. Conger had designated William Hartley (1879–1955) as his successor, but the cabinet acknowledged James A. Long (1898–1971) as leader instead, the argument being that the original document containing Col. Conger's declaration was not produced, only a photostatic copy. As a result, Hartley, together with his followers, left Covina and established their own Theosophical Society, which is now head-quartered in The Hague, Netherlands.

Long undertook a number of actions disengaging the society from a number of activities and properties. The Theosophical University was closed, as were all the lodges chartered during the tenure of Dr. de Purucker, and Swedish property in Visingsö was sold.[64] On a somewhat more positive note, he established the monthly magazine, *Sunrise,* which is published to this day. He also went on extensive lecture tours overseas and set about visiting the membership both within and outside the United States. Upon his death in 1971, Miss Grace F. Knoche became the leader of the Theosophical Society and remains so as of this writing.[65]

Two other organizations of note arose out of the Pasadena Theosophical Society. The first, the Temple of the People, arose from the Syracuse (New York) Lodge of the Universal Brotherhood and Theosophical Society in order to lay the "mental, physical, and spiritual foundations of the coming sixth race." This group, founded by Dr. William H. Dower (1866–1937) and Mrs. Francia LaDue (1849–1922) in 1898, moved to California in 1904 and established its headquarters, known as Halcyon, near Oceano. Dr. Dower soon opened a sanitarium so he could continue to practice medicine. A colony, the Temple Home Association, was established in 1905 with the leadership Mrs. LaDue as Guardian in Chief. She was to head the association and the temple until her death in 1922. Dr. Dower then took over the duties formerly held by Mrs. LaDue and built the Blue Star Memorial Temple. Following Dr. Dower's death, all responsibilities passed on to Mrs. Pearl Dower, who organized the property according to its present specifications, a ninety-five-acre property consisting of fifty-two homes, thirty of which are owned by the temple; the William Quan Judge Library, which also houses the temple offices; and an apartment for visitors. Harold Forgostein succeeded her in 1968; his main contribution was the painting of twenty-two pictures at the behest of Dr. Dower. These paintings depicted the Native Americans' contributions to understanding the balance in nature and scenes from the life of Hiawatha, both important in temple teachings. These paintings are now in the temple's University Center. Following Mr. Forgostein's death in 1990, Eleanor L. Shumway assumed the leadership role of the community and remains the Guardian in Chief as of this writing. There are about 250 members worldwide.[66]

Another association, the United Lodge of Theosophists, was organized by a former member of both the Universal Brotherhood and Theosophical Society at Point Loma and Hargrove's Theosophical Society. Robert Crosbie (1849–1919), a Canadian living in Boston who became a Theosophist under the influence of W. Q. Judge, originally lent his support to Mrs. Tingley as Judge's successor and followed her to Point Loma around 1900 in order to help in the work she initiated there. By 1904, he lost confidence in her leadership and methods for private reasons, left Point Loma for Los Angeles, where he associated for a time with Hargrove's Theosophical Society and with a number of Theosophists who were later to support the his organization. In 1909, Crosbie, with a number of acquaintances who shared his view that only the Source Theosophy of Blavatsky and Judge contained the teachings of Theosophy as it was intended to be delivered in modern times (that is, from the latter decades of the nineteenth century), formed the United Lodge of Theosophists in Los Angeles. What set this group apart from other Theosophical societies was and is its stress on Source Theosophy and those writings in philosophical accord with Blavatsky's and Judge's interpretation of Theosophy. Unlike other Theosophical organizations, leaders and teachers are rejected in favor of the view that all members (associates) are students. Anonymity is stressed, conforming to the Hargrove Theosophical Society proclivity for this trait, but to a greater degree.

A few years following Crosbie's death, the United Lodge of Theosophists in Los Angeles established the Theosophy Company in 1925 to serve as fiduciary agent for the associates. No leader was recognized, but John Garrigues, one of the early acquaintances of Crosbie, was acknowledged as a leading figure in the lodge until his death in 1944, along with Mrs. Grace Clough and Henry Geiger. It was under the influence of another student, the Indian Parsi B. P. Wadia (1881–1958), that the lodge was organized into an international association of study groups. Such is the nature of the United Lodge of Theosophists to this day—a group of lodges and study groups organized in several countries, including Belgium, Canada, England, France, India, Italy, Mexico, The Netherlands, Nigeria, Sweden, and Trinidad.[67]

Neo-Theosophy, the World Teacher, and the Liberal Catholic Church

Although the Adyar Society was not free from controversies of its own, the ensuing discord took place primarily within the Theosophical Society, with some notable exceptions. One of the issues concerned adherence to Blavatsky's Theosophical teachings. Although many Theosophists, from the leaders on down, believed they were reflecting her teachings, discrepancies were clearly perceptible in their writings, if not to them certainly to the Blavatskyites. Disapproval of the new teachings was a long time in coming. The Back to Blavatsky movement was first mentioned in 1917 by the editor of a Theosophical magazine devoted to prison-related topics entitled the O. E. Library Critic, Henry Newlin Stokes (1859–1942), and the movement developed thereafter throughout the Theosophical world. This movement was in reaction to the neglect by Theosophical Society leadership (referring primarily to Mrs. Besant, who became president in 1907, and her colleague, C. W. Leadbeater) of Blavatsky's works in favor of their own.[68] For many years, both Besant and Leadbeater engaged in activities that gradually shifted Theosophy from a study to a practice. Both collaborated in supraphysical phenomena, including gaining evidence of reincarnation and participating in the astral plane. A number of books followed from these studies, including *Occult Chemistry* (1908), *Talks on the Path of Occultism* (1926), *Thought Forms* (1901), and *The Lives of Alcyone* (1924).[69] This collaborative work was halted because of charges of immoral conduct perpetrated by Leadbeater on young boys, thereby presenting the specter of pederasty. The charges led to his resignation in 1906, once they were made public. Within three years (1909), however, Mrs. Besant reinstated him in the Theosophical Society and their work continued.

Within a short time of his reinstatement in the Theosophical Society, Leadbeater, allegedly through his psychic powers, discovered a young Brahmin boy, Jiddu Krishnamurti, whom he claimed would become the vehicle of a great spiritual force, the World Teacher, the Lord Maitreya or the Christ to prepare for the coming sixth subrace of humanity: the next stage in the evolution of humanity. Such a claim was first made by Blavatsky, but Leadbeater and Besant modified her teaching so that it became one associated more with their version of Theosophy, called disparagingly Neo-Theosophy by F. T. Brooks.[70] Over the next twenty years, Mrs. Besant and the Theosophical Society leadership were immersed in furthering this millenarian teaching by training and preparing the young man for his eventual overshadowing by the World Teacher, and by preparing the members of the society for his coming. The promotion of the idea of the coming World Teacher was further enhanced by the formation of a new organization—the Order of the Star in the East—which was established in Benares in 1911 by George Arundale (1878–1945) for the express purpose of preparing for the coming of the World Teacher. Over the next twenty years, the movement looked promising, with reports of Krishnamurti showing evidence of a personality other than his own.[71] Yet there was some displeasure with this attempt at creating and sustaining a millenarian movement, especially with the increasing role of the Liberal Catholic Church in the society after 1914. Even before the society's alliance with the Liberal Catholic Church, a major breach within the society took place in 1913 with the departure of the influential general secretary of the German Section, Rudolf Steiner (1861–1925), who took with him fifty-five of the sixty-nine German lodges under his leadership. Because of his antagonism to the teachings surrounding the World Teacher and the establishment of the Order of the Star in the East, he created a new society in early 1913, the Anthroposophical Society, after the charter of the German Theosophical Society was revoked. From that point on, Steiner pursued his own interests: esoteric Christianity, education (the Waldorf schools), agriculture (biodynamics), and eurythmy (translating "the sounds, phrases, and rhythms of speech or the dynamic elements of music into movement and gesture").[72]

The increasing role of the Liberal Catholic Church in the Theosophical Society would further separate Neo-Theosophical teachings from the Blavatskyite understanding of Theosophy. The church was part of the Old Catholic Church movement that went back to the Catholic Church in Holland, a movement that separated from Roman Catholicism in 1704. The church remained in Holland until Arnold Harris Mathew (1852–1919) came to Great Britain following his consecration in 1908 as the Old Catholic Bishop for Great Britain and Ireland. In the ensuing years, most of the clergy of the church in Britain were Theosophists, including its future leader, Bishop James Ingall Wedgwood (1883–1950). Wedgwood consecrated Leadbeater as bishop on July 22, 1916, thus ensuring Theosophical leadership and a close alliance with the Theosophical Society. Not only did Wedgwood introduce Theosophical teachings into church doctrine he also allied the church with the World Teacher and Krishnamurti. The involvement of the Liberal Catholic Church (so renamed in 1918) in the Theosophical Society carried no official or administrative connection; rather, the church served as a viable contributor to the society's most important work at hand, the World Teacher movement. In addition, the church served as a source of ritualism that became part and parcel of Neo-Theosophical teaching.

The great promise of the coming of the World Teacher abruptly came to an end when Krishnamurti announced the dissolution of the Order of the Star (the new name of the Order of the Star in the East) in 1929 and his own resignation from the Theosophical Society. This created a significant blow to the popularity of the society. Its membership, which had grown considerably over the previous decade to well over 40,000 members, quickly pummeled to a little over 20,000. The shock certainly affected Besant's health, which declined over the next four years, resulting in her death on September 20, 1933. She was soon followed (in 1934) by her cohort, Leadbeater, leaving a group of loyal followers who made every effort to follow their teachings. George Arundale served as president of the Theosophical Society from 1934 to 1945 after Besant's death, and carried on a more Theosophically oriented activism rather than the eclectic activism of Mrs. Besant. One immediate result was the establishment of the Besant Educational Trust and the Besant Memorial School in Adyar, both in 1934, and the foundation of the International Academy of the Arts (later known as Kalakshetra, "the field or holy place of arts"), in 1936 by Dr. Arundale's wife, Srimati Rukmini Devi (1904–1986).

Following Dr. Arundale's death in 1945, a protégé of Leadbeater, C. Jinarajadasa (1875–1953), the Outer Head of the Eastern School of Theosophy, carried on in that post after Leadbeater's death, and became president in 1946. Noted as a prolific author and lecturer, one notable contribution he made in that office was to inaugurate the School of the Wisdom in 1949.

Succeeding Jinarajadasa were Nilakanta Sri Ram (1889–1973) who, during his presidency of twenty years (commencing in 1953), was responsible for the construction of the new Adyar Library building; John S. Coats (1973–1979); and the current president, Radha Burnier (1980–).

Quasi-Theosophical Organizations

A number of movements provided teachings that were partially based on Theosophical concepts. These include the Anthroposophical Society of Rudolf Steiner (mentioned above), the Arcane School of Alice Bailey (1880–1949), the "I AM" Religious Activity of Guy Ballard (1878–1939), and the Church Universal and Triumphant (formerly the Summit Lighthouse), founded by Mark Prophet (1918–1973). Aside from the Anthroposophical Society, which is based on the esoteric Christianity of Rudolf Steiner, the other groups share the common feature of including Masters or Mahatmas to provide legitimacy to the teachings propounded. Superior beings who guide humanity have been acknowledged from earliest times: angels in the Judeo-Christian tradition, bodhisattvas in the Buddhist tradition, the initiated brotherhoods of Rosicrucianism and later Rosicrucian organizations, the spirits in the spiritualist movement, the Masters or Mahatmas of Theosophy, the Tibetan master (Djwhal Khul) of Alice Bailey (1880–1949), Blavatsky's Mahatma Morya, and the Ascended Masters of both the "I AM" Religious Activity and the Church Universal and Triumphant.

Alice Bailey became a member of the Theosophical Society in 1915 and from that time on was very much under the influence of Blavatsky's teachings, especially those contained in *The Secret Doctrine,* and of the president of the society, Annie Besant. A new Theosophical influence came into her life in 1919, however: the Master Djwhal Khul or simply the Tibetan. This contact with a Master was not totally unexpected, however, for twenty years earlier, at the age of fifteen, Bailey claimed to have been visited by another Master of Wisdom, Koot Hoomi, who declared that she would work in the world on his behalf. This was to come to fruition with the publication of her first received book in 1922 in her role as amanuensis to her Master, followed by a series of books that ended only with her death in 1949.[73] In addition to her role as amanuensis, she, with her husband Foster Bailey, established a correspondence school in April 1923. This school, known as the Arcane School and modeled after the Esoteric Section of the Theosophical Society, was set up to answer the questions raised by readers of her publications.

The principal teachings of the Arcane School are described as follows: one, that the Kingdom of God, the Spiritual Hierarchy of our planet, is already invisibly present and will be materialized on earth; two, that there has been a continuity of revelation down the ages and that from cycle to cycle God has revealed himself to humanity; three, that God Transcendent is equally God Immanent, and that through human beings, who are in truth the sons of God, the three divine aspects—knowledge, love, and will—can be expressed; four, that there is only one divine Life, expressing itself through the multiplicity of forms in all the kingdoms of nature, and that the sons of men are, therefore, ONE; five, that within each human being there is a point of light, a spark of the one flame—this is believed to be the soul, the second aspect of divinity, "the *demonstration* of the divine livingness in each person which is our goal, and discipleship is a step upon the way to that attainment"; six, that an ultimate perfection is possible for the individual aspirant and for humanity as a whole through the action of the evolutionary process (involving a "myriad of developing lives, each with its place within the scheme . . . [leading] to those exalted spheres where the Lord of the World works out the divine Plan"); seven, that there are certain immutable laws governing the universe, and man becomes progressively aware of these as he evolves, these laws being expressions of the will of God; and eight, that the basic law of our universe is to be seen in the manifestation of God as *Love.*

The Arcane School remains an active organization, although a number of other groups have developed from the Bailey-inspired teachings. Among these groups are the Meditation Groups, Inc., and the School for Esoteric Studies.

Nine years following the foundation of the Arcane School arose another group that claimed to have received teachings from a higher realm from Ascended Masters. This group, known as the I AM Religious Activity, was founded in 1931 by Guy W. Ballard (1878–1939) and his wife Edna Wheeler Ballard (1886–1971) for the purpose of releasing the teachings of the Great White Brotherhood or the Ascended Masters.[74] The Messenger of the Ascended Masters was at first Guy Ballard, who was allegedly chosen by the Ascended Master Saint Germain on Mount Shasta in 1930. The purpose of the Masters, in the words of Godfré Ray King [Guy Ballard], is to help us realize our own divine nature (known as "The Mighty I AM Presence" or the Individualized Presence of God) and to cause individuals to emanate Divine Love.[75] In a broader context, these teachings, known as the Great Law of Life, promulgated by Saint Germain through his Messenger, Guy Ballard, were intended to initiate the Seventh Golden Age or the "I AM" age of eternal perfection.[76]

When Ballard died, he was declared to be an Ascended Master by his wife and successor, Edna, who led the organization until her death in 1971. A highly publicized trial was held in 1940, when charges of mail fraud were brought by members of Ballard's personal staff. One of the charges that deserves mention, typical in the 1940 court case in the District Court of the United States (Southern District of California, Central Division, No. 14496), is as follows:

That the defendants falsely represented that Guy W. Ballard, now deceased, alias Saint Germain, Jesus, George Washington, and Godfre Ray King, had been selected and thereby designated by the alleged "ascended master," Saint Germain, as a divine messenger; and that the words of "ascended masters" and the words of the alleged divine entity, Saint Germain, would be transmitted to mankind through the medium of the said Guy W. Ballard; whereas in truth and in fact the defendants well knew that the said Guy W. Ballard was not a "divine messenger" and all of said representations so made were false and fraudulent, and the defendants and each of them well knew that defendant Guy W. Ballard had no such divine or supernatural power.

This charge, based upon the presupposition that the teachings were so bizarre that no one could possibly accept them as true, led to the revocation of the organization's use of the mail. The conviction of Edna, her son Donald, and others was appealed and overturned in the Supreme Court on April 24, 1944. This was a significant judgment because the court states that religious belief cannot be made an issue in a court of law. In other words, the court agreed with the ruling in *Watson v. Jones* (13 Wall. 679, 728): "The law knows no heresy, and is committed to the support of no dogma, the establishment of no sect."[77]

The parent organization, the Saint Germain Foundation, has its world headquarters at Schaumburg, Illinois, but Mount Shasta is still a major center for the I AM Religious Activity. A board of directors is currently in charge of the I AM Religious Activity. Perhaps its most publicized event at present is a pageant on the life of Jesus. Known as the "I AM COME!" it is held on Mount Shasta in the G. W. Ballard Amphitheater.[78]

The connection between the I AM Religious Activity and the Church Universal and Triumphant is through a splinter group that arose out of the former. This group, the Bridge to Freedom (currently called The Bridge to Spiritual Freedom, Inc.), was founded in 1952 by Geraldine Innocente (?–1961) and her mother, Mary Innocente. Geraldine was recognized as a Messenger of the Ascended Master El Morya, and brought forth many dictations from this Master. Soon after the foundation of the Bridge to Freedom, other Messengers appeared, one of whom was to become well known in the Bridge to Freedom with the publication of dictations received from the Masters. These dictations were publicized through the efforts of Frances Ekey, who, with this Messenger, established a Philadelphia-based organization, Lighthouse of Freedom, in 1958. In the same year, this Messenger, Mark L. Prophet, founded his own group in Washington, D.C., the Summit Lighthouse, in order to disseminate the Masters' teachings. By the early 1960s, Prophet assumed complete independence from the Lighthouse of Freedom. In 1961, Mark met a recently married student from Antioch College in Ohio, Elizabeth Clare Wulf Ytreberg (1939–), at a Summit Lighthouse service.[79] Soon after she became his disciple, they carried on a love affair that led to their marriage in 1963 after they divorced their spouses. By 1964, Elizabeth became a Messenger, her position given legitimacy since it is alleged that she was anointed by Saint Germain. Over the next few years, Elizabeth and Mark Prophet oversaw a growing movement, due in large part to Elizabeth's marketing ability and Mark's sermons.

In 1966, the headquarters of the Summit Lighthouse was moved to Colorado Springs, Colorado on a property known as La Tourelle. Two significant events during this time were the founding of Summit University in 1971 and the publication of one of the Prophets' more important works, *Climb the Highest Mountain*, in 1972.[80]

In 1973, Mark died of a massive stroke. The event was interpreted as an ascension, with Mark now known as the Ascended Master Lanello. Lanello has dictated a number of messages to Elizabeth that were published as *Cosmic Consciousness: The Putting On of the Garment of the Lord* in 1976.

Two years previously (1974), the Church Universal and Triumphant was established, with the Summit Lighthouse now identified as the publishing arm of the church. In 1976, the headquarters was first moved to southern California on the campus of the former Pasadena College and then to Malibu on the former campus of Thomas Aquinas College, which it renamed Camelot in 1978. Four years later (1981), the church bought property in southwestern Montana on a 12,000-acre parcel of land known as the Royal Teton Ranch.[81] It formally moved its headquarters there in 1986, where it operated Summit University, conducted retreats, and engaged in farming, ranching, publishing, and education.[82]

The move to Montana seems to have been occasioned by Mrs. Prophet's fear of a coming nuclear holocaust. This was occasioned by predictions of a nuclear war in March and April of 1990, as discussed in her 1991 *Gnosis* interview with Jay Kinney and Richard Smoley, wherein she speaks of a power elite in the U.S. government that is responsible for "heinous crimes" and the failure of nuclear war with the Soviet Union to occur. Her response to the latter was that "the danger of nuclear war *was* heightened" and that this danger would not end until 2002.[83] In expectation of this coming war, nuclear shelters were constructed on the property and arms were purchased to prepare for post-nuclear chaos.[84] The possession of firearms led to the arrest of two officials in 1989 for illegally purchasing the same.[85] Also, about two thousand church members moved to the headquarters, fearing an imminent attack. The outcome of this episode was the disillusionment of a number of church members, their leaving the church, the resignation of a number of church officials, and discussions within the larger community whether the Church Universal and Triumphant was in fact a dangerous or destructive cult.[86]

In the mid-1990s, Elizabeth Clare Prophet turned over her administrative duties to Gilbert Cleirbaut, a former director of human resources for Union Carbide, British Petroleum, and the government of Alberta, who had to meet the challenge of solving the financial difficulties of the church. Cleirbaut remained president until 1999, when duties were taken over by the Church's board of directors and management.[87]

For years there was the suspicion that Elizabeth Clare Prophet had been suffering from memory lapses in addition to the diagnosis of epilepsy in 1998.[88] It was then confirmed that Mrs. Prophet was suffering from Alzheimer's Disease, causing her to retire as spiritual leader.[89]

The teachings of the Church Universal and Triumphant have recently been summarized in a publication titled *Keys to the Kingdom and New Dimensions of Being*.[90] A few of the more fundamental teachings are as follows:

(1) We humans have a Higher or Divine Self. There is a God Within or the I AM Presence, the Christ Self or the Inner Teacher that mediates between God and humans and who speaks within—our conscience so to speak, and the soul evolving on earth. It is the soul that reincarnates and so evolves through time and space, that determines your essence or character. It is also the soul that returns to God. This return is known as the ascension or reunion with God.

(2) Life is like a classroom. We are put on earth to learn lessons and to move on. Free will allows us to make decisions and to undo decisions that we learn are wrong. Whatever we do will have a consequence, and this we identify as karma or "deed." What is performed in the past affects us in the present. What we do now will affect our future, including our future lives. Connected to karma is reincarnation, or the passage of the soul from life to life. It is looked upon as good because it allows us to experience our past actions and to make amends for our past mistakes.

(3) Because of the human karma, the "astral effluvia" or the "misqualified energy" of God's lifestream that flows from our I AM Presence and the planetary karma that we bear prevents us from being reunited with God until all are counteracted with positive energy.

(4) As spiritual beings, our bodies contain seven energy centers or *cakras*, the latter defined as "internal step-down transformers that regulate the flow of God's energy according to the needs of the four lower bodies."[91] The *cakras* are located from the crown to the base of the spine: the *crown cakra* is the location of thinking and cogitation; the *third eye cakra* is the location where we experience God as concentration and so see creation as God sees it; the *throat cakra* refers to the power of speech; the *heart cakra* is the location of our experience of God as love; the *solar-plexus cakra* is the location of peace; the *seat-of-the-soul cakra* is the location where the soul is anchored in the body.

(5) Within the heart is a secret chamber containing a threefold flame, the spark of life that projects from the Higher Self. The flame consists of three colors: blue, yellow, and pink, referring respectively to power, wisdom, and love (or faith, hope, and charity). This is the Trinity within: the power of the Father, the wisdom of the Son, and the love of the Holy Spirit. The flame within the human heart is the divine spark and potential of one's divinity.

(6) The third aspect of the Trinity, the Holy Spirit, is the vehicle through with all the teachings of Jesus, not preserved in the scriptures, will once again be brought forth in the age of Aquarius, the age of the Holy Spirit. What the Holy Spirit will bring is enlightenment specifically by transmuting hatred into love, which is manifested by the dispensation of the violet flame.

(7) There is a heavenly hierarchy consisting of masters, angels, and cosmic beings. Among these figures are members of the Great White Brotherhood who have come forth to assist humanity in its spiritual evolution. Of special importance is Saint Germain, the patron of the United States and the hierarch of the Aquarian age. He is the founder of the keepers of the Flame Fraternity, an organization of individuals who serve with members of the heavenly hierarchy. Important also are the World Teachers, Jesus and Kuthumi, the holder of the office of Cosmic Christ and Planetary Buddha, Lord Maitreya.

Taking the above into account, the overarching teaching centers on a separation and return: the separation of sparks of the light—the I AM Presences—from the Central Sun or God and the eventual return of the sparks through countless reincarnations of steady progress. The Great White Brotherhood (or Ascended Masters) aids in this progress by guiding humanity through its journey. The ultimate goal is to return to the Divine Source through the ascension.

NOTES

1. The minutes of the meeting held at 46 Irving Place in New York City on September 8, 1875.

2. Antoine Faivre, "Questions of Terminology Proper to the Study of Esoteric Currents in Modern and Contemporary Europe," in *Western Esotericism and the Science of Religion*, edited by Antoine Faivre and Wouter J. Hanegraaff (Leuven: Peeters, 1998), 2.

3. Henry Steel Olcott, *Old Diary Leaves: First Series America 1874–1878*, second edition (Adyar, Madras: Theosophical Publishing House, 1974), 13. Originally published in 1895. Hereafter abbreviated *ODL*). I, 114. This is a six-volume set of the reminiscences of Henry Olcott. The reminiscences surround the activities of Blatavsky, Olcott, and others vis à vis the Theosophical Society. The dates extend from 1874 to 1898.

4. On Felt's connection to Stevens, see Michael Gomes, "Studies in Early American Theosophical History: VI. Rev. Wiggin's Review of George Henry Felt's 1875 Lecture on the Cabala," *Canadian Theosophist* 71/3 (July–August 1990): 67. It is also confirmed by Henry J. Newton, who was to become the first treasurer of the Theosophical Society, in the article "Theosophy's Origin Exposed," which appeared in the New York *Herald*, November 10, 1895. On the subject of the presentation, see Olcott, *ODL*, I, 115; and *The Liberal Christian*, 25 September 1875, reprinted in Michael Gomes's "Studies in Early American Theosophical History," 63–69.

5. Felt was a 32° member of the Scottish Rite who later (1877) joined the Ancient

Arabic Order of Nobles of the Mystic Shrine (popularly known as the Shrine and its members the Shriners). He was also an inventor and by profession a civil and mechanical engineer. For his Masonic connection, see John Patrick Deveney, "Nobles of the Secret Mosque: Albert L. Rawson, Abd al-Kader, George H. Felt and the Mystic Shrine," *Theosophical History*, 8/9 (July 2002): 250 and 255; for his career as inventor and engineer, see James A. Santucci, "George Henry Felt: The Life Unknown," *Theosophical History*, 6/7 (July 1997): 248–52. His lecture, "The Kaballah of the Egyptians and Canon of Proportions [sic] of the Greeks," appeared in the New York *Dispatch* on May 26, 1872.

6. Compare Olcott, *ODL*, I, 115. Therein, Olcott mentions that the lecture was accompanied by "drawings to illustrate his theory that the canon of architectural proportion, employed by the Egyptians as well as by the great architects of Greece, was actually preserved in the temple hieroglyphics of the Land of Khemi." He claimed that the "secret of the geometrical problem of proportion" could be read on a temple wall that agrees with the actual "pictures, statues, doors, hieroglyphs, pyramids, planes, tombs and buildings of Ancient Egypt."

7. Prospectus for *The Kaballah of the Egyptians and the Greek Canon of Proportion*, issued by J. W. Bouton (N.Y.: J. W. Bouton, 1877). On file at the Library Company of Philadelphia. Here is what Josephine Ransom wrote in *A Short History of the Theosophical Society* (Adyar: Theosophical Publishing House, 1938), 77: "This diagram not only unlocked the secrets of the Kabala, but when applied to ancient Egyptian architecture as well as to the Greek, showed how all masterpieces of both were constructed, even the statues. In music, in prismatic colours, in the configuration of leaves, and in the world's circumference, he found the same law of proportional harmony. This diagram, applied to the Egyptian table of hieroglyphics, indicated the parts to be read, and revealed startling correspondences. He applied it also to the Mosaic account of creation and the story of Eden, and showed here also the correspondences, all pointing to a common knowledge in the Kabalistic schools of the long past."

8. Prospectus for *The Kaballah of the Egyptians*.

9. One of the attendees, Henry J. Newton, stated in the New York *Herald* many years later (November 10, 1895) that the "lecture was very disappointing, as it was not at all what was expected, but was a dry dissertation on geometry and ancient mathematics generally without reference to cabbala." Newton, who was to become the first treasurer of the Theosophical Society, claimed it was he, not Olcott, who "moved a committee be appointed to investigate the phenomena referred to [by Felt], and made a statement quite at length, setting out the importance of the information received, if true, and our duty to determine whether or not it was true." This claim also appeared in other publications, including *Light* (a spiritualist journal) in the November 23 and 30 (1895) issues, and reprinted in *Theosophical History*, 1/7 (July 1986), 175–85, which published an article by "QuÆstor Vitæ."

10. Olcott, *ODL*, I, 117. Felt's own extensive account of his researches appears in this letter, reprinted in Olcott, *ODL*, I, 126–31.

11. One early source states that Paracelsus borrowed from Plato's *Phædrus*, Faust's "Compulsion of Hell," and Petro de Albano's *Heptameron*. See Joseph Ennemoser, *The History of Magic*, translated by William Howitt (New Hyde Park, N.Y.:

University Books, 1970), I, 6 (originally published in German under the title *Geschichte der Magie* [Leipzig]: F. A. Brockhaus, 1844).

12. "Inaugural Address of the President, Delivered before the Society, November 17, 1875," Archives of the Theosophical Society, Pasadena, Cal. 17.

13. Ibid., 23, 24.

14. Ibid., 16, 17.

15. My thanks to Joscelyn Godwin for giving additional information on the elementals in an e-mail dated April 30, 2003.

16. "Preamble and By-Laws of the Theosophical Society," Archives of the Theosophical Society, Pasadena, Cal., 5: "to obtain knowledge of the nature and attributes of the Supreme Power and of the higher spirits *by the aid of physical processes.*"

17. Compare this definition with Antoine Faivre's understanding of "theosophy" in Faivre and Hanegraaff, *Western Esotericism and the Science of Religion*, 23: "Theosophy is a gnosis that has a bearing not only on the salvific relations the individual maintains with the divine world, but also on the nature of God Himself, or of divine persons, and on the natural universe, the origin of that universe, the hidden structures that constitute it in its actual state, its relationship to mankind, and its final ends."

The lecture was also delivered on December 1, 1875, before the Theosophical Society and later published in the *Spiritual Scientist* (Boston) in nine installments: 4/6 (April 13, 1876): 61–62; 4/7 (April 20, 1876): 76–77; 4/8 (April 27, 1876): 88; 4/9 (May 4, 1876): 101; 4/10 (May 11, 1876): 116–17; 4/11 (May 18, 1876): 124–25; 4/12 (May 25, 1876): 140–41; 4/13 (June 1, 1876): 1,148–49; 4/14 (June 8, 1876): 161.

18. John Patrick Deveney, *Astral Projection or Liberation of the Double and the Work of the Early Theosophical Society* (Fullerton, Cal.: Theosophical History, 1997) (Theosophical History Occasional Papers, vol. 6). In a letter from Olcott to W. Stainton-Moses (1839–1892), dated May 18, 1875 (reprinted in W. Stainton-Moses, "Early Story of the Theosophical Society," *Light* [July 9, 1892]: 331), Olcott remarked that he believed that his spirit did travel outside his body while asleep. Also, W. Q. Judge, in a lecture given in 1876 (reprinted in John Patrick Deveney, "An 1876 Lecture by W. Q. Judge on His Magical Progress in the Theosophical Society," *Theosophical History* 9/3 [July 2004]: 12–20), claimed the abilities of engaging in out of body experiences, of influencing others by impressing his thoughts upon them, of precognition, and of clairaudience.

19. Deveney, *Astral Projection*, 65–73.

20. H. P. Blavatsky, *Isis Unveiled* (N.Y.: J. W. Bouton, 1877; reprinted Los Angeles: Theosophy Company, 1931).

21. Blavatsky, *Isis Unveiled*, I, vii. The Wisdom Religion is identified with magic in *Isis Unveiled*, II, 590: "MAGIC is spiritual WISDOM; nature, the material ally, pupil and servant o the magician."

22. Blavatsky, *Isis Unveiled*, II, 216.

23. *H. P. Blavatsky Collected Writings: 1874–1878*, compiled by Boris de Zirkoff. Volume I, 3rd edition (Wheaton, Ill.: Theosophical Publishing House, 1988), 193–94.

24. Circular composed chiefly by Olcott and dated May 3, 1878. It was reprinted in *H. P. Blavatsky Collected Writings: 1874–1878*, I, 375–78.

25. Ransom, *A Short History of the Theosophical Society*, 548.

26. Olcott, *ODL*, I, 396–97. The council's statement was recorded by Augustus Gustam, the recording secretary, dated May 22, 1878. Swami Dayananda was recognized as "its lawful director and chief" (ibid.). See also *ODL*, I, 397–98 and Ransom, *A Short History of the Theosophical Society*, 105–106. Dayananda's goal was to promote the Vedas—the ancient compositions of the north Indian Aryan tribes composed between 1600 and 500 B.C.E.—as the font of Truth. This served as the basis of his attempt to return Hinduism to a more pristine form devoid of later corruptive teachings and practices such as polygamy, child marriage, caste, *sati* [suttee], and polytheism. For the relationship of Swami Dayanand and the original object of the Society, see Deveney, *Astral Projection*, 61–65.

27. Henry Steel Olcott, *Old Diary Leaves: Second Series, 1878–83* (Adyar: Theosophical Publishing House, 1974 [originally published in 1900]), 28; Alfred Percy Sinnett, *Autobiography of Alfred Percy Sinnett* (London: Theosophical History Centre, 1986), 16. See Michael Gomes, "Theosophy in A. P. Sinnett's *Pioneer*," *Theosophical History* 8/5 (January 2001): 155–58.

28. *H. P. Blavatsky Collected Writings: 1879–1880*, compiled by Boris de Zirkoff. Volume 2 (Wheaton, Ill.: Theosophical Publishing House, n.d. [1967]), 83–84.

29. *The Theosophist* 1/1 (October 1879): 2–5 and 5–7. Reprinted in the *H. P. Blavatsky Collected Writings: 1879–1880*, 87–106.

30. A. P. Sinnett, *The Occult World*, 8th ed. (London: Theosophical Publishing Society, n.d. [reprinted 1906; originally published in 1881]), 21; A. P. Sinnett, *Esoteric Buddhism*, 5th ed. (San Diego: Wizards Bookshelf, 1981 [originally published in 1883]), 11.

31. W. Q. Judge, *The Ocean of Theosophy* (Los Angeles: Theosophy Company, 1971 [originally published in 1893]), 11.

32. See also H. P. Blavatsky, *The Key to Theosophy* (Los Angeles: Theosophy Company, 1973 [originally published in 1889]), 215–18; H. P. Blavatsky, *The Secret Doctrine*, two volumes in one (Los Angeles: Theosophy Company, 1974 [originally published in 1888], I, 273; Annie Besant, *The Theosophical Society and the Occult Hierarchy* (London: Theosophical Publishing House, 1925), passim; Annie Besant, *H. P. Blavatsky and the Masters of the Wisdom* (London: Theosophical Publishing House, 1907), 10–21; Robert Ellwood, *Theosophy* (Wheaton, Ill.: Theosophical Publishing House; Quest Books, 1986), 118–44 ; Ransom, *A Short History of the Theosophical Society*, 42–56; and G. de Purucker, *Occult Glossary*, 2nd ed. (Pasadena: Theosophical University Press, 1996 [originally published in 1933]), 94–95. For a personal and antagonistic account of the Masters in a number of esoteric movements, see Kenneth Paolini and Talita Paolini, *400 Years of Imaginary Friends* (Livingston, Mont.: Paolini International, 2000).

33. First and second edition (London: Trubner). Both were reprinted several times thereafter. The Mahatma letters, number around 270 letters if letters besides those to Sinnett are counted. An e-mail message from Jerry Hejka-Ekins, dated January 21, 1998, gives a rough count of 149 letters to Sinnett (sent between 1880 to 1885), plus some 129 letters that were published by C. Jinarajadasa in two series (*Letters from the Masters of the Wisdom: First Series* [Adyar: Theosophical Publishing House, 1924] and *Second Series* [Adyar: Theosophical Publishing House, 1925]). These letters were to a number of individuals, including Col. Olcott, W. T. Brown,

E. W. Fern, Subba Row, John Smith, R. Keshava Pillai, S. Ramaswamier, Dr. Hübbe-Schleiden, Mary Gebhard, Franz Hartmann, and many more.

Tony Hern, in an e-mail message dated January 29, 1998, writes that 176 Mahatma letters are held at the British Museum, placed there in 1939 by the literary executor of Mr. Sinnett's estate, Maud [Mr. Sinnett's spelling] Hoffman (?–1953) (Mr. Sinnett died on June 26, 1921). After having the letters examined by handwriting experts, the British Museum accepted them. In 1952, they were bound in seven volumes and microfilmed on four reels. According to James Moore ("The Blavatsky-Gurdjieff Question: A Footnote on Maude Hoffman and A. T. Barker," *Theosophical History* 3/3 [July 1990]: 77), Miss Hoffman decided to make the letters public because of differences between Mr. Sinnett and the president of the Theosophical Society, Annie Besant. It was Miss Hoffman also who chose her personal friend, A. T. Barker, to serve as editor.

The copyright of the letters is currently held by the Mahatma Letters Trust, set up by Christmas Humphreys as the first trustee and currently headed by Tony Maddock. My thanks again to Tony Hern for the above information.

34. The Five Precepts include refraining from taking a life, from taking what is not given, from incontinence, from speaking falsehood, and from any state of indolence arising from the use of intoxicants.

35. Both, however, claimed to have already been Buddhists, so the ceremony was actually a confirmation rather than a conversion. See Olcott, *ODL,* II, 167–68.

36. Information based upon Michael Gomes's "The Coulomb Case" (to be published in 2004 as volume 10 of Theosophical History Occasional Papers).

37. London: Field and Tuer, 1882.

38. Henry Steel Olcott, *Old Diary Leaves: Third Series, 1883–87,* 2nd ed. (Adyar: Theosophical Publishing House, 1972 [originally published in 1904, 2nd ed. in 1929], 101. Gomes, "The Coulomb Case."

39. Quotation from the 1885 Constitution and Rules, section 2 (located in the *Proceedings of the Society for Psychical Research,* 3 (London: Trubner and Co., 1885), 492.

40. 1885 Constitution and Rules, section 2.

41. "Report of the Committee appointed to Investigate Phenomena Connected with the Theosophical Society," 201–3. Published in the *Proceedings of the Society for Psychical Research* 3 (1885).

42. This board was established on February 19, 1884, to run the society's everyday affairs. The Board was needed because Olcott and Blavatsky were leaving for Europe: Blavatsky for medical reasons, Olcott on society business and as an advocate for the Buddhist cause in Ceylon.

43. William T. Brown, *Some Experiences in India* (London: London Lodge of the Theosophical Society, 1884). Quoted in *The Esoteric World of Madame Blavatsky,* collected by Daniel H. Caldwell (Wheaton, Ill.: Quest Books, Theosophical Publishing House, 2000 [originally published as *The Occult World of Madame Blavatsky,* 1991]), 221.

44. The conclusions are given on pages 312–17 of the Hodgson Report (*Report of the Committee Appointed to Investigate Phenomena Connected with the Theosophical Society, Proceedings of the Society for Psychical Research* 3 [1885]).

45. Helena Petrovna Blavatsky, *The Secret Doctrine*, 2 vols. (Los Angeles: Theosophy Company: Los Angeles 1974 [originally published in 1888]).

46. Anonymous (perhaps Annie Besant), "The Eastern School of Theosophy: Historical Sketch," reprinted in *Theosophical History* 6/1 (January 1996): 11. It was originally printed in Madame Blavatsky's journal, *Lucifer* 3/14 (October 15, 1888).

47. *The Perfect Way, or, The Finding of Christ* (Boston: Esoteric Publishing, 1888); *Théosophie universelle*, vol. 1: *Theosophie chrétienne* (Paris: Carré, 1886).

48. Letter to William Q. Judge from H. S. Olcott, dated February 7, 1894, quoted in Anonymous, *The Theosophical Movement: 1875–1950* (Los Angeles: Theosophy Company, 1951), 205.

49. Henry Steel Olcott, *Old Diary Leaves: Fifth Series (January, 1893–April, 1896)* (Adyar: Theosophical Publishing House, 1932; reprinted 1975), 175.

50. Judge based his statement on Article 13, section 2 of the society's constitution, which read: "2. No Fellow, Officer, or Council of the Theosophical Society, or of any Section or Branch thereof, shall promulgate or maintain any doctrine [e.g. existence of the mahatmas] as being that advanced or advocated by the Society" (*The Theosophical Society. European Section. General and Sectional Constitution and Rules* [London: General Secretary's Office, 1894], 21). See Brett Forray, "William Q. Judge's and Annie Besant's Views of Brahmin Theosophists," *Theosophical History* 10/1 (January 2004): 25 note 7. See also Olcott, *ODL: V*, 181–89.

51. Anonymous, *The Theosophical Movement: 1875–1950*, 228.

52. Walter Old, known as Sepharial to most astrologists (March 20, 1864–December 29, 1929), was one of the Inner Group pupils of Blavatsky, a vice president of the Blavatsky Lodge, and a general secretary of the British Section of the Theosophical Society. It was he, together with Sidney Edge, who suspected Judge of forging the Mahatma letters that he supposedly received. See Kim Farnell, "Walter Richard Old: The Man Who Held Helena Blavatsky's Hand," *Theosophical History* 8/2 (April 2000): 71–83.

53. Anonymous, *The Theosophical Movement: 1875–1950*, 237–38.

54. Duplicated on Blavatsky Archives Online at www.blavatskyarchives.com/ judgebmd1894.htm. "These Black Magicians have succeeded in influencing certain Brahmans in India through race-pride and ambition, so that these, for their own advantage, desire to control and manage the T.S. through some agent and also through the E.S.T. They of course have sought, if possible, to use one of our body, and have picked out Mrs. Besant as a possible vehicle."

55. "All her vast work in the West, with western people, upon western religions and modern science, was toward this end, so that when she comes again as Messenger—as hinted at in the *Key to Theosophy*—much of the preparatory work should have been done by us and our successors. It is, *the establishment in the West of a great seat of learning where shall be taught and explained and demonstrated the great theories of man and nature which she brought forward to us, where western occultism, as the essence combined out of all others, shall be taught*" (www.blavatskyarchives.com/judgebmd1894 .htm). The most recent study on this case appears in Brett Forray's "William Q. Judge's and Annie Besant's Views of Brahmin Theosophists," *Theosophical History* 10/ 1 (January 2004): 5–34.

56. "By Master's Direction," in www.blavatskyarchives.com/judgebmd1894.htm; Olcott, *ODL V*, 252–60; Ransom, *A Short History of the Theosophical Society*, 297–306; Anonymous, *The Theosophical Movement: 1875–1950*, 241–45.

57. Olcott, *ODL: V*, 266–302; Ransom, *A Short History of the Theosophical Society*, 307–308; Anonymous, *The Theosophical Movement: 1875–1950*, 246–47.

58. Anonymous, *The Theosophical Movement: 1875–1950*, 250–51.

59. Anonymous, *The Theosophical Movement: 1875–1950*, 252–53; Ransom, *A Short History of the Theosophical Society*, 310–11; Olcott, *ODL V*, 310–20; Michael Gomes, "From the Archives," *Theosophical History* 10/1 (January 2004): 37.

60. John Cooper, "The Esoteric School within the Hargrove Theosophical Society," *Theosophical History*, 416–7 (April-July 1993): 179.

61. The last document ascribed to the Esoteric School of Theosophy is *Aids and Suggestions* No. 18, dated December 7, 1907. See Cooper, "The Esoteric School within the Hargrove Theosophical Society," 185. The "indrawal" most likely took place in the latter part of 1938, although John Cooper (180) considers 1935 to be the actual date. *The Theosophical Quarterly*, the major magazine of the society, ended its publication run in October 1938.

62. On Col. Conger's life and role as leader of the Theosophical Society, see "Colonel Arthur L. Conger," *Theosophical History* 7/1 (January 1998): 35–56

63. James Santucci, "Editor's Comments," *Theosophical History* 8/1 (January 2000): 1–3; "The Conger Papers 1945–1951: Part 1," introduced by Kenneth R. Small, *Theosophical History* 8/1 (January 2000): 11–34.

64. The Theosophical University was chartered by Katherine Tingley in 1919. Although closed in 1951, its charter has been kept current by its trustees. My thanks to Mr. Will Thackara of the Theosophical University Press (Pasadena).

65. For an account of Point Loma and the subsequent history of the Theosophical Society, see Emmett A. Greenwalt, *California Utopia: Point Loma: 1897–1942*, 2nd ed. (San Diego, Cal.: Point Loma Publications, 1978 [originally published in 1955]).

66. This information is derived from the entry "Temple of the People" by James Santucci in *The Encyclopedia of Cults, Sects, and New Religions*, 2nd ed. edited by James R. Lewis (New York: Prometheus Books, 2002), 722–723.

67. Derived from "United Lodge of Theosophists (U.L.T.)," in *Encyclopedia of Cults, Sects, and New Religions*, 760–762.

68. On H. N. Stokes, see my article "H. N. Stokes and the *O. E. Library Critic*," *Theosophical History* 1/6 (April 1986): 129–139.

69. *Occult Chemistry* (Adyar: Theosophical Publishing House, 1908); *Talks on the Path of Occultism*, 3 vols.: vol. 1, *At the Feet of the Master* (6th ed., Adyar: Theosophical Publishing House, 1971); vol. 2, *The Voice of the Silence* (6th ed., Adyar: Theosophical Publishing House, 1973); vol. 3, *Light on the Path* (2nd ed., Adyar: Theosophical Publishing House, 1931); *Thought Forms* (Adyar: Theosophical Publishing House, 1901); *The Lives of Alcyone*, 2 vols. (Adyar: Theosophical Publishing House, 1924).

70. A review of the evidence on Krishnamurti appears in James Santucci, "Foreword," to *Krishnamurti and the World Teacher Project: Some Theosophical Perceptions*, Theosophical History Occasional Papers 5 (Fullerton, Cal.: Theosophical History, 1997), vi–vii, xi–xiii (notes 24–27 and 29). The term "Neo-Theosophy" was first introduced by Ferdinand T. Brooks (1873–1916) in his book *Neo-Theosophy Exposed* (1914,

reprint Edmonton: Edmonton Theosophical Society, 1991). For an overview of his life, see Michael Gomes, "Nehru's Theosophical Tutor," *Theosophical History* 7/3 (July 1998): 99–108.

71. Santucci, "Foreword," i–ii.

72. "Anthroposophical Society in America," in *The Encyclopedia of Cults, Sects, and New Religions*, 63.

73. *Initiation, Human and Solar* (New York: Lucis Press, 1972 [first published 1922]. *Esoteric Psychology*, 2 vols; vol. 1 (New York: Lucis Press, 1991 [first published 1936]); vol. 2 (New York: Lucis Press, 1970 [first published 1942]). See also *The Externalisation of the Hierarchy* (New York: Lucis Press, 1989 [first published 1957]).

74. According to Robert Ellwood, "Making New Religions: The Story of the Mighty 'I AM'," *History Today* 38 (June 1988): 20–21, Ascended Masters are those who have ascended beyond the physical realm and who possess within them the individualized "I Am Presence," that is, the individualized God within. For the summary statement of this teaching, see Mrs. Guy W. Ballard and Donald Ballard's *Purpose of the Ascended Masters "I AM"* (reproduced in Paolini and Paolini, *400 Years of Imaginary Friends*, 209. See also J. Gordon Melton, "The Church Universal and Triumphant: Its Heritage and Thoughtworld," in *Church Universal and Triumphant in Scholarly Perspective*, edited by James R. Lewis and J. Gordon Melton (Stanford: Center for Academic Publication, 1994), 8–12.

75. Godré Ray King, *The Magic Presence*, 5th ed. (Schaumburg, Ill.: Saint Germain Press, 1982 [first published in 1935]), 173–75. Godré Ray King is the pseudonym of Guy Ballard.

76. Melton, "The Church Universal and Triumphant," 7–8. James Lewis, ed., *Odd Gods: New Religions and the Cult Controversy* (Amherst, N.Y.: Prometheus Books, 2001): 294.

77. Pertinent quotes from the 1944 case are given on the Web site "The Witches Voice, Inc." at www.witchvox.com/white/wballard.html.

78. For information on this pageant, go the Saint Germain Foundation Web site, www.saintgermainfoundation.org/pageant.htm.

79. Ytreberg was her married name. Elizabeth married Dag Ytreberg in 1960.

80. Melton, "The Church Universal and Triumphant," 16.

81. Ibid., 16.

82. One article on the church's ranching activities is "Church Universal and Triumphant to Sell Ranch: Sect's Annual Report said Contributions Fell by nearly $1 million between 1997 and 1998," *Spokane Spokesman Review*, October 9, 2000. Available on the Ross Institute Web site at www.rickross.com/groups/cut.html. Its headquarters are now at the "North Ranch" near Livingstone, Montana.

83. Jay Kinney and Richard Smoley, "War on High: The *Gnosis* Interview with Elizabeth Clare Prophet," *Gnosis* vol. 21 (Fall 1991): 32, 34, 35.

84. This is known as the "shelter cycle" (1989–1990). See Scott McMillion, "Prophet's Daughter is Writing a Book about CUT," *Bozeman Chronicle*, March 16, 1998. Available on the Ross Institute Web site at www.rickross.com/groups/cut.html.

85. The officials were Mrs. Prophet's then husband, Edward Francis, and church member Fernon Hamilton. They were "indicted on federal conspiracy charges for using false names to purchase $150,000 in weapons—including .50-caliber rifles de-

signed for combat." See Philip J. LaVelle, "Disputes, Legal Woes Dog Church," San Diego *Union Tribune*, November 12, 1997.

86. W. Michael Ashcraft and Leah Shaw, "Church Universal and Triumphant," in *Religions of the World: A Comprehensive Encyclopedia of Beliefs and Practices*, vol. 1, edited by J. Gordon Melton and Martin Baumann (Santa Barbara: ABC CLIO, 2002), 347.

87. Joe Kolman, "Cleirbault Cites Lack of Family Time as One Reason for Leaving," *Gazette Bozeman Bureau*, July 3, 1999. Available on the Ross Institute Web site at www .rickross.com/groups/cut.html.

88. Scott McMillion, "Prophet Family Struggles with Problems Right at Home," *Bozeman Chronicle*, March 16, 1998, and "Elizabeth Clare Prophet Diagnosed with Epilepsy," *Religion Briefs*, January 8, 1998. Both available on the Ross Institute Web site at www.rickross.com/groups/cut.html.

89. Scott McMillion, "Prophet Stepping Down as Spiritual Leader of CUT," *Bozeman Chronicle*, January 3, 1999. Available on the Ross Institute Web site at www .rickross.com/groups/cut.html.

90. Compiled from the works of Mark L. Prophet and Elizabeth Clare Prophet (Livingston, Mont.: Summit University Press, 2003).

91. *Keys to the Kingdom*, 61. The four lower bodies are the emotional, physical, mental, and etheric bodies. These bodies clothe the soul. The *etheric body* has within it the "blueprint of the soul identity, the blueprint that will manifest as consciousness, as mind, as emotion and as the physical matrix itself" (45). This body has a lower and higher body: the higher refers to the superconscious mind and the lower body refers to the subconsious records and patterns of all we have ever experienced in the material cosmos. The *mental body* is an instrument intended as the vehicle of the mind of God and the mind of the Christ and the Buddha. The *desire body* is to express the desire of God, and the *physical body* is intended to be the vehicle of the soul and spirit.

13

The Solar Temple "Transits": Beyond the Millennialist Hypothesis

James R. Lewis

[Various] problems, internal and external, are crucial in understanding the OTS's gradual distortion and disintegration. Di Mambro had gathered around him a group that lent an appearance of reality to the fictions he created. And now this imaginary universe began to come under critical scrutiny. The head of the Solar Temple apparently decided to respond by taking himself and his followers away from the scene altogether.

> —Jean-François Mayer, "Our Terrestrial Journey Is Coming to an End"

In October 1994, fifty-three members of the Order of the Solar Temple (Ordre du Temple Solaire, or OTS) in Switzerland and Québec were murdered or committed suicide. On October 4, a fire destroyed the villa of Joseph Di Mambro (the group's leader) in Morin Heights, Canada. Police found five charred bodies in the ruins. Three had been stabbed to death before the fire. At 1:00 A.M. on October 5, a fire started in Ferme des Rochettes, near Cheiry, in the Canton of Fribourg, one of the centers of the Solar Temple in Switzerland. Police found twenty-three bodies in a room that had been converted into a temple. Some had been shot; many others were found with their heads inside plastic bags. At 3:00 A.M. the same day, three chalets inhabited by members of the Solar Temple caught fire almost simultaneously at Les Granges sur Salvan, in the Valais Canton. Police found twenty-five bodies, along with the remains of the devices that had initiated the fires as well as the pistol that had shot the people near Cheiry.

For many months prior to this initial spate of murder-suicides, rumors of financial mismanagement had been circulating among Solar Temple members. On September 30, shortly before the group's dramatic final "transit," a three-month-old infant was killed in Canada by a wooden stake driven through its heart. The parents, who were ex-members of the Temple, were also brutally murdered. Surviving members explained that Di Mambro had ordered the killing because the baby was the Anti-Christ. Several days later, Di Mambro and twelve followers convened a ritual Last Supper. The murder-suicides took place not long after this meeting. Fifteen members of the inner circle—referred to as the "awakened"—took poison. Thirty others—the "immortals"—were shot or smothered to death. Eight others—termed "traitors"—were also murdered.

The plan seems to have been for the fire to more or less completely destroy everything in the Swiss centers. This would have compelled investigators to focus on the group's self-interpretation of their actions—a self-interpretation embodied in four letters or "Testaments" sent to sixty journalists, scholars, and government officials. However, because the incineration devices at the main center in the Cheiry farmhouse failed to ignite, many documents and other artifacts were left intact. One of the testaments, addressed "To All Those Who Can Still Understand the Voice of Wisdom," issued a call for other Solar Temple members and sympathizers to follow their example: "[F]rom the Planes where we will work from now on and by a just law of magnetism, we will be in the position of calling back the last Servants capable of hearing this last message . . . may our Love and our Peace accompany you during the terrible tests of the Apocalypse that await you. Know that from where we will be, we will always hold our arms open to receive those who are worthy of joining us" (*Gnosis Magazine* 1995: 90).

This invitation to join them in the beyond found a receptive audience. On December 16, 1995, sixteen of the remaining European members disappeared from their homes in France and Switzerland. Four left notes hinting at a second mass suicide. Thirteen adults and three children were later found dead in a remote forest in southeast France. Investigators concluded that at least four of the sixteen did not die willingly. Most had been drugged. Two of the sixteen shot the others, poured gasoline over their bodies, set them on fire, and then shot themselves so they would fall into the flames.

Finally, five additional adult members and three teenage children tried to commit suicide on the spring equinox of March 20, 1997, in Quebec, Canada. The attempt initially failed due to faulty equipment. The teenage sons and daughter of one of the couples convinced their parents that they wanted to live. They were then allowed to leave, and the adults subsequently succeeded in burning down the house with themselves in it. Four of the bodies were arranged to form a cross. The teens were found drugged and disoriented, but otherwise safe, in a nearby building. A note was found that described the group belief that death on earth leads to a transit to a new planet where their lives would continue.

More than a few serious observers have analyzed the OTS in detail, giving particular attention to the factors that seem to have precipitated the murder-suicides. Especially in studies comparing different alternative religions that have been involved in violence, explanations tend to emphasize these groups' millennialist belief systems—implicitly or explicitly portraying such beliefs as the key to understanding their violence. In this chapter, I will present an overview of the Solar Temple; in the latter part I will argue against, among other things, the primacy of millennialism as an explanatory factor for understanding group suicide.

Neo-Templarism and Esotericism

Di Mambro had sampled a variety of different esoteric groups, including the Ancient and Mystical Order Rosae Crucis (AMORC), which he joined in 1956, and of which he was a member until at least 1968. He would later incorporate some of this group's ideas and vocabulary into the OTS; for instance, the term "transit" comes directly from AMORC, which "uses the word 'transition' as an equivalent for death" (Mayer 2001: 437, note 2). In the 1960s, he came into contact with several persons who would later play a role in Solar Temple history, including Jacques Breyer, who had initiated a "Templar resurgence" in France in 1952. Several groups, including the Order of the Solar Temple, have their roots in Breyer's work.

"Templar" in this context refers to the Knights Templar, the medieval order to which groups in the Neo-Templar tradition ultimately trace their lineage. (This claimed lineage is almost certainly spurious; instead, Neo-Templar groups are esoteric organizations in the theosophical tradition.) A wealthy, powerful order, the Knights Templar had inspired envy among European rulers. As a consequence, in 1307 the Templars were accused (probably falsely) of heresy and arrested en masse. In 1310, fifty-four knights who had recanted earlier confessions were burned alive at the stake. And four years later, the Grand Master of the order and a provincial leader were similarly burned alive. The fires set or attempted by Solar Temple members during all of the murder-suicide incidents seem to have been inspired by the fiery deaths of the original Templars. According to Introvigne (1995: 279), the fifty-three initial OTS deaths also represented an attempt to mimic the fifty-four Templar deaths—an attempt frustrated by the last-minute escape of Theirry Huguenin, a Swiss dentist and ex-member who had "sensed trouble at the Granges sur Salvan and fled" before he could be murdered (Harriss 1997).

Though a secretive organization, the original Knights Templar were almost certainly orthodox Christians. Their secrecy, however, in combination with the charges of heresy leveled against them in the fourteenth century provided fertile grounds for speculation, allowing later esotericists to construct a hypothesis that the order was secretly an esoteric-magical group. This line of speculation—bolstered by the unlikely claim that the order secretly survived into modern times—underlies contemporary neo-Templarism.

Massimo Introvigne, a scholar of the Western magical milieu (Introvigne 1990), observes that most modern neo-Templar groups trace their origin to the Order of the Temple founded in 1805 by Bernard-Raymond Fabré-Palaprat. "This French physician and Freemason claimed to represent an uninterrupted succession of Templar 'Grand Masters' operating secretly since the suppression of the medieval Order in the fourteenth century" (Introvigne 2000: 140). It was this tradition that Breyer revived in the mid-twentieth century.[1]

The Cult Stereotype and "True Lies"

The Solar Temple tragedies played a pivotal role in inflaming the cult controversy in Europe. Although European anticultists had been active for decades, the spectacle of the murder-suicides influenced public opinion to support harsher actions against new religious movements. Interestingly, this came about at around the same time the North American anticult movement suffered a severe setback as a consequence of the bankruptcy of the Cult Awareness Network (Melton 1999: 229). The Solar Temple incidents were directly responsible for prompting European governments to begin issuing official reports on the dangers posed by nontraditional religions (Introvigne 2004: 207) and, particularly in France and Belgium, a growing campaign to "combat" alternative religions (Hervieu-Léger 2004: 49; Palmer 2004: 65; Lucas 2004: 346). The incidents also helped bolster the North American anticult movement, which supplied consultants for European governments, as well as the mind-control ideology that became a central element of European reports and subsequent legislation (Shupe et al. 2004: 198).

Mind-control ideology and the tendency to lump all nontraditional religions into the same stereotype have been extensively critiqued by the present writer and others (for example, Lewis 1998; Dawson 1998; Anthony and Robbins 2004), and there is no need to repeat these arguments here. There is, however, an aspect of the cult stereotype that seems to apply with particular force to the Solar Temple and that merits attention in this case, namely, the flawed character of the leadership (Mayer 2001: 448–449).

One of the standard accusations hurled again nontraditional religions is that founder-leaders are egotistical, self-seeking charlatans who cynically concoct pseudo religions for the purposes of self-aggrandizement and the exploitation of converts, both financially and sexually. "Cult leaders" are also often portrayed as mentally imbalanced, paranoid, manipulative, and rigidly authoritarian (Dawson 2002: 80). This portrayal obviously represents a caricature—so overstated as to be useless for analytical purposes—but even stereotypes sometimes contain an element of truth. The founder of the Solar Temple fit this stereotype more closely than most, but, despite his deceptions, even Joseph Di Mambro was not totally insincere. We can gain a more nuanced understanding of Di Mambro if we first discuss the more general pattern of certain new religious movement leaders to dissimulate and to act from mixed motives.

Having interacted with more than a few leaders of nontraditional religions, I have the strong impression that almost all are sincere (though a critic might say they are sincerely deluded), whatever their personal foibles. Despite the personal benefits—so obvious to outside observers—of being a spiritual leader, the demands of running even a small religious group are simply too burdensome and involve too many personal sacrifices to attract individuals intent on fulfilling purely selfish goals.

However, I also have the impression that some of the leaders of such groups frequently act from mixed motives, though they may convince themselves that they are acting from pure motives. The polygamous arrangement David Koresh established at Mt. Carmel among his closest followers (Bradley 1994: 166–167) appears to be an example of this mixing of motives. In other words, even assuming Koresh sincerely believed that God commanded him to take additional wives, it is difficult to dismiss the impression that carnal motives (unconscious though they may have been) played a role in shaping this particular revelation.

More problematic for assessing the ethics of new religious movements are cases in which leaders consciously utilize deception. For example, a spiritual leader can straightforwardly request a follower to make a hefty donation without invoking divine sanction. Alternately, a leader might feel an inner prompting he interprets (correctly or incorrectly) as a prompting from a (typically disembodied) spiritual personality to ask the follower to make a sizeable donation—for example, "Master D. K. tells me that you should immediately donate $5,000." Yet another scenario would be a case in which the leader wants the follower to make a big donation, but feels he needs to invoke divine sanction in order to realize his request. In this case, he might *say* "Master D. K. tells me you should donate $5,000," but in fact the request has nothing to do with any spiritual prompting. Even this, however, need not be entirely cynical.

Perhaps the leader feels his disciple has plenty of money, the group needs the donation to pay this month's bills, and Master D. K.—assuming the leader truly believes in the real existence of Master D. K. on the inner planes—obviously would not want the group to go into debt. Therefore, Master D. K. would certainly approve of the leader's request for a donation. Hence telling the disciple that "Master D. K. has told me you should donate $5,000" is, from the leader's perspective, a mostly true statement. Though I do not have empirical evidence to support this (and it is frankly difficult to imagine how one would collect such evidence) beyond informal impressions from my fieldwork, my sense is that some new religious movement leaders engage in these kinds of "slippery" inferences on a regular basis.

Another related phenomenon is what I have elsewhere called the "true lies" pattern. With respect to the legend of Jesus' trip to India, I have argued that a succession of otherwise honorable men verified the existence of a non-existent manuscript, *The Life of Saint Issa*, because it expressed (or expressed after some massaging of the text) what they felt were profound truths (Lewis 2003: 73–88). Some of the documents created by Gerald Gardner, the founder of modern Wicca, exemplify the same phenomenon (Lewis 1999: 345–352). In these cases, the motive behind the various deceptions is to add a degree of legitimacy to the ideas expressed in fabricated documents. Before we judge this legitimation strategy too harshly, we should remember that the history of religion contains innumerable examples of forged scriptures—including documents in the scriptural canons of some of the major world religions. Many of the principal scriptures of Mahayana Buddhism, for instance, claim to have been authored by the historical Buddha, despite the fact that they did not appear until many centuries after his death.

It is also generally accepted among mainstream biblical scholars that some of the epistles supposedly authored by Paul were simply forged. In both of these cases, the respective authors' strategy was to draw on the prestige of a great religious figure to legitimate particular doctrines and associated practices. In *The Gnostic Gospels*, for example, Elaine Pagels notes that a number of the pseudo-Pauline letters pick up on and amplify the antifeminist tenor of Paul's own views, presumably to legitimate the repression of uppity women in their congregations; for example, I Timothy 2: 11–12: "Let a woman learn in silence with all submissiveness. I permit no woman to teach or to have authority over men; she is to keep silent" (Pagels 1989: 63). A variation on this strategy is to forge a narrative in which an authoritative figure is reported as advocating a particular ideology.

The true lies pattern may, however, be extended to nontextual examples. In neo-Templarism, for example, different individuals claimed to have secretly met, and to have been initiated by, representatives of the underground Knights Templar. For instance, Jacques Breyer, the founder of the "Templar Renaissance" that ultimately inspired the OTS, claimed to have received such an initiation on June 12, 1952, in the ruins of the Arginy Castle. Raymond Bernard, founder of the Renewed Order of the Temple, made a similar claim about being initiated in the "crypt" of the Abbey of St. Nilus in the 1960s. Thirty years later, Bernard admitted that his account was fictional, though "based upon deeply moving personal mystical experiences" (Introvigne 2000: 142). Again this is a legitimation strategy—in these cases to legitimate the authority of Breyer and Bernard as neo-Templar leaders.

Though we may judge the actions of these men harshly, the purpose behind the claims of Breyer, Bernard, and others is to amplify their authority so they can be in a better position to propagate what they feel are profound truths. In other words, in most cases of this sort, my impression is that such leaders are otherwise sincere. As argued above, the demands of founding and leading a religious community are such as to make the existence of a completely cynical leader unlikely. Nevertheless, a lack of total cynicism does not mean that the founder-leader of a religious group is thereby necessarily *good*.

Joseph Di Mambro

Joseph Di Mambro was born August 19, 1924, in Pont-Saint-Esprit, France. From the age of sixteen, he was apprenticed as a watchmaker and jeweler and seems to have pursued this profession during the first part of his life. Not much is known about this period except that from a young age he was deeply interested in esotericism, as previously noted.

We first catch a glimpse of the unsavory side of his character from a 1972 conviction on charges of fraud "for impersonating a psychologist and passing bad checks" (Hall et al. 2000: 120). John R. Hall and Philip D. Schuyler speculate that a 1979 fire at La Pyramide, an early communal farm founded by Di Mambro near Geneva, was possibly an insurance swindle. Hall and Schuyler seem to imply that the insurance money from the fire enabled Di Mambro to obtain a mansion in Geneva where he started the Golden Way Foundation (ibid.: 120). The Golden Way was the immediate predecessor organization to the Solar Temple.

The International Chivalric Order Solar Tradition (Solar Temple) was founded in 1984. Solar Temple groups were organized in Quebec, as well as in Australia, Switzerland, France, and other countries. The leadership saw themselves as playing a pivotal role on the world stage. Partially as a consequence of this view, they felt that the Solar Temple was being systematically persecuted by the various governments with whom they were having relatively minor problems. A grandiose self-image is not, of course, unique to the OTS; many other small new religious movements perceive themselves as being at the fulcrum of world history (Mayer 2003: 155–156). Nevertheless, this attitude does not speak well for the Solar Temple's sense of social reality.

On the one hand, Di Mambro was realistic enough about his own lack of charisma that he brought Luc Jouret into the OTS to become the public face of his organization. Intelligent and charismatic, Jouret had been trained as a medical doctor and was an accomplished practitioner of homeopathy. He also lectured on naturopathy and ecological topics and was active in the wider circuit of the French-speaking New Age movement. He spoke in New Age bookstores and to eclectic esoteric groups in France, Switzerland, Belgium, and Canada, recruiting people for the Solar Temple.

On the other hand, Di Mambro was far from humble and claimed to be the reincarnation of Osiris, Akhnaton, Moses, and Cagliostro (Wessinger 2000a: 220–221). He identified various OTS members as having been such famous individuals as Bernard de Clairvaux, Joseph of Arimathea, Queen Hapshetphout, and Rama (Palmer 1996: 308).[2] He was also regarded by his followers "as the only one on Earth who had access" to the Masters (Introvigne and Mayer 2002: 183). Furthermore, Di Mambro saw the OTS as producing "cosmic children" who would shape the future destiny of the planet. Chief among these was his own daughter Emmanuelle, who was to be the messiah-avatar of the New Age. Di Mambro required her to wear gloves and a helmet to protect her purity, and she could only be touched by family members.

Although it is almost certain that Di Mambro believed most of what he taught about Cosmic Masters and the like, he "pretended (since at least the late 1970s) to represent the 'Mother Lodge' and to receive his orders from mysterious 'Masters' " (Mayer 2003: 160; also refer to Mayer 1999: 217). The concept of Masters was codified within Theosophy in the 1880s, and from there was passed on to various religious groups descended from the Theosophical Society. The Masters, in turn, had been derived from the earlier notion of "secret chiefs" (Hutton 1999: 58) to which a wide variety of different occult lodges—including the well-known Hermetic Order of the Golden Dawn—appealed as their primary "source of legitimation" (ibid.: 76). Many people in the occult/metaphysical/New Age subculture believe that a "Great White Brotherhood" of such Masters guide the spiritual progress of the Earth.

Di Mambro deceived his followers into believing that these exalted spiritual personages would deign to manifest themselves during Temple initiations. These manifestations were accomplished by means of hidden technology: holographic projections of the Masters, "together with the robes, candles, incense, and music, created a powerful sacred tableau" (Hall et al. 2000: 126):

> Solar Temple ceremonies were held in darkened inner sanctums. "During ceremonies we would hear sounds from the star Sirius, followed by apparitions of chandeliers, swords and so on, leading up to the appearance of the Masters," recounts a former Canadian member. Sometimes the Master held a sword and tapped the floor in a coded message. Or it could be King Arthur's sword, Excalibur, that materialized before the members' ecstatic eyes. Or the slow, hovering appearance of the Holy Grail, the chalice Christ used at the Last Supper. The apparitions were cleverly designed holograms. "Di Mambro would tell us, 'Do you realize that we are the only people on the planet to see these things?' " (Harriss 1997 [an unpaginated electronic work])

A *Readers Digest* reporter was able to examine some of the ritual stage props confiscated by the Canadian police in the wake of the initial transits. He reports that "King Arthur's Excalibur was a large, tinny broadsword crudely painted with fluorescent green and red. In a dark room, black light made it appear suspended in midair, blood dripping from its tip. Another sword had a small nine-volt battery taped to its hilt. Electrical wires, masked with black tape, led to a tiny read light at the tip" (ibid.). The effects of this technology may also have been enhanced by having participants drink coffee that was "laced with stimulants and hallucinogens" (Palmer 1996: 313).

The apparitions and gimmicks convinced members that Di Mambro really held the special status he claimed. When his son Elie discovered the technological nature of these manifestations in 1990, he began to speak openly of his father's trickery. The Order's chief "special effects" technician, Tony Dutoit, also initiated rumors about the holograms. But Tony and his wife Nicki Dutoit went further: They not only defied Di Mambro's order that they not have a child, they also provocatively named their son Christopher Emmanuel in what seemed to be an implicit challenge to Emmanuelle's messianic status. Enraged both by the Dutoits' disobedience and by their challenge to Emmanuelle, Di Mambro ordered their baby son executed as the Anti-Christ shortly before the group transit.

This incident provides us with yet another window into Di Mambro's flawed character: an authoritarian leader, he directed his followers' personal lives in ways that went far beyond the proper bounds of pastoral care. Of particular note was the Temple's practice of "cosmic coupling" that routinely broke up married couples and paired them with other followers, often resulting in pairs with significant age differences (Palmer 1996: 309). The authorization for these intrusions into the personal lives of members was attributed to the will of the Cosmic Masters, as indicated by Bruno Klaus's announcement to his wife that he was leaving her because, "The Masters have decided. I am going to live with another woman" (cited in Hall et al. 2000: 128). Although Di Mambro may have mistakenly imagined that his personal whims were actually spiritual promptings, it is difficult to avoid the impression that—especially in the later days of his career—he simply asserted that all of his decisions were the will of the Masters, whether he believed so or not.

It should finally be noted that Di Mambro was defensive and paranoid—someone who could never accept responsibility for any of the problems the OTS experienced during the last few years before the transit. It was, for example, his decision to "uncouple" Bruno Klaus from his wife that produced the Temple's most persistent critic. Rose-Marie Klaus doggedly sought to revenge herself against the OTS, an effort that eventually paid off after two Canadian members were arrested while attempting to buy silenced semiautomatic pistols (illegal in Canada). Although the court handed out only one year of unsupervised probation and a token fine, Klaus made tabloid headlines a few days following the arrests, in interviews in which she recounted the hidden "horrors" of the OTS (Hall et al. 2000: 132).

The news coverage in combination with the gun charges set in motion police investigations that led Di Mambro to conclude the group was a target of an international conspiracy. As his wife wrote at the time, "Our file is the hottest on the planet, the most important of the last ten years, if not of the century." Additionally, she recorded a message on an audiotape in 1994 in which she stated, "We are rejected by the whole world" (cited in Wessinger 2000a: 225). One of the testaments left behind after the transit even asserted that the OTS had been the target of "systematic persecution" by authorities on three continents.[3] Di Mambro also bitterly accused Jouret of having brought ruin on the OTS by his bungling. This exaggerated, paranoid attitude plus his blaming of everyone else for the Solar Temple's problems was, unfortunately, typical of Di Mambro.

"Suicide Cults"

The Solar Temple murder-suicides are frequently compared with violent incidents involving other alternative religions, especially the Jonestown murder-suicides (1978), the ATF/FBI raid on the Mt. Carmel community (1993), the Tokyo subway poison gas attack (1995), and the Heaven's Gate suicides (1997). The sensational violence associated with the murder of members of the Movement for the Restoration of the Ten Commandments of God (2000) is often not included in these comparisons, partly because it took place more recently and partly because it seems to have been a somewhat different phenomenon. (For a brief overview, refer to the discussion in the introduction to the present volume.)

Two major monographs that appeared in 2000—John R. Hall et al., *Apocalypse Observed*, and Catherine Wessinger, *How the Millennium Comes Violently*—developed analyses of new religious movement–related violence that included thick descriptions of some of the more controversial groups, including the People's Temple, Branch Davidians, Solar Temple, AUM Shinrikyo, and Heaven's Gate. Many other observers have taken similar approaches (for example, Robbins and Palmer 1997; Daniels 1999; Wessinger 2000b; Bromley and Melton 2002). As reflected in such titles as *How the Millennium Comes Violently* (Wessinger 2000a), *Millennialism, Persecution, and Violence* (Wessinger 2000b), *Millennium, Messiahs, and Mayhem* (Robbins and Palmer 1997), and numerous scholarly articles, millennialism has been central to these discussions—though it should immediately be noted that contemporary analysts of new religious movements and violence are generally careful to "eschew single-factor explanations" (Bromley 2004: 154). Other factors usually considered in attempts to construct a general model of high-demand organization (meaning that participants do not have the option of being casual, part-time members), charismatic leadership, isolation from the surrounding society, and the threatening role played by external forces such as hostile apostates and intrusive governmental authorities. (For a comprehensive discussion, refer to Bromley and Melton 2002.)

At the present juncture, the relatively mature state of this body of literature makes it possible to ask different sorts of questions. Specifically, rather than a straightforward comparison of the five principal groups, what if one focused instead on the three groups that imploded in group suicides—People's Temple, Solar Temple, and Heaven's Gate? Although it is true that both the People's Temple and the Solar Temple also engaged in acts of murder, it could be argued that these violent acts were aspects of the suicide event. It is thus possible to distinguish such suicide-related murders from the otherwise comparable violence initiated by the leadership of AUM Shinrikyo and other groups. The balance of this chapter will examine the three "suicide cults."[4]

It is often more illuminating to "complexify" rather than to simplify certain phenomena, but for my purposes I will focus on distilling the details of these three groups down to a common core of shared traits. Though this approach is open to criticism—and would certainly never do for a comprehensive explanation—it nevertheless bears fruit as an analytical strategy, as will be demonstrated.

As a preliminary move, it should be noted that neither Shoko Asahara nor David Koresh seriously contemplated suicide. When authorities finally located Asahara in a secret room at AUM's Mt. Fuji center, they also found him with an abundant stash of money (not unlike Saddam Hussein) that he planned to support himself with into the foreseeable future. And though Koresh seems to have been willing to die a martyr's death, it also appears he was ready to embrace martyrdom only if all other options (or, perhaps more accurately, all other reasonable options within the horizon of his religious ideology) were closed. The fact that during the siege of Mt. Carmel Koresh retained a literary attorney to handle his story (Lewis 1994: 117; Hall 2002: 166) should be enough to indicate that he envisioned himself living into the post-siege future—not to mention his explicit assertion to FBI negotiators a few days before the final assault that "I never intended to die in here" (cited in Wessinger 2000a: 105). (Also refer to Palmer 1994 in this regard.)

Millennialism

To turn our attention to the People's Temple, the Solar Temple, and Heaven's Gate, what happens when we ruthlessly cut away everything except the barebones structure shared by the three "suicide cults"? Surprisingly, the first trait to drop out is millennialism. Though it is quite possible to argue that Jim Jones was millenarian (see, for example, Chidester 1988; Wessinger 2000a), in point of fact he had no theology in the proper sense, much less a developed eschatology. Well before the establishment of Jonestown, he had become little more than a secular socialist in religious garb. Even as people lined up to drink a mixture of cyanide and Kool-Aid during the final drama, Jones exhorted his followers with the assertion that "This is a revolutionary suicide; this is not a self-destructive suicide" (Hall et al. 2000: 37), rather than consoling them with visions of the afterlife—though, as Jonathan Z. Smith notes (1982: 117), one can also point to portions of the audiotape made during the event that intimate they would be reunited in a postmortem state.[5] Dismissing millennialism, however, flies in the face of other scholarly approaches to the Jonestown suicides. The point being made here thus calls for more discussion.

Millennial movements in the proper sense, to cite Norman Cohn's classic study, always picture the millennium as something "that is to be accomplished by, or with the help of, supernatural agencies" (1970: 15). Even current definitions of millennialism typically mention such agencies. However, as in the following excerpt from a recently published encyclopedia of new religious movements, the People's Temple is included as a example of a millenarian group, despite Jim Jones's nonbelief in divinities of any sort:

> The terms "millenarianism" and "millennialism" are usually applied to the study of apocalyptic beliefs. They refer to the expectation of imminent world transformation, collective salvation, and the establishment of a perfect, new world of harmony and justice to be brought about by otherworldly beings acting in accordance with a divine or superhuman plan. . . . Millenarian ideas associated with new religions often include the belief that the transformation of the present world will be cataclysmic; the worldview (referred to variously as catastrophic millennialism, apocalypticism or premillennialism), expresses a pessimistic view of humanity, maintaining that the world is fatally flawed and unredeemable by human effort, and that only a divinely ordained world cataclysm can usher in a millennial age of peace and prosperity. Groups such as the Branch Davidians, Aum Shinrikyo and the People's Temple exemplify catastrophic millenarian views. (Wojcik 2004: 388)

One can, of course, redefine religion to encompass secular visions (as Wessinger does via Tillich's notion of "ultimate concern" [2000a: 15]), or redefine millennialism to include secular phenomena [as the editors and some of the contributors do in Robbins and Palmer 1997]). The problem with such approaches is that as soon as one expands millennialism to include nonreligious phenomena, then one can legitimately ask, Why stop with survivalism, feminism, and radical environmentalism (three movements examined in the Robbins and Palmer collection)? Almost any group of people who look forward to a better tomorrow—including educators and mainstream political parties—

could conceivably be viewed as millennialist. At this level of generality, however, millennialism becomes almost meaningless as a category of analysis.

We should also note that millennialism in the primary sense described by Norman Cohn involves a salvation that is "terrestrial, in the sense that it is to be realized on this earth and not in some other-worldly heaven" (1970: 15). At the time of their dramatic "exits," however, *not one* of the three suicide groups examined here envisioned returning to a paradisal era on this planet. For example, as Mayer observes with respect to the OTS, describing "the Solar Temple as a 'millennial group' may be misleading if millennial salvation is seen primarily in earthly terms" (2001: 441).

In spite of the line of argument I have been pursuing, I am not necessarily opposed to redefining millennialism to encompass either secular phenomena or extraterrestrial millennia. Rather, my purpose is simply to call into question the axiomatic assumption of many analysts that millennial ideology is a *core* characteristic of contemporary violent groups, *essential* for understanding their violence (for example, Dawson 1998; Hall and Schuyler 1998; Wessinger 2000a; Robbins 2002).[6] And though readers may be hesitant to restrict the scope of millennialism, the issues raised in the present discussion should nevertheless cast doubt on the adequacy of this concept as a primary category for interpreting violence related to new religious movements—especially if we are able to find other, more compelling factors that can explain group suicides without invoking millennialism.[7]

External Provocation and Social Isolation

Shifting our attention from the People's Temple to Heaven's Gate, we encounter another surprise when we subject Marshall Applewhite and company's dramatic exit to the same kind of analysis: namely, pressing external threats, whether real or imagined, are not one of the essential factors necessary for a group suicide (Wright 2002: 104). In all four of the other new religions to be engulfed by violence, hostile outsiders were a major factor precipitating each tragedy—though none was quite as dramatic as the military assault on Mt. Carmel. The press criticism and government scrutiny directed against the Solar Temple and the People's Temple were mild by comparison.

In the case of Heaven's Gate, the group suicide was set in motion by the seemingly innocuous speculation of UFO buffs that a large UFO was approaching earth in the wake of the Hale-Bopp comet. It seems that Applewhite had already decided some years prior that he and his followers would make their exit via a group suicide. Thus he was predisposed to interpret any indication that the space brothers were coming as a sign that it was time to leave (Lewis 2003: 129). Although "The Two" (as Applewhite and his partner Bonnie

Sue Nettles often referred to themselves) had received hostile media coverage in their early years and even feared assassination—at one point they purchased weapons for fear of being attacked (Hall 2000: 171)—these were not factors in March 1997, when Applewhite decided they would exit the planet (Chryssides 2005). This is not, of course, to downplay the important role hostile external forces play in the precipitation of most violence related to new religious movements. Rather, the point here is that this kind of intrusion by the outside world is not *essential* to all such violence.

To finally shift our attention to the Solar Temple, yet another trait seemingly shared by all of the principal new religions involved in violence drops out—namely, the group's social isolation. It is the social dynamics of the segregated (usually communal) worlds of certain alternative religions that allow extreme actions to be contemplated, whether the internally directed violence of Heaven's Gate or the externally directed violence of AUM Shinrikyo. The Solar Temple, in contrast, was only semi-segregated from the larger society. Although Di Mambro established his early Pyramid group as a communal organization, the Solar Temple tended to be only partially communal. Thus, for instance, when the Temple was establishing a "survival farm" in Canada, only a half-dozen members actually lived in the group's headquarters. The rest lived outside the house and took their meals there. Yet other members scattered about Quebec traveled to the house once a month for a meeting that took place on the full moon (Hall et al. 2000: 125). Perhaps more important, many Solar Temple members were wealthy and socially established—belonging to "the elite of the Francophone west" (Daniels 1999: 147)—people who could have been only partially separated from the larger society without arousing suspicion.[8]

Nevertheless, one could argue that the leader's distance from the voices of all but his closest followers was an essential factor contributing to his radical actions. In fact, Di Mambro tended to stay behind the scenes surrounded by a core of staunch loyalists, and even brought Jouret into the Temple for the purpose of interacting with outsiders.[9] This finally brings us to a core trait of suicide cults, namely, a charismatic leader who surrounds himself with absolutely loyal followers and who does not permit any overt disagreement with the group's ideology.

Here the analysis begins to sound rather like a cult stereotype. Focusing on the personality of the leader—usually portrayed, as we have seen, as a warped megalomaniac—is a staple in anticult discussions. In contrast, mainstream scholars tend to include an analysis of the leadership as but one factor among others, such as a given group's social dynamics, ideology, and other less personal factors. Of course the leadership must interact with the membership in order to have any kind of organization at all. But, in the new religious movements we have been discussing, the leader is clearly the epicenter. And the quest for commonalities among suicide groups has boiled down to commonalities among their leaders. So though I am not unmindful of group dynamics, and would never downplay the importance of "exogenous" factors (Robbins 2002: 58; Robbins and Anthony 1995), for the sake of simplifying this analysis I will focus narrowly on the leadership.

Di Mambro, Jones, and Applewhite

What can we say about Jim Jones, Joseph Di Mambro, and Marshall Applewhite? If we again try to eliminate everything except shared traits, Applewhite undermines the stereotypical image of the cult leader because he neither demanded to live a better lifestyle than his followers nor did he attempt to seduce any of them (even before he was castrated). It also seems that Applewhite did not feel particularly bitter toward the people who left Heaven's Gate. And he apparently did not cultivate a distance between himself and his followers. In all of these particulars, he was quite different from Jones and especially from Di Mambro.

What all of these men *did* share was first, an intolerance of any perspective other than their own; second, a need for total commitment—if not absolute obedience—from their followers (all three seem to have been "control freaks" to a greater or lesser extent); and third, a greater or lesser paranoia about external forces threatening them or their group. And although, as we saw with the Solar Temple, it is not essential that the entire group be segregated from the larger society, self-destructive leaders typically surround themselves with loyalists who effectively isolate them from external input. At this point, however, we are faced with the problem of finding what makes these men *different* from other new religious movement leaders. Although, unlike the three suicide group leaders, David Koresh seems to have regularly interacted with people outside of his community, Shoko Asahara was every bit as isolated from external reality as Di Mambro, Applewhite, and Jones. Furthermore, Asahara demanded total obedience, was extremely intolerant of other views, and was paranoid about real and imagined enemies. Yet Asahara apparently never contemplated suicide.

So where does that leave us? Though we have managed to identify some essential common traits via comparison and contrast, a factor that sets the Solar Temple, the People's Temple, and Heaven's Gate apart from AUM Shinrikyo and the Branch Davidians seems to have eluded us. Discovering this additional factor requires that we shift our focus away from traits frequently discussed in the literature and focus instead on less commonly discussed characteristics. What did Di Mambro, Applewhite, and Jones share that distinguishes them from Koresh and Asahara?

Some years ago while researching Heaven's Gate for an analysis of the strategies by which Marshall Applewhite legitimated suicide, I came across several sources that mentioned that his health was failing (for example, Perkins and Jackson 1997: 81). Although his autopsy demonstrated otherwise, he believed he was dying of cancer (Balch and Taylor 2002: 221). Also, Wessinger points out that Applewhite never considered the option of appointing a successor who could lead the group after his passing, which probably made the group suicide option more attractive (2000a: 81). At the time these seemed like minor factors in explaining the Heaven's Gate tragedy, so they were mentioned only briefly in my study of legitimation strategies (Lewis 2003: 129).

In the context of the current discussion, however, these become major factors because they are precisely the traits that set the suicide groups apart from the others. In terms of health, Di Mambro was "suffering from kidney failure and incontinence as well as severe diabetes, and he believed he had cancer" (Wessinger 2000a: 221). And Jones—either because he was sedating a genuine physical problem or because he had become a self-destructive addict—was gradually destroying himself with excessive prescription tranquilizers (Templer 1998: 8). Thomas Robbins emphasized the importance of a charismatic leader's health in a personal communication to Hall when the latter was researching and writing *Apocalypse Observed*, though Hall quickly passes over the subject after mentioning Robbins's communication in the latter part of his book (2000: 193).[10] It is easy to understand how Hall, focused as he was on other aspects of new religious movements, would have failed to perceive the health of the charismatic leader as a major explanatory factor. In the context of the current discussion, however, the observation that Applewhite, Di Mambro, and Jones were in failing health, whereas Koresh and Asahara were not, makes this factor suddenly stand out as important: If the three suicide leaders all perceived themselves as dying, then the notion of bringing the whole group—perceived narcissistically as an extension of themselves (Oakes 1998)—along on their postmortem journeys might strike them as attractive. As Palmer observes with respect to Di Mambro, "Perhaps he chose to stage a Pharaoh's funeral so that he could . . . take his retinue with him into the afterlife" (1996: 315).

In addition to their physical deaths, all three men knew their respective groups had not only stopped growing but were also likely to decline precipitously in the future. The Solar Temple, for instance, "was a group in decline, which was losing members at an increasing rate" (Mayer 2001: 444). The number of Heaven's Gate followers had dropped to thirty-eight, and efforts to spread the message "were hitting a dead end . . . the main response was ridicule" (Balch and Taylor 2003: 233). Neither Applewhite (as noted) nor Jones (apparently) had given serious thought to grooming a successor. Di Mambro, on the other hand, seems for many years to have anticipated that his daughter Emmanuelle would inherit his mantle. By twelve years of age, however, she was already rebelling against the script her father had imagined her fulfilling (Palmer 1996: 315), effectively frustrating whatever desire he might have had for a legacy. By the time of the Transit, he had also come to nurse an exaggerated hatred for the "barbarian, incompetent and aberrant" Jouret (Introvigne and Mayer 2002: 177), an obvious person to take over should Di Mambro pass from the scene.

To summarize the above discussion into a list of traits, we can say that, based on an analysis of the People's Temple, the Solar Temple, and Heaven's Gate, the essential characteristics of a suicide group are:

1. Absolute intolerance of dissenting views.
2. Members must be totally committed.
3. Exaggerated paranoia about external threats.
4. Leader isolates him/herself or the entire group from the nonbelieving world.
5. Leader's health is failing—in a major way, not just a transitory sickness; or, alternately, the leader believes he or she is dying.
6. There is no successor and no steps are being taken to provide a successor; or, alternately, succession plans have been frustrated.
7. The group is either stagnant or declining, with no realistic hopes for future expansion.

As noted earlier, there are numerous points of overlap with AUM Shinrikyo and the Branch Davidians. However, despite major areas of overlap, both of these groups lack several essential traits. Specifically, David Koresh did not segregate himself from unbelievers (Dawson 2002: 86–87) and was in good health immediately prior to the ATF raid on Mt. Carmel. Koresh had also fathered a number of children he believed would eventually rule the earth—in effect, his successors. Asahara seems to have been in reasonably good health as well, and he had already indicated to followers that his children would be his spiritual successors (though it should be noted that this successorship was rather vague at the time of the subway attack and only clarified later). Finally, though neither AUM in 1995 and nor the Davidians in 1993 were experiencing rapid growth, they were also not stagnant; both could have reasonably anticipated future growth.[11] In other words, the Davidians lacked traits 4, 5, 6, and 7, whereas AUM lacked 5, 6, and 7.

In contrast to recent theorizing focused on the relational and processual aspects of violence (for example, Bromley and Melton 2002), the approach of distilling a list of traits will probably strike some observers as static and regressive. Also, confining the discussion to specific internal factors seems to reproduce the flaws of anticult theorizing about cults (Hall 2002: 167), especially when that theorizing focuses on charismatic cult leaders (Melton and Bromley 2002: 46–47). So, to make certain my analysis is not misinterpreted, let me explicitly restate that my goal here was a very narrow one, not intended to constitute anything like a general theory—either of violence related to new religious movements or of suicide cults. Producing a truly comprehensive account of religious groups that have committed acts of mass suicide would necessarily go beyond the factors discussed above.

Another potential criticism is that the Movement for the Restoration of the Ten Commandments (MRTC), the Ugandan group murdered by its leaders in 2000, refutes my analysis. Although the remains of leaders have never been identified, some observers have concluded that they committed suicide after murdering their followers (Bromley and Melton 2002: 238). If this is the case, then the MRTC—which does not seem to have had an ailing leader—constitutes an exception to the pattern outlined above. However, given how little we really know about the group, it is difficult to even begin to respond to this hypothetical critique. On the one hand, it is quite possible that one or more of the group's leaders survived, and are in hiding somewhere living off the donations of murdered followers. On the other hand, it may be that the primary leader was suffering from a terminal illness, though we will probably never know for certain. We should finally consider that the African cultural context places the MRTC in a somewhat different category from that of the other groups analyzed here, making comparisons problematic. In any case, too little information is currently available to bring the MRTC to bear on this discussion in a meaningful way.

One last point that needs to be addressed is the problem raised by the suicides of other Solar Temple members in the years following the original transit. As Introvigne and Mayer argue, "After the second and third tragedies of 1995 and 1997, it became even more apparent that Di Mambro's manipulative behavior could not have been the only explanation for the OTS process of self-destruction" (2002: 178). There were also several Heaven's Gate members who took their own lives in the years following the mass suicide of that group.

These later suicides could be marshaled to support a position that the role of the leadership is less central for interpreting the original group suicides than I have been arguing here. However, this hypothetical position ignores the fact that a number of *new* influences come into play that are *more* important for understanding the actions of members who survived the initial suicide event. Perhaps most important, participants who had been deeply involved in the Solar Temple or Heaven's Gate would have felt that a vital part of their lives had been lost in the wake of the departure of the group. They would also have felt that their group "was entirely misunderstood and vilified by the rest of the world" (Mayer 2001: 447, note 49), and would have had to have endured the stigma of being "survivors" (Palmer 1996: 304).[12] Finally, in the exit videos left behind by Heaven's Gate and in the Solar Temple testaments, survivors were explicitly invited to follow the group into the beyond—as we noted in the OTS testament cited in the introductory section of this chapter. In other words, surviving members were acting under a new constellation of influences that make their suicides highly problematic as a basis for interpreting the original suicides.

Conclusion

I have focused this chapter on the founder of the OTS because his idiosyncra-cies provide keys for understanding the Solar Temple's final "transit." Leaders of many religions (not excluding traditional religions) have utilized question-able legitimation strategies, such as fabricating documents that claim special authority for the teachings they contain. The Solar Temple's holographic fab-rications, however, put Di Mambro in a class by himself. Nevertheless, though he "acted at times like a common swindler . . . he very likely remained con-vinced of his message and mission until the end" (Mayer 2003: 174). A deeply flawed character, Di Mambro had founded a fatally flawed organization. And although the murder-suicides were probably not inevitable, it seems that the Solar Temple was early set on a collision course that would eventually have led to an unhappy outcome of some sort.

The focus on Di Mambro feeds into a broader analysis of the three primary suicide cults examined by contemporary scholars of alternative religions: the People's Temple, the Solar Temple, and Heaven's Gate. The final sections of the chapter argued that some of the factors normally given pride of place in discussions of violence associated with new religious movements—especially millennialism and external provocation—were not as central for understand-ing mass suicides as previous analysts have suggested. Instead we found that a leader with failing health, in combination with certain other characteristics of intensive religions, are more important factors for predicting which groups are predisposed to suicide.

NOTES

1. There is a good summary of neo-Templarism in Introvigne 1995, and a short but illuminating discussion of the magical milieu, its relation to the alternative spiri-tual subculture, and the immediate precursors to the Solar Temple in the first section of Introvigne 2000. The OTS appropriation of this tradition is reflected in *The Tem-plar Tradition in the Age of Aquarius* (Delaforge 1987), a publication that, it was hoped, would bring English-speaking North Americans into the Solar Temple. This effort to attract non-Francophones failed miserably.

2. Past-life claims as a strategy for legitimating charismatic authority appears to be widespread, as noted by Dawson (2002: 82–83).

3. In this regard, refer to the discussion under the section heading "A Persecu-tion Mania" in Mayer (2003: 167–170).

4. Introvigne and Mayer (2002) compare these same three movements in the

concluding section of their analysis, though they do not explicitly note group suicide as the principal shared trait.

5. Also refer to Chidester's (1988: 106) application of Lifton's (1968) notion of "revolutionary immortality" to Jonestown.

6. For a critique of this view, refer to Bromley and Melton (2002: 47–48).

7. Though in the case of certain nonsuicidal new religious movements such as AUM Shinrikyo, millennialism may be a significant factor for understanding their violence (Mullins 1997).

8. In this regard, also refer to the discussion in Introvigne and Mayer (2002: 176).

9. Mayer observes that by the time of the transits, Di Mambro was mentally imbalanced and "had lost touch with reality" (Mayer 2001: 448).

10. Robbins has elsewhere called attention to the poor health of the leader as a factor in violence related to new religious movements. In a recent publication, for example, Robbins observes that, among other factors, the "personal deterioration of the prophet, set the stage for a gigantic tragedy of mass suicide and homicide" at Jonestown (2002: 64–65).

11. Though not growing—or growing only very slowly—in Japan, AUM Shinrikyo had been expanding in Russia (Reader 2002: 195).

12. Though these two references are specifically referring to Solar Temple survivors, it is reasonable to extend their observations to Heavens Gate survivors as well.

WORKS CITED

Anthony, Dick, and Thomas Robbins. 2004. "Conversion and 'Brainwashing' in New Religious Movements." In *The Oxford Handbook of New Religious Movements,* edited by James R. Lewis, 243–297. New York: Oxford University Press.

Balch, Robert W., and David Taylor. 2002. "Making Sense of the Heaven's Gate Suicides." In *Cults, Religion, and Violence,* edited by David G. Bromley and J. Gordon Melton, 209–228. New York: Cambridge University Press.

———. 2003. "Heaven's Gate: Implications for the Study of Commitment to New Religions." In *The Encyclopedic Sourcebook of UFO Religions,* edited by James R. Lewis, 211–237. Amherst, N.Y.: Prometheus Books.

Bradley, Martha Sontag. 1994. "A More Righteous Seed: A Comparison of Polygamy among the Branch Davidians and the Fundamentalist Mormons." In *From the Ashes: Making Sense of Waco,* edited by James R. Lewis, 165–168. Lanham, Md.: Rowman and Littlefield.

Bromley, David G. 2004. "Violence and New Religious Movements." In *The Oxford Handbook of New Religious Movements,* edited by James R. Lewis, 143–162. New York: Oxford University Press.

Bromley, David G., and J. Gordon Melton, eds. 2002. *Cults, Religion, and Violence.* New York: Cambridge University Press.

Campiche, Roland. 1995. "Quand les sects affolent: Ordre du Temple Solaire, médias et fin du millénaire." *Entretiens avec Cyril Dépraz.* Geneva: Labor et Fides.

Chidester, David. 1988. *Salvation and Suicide: An Interpretation of Jim Jones, the Peoples Temple, and Jonestown.* Bloomington: Indiana University Press.

Chryssides, George D. 2005. " 'Come On Up, and I Will Show Thee': Heaven's Gate as a Postmodern Group." Chapter 16 in the present volume.

Cohn, Norman. 1970. *In Pursuit of the Millennium*. New York: Oxford University Press.

Daniels, Ted, ed. 1999. *A Doomsday Reader: Prophets, Predictors, and Hucksters of Salvation*. New York: New York University Press.

Dawson, Lorne L. 1998. *Comprehending Cults: The Sociology of New Religious Movements*. Toronto and New York: Oxford University Press.

———. 2002. "Crises of Charismatic Legitimacy and Violent Behavior in New Religious Movements." In *Cults, Religion, and Violence*, edited by David G. Bromley and J. Gordon Melton, 80–101. New York: Cambridge University Press.

Delaforge, Gaetan. 1987. *The Templar Tradition in the Age of Aquarius*. Putney, Vt.: Threshold Books.

Hall, John R. 2002. "Mass Suicide and the Branch Davidians." In *Cults, Religion, and Violence*, edited by David G. Bromley and J. Gordon Melton, 149–169. New York: Cambridge University Press.

Hall, John R., and Phillip Schuyler. 1997. "The Mystical Apocalypse of the Solar Temple." In *Millennium, Messiahs, and Mayhem: Contemporary Apocalyptic Movements*, edited by Thomas Robbins and Susan J. Palmer, 285–311. New York: Routledge.

———. 1998. "Apostasy, Apocalypse and Religious Violence." In The Politics of Religious Apostasy, edited by David G. Bromley, 141–170. Westport, Conn.: Praeger.

Hall, John R., with Philip D. Schuyler and Sylvaine Trinh. 2000. *Apocalypse Observed: Religious Movements and Violence in North America, Europe, and Japan*. London: Routledge.

Harriss, Joseph A. 1997. "Mystery of a Killer Cult." *Readers Digest,* International Edition (December). http://perso.wanadoo.fr/joseph.harris.cult.htm.

Hervieu-Léger, Danièle. 2004. "France's Obsession with the 'Sectarian Threat.' " In *New Religious Movements in the 21st Century: Legal, Political, and Social Challenges in Global Perspective*, edited by Phillip Charles Lucas and Thomas Robbins, 49–59. New York: Routledge.

Hutton, Ronald. 1999. *The Triumph of the Moon: A History of Modern Pagan Witchcraft*. New York: Oxford University Press.

Introvigne, Massimo. 1990. *Il cappello del mago. I nuovi movimenti magicci dallo spiritismo al santanismo*. Milan: Sugar Co.

———. 1995. "Ordeal by Fire: The Tragedy of the Solar Temple." *Religion* 25, 267–283.

———. 2000. "The Magic of Death: The Suicides of the Solar Temple." In *Millennialism, Persecution, and Violence: Historical Cases*, edited by Catherine Wessinger, 138–157. Syracuse, N.Y.: Syracuse University Press.

———. 2004. "Something Peculiar about France: Anti-Cult Campaigns in Western Europe and French Religious Exceptionalism." In *The Oxford Handbook of New Religious Movements*, edited by James R. Lewis, 206–220. New York: Oxford University Press.

Introvigne, Massimo, and Jean-François Mayer. 2002. "Occult Masters and the Temple of Doom: The Fiery End of the Solar Temple." In *Cults, Religion, and Violence*, edited by David G. Bromley and J. Gordon Melton, 170–188. New York: Cambridge University Press.

Lewis, James R. 1994. "Fanning the Flames of Suspicion: The Case against Mass Suicide at Waco." In *From the Ashes: Making Sense of Waco,* edited by James R. Lewis, 115–120. Lanham, Md.: Rowman and Littlefield.

———. 1999. *Witchcraft Today.* Santa Barbara: ABC-Clio.

———. 2003. *Legitimating New Religions.* New Brunswick: Rutgers University Press.

Lifton, Robert Jay. 1968. *Revolutionary Immortality: Mao Tse-Tung and the Chinese Cultural Revolution.* New York: Random House.

Lucas, Phillip Charles. 2004. "Conclusion." In *New Religious Movements in the 21st Century: Legal, Political, and Social Challenges in Global Perspective,* edited by Phillip Charles Lucas and Thomas Robbins, 341–357. New York: Routledge.

Mayer, Jean-François. 1996. *Les Mythes du Temple Solaire.* Geneva: Georg.

———. 1999. "Les Chevaliers de l'apocalypse: L'Ordre du Temple Solaire et ses adepts." In *Sects et Démocraties,* edited by Françoise Champion and Martine Cohen, 205–223. Paris: Editions du Seuil.

———. 2001. "The Dangers of Enlightenment: Apocalyptic Hopes and Anxieties in the Order of the Solar Temple." In *Esotérisme, gnoses et imaginarie sybolique: Mélanges offerts à Antoine Faivre,* edited by Richard Caron, Joscelyn Godwin, Wouter J. Hanegraaff, and Jean-Louis Vieillard-Baron, 437–451. Leuven: Peeters.

———. 2003 [1999]. " 'Our Terrestrial Journey Is Coming to an End': The Last Voyage of the Solar Temple." In *The Encyclopedic Sourcebook of New Age Religions,* edited by James R. Lewis, 155–178. Amherst, N.Y.: Prometheus Books. (Originally published in *Nova Religio* 2, no. 2: 172–196.)

Melton, J. Gordon. 1999. "Anti-Cultists in the United States: An Historical Perspective." In *New Religious Movements: Challenge and Response,* edited by Bryan Wilson and Jamie Cresswell, 213–233. London: Routledge.

Mullins, Mark. 1997. "Aum Shinrikyo as an Apocalyptic Movement." In *Millennium, Messiahs, and Mayhem: Contemporary Apocalyptic Movements,* edited by Thomas Robbins and Susan J. Palmer, 313–324. New York: Routledge.

Oakes, Len. 1998. *Prophetic Charisma: The Psychology of Revolutionary Religious Personalities.* Syracuse: Syracuse University Press.

OTS. 1995. "To All Those Who Can Still Understand the Voice of Wisdom . . . We Address This Last Message." *Gnosis Magazine* no.34 (winter).

Pagels, Elaine. 1989 [1979]. *The Gnostic Gospels.* New York: Vintage.

Palmer, Susan J. 1994. "Excavating Waco." In *From the Ashes: Making Sense of Waco,* edited by James R. Lewis, 99–110. Lanham, Md.: Rowman and Littlefield.

———. 1996. "Purity and Danger in the Solar Temple." *Journal of Contemporary Religion* 1, no. 3: 303–318.

———. 2004. "The *Secte* Response to Religious Discrimination: Subversives, Martyrs, or Freedom Fighters in the French Sect Wars?" In *New Religious Movements in the 21st Century: Legal, Political, and Social Challenges in Global Perspective,* edited by Phillip Charles Lucas and Thomas Robbins, 61–73. New York: Routledge.

Perkins, Rodney, and Forrest Jackson. 1997. *Cosmic Suicide: The Tragedy and Transcendence of Heaven's Gate.* Dallas: Pentaradial Press.

Reader, Ian. 2002. "Dramatic Confrontations: Aum Shinrikyo against the World." In *Cults, Religion, and Violence,* edited by David G. Bromley and J. Gordon Melton, 189–208. New York: Cambridge University Press.

Robbins, Thomas. 2002. "Sources of Volatility in Religious Movements." In *Cults, Religion, and Violence*, edited by David G. Bromley and J. Gordon Melton, 57–79. New York: Cambridge University Press.

Robbins, Thomas, and Dick Anthony. 1995. "Sects and Violence: Factors Enhancing the Volatility of Marginal Religious Movements." In *Armageddon in Waco: Critical Perspectives on the Branch Davidian Conflict*, edited by Stuart A. Wright, 236–259. Chicago: University of Chicago Press.

Robbins, Thomas, and Susan J. Palmer, eds. 1997. *Millennium, Messiahs, and Mayhem: Contemporary Apocalyptic Movements*. New York: Routledge.

Shupe, Anson, David G. Bromley, and Susan E. Darnell. 2004. "The North American Anti-Cult Movement: Vicissitudes of Success and Failure." In *The Oxford Handbook of New Religious Movements*, edited by James R. Lewis, 184–205. New York: Oxford University Press.

Smith, Jonathan Z. 1982. *Imagining Religion: From Babylon to Jonestown*. Chicago: University of Chicago Press.

Templer, Robert. 1998. "Jonestown." In *The Richmond Review*. www.richmondreview .co.uk/features/temple02.html.

Wessinger, Catherine. 2000a. *How the Millennium Comes Violently: From Jonestown to Heaven's Gate*. Chappaqua, N.Y.: Seven Bridges Press.

———, ed. 2000b. *Millennialism, Persecution, and Violence: Historical Cases*. Syracuse, N.Y.: Syracuse University Press.

Wojcik, Daniel. 2004. "Apocalypticism and Millenarianism." In *Encyclopedia of New Religions: New Religious Movements, Sects, and Alternative Spiritualities*, edited by Christopher Partridge, 388–395. Oxford: Lion Publishing.

Wright, Stuart A. 2002. "Public Agency Involvement in Government-Religious Movement Confrontations." In *Cults, Religion, and Violence*, edited by David G. Bromley and J. Gordon Melton, 102–122. New York: Cambridge University Press.

14

From Atlantis to America: JZ Knight Encounters Ramtha

Gail M. Harley

For the past century and a half, there have been remarkable transformations in our images of the Divine. Women have been the catalysts for several major shifts that challenge the parameters of traditional thinking. JZ Knight (b. 1946) shares an enigmatic relationship with her knight in shining armor—Ramtha—who dwells in the invisible realm. Knight was one of the first channelers to find public success in this arena. Jane Roberts, who claimed to be channeling an entity called Seth, developed her channeled teachings in 1974, slightly ahead of the emergence of Ramtha in 1977. The channeling sessions of Roberts (who was somewhat reclusive) were conducted at home, and the transcribed communications disseminated primarily through books. Knight and Ramtha went public in 1978 after one year of working together under the mentorship of a spiritualist medium.[1] They conduct classes and seminars not only in Yelm, Washington, where they are headquartered, but also in the international arena, attracting students from all over the world.

Certain nineteenth-century women religious leaders provide interesting contrasts to Knight. Helena Blavatsky (1837–1891), cofounder of Theosophy, claimed to be sending messages back and forth to a celestial hierarchy she referred to as the White Brotherhood. Her shift from the Spiritualist tradition of talking to the mundane dead to communicating with celestial dieties and spiritual masters helped focus the idea that communication between spheres was possible through the revelations of invisible masters who chose to speak through living people. Another avant garde woman religious leader, Mary Baker Eddy (1821–1910), claimed that God had miraculously healed her in 1876 while she was reading the Bible. She thought that she was specially selected and that she alone had been chosen by God to deliver a special message about spiritual healing. She founded the Christian Science Church based on her unique revelations. According to Catherine Wessinger, Eddy fits the paradigm of "extraordinary charisma."[2] This means that direct revelation from the Holy is available to the leader and not the other members of the group. Madame Blavatsky also established herself as the primary person to manifest "extraordinary charisma" in the Theosophical Society when she was the paramount channeler of spiritual messages from the mahatmas of the spiritual realm.

These two religious entrepreneurs projected extraordinary charisma. In contrast, Emma Curtis Hopkins (1849–1925), founder of New Thought, did not publicly claim for herself any special revelation from God that others could not access. Wessinger asserts that a leader who makes no special claims and operates through "ordinary or democratic charisma" makes it permissible for other members of the group to receive direct revelations. Hopkins is an example of a powerful figure demonstrating "democratic charisma," while her students, her followers, and disciples thought that this saintly woman who believed she was married to God possessed "extraordinary charisma."[3] All of these women believed they held a divine charter from the Holy and devoted their lives to the teachings of their perceptions of the Divine.

JZ Knight of the Ramtha School of Enlightenment expresses extraordinary charisma. Knight adds a distinct facet to her being the chosen one reflecting extraordinary charisma. In fact, Knight reveals in her autobiography, *A State of Mind: My Story*, that she was especially chosen by Ramtha because she was not able to go to college. Academic and worldly innocence are factors believed to make one a better, clearer conduit for spiritual communiqué.[4]

Knight believes her revelations from Ramtha are unique and that she has a divine charter to teach others who seek spiritual success. All prophets, if they are going to be successful, must survive in the cultural milieu of their times. Religious entrepreneurs operating outside of or marginally within mainstream denominations receive little legitimation and are frequently ostracized by congregations and the clergy of traditional churches.

The industrial revolution, concomitant with the advent of more sophisticated technology, impacted religious ideas. Innovative prophets, seizing upon the zeitgeist, quickly appropriated scientific terminology to explain their revelations. The science in Christian Science, Divine Science, and Religious Science designates certain religious groupings within the metaphysical family of religion. They insisted that the newer made-in-America religions warranted empirical endorsements. This tradition of wedding religion to science continues down to the present. Knight advances this notion. Hers is among those whose conception of religion includes a religious *technology*.[5] More than a century later than Christian Science and New Thought, the wedding drums synthesizing religion and science are beating out a similar yet staccato rhythm for the Ramtha School of Enlightenment.

Knight is a modern-day benefactor of this urge toward technological armament for her religious vision. Scientists such as Amit Goswami offer a new paradigm for understanding the invisible world and the method by which it can operate in tandem with what is conceived of as the finite world. Goswami argues that what changes ideas about what is possible into reality is the consciousness of the individual. If consciousness is assumed to be the pivotal point around which human life revolves, then a new science evolves that is "permissionary," taking into consideration paranormal phenomenon such as channeling and telepathy.[6]

Ancient Gnosticism and the New Sciences

Ancient gnosticism resonates with concepts uniting human and divine natures. In this system of unification, God is immanent (within the individual), whereas God as the transcendent Other who operates outside of and apart from humanity is emphasized in the traditional monotheistic faiths. The notion of the unity of god and humanity is quite old. For instance, Plato and his teachings received a gnostic interpretation under the tutelage of Plotinus (295–270 BCE). From that time onward, threads of gnosticism have run through Western theology.

Although gnosticism has been largely rejected by the mainstream, the ideas continue to be revisited by new religious movements, particularly by the New Age. The gnostic idea underwrites Christian Science, New Thought, and a number of Asian religions. Ramtha clearly advocates gnostic ideals. Today's religious entrepreneurs are reviving ancient ideas of the divine in order to join religious thought with cutting-edge postulations such as quantum physics. They believe that at some point down the theological turnpike, science will become a decisive voice for explaining the consciousness of spiritual wholeness. As Goswami has noted, permissionary ideas of consciousness give these movements room to grow.

Ramtha's teachings represent the new science of the new millennium as well as the gnostic thread of antiquity. The conventional scientific establishment might assert that quantum mechanics remains at the experimental stage, attempting to establish sanction within mainstream scientific circles. Other writers and scholars such as Ken Wilber already unify various approaches to spiritual consciousness. His particular model of consciousness "unites mysticism, Eastern and Western psychologies in general [and] also clarifies Western approaches to psychotherapy."[7]

Ramtha selectively appropriates some of the theories from perennial philosophers and synthesizers such as Wilber. He weaves quantum physics and cutting-edge psychology and utilizes them engagingly in his dialogues as scientific paradigms for personal transformation. Ramtha's message is about transformation of the little self into the larger Self through mastery of the world-at-large. Spiritual competence allows one to play an active part in one's own personal fulfillment and change behavior patterns that have been destructive, unrewarding, or otherwise disadvantageous.

This eclectic, unified approach combining science with spirituality propels religious technology forward, advancing innovative developments. Pioneers who changed paradigms interfacing science and religion served to promote a foundational infrastructure that has found acceptance by a public who believes that science and religion are not mutually exclusive. These tenets support contemporary spirituality, undergird the New Age movement, and become permissionary for channeling as a method of communication between worlds.[8]

Different from the older spiritualist mediums who seanced and spoke to the ordinary or not-so-ordinary deceased, this elevated idea of talking to the major players of the spirit world developed anew in the 1970s. Those considered holy enough emerged as human conduits for the prophecies of exalted deities. This shift in focus changed the face of mediumship. Mediums comfort with messages of deceased loved ones perceived to be in the spirit world. However, it is the channelers of the divine who are receiving the most acclaim today.

Religion in America has been shaped by women who spoke before modern-day channelers appeared on the scene. At the end of the twentieth century, Mary Farrell Bednarowski wrote that women were becoming more assertive about their theological needs, and are definitely moving on with their ideas about immanence, community, and the spirituality of the earth as Divine Mother.[9]

A Troubled Past

JZ Knight, was born Judith Darlene Hampton in Roswell, New Mexico, a younger child in a large family of poverty-stricken farm workers. She suffered emotional and sexual abuse as a child: She was abandoned by her father and suffered with her stepfather. Knight became a victim. Robbed of her innocence and without a male authority who was kind and supportive, she dreamed of finding a loving, caring man. After she graduated from high school, she attempted to attend college. However, through no fault of her own, she failed due to severe health issues, partially brought about by trying to support herself and earn enough money to obtain a higher education.

She married shortly after her aborted attempt to go to college. Her husband was reported to have been emotionally abusive and exploited her as a person and woman. She eventually divorced him, and sought a way to create a more prosperous and harmonious life for herself and her two sons. She found success in California with the early cable franchise networks. Working hard and fast, she earned enough money to have a housekeeper help with the children. Knight married again to Jeremy Wilder, a dentist who settled down with her and her children to an upper-middle-class life in Tacoma, Washington. In the mid-1970s, intrigued with ideas of pyramid power, she experimented by placing pyramids throughout her house. Ramtha then appeared to her.

Ramtha was a larger-than-life spiritual being visible only to Knight. Ramtha told her he was a 35,000-year-old warrior, a survivor of a cataclysmic destruction on Lemuria who fled to Atlantis for safety. Knight's husband Wilder became entranced with Ramtha and with the transformation of Knight that took place when she allowed Ramtha to control her body and speak through her. Wilder, once galvanized by the beauty of his wife, now became enamored with Ramtha and promoted him as an enigmatic figure from another world. Knight had become number two in his life.

Knight lost again as her personhood and integrity were no longer valued. She had become a commodity for her spouse. Deprived of her sanctity as a child, she became an object for her second husband, which dehumanized her even more. Ramtha had enthralled him more than she had. She subsequently divorced Wilder.

Knight married again; she thought Jeffery Knight was her soul mate. By this time she had achieved celebrity status as the channel for Ramtha. Jeffery was a homosexual whose basic romantic interests were with other men, and he did not appreciate the extraordinary charisma of JZ. Traumatized again by the oversights and violation from men in her life, she again lost. Her needs for a marital partner committed to her as a soul mate led to their separation and eventual divorce. Jeffery eventually died of AIDS. Both Wilder and Jeffery Knight had taken advantage of her celebrity status to enrich themselves. She and Ramtha were reified in the process.

Despite the distress in her personal life, she continued her relationship with Ramtha. He emerged as a powerbroker in her life. He was a larger-than-life, spiritually energized warrior, a male protector who never abused or left her. He was there to advise her and coach her in esoteric lessons about life, and through the years he had shared these lessons or "Dialogues" with her burgeoning community of disciples. What became successful for her was disseminated to her followers.

Extraordinary Charisma

According to Robert Ellwood and Catherine Wessinger, women with extraordinary charisma had "innate gifts of spiritual leadership or theological articulation" that were not accepted or respected by mainline theological institutions in part because of their gender.[10] The creativity of women explorers of the spiritual realms side-stepped the conventional for the nonconventional. The oratorical power awarded to the sacred speaker found a home in channeling, while the status of theological articulation was raised to heightened levels with the advent of the New Age. Looking for ways to create innovative pathways of power through divinity with their emerging spiritual proclivities became the focal point for gifted women. The union of science and technology—at least in the mind of the believer—was a unique aspect of this development. These religious entrepreneurs initiated and orchestrated new religious movements that became the focal point for their extraordinary talents. Such ventures into the world of religion were controversial not only because they were women but also because they seized the theological authority normally accorded only to men.[11]

Eddy, Hopkins, and Blavatsky claimed that God was immanent—meaning that God dwelled within each person, male or female. This foundational theme of immanent deity seems to many to have been a way of proving that women were not separate from but identical with the divine. In line with the historical precedents set by women such as Hopkins and Blavatsky, Knight claimed direct power linkages to a divine entity—in Knight's case, to the former warrior of Lemuria, Ramtha, who in a prior lifetime was the Hindu god Rama. Knight seized divine sanction and empowered herself through her channeling of Ramtha's teaching.

J. Gordon Melton has suggested that the emergence of Hopkins and Blavatsky and other women who founded significant religious movements in the late nineteenth century cannot be understood without recognizing the new space created for women in the religious community by the earlier revivalists and the holiness movement.[12] Hopkins, Eddy, and Blavatsky were the late-nineteenth-century recipients of this new idea of seizing divine authority. However, it would be Hopkins who heralded the new ideas by assuming the role of bishop and ordaining twenty women and two men to the New Thought ministry in the 1880s.[13] The trail had been blazed and those riding point claimed it.[14] Today, Knight and her contemporaries benefit from their boldness. Knight, of course, has developed her own version of a religion of synthesis.

These new religious movements, including the Ramtha School of Enlightenment, proselytized for women's empowerment through mastery of one's own lifestyle through harmony, prosperity, and spiritual serenity. Divine sanction and religious technology provided women with the metaphysical tools to create their reality and short-circuit the social construction of deity established by mainline churches. In other words, they seized the power to reconstruct deity to include them.

Ramtha and JZ Tell His Story

In his past life as a warlord, Ramtha was victimized and orphaned. Through violence and bloodshed, he eventually learned he was divine. According to his teachings, he has a unique history and a noteworthy heritage. His Hindu line-age—he claims to have been incarnated as Rama, the Hindu avatar—legitimates him by connecting him with one of the oldest religious traditions in the world. He has evolved through many lifetimes, acquiring credentials in the spiritual world partly through the complexity of traumatic experiences that allowed him to ascend into the ethereal realms. He transcended a world filled with horror and war after the fall of Atlantis. He escaped after earning his self-taught freedom to the divine realms of pure spirit. Later he emerged as a member of the Great White Brotherhood of Theosophy and its esoteric off-shoots. Ramtha, wanderer of many worlds, remains eclectic.

The Experimental Quest

In late 1978, Knight forged a public persona combining New Age concepts with her extraordinary charisma and began to do public sessions channeling Ramtha. This led to private appointments with individuals, which were eventually discontinued in favor of more structured group teachings and organized fieldwork classes through the American Gnostic School.

Knight organized the Church I Am in the mid-1980s and then dissolved it. Through trial and error, much like Eddy and Hopkins, she disbanded her initial ventures in favor of other highly structured models. This initial organization may be a necessary experimental stage for fledging new religious movements. For instance, Eddy reorganized her first Christian Science Association in 1882 and Hopkins her college in Chicago in 1886. Both developed their organizations into more sophisticated, ecclesiastically oriented forms. As these women grew into their new leadership roles, they naturally wanted the expression of what they were doing to reflect the values they supported and the divine avenue they would embrace. Experimentation with structures and systems proved advantageous for them.

The Oneness of All

Hopkins as perennial philosopher was a significant forerunner of the contemporary evolution of psychological thought that postulates that humans are at one with or identical with Holy Spirit. Although this was not a new idea in human history, she masterfully made it work in her New Thought religion.

Hopkins and Eddy, as well as many other Christian Science and New Thought writers, wrote extensively about this premise and affirmed that "All is one, All is God." Hopkins took this a step farther and verbally decreed the at-one-ment. Today Knight has reached a pinnacle of success throughout the New Age movement that in part springboards from the religious ideas of her theological mothers. Her innovative evolution and the eclectic mix of Hinduism and gnosticism as well as creative visualization add a new twist to the old. Esoteric traditions as well as her own developments, such as the highly structured disciplines contained in the Consciousness and Enlightenment portions of her curriculum, have demonstrated that her students find something meaningful in the exercises that lead them to positive-oriented growth in their personal life.

The religion taught by Ramtha is inclusive of both genders and all races and ethnic groups. Ramtha claims to have a scientifically based methodology, integrated with age-old wisdom for students to learn to be the maestro of their lives by taking charge and making changes. Ramtha calls the students "master," buttressing their self-esteem, and implying they, too, are on the road to adeptship and are his equals. This attempt to empower the students through spirituality gives them an anchor replete with esoteric tools to grapple with an ever-changing and demanding world that speaks of the values and ethics of religion but operates primarily in a secular fashion.

Nature Religions and Ramtha

The neopaganism integrated into the Ramtha School of Enlightenment seems to reflect the desire to return to primordial times, when nature was the basis of religion and animism was the cultural and religious norm. This component of the Ramtha School supports Wessinger's theory that the metaphysical movements furnish a monistic worldview that presents "animism packaged for industrialized consumption by people tired of western theism and scientific materialism."[15]

This religious position has become a focal point for some new religious movements. Seizing the idea based on immanence from the New Thought movement and Native American religions as well as others allows God into the human through immanence. Hence, all life is holy. Knight in this case becomes the channeler of the Great Holy and expresses her extraordinary charisma through this avenue of divinity.

Pagan Elements: The Earth Counts

Pagan dancing (honoring life forms connected to nature) has been creatively appropriated at the Ramtha School of Enlightment as a celebratory energy-release dynamic and central fusion point. After flying high with Ramtha, the students then come down to earth to embrace their kinship with the earth mother. Members of the School can choose to create costumes reflecting creatures of the sky, earth, or water. Some of the costumes are artfully and innovatively put together. A colorful painting depicting Shiva is prominently displayed upon one wall of the arena hosting Ramtha School events. He is often understood as the destroyer deity of the Hindu trinity. Hinduism is noted for the female consorts or goddesses who accompany each male deity. In his portrayal at the Ramtha School of Enlightment, Shiva underwrites new birth—the ultimate symbol of the destructive forces that destroy the old and decadent to make way for the new rejuvenation that changes life from one dimension to another. The mythological concept that he is sometimes half male and half female provides a role model for the integration of masculine and feminine energies in each person. Androgyny has found a home here.

Women and their achievements and accomplishments find acceptance in the Ramtha School of Enlightenment. The senior students, business office personnel, and musicians are clearly visible, having attained positions of some responsibility and authority within the School. Pagan elements subtly associate women with the earth mother while Ramtha reigns as sky father. When Ramtha is not present, advanced students exert bits of autonomous control over the daily curriculum and student body. Knight seems to be comfortable with their on-site decisive abilities.

Conclusion

The quest for women's equality in mainstream religion has been an ongoing struggle. However, the women addressed in this analysis—Knight, Hopkins, Eddy, and Blatvastsky—show some adjustments to the male power structure while seizing individual power based on their special charismatic roles as revelatory prophets of the divine. Blavatsky's invisible spiritual hierarchy is male. Ramtha is male, and through Shiva—understood as the hermaphrodite god of the Hindu pantheon—validates women.

Even in the atmosphere of today's advanced ideas about gender rights, channelers must still work through the male voice. Women have seized the authority to communicate with Deity, though images of divinity tend to remain male. It is only very recently that popular religious culture has begun to accept female images of the divine, such as neo-pagan goddesses. The Ramtha School promotes women's rights as well as beauty of attainment and creativity. Would channeling a female deity disempower the channel? Would it be thought inappropriate? It will be interesting as the new century continues to see exactly when the paradigm shift occurs at which channeling female deities becomes the norm, if it ever does.

Channelers, being human, are reflections of a society, mirroring not only the religious ideals of a population but the unconscious conflicts within a culture—in this case, a culture ambivalent about giving women too much power. Channeling activity allows them to become empowered in a universe that does not promote women as religious authorities. So success still tends to come through male validation.

Perhaps the best of what is available to women and to female prophets is to dictate their personal and professional life on their own terms as much as possible. Hopkins, Eddy, and Blavatsky certainly were examples of women who carved innovative domains within the larger social structure of the Victorian era. Knight has created a large ranch, her personal domain in which to teach her channeled material. Surrounded by high walls, security guards, and watch dogs, she attempts to serenely order her universe close to her own personal standards and the need for privacy. Enthusiastic students clamor for more of Ramtha, and the townspeople, eager to catch a glimpse of Knight, sometimes gather outside the fence. Her controversial religion has not been fully accepted by the mainstream religions in her area. Success for her has had a downside. Yet her domain bears witness that her lifestyle is in many ways orchestrated on her own terms.

As a trailblazer for technological gnosticism, Knight has fought for the acceptance and legitimation of her particular school of enlightenment. She is a multifaceted personality unique in several respects. She has challenged the frontiers, synthesizing the age-old wisdoms with New Age science and psychology. The religious technology of New Thought has found a home in New Age communities. Ideas about what is permissible yield a metaphysical framework interfacing the visible and invisible that is a workable paradigm for her followers.

Democratic charisma advances the goals of the group and the individuals who wish to share spiritual empowerment. The fascination with the phenomenon of prophets and channelers rivets the attention of searchers and seekers. Knight has earned her place in religious history at the forefront of innovative religious activity, and has left a legacy of spiritual entrepreneurship for those who will march on behind them to the beat of a different drummer.

NOTES

1. See Ann Braude and her insights about the "Perils of Passivity: Womens Leadership in Spiritualism and Christian Science" found in Wessinger, Women's Leadership, 55–67. Braude's salient comments about women providing the vessel for the divine are stimulating and provocative.

2. See Wessinger in Women's Leadership. I am particularly indebted to Catherine Wessinger for her coinage of the terms "extraordinary charisma" and "democratic charisma."

3. See Harley in *Emma Curtis Hopkins*.

4. Braude in Wessinger, *Women's Leadership*, 57.

5. See Dell de Chant, "New Thought and the New Age," in Melton, *New Age Encyclopedia*, 326–331.

6. Amit Goswami, "Channeling the Ramtha Phenomena and Esoteric Teachings: A Quantum View from a New Science" paper presented at the "In Search of Self Conference," Yelm, Washington, February 8–9, 1997.

7. Wilber, *Spectrum of Consciousness*, 198.

8. See Tishken, "Metaphysical Paradigms in Contemporary Channeled Literature."

9. For a thoughtful discussion that is groundbreaking for understanding how women express religion, see Mary Farrell Bednarowski in "Outside the Mainstream: Womens Religion and Women Leaders in Nineteenth-Century America," *Journal of the American Academy of Religion* 48 (June 1980): 207–231. Women of the twentieth century were provided an infrastructure by women of the nineteenth century. Those intrepid advocates of women's empowerment rocked the proverbial boat so that paradigm shifts propelling women forward could be parlayed into today's religious arena.

10. See Catherine Wessinger and Robert Ellwood, "The Feminism of Universal Brotherhood: Women in the Theosophical Movement," in Wessinger, *Womens Leadership*, 68–87.

11. See *The Alphabet and the Goddess* for a compelling look at how the Goddess and priestess religions lost power as the alphabet emerged to fortify and advance logical linear left-brain function. Author Leonard Schlain is a neurosurgeon offering thought-provoking evidence (not in technical jargon) about what is masculine and feminine thinking and how it shapes society, education, and culture.

12. See J. Gordon Melton's position in "Emma Curtis Hopkins: A Feminist of the 1880s and Mother of New Thought" in Wessinger, *Women's Leadership*, 88–101.

13. Ibid., 90.

14. See the *Journal for the Society of the Study of Metaphysical Religion*, edited by Dell deChant. Of particular interest is the thought-provoking article by John Simmons, "The Eddy-Hopkins Paradigm: A Metaphysical Look at Their Historic Relationship," vol. 8.2: 129–151. This particular edition is devoted to thought-provoking commentary about *Emma Curtis Hopkins: Forgotten Founder of New Thought*, by Gail M. Harley.

15. See Wessinger, "Introduction," *Women's Leadership*, 8.

WORKS CITED

Harley, Gail M. *Emma Curtis Hopkins: Forgotten Founder of New Thought*. Syracuse: Syracuse University Press, 2002.

Kerins, Debra. *Spinner of Tales*. Yelm, Wash.: New Horizon, 1991.

Knight, JZ. *A State of Mind: My Story*. New York: Warner Books. 1987.

Melton, J. Gordon, ed. *Finding Enlightenment: Ramtha's School of Enlightenment*. Hillsboro, Ore.: Beyond Words Publishing, 1998.

———. *New Age Almanac*. New York: Visible Ink Press, 1991.

————— ed., *New Age Encyclopedia*. Detroit: Gale Publishing, 1990.

Miller, Timothy, ed. *America's Alternative Religions*. Albany: State University of New York Press, 1995.

Satter, Beryl. *Each Mind a Kingdom: American Women, Sexual Purity, and the New Thought Movement, 1875–1920*. Berkeley and Los Angeles: University of California Press, 1999.

Schlain, Leonard. *The Alphabet and the Goddess: The Conflict between Word and Image*. New York: Viking, 1998.

Tishken, Dennis. "Metaphysical Paradigms in Contemporary Channeled Literature: A New Revelation or a Revival of Perennial Philosophy?" Ph.D. dissertation, Florida State University, 1998.

Wessinger, Catherine, ed. *Women's Leadership in the Marginal Religions: Explorations Outside the Mainstream*. Urbana: University of Illinois Press, 1993.

Wilber, Ken. *The Spectrum of Consciousness*. Wheaton, Ill.: Theosophical Publishing House, 1993.

15

Heart and Soul: A Qualitative Look at the Ethos of the Movement of Spiritual Inner Awareness

Diana G. Tumminia

This descriptive study of the Movement of Spiritual Inner Awareness (MSIA) centers on the cultural ethos of the group. Information presented here was gathered by participant observation, interviews, examination of MSIA literature, and statistics provided by the organization. The main emphasis of this chapter involves a qualitative look at the ways MSIA members use their meaning system in their lives. Earlier studies (Ellwood 1999; Jones 1999; Lewis 1994, 1998a, 1998b; Zonta 1997; Introvigne 1998) have provided some information about this relatively new religion's practice and its history.[1] Since so little is known about the group other than these earlier works and very public criticisms (Lane 1994), this description may add to the knowledge about its cultural practices and everyday understanding of how the reality works within this worldview.

In addition to giving background information on MSIA, this chapter seeks to delineate the interpretive frameworks of the organization and its members. Frame-alignment theory derived from the work of Erving Goffman (Benford and Snow 2000) stresses the normative nature of meaning as a vehicle for group action. Each group creates an ethos comprising characteristic cognitive and emotional accommodation to cultural expectations through socialization. Relying on presumptions that an invisible spiritual world orchestrates the meaning of the visibly mundane reality, followers of any religion enact their participation based on relevancy constructed through social interaction. But cultural meaning plays an even more important part in new religions because members are rarely born into these belief system. Rather they choose the group based upon its appeal, that is to say, how well the belief system makes sense to them and serves their cognitive and emotional needs.

The Movement

The former high school teacher John-Roger Hinkins (called J-R) founded MSIA in 1968 and incorporated it as a church in 1971 as a vehicle to teach spiritual love and soul travel. A pivotal portion of the MSIA worldview proposes that the loving energy of the soul can become an attainable experience in life. Purportedly aided by divine forces, John-Roger based his authority upon his personification of the Mystical Traveler Consciousness.[2] In 1988, he passed the "keys" to that consciousness to John Morton, a former park ranger and prominent minister in MSIA, who now heads the church and continues to work alongside his mentor (Anonymous 1999). As an educational arm of MSIA, Peace Theological Seminary and College of Philosophy offers various courses in MSIA theology in addition to a master's and doctoral program in spiritual science. Two charitable organizations, the Institute for Individual and World Peace and the Heartfelt Foundation, implement the group's compassionate service orientation.[3] Based in Los Angeles, MSIA functions alongside relatively more secular sister organizations, the University of Santa Monica and Insight Training Seminars, which teach holistic psychology.

MSIA requests that members daily perform at least fifteen minutes or ideally two hours of meditation, called *simran* or spiritual exercises (John-Roger 1997). Typical members attend talks given by John-Roger and John Morton (called seminars); in the absence of "live" seminars, adherents listen to audio and videotapes of past talks. Commonly MSIA members call in the Light, then they meditate ("do spiritual exercises") on the Sound of God. Participants chant "Hu" (an ancient name for God) and "Ani Hu" (empathy for God's people) in public gatherings. After initiations, adherents silently chant secret "tones" (spiritually charged words given to them during the initiation process). At home, they do not normally set up altars, as some groups do, although they often display pictures of their spiritual teachers. Some followers fashion specialized spots for meditation at home, while others do not put much effort into this. Movement participants are encouraged to live from their hearts and to express loving feelings believed to be the true expressions of their souls. They frequently engage in charitable service projects as part of their spiritual practice. The group highlights the significance of compassionate service and love as part of a higher calling.

MSIA practices present a blend of Eastern mysticism with Western prag-

FIGURE 15.1. MSIA Spiritual Director John Morton sharing with students at the Master of Spiritual Science class in Santa Monica, California.

matism, called "practical spirituality." The organization does not require any special clothing or dietary restrictions, such as vegetarianism. However, those people physically closest to John-Roger (such as the MSIA staff) do not eat onions or garlic because he is allergic to those foods and the smell of those foods. The church suggests that its supporters not eat pork due to its "low" energy, although there are no real restrictions against it. MSIA also asks its members not to use illicit drugs, including marijuana. The group retains a modernized Western orientation toward gender and women's rights, and it makes no pronouncements about sexual orientation or lifestyle. MSIA ordains women and gays as ministers without fanfare or discussion, in line with its notion of universality and its commitment to minister to "all regardless of circumstance." According to Lewis (1998b), about two-thirds of MSIA members are women, and approximately 74 percent are baby-boomers.

The church professes a belief in karma and reincarnation within a modified Westernized context unbound by the Eastern implications of caste and gender inferiority (John-Roger 1975). Despite its emphasis on karma, MSIA also promotes a philosophy of life choices and self-accountability, saying in effect "it is not what happens to you, but how you handle it that is important." References to the existence of karma come up frequently as a topic in conversations, although MSIA's view of it may differ somewhat from that of other groups. Their concept connotes a karmic debt held within a multidimensional concept of the self, as well as in the positive or negative events that happen in one's life.

Members refer to MSIA as the "Movement" and to themselves as "people in the Movement" or students of the Traveler. MSIA identifies itself as an ecumenical church, referring to its use of eclectic metaphysical narratives; however, some members bristle at the term "church," preferring to define it differently, for example as a mystery school, a spiritual journey, or an inner experience. Some of this discomfort with the definition comes from members who were raised Jewish or rigidly Christian, and also from believers who prefer a New Age approach that would break with former conceptions of spirituality. As one minister wrote me in an e-mail, he did not think of MSIA as a religion but rather as way to experience "God as a living presence." Many members convey dissatisfaction with conventional religion; as one member put it, he wanted an "un-religion," if possible. Although MSIA members recognize the necessity of the legal status of the church, many find the term too constraining for their "experience" in the organization. Various followers say they joined because of "the loving" expressed in the Movement, evidenced in part by the typical MSIA greeting—the hug.

Generally in line with its emphasis on tolerance and flexibility, MSIA makes suggestions and guidelines as opposed to rules and restrictions. According to the church, the central teachings (Peace Theological Seminary 2000) are:

- God loves all of its creation.
- Not one Soul will be lost.
- Don't hurt yourself, and don't hurt others.
- Take care of yourself, so you might take care of others.
- Use everything for your upliftment.

The Movement's teachings also involve a complicated mix of esoteric topics (Santucci 1999) that can include discussions of auras, chakras, Masters of the Color Rays of light, and Lords of the Realms, to name a few subjects. Before the 1980s, when the Movement started to expand and to take on a more mainstream look, it was more likely to emphasize the esoteric. As one long-time member said, "The Movement used to be a lot more funky, full of flower children and nonconformists, but we changed with the times." This roughly correlates with the development of Insight Seminars and the University of Santa Monica, which concentrate on broadly accessible life philosophies and practical self-help spiritualities. This change reflected some of the modification in thematic direction as MSIA became more internally focused, drawing upon its own established identity. John A. Saliba (1998) observed a historical shift in the contents of the Movement's official newspaper, which used to print interviews with other spiritual teachers like Rajaneesh and Sathya Sai Baba and a column on astrology during the 1970s. Saliba contends that the historical

MSIA gradually changed its focus from the broadest context of spirituality to a focus on its own organizational accomplishments. James R. Lewis (1998b: 128) also cited this discernible transition: "In line with this maturation process, the focus of the learning that is the essence of the MSIA path has gradually shifted from esoteric education to an emphasis on self-understanding and personal growth."

I would argue that MSIA has never really shifted away from the esoteric, except in a cosmetic sense. As members aged, they may have become more concerned with social integration and material comfort, which could account for the historical change in appearance, as does the influence of the Reagan years on American culture in general. According to MSIA folk wisdom, John-Roger created the self-help focus to "assist" people with their "10 percent levels" (their physical lives in contrast with their spiritual lives) because it was an important need among his followers.

A Pastiche of Theology and Philosophy

MSIA combines Christian imagery with Indian Sant Mat practices (Jurgensmeyer 1991) in addition to its emphasis on the "practical spirituality" of self-help psychology. David Lane (1992) and Andrea Diem (1995) categorize MSIA as one of the newer offshoots of the Sant Mat religion, like Eckankar or Divine Light Mission that are also based on the Radhasoami tradition of India. Somewhat like these other Surat Shabd Yoga groups, the Movement teaches "soul transcendence" through soul travel in the "Light and Sound" of God. James R. Lewis (1998b) and John A. Saliba (1998) both noticed a marked tolerance toward other religions by MSIA, despite its generalized cautions toward overtly occult practices such as black magic (John-Roger 1976b). Saliba (1998) stresses the decidedly Christian theology of the Movement, while also noting the incorporation of Buddhist and Taoist philosophy, for example, John-Roger's book *The Tao of Spirit* (1994) and Peace Theological Seminary retreats in Japanese Zen temples. MSIA asserts that Christ serves as the head of their church, and that they as a group work with the Holy Spirit (usually referred to as the "Spirit"). Using Christian terminology, members aspire to live in "grace," and they often tell stories about the "miracles" happening in the their lives. Many followers talk about angels, and in accordance with Christian teachings they practice forgiveness of self and others (John-Roger 2000). Absent from their Christian-like orientation is the notion of original sin; to the contrary, MSIA claims that no one is ever separate from God. Rather than seeking the Light (Lewis 1998b), the teachings remind members that they are the Light, encouraging them to use the Light in their daily process of living.

A central theme utilized within the Movement pertains to the existence of alternative ways of knowing. As a general assumption, MSIAers can tap into their higher selves for a greater access to self-knowledge and information about what is happening around them. This type of experiential knowledge is considered a sacred gift of reawakening to the guidance provided by the soul and the Spirit. As a generalized pattern, MSIAers entertain interpretations based on dreams, visions, paranormal phenomena, and intuition as legitimate supplements to rationalized Western forms of knowledge. Some believers mistrust traditional forms of education, science, religion, and politics and presume that Spirit is manifesting newer and higher forms of these institutions to allow for more freedom, love, and spontaneity.

Saliba (1998) notes that MSIA people honor the Holy Bible in the same vein as *The Aquarian Gospel of Jesus Christ*, a very unofficial Christian book circulated in New Age circles. But true to its eclectic nature, MSIA also draws "life lessons" from Hollywood movie plots or television shows along with frequent references to personal experience and folk wisdom. In everyday practice, followers pick and choose their own readings and influences in a philosophy that the individual has free rein. Privileging personal experience over doctrine, members are encouraged to explore to "see what works for them."

From my own observations, typical MSIA members show histories of experimentation with and tolerance toward alternative spiritual practices. They are so likely to see alternative healers or body workers, like homeopaths and holistic chiropractors, that many Movement people themselves joke about the plethora of alternative diet plans or therapies they follow. Unlike Saliba (1998), I have observed individuals working with crystal pendulums and astrology when a fad moved through a local community. Since many MSIA local communities are tightly knit, news of any sort moves swiftly; this may account for the minifads that wash through the population (such as angel pins, the blood-type diet, special meditation chairs, vitamin supplements, red velvet hearts, and so on). Although I must agree with Saliba that such practices are not the focal point of MSIA, members are free to experiment, and they are frequently networked to other members with entrepreneurial enterprises that involve various holistic therapies and products for sale.

The Movement's theological eclecticism reflects a postmodern sensibility that evades the totalistic absolutism of established world religions in favor of a nonscriptural pastiche of various philosophies. Thus, MSIA subject matter can touch on any number of topics from nature spirits (devas and trolls) to the Christ Consciousness or out-of-the-body experiences to how to deal with your mother-in-law. True to its adaptive syncretism, MSIA has been known to organize a mass meeting for their version of the Jewish Seder (Passover) followed by an Easter celebration the next day. This distinctive process of refashioning and combining spiritual themes is a hallmark of their activities and teachings.

Social Organization

In 2003, MSIA had about five thousand active members who subscribe to monthly teachings called Soul Awareness Discourses or tapes called Soul Awareness Tapes. Deferring to the charismatic authority of John-Roger and John Morton, typical organizational bureaucracies with officers and departments run the church and its aligned groups. Moreover, large numbers of volunteers carry out specific tasks on all levels of involvement. MSIA has representatives in about thirty-two countries, with its largest following in the United States, Australia, Colombia, Brazil, and Nigeria, respectively. The Movement translates a significant amount of its literature into Spanish, and it maintains translators at most public events.

Its principal vehicle for organizing and carrying out projects rests with its ministers, who number about 2,600. Most ministers do not receive any pay from MSIA unless they have a staff job with the organization, only a tiny fraction of the whole. Meeting monthly to chant, ministers play a special role as a volunteer labor force that organizes and staffs MSIA events centrally and locally. Although nonministers also volunteer, ministers make up the bulk of this type of service.

The church ordains a minister on the basis of an approved application that is accompanied by recommendations from others. Other requirements include initiation, at least two years of study in MSIA, good character including economic self-sufficiency, and no use of drugs. In this process the applicant articulates a spiritual calling, the content of which is open and flexible. A typical ministry can be broadly based (such as serving one's family and community) and can also be specific (such as teaching or counseling). Most ministers hold jobs outside the church, because ministry does not fit the model of a salaried preacher. Rather the ministry is viewed as an individualized calling to act from the heart with loving service. As a case in point, noted MSIA minister and actress Sally Kirkland gives yoga classes while she also directs her ministry toward women who have had breast implants removed.

The informal organization of MSIA lies imbedded in its webs of social networks that are formed through seminar and class attendance. Such social networks influence members to attend MSIA events and to take "trainings" around the same time, establishing plausibility structures (Snow and Machalek 1982) of interpretive reference and physical exchange. Local members communicate through meetings, phone trees, and e-mail, in addition to established friendship connections. MSIA social networks serve as a primary community of interaction, although those networks closer to Los Angeles provide more intense integration with central church activities.

Massimo Introvigne (1998) equates MSIA with Paul Heelas's concept of a New Age seminar religion (1996), a type of spirituality that focuses on personal experience and psychological exercises aimed at self-knowledge and self-improvement. At the grass-roots level, local MSIA groups hold meetings (called seminars) and classes in spiritual and personal awareness. In addition to live sessions, seminars are also available on cassettes, video, and through the Internet. In a postmodern sensibility, Movement people regard the electronic connection as the same as the physical presence of their teacher.[4] By supplementing the transmission of its ideas with the use of an up-to-date electronic means, MSIA gets its message out by means of monthly Internet broadcasts, as well as sales of tapes, books, and videos. Although social interaction remains primarily facilitated through local seminars, workshops, and community service projects, such electronic media (Internet, tapes, and video) provide connection even at a distance from the main social activities.

The Norm of Positive Focus

The Movement exhorts its followers to be loving in their expressions, and it deems joy an indication of the presence of the Spirit and the true manifestation of God's energy. "Positive" emotions and speech wax normative in the group's worldview, which also cultivates spontaneous humor and expressive elation. Movement people eschew "negativity." As part of its norm for a positive focus, MSIA asserts that thought creates action in the world, a belief characteristic of several influences. It owes some of its belief system to the New Thought Movement and religions like Unity or Science of the Mind, which have influenced so many self-help modernists in the Human Potential Movement and New Age healing arts (DeChant 1999). If stripped of its metaphysical assumptions about karmic cause and effect, this philosophy also coincides with the psychological paradigm of Rational Emotive Therapy. From the Movement's point of view, positive thoughts and words create positive experiences, thus forming a normative verbal goal for members.

In keeping with its normative ethos, followers often correct themselves when they talk in a less than "positive" fashion, saying "deflect" if they have uttered a negative statement. For instance, one woman complained to me about another member in the group, but caught herself in mid-sentence. She said, "Oh, I can't take it anymore. He's a jerk. I can't stand it. Deflect. Ok, deflect on that!" After she composed herself she began again, "I am handling this with ease and grace. There, that's better."

Like many newer religions, especially those with New Age influences, MSIA interprets the earth as a teaching school that facilitates the learning of life lessons. In this vein, every life experience holds key lessons in spiritual living, from trivial traffic tickets to the tragedy of terminal cancer, and for that matter any emotional turmoil like anxiety or anger offers "opportunity" for growth. This is what is meant in terms of the MSIA teaching, "Use everything for your upliftment." Movement people pride themselves on being adaptive and living their lives without "limitations." By taking so-called negative experiences and cognitively redefining them as "learning experiences," they are able to get "above" their karma and reconstruct these events into positively viewed occurrences. They realign their perceptions away from "negativity," which is the normative frame-alignment in MSIA.

For example, I listened to a local member talk about her illness, a spinal injury requiring surgery, which eventually put her on disability payments. She explained to me how the pain she suffered, which now includes periodic migraines, led to her divorce. Since she now lives alone and experiences loneliness, she did not want to focus on her loneliness. This is also in line with a Movement aphorism, "Focus on what you want, not what you do not want." Putting emphasis on a positive interpretation, she said, "This has all been an incredible learning experience for me. Since I am by myself now, I can spend more time in my spiritual practice. A definite plus! My pain helps me have compassion for other people. This has all been a wonderful blessing taking me to a higher level."

Another example can be found in the perceptions of one follower about being a member of MSIA. Hardships are normally restated as blessings in disguise. I was privy to a conversation between two members who were talking about their lives after joining the group. When one asked if his life was better after joining, the other laughingly replied, "I wouldn't put it that way. My life has been a lot harder since I joined, but that is because I am working out my karma. I wouldn't want to think of what it would be like if I didn't have the Traveler. When I think of it that way, I feel really blessed."

The Movement states its guidelines for living within a "positive" linguistic framework. They avoid thou-shall-not statements, because that would be a "negative" way of putting things. True accomplishment of membership shows up in the way people frame their speech. Side-stepping the baser emotions of fear, envy, hate, and anger, members endeavor to speak in "loving ways" in order to be true to the Movement maxim, "Always use love, always." MSIA explains that this stance ought not be confused with the power of positive thinking that other groups use; rather they state that they practice a positive focus for their own spiritual advancement.

As part of its general cultural tenor, the Movement encourages humor and laughter. One initiate sent me an e-mail description of a live seminar she attended in which people broke out into a typical MSIA laugh fest: "The meeting was totally awesome. John Morton got up to speak, and he had serious things to communicate. But the crowd went wild with laughter every time he tried to talk. It was like Spirit was just dancing across the room causing giggles."

Prayer

People in the Movement pray by invoking the Light. All Movement events begin by "calling in the Light," as do many mundane activities like driving a car or finding a parking space. The act of calling in the Light for mundane purposes varies, of course, from member to member, but "putting things in the Light" remains as a consistent theme. The Light serves as a member's constant spiritual companion and protector, as well as the conduit for wishing others well. For example, "I place my husband in the Light for the Highest Good." Or one might say, "I place the situation in the Middle East in the Light for the Highest Good." Members pray in terms of putting any and all situations (such as illness or job searches) in the Light and asking for the highest good of all concerned. MSIAers frequently qualify sentences by saying, "for the highest good" because of the caution that "you might just get what you pray for." In their view, "for the highest good" provides a spiritual protection for any prayer or wish.[5]

As many people around the world do, MSIAers turn to prayer in order to solve personal problems or troubling issues. The church cautions against trying to control things and other people in the world, but encourages members to "put the Light on" situations using the highest good proviso, part of the reasoning being that few people understand the "karma involved." Members frequently pray for healing of physical conditions. Although the group makes no medical claims, members often expect healings and miracles, an expectation found in many other religions. Other frequently voiced prayers are for prosperity—"health, wealth, and happiness." Money is considered a "mirror of consciousness" or a feedback mechanism for how one is doing to support oneself inwardly. Besides more material concerns, members often express the desire to return home to God or other related spiritual intentions; for instance, "Light, bless me on all levels of my consciousness, awareness, and existence. And, Light, please help me to do better with my s.e.'s [spiritual exercises]."

The Relationship with the Spiritual Teacher

Like other Eastern religions organized around surrender to the guru, the Movement offers a spiritual master as the teacher of the sacred path, called the Traveler. Westerners and anticult sympathizers can confuse this concept with slavish obedience to a mortal man, who from their perspective lacks rational authority or personal integrity. In contrast, those amenable to this form of Eastern religiosity find the spiritual master a great source of comfort, sometimes described as "shelter" from the illusions of the material world. For some he becomes a father figure, even a divine loved one. According to MSIA (Peace

Theological Seminary 2000: 1), the Traveler serves as a spiritual friend: "Imagine that you had a perfect friend and guide to help you navigate a journey into unchartered territory—territory unlike anything you have experienced in your time on Earth."

Some participant observers of religious phenomena concern themselves with how participants recognize charisma in spiritual leaders. According to Lucy DuPertuis (1986), who studied Radhasoami and the Divine Light Mission, the power of the guru could be found in the perceptions of the students. To paraphrase DuPertuis's Weberian analysis, charisma is found in the eyes of beholders. Typically, followers presume special spiritual communication and power that flows from the presence of the master or image of the teacher.

Although there are exceptions, most MSIA members develop a strong relationship with their spiritual teacher as they endeavor to be released from karma in order to go home to God. Those members initiated before 1988 generally come under the auspices of John-Roger, and those initiated later come under the authority of John Morton. They are both called the Traveler. Essentially MSIA draws on older customs involving gurus and living masters coming from the Sant Mat tradition, but it does not impose any absolute deference. True to its penchant for innovation, it has created a new synthesis that defines the teacher as a Wayshower rather than a god. According to Mark Lurie, an MSIA minister who researched Movement transcripts on the subject, John-Roger very rarely used the Indian terms *guru* and *chela* (devotee); if at all, it was when he referred to someone other than himself. *Sri* is an honorific Indian title given to gurus. Initially members called him Sri John-Roger before he asked them to stop, early in the Movement's history.

In league with their mixture of approaches, MSIA members usually accord remarkable deference toward their teachers, tempered by casual familiarity. On the one hand, an initiate may entrust his or her total spiritual welfare to the teacher, and on the other hand, approach him informally to tell a joke or receive a hug. Followers exhibit no bowing or scraping to the spiritual master, but they do listen attentively and express delight at the sight of their teachers. Receiving a hug is a prized event evidenced by the fact that members usually report it with glee, saying something like, "I got a hug from the Traveler." Also anticipated and valued is the *twaji*, the gaze of the spiritual master. For instance, one member said, "When he looked at me, I thought he was looking right into my soul."

Members write "tone reports" once after each initiation, in which they describe their experiences in meditation and in any pertinent dreams. Experiences acquired through meditation and dreams comprise part of the process of knowledge acquisition. Followers also convey questions about their spiritual practice and include queries about their personal lives in tone reports or general letters. In what some students of the Movement consider the shedding of the ego, they unburden themselves about the most intimate details of their lives in the hope of receiving guidance and releasing their karma. Although not all letters receive "physical" answers due to the great volume of mail, members usually find the process of letter writing therapeutic. Sometimes members burn the letters without ever sending them, because they "know" the answers will be received spiritually.

MSIA members are said to be able sometimes to see the Traveler during their meditations (spiritual exercises). As an "inner master," their teacher may appear as a purple light or in a form they could recognize, like the face of Buddha among other appearances. In that vein, members also receive visitations from their spiritual teacher during the dream state, a notable event in the MSIA experience, which may motivate a person to write a letter about the dream. Although adherents rarely talk about what they encounter during spiritual exercises, they may speak about their dreams. Said one initiate about her vivid dream, "I opened a door and there stood Jesus, only I couldn't see his face, because it was just an outline. But within the outline shone all this light. After that dream I wrote MSIA to see if I could get an initiation."

From a Weberian perspective (Gerth and Mills 1946, Eisenstadt 1968), outsiders rarely understand what insiders "see" because followers, in contrast to nonbelievers, endow the charismatic leader with perceived gifts of grace. Adherents often attribute supernatural qualities to the teachers; as a minister disclosed to me, "When I first saw J-R, I didn't know who he was, but he had this big purple light around his head. So I thought, wow, I gotta find out who this guy is!"

Religion scholar James R. Lewis (1998b) found John-Roger remarkably uncharismatic, but reported a dream experience that allowed him to empathize with the ways MSIAers interpreted their connection to their teacher. MSIA offers a course on dreams, and it sells *Dream Voyages* by John-Roger that explains the meanings of dreams. According to the teachings, flying dreams may represent soul travel, a high level of consciousness. A member who took the dream course said, "Yeah, the Traveler took my hand and we flew through the stars. Just me and the Traveler—that's bliss."

Subjectivity and Self

All religions idiosyncratically define the self within their own worldviews (Pandian 1991). In what might at first sound contradictory in view of a follower's devotion to the spiritual teacher, MSIA places great importance on the individual and the self. From the worldview of Eastern mysticism, the spiritual master reflects the divine for the student; what the student sees is his/her own spark of divinity, a connotation that can also be construed as yet another interpretation of MSIA's Traveler. As one follower put it, "I just saw his picture, and it pulled me right in like an irresistible force. Then I saw my face in his face, and we were one thing. I'll never forget that, and that is why I joined the Movement."

MSIA emphasizes the exploration of one's relationship with the self and the process of interpreting personal experience as a path for spiritual enrichment, as do many groups with a New Age inclination (Heelas 1996). The very name of the organization, Movement of Spiritual Inner Awareness, refers to the implied sovereignty of subjective experience within the group's understanding of reality. Members seek an inner awareness and experience of what they believe in, hence the saying, "Go inside and check it out." Since MSIA considers the soul or the true self as divine, they exhort students of Traveler to reconnect with their higher natures (John-Roger 1984). Nevertheless, it teaches that experience may involve the awareness of three selves: the High Self, the Conscious Self, and the Basic Self (roughly equivalent to a lower self). MSIA warns against the delusions of the False Self, and promotes the experience of the True Self. Self and consciousness are considered to be multilayered and multidimensional, providing transcendent mystical knowledge in addition to mundane perception.

Since individual choice and perception are so strongly encouraged, members often talk in tentative ways suggesting the primacy of free will in all interactions. In normal everyday interaction, little formal sanctioning occurs, because MSIAers prefer to place common disputes in the Light ("I put this situation in the Light") in a hope of finding peaceful solutions. They utter phrases like, "You might find this helpful." Then there is the oft-spoken, "You might want to look into this." They avoid saying the word "should," as that would be controlling and oppressive to the consciousness. In line with this reasoning, members rarely if ever proselytize or preach in the traditional sense of these words, preferring rather to "share" their experiences. As a norm, MSIAers do a lot of "sharing."

As previously mentioned, MSIA provides countless books on self-improvement and psychological exploration of dealing with "issues." Many MSIAers write and repeat affirmations about having positive self-images or creating wealth and success.[6] The journaling of personal experiences serves as a very popular preoccupation in the Movement, indicating the emphasis placed upon internal dialogue and self-examination (John-Roger 1998). Because adherents spend a great deal of time examining their individual perspectives, they sometimes indulge themselves with lengthy stories about their inner processes. In response to this time-consuming interactional problem, they can be asked to "laser it," meaning cut the story short and get to the point. They often begin sentences with the qualifier, "In my experience, ————." In an attempt to avoid judgments of other people, a follower might say, "I experience you as ———— [fill in the blank]," in an attempt to take full responsibility for one's perception.

Another spiritual motivation for self-help comes from Movement teachings about self and karma. Members learn they do not have karma with other people, but rather have karma with themselves. Since presumably much karma stems from judging oneself (and others), a typical member may state self-forgiveness by saying, "I forgive myself for judging myself."

Another aspect of self and experience that MSIAers often articulate is their interpretation of synchronicity, the analysis of meaningful coincidence. In their minds, "there are no accidents," and everything happens for the spiritual reason of learning. The stories about these learning experiences account for much of the "sharing" that goes on. MSIAers attribute the causal factor of synchronicity to the orchestration of events that happen in their daily lives.[7] Chance meetings, job acquisitions, marriages, and divorces are often explained as the divine machinations of personal lives, as are other events like receiving money at a certain time or moving to a new location. In the recounting of these incidences, they often say, "I can see now that everything had been set up by Spirit." For instance, one initiate explained the synchronicity involved in choosing MSIA instead of another group: "I lived with my mother who was and still is very controlling. MSIA was the only group where you didn't have to dress differently or just eat vegetables. I could sneak out and go to the seminars without her knowing. So you see her being uptight just helped Spirit lead me to the right group after all."

Conclusion

Qualitative sociology endeavors to convey the ways that members of groups see their reality. Through participant observation, I studied the cultural ethos and uses of meaning in the Movement of Spiritual Inner Awareness, a relatively new religion that displays a syncretistic postmodern assortment of religious traditions and spiritual innovations. Although MSIA departs from conventional religions in some ways, it also shares a great deal with established traditions. In many ways, Movement members do what other people around the world do. They pray, and they worry about their families and finances, looking to spiritual intervention for comfort and relief. They yearn for miracles and healing, and relate to the mystical promise of supernatural contact. They hope to feel more peace and to go to a better place when they die.

Any religion erects boundaries of beliefs not shared with outsiders; within every religion meaning systems create differentiated worlds of experience. In the cultural atmosphere of MSIA, followers value love and spiritual energy believed to be emanating from the soul. As an extension of this value system and imagery, norms aimed at fostering positive expression frame the way members communicate and order their thinking. As in any utopian vision, the results may be less than perfect, but Movement people hold to the normative structure in order to "experience the loving." In visions of self or of the spiritual teacher, the notions of unconditional love extend to the others and take precedent in internal dialogues. Because of the human difficulty of maintaining such expression, MSIAers take classes aimed at psychological introspection and self-improvement, which is believed to be fueled by spiritual energy.

Although considered controversial by some because of its unconventional approach, MSIA endures because members still relate to its philosophy that utilizes many types of alternative knowledge and experiential interpretation heretofore rejected by the Western mind-set. Its amalgamation of previously disparate themes, such as Christianity, folk animism, Eastern religion, and New Age thought, exemplifies a postmodern acclimatization facilitated technologically by electronic means and interactionally by communal engagement. This adaptive process of reformulating and synthesizing ancient spiritual themes into contemporary approaches characterizes MSIA activities, and it remains a key factor in its appeal to those who choose it as a spiritual practice. Moreover, this type of synthesis may indicate an embryonic evolutionary trend in twenty-first-century religion. Despite public criticism, Movement members continue to find its philosophy salvational at the most and pragmatic at the least. MSIA appears to be in a period of stability, without any significant growth in the number of members in the last five years. When and if MSIA will be shifted from the category of new religions into an accepted religious sect is still unknown. Other questions remain. Will children born into the Movement stay in the group when they come of age? What will happen after the death of their founder? Will the MSIA prove adaptive and resilient to future trends in religion?

NOTES

1. The categorization of MSIA as a controversial religion stems from the nature of the polarized debate about the labeling of incipient groups as cults. Before the emergence of the anticult movement (Needleman 1972; Glock and Bellah 1976; Stoner and Parke 1979; Shupe and Bromley 1980; Bromley and Shupe 1981; Lewis 1994), new religions mushroomed within a sense of experimentation and amid an atmosphere of searching for new meaning. California played a strong role in the development of new religious movements because of its proximity to Asia and its population that had broken with many established traditions by means of extended migration. Upstart religions influenced by Eastern traditions found audiences especially among disenchanted youth. Public sentiment shifted somewhat by the mid-1970s, when abuses from some organizations became known and suspicions toward all new groups began to grow. While the anticult movement (Lewis 1994; Dawson 1998; Zablocki and Robbins 2001) highlighted important public issues, it also orchestrated the development of the cult stereotype by virtually erasing the notion of religious innovation and by substituting an absolutist label synonymous with social pathology. Stereo-

typically, internal disputes within organizations became redefined as automatically indicative of cultic misconduct. Today the dialogue and research seems to be polarized between anticult crusaders and cultural relativists who are more likely to use the term, "new religious movements" (Saliba 1995).

Historically, MSIA flew low on the anticult movement's radar until about 1988, when a series of *Los Angeles Times* articles focused on John-Roger and the allegations of disaffected members, some of whom were prominent ministers (Lewis 1994). Massimo Introvigne (1998) attributes much of the literary interpretation of MSIA as a cult to sociologist David Lane, who conferred with several authors, from the *Los Angeles Times* writers to the now-deceased Peter McWilliams. Popular author and former minister in MSIA, McWilliams (1994) launched an informational campaign against John-Roger with the book *Life 102: What to Do When Your Guru Sues You,* which involved legal battles and settlements. Lewis (1994) and Introvigne (1998) detail the waves of controversy. Introvigne (1998; CESNUR no date) further contends that Lane maintains anti-MSIA Web sites, some of which have been successfully legally challenged. How much such activities affected MSIA's membership is not known by this researcher. However in 1998, I did observe one woman at a local seminar who tearfully reported that her husband would not allow her to attend MSIA functions anymore because of what he had read on the Internet about the group.

When I talked to and e-mailed several long-time members who had stayed with the organization despite the charges, they generally said that they had thought about and considered the allegations, but found in them no compelling reason to leave. All cited their "experience" with MSIA as the motivation for staying. These experiences usually defy definition and include what MSIA calls multidimensional awareness, although people often ventured that the feelings of love for self, others, and God were part of what they perceived. One minister wrote in an e-mail that at the time he confided his misgivings to a friend who was also in the group, "As he spoke of his experiences, my own experience of the truth I knew came alive inside of me. . . . I found myself free of emotional speculations of disaster and standing solidly on a foundation of my experience."

2. The Mystical Traveler Consciousness and the Traveler are terms used in MSIA in a number of ways. In its spiritual essence, the Traveler serves as the "Wayshower" who guides the initiated through the other realms of existence so they may return to the "soul realm" and ultimately may become one with God. This consciousness, the Mystical Traveler, "anchors" itself with John-Roger and John Morton, who play the role of intermediaries with the divine. In its metaphysical sense, the Traveler refers to the true spiritual teacher who works through them and ultimately through all people. Sometimes the Traveler means an inner master seen in meditations or dreams; for example, "I had dream last night where I saw the Traveler." MSIA (Peace Theological Seminary Web site 2000: 1) describes the term as, "Traveler refers to mobility of consciousness. The Traveler is a consciousness that is present and available to all people." The term Mystical Traveler implies that this movement happens in "mysterious" ways. Sometimes people use the word to mean either John-Roger or John Morton, as when someone says, "I just saw the Traveler and asked him for a hug." The Mystical Traveler Preceptor Consciousness is a special dispensation associated with John-Roger.

3. The Institute for Individual and World Peace, the Heartfelt Foundation, University of Santa Monica (private accredited graduate school in counseling) and its division Insight Seminars are not legal subsidiaries of MSIA. However, John-Roger established them, and they are socially networked together as part of the MSIA culture. They also afford venues for educational and charitable events outside MSIA proper.

4. In this context of the seminar, the spiritual teacher holds *satsang*, a gathering of souls in the form of students around the master. During seminars, the Traveler is believed to communicate to each soul present, whether he is physically present or speaking through a tape recording. A typical member might attend a local taped seminar about once a week or at least at regular intervals, and privately listen to tapes at his or her leisure. An average member owns a large number of MSIA tapes. Those interested can attend an annual conference in Los Angeles with "live" seminars, and they might possibly sign up for classes at various cities in the United States and in certain other countries where MSIA has followers. Although John Morton and John-Roger may physically preside at only a portion of these events, the energy of the Traveler is believed to be present.

5. The Movement teaches a distinction between the Light, the spiritual energy, and *magnetic* light, a lower form of energy (John-Roger 1976a). The energy below the soul realm consists of the psychic-material worlds that utilize magnetic light. This magnetic light is part of the emotional or imaginative energy of a person. Magnetic light as controlling energy toward other people can cause harm. This negative state is avoided by placing people and things in the spiritual Light without attachment to the results, called "letting the Light work."

6. People say they "do" affirmations. For example, "I do affirmations. She does affirmations." An affirmation is a self-statement such as, "I am strong, rich, and successful. I am loving you and loving me."

7. Believers say they "attract" situations for learning. For example, "She attracted a boyfriend. She attracts success. He attracts disappointment."

WORKS CITED

Anonymous. 1999. *Interviews with John-Morton and John-Roger: Religious Scholars Interview the Travelers.* Los Angeles: Mandeville Press.

Benford, Robert D., and David A. Snow. 2000. "Framing Processes And Social Movements: An Overview And Assessment." *Annual Review of Sociology* 26: 611–39.

Bromley, David G., and Anson D. Shupe. 1981. *Strange Gods: The Great American Cult Scare.* Boston: Beacon Press.

CESNUR (Center for Studies on New Religions) Web site. No date. "MSIA v David Christopher Lane—Opinion of August 19, 1998, and Judgment of September 1, 1998." http://www.cesnur.org/testi/msia_lane.htm.

Dawson, Lorne L. 1998. *Comprehending Cults: The Sociology of New Religious Movements.* Toronto: Oxford University Press Canada.

DeChant, Dell. 1999. "New Thought and the Movement of Spiritual Inner Awareness." Paper presented at the meeting of CESNUR (Center for Studies on New Religions) in Bryn Athyn, Pa. June 2–4, 1999.

Diem, Andrea Grace. 1995. "Shabdism in North America: The Influence of Radhasoami on Guru Movements." Ph.D. dissertation, University of California at Santa Barbara.

DuPertuis, Lucy. 1986. "How People Recognize Charisma: The Case of Darshan in Radhasoami and Divine Light Mission." *Sociological Analysis.* 47(2): 111–124.

Eisenstadt, S. N. 1968. *Max Weber: On Charisma and Institution Building.* Chicago: University of Chicago Press.

Ellwood, Robert. 1999. "The Americanization of Asian Religion: The Case of MSIA." Paper presented at the meeting of CESNUR (Center for Studies on New Religions) in Bryn Athyn, Pa. June 2–4, 1999.

Gerth, H. H., and C. Wright Mills, eds. 1946. *From Max Weber: Essays in Sociology.* Translated by H. H. Gerth and C. Wright Mills. New York: Oxford University Press.

Glock, Charles Y., and Robert N. Bellah, eds. 1976. *The New Religious Consciousness.* Berkeley: University of California Press.

Heelas, Paul. 1996. *The Celebration of the Self and the Sacralization of Modernity.* Oxford: Blackwell.

Introvigne, Massimo. 1998. "The Origins of the Movement of Spiritual Inner Awareness (MSIA)," www.cesnur.org/testi/msia.htm.

John-Roger. 1975. *The Journey of a Soul.* Los Angeles: Mandeville Press.

———. 1976a. *Awakening Into the Light.* Los Angeles: Mandeville Press.

———. 1976b. *Psychic Protection.* Los Angeles: Mandeville Press.

———. 1984. *The Power within You.* Los Angeles: Mandeville Press.

———. 1994. *Tao of Spirit.* Los Angeles: Mandeville Press.

———. 1997. *Inner Worlds of Meditation.* Rev. ed. Los Angeles: Mandeville Press.

———. 1998. *Spiritual Warrior: The Art of Spiritual Living.* Los Angeles: Mandeville Press.

———. 2000. *Answers to Life's Questions.* Los Angeles: Mandeville Press.

John-Roger, and Peter McWilliams. 1988. *You Can't Afford the Luxury of a Negative Thought.* Santa Monica: Prelude Press.

Jones, Constance. 1999. "The Americanization of Asian Religion: The Case of MSIA." Paper presented at the meeting of CESNUR (Center for Studies on New Religions) in Bryn Athyn, Pa. June 2–4, 1999.

Jurgensmeyer, Mark. 1991. *Radhasoami Reality.* Princeton: Princeton University Press.

Lane, David C. 1992. *The Radhasaomi Tradition.* New York: Garland.

———. 1994. *Exposing Cults: When the Skeptical Mind Confronts the Mystical.* New York: Garland.

Lewis, James R. 1994. "The Cult Stereotype as an Ideological Resource in Social Conflicts: A Case Study of the Movement of Spiritual Inner Awareness." *Syzygy* 3(1–4): 23–37.

———. 1998a. *The Encyclopedia of Cults, Sects, and New Religions.* New York: Prometheus.

———. 1998b. *Seeking the Light: Uncovering the Truth about the Movement of Spiritual Inner Awareness and Its Founder John-Roger.* Los Angeles: Mandeville Press.

McWilliams, Peter. 1994. *Life 102: What to Do When Your Guru Sues You.* Los Angeles: Prelude Press.

Needleman, Jacob. 1972. *The New Religions: The Teachings of the East—Their Special Meaning for Young Americans*. New York: Pocket Books.

Pandian, Jacob. 1991. *Culture, Religion, and the Sacred Self: A Critical Introduction to the Anthropology of Religion*. Englewood Cliffs, N.J.: Prentice-Hall.

Peace Theological Seminary Web site. 2000. "Key Teachings of MSIA and Terms of Reference," www.pts.org/keyteachings.html.

Saliba, John. 1998. "The Movement of Spiritual Inner Awareness and Other Religions." Paper presented at the annual Meeting of the Society for the Scientific Study of Religions in Montreal.

Santucci, James. 1999. "Esoteric Themes in MSIA Thought." Paper presented at the Meeting of CESNUR (Center for Studies on New Religions) in Bryn Athyn, Pa. June 2–4, 1999.

Shupe, Anson D., and David G. Bromley. 1980. *The New Vigilantes: Deprogrammers, Anti-Cultists, and the New Religions*. Beverly Hills: Sage.

Snow, David A., and Richard Machalek. 1982. "On the Presumed Fragility of Unconventional Beliefs." *Journal for the Scientific Study of Religion* 21(1): 15–26.

Stoner, Carroll, and Jo Anne Parke. 1979. *All God's Children: The Cult Experience—Salvation or Slavery?* New York: Penguin.

Zablocki, Benjamin, and Thomas Robbins, eds. 2001. *Misunderstanding Cults: Searching for Objectivity in a Controversial Field*. Toronto: University of Toronto Press.

Zonta, Micela. 1997. "The Church of the Movement of Spiritual Inner Awareness: A Demographic Profile." *Syzygy* 6(1): 7–32.

PART IV

Other Groups
and Movements

16

"Come On Up, and I Will Show Thee": Heaven's Gate as a Postmodern Group

George D. Chryssides

And I will give power to my two witnesses, and they shall prophesy . . . clothed in sackcloth. . . . And when they have finished their testimony, the beast that ascendeth out of the bottomless pit shall make war against them and shall overcome them and kill them. And their dead bodies shall lie in the street of the great city. . . . And the people . . . shall see their dead bodies three days and an half. . . . And after three days and an half the spirit of life from God entered them and they stood upon their feet and great fear fell upon them which saw them. And they heard a great voice from heaven saying unto them, Come up hither. And they ascended up to heaven in a cloud; and their enemies beheld them. And the same hour there was a great earthquake, and the tenth part of the city fell . . . and the remnant were affrighted and gave glory to the God in heaven. (Revelation: 11:3–13)

The enigmatic nature of the Book of Revelation has enabled a variety of improbable interpretations. Most people, and certainly all serious academic interpreters of the book, would agree that St. John the Divine was not talking about spaceships, the Hale-Bopp comet, the Heaven's Gate leaders Marshall Applewhite and Bonnie Nettles, or how to gain transition from the realm of human existence to "the next level above human." Why, then, should an iconoclastic interpretation of the book by two leaders, both devoid of any formal qualifications that enabled them to pronounce authoritatively on its meaning, not only gain credence by their followers, but persuade them to commit collective suicide, in the certainty that this interpretation was true?

Mass suicide can be difficult to comprehend, particularly in a group like Heaven's Gate, which was under no immediate threat—unlike the Peoples Temple or the Branch Davidians at Waco. Those of us who are in positions of authority know only too well how difficult it can be to secure compliance, even on small matters; how, then, could Applewhite apparently gain such a hold over his followers as to make such a supreme sacrifice? This essay explores the question by considering the worldview of Heaven's Gate, and how Applewhite's interpretation, strange as it might seem to those outside the organization, succeeded in gaining credence.

In what follows I do not intend to take up such issues as brainwashing or charismatic leadership. Although I acknowledge that many religious groups exercise psychological pressure on their members, "brainwashing" is an imprecise and emotive term, lacking a clear or agreed definition, and brainwashing theories were largely discredited in Eileen Barker's important study *The Making of a Moonie*. Robert Balch, who covertly joined Heaven's Gate in 1975, together with his collaborator David Taylor, concluded that seekers were more inclined to come into the movement through a process of "social drift," while retention within the movement was a result of "social influence" (Balch, 1995). Likewise, charismatic leadership is a problematic concept. I have argued elsewhere that there are important different types of charismatic leader, and that charisma is better regarded not an inherent quality of a leader but as something that is generated by a group as much as by the supposedly charismatic leader (Chryssides, 2001). I know of no one, apart from the members of Heaven's Gate, who regarded Applewhite as remotely charismatic, and the members of the fated community were not impressionable young people; in fact, only two members were in their twenties, and the average age was forty-seven.

If we want to understand Heaven's Gate, we must examine the group's worldview, and I shall do this by arguing that the group exhibited a number of features associated with postmodernity. Postmodernity, of course, differs from postmodernism: the former is the set of characteristics that are supposedly attributable to humanity's present condition, whereas the latter consists of the ideas of various thinkers such as Roland Barthes, Michel Foucault, Jacques Lacan, Jacques Derrida, and Jean François Lyotard. The present study will draw on the features of postmodernity rather than endorse the ideas of any of the postmodernist writers.

Regarding methodology, I intend to outline the key ideas from the Bible, principally—but not exclusively—the Book of Revelation, on which the group drew. I shall sketch out some of the issues arising from these passages that would typically elicit comment by present-day biblical scholars, contrasting these with Applewhite's interpretation. The Heaven's Gate group is, of course, no longer in existence to corroborate or comment on interpretations; the one survivor, Chuck Humphrey (known as Rkkody, pronounced "Ricody") committed suicide a year later, in an attempt to join the rest of the "crew." Sources that remain are twofold: the Heaven's Gate Web site, which has been mirrored and is still accessible on the Internet, and some early accounts of the organization in the 1970s, written by Balch and Taylor.

The History of Heaven's Gate

A brief outline of the history of Heaven's Gate, leading up to the tragic events of 1997, may be useful at this juncture. The organization was founded by Marshall Herff Applewhite (1931–1997) and Bonnie Nettles (1927–1985). Applewhite was the son of a Presbyterian minister, and decided to study philosophy, gaining his degree in 1952. Intending to follow in his father's footsteps, he embarked on a theology course at Union Theological Seminary and Presbyterian School of Christian Education, at Richmond, Virginia. He soon abandoned his studies, deciding to embark on a musical career, and completed a master's degree in Music at the University of Colorado. He held two university posts: first at the University of Alabama, and subsequently at St. Thomas University, Houston, from which he was dismissed in 1970. Applewhite had experienced problems regarding his sexual orientation; he was married, but had a number of homosexual affairs. In 1965 he left his wife, and the couple were divorced in 1968. His father's death in 1971 compounded Applewhite's emotional problems, and it was in a state of confusion and depression that he met Bonnie Nettles in 1972.

Nettles was born a Baptist, but was little interested in mainstream Christianity. A member of the Houston Theosophical Society, she believed in the existence of the Masters, and attended a meditation group that claimed to channel discarnate spirits. The circumstances of her meeting Applewhite are unclear. According to most accounts, Nettles was a pediatric nurse who was filling in at a hospital where Applewhite was seeking a "cure" for his homosexuality. Other accounts state that Applewhite had a heart condition, and had a near death experience in the course of his treatment. One source suggests he was simply a visitor to the hospital, while another suggests that he suffered the more mundane ailment of hemorrhoids. I do not propose to adjudicate these competing explanations for the meeting. Whatever happened, Applewhite and Nettles established a rapport. Both had recently experienced personal traumas, and regarded their meeting as divinely ordained. Their subsequent relationship was not a sexual one; they believed that it was somehow connected with fulfilling biblical prophecy, and providing some new understanding of the world and human destiny. They came to attribute their personal traumas to the possession of their bodies by "Next Level" minds.

After spending some six weeks at a Texas ranch, the two decided to take their message "on the road." After a brief encounter with Ananda Marga, a Hindu yoga group, which did not appeal to them, they reached the conclusion that they were the "two witnesses" mentioned in the Book of Revelation (Revelation 11:1–2), and announced their identity on 11 August 1973. They hired a car, and traveled through Canada, buying their necessities with a credit card, which Nettles had "borrowed." Their technique of propagating their message appears to have consisted largely of leaving notes in churches announcing that the "two witnesses" had arrived. At one point, the two alighted at a New Age center, only to discover two members of the community already claimed to be the "The Two." When Applewhite failed to return the car, and the police discovered Nettles's credit card fraud, the two were arrested and served prison sentences. It was during his six-month period in prison that Applewhite appeared to shape his theology. From this point onward, there was little reference to the occult, but more on UFOs and the Next Level Above Human. Applewhite taught that there would soon be a "demonstration"—empirical proof of the existence of extraterrestrials, who would arrive to collect their crew.

Having been released from prison, the two met up again, and, having convinced themselves that their mission was somehow connected with extraterrestrials and space travel, they attempted to select a "crew." This time, they decided to organize a series of public meetings, producing advertisements, the first of which read as follows:

UFO'S

Why they are here.

Who they have come for.

When they will leave.

NOT a discussion of UFO sightings or phenomena

Two individuals say they were sent from the level above human, and are about to leave the human level and literally (physically) return to that next evolutionary level in a spacecraft (UFO) within months! "The Two" will discuss how the transition from the human level to the next level is accomplished, and when this may be done.

This is not a religious or philosophical organization recruiting membership. However, the information has already prompted many individuals to devote their total energy to the transitional process. If you have ever entertained the idea that there may be a real, PHYSICAL level beyond the Earth's confines, you will want to attend this meeting. (Cited in Chryssides, 1999, p. 69)

The group assumed various names. Applewhite called it the Anonymous Sexaholics Celibate Church, but perhaps unsurprisingly this name was

dropped after a very short period. The press gave it the name Human Individual Metamorphosis, which was Applewhite's jargon for the evolutionary process that their crew were expected to undergo in order to arrive at the Next
Level. "The Two" initially assumed the names of Guinea and Pig—an allusion
to their belief that they were participants in a cosmic experiment, designed by
the inhabitants of the Next Level. The Two invariably abandoned conventional
human names, in order to emphasize their "Next Level" identity and, being
"The Two," their names—which changed through time—were invariably those
of matching pairs, such as Bo and Peep, Do and Ti (or Te), and even Nincom
and Poop.

Nettles and Applewhite organized a total of 130 such meetings in various
locations in the United States and Canada. At one meeting—at Waldport, near
Eugene, Oregon, in September 1975—two hundred people turned up to hear
Bo and Peep, and thirty-three joined, giving up their attachments to the human
world. At the group's height some two hundred followers accepted The Two's
message.

In 1975, however, Applewhite and Nettles split the group up into small
cells, assigning each member a partner, and sending them to various locations
throughout the United States while Applewhite and Nettles withdrew from
public view. It was during this period that the really stringent membership
requirements were imposed. Members were not allowed contact with family
or friends; reading newspapers and watching television were forbidden; members had to renounce drugs and alcohol; men had to shave off their beards and
women had to give up wearing jewelry; sex was prohibited; and friendships
and conventional forms of socializing were to be given up. Members were
required to assume new names, all of which had to end in "-ody." This austere
period, which lasted until February 1976, resulted in mass apostasy, and the
organization lost approximately half its members.

In February 1976, Applewhite and Nettles reappeared, now known as Ti
and Do, and that summer the group moved to a remote camp near Laramie,
Wyoming. Nettles at first informed the group that they would receive a "demonstration" of the events The Two had predicted—by which she meant a firm
sighting of a spacecraft—but the group was later told that this "demonstration"
was cancelled. (Nettles seems to have made a practice of tantalizing the group
with such prospects, which did not materialize.) The group was then divided
into small units, or "star clusters," each named after a stellar constellation. It
was at this time that "uniforms" began to be worn, consisting of a nylon anorak
and hood, making members appear rather like Christian monks. In 1978 the
group's finances took a dramatic turn for the better. The exact details are unclear. An ex-member informant of Balch's mentioned a legacy of $300,000
that the leaders inherited; John R. Hall, on the other hand, attributes the
group's financial success to external jobs that were taken up by members,

principally in auto repair, technical writing, and computing. (It is an agreed fact that members had been undertaking external work immediately before they communal suicide; some of the group had expertise in Web design.)

The progress of the Heaven's Gate group from 1979 onward is not so well documented. Balch and Taylor left the group in 1975, and Balch stopped collecting information in the early 1980s. However, we know of two events that were of key significance. Nettles was diagnosed as having cancer in the early 1980s, and in 1983 had to undergo surgery, in which one of her eyes was removed. She died in 1985. Applewhite's interpretation of this event was that she had abandoned her earthly body in order to return to the Next Level to await the rest of the group. Applewhite remained to lead the group single-handedly.

The second event of import was in 1992, when the group resurfaced publicly, this time with the name Total Overcomers Anonymous. Despite their previous claim that the crew was complete, they made a "final offer" the following year, putting out a satellite broadcast, and taking out a full-page advertisement in USA Today, part of which read: "The Earth's present 'civilization' is about to be recycled—'spaded under.' Its inhabitants are refusing to evolve. The 'weeds' have taken over the garden and disturbed its usefulness beyond repair." (USA Today, 27 May 1993; quoted in Balch, 1995, p. 163). This final call was essentially for the "lost sheep" to reestablish contact with the group. About twenty of them did, and were readmitted.

This final period of the group's life was characterized by renewed vigor. There were renewed attempts to curb sensual desire, and when some male members found this unduly difficult, they discussed the possibility of castration. Seven members, and Applewhite himself, underwent surgery. The group continued to proclaim that the Earth was about to be "spaded under," and that humanity had a "last chance to advance beyond human," but this time with a much greater urgency than ever before. Balch comments that one of their advertisements "had an apocalyptic tone that was much more dramatic than anything I had heard in 1975" (Balch, 1995, p. 163; cited in Hall et al., 2000, p. 170).

The final incidents are well known. Applewhite and his followers rented Rancho Santa Fe, a mansion situated some thirty miles to the north of San Diego. Members of the group continued with their computer consultancy work, under the name "Higher Source," and led a highly regimented quasi-monastic life. Reports about the Hale-Bopp comet began in November 1996, and rumors of another object behind it were propagated by Courtney Brown, a university professor who had written the book Cosmic Voyage. Brown claimed to have communicated with psychics who affirmed that this object was a large alien spacecraft. Brown averred that it was arriving not for the purpose of invading Earth but to facilitate "galactic evolution." Members of Heaven's Gate took a keen interest, studying the skies and listening to reports of the comet's progress.

The third week in March was Holy Week in the Christian calendar, and the group requested that there be no visitors. The week was spent recording farewell videos and preparing for the transition. They packed suitcases, put money and identification in their pockets, and committed suicide, as planned.

The Book of Revelation

The Book of Revelation, as well as a few other biblical passages, featured significantly in Applewhite's teachings. Although seemingly scientific, UFO-religions are remarkably biblical in their teachings. Some, like Unarius (the first UFO-religion to gain attention, founded in 1954 by Ernest L. Norman) and the Aetherius Society (founded by George King in 1955) place biblical teachings in a wider world-ecumenical religious context, as did Erich von Däniken, in his well-known and influential *Chariots of the Gods?* (1969). Others have focused more exclusively on the Bible, for example the Raëlian Chuch (founded by Claude Vorilhon in 1974) and Heaven's Gate. In what follows, I propose to examine the interpretations of the "Two Witnesses" passage in Revelation that are generally found in mainstream Christian academic writing, and then to compare them with the meanings that members of Heaven's Gate ascribed to it.

Unsurprisingly, there are significant differences among mainstream scholarly interpretations of the Revelation passage. The book's historical context, and hence its dating, are contested, some scholars favoring a date around 68 CE, when the Roman emperor Nero was persecuting the Jewish and Christian communities, while others favor a later date, between 92 and 96 CE, during Domitian's rule. Although much used by fundamentalist Christian apocalyptists, it is not at all certain that the bulk of the text was written with a Christian readership in mind. It may have been originally a Jewish and not a Christian apocalyptic work, lightly edited, with the insertion of a few specifically Christian interpolations. One example is found in the passage under discussion (Revelation 11:8), in which the clause "where also their Lord was crucified" follows the phrase "the great city" (the passage is omitted from the opening quotation here): this could easily be a Christian insertion into a text that reads very adequately without the expression. The central spiritual figure in the book is "the Lamb," whom Christians popularly assume to be Jesus. This is never explicitly stated, however, and there is only one identification of Jesus as "the lamb of God" by John (almost certainly not the same author as that of Revelation) in his gospel: "Look, the Lamb of God, who takes away the sin of the world!" (John 1:29).

Although the author makes it sound like a personal vision in which John gains access to heaven and sees God's throne, this is more likely a literary device, serving as a framework for the book's message. Revelation is certainly a composite work, not something revealed in one single moment, when the author was "in the Spirit on the Lord's Day" (Revelation 1:10), since much of it is drawn—not to say plagiarized—from Hebrew scripture and Jewish apocaplytic writings of the intertestamental period. Indeed, the composite nature of the work may well be the cause of apparent discrepancies that relate to dating.

The passage under discussion is situated in the center of the book, and is a pivotal chapter. The main substance of the book up to this point has been a vision given to John of a door opening up into heaven, through which he was taken and afforded a view of God's throne. He sees a scroll, which has seven seals firmly protecting it. The "Lamb" sits on God's right hand: he is unusual in having seven horns and seven eyes, and he looked "as if he had been slain" (Revelation 5:4). The ensuing chapters describe the progressive opening of the seals, and this is followed by seven angels successively blasting their trumpets. By the end of the ninth chapter, the seventh angel is expected, but the text breaks off with a parenthetical chapter and a half (Revelation 10:1–11:14). Although it is probably an interpolation, it serves to increase the suspense before the seventh trumpet and the final opening of the scroll.

In this hiatus, a "mighty angel," who has a face like the sun, and legs like fiery pillars, presents John with a "little scroll." John is asked to eat the scroll; this seemingly strange injunction is reminiscent of the prophet Ezekiel, who was given a similar command (Ezekiel 2:9–3:3). The importance of this seemingly strange instruction is that it heralds a prophetic message, which the prophet has quite literally had to "read, mark, learn and inwardly digest." John is then asked to measure God's temple and altar; again, this harks back to Ezekiel, who has a vision of "a man whose appearance was like bronze" measuring the Temple area (Ezekiel 40). John is instructed not to measure the Court of the Gentiles, since they are excluded from God's dwelling; we are to understand that they are either the Roman persecutors or else the heretics that John has condemned earlier in this writing (Revelation 2:6, 14). The New Jerusalem will be designed without a Gentile court, thus ensuring their exclusion.

"Two witnesses" will prophesy, reminding their hearers of the impending doom. The identity of "the two" is crucial for understanding the passage (and of course Heaven's Gate). Two witnesses were needed in order to accord with Jewish law, which required at least two witnesses in order to convict someone of a crime (Deuteronomy 19:15). This passage predicts judgment either on Rome for its persecution or on the Jews for their disobedience. The vast majority of commentators agree that the "two witnesses" are Moses and Elijah, being the personification of the Law and the Prophets, respectively. At the scene of Jesus' transfiguration (Mark 9: 2–13), Moses and Elijah appear as witnesses to attest God's designation of Jesus as his Son. Both confronted the Israelites' idolatry, as evidenced by Moses' anger at the golden calf incident (Exodus 32) and Elijah's admonition of Queen Jezebel (1 Kings 21:23–24). The reference to fire coming from their mouths to devour enemies is more obscure; the allusion may be to Elijah's miraculous kindling of fire on Mount Carmel (1 Kings 18: 16–39), although it is more difficult to find an incident relating to Moses. Some commentators suggest the allusion metaphorically relates to the plagues of Egypt, but it may refer to Moses' fiery serpent (Numbers 21:8).

The numerology in the chapter is not easy to decode. The passage refers to 42 months (11:2), 1,260 days (11:3) three and a half days (11:9, 11) and seven thousand people who are killed in the ensuing earthquake. The first three numbers are inherently connected: 42 months and 1,260 days are both three and a half years. Whatever the explanation, the numbers are derived from Daniel 12:7, an equally obscure passage in which Daniel asks the question, "How long will it be before these astonishing things are fulfilled?" and is told by "a man clothed in linen," "It will be for a time, times and half a time" (Daniel 12:6). As Preston and Hanson point out, the significance of three and half may derive from its being half of the perfect number (seven), and hence appropriate to designate a period of duration of evil power. Certainly, both Daniel and John are speaking of a period of tribulation—John in fact calls it the "Great Tribulation" (Revelation 7:14)—and Daniel is probably alluding to the persecution of the Jews under Antiochus some two centuries previously. The period designated by the number three and a half is, however, a period in which good will triumph over evil, and John speaks of the resurrection of the two witnesses and their ascension into heaven, having been taken up into a cloud (Revelation 11:12) at the final end, followed by the ascent of God's chosen ones, leaving the rest of humanity behind amid total chaos and disaster.

Heaven's Gate's Exegesis

Scholarly interpretation of Revelation did not interest Nettles and Applewhite or their followers. Applewhite's message lacked any formal theological vocabulary; the metaphors he used were of two main types. The first are essentially derived from science fiction, especially TV series and films such as "Star Trek," *Star Wars*, and *E.T.* Applewhite frequently refers to an "away team"—a concept used by the crew of the Starship Enterprise in "Star Trek" to refer to those who had temporarily left their spaceship to embark on a special mission. Applewhite used this term to refer to the space aliens who had left their home planet, and who were engaged in the mission of "tagging" designated individuals, with a view to enabling the transition from Earth to the Next Level Above Human.

The second type of metaphor that Applewhite employed was horticultural.

He spoke of the Earth as a "garden" which was now so smothered with weeds that it had to be "spaded under." In order to be transported to the Next Level, "grafting" was needed: the members of Heaven's Gate had to be "grafted" onto the two leaders, Nettles and Applewhite. Horticultural metaphors derive principally from the Bible, where Jesus speaks of himself as the "real vine" whose gardener was his father and whose branches were his disciples, deriving their power from Christ, the principal stem (John 15:1). Engrafting is a metaphor used by Paul to indicate how the Gentiles can become part of God's covenant, which was originally given to the Jews (Romans 11:11–24). Parables of sowing seed, harvesting crops, uprooting weeds, and working in vineyards feature prominently in Jesus' teaching.

Some commentators have suggested that Applewhite used other sources, notably Hinduism and "Gnosticism." Writing on behalf of the Dialog Center, Helle Meldgaard states, "The mythology of 'Heaven's Gate' has echoes of both classical Hinduism, Christian ideas, and not least clear Gnostic traits" (Meldgaard, n.d.). It is unlikely that either of The Two had read any Hindu texts, and the suggestion of a Hindu connection has angered several Hindu teachers (Brahmavidyananda, 1997; Atmarupananda, et al., n.d.). Catherine Wessinger suggests that their idea that the body was a suit of clothes that the soul casts off upon death comes from the *Bhagavad Gita*, possibly through Helena P. Blavatsky's *The Secret Doctrine*. Even this is doubtful; the idea of the body as a suit of clothes is to be found in Plato's *Phaedo*, which Applewhite would be likely to have encountered as a philosophy student.

The influence of Gnosticism can be readily dismissed, too. Again, there is no evidence of ideas from either ancient Gnostics or modern revivalist groups that use the name. If "Gnosticism" is used in a generic sense to indicate that the Heaven's Gate group believed in a higher level of existence to which only initiates could gain access, then any claim that the group is Gnostic is merely descriptive, and gives no clue to any real or supposed influence. The group never used the term, and the notion of a Next Level Above Human can be easily accounted for by reference to UFOlogy and science fiction; there is no need to look to Gnosticism for any explanation. Applewhite's ideas can largely be accounted for in terms of his idiosyncratic understanding of the Bible.

Applewhite's reading of Revelation has some common elements with mainstream Christianity. There is an acknowledgment of two classes of people: those who are chosen to ascend, and those who are left behind on the earth. He perceived those destined for the Next Level as being confronted by forces of evil—the Luciferians, in his terminology—who had misled humanity and created evil on the Earth, to the extent that it was now beyond any redemption. He acknowledged a period of tribulation that would anticipate the final culmination in which good would triumph over evil for those destined to proceed to the Next Level.

His own distinctive interpretation of the passage is fairly evident. First, there is the identity of The Two, which, as I have already mentioned, was none other than the two leaders Nettles and Applewhite. Importantly, the interpretation of the passage is physicalistic rather than spiritual. "Come up here" means literal ascent; as Applewhite taught, heaven is not a metaphysical realm but rather the Next Level is located within physical space, to be reached by the spacecraft that was coming to collect its crew. The reference to overpowering and killing (11:7) again is literal; the only way to gain access to the spacecraft is through death, three and a half days after which a resurrection and ascension would follow. As events turned out, the picture of the rest of humanity gazing on the dead bodies was fulfilled in the enormous media coverage that the group received. Mention of earthquakes, particularly in the San Diego area, could understandably be taken as literal, since San Diego County is located amid a number of earthquake faults, and the whole area of California is particularly prone to seismic disturbance. Indeed, this is sometimes adduced as an explanation for the popularity of apocalyptic sects in that region.

The reference to the three and a half days is nonetheless associated with Jesus. Applewhite taught that there were several windows of opportunity for human beings to ascend to the Next Level, and that such windows appeared approximately every two thousand years. It is not without significance that the year 1997 was two thousand years on from the year 4 BCE, a date commonly given for the birth of Jesus of Nazareth. As well as being a reference to Applewhite's "crew," the verse also refers to Jesus' death and resurrection. Applewhite taught that Jesus was a "tagged" human individual, born of a human mother but conceived by an extraterrestrial. The purpose of his appearance on earth was to show how it was possible to change one's physical body "into a body of the kingdom of heaven through a *natural* process" (Steiger and Hewes, 1997, p. 179; their italics). This new body had remarkable properties; for example it appeared to be capable of suddenly appearing and vanishing, and was able to pass through closed doors. However, it was still a body of flesh and blood, as evidenced by Jesus' ability to eat and drink, and his invitation to Thomas to feel his wounded side (Steiger and Hewes, 1997, p. 180). The final incident in Jesus' life was his ascension, in which it is recounted that a cloud took him back up into heaven; predictably, Applewhite took "cloud" to mean "spaceship," and hence Jesus' ascension was his reclamation by the space crew from the Next Level.

Just as Jesus obtained his kingdom of heaven through death and resurrection, and forty days later was taken back up into the Next Level, so Applewhite's "crew" could expect to receive their new bodies by their own death and subsequent resurrection, after which their new "kingdom of heaven" bodies would be taken up into the spacecraft that awaited them.

Postmodern Analysis

Although such an interpretation of the Bible would be laughed out of court by mainstream scholars, Applewhite was not theologically illiterate, having experienced some formal training in theology, albeit briefly, as we have seen. It is unlikely that he formally studied the Book of Revelation, but at least he would be aware of the kind of approach that was characteristic of mainstream Christian scholarship. Why, then, did he offer an interpretation of parts of the Bible to which no reputable scholar would give the slightest credence?

What follows is somewhat more exploratory than what has gone before. I intend to analyze the reasons for Heaven's Gate's distinctive interpretations of the Book of Revelation by using the concept of postmodernity. It is important not to confuse postmodernity with postmodernism. The latter is a school of thought, or—more accurately—a number of related currents of thinking. Postmodernity is the condition that is attributed to society in the late twentieth century and early twenty-first century.

James Beckford identifies four key features of postmodernity:

1. A refusal to regard positivistic, rationalistic, instrumental criteria as the sole or exclusive standard of worthwhile knowledge.
2. A willingness to combine symbols from disparate codes or frameworks of meaning, even at the cost of disjunctions and eclecticism.
3. A celebration of spontaneity, fragmentation, superficiality, irony, and playfulness.
4. A willingness to abandon the search for overarching or triumphalist myths, narratives, or frameworks of knowledge. (Beckford, 1992, p. 19; cited in Woodhead and Heelas, 2000, p. 4)

Beckford's first set of criteria are plainly evident in the Heaven's Gate worldview. Like the vast majority of new religions, its worldview had an internal coherence, and hence, it might be argued, a rationality of its own. Nonetheless, Applewhite's methods of biblical interpretation were such as would be totally rejected by any serious student of the Bible. For a start, he seems to pay no regard to the quality of the English translation. At times he uses the King James Version (1611), which is now seldom used in mainstream churches, and which would be judged totally inappropriate for providing an accurate rendering of the original texts. At other times, and more usually, he uses the Amplified Bible, sometimes including its amplified glosses on the translation, and at other times omitting them for no obvious reason.

Although Heaven's Gate may appear to be an empirical religion, having dispensed with supernatural entities such as gods, the idea of a "demonstration" is something from which Nettles in particular held back. Members never became party to a sighting of the alien spacecraft, and even in the scenario of the communal suicide, belief in the existence of a craft hiding behind the Hale-Bopp comet was only accepted on Applewhite's authority. Followers were therefore not allowed to be wholly empirical in their reception of The Two's message, and firm verification was discouraged.

The group's synthesis of different frameworks of meaning is interesting. Heaven's Gate was not the first group to have combined UFOlogy with the Bible. As I have said, this had already been done by several UFO-religions. Unlike organizations such as the Jehovah's Witnesses, who have sought to expound the Book of Revelation systematically, and indeed to harmonize its ideas with the entirety of all the other books of Judaeo-Christian scripture, Applewhite made no attempt to explain the book systematically, to discuss its relationship with other parts of scriptures, or indeed to study it as a whole. The totality of his exegesis consisted of using a very small number of verses of Revelation for his own purposes, and combining them with his other cosmological ideas about spacecraft and beings from the Next Level.

In line with the second feature of postmodernity—eclecticism—Applewhite pieced together fragments of information from a variety of disparate sources. The idea of combining biblical exegesis with belief in space aliens is, of course, not new, and has its pedigree in organizations like Unarius and the Aetherius Society, and, more popularly, in the writings of Erich von Däniken. Applewhite showed no interest in making his ideas part of a school of thought, however, or in developing a philosophical or theological system to legitimate them. Unlike certain new religious movement, such as the Unification Church or ISKCON (International Society for Krishna Consciousness), the group was uninterested in developing a way of thinking that was capable of being defended in academic circles. Consistent with postmodernity, there were no grand theories to explain or legitimate, or inherent connections between the disparate ideas, only fragments blended together. The phenomenon is somewhat reminiscent of the well-known advertisement that associates a man smoking a cigar with Bach's Air on a G-String: there is no intrinsic connection, but they are drawn together for the advertiser's own immediate purpose.

The third feature of postmodernity (celebration of spontaneity, fragmentation, superficiality, irony, and playfulness) may initially seem inappropriate on account of the tragic events that brought Heaven's Gate to its end. Although the members themselves were subject to a highly structured existence within the organization, however, and exercised no originality or spontaneity of their own but thoroughly complied with Ti and Do's instructions, Ti and Do were themselves unpredictable and spontaneous, changing the group's structure as it progressed, issuing sudden instructions for members to convene at Wyoming, and teaching a message from Judaeo-Christian scripture that was largely Applewhite's own creation. A degree of playfulness and frivolity can be perceived, too, in the adoption of the various silly names by the leaders, and their notion that affairs on the planet Earth are not intrinsically valuable but are the results of a failed experiment by extraterrestrials.

The final notion—the abandonment of triumphalist and overarching myths—can be demonstrated in a number of ways. First, Applewhite was not seeking a form of scriptural exegesis that was valid for all time but only for the here and now. It is not an exegesis that looks for the original meaning of a set of doctrines or a sacred text, traces its meaning through time, and perceives itself as standing within a continuous unbroken tradition.

A feature of "modernism" is the attempt to analyze narratives diachronically rather than synchronically. For example, students of Christianity are typically taught to understand the Nicene Creed by examining the early debates between Arius and Athanasius; the early "ecumenical" councils of Nicaea, Constantinople, Ephesus, and Chalcedon; the meaning of Greek philosophical concepts such as *ousia* (being or substance), *homoousia* (of the same being), and *homoiousia* (of like substance), and so on. The scholar is meant to look at the origins in order to ascertain the meaning. This activity is not confined to Christian theology, but belongs also to a variety of academic disciplines. For example, in music the subject of musicology has been employed to ascertain what an "authentic" performance of a piece of music ought to be like—"authentic" meaning a definitive performance in the way the composer originally intended. Close examination has therefore been given to the musical conventions of the composer's time, establishing the true text, free from editorial interpolations, and often ensuring that the original instruments (or at least replicas) were employed in the performance.

The underlying rationale of this thinking was that there were components of meaning: the author's meaning and the user's meaning. Ideally, one should prise off the latter, leaving the former behind in its "pure" form. This way of thought underlies the phenomenological method in religious studies, in which early proponents such as Gerard van der Leeuw advocated *epochē*—the holding back or bracketing of one's assumptions in order to achieve "eidetic vision," or the perception of the pure form of the phenomenon, unclouded by one's own prejudices and preconceptions.

Subsequent thinking has indicated that such a quest is an impossibility. As Bakhtin and others have suggested, the knower is inextricably in the known. This is all the more true of religious communities than of scholars; the latter professedly aim to approach texts diachronically as well as synchronically, but in the case of religious communities, a diachronic approach to texts can often be positively unhelpful. The Heaven's Gate group was not a community of scholars examining the Book of Revelation against the history of early Jewish and Christian persecution, but a community that used selected texts to reinforce their own particular worldview. Given the presuppositions of Heaven's

Gate, the Book of Revelation appropriately reinforced the ideas of two leaders having been specially selected for the important mission of bringing together the "tagged" individuals—their "crew"—and enabling them to find the spacecraft that supposedly awaited them. The injunction to "Come on up" could therefore be interpreted as entailing physical ascension rather than metaphysical transformation.

The practice of reinterpreting texts to suit one's particular set of doctrines is not, of course, unprecedented. Arguably, early Christian thinkers did substantially the same with Jewish texts, construing many as cryptic prophecies foretelling their newly announced messiah. Understandably, present-day Jewish writers such as Michael Hilton, Hyam Maccoby, and others protest that such interpretations often wrench the text out of its context, doing violence to its original meaning. No doubt they are right, but meanings are adapted within religious communities, who put their own key doctrines into the texts, rather than bracket them and try to ascertain the author's original meaning. To take an analogy, there is a difference between buying a historical building that one must preserve, museumlike, in its authentic form, and buying a home in which one intends to reside, making the necessary adaptations for one's personal convenience and comfort. Traditionally the scholar is more like the museum curator, attempting to preserve the authentic original form, whereas the follower of a religion is more like a homeowner, who adapts and makes changes as necessary.

It therefore follows that understanding a religious community involves more than an understanding of its texts, as traditionally understood. As Wittgenstein argued, "the meaning of a word is its use in language" ([1953] 1963, I: 43), and to understand the meaning of any discourse one must understand the language game that is being played, and the "form of life" that is associated with the discourse. It is the community that ultimately decides what its religious texts mean, even if such texts are borrowed (as is often the case) from a different community that existed at a previous time and place in human history. Biblical scholars are now increasingly emphasizing the notion of reader criticism as a tool for understanding the meaning of a text, contending that in previous periods there has been somewhat too much emphasis on the background of the original author and his or her community, to exclusion of those who have used the texts. In some cases, such as Jewish scripture, there can be more than one category of user; hence interpreting Jewish prophetic writing can involve ascertaining how Jewish and Christian communities alike have regarded a particular passage.

Similar considerations pertain to new religious movements such as Heaven's Gate. Like the early Christians, they devised their own distinctive meanings of sacred texts. There is therefore limited force in countercult critiques that seek to demonstrate the ways in which such movements do violence to the meaning of scripture. The meaning of scripture is the meaning *for them*, and whether this is congruent with the text's original meaning is often a matter of little concern.

Finally, what is to be gained by analyzing Heaven's Gate's teachings in terms of postmodernity? Most obviously, any theoretical model facilitates explanation of a set of ideas and events rather than simply "telling the story." More specifically, such analysis helps us to identify a number of societal factors that were at work in the Heaven's Gate phenomenon: apocalyptic ideas, attempted separation from the world, and fragmentary knowledge of philosophy, religion, and space science. To the vast majority of people who remained outside the Heaven's Gate movement, it is not obvious how significant numbers of people could be persuaded to follow two leaders who used silly names, who claimed to be the unique fulfilments of biblical prophecy, and who had superficial knowledge of the subject areas relevant to their teachings. The analysis I have offered, I hope, helps to demonstrate how an intellectual climate of superficiality and fragmentary knowledge helps to make this possible, and how a group's attempt to find life's purpose entails seeking a "meaning for them" in a religious text, rather than a more overarching comprehensive historical meaning of the kind found within academia, from which Applewhite had long since been excluded.

WORKS CITED

Amplified Bible, The (1965). Grand Rapids, Mich.: Zondervan.

Anon (1997). "List of Mass Suicide Victims" *New York Times*, 29 March, www .rickross.com/reference/heavensgate/gate3.html. Accessed 8 June 2003.

Atmarupananda, Swami et al. (n.d.). "Suicide: Upside/Downside: Five Swamis Critique Media, Spaceships and Suicide" *Hinduism Online*, www.himalayanacademy .com/Resources/Suicide/LeadersViews.html. Accessed 8 June 2003.

Bakhtin, Mikhail (1981). *The Dialogic Imagination*. Austin: University of Texas Press.

Balch, Robert W. (1980). "Looking behind the Scenes in a Religious Cult: Implications for the Study of Conversion." *Sociological Analysis* 41.2: 137–143.

———. (1995). "Waiting for the Ships: Disillusionment and the Revitalization of Faith in Bo and Peep's UFO cult." In James R. Lewis, ed., *The Gods Have Landed* (Albany: State University of New York Press, 1995, pp. 137–166.

Balch, Robert W., and David Taylor (1977). "Seekers and Saucers: The Role of the Cultic Milieu in Joining a UFO Cult." *American Behavioral Scientist*, 20.6 (July/August): 839–860.

Barker, Eileen (1984). *The Making of a Moonie*. Oxford: Blackwell.

Barton, John, and John Muddiman (2001). *The Oxford Bible Commentary*. Oxford: Oxford University Press.

Beckford, James A. (1992). *Religion and Advanced Industrial Society*. London: Routledge.

Brahmavidayananada Saraswati, Swami (1997). "This Suicide Got No One to Heaven: Blame the Wrong-Thinking Philosophy of Heaven's Gate, Not the Eastern

Faiths" (1997). *Hinduism Today*, www.hinduismtoday.com/archives/1997/7/1997 -7-07.shtml. Accessed 8 June 2003.

Brown, Courtney (1997). *Cosmic Voyage: A Scientific Discovery of Extraterrestrials Visiting Earth*. London: Hodder and Stoughton.

Caird, G. B. (1984). *A Commentary on the Revelation of St. John the Divine.* 2nd ed. London: Black.

Chryssides, George D. (1999). *Exploring New Religions*. London: Cassell.

———. (2001a). *Historical Dictionary of New Religious Movements.* Metuchen, N.J.: Scarecrow.

———. (2001). "Unrecognized Charisma: A Study of Four Charismatic Leaders— Charles Taze Russell, Joseph Smith, L. Ron Hubbard, and Swami Prabhupada." Revised conference paper, London School of Economics, April. *CESNUR Library Texts and Documents*, www.cesnur.org/2001/london2001/chryssides.htm.

CNN Interactive (1997). U.S.News Story Page, www.cnn.com/US/9703/28/mass .suicide/links.html. Accessed 8 June 2003.

Court, John M. (1994). *Revelation* Sheffield: J.S.O.T. Press.

Deméré, Thomas A. (2003). "Faults and Earthquakes in San Diego Country." Biodiversity Research Center of the Californias, San Diego Natural History Museum, www.sdnhm.org/research/palaeontology/sdfaults.html. Accessed 12 May 2003.

Garrow, A.J.P. (1997). *Revelation*. London: Routledge.

Hall, John R., Philips D. Schuyler, and Sylvaine Trinh (2000). *Apocalypse Observed: Religious Movements and Violence in North America, Europe and Japan.* London: Routledge.

Harvey, A. E. (1973). *The New English Bible: Companion to the New Testament.* Cambridge: Oxford and Cambridge University Presses.

Humphrey, Chuck (1997). "Who Is Rkkody??" June, www.clas.ufl.edu/users/ gthursby/rel/gate/rkkstory.htm. Accessed 8 June 2003.

Introvigne, Massimo (2002). "There Is No Place for Us but to Go Up." *Social Compass* 49.2: 213–224.

Kurtz, Josh (1994). "Of UFOs and Hemmorrhoids." *Santa Fe Reporter*, April 27, www .rickross.com/reference/heavensgate/gate23.html. Accessed 8 June 2003.

Lewis, James R., ed. (1995). *The Gods Have Landed: New Religions from Other Worlds.* Albany: State University of New York Press.

———. (2003). *The Encyclopedic Sourcebook of UFO Religions.* Amherst, N.Y.: Prometheus Books.

Meldegaard, Helle (n.d.). "Exit Heaven's Gate." Aarhus, Denmark, Dialog Center, www.dci.dk/en/mtrl/heaven.html. Updated 14 February 2003; accessed 8 June 2003.

Partridge, Christopher (2003). *UFO Religions*. London: Routledge.

Preston, Ronald H., and Anthony T. Hanson (1962). *The Revelation of Saint John the Divine.* London: S.C.M.

Robinson, Bruce A. (1997). "Heaven's Gate: Christian / UFO Believers," 25 March. www.religioustolerance.org/dc_highe.htm. Updated 25 March 1997; accessed 8 June 2003.

Spacestar Communications (2000). "Red Alert: Hale-Bopp Comet Brings Closure to

Heaven's Gate," www.trancenet.orgshheavensgate. Updated 29 October 2000; accessed 8 June 2003.

Steiger, Brad, and Hayden Hewes (1997). *Inside Heaven's Gate: The UFO Cult Leaders Tell Their Story in Their Own Words*. New York: Penguin.

Thompson, Leonard L., (1990). *The Book of Revelation: Apocalypse and Empire*. New York: Oxford University Press.

Von Däniken, Erich (1969). *Chariots of the Gods? Was God an Astronaut?* London: Corgi.

Wessinger, Catherine (2000). *How the Millennium Comes Violently: From Jonestown to Heaven's Gate*. New York: Seven Bridges.

Wittgenstein, Ludwig ([1953] 1963). *Philosophical Investigations*. Oxford: Blackwell.

Woodhead, Linda, and Paul Heelas, eds. (2000). *Religion and Modernity*. Oxford: Blackwell.

17

The Raëlian Movement: Concocting Controversy, Seeking Social Legitimacy

Susan Palmer

The Raëlian movement appears to be the largest and fastest-growing UFO religion of the decade, reaching up to sixty thousand members—according to their own statistics released in January 2003—after the "baby Eve" cloning controversy had subsided. And it is controversial, like many other successful, evangelistic, apocalyptic new religions. But on closer examination, the source of the notoriety appears to be in their policies regarding the media. Since the early 1990s, the Raëlians have launched a series of publicity campaigns that were designed to shock, titillate, and capture the media's imagination.

What are the characteristics of new religions that tend to provoke conflict and controversy? The most common complaints against "cults" are that they split up families, they are closed communities, they drain members' financial resources, they deprive members of medical care and chidren of a broad education, and, finally, they sexually maniplate and exploit their members.

Many new religions invite conflict with members' families, almost inevitably, as a by-product of their "defamilialization" processes (Bromley and Shupe 1981). But the Raëlian Movement (unlike the early Children of God, Unification movement, and ISKCON) is not "world rejecting" (Wallis 1984) and does not offer a communal way of life. It even offers courses to assist members to plan their careers, higher education, and worldly success. Raëlian membership fees are minimal ($150 in Canada), their two-week summer camp is inexpensive, and the 11 percent tithing is suggested rather than enforced. Many new religious movements provoke controversy through refusing medicine or surgery (like Christian Scientists), but the Raëlians opt for modern medicine—indeed they might appear overly enthusiastic in praising science's utopian potential and the promise of human immortality through cloning. Raëlians do not set up parochial schools or practice homeschooling; indeed, parenthood is not encouraged, and the children of Raëlians are encouraged to explore other religious traditions before making their own choice.

Although the Raëlians' stance on "free love" and public nudity have generated some excitement in the press, this cannot compare with the punitive backlash against other new religious movements that espouse open sexuality. The Children of God/the Family were the target of a series of raids on their international colonies in the 1970s and 1980s, partly due to their missionary strategy of "flirty fishing" that was often mistaken for a prostitution racket, and partly as the result of their prophet, Father David's antinomian stance on children's sexuality (Melton 1994). Bhagwan Shree Rajneesh (dubbed the "sex guru") presided over an ashram in Poona, India, where avant-garde cathartic therapy groups encouraged group sex and cathartic self expression of erotic and aggressive impulses that led to broken bones and allegations of public orgies and rape (Belfrage 1981). The Raëlians' free sexual expression has, thus far, evoked a public reaction of amused tolerance rather than outrage—except in France, where many of "les sectes" have become the targets of rumors and unfounded allegations of pedophilia since the 1996 Guyard Report (Introvigne 2001).

The Raëlians' strategy for gaining social acceptance and free publicity might be compared to that of the infamous Church of Satan, which rose rapidly to prominence by the early 1970s, as their prophet, Anton Szandor LaVey, "seized opportunities for publicity" (Lewis 2002: 214)—publicity that relied on his theatrical sense (wearing devil costumes) and shock value (preaching antinomian values). The result of this was that Anton LaVey became an American icon, a pop culture hero, who appeared in the film *Rosemary's Baby*, and whose photograph still appears in tabloid stories on devil worship.

Paradoxically, it is through stirring up, then carefully monitoring a mild level of cultural conflict that the Raëlian movement has won a measure of public tolerance and acceptance. Raël, with his samurai topknot and white padded suit, is well on his way to becoming an international celebrity due to his controversial stance on cloning.

Raël's climb from charismatic prophet toward pop idol was achieved through periodic press conferences, where the Raëlian stance on a public issues such as deforestation, vote for minors, condom machines in Catholic High schools, anticlericalism, genetically modified foods, and nuclear testing would be voiced. After the controversy died down, spin-off articles would appear on Raël's clothes, Raëlian women's sexy Raëlian fashion, and on Raël's futuristic theme park, UFOland.

This chapter will demonstrate how the Raëlian movement (in my view, a harmless new religious movement with "deviant" beliefs that are no more or less irrational than those of mainstream religions) "inoculates" the public by feeding them selective doses of entertaining weirdness and mild controversy, in order to promote a greater familiarity with and tolerance of Raëlian beliefs—and, it is so hoped, to win a place in the public realm. In this way, the Raëlians are prudently working to forestall the kind of massive allergic reaction against unconventional religions that is currently sweeping through France, China, and Eastern Europe (Baubérot 2001).

Brief Overview of the Raëlian Movement

Raël, born Claude Vorilhon in 1946 in Vichy, France, was a race-car driver and journalist before founding the Raëlian movement in 1973. The movement began after Raël's encounter with extraterrestrials during a walking tour of the Clermont-Ferrand volcanic mountains in France. These beings, whom Raël describes in his book *Space Aliens Took Me to Their Planet*, entrusted him with a message for humanity. This message concerns our true identity: we were "implanted" on earth by a team of extraterrestrial scientists, the "Elohim," who created us from their own DNA in laboratories. Raël's mission is to warn humankind that since 1945 and Hiroshima, we have entered the Age of Apoc-

FIGURE 17.1. Publicity shot of Raël, founder of the Raëlian movement.

alypse, in which we have the choice of destroying ourselves with nuclear weapons or making the leap into planetary consciousness.

Denying the existence of God and the soul, Raël presents as the only hope of immortality a regeneration through science, and to this end members participate in four annual festivals so that the Elohim can fly overhead and register the Raëlians' DNA codes on their machines. This initiation ritual, called "the transmission of the cellular plan," promises a kind of immortality through cloning. New initiates sign a contract that permits a mortician to cut out a piece of bone in their forehead (the "third eye") after they die, and mail it packed in ice to Raël, who in turn relays it to the Elohim.

Members are encouraged through summer courses to achieve worldly success in their careers, to have better health through avoiding all recreational drugs and stimulants, and to enlarge their capacity to experience pleasure, which, Raël claims, will strengthen their immune system and enhance their intelligence and telepathic abilities. Raël advises Raëlians not to marry or exacerbate the planetary overpopulation problem, but to commune with the wonder of the universe by exploring their sexuality. To this end, Raëlians participate annually in the Sensual Meditation Seminar in a rural setting that features fasting, nudity, and sensory deprivation/awareness exercises and sexual experimentation, the ultimate goal being to experience "cosmic orgasm."

Getting Attention

A study of Raëlian history reveals a pageant of colorful controversies. These include the Masturbation Conference, their funeral practice of "lifting the frontal bone," "Operation Condom," and the Jews' response to their swastika medallion.

Most of these controversies seem to be deliberately provoked, and might be analyzed as practice drills in the Raëlians' twenty-five-year apprenticeship in riding the media. They have succeeded to a remarkable degree in reeling in journalists to attend their provocative press conferences, and in shaping the substance of news reports concerning the "UFO cult." With their Boxing Day 2002 announcement of Clonaid's (the Raëlians' cloning company) successful production of a cloned baby, they demonstrated their ability to coopt the organs of the international mass media to broadcast their own, quintessentially religious message.

Raël's taste for media attention is no mere narcissistic indulgence. It is simply the most efficient way to spread the "Message" given to him by an extraterrestrial named YAHWH, that fateful day in 1973 when he was climbing the volcanic mountain range of Clermont-Ferrand in central France. On December 13, 1973, a twenty-seven-year-old sports journalist, Claude Vorilhon, claimed he was dubbed Raël by the Elohim, and was given a mandate as the extraterrestrials' chosen prophet to inform humanity about its origins and the loving presence of "Our Creators."

Raël commenced to establish his movement by publicizing his book, *Le livre qui dit la verité* (1974), in which he describes his first encounter of the third kind, and offers a "scientific" interpretation of the Bible, with an urgent warning concerning humanity's potential to destroy life on this planet through the misuse of science by building nuclear weapons. He was interviewed by Jacque Chancel on his popular talk show, and after that Raël was besieged by journalists. Raël gave his first lecture at the Salle de Pleyel in September 1974, then in November rented a larger hall to seat one thousand. Raël first set up what Saliba (1995) terms a "platform society" called MADECH. Its stated mission was to demystify and demythologize the world's religions and to "spiritualize" science—without lapsing into "occultism or the pseudo-sciences" (Terrusse and Richard 1994: 39–40). By 1976, Raël had dissolved MADECH, and from its ashes a new religious movement arose. The International Raëlian Movement depended upon the authority of Raël, the "the Guide of Guides," who presided over a six-level pyramid of Guides. The Bishop and Priest Guides were empowered to perform initiations and publically represent the Raëlian movement, and under them were the Animators, Assistant Animators, and Propationers, who worked on a voluntary basis to set up meetings, organize lectures and social events, to sell Raël's books, and generally promote the "message."

The first deliberate strategy to manipulate the media was Planetary Week, held for the first time in April 1992. As a Guide explained to me, "we are planning a global action calculated to attract media attention, and demonstrate to the public what Raëlians believe and stand for." One of their first actions elicited strong media support—Operation Condom. This project was launched in December 1992 to protest against the Montreal Catholic School Commission's decision to veto the proposal to install condom machines in their high schools. A pink van dubbed the "condom-mobile," painted with UFOs, swastikas, and condoms toured Quebec and Ontario, stopping outside Catholic high schools during their lunch recess (Casgrain 1992). White-garbed, long-haired Guides, wearing their medallions of a swastika inside the star of David, leaped out and handed out free condoms; they distributed ten thousand condoms and pink buttons with the slogan, "Oui aux condoms a l'école" to the bemused high school students. "The Elohim don't want you to die!" the Guides told them. "They want you to live for ever! They created us to have pleasure!" The project was directed by a transexual Raëlian Guide who explained to the press that he/she was protesting the "ostrich-like stance" of the Montreal Catholic School Commission, and quoted daunting statistics concerning teenage pregnancies and sexually transmitted diseases in Quebec.

The next media blitz was in response to the July 7, 1993, Masturbation Conference. This event was the brain child of Raëlian bishop Daniel Chabot,

Ph.D., a psychology professor at a Montreal college. "Oui à la masturbation" buttons were handed out during the Montreal Jazz Festival to attract an audience, and the keynote speaker was the famous California feminist postmodernist pornographer-photographer Betty Dobson, who gave a lecture titled "Sex for One" and showed her film of overweight ladies masturbating therapeutically in a circle. Raël gave a rousing speech on the importance of self-love, and Chabot spoke about the psychological and health benefits of masturbation, expounding a neurophysiological theory about how pleasure stimulates the growth of new brain cells, leading to increased intelligence and spiritual awareness. The religious subtext of this event was that the Elohim created humans to enjoy pleasure without guilt. (One Guide, in reponse to my query, "why masturbation?" claimed that even Jesus himself preached masturbation. When I asked, "where . . . in the Bible?" he quoted Jesus's commandment, "Love thy neighbor as thyself.")

This conference sparked some negative news reports criticizing the Raëlians for luring innocent youth into their "esotique-erotiqur" sect, and Dr. Daniel Chabot became embroiled in a long-drawn-out lawsuit with the Corporation Professionnelle des Psychologues du Quebec who held a *deontologie* enquiry to determine whether Chabot was using his professional status to attract converts to his "secte" (*La Presse*, July 9, 1993: 4). Chabot retaliated by suing the corporation, and sent out a letter to all the psychologists in Quebec protesting the director's statement to the press that "Chabot was contaminated by his religious beliefs" (*La Presse* September 7, 1993: A4). Chabot lost his case, but proceeded to charge the corporation with violation of human rights.

Antisect Persecution in France

The Canadian and U.S. media have consistently tended to portray the Raëlians as harmless, good-looking eccentrics—or, at worst, as gullible nitwits. Raël, who recently only grants interviews to journalists who address him as "His Holiness," has become a media star, a celebrity, although he has been the target of the usual aspersions cast against "cult leaders." In France, however, the Raëlians have experienced serious opposition. Their playful experiments have been met with draconian responses of social control, including police raids, arrests, and lawsuits.

The first rumbling of controversy was over the "geniocracy." In Raël's 1977 book, *La geniocratie*, he lays out the political system on which the Elohim's utopia is based, which he observed on October 7, 1975. He claims the Elohim invited him aboard their spaceship and flew him to their planet for a brief tour. There he was introduced to a "geniocracy" of intelligent scientists and creative artists, who were awarded political leadership on the basis of intelligence test results.

This was more than a mere utopian fantasy; it became an urgent political movement. When Raël returned to earth, he called for support from his followers to "participate in the creation of a worldwide political party advocating humanitarianism and geniocracy, as they are described in the first message of the Elohim, and you will support its candidates. Only via geniocracy can humanity move forward into the golden age" (1998: 85–104).

In 1978, the Raëlians held a press conference to announce the creation of a new political party, "le mouvement pour la geniocratie mondiale." Three candidates were presented for the legislature, and in March 1978 they managed to vote in a Raëlian named Marcel Terrusse as city councillor in the town of Sarlat. While Raël was on tour in December 1977, the gendarmes searched his house and seized his files. Some of the top Guides' homes were also raided, and several Raëlian Guides were arrested and held for questioning (Terrusse and Richard 1994: 53). It seems that the combination of a swastika symbol (which by error was printed backward, thus conforming to the Nazi symbol on one of their posters) and the geniocracy, interpreted as a "fascist" political platform, evoked this extreme reaction from law enforcement.

Raël's reaction to society's hostile overreaction was both rational and prudent. He ordered his followers to abandon the pursuit of geniocracy, explaining that "we must chose between spreading the message and the Geniocracy. We are not ready to fight on two fronts. . . . [At any rate] thus far we lack a tool to measure the intelligence of an individual" (Terrusse and Richard 1994: 56).

In 1992 Raël and his Guides responded to the mounting anticult pressure in France, headed by the powerful anticult organization l'Association de Defense de la Famille et de l'Individu (ADFI), by adopting a defensive course. This involved suing the media for libel, public protest marches, and finally, the founding of FIREPHIM (Federation Internationale des Religions et Philosophies Minoritaires). FIREPHIM's aim was to protect the rights of religious, philosophical, sexual, and racial minorities (Vorilhon 1992).

FIREPHIM was the direct outcome of the assassination of a fellow French contactee named Jean Migueres. Migueres was the author of several popular books on extraterrestrials and near death experiences (NDEs), and had been brutally gunned down in the street by his father-in-law (Auque 2001). Raël, although he disagreed with Migueres's ideas on extraterrestrials, upheld his freedom of speech, and urged his followers to sign a form protesting the French government's granting of financial support to anticult groups that promote hatred toward religious minorities. He wrote a book denouncing the French government's support of anticult organizations, *Le racisme religieux financé par le gouvernement socialiste* (1992), and simultaneously founded FIREPHIM.

On March 29, 1992, FIREPHIM staged a week-long demonstration against the Montreal anticult center Info-Cult, carrying placards proclaiming "NO TO (anti-secte) RACISM!" and "Protect the Rights of Religious Minorities!" They stood outside the office of Info-cult, denouncing it in their interviews with journalists as "an antireligious criminal organization."[1] They did this in response to Info-Cult's published expose of Raël's "fascist" ideas on government, which warned the public about Raël's geniocracy as representing "a serious threat to democracy" (Casgrain 1992).

Raëlians joined in these publicity-seeking events initially as fun social gatherings, but they were soon confronted with a serious controversy: the Christophe Dechavannes affair.

In October 1992, Raël became the victim of ambush journalism when he appeared on a popular live talk show (Terrusse and Richard 1994: 152). Christophe Dechavannes, the host of "Ciel mon Mardi" put Raël on a panel of guests that included a priest, a psychologist, and a social worker. All expressed their disapproval of Raël's liberal views on sexuality and family. Then a surprise guest came on; an ex-Raëlian named Jean Parraga, who launched into a diatribe against Raël, accusing him of breaking up his family, brainwashing his wife, and incarcerating his little daughters at the Raëlian summer camp. Parraga projected an image of a respectable, concerned family man to the television audience, and his criminal record for smuggling stolen cars stuffed with hashish across the Algiers border was not mentioned. Similarly, his assassination attempt on Raël and his kidnapping of his daughters were not brought up.

It was quite clear whose side Dechavannes was on. As the result of this defamatory broadcast, Raël received hate mail and death threats, and found it expedient to move to Quebec and apply for Canadian citizenship. Raëlians protested this shabby treatment of their Beloved Prophet by flooding the TV station with letters demanding an apology and the right of reponse. Dechavannes countered by charging Raël with "incitement to violence." Raël agreed to ask his members to stop sending letters but demanded a public apology, and the two parties agreed to drop the feud. Parraga went on to found an anticult movement and raised funds for it by operating a prostitution ring on the Franco-Spanish border during the Olympic Games. He was arrested for "aggravated procurement" and received a five-year prison sentence.

The Dechavannes show precipitated a series of articles in the French media alleging that Raël preached pedophilia. In an article, "La curieuse leçon des petits hommes verts" [The curious lesson of little green men] that appeared in the Montreal newspaper Le Devoir (July 12, 1993), the journalist Stephane Baillargeon wrote that the Raëlians "defend pedophilic opinions" and that "certain old Raëliens accuse the guru of liking very young girls a little too much," and recommended that the Quebec government set up an investigation into the Raëlian movement. When Raël wrote a letter of protest clarifying his position, Le Devoir refused to publish it. Raël then launched a legal action for defamation and publishing "lying, malicious, injurious, and calumnious remarks" (Decision, Dossier 95–05–23, Roland, The Canadian Raelian Movement versus Bailar-

geon). After some negotiation, the newspaper published Raël's letter (*Le Devoir* September 7, 1994: A7), which states that the rumor is an ignominious defamation, and that Raël and the Raëlian movement "have always condemned pedophilia and promoted respect for laws that justly forbid the practices that are always the fault of unbalanced individuals."

It has become customary for the French media to refer to prophets of new religious movements as "pedophiles," and Raëlians have been often labeled "pedophiles" in spite of the absence of children at their gatherings and lack of evidence that their sexual practices include anyone besides consenting adults. The French anticult organization, ADFI, rooted out one Raëlian member out of sixty thousand with a troubled history of pedophile allegations, and relayed that information to the press, thereby stimulating a rash of Raëlians-as-pedophiles stories. As a response to this unfair stigmatization, the Raëlians adopted a proactive stance, and founded NOPEDO, an organization dedicated to educating parents on the dangers of pedophilia.

NOPEDO stirred up controversy in July 2001 by handing out flyers on the street in Italy and Switzerland warning parents of the dangers of pedophile Catholic priests in the confession boxes, claiming that one hundred priests in France alone had been already convicted of child molestation. When I interviewed a Raëlian Guide in Paris, he explained their strategy as follows: "We're not pedophiles, and were sick of being called that. So we want to make people aware of the double standard." The International Raelian Movement was promptly sued for libel by the Vicariat Episcopal of Geneva.

Today, in spite of the fact that only two Raëlians out of fifty-five-odd thousand members have been convicted—not of rape, but of inappropriate touching of a minor—the Raëlian movement in French-speaking Europe has, through the "rumor effect," gathered infamy as a dangerous sect that preaches and promotes sex with minors.[2] This has had a devastating impact on the lives of many Raëlians. Several have lost their children in custody battles. Two Raëlian bishops who offer sales personnel training workshops in France had their contracts cancelled. A Raëlian ophthamologist at a hospital in Roanne, France, held a three-week public fast in September 1992 to protest being fired, stripped of his title as "chef de service." He was reinstated after attracting considerable publicity, with the help of fellow Raëlians (Terrusse and Richard 1994: 160). Raëlian bishop and director of the Clonaid Company, Dr. Brigitte Boissellier, was fired from her job as the director of a research project for a French chemical company, Air Liquide, in 1997, after she "came out" as a Raëlian on the media supporting human cloning. She also lost the custody of her youngest child when her ex-husband sued successfully for sole custody and restricted visitation due to her involvement in a "dangerous sect" (interview with Boissellier at UFOland, Quebec, July 1998).

Stirring up Controversy

Although it is fair to state that the Raëlians are innocent victims of anticult forces in France, it is also true that they deliberately stir up controversial situations in Canada. Their periodic attacks on the Catholic Church are a good example of this.

The Raëlians' recurring anti-Catholic campaigns are one of its puzzling features. These actions would appear on the surface to contradict Raël's message of universal tolerance and "respecting differences"—racial, religious, cultural, and so on. But the Raëlians' anticlerical, pope-bashing crusades are, from their perspective, a necessary step toward correcting the message of Jesus (who, like Raël, was the son of an extraterrestrial) and toward realizing their millenarian goal. In Raël's, view, the Catholic Church has failed and has no reason to exist any longer, for it has failed to spread Jesus' message and prepare for the Age of Apocalypse. "Yes to Jesus, No to the Catholic Church" is a Raëlian motto, and Raël proposes that the Vatican be forced to compensate the descendants of Huguenots and Muslims in Jerusalem, whose property was "illegally seized." Raëlian Guides were dispatched to Rome to collect signatures on the street for their petitions to dissolve Vatican City and take back the land and all the wealth of St Peter's for the Italian people.

During the first week of October 2002, the Raëlians stood outside Quebec high schools handing out crosses to the students, inviting them to attend a cross-burning party in Jeanne Mance Park. The students were also given letters of apostasy to sign and send in to the Catholic Church renouncing their baptisms. The Quebec Assembly of Bishops accused them of "incitement to hatred." Several school boards tried to ban the Raëlians from "consorting with students" (*The Gazette*, October 2002: A6). Apostasy marches were staged in Quebec in the spring of 2002 to encourage Catholics to formally defect from their religion. The Catholic Church in Quebec has thus far received over five thousand letters proclaiming the "act of apostasy," whereby former Catholics renounce their baptism and proclaim their new allegiance to Raël and the extraterrestrials.

Raël's bishops demand that equal respect be paid to Raël as to the pope or the Dalai Lama, so in January 2003, shortly after the cloned baby announcement, journalists who wished to interview Raël were told that they must bow in his presence and address him as "His Holiness" (personal communication).

The Struggle to Control the Media

Although the Raëlians invite the media to cover their controversial antics, at the same time they demand respect. There is always a Guide in charge of collecting media reports on Raël and his religion, and of sending out "right of response" letters demanding apologies and corrections. Before 1992, most news reports were tongue-in-cheek, or even favorable, but since then anticult organizations have influenced the media's portraits of Raël so that he conforms to the stereotypical model of the "cult leader" who is a sexual libertine enjoying a luxurious life at the expense of his followers' pocketbooks. To illustrate the anticult movement's stranglehold over the media, I have found that since the December 2002 announcement of Baby Eve, four journalists have phoned me and asked if I think Raël fits the same psychological profile as Jim Jones and David Koresh, and if there is any chance the Raëlians might be planning a mass suicide.[3]

The Raëlian movement has pursued a litigious strategy of aggressive self-defence towards the more stigmatizing news reports written by irresponsible journalists. As a Raëlians' lawyer explained, "We are on our guard when we see journalists . . . we sue them because we demand respect . . . we are not con artists or nutcases" (personal communication).

Paul Toutant, a Radio Canada journalist, was sued for suggesting on his December 12, 1979, report that Raël was motivated by greed, and that donations toward the embassy for the Elohim that Raël is trying to establish were lining his pocket. Referring derisively to Raël's prediction of the aliens' arrival, Toutant hoped Raël would have enough time to spend his ill-gotten gains." When the case was tried in the Superior Court, Judge Jean Provost stated that Tournant's report that Raëlians contributed over a million dollars a year was accurate, but that did not give him the right to conclude that Raël pocketed the proceeds. Another libel suit was slapped on a publishing company, Spiromedia (associated with a Catholic countercult group), for publishing articles with titles like *Une escroquerie financière* (A financial scam). When journalist Jean-Luc Mongrain attacked the Raëlians on his program on Tele-Metropole in early December 1993, FIREPHIM responding by sending seventy Raëlians to the station to stage a protest demonstration (*Journal Vedettes* 9 [November/December 1993]:1).

Around the New Year of 2003, Raël's bittersweet love affair with the media came to a climax with Clonaid's dramatic announcement of the first human clone. (Clonaid is inspired by Raël but is not a formal part of the Raëlian religion.) This was a tense moment with high stakes. If "Baby Eve" proved to be an authentic clone, the Raëlians would gain social prestige associated with a major scientific breakthrough. But success could also render Raël and Clonaid's staff vulnerable to litigation, religious persecution, and terrorist acts perpetrated by outraged fundamentalists. And if Baby Eve proved to be a hoax—a preemptive scoop and bid for fame to one-up rivals in the cloning race—the Raëlians risked public exposure as perpetrators of a worldwide hoax that could damage their future relations with journalists and scientists.

Moderate Controversy—the Recipe for Success

Five cloned babies later, no testing had been arranged. The media has reached a consensus that the whole announcement had been, as Dr. Michael Guillen (former science editor of ABC News who had agreed to oversee the testing) put it, "an elaborate hoax . . . to bring publicity to the Raëlian Movement." But the movement gained free advertising on an international scale. As Raël said at the subsequent January 2003 meeting, "It's done. I've informed the entire planet of the message." The Raëlians' membership suddenly jumped from fifty-five to sixty thousand.

The Raëlian movement's conspicuous success in terms of growing membership and survival into the future appears likely at present, at least according to the eight conditions for the success of a new religious movement proposed by Rodney Stark (1987). Stark bases his criteria for success on his study of the Mormons, who were a small, persecuted minority in the nineteenth century, but who evolved into a large, international congregation that is still denounced as heretical, but is firmly established as a respectable minority church in most countries. The Raëlian movement satisfies seven out of eight of Stark's conditions, and Stark claims that if a new religious movement exhibits only five or more, its success is probably assured. The most significant condition for our purposes is that of "medium tension." Stark claims that a high level of tension between an new religious movement and society tends to invite repression and stigmatization, and can result in the destruction of that religion (as, for example, David Koresh's Branch Davidians in Waco in 1993). Low tension, on the other hand, tends to result in members' attrition and secularization, as seen in Christian Science. The International Raëlian Movement, as their history of controversy indicates, has managed to maintain a delicate balance between deviance and conformity, conflict with their host society and accommodation or deescalation of conflict (see Palmer, 1998). Some of their actions seem designed to provoke and shock, but others are calculated to appease and please. Their history shows a gradual movement toward social respectability and accommodation. Their *Apocalypse* magazine, for example, no longer features nudity in its photographs. The swastika medallion has been watered down to resemble a daisy. Children are not permitted to enter the Sensual Meditation of the camp areas, so as to avoid allegations of indecent exposure or child molestation. Raël urges members to obey the local laws of whatever country they live in.

So today Raël has achieved what every "cult leader" aspires to: some measure of social recognition, if not respect. Despite society's overwhelming prejudice against new, upstart prophets, and a strong anticult agenda in his native land, Raël has spoken before the U.S. Senate, he has rubbed shoulders with some of the world's top scientists in the field of genetics, and has shaken hands with the president of Zimbabwe. He has appeared on television countless times, and granted interviews to the world's most prestigious newspapers and magazines. His career reveals a steady and gradual escalation in his charismatic role. Claude Vorilhon started out as just another French contactee in the UFOlogical milieu, from the public's point of view, but his followers believed his claim that the Elohim had made him their prophet, indeed "the last prophet" in the "Age of Apocalypse." He later reveled himself to be a space traveler and a messiah (begat by a father who came from the sky). Today Raël demands the respect awarded to a world spiritual leader who must be addressed as "Your Holiness."

It is not unusual for the prophet-founders of new religions to be surrounded by a congregation of tens, even hundreds of thousands of adoring followers—and yet find themselves demonized in the media, and ostracized and often persecuted by the larger society. L. Ron Hubbard, Reverend Sun Myung Moon, Moses David, and Bhagwan Shree Rajneesh are examples of this paradox. The public's awareness and almost exclusive source of information on these religious innovators has been through the media, its stigmatizing news reports and hostile deviance labeling ("cult," "sect," "brainwashed," "mind control")—words that indicate journalists' heavy reliance on the anticult movement.

Raël has managed to overcome this hurdle by bearding the lion in his den, so to speak. Instead of waiting until journalists noticed his burgeoning new religion and wrote the usual snide cult stories on the wealthy leader, the gullible brainwashed zombies, rumors of sexual and financial abuse, and the kinky, kooky beliefs, Raël invited them to press conferences that highlighted an issue or a controversial stance. The news stories that emerged would then would be about the weird cult that was saying or doing something interesting and relevant, not just about the weird cult that was perceived as potentially dangerous because it happened to be a "UFO cult" like Heaven's Gate.

Despite their efforts to provoke and generate controversy, the Raëlian Movement's conflict with society has remained at a low level. Raël responds in a prudent fashion to signs of escalating hostility. For example, at the time of this writing, he is publicly distancing himself from Clonaid's enterprise, and claims he never personally viewed the cloned baby. Despite the failure of Baby Eve to materialize in the public realm, Raël is forging ahead. He has instructed Dr. Boisselier to build a "babytron"—a machine in which the cloned babies might be placed in order to undergo accelerated growth. Thus, Raël continues to pursue his religious quest for immortality.

NOTES

1. "Info-Secte n'a pas sa place dans une societé démocratique, disent raëliens et scientologistes," La Presse, April 14, 1993: 4.

2. Oddly enough, Raël's own marriage to a sixteen-year-old, which began as a courtship while she was still fifteen, has received no comment in the press.

3. Since the mass suicide-homicides of the Ordre du Temple solaire in October 1993, the climate of religious tolerance in France has plummeted. The French media receive faxes relating the lastest *secte* scandal daily from the countercult agancy ADFI, and relies almost exclusively on anticult sources. Dissenting, more tolerant opinions regarding new religions are not heard in the public forum, and the degree of persecution leveled against religious minorities appears astonishing to North Americans accustomed to the assumptions regarding religious freedom and toleration that are built into our Constitution.

WORKS CITED

Augue, Roger. 2001. "Au nom de la loi, rien de l'arrête!" *Le Figaro Magaziner,* June 22, 23.

Baubérot, Jean. 2001. "La laicité française face à un pluralisme et ses mutations." Pp. 169–182 in *Chercheurs de Dieux dans l'espace publique,* edited by Pauline Cote. Ottawa: University of Ottawa Press.

Belfrage, Sally. 1981. *Flowers of Emptiness.* New York: Dial Press.

Bromley, David G., and Anson Shupe. 1981. *Strange Gods.* Boston: Beacon Press.

Introvigne, Massimo. 2001. "Le famtôme de la Liberté: Les controverses sur les sects et les nouveaux mouvements religieux en Europe." Pp. 57–82 in *Chercheurs de Dieux dans l'espace publique,* edited by Pauline Cote. Ottawa: University of Ottawa Press.

Lewis, James R. 2002. "Diabolical Authority: Anton LaVey, The Satanic Bible and the Satanist Tradition." *Marburg Journal of Religious Studies* 7:1. [An unpaginated electronic work.]

Melton, J. Gordon. 1994. "Sexuality and the Maturation of the Family." Pp. 71–96 in *Sex, Slander and Salvation,* edited by James R. Lewis and J. Gordon Melton. Stanford, Cal.: Center for Academic Publication.

Palmer, Susan. 1998. "The Raëlians Are Coming: The Future of a UFO Religion." Pp. 139–46 in *Religion in a Changing World,* edited by Madeleine Cousineau. Westport, Conn.: Praeger.

Saliba, John A. 1995. "Religious Dimensions of the UFO Phenomena." Pp. 15–64 in *The Gods Have Landed,* edited by James Lewis. Albany: State University of New York Press.

Stark, Rodney. 1987. "How New Religions Succeed: A Theoretical Model." Pp. 11–29 in *The Future of New Religious Movements,* edited by David G. Bromley and Phillip E. Hammond. Macon, Ga.: Mercer University Press.

Terrusse, Marcel, and Michèle Richard. 1994. *20 ans: La génération temps des Pionniers.* Nimes: Éditions DIFRA, Mouvement Raëlien.

Vorilhon, Claude [Raël]. 1974. *Le livre qui dit la verité.* Vaduz: Fondation Raëlienne.

———. 1977. *La geniocratie.* Brantome: L'édition du Message.

———. 1992. *Le racisme religieux financé par le gouvernement socialiste: Halte à la violation des droits de l'homme en France.* Geneva: La Fondation Raëlienne.

Wallis, Roy. 1984. *The Elementary Forms of the New Religious Life*. London: Routledge and Kegan Paul.

REFERENCES

Décision Dossier 95-05-23, Roland, Mouvement Raëlien Canadien et Raël contre Baillargeon et *Le Devoir*. Conseil de Presse du Quebec.

Le Devoir, 4 December 1992, B-7. "Le condom raëlien: une initiative prophylactique anti-democratique," by Yves Casgrain.

La Presse, Montreal, 9 July. "Raël et la masturbation: les psychologues enqueteront sur la participation d'un des leurs a une conference."

La Tribune, Sherbrooke, 21 May 1993. "Raël plaide pour le respect des differences."

18

White Racist Religions in the United States: From Christian Identity to Wolf Age Pagans

Mattias Gardell

Among the controversial new religions transforming the spiritual landscape of the United States are white racist religions, which recruit adherents from the "white power milieu."[1] White religious racism is not a unified creed but a heterogeneous category that comprises many different congregations and philosophies, ranging from racist recasts of Christianity to a plethora of racist pagan, occult fascist, and Satanist constructs. Racist interpretations of religion are obviously not unique to white Americans but may be found among Americans of every "race"—as evidenced, for example, by the inroads made by black nationalist Islam among African Americans (Gardell 1996). Neither are racist readings of religions new, as evidenced by the contribution of theological reflection to the invention of race and racism in the sixteenth and seventeenth centuries and the utilization of biblical arguments to legitimize slavery and white world supremacy.

To a certain extent, the white racist religions presented in this essay represent a continuation of religious racist thought from the past, cultivating the legacies of racist Christianity in antebellum America and racist pagan/occult protofascist philosophy prevalent in the national romantic *völkisch* culture of continental Europe at the turn of the last century. What makes these belief systems "controversial" is linked to the gradual reevaluation of racism in mainstream America. Once considered a divinely created order of nature confirmed by science, racism is today cast in the garbage dump of obsolete ideas, at least publicly. Whereas a white religious racist in pre-Brown America could come across as a "good citizen," today he would be seen as a social villain. Along with the process by which racism was challenged as a constitutionally protected pillar of American society, white racist attitudes toward the federal government to be transformed from the "patriotic" celebration of "hundred percent Americanism" of the classical Ku Klux Klan to the present-day declaration of war against an American administration seen as a primary enemy of the white man. From this shift stem occasional outbursts of violent words and deeds that contribute toward making many if not all of these racist religious groups qualify as controversial or even criminal in the public eye.

The racist religions presented here fall into three main categories: racist Christianity, religious national socialism, and racist paganism. To a certain extent, their emergence reflects a gradual radicalization of white-racist thought in the United States. As they are all linked with the formation of a white-power underground culture, a brief introduction to this milieu will set the stage for the subsequent discussion of the three categories of white racist religious thought.

White Power

Coined in 1966 by George Lincoln Rockwell, founder of the American Nazi Party and chairman of now defunct World Union of National Socialists, the concept of White Power was formulated in response to the black civil rights movement's fight to end racial segregation, and in the face of more radical demands for Black Power (coined by Adam Clayton Powell and popularized by H. Rap Brown earlier the same year).[2] With the concept of White Power, Rockwell initiated a national socialist shift away from the narrow Aryan/Germanic ultranationalist position of Hitler toward the inclusive pan-Aryan-race nationalist perspective that informs much of the current white-racist culture. At the time, Rockwell's willingness to include non-Nordic people such as Poles, Russians, Greeks, Turks, Spaniards, and Italians as white provoked ideological resentment from both Hitlerite Nordic purists and believers in the legacy of Anglo-Saxon supremacy that long had dominated the alchemy of race and nation in American society. Informed by the then culminating process to construct a monolithic white race—whereby the previously distinct Nordic, Alpine, Mediterranean, and such "races" metamorphosed into a plethora of different "ethnics"—to secure white power over black people in American society, Rockwell's thinking was in line with the times and his position would eventually secure the largest following.

At its heart, invoking the concept of white power involves a notion of powerlessness, of having been deprived of an exalted position conceived of as a birthright privilege. Issued at the height of the conflict over racial segregation,

Rockwell's call for white power came at a time when white racists felt their claims of supremacy threatened but not yet lost. Although he called himself a revolutionary, Rockwell insisted on loyalty to the Constitution and the laws of the United States and believed that the imagined Jewish conspiracy for world dominion could be halted, as it was not yet complete. None of Rockwell's organizational efforts achieved any resemblance of importance before his assassination in 1967. The significance of Rockwell lies rather in the legacy he bequeathed the white-racist scene, for which the concept of white power became a unifying tool in the decades to come.

As the 1960s gave way to the 1970s, racial desegregation became more of a reality than a threat, and mainstream American society turned decisively toward a multicultural conception of the American nation. National liberation movements all over Africa and Asia successfully braved the colonial world order and a series of new states achieved independence. Racism gradually lost its adequacy as a mode of social classification and was seriously challenged in science, education, religion, politics, sports, media, and culture. Organized white-racist opposition to this overall process grew increasingly more radical, desperate, and fragmented after each defeat. How could white racism, long thought of as mandated by God and the laws of nature, now suddenly be stigmatized as false and unwanted?

Cast into a state of confusion, white-racist ideologues developed various conspiracy theories alleging that an evil cabal of racial enemies, often though not exclusively known under the acronym ZOG (Zionist occupational government) had usurped the power of the U.S. administration and all the governments of the "once white world." This perspective involves the elevation of Jews as an omnipotent body of malicious power, a key component in the conspiracy for world dominion that may also include assorted others such as bankers, plutocrats, aliens, or the illuminati. The cabal is typically thought to have masterminded a plan to eliminate the one force with innate qualities strong enough to thwart their scheme: the freedom-loving white race. Pushing racial equality, multiculturalism, immigration, and relocation of industries from "white" nations to nonwhite countries, the imagined cabal is alleged to be trying to blend all the cultures of the world into one, soulless, mongrel race of easily manipulated and exchangeable units of production. The white man is accordingly believed to be a rapidly diminishing minority at the brink of extermination. White power activists see themselves as the "last resort" of a righteous resistance. The brave heroes who dare to resist ZOG rule risk being assassinated or unjustly thrown away in the "federal dungeons." With a logic that might seem bizarre from the perspective of an African, Asian, or Latin American, white racists have hereby come to adopt an *underdog* position from which their call for white power assumes a revolutionary dimension in the mental universe of Aryan activists.

Emerging in the late 1970s and early 1980s, the ZOG theory gained ground following the dismantling of the Soviet Union, whereby communism disappeared as a distracting foe to the radical right, home to many—but far from all—white-power activists. The radicalization of the white-racist scene in the United States involved a dismissal of the traditional far right as CRAP (Christian Rightwing American Patriots), a phrase coined by Odinist white-power ideologue David Lane, imprisoned member of the notorious guerrilla group *Brüders Schweigen* (known as the Order after the fictional group featured in the best-selling race-war novel *Turner Diaries* by the late William Pierce). Claiming that the traditional far right has been blinded by their patriotism to swear allegiance with an administration controlled by racial enemies, the CRAP stance involves two important aspects of the current white-power scene.

First, the declaration of war against the federal government established a link between the U.S. scene and European fascism, which has been anti-American since the U.S. intervention in the Second World War, thus facilitating the construction of a global white-power culture. Second, it demonstrates the distinction between, as white-power activists put it, the "right wing" and the "white wing." White-power ideologies typically feature anticapitalist as well as anticommunist sentiments, not infrequently presenting their alternative as the "third position," reflected in the slogan "neither left, nor right, but forward." Politically, white power ideologues adopt elements from both the right and the left. Hailing god, nation, patriarchy, heterosexuality, social Darwinism, and anti-egalitarianism, white power activists may also address white-working-class issues and environmental concerns, and may want society to provide for the elderly poor and single mothers as practical points derived from their ideals of racial solidarity. They may want to curtail corporate power and reorganize production to serve the interest of the people (that is, the Aryan Folk) rather than the (Jewish) plutocrats. This populist blend of rightist and leftist themes is characteristic of the political dimension of most white race–nationalist creeds presented below.

The related factors of a generational shift, the rise of the white-power music industry, and the revolution of communication technology accompanied the radicalization of the white-power scene. The past two decades have witnessed the influx of a new generation of racist activists into a scene that had begun to look like a home for retired people. Defined by its lyrics, white-power music covers a wide range of genres, including ska, oi, noise, hatecore, metal, and folk. Transnational since its inception in the late 1970s and early 1980s, white-power music is today a global industry with several hundred contributing acts from all continents, and has become a prime recruitment tool that has also proved financially profitable. Across the world, white-racist concerts organized on April 20 (Hitler's birthday), August 17 (death of Rudolf Hess), or December 8 (Day of Martyrs) function as revivalist white-power meetings, with the musicians acting as high priests who invite born-again Aryans to accept the transformative truth of white power.

White-power music fanzines, such as *Resistance, Nordland,* or *Blood & Honor* blend reviews of white-power bands with ideological articles and carry advertisements from white-power record labels. Former Ku Klux Klan leader Louis Beam pioneered white-power cyber activism, and in 1984 constructed the Aryan Nations Liberty Net, which linked a dozen computerized white-racist information bases to facilitate communication exchange. With the first white-power Web site *Stormfront* (launched in 1996 by former Imperial Wizard Don Black), white-power cyber activism exploded with several hundred white-power Web sites, electronic newsletters, e-zines, dating pages, and chat groups. A main avenue of white-power ideology production and dissemination, the Internet offers even the loneliest white-racist believer a sense of belonging to a worldwide web of white-power activism.

Although there are women activists and a few female organizations and auxiliaries, the white-power scene is predominantly populated by white males. Through race-war novels, white-power music, and the art of white power, a romanticized warrior ideal is created that is frequently added to the construction of an Aryan male identity. Knightly values such as courage, strength, honesty, honor, and valiance are hailed as primary Aryan virtues. The white woman is presented as an endangered species, a shining jewel of pristine cleanliness surrounded by dribbling perverts at a sinking island in an ocean of filth, setting the stage for the Noble Aryan Warrior to come to her rescue. Frequently illustrated with medieval knights and raging Vikings, Aryan revolutionary tabloids, Web pages, and white-power CDs feature a bombastic language more suited to heroic legends of the past than contemporary politics. Aryan activism provides its adherents with an opportunity to be part of a grand narrative by which they can rise above the trivialities of the everyday commoner and emerge in shining armor at the battleground for the final conflict, lifting their swords for race, nation, blood, and honor.

A class analysis of the U.S. scene shows that the majority of white-power activists come from families where the father had been a military officer, farmer, small businessman, policeman, lower-white-collar or skilled worker. Activists typically see themselves as descended from those who "built this country" and thus entitled to certain "birth-right privileges" now being "negated." Surprising to those accustomed to the "white trash" thesis, this well matches the constituency mobilized by the German National Socialist Party in the 1930s. The popular stereotype of the barely literate white-power activist does not match the U.S. scene, in which the level of education is slightly above average. Moreover, the milieu hails the ideals of classic Western learning, and most groups expect the members to increase their learning by studying classic philosophers and ideologues, ranging from Nietzsche to Hitler.

The white-power scene revolves around a mythic notion of racial rebirth, typically specifying rejuvenation through violence as the route of redemption. Transcending national borders, music and electronic communication have facilitated a global flow of ideas, engaging racist radicals across the world in a vision of a future in which race will define nation. Meaning rendered according to context, the notion of white power has divided the scene in two distinct, albeit not necessarily exclusive, orientations: a narrower ultranationalist project to cleanse an already defined white American nation state of all who are considered aliens, and a more ambitious race-nationalist object that transcends existing national borders, aiming at establishing a transatlantic or even global "white homeland." The mythic core of white-power ideologies may also lend itself to religious interpretations. The mushrooming alternative religions competing for the souls of Aryan activists reflect a final important feature of the current white-power scene: its high level of infighting and fragmentation. Scattered into literally hundreds of mainly dysfunctional and microscopic parties, congregations, secret societies, and armed cells that form and dissolve with astonishing speed, the Aryan "resistance" is anything but united and spends more time attacking each other than the perceived "racial enemies." This further underscores the importance of the concept of white power as a core concept that enables an otherwise fundamentally factious world to take on a resemblance of unity by offering a symbol vague enough for every believer. Revolving around the notion of white power is the plethora of white-racist religions to which we now turn our attention.

Christian Identity: The Gospel of Aryan Israel

Christian Identity is a racist recasting of British-Israelism, a lay school of theology that identified the peoples of northern Europe with the lost tribes of Israel. Introduced into the United States at the turn of the century, British-Israelism resonated with the Puritan legacy that identified America as the New Israel to which Providence had brought the chosen through an Exodus from European bondage. Substituting analogy with biology, British-Israelism carried the argument further by insisting on a genealogical identity with the Chosen People. A creed of Anglo-Saxon-Nordic supremacy, American British-Israelism attracted laymen with anti-Semitic and pronational socialist leanings and began transforming into Christian Identity, as detailed by Barkun (1997). During the 1970s, Identity contributed to the radicalization of the white-racist underground as key Identity preachers came to occupy leadership positions in Ku Klux Klan organizations (Rich 1988).

Far from being a cohesive creed, Identity is highly fragmented theologically and organizationally. At present, there are about forty "open" Identity ministries, the majority of which are primarily "cassette ministries," which spread the gospel of the Aryan Christ by mail order sales of audio- and videocassettes, Bible study material, talk radio, and the Internet. Believers are not necessarily members of an Identity congregation, but may form Bible study groups that convene in the readers' homes. Reflecting their Israeli identity, families may name their children Seth, Elisheba, Levi, Rebekah, Melchizedek, or Sarai, and adopt Israeli surnames, such as Weisman or Neuman. To distance themselves from corrupted Judeo-Christianity, believers prefer the ancient Israeli YHWH or Yahweh for God and Yahshua or Yahweh-Yahshua for Jesus. Many observe the Sabbath, celebrate Passover and Purim, follow the dietary laws of Deuteronomy and Leviticus, and practice male circumcision to symbolize the Covenant. Given the anti-Semitic attitude typical of the white-power scene, this may be a source of confusion. Not every Aryan warrior understands or appreciates the activities of a "Mission to Israel," a white-racist church, or an "Army of Israel," a racist-skinhead tribe. Estimates of the combined membership vary considerably, but it is thought to be less than one hundred thousand, a number Barkun (1997: viii) suspects could be reduced by half. Peaking in the 1980s, Identity now seems on the decline. Although some white-power bands refer to Identity themes, and Identity summer camps may still attract hundreds of youth, Identity has the ring of an old man's religion about it.

Christian Identity is best understood as an umbrella concept for a wide variety of different theologies. Ministries and laymen differ considerably in matters of dogma and religious observance. During the 1980s and 1990s, a series of violent events brought Identity to public attention with chilling reports of fortified compounds, armed underground activities, and leaders paying homage to Jesus and Hitler. This contributed to the crystallization of two major Identity Christian "schools," here termed *hard-core* and *soft* Identity. Major differences involve conflicting notions of how to understand Counterfeit Israel (the Jews), Aryan Israel's relation to Gentile races, national socialism, and apocalyptic expectations. In the 1990s, influential ministers of the soft school began to distance themselves from the hard core by rejecting the Identity label in favor of nonstigmatized terms like Kingdom Israel or Covenant People. Although there are still areas of crossovers, polarization is likely to continue and may result in two separate religions of Aryan Israel.

At the core of Identity is the belief that only whites are descendants of Adam. In Genesis 2:5–7, God contemplated his creation. As there was no man to till the ground, God created Adam out of dust, gave him the "breath of life; and man became a living soul." Correctly translated, *Adam* means "White Man," according to Identity Christians, citing as evidence Adam's derivative meaning to "show blood in the face." "The colored races, not having been endowed with God's Spirit, have no abstract sense of right or wrong," Identity minister Thomas O'Brien (n.d.: 7) claims, "and consequently are never embarrassed." Similarly, Jack Mohr, a seminal producer of anti-Semitic ideology, (interview 1997) emphasizes the innate spiritual and moral superiority of the white man. God "placed His law in our heart," thereby making Aryan man the holy people of God.

This notion forms the basis of a racial gnosis in the Ariosophic undercurrent of Christian Identity. Gary Yarbrough—an imprisoned Identity Christian member of the Aryan guerilla band "the Order"—asserts (interview 1997) that there "is a spark of life, divine life, in the DNA" of Aryan man. A united race equals a unified God-force, known as the Second Coming of Christ. Aryan man is accordingly "holy," that is, "set apart" as the embodiment of God, his body being a container for the spark of divinity. As the "Temple of God," Aryan man must be separate from the contaminating influences of Babylon. Above all, the God within must be protected from the bodily fluids of other races. The divine spark cannot be corrupted, Yarbrough explains. If a white "becoming-God" takes a nonwhite partner, the offspring will not be half God, half beast. The divine spark dies if it comes in contact with the impure genes of nonwhite "mud races," making biracial love the highest of capital crimes.

Nondivine races divide into two categories: the pre-Adamic "colored" races and the post-Adamic "serpent" race. The thought that there existed humans on earth prior to Adam and Eve is not novel to Identity but has been part of Christian speculation since at least the seventeenth century. If Genesis is to be believed, how else could one explain the wife Cain married when he dwelt in the land of Nod, east of Eden? At the bottom ladder of pre-Adamic races is the black "servant race." Hard-core Identity members identify blacks with the beasts of Genesis 1:24–25, where God "made the beast of the earth after his kind, and the cattle after their kind," prior to making man in his image. "The Adamic Race is to have dominion over every form of life previously created," O'Brien comments. "This includes not only the four-legged beasts, but the two-legged as well. The negro is merely an articulate member of this beast creation." According to Richard G. Butler (interview 1996), pastor in the hard-core Church of Jesus Christ, Christian/Aryan Nations, the subhuman black race has been the "white man's burden." "God put His [white] people here to bring light to the world. We taught the blacks everything they know. We gave them clothes and shoes and some education. It didn't come out of them—it came from us. We trained that animal, and learned that animal to do certain things; it's like, you can take a monkey and train it to ride a bicycle, same thing with negroes. So, as for the black man, whatever he can do, a white man has taught him. Take football and basketball; they didn't invent it, they didn't think out the rules for it, whites did. They've been trained to play it to entertain us. We are the light of the earth."

Inferior by nature, pre-Adamic people cannot, Identity doctrine claims, challenge white world dominion. The formidable enemy entered the scene after Adam: the Jews. Hard-core Identity believes that Satan literally seduced Eve, who fathered his evil son Cain, progenitor of the Jewish race. Earth was thenceforth populated by two ontologically distinct "seedlines," the divine Aryan race and the diabolic Jewish race. The two-seedline theory was in different versions developed by first-generation Identity theologians Wesley Swift, Conrad Gaard, William Potter Gale, and Bertrand Comparet. In its mild version (reminiscent of nineteenth-century racist theologian Charles Carroll), Gaard and Comparet suggest that a pre-Adamic man had seduced Eve. The Original Sin, therefore, was miscegenation, transgressing God's order of creation that every living thing should only be with its own kind. Eve bore the bastard Cain who, after slaying his half-brother, the racially pure Abel, continued the evil pattern of miscegenation by marrying a pre-Adamic wife. The original sin became part of the genetic makeup of all subsequent descendants, the mongrelized Jewish race, constantly defiling the purity of the original classificatory order.

In its stronger version, the seducer is the Devil himself. Gale and Swift introduced Gnostic visions of preexisting good and evil beings, and made the earthly racial battle key to a larger intergalactic space war. Swift taught that the divine white race is of God's own household, "His Elohim, which is plural for God." This explains the Lord's words in Psalms 82:6: "Ye are gods; and all of you are children of the most High." Originally, the white race was a race of "celestial beings" who assisted God in his creation, when a fleet of space ships piloted by Lucifer and his demons attacked. Returning fire, the Space Aryans won the battle, and surviving demons sought refuge on earth. Lucifer, with his "fallen angels" and demonic soldiers, now roamed among the earth's inhabitants. The "dark and curly-headed [demonic race that] we call Negroes today . . . came in with the warring ships and the fallen angels whom they served," Swift explains, and "started to mix races." The second extraterrestrial race was the fallen Luciferian Angels who by race mixing produced a race of pure evil, the Jews. To combat the evil mongrels, God provided carnal hues to his divine warrior race. He commanded Adam and Eve not to eat from the "racial tree" of good and evil. "You can't touch that one," Swift explains. "You are not to mongrelize. You are to maintain a holy seed." Satan now seduces Eve and fathers an evil son. Accordingly, when Cain killed Abel it was not fratricide but the first attempt of the devil's spawn to exterminate the children of god. World history has since been an escalating race war.

Swift's view of Jews as the mongrelized offspring of Satan and Eve became part of standard doctrine to hard-core Identity. The influential American Institute of Theology (AIT) points to John 8:44, where Jesus charges his Jewish adversaries, "ye are of your father the devil." "In this," AIT explains matter-of-factly, "He was simply stating a biological fact with scientific precision and identifying the persons with this ancestry." Aryan Israel disregarded the wisdom of Jesus, which left the House of God in peril. "He told us to arm ourselves (Luke 22:36) and utterly destroy that evil serpent race (Luke 19:27)," said Pastor Mark Thomas (then head of the Christian Posse Comitatus of Pennsylvania). "We failed to obey His commandment and we now serve the jews [sic] as their slaves" (Thomas internet 1996a). The evil seed may temporarily rule the earth, but the Aryan Christ did not die in vain. "Christ, Who was God Incarnate was perfected along with the rest of the Adamic race by His crucifixion," Thomas explains (ibid.). "God lives with us and our entire race is one living organism, the body of Almighty." This balances the fact that "Satan became a man." Whites are "locked in mortal combat with his children who are incarnate among us. They are found among the jews as the progeny of Cain" (Thomas 1996b). Hailed as the "greatest White man to stand on this earth since Jesus Christ," Adolf Hitler serves as a role model instilling a sense of duty in the Aryan warrior-gods (Thomas 1996c). "We are born to throw down this wicked murdering system of jew-inspired globalism," Thomas exclaimed (1996d). "Do not speak with me of building the Kingdom of God on any other foundation than the blood-soaked ashes of Babylon!"

Linked with the Aryan Nations, the ministry of Mark Thomas was characterized by a repeated call to arms. "White man, this is your final call; there is nowhere else to run or hide. Either fight or prepare to turn your daughters over to the mongrelized descendants of dusky two-legged beasts. The choice is yours" (Thomas 1996e). Inspired by the inflammatory rhetoric of Thomas, Peter K. Langan and Richard Lee Guthrie, Jr., in 1993 established the Aryan Revolutionary Army (ARA). Modeled on the Order, ARA built a war chest in a series of twenty-two robberies in the Midwest. "Our basic goal," the hooded commander said in an ARA recruitment video, "is to set up an Aryan republic." When police in 1996 made a deal with an ARA turncoat, the guerrilla group was finally apprehended. When in Babylonian custody, Mark Thomas lost his bravery. He turned against his Aryan brethren and disappeared into the Protected Witness Program.

Soft Identity rejects the seedline theory as "unbiblical" in favor of alternative theories, suggesting that Jewish people descend from the biblical characters Esau and Edom and/or from the historical Khazars. In Genesis, God informs Rebekah that she would give birth to two nations that would fight each other, adding that He would elevate the younger Jacob (Israel) over Esau. Identity explains Esau's degradation by his desire for women of other races. God therefore hated Esau and his mongrel offspring called Edom. When God exalts Jacob to be Israel, Esau desires to kill his brother, an obsession supposedly inherited by his offspring. Esau means red, which to Identity believers links Edom with Communism, Babylon, and the Antichrist. This school of thought emphasizes the biblical promise that the enemies of Aryan Israel will be exterminated at the Day of the Lord, citing Obadiah 18: "and there shall not be *any* remaining of the house of Esau." The resemblance to the Final Solution has not been lost to Identity. Weisman observes that the Bible "actually prophesies the genocide of Esau-Edom!" To Charles Weisman (1991: 115–117), this explains the Jewish concern with the Holocaust. "It is because in God's Script for the world, the Jews are scheduled to be exterminated, and that impending reality is why they are so paranoid about 'genocide.' "

The Khazars once populated the steppes between the Black and Caspian Sea, north of the Caucasus Mountains. Squeezed between the Byzantine

Empire and the Umayyad Caliphate, the Khazar ruler reportedly converted to Judaism about the middle of the eighth century. With the thirteenth century Mongol invasion, the Khazar Empire declined, and the history of the Khazars was lost in obscurity. In the nineteenth century, scholars of philology and anthropology suggested that Ashkenazi Jewry were largely of Khazar ancestry, an idea seized upon in British-Israelite circles. By the turn of the century, the theory was adopted by nativist Anglo-Americans who called for immigration restriction. The theory circulated in the Ku Klux Klan, featured in the writings of Lothrop Stoddard and Wilmot Robertson, and was readily embraced by Identity activists. In 1976, the Jewish novelist Arthur Koestler published *The Thirteenth Tribe*, a work received with enthusiasm by Identity people. Koestler claims that a substantial number of Eastern Jewry are of Khazar-Turkish rather than Semitic origin. "If so, this would mean that their ancestors came not from the Jordan but from the Volga, not from the Canaan but from the Caucasus . . . and that genetically they are more closely related to the Hun, Uigur and Magyar tribes than to the seed of Abraham, Isaac and Jacob" (Koestler 1976: 17). Koestler (223) argues that Israel's right to exist is not based on the "hypothetical origins of the Jewish people" or "on the mythological covenant of Abraham with God," but rather on international law, that is, on the United Nations decision of 1947. This secular argument was lost completely to Identity ideologues, who triumphantly declared that "counterfeit Israel" had been exposed by one of their own. "The Jews have never been part of Israel," Pastor Butler asserted (interview 1996). "The Jew Koestler [admits that they] are tribes from central Russia, the Khazar kingdom" who are "trying to say that they are the Chosen People but the Bible says we are the Chosen."

Christian Identity preachers generally adopt an underdog perspective alien to their British-Israelite predecessors, who saw the British Empire as confirmation of their claim of being the Chosen People. A century later, colonialism was gone and the interpretation of global politics reversed. "It is important to understand that Satan has dominion over this world," an Identity Bible course informs its students. All the once-white nations suffer under the yoke of the Jew World Order. The root of it all, Identity teaches, is spiritual corruption. Challenged by the Aryan Christ, the Jews engaged in a conspiracy to turn the racial gospel into degenerated Judeo-Christianity which, Thomas claims, has "been the ruin of every civilization that has adopted it." It teaches that God loves all of humanity and hates discrimination, when God in fact is a racist and discrimination the bedrock of divine Law. "One of the greatest mistakes made by the Third Reich was the burning of only the synagogues," Thomas concludes (1996b). "How utterly tragic because this mistake cost Germany and our entire race the war; [Hitler] should have . . . leveled every church in Germany."

The global reign of Antichrist is a sign of the end of time. Identity has no equivalent to the rapture doctrine of evangelical Christianity in which God will provide a heavenly refuge to spare the righteous. Identity believers instead pattern their understanding of the approaching Armageddon on the Old Testament, where God descends to command his people in earthly warfare. "The ideal government of the world is God's government with Christ as the King," Klan leader and hard-core Identity believer John Baumgardner explains (interview 1996). "And I think that God uses His people to accomplish that. He has historically used His people to overthrow governments. And so we're entering this so-called Messianic Age. We're not going to be pulled off into the sky and saved from a world of destruction; we're gonna see an apocalyptic change on this planet, the dawn of God's government. It's gonna be a total war, a revolutionary war, and [Israelis] gonna have to fight! We need people to be preparing for guerrilla war, we need terrorists, we need that, because a system that breeds violence, practices violence, only understands violence."

Identity generally sees American history as reflecting the stories of the Bible. In Joshua, God intervenes to command the army of Israel in taking possession of the Holy Land, ransacking thirty-two cities and wiping out its inhabitants. Joshua "left none remaining, but utterly destroyed all that breathed, as the Lord God of Israel commanded." According to Baumgardner, this history was repeated when God ordained Aryan man to establish the New Israel in North America. "God said to Israel: 'Go in and kill every human being and then possess the land.' And we did. We obtained this land by divine conquest. This land does not belong to the Indians. This land was given to us." In return, Israel was to remain pure of foreign influences or suffer the wrath of God. "The Bible teaches us that when we bring strangers and aliens into our land, people of other religions who worship other gods, we begin to take their gods as our own," Baumgardner said. "We, who are part of Israel, are punished today for that very reason, the same reason that ancient Israel was punished! We haven't learned yet."

In 1990, hardcore Identity ideologue Richard Kelly Hoskins suggested that individual zealots could atone for Israel's transgressions by assassinating homosexuals, interracial couples, and prostitutes. Hoskins believed they belonged to an underground tradition of racial purists, the Phinehas Priesthood, tracing its history back into antiquity. In Numbers 25, God finds Israeli men engaged in miscegenation with Moab women and is ready to consume them when Phinehas dashes into the tent and throws his javelin through the transgressors' bodies. Pleased, God announces, "Phinehas hath turned my wrath away from the children of Israel" and bestows "Phinehas" and "his seed" a "covenant of an everlasting priesthood because he was zealous." During the 1990s, individual hard-core activists embraced Hoskin's fantasy. Self-proclaimed Phinehas Priest Walther E. Thody was sentenced to life and 125 years for twenty robberies in 1990–91 made to finance a squad of Identity assassins; in 1993, Paul Hill wrote an article advocating Phinehas actions and proved himself by assassinating doctor John B. Britton outside his Florida abortion clinic; Charles Barbee, Robert Berry, and Jay Merrell were convicted for a 1996 Spokane bank robbery where they left a letter signed with the Phineas Priesthood symbol.

Horrified that racist vigilantes with "as much spiritual insight as the length of their bullets" would justify "unlawful deeds" with reference to the God of Christian Israel, Ted R. Weiland of the soft Identity project Mission to Israel launched a campaign of correction. Weiland argued that it is impossible for anyone to prove a Phinehas ancestry. There is no biblical sanction for the thought that a "Phinehas act" qualifies a man for the priesthood, and nowhere does God authorize vigilantism. "The Phinehas priesthood," Weiland concludes (interview 1999), "essentially are 'Phinehas hoods' because they themselves are in contradiction to the laws of Yahweh. They're looking for a quick fix, but there are no shortcuts, and there are no Phinehas priests." Divided over the Phinehas Priesthood concept, hard-core and soft Identity also part ways concerning the approaching apocalypse. While believing that "God's law require us to be armed," Weiland dismisses the notion that God commands Israel to launch guerrilla warfare at this point in time. "I know that some people believe that that's the only thing left, an armed revolution, but right now it is naïve to believe that we can win this battle with arms. It's nowhere close to that."

Hard-core militancy has occasionally manifested in establishments of armed communal settlements. In 1976, Covenant, Sword, and Arm of the Lord (CSA) founder "King" James Ellison set up the paramilitary commune Zarephath-Horeb at a 224-acre-tract in the Ozark wilderness in northern Arkansas. Ellison believed that Aryan Israel literally was a divine race predestined to inherit the earth. "As Sons of God," a CSA 1982 article exclaimed, "we shall drive out those tenants who now occupy our possession and shall therefore rule our enemies under our footstool." Convinced that "Jesus is building an army which shall show forth the Arm of the Lord, bringing judgment against the enemies of God," Ellison organized paramilitary training and prepared to advance into enemy territory. "Warfare is in the genes of every true son of God," CSA declared (1982b). The CSA commune became a refuge for racist activists. In return for funding received by the Order, it provided shelter for the likes of wanted David Tate and Richard Snell, but would not stand the test when challenged by federal authorities. Surrounded by the ATF in 1985, the CSA gave up without resistance. Ellison was sentenced to twenty years and would then appear as a government witness in the Fort Smith sedition trial in exchange for a sentence reduction.

The failure of high-profile Christian Identity leaders to show up and to take action would contribute to the fading image of Aryan Christ in the white-power culture. By and large the religious dimension of revolutionary white racism in the 1980s, Identity was soon challenged by alternative white racist creeds. In the 1980s, Richard G. Butler, pastor of the Church of Jesus Christ, Christian, could summon several hundreds of Aryan leaders and activists of different streams at his yearly Aryan World Congresses at the Aryan Nations' Hayden Lake headquarters. In the mid-1990s, Aryan Nations remained, perhaps, an important symbol of white power, but was in practical respects a star of the past. By then, no armed guards regularly patrolled Aryan Nations property. Few would dare the hazardous climb up the crumbling watchtower. No electricity charged the fencing wire; the church badly needed repainting, and the "Whites Only" sign was askew. Butler continued to host Aryan World and Youth Congresses, but fewer showed up since white power activists had come to see Aryan Nations meetings as an infiltrators' haven, and believed the buildings to be jammed with bugs and hidden video cameras.

By 1998, conditions had deteriorated to such a point that local youth found pleasure in embarrassing the Aryan world headquarters by sneaking into the property to spray-paint buildings or steal the Aryan Nations' banner. Infuriated, Butler ordered heightened security, a move that contributed to his final downfall when his guards mistook a passing mother and son for intruders. After a two-mile car chase with blazing guns, the guards shot out a tire and forced the chased car into a ditch. Interrupted by approaching neighbors, the Aryan Nations guards made a Hitler salute and took off. Represented by Morris Dees's Southern Poverty Law Center (SPLC), the mother and son were awarded 6.3 million dollars in damages by a civil court jury in 2000. Vincent Bertollini of the hard-core eleventh *Hour Ministry* provided Butler with a new residence, but the Aryan Nations headquarters was gone. On September 27, 2001, Pastor Ray Redfearin of Ohio was named Butler's successor and Aryan Nations national director. Pastor August B. Kreis III, formerly of the Sheriff's Posse Comitatus, was named new Aryan Nations minister of information. The future will see the extent to which they manage to revive the Aryan Nations which for all practical purposes was long since dead when the SPLC closed down its Hayden Lake headquarters.

Religious National Socialism

The national socialist project revolves around a palingenetic myth of racial rebirth and renewal. The German National Socialist revolution aimed at ridding society of parliamentary democracy, liberal humanism, capitalist economy, and communist class struggle, which were all considered antithetical to the interest of the organic race. Purified by a baptism of fire, the German Eagle would emerge from the smoldering ruins to usher in a millenarian New Order and a New Man. Attracted to this myth were different ideologues and groups with divergent views concerning what exactly this dream was supposed to mean and how it translated into political practice. A significant tendency saw national socialism as essentially a spiritual project, a perspective represented in the National Socialist leadership by Heinrich Himmler, Rudolf Hess, and Alfred

Rosenberg. While Hitler accepted the support of esoteric societies in his bid for power, he remained largely indifferent to the project of Aryan self-theomorphosis, finding the loyal soldier more useful than the wandering mystic (Goodrick-Clarke 1992). This religious interpretation of the national socialist project also found its way to the United States. The Aryan Christ addressed in Rosenberg's ariosophic Christianity would inspire hard-core Identity and the pagan beat of Himmler's occult National Socialism came to influence racist heathens. A third category interprets the millenarian New Order and the legacy of Hitler in spiritual terms that are neither Christian nor pagan. This category may be further subdivided into two major tendencies. The first looks to Hitler as a divine messenger or savior, while the second takes a nondeist or even atheist path and celebrates the white race itself with religious zeal.

A religious dimension was already present with Rockwell, who claimed to have received a calling from Adolf Hitler and kept a Hitler shrine at American Nazi Party headquarters. His rival James H. Madole, eccentric leader of the (now defunct) National Renaissance Party, interpreted national socialism from the perspective of theosophy and the occult. Insisting that America is the "New Atlantis" and the "cradle of a new God-like race," Madole (1977) developed contacts with Satanists, warlocks, witches, and esoterics, but received far fewer sympathizers than sensationalist media coverage. Following the 1967 assassination of Rockwell, his successor Matt Koehl would rework the classical vehicle for American National Socialism into a new religion, stressing that "all the problems we face here in North America today are fundamentally spiritual in origin." Shortly before his death, Koehl (1985a) claimed, Hitler declared that national socialism as a political phenomenon was over, but thought it could "be resurrected as a religious Movement." Koehl now realized why the American Nazi Party had completely failed to reach the masses. "A movement which bore an essentially religious mission could not successfully pursue a political program." In 1983, Koehl remade Rockwell's party into a "holy" New Order, conceived of as a "community of faith" and a "spiritual SS" (Koehl, 1982). Hitler "came to offer hope and salvation for an entire race," Koehl (1985b) claims. "Adolf Hitler was a gift of Almighty Providence. And in rejecting him, we rejected God himself," Koehl stated, pushing a Hitler–Jesus analogy. "Adolf Hitler came into the world in human form. He was born, and he died. He gave his very life in a supreme act of devotion of sacrifice" (Koehl 1985c). Rejecting the "escape legend," popular among contemporary Nazis, that tells of Hitler's post-1945 adventures and present whereabouts, Koehl insists that Hitler did die on May 8, 1945, the "Good Friday" of religious National Socialism. "And we all know what comes after Good Friday." "Just before His immolation," Koehl jubilantly declares, "the Leader uttered these fateful words: 'It is necessary that I should die for my people; but my Spirit will rise from the grave, and the world will know that I was right.' The cycle of life and death was to be perfected through His reappearance on Earth—not in flesh and blood, but in spirit: *His* immortal spirit." Yes, "our immortal Leader," Adolf Hitler, "has risen from the grave. He lives! We sense it; we recognize it. . . . This is the spiritual dynamic of our time; this is the good news of the age" (Koehl, 1985d). The New Order itself seems, however, less dynamic and has remained a quite miniscule effort.

Among Rockwell's associates was Savitri Devi (born Maximiani Portas in 1907), whose Hindu-Aryan esoteric Hitlerism has made an increasing impact in the worlds of occult national socialism and New Age spirituality since the 1970s (Goodrick-Clarke 1998). Impressed by the Hindu caste system that she interpreted as based on racial hierarchy, Devi concluded that modern Hinduism was the only living Aryan heritage. During a spiritual quest in the 1930s, she converted, married the pronational socialist Brahmin Asit Krishna Mukherji, and became instrumental in the construction of a pro-German Hindu nationalism. Following the war, Savitri Devi proceeded with an international national socialist career, cofounding the World Union of National Socialism in 1962 and becoming a widely read spokeswoman for esoteric Hitlerism. Upon her death in 1984, Devi's portrait was decked with Hitler's funeral sash and her ashes placed besides Rockwell's and the eternal flame of National Socialism in the sanctuary housed by the above-mentioned New Order in Arlington, Virginia.

Based in part on Hindu cosmology and concepts, Devi's occult National Socialism is outlined in a series of books, chief of which is The *Lightning and the Sun* (1958). Hindu cosmology operates with the concept of time moving in eternal cycles of birth, death, and renewal. Puranic Hinduism divides cosmic time into four *yugas* (eras). Life commences in a stage of perfection in Satya or Krita yuga and progress through Treta and Dvapara yuga, eras of diminishing enlightenment and duration, ending in Kali Yuga, a miserable era of negated enlightenment that ends with a cleansing apocalypse and the birth of a new golden age. During the turning wheels of cosmic history, the divine descends into the world in various avatars or incarnations, either in superhuman, human, or animal form. In Vaishnava Hindu literature (the Epics and the Vishnu Puranas), the transcendent Lord Vishnu descends as an avatar ten times in the successive forms of a fish, tortoise, boar, man-lion, dwarf, Rama-with-an-axe, Rama, Krishna, Buddha, and Kalki. Vishnu enters Kali Yuga twice, in its beginning as the redeeming Lord Krishna and in its ending as Kalki, the fiery sword-wielding Destroyer, cleansing the world to usher in Satya Yuga. To Savitri Devi, this was the proper context to fully appreciate the nature of national socialism and Adolf Hitler.

Devi proceeds by developing a distinction between three types of uniquely gifted historical actors, representing three different responses to the bondage of time most of mankind might dimly feel but unconditionally submits to: Men in Time, Men above Time, and Men against Time. Men in Time embody the characteristics of their age. In the dark age of Kali Yuga, Men in Time (exemplified by Gengis Khan and Stalin) are possessed by the destructive forces of Nature, remorselessly exacted to further goals of self-gratification and enrichment, and represent the "lightning" in the title of her work. The enlightened Men above Time sense the Reality beyond Time and embody ideals of the golden age, but their message can only be received according to the imperfections of the time they are presented in. Representing the "sun" of her theory, these men are exemplified by Buddha, Akhnaton, and Jesus Christ. Men against Time partake in both the lightning and the sun by ruthlessly employing all the destructive forces of Kali Yuga to further the realization of the golden age ideals they are animated by. To Savitri Devi, "Adolf Hitler is a typical Man against Time" (Devi 1958: 256). He was possessed by Cosmic Truth, the national socialist ideal of the Golden Age, and was prepared to make brutal force to forward the reestablishment of society in harmony with cosmic Order. Hitler was to Savitri Devi an avatar of Vishnu, coming like Krishna in Kali Yuga to pave the way for the last incarnation, Kalki, the Destroyer. She believes that Hitler probably was aware of his incarnate divinity, but claims that he was of too benign a character, had too many "sun" qualities, to make use of all the destructive Dark Age forces. Referring to a 1928 statement by Hitler, "I am not he, but while nobody comes forward to prepare for him, I do so," Savitri Devi comforts her fellow believers that the last avatar of Vishnu is bound to come. He will incarnate as Kalki, and completely destroy the Jewish Dark Age regime to restore the golden age of true cosmic National Socialism (Devi 1958: 417ff.).

Among those inspired by Devi's esoteric Hitlerism is Miguel Serrano, one of the most important occult fascists in the Latin-speaking world. Serrano construed an occult ariosophy outlined in several works, including a trilogy on esoteric Hitlerism and the hermetic *Nos: Book of the Resurrection*. A gifted writer, Serrano outlines an epic hierohistory of a scale comparable to Blavatsky or Tolkien that has made an inroad among esoterics and fantasy lovers outside the world of ariosophic national socialism. In the white-power culture proper, Serrano has inspired numerous race mystics, an impact bound to expand as his main works are now being translated by Katja Lane, founding member of the Wotansvolk project. In line with classic ariosophic speculation, Serrano expounds the polar myth of Aryan origin (Godwin 1996). According to Serrano, the divine Aryan race has an extraterrestrial origin in the spiritual Hyperborean civilization in times immemorial. Entering a holy war against Yahweh, the evil demiurge that rules this material planet, the divine Aryans created a Second Hyperborean civilization, Asgård or Ultima Thule at the North Pole. During the golden age, Satya Yuga, the ancestral Aesir began to spiritualize the earth and developed consciousness-raising techniques by which man could ascend into divinity. Descending cosmic time cycles, the fall of a giant comet and mongrelization between the divine Aryans and the carnal races of the demiurge caused the downfall of the aboriginal Hyperborean civilization. Some immortal Ariosophic masters relocated to Agartha, the legendary subterranean city somewhere in the Himalayas, while others eventually found the north and south polar entrances to the Inner Earth. Adolf Hitler is thought to be simultaneously a personification of the Wotan archetype in the Aryan racial unconscious and an avatar of Vishnu (also identified as Wotan) who came at the end of the present Kali Yuga to usher in a new golden age.

A believer in the escape legend, Serrano claims that Hitler left Berlin in a German flying saucer to a secret National Socialist base in Antarctica. Eventually, Hitler transferred to the super-Aryan civilization inside the Hollow Earth from where he leads the Esoteric War that has followed the end of the Exoteric War. Serrano is consciously ambiguous concerning the nature of the Inner Earth, which need not necessarily be a physical location but is described as simultaneously a subterranean and an extraterranean realm, a paradise land that is no longer and yet exists as "the inner earth, the Other Earth, the counterearth, the astral earth, to which one passes as it were with a 'click,' a bilocation, or trilocation of space" (Serrano 1984a). Based on a complex series of micro-macrocosmic correspondences, Aryan man can make his contribution to this Esoteric War by adding the strength of a self-realized Nietzschean *übermensch* to the cosmic will to power. By using ancient Aryan Yoga techniques, he might reawaken Kundalini, the astral fire sleeping at the base of the spinal chain of runic chakras, and progressively raise his consciousness, ascending into divinity. This path is exclusive to Aryans of unmixed lineage, as undefiled blood is a condensation of the Green Ray, the light of the Black Sun, and carries memories of the Hyperborean race. The advanced Aryan yogi might thus reach a point at which he goes through the mystical death and "clicks" into the Hyperborean dimension parallel to ours. The occult national socialist quest of Miguel Serrano and Savitri Devi, with its reference to Arthurian mysteries, lost worlds, tantric techniques, and esoteric lore, would during the 1990s attract a growing audience in the ariosophic undercurrent of white-power believers, not least among those inspired by pagan, occult, or New Age philosophies.

However, not all religious national socialists would appreciate the esotericism of Devi and Serrano. Among those who dismiss them as an unwanted diversion from the project of racial survival and expansion are the spokespersons involved with the race-as-religion tendency in the contemporary white-power culture. Crystallized during the radicalization process of the 1980s, this tendency formed in opposition to Christian Identity, a creed they rejected as historically unsubstantiated and basically nonsensical. Paving the way for the subsequent rise of racist paganism was an anti-Christian, nondeist tendency to focus on the Aryan "race" with religious devotion. Tom Metzger of the White Aryan Resistance (WAR) aptly summarizes the position in his declaration of WAR: "Our race is our religion. WAR condemns priest craft and all religions. WAR will not allow religious theories and unproven myths to interfere with Aryan survival and advancement. Whites must deal with reality and the world around them. We must demand evidence of those who attempt to control us with unsubstantiated stories from the Middle East." This tendency could be elaborated along the lines of either racist atheism or pantheism, here represented by its most successful vehicle, the Church of the Creator.

Founded by Ben Klassen in 1973, the Church of the Creator gained momentum in the white-power culture in the 1980s and 1990s. Ukraine-born businessman Klassen briefly served as a Florida state legislator in 1966 (on an anti-busing Republican platform) and founded the dysfunctional White Nationalist Party before abandoning secular politics in favor of a religious approach to secure a white-racist revolution. Convinced that the white race was embroiled in a racial war against the Jews, Klassen taught that Christianity was a Jewish creation designed to derange the white intellect. Based on superstitious beliefs in "spooks in the sky" and unsubstantiated theories about life beyond death, Christianity was to Klassen (1981: 311ff.; 350ff.) a compilation of suicidal advice to "love your enemy" that needs to be overcome to secure racial survival. Ridiculing Christianity with an iconoclastic fever, Klassen dismissed as idiocy the Identity creed as it retained delusions of a heavenly Superspook and wasted energy on irrelevant theories of an imaginary ancient past. "There is not a shred of historical evidence that there ever were any Ten Lost Tribes of Israel, and if they ever existed and got lost, all I can say is GOOD RID-DANCE," Klassen wrote (1987: 125), wondering why "any sane, intelligent white man [wants] to break [his] neck to distort history [only to pose as] a descendant of such trash." Rejecting any notion of gods, demons, spirits, and souls, the Creators do not believe in heaven and hell, immortality after death, or the "hereafter," however imagined. "We have dispensed with that nonsense," Klassen wrote (1981: 360), "and can better concentrate our thoughts and energy on living in the here and now, the only life we will ever experience." The rational Creator does not worship anything, or anybody; his sense of purpose and morals is based on racial loyalty and the laws of nature.

Klassen outlined the basic creed of Creativity in the three "holy books," *Nature's Eternal Religion* (1973), the *White Man's Bible* (1981), and *Salubrious Living* (1982) (the last was co-authored with Arnold DeVries), and a rich production of secondary writings. Terming his religion Creativity and the members Creators to capture the essence of the white soul, Klassen ([1973] 1992: 253) aimed at substituting for Christianity a religion based on "Nature's Law" to "propagate, advance, and expand the White Race, the highest pinnacle reached in the handiwork of Nature." Following racist historian Arthur Gobineau, Klassen believed that the white race is the founder of every high culture of antiquity—China, India, Egypt, Sumeria, Greece, Rome, the Aztec and Inca—all of which were destroyed by miscegenation. Whereas other modern readers of Gobineau conclude that imperialism was a mistake and advocate white separatism instead of supremacy, Klassen regards any such strategy racial treason. Issuing the battle cry *RaHoWa* (Racial Holy War), Klassen (1987: 12) held the "winning of the west" as "prototype for the winning of the world," in the Church of the Creator (COTC) program to "expand the White Race, shrink the colored races, until the White Race is the supreme inhabitant of the earth" (Klassen [1973] 1992: 262). In line with the health fad of the 1980s, Klassen issued a "salubrious living" program for keeping the body fit and free from diseases, prescribing fasting, physical exercise, sufficient rest, and a fruitarian diet of organically grown uncooked and unprocessed fruits, vegetables, grains, and nuts. Building a COTC elite of healthy racial loyalists, Klassen hoped to set the stage for a worldwide white revolution. According to the secular millenarianism of the COTC, a racial golden age will commence by ridding the earth of the mud races and perfecting Nature's finest by enforced eugenics and salubrious living. Inspired by romanticized notions of the Roman Empire and the statecraft of Hitler Germany, Klassen envisioned the government of the future as "racial socialism" defined as an authoritarian collectivism based on the "leadership principle," an orchestrated teamwork for the welfare of the globally united race, communicating in revised Latin as its universal language.

Investing his personal fortune, Klassen in 1982 established a World Creativity Center at Otto in the Blue Ridge Mountains of North Carolina, founded the *Racial Loyalty* tabloid, and distributed his books, often free of charge. A mail-order seminar offered members the chance to become Reverends for a small fee. Continuing education and military training in the paramilitary White Berets was offered at headquarters. By the late 1980s and early 1990s, COTC began attracting the new generation of Aryan activists. Spread via the white-power music scene, its membership increasingly became dominated by youth, skinheads, and prisoners. Abroad, COTC missionary activities produced chapters in Western Europe, Australia, New Zealand, and South Africa. Yet the COTC remained miniscule with a worldwide membership of fewer than five thousand, out of which a couple of hundred were ordained ministers. Organizationally, the effort was hampered by financial difficulties and Klassen's stubborn reluctance to delegate power and responsibilities. By 1993, Klassen concluded that he had done his chore. The *White Man's Bible* recommends suicide as a dignified way to die, much preferable to prolonging a life that, for any number of reasons, is no longer worth living—and he acted on his belief. Following the death of its founder, COTC split into several competing factions. In July 1996, a rebuilding process commenced with four out of five "Guardians of Faith" recognizing law student Matt Hale of the World Church of the Creator (WCOTC) as the new Pontifex Maximus.

Born 1971 in East Peoria, Illinois, as the youngest son of a police officer, Hale had operated the dysfunctional American White Supremacist Party and the equally unsuccessful White America National Socialist Party, when he stumbled onto the *Racial Loyalty* tabloid in the early 1990s. Finding Creativity a perfect blend of National Socialism and Nietzschean social Darwinism, Hale applied for membership in 1995 (Hale interview 1999). Despite being a late

convert, Hale managed to reunite a majority of the competing Creativity factions in the United States, and a number of new, youth-dominated local chapters were founded. In 1998, Hale earned a law degree and passed the Illinois
bar. Citing his racist worldview, however, the state of Illinois denied him a
license to practice law. On July 2, 1999, a state panel denied his appeal. That
night, World Church of the Creator member Benjamin Nathaniel Smith
launched a three-day shooting spree in Indiana and Illinois, killing two and
wounding nine Asians, blacks, and Jews before committing suicide. Boasting
a membership increase by 10 to 15 percent because of the attention the serial
killings had given Creativity, Hale (interview 1999) said that although he did
not "agree with [Ben's] actions," he "could not say anything bad about" such a
"loyal friend." As of 2000, seventy (more or less functional) chapters distributed over twenty-eight states were affiliated with the WCOTC.

Noting that "most pro-White organizations today do not make a focused
effort to recruit women" or "encourage women to pursue leadership roles" in
the racial struggle, WCOTC in 1998 launched the Women's Frontier led by
(now defected) Lisa Turner. The white revolution could hardly benefit from
engaging only half of its population, Turner argued. This should not be confused with feminism, Turner (internet 1999) specified. "We recognize, in accordance with Nature's eternal laws that men and women are vastly different
genetically and biologically and are in no way equal." Solidarity belongs to the
racial nation and not to a universal womanhood. Although "lone wolf" Kathy
Ainsworth (bomber of synagogues and private Jewish residences) was included
alongside Eva Braun and Katja Lane in the White Women's Hall of Fame,
female participation in the white revolution does not necessarily imply military
service, and Turner stressed that a white woman's primary role is that of wife
and mother. By the year 2000, some ten chapters of the Sisterhood of the
WCOTC had been established locally, and the Women's Frontier expanded in
cyberspace with an e-zine, kid pages, and articles by and about female revolutionaries. In January 2003, Matt Hale was arrested for soliciting an assassin
to murder U.S. district judge Joan H. Lefkow, a charge that could render him
a thirty-year sentence. Hale pleaded not guilty, but was denied bail. His trial
was scheduled for September 2003 but subsequently moved to April 2004.
Whatever the outcome, Creativity is likely to be around, at least as a distributor
of Klassen classics. By the time of Hale's arrest, Creativity had been dwarfed
by the rise of racist paganism, a phenomenon to which we now will turn.

Wolf Age Pagans

The late 1990s saw the rise of racist paganism to become one of the most
dynamic religious expressions of the white-power culture. This fact should not
mislead the reader to assume that racism is inherent in paganism or that all

pagans are racists. The invention of the classificatory categories "race" and "nation" are products of modernity and were, probably, unknown to the pagan cultures of pre-Christian Europe. Pagans of today, however, live in social realities long governed by these classificatory categories as organizing principles, which are impossible to avoid. In fact, a perennial conflict among today's pagans involves different understandings of what paganism is and for whom a certain tradition is appropriate. Is it necessary to be an American Indian to practice Native American religion, or could anybody become a shaman? May an African American be part of an Asatrú guild or is Norse religion only for those who claim a northern European ancestry? On this issue, today's paganism has taken three distinct positions: a non- or even antiracist position, an explicitly racist, and an ethnic position.

This is illustrated with Asatrú or Odinism, the pagan milieus involved with reviving the pre-Christian traditions of northern Europe. Nonracist Asatrú is a polytheist spiritual path that welcomes any genuinely interested person irrespective of race or ethnicity. Dismissing nonracist Asatrú as an effeminate New Age corruption, the racist position defines Asatrú/Odinism as an expression of the Aryan racial soul and hence an exclusive creed open to whites only. In fact, many but not all who adhere to the racist position prefer to call their warpath of spiritual politics "Odinism" or the Germanic "Wotanism" rather than risk being lumped together with nonracist Asatrúers.

Attempting to get beyond the issue of race, the third position defines Asatrú as an ethnic religion, native to northern Europe and therefore "natural" to Americans of northern European ancestry. The notion of an "organic" link between ethnicity and religion obviously implies an assumption that genetics somehow determine the spiritual disposition of man. Accordingly, although most take exception to racism, adherents of the ethnic position share certain presuppositions with racist paganism. This unresolved element of philosophical ambiguity has left ethnocentric Asatrú open to criticism from both nonracist and racist pagans. Simultaneously being denounced as racists and race-traitors, ethnic Asatrúers argue that they are neither, and insist that partisans should leave their politics out of pagan activities. Numerically, the nonracist position seems to be the strongest, although there are no reliable statistics available. The reader is encouraged to keep this in mind during the following presentation of racist paganism. Just as the activities of Identity Christians do not make all Christians racists, the existence of racist pagans should not taint all pagans.

The surge of racist paganism is related to a process of radicalization of the white-power culture. As such, it is a continuation of the refutation of Christianity that took hold in the Aryan underground in the 1980s. As with the iconoclastic rhetoric of Creativity, many racist pagans single out Christianity as a key to the perceived demise of white power and Western civilization. Racist pagans tend, however, to be dissatisfied with the basically atheist outlook of the Church of the Creator. Opting to replace Christianity with an alternative native to white people, racist pagans see the future in the past, and aim at reconstructing some pre-Christian tradition of ancient Europe as the white man's "true" religion. This project may take many different, though not necessarily exclusive, forms, and the white-power culture abounds with symbols, divinities, and mythologies found among the archeological remnants of the ancient cultures of Europe (such as the Greek, Slav, Roman, Etruscan, Celtic, Saxon, Manx, or Scandinavian). As the efforts to revive pre-Christian traditions of northern Europe have so far been proven to be the most viable, we will here focus on this project.

With important predecessors among the racist mystics and philosophers in the pan-Germanic *völkisch* milieu vibrant in continental Europe at the turn of the twentieth century, racist paganism has since come in two waves; one in the late sixties and early seventies, and one in the late eighties and nineties. During the flower-power era, racist Americans were still very much Christian and mainly caught up with the Klan project of 100 percent Americanism, and most counterculture pagans tended to be left-leaning hippies. Comparatively more racist pagans came with the second wave, when flower power had given way to the more reactionary winds of the Reagan/Bush era and many white racists had made the transition to the underground white-power scene. We will facilitate an understanding of racist paganism by focusing on one significant racist pagan vehicle of each wave: the Odinist Fellowship and Wotansvolk.

Established in 1969, the Odinist Fellowship is the oldest existing organization on the Norse pagan scene. Primarily a ministry by mail, it was long based in founder Else Christensen's mobile home at Crystal River, Florida, and is now relocated to her small trailer in Parksville at Vancouver Island, British Columbia. As the Grand Mother of racist Odinism, Christensen introduced significant elements later adopted by many racist pagans, including her identification of Norse paganism as the "racial soul" of the Aryan Folk; her Jungian view of the heathen gods and goddesses as race-specific, genetically engraved archetypes; her politics of "tribal socialism"; and her focus on prison outreach ministries as a prime recruitment avenue. Through Christensen, many of the current Asatrú and Odinist ideologues first became acquainted with Norse traditions, although many of them would later embark on independent routes. Although some express impatience with her insistence on a low political profile, others would explore in more depth the ritual and magical paths Christensen was less inclined to tread.

Born in Denmark in 1913, Christensen began as an anarchist before converting to the national-bolshevist (Strasserite) wing of the Nazi movement. Her husband Aage Alex Christensen was a top lieutenant in the minuscule Danish National Socialist Workers' Party. Ousted along with the Strasserite faction, he was later arrested when Germany occupied Denmark, and served six months in a detention camp. Following the war, Christensen moved to Toronto, and developed contacts with the emerging white-power scene across the border. Among her close associates was the seminal populist anti-Semite Willis Carto and American Nazi Party organizer James K. Warner. Later an influential Identity Christian minister and Klan leader, Warner had made an aborted attempt to launch Odinism as the religious dimension of revolutionary national socialism. Disappointed by the failure of his (Sons of Liberty) Odinist Religion, Inc., Warner gave Christensen all his leftover Norse material, including a pamphlet by the Australian lawyer and Church of Odin founder Alexander Rud Mills, the *Call of Our Ancient Nordic Religion*.

At the time, Christensen was greatly influenced by Spengler and his national socialist interpreter, Francis Parker Yockey, whose *Imperium* became a white-power culture staple. Following Yockey, Christensen concluded that the Aryan civilization had reached its "senility phase," deranged by the combined effects of Christianity, capitalism, and communism. Christianity promotes the "unnatural" idea "that all people are equal" and its corollary, "universal brotherhood"; capitalism favors individual enrichment over folk solidarity and exploits nature for short-term profit; and communism destroys the organic unity of a race by its call for class struggle and international solidarity. Following Mills, Christensen (interview 1998) argued for a spiritual remedy: a revival of Norse paganism; identifying Odinism as a primordial expression of the Aryan "folk soul," understood in Jungian terms as a genetically transmitted collective unconscious. To Christensen (1984), the "primary source" of Odinism is biological: "its genesis is in our race, its principles encoded in our genes."

Convinced that any overt racist agenda would attract unwanted attention, Christensen (interview 1998) claims the advantage of a pagan approach: "You have to go in the back door! You have to sway with the wind. . . . I don't think that anybody mistook my opinions from what we wrote in *The Odinist*, but nobody could put a finger on what we said, because we said it in such a way that it couldn't be clamped down at. We still have to do that." A carefully veiled racialist pagan message will, Christensen argues, prevail where others fail: "Metzger thought he could twist the noses of the Jews, but you can't do that, so he collapsed. He just disintegrated. It was the same with Klassen. . . . You cannot repeat the mistake that Hitler made. . . . Everybody knows that the Jews rule the whole damned world, so you cannot fight their combined power. You need to watch your step."

Exactly how carefully "veiled" the message really was might be doubted. A couple of nonracist Odinists charged the editors of Christensen's tabloid, the *Odinist*, with "doing a disservice to paganism by promoting religious zealousness in the form of politics, especially 'Nazi politics' and [printing articles with] offensive racial overtones." In a 1985 rebuttal, the *Odinist* editor claimed that the "Nazi charge was the cheapest of all cheap shots that can be aimed against anyone who finds something positive to say about National Socialism." "If any Odinist is ashamed of the 'racial overtones' of being Aryan, of standing up for

Aryan rights, then we wonder why such a skittish a person ever want to be an Odinist," the editorial stated. "We, as Odinists, shall continue our struggle for Aryan religion, Aryan freedom, Aryan culture, Aryan consciousness and Aryan self-determination" ("Odinism" 1985).

Christensen urges American racists to learn from the history of fascism. Saluting the early left-oriented ultranationalist ideology of Mussolini's *Fasci*, Christensen claims that Mussolini betrayed the cause by "collaborating with the capitalist element." Similarly, she regrets that the "true, socialist and folkish, potential" of national socialism never became realized as Hitler purged the movement of the national bolshevist faction and aligned with the far right. Key to the historical failure of fascism was, to Christensen, its centralized totalitarianism. In this argument, the anarchist leanings of her youth shine forth. Anarchism seeks the dissolution of authoritarian government, the decentralization of responsibility, and the replacement of states and similar monolithic forms of political administration with a radically decentralized federalist organization of society. This will "return" sovereignty to the individual and the local community in a society governed by direct democracy. Christensen departs from the mainstream of anarchist philosophies by her insistence on the primacy of race. Whereas the contemporary anarchist scene generally is antifascist and antiracist, Christensen describes anarchism as a fundamentally Aryan ideology. She believes that anarchism originated in the "nature" of Aryan man and wants a decentralized society based on the voluntary cooperation of free Aryan individuals. Christensen upholds as ideal a decentralized folkish communalism, modeled on self-sufficient communes such as the Amish or the early National Syndicalists in Spain, described as an effort "to unite Anarcho-Syndicalist ideals with the nationalist spirit," which was later suppressed by "reactionary Francoite authoritarianism" ("Aryan" 1983; Christensen interview 1998).

Projecting her ideals back into legendary times, Christensen claims that pre-Christian Norse society practiced "tribal socialism," a system that supposedly combined "freedom of self-expression," "private enterprise," and "encouragement for every member of the tribe to reach his fullest potential" with socialist concerns of sharing resources and responsibilities, and caring for the young, the elderly, and the disabled of the tribe. A "race-conscious" free society will put the "interest of the racial community before those of any individual" as "individuals will die [whereas] the Race has the potential for immortality" ("Neo-Tribalism 1979; "Racial Consciousness" 1984). Christensen (interview 1998) argues that this has "nothing to do with fantasies of white supremacy." The doctrine of supremacy, the argument runs, leads invariably to ambitions of world dominion and thus to racial coexistence and race-mixing. Better then to keep the races apart to develop according to their unique racial souls in relation to their various ecological habitats.

Christensen connects the imperative of racial consciousness with the necessity of environmental awareness. Materialism, consumerism, and the capitalist exploitation of nature have brought on an ecological crisis of global magnitude she believes could only be reversed by implementing a pagan back-to-earth program of retribalization and ecologically sustainable production. Through Christensen's philosophy runs a streak of preoccupation with purity, peculiar to the national socialist version of environmental concern. A chain of idealized pure entities links macro and micro cosmos, emphasizing the postulated interdependence of the purity of the mind-body-race environment. Thus, a pure individual nurtures a pure mind in a pure body and lives in purity with an equally pure partner in a pure, that is, heterosexual and monoracial, relationship. This pure family provides a wholesome environment for bringing up pure and healthy children and is the primary building block of a pure racial organism living in harmony with a pure, unpolluted ecological system.

In line with the all-American longing for the simple life style of the free yeoman in the "good old days," Christensen envisions a future return to "small-town America" without monstrous cities and industrial pollution. Small-scale family farms would replace agribusiness and, freed from federal tyranny, white Americans would secure individual happiness through their natural industriousness in a Jeffersonian—though folkish pagan—utopia. To get there, Christensen outlines a long-term strategy of establishing small intentional communities of racist pagans that should avoid federal attention by keeping a low political profile. Regional networks of independent folk communities could then serve as springboards to meaningful activism. Self-sufficient, ecologically sustainable monoracial tribes would, Christensen suggests, be a practical avenue to redefine American federalism aiming at establishing an Odinist union of Aryan republics.

In the early 1980s, Christensen began a prison outreach ministry. Within a few years, she got Odinism to be officially accepted as a legitimate religion in the state of Florida, which enabled her to send in literature and hold services. Serving at seven Florida prisons with Odinist congregations ranging from 5 to 50 members, Christensen was a forerunner whose example has been emulated by other racist pagans. In 1993, Christensen was sentenced to five years in prison for drug trafficking—a sentence widely believed to be political in the racist pagan community—and was then deported to Canada. Upon her release, Christensen adopted an even lower political profile. Members of the revived Odinist Fellowship now have to sign a statement affirming that they intend to stay "within the legal laws of the country" of residence, and the Odinist Federation avoids the word "Aryan" in public communications. Thus distancing herself from the racist pagan milieu she was part of establishing, Christensen would probably rather be a revered icon than make a comeback at the forefront; the banner of radical racist paganism will be carried further by more outspoken ideologues, including the Wotansvolk.

A prominent voice of racially based Odinism is Wotansvolk, established in early 1995 by David and Katja Lane and Ron McVan. With headquarters at a mountain outside St. Maries, a small lumber town southeast of Coeur d'Alene in northern Idaho, Wotansvolk evolved into a dynamic propaganda center that spread its message throughout the United States and abroad and ran a quite successful prison outreach program catering to several thousand heathen prisoners in U.S. penitentiaries. A number of pagan white-power bands have put Wotansvolk lyrics to music, including Darken's *Creed of Iron* album and Dissident's song "Roots of Being" on the album *A Cog in the Wheel*. In line with the white-power pattern of fragmentation and infighting, Wotansvolk split in 2002, when administration was transferred to John Post in Napa, California. Based on fieldwork in the late 1990s and early 2000s, the presentation herein is confined to its first phase.

Wotansvolk combines an Aryan call to arms with an esoteric teaching, based in part on Jungian psychology, *völkisch* philosophy, and occult national socialism. An early proponent of the ZOG theory, Lane believes that the U.S. administration is controlled by racial enemies, using its military might to establish a global Jewish dictatorship. Convinced that Aryan man is an endangered species, Lane coined the "fourteen words" as a rallying point for a pan-Aryan uprising: "We must secure the existence of our people and a future for White children." The motto has taken hold in the global white-power scene, as evidenced by the almost universal reference to the fourteen words in poems, lyrics, articles and books and to the common racist habit of signing a letter *14/88* (meaning the 14 words and Heil Hitler).

Aiming at a white revolution, Wotansvolk endorsed the "leaderless resistance" strategy originally developed by Klan veteran Louis Beam, a longtime friend of the Lane family. In its Wotansvolk version, it involves the tactical separation between an open propaganda arm and a paramilitary underground. The function of the overt part is to "counter system-sponsored propaganda, to educate the Folk, to provide a man pool from which the covert or military arm can be [recruited]." Since the open racial propagandist "will be under scrutiny," Lane (1994: 26f.) emphasizes that cadres involved need to "operate within the [legal] parameters" and keep "rigidly separated" from the military underground. The paramilitary "must operate in small, autonomous cells, the smaller the better, even one man alone." Revolutionary activity means utilizing "fire, bombs, guns, terror, disruption and destruction. Weak points in the infrastructure of an industrialized society are primary targets. Whatever and whoever perform valuable service for the system are targets, human or otherwise. Special attention and merciless terror are visited upon those White men who commit race treason." Lane (interview 1996) is indifferent that his message might inspire the likes of Timothy McVeigh (who was convicted for the Oklahoma City bombing that killed 168 persons, including 15 children). "In the coming revolution there will be no innocents. There are only those who are for our cause and those who are our enemies. [The masses] will either follow us or follow them. They are now following their terrorism. When the time comes that our terrorism is superior to theirs, they will follow us. They will worship and adore whoever is the greater tyrant. That's the nature of the masses." The current weakness of Aryan man is attributed to Christianity, a creed "diametrically opposed to the natural order" (Lane interview 1996). "God is not love. God the Creator made lions to eat lambs; he made hawks to eat sparrows. Compassion between species is against the law of nature. Life is struggle and the absence of struggle is death." If Aryans are to survive, the otherworldly and self-denying Christianity must be abandoned in favor of Odinism, a religion based on nature's order—"a natural religion" that "preaches war, plunder and sex."

This uncompromising rhetoric designed by Lane to reach the lowbrow warrior caste of the white-power scene is combined with an esoteric teaching that at its core is race mysticism. Developed by Ron McVan, an artist and former associate of Ben Klassen, Wotansvolk ariosophy is outlined in *Creed of Iron* (1997) and *Temple of Wotan* (2000). Dissatisfied with the multiracial re-working of the American nation, Wotansvolk aims at "reaching deep into the ancestral past" to reconnect with the "roots of the Aryan race" in order to redevelop a lost "folk consciousness" (McVan interview 1996). Wotanism is presented as "the inner voice of the Aryan soul, which links the infinite past with the infinite future" (McVan 1997: 2). Accordingly, McVan (1997: 29) be-lieves that "all Aryans today retain an element of Wotan consciousness," a revival of which would liberate the white man. To Wotansvolk, Wotan (the Germanic name for Odin) symbolizes "the essential soul and spirit of the Aryan folk made manifest" (McVan interview 1999). As an iron-willed warrior god, Wotan is said to instill in the white race the determination and heroic qualities necessary to arise victoriously in the ongoing race war. Wotansvolk cast their work as a continuation of the efforts of turn-of-the-century ariosoph-ist Guido von List, philosopher Friedrich Nietzsche, and psychoanalyst Carl Gustav Jung, aiming at returning Aryan man to his perceived true nature.

Wotansvolk teaches that each race is by nature unique and given distinct qualities truly its own. To survive and evolve along the desired path of racial greatness, a race must be animated by its "racial soul," a genetically transmitted spiritual heritage, understood as a race-specific Jungian collective unconscious. "Every race has its soul and every soul its race" (McVan n.d.). Engraved in each racial member are powerful archetypes that may be reached through perform-ing the rituals and ceremonies developed by the ancestors in times imme-morial. These archetypes are the Gods of the Blood, who will exist as long as there are living members of the race. To the individual Aryan, the meeting with these archetypical forces recharges divine energy that man may evolve into the realization of the Nietzschean superman. Odinism here equals the rope over the abyss, connecting man the Beast with the Superman. "Through

Wotanism one may experience the infinitude of life mysteries and the divine completion of [Aryan] man," McVan (1998) asserts. There is no ontological distinction separating Aryan man and Aryan gods. They are conceived of as kin, differing in power rather than nature. Personifying the divine essence of Aryan man, the significance of Wotan expands beyond his warrior aspect. He is the master of gnosis who invites man to pursue the upward ariosophic path of perfection. In the occult National Socialist tradition of Serrano and Rosenberg, McVan cultivates the "mystery of the blood," believing that unmixed Aryan blood carries genetic memories of the racial lineage with all its gods, demigods, and heroes of the aboriginal golden age. Reconnected with the archetypical gods of the blood and developing his mental powers, "man is able to awaken to a divinity which flows within him" (McVan n.d. "Mind"). To the race, the rapport with its collective unconscious is a necessary prerequisite for keeping its identity and mission as a unique spiritual being. "A race without its mythos and religion of the blood shifts aimlessly through history" (McVan 1997: 16).

Operating with a less complex concept of cyclical time than Blavatsky, Serrano, and Devi, McVan's ideas still reflect the basic structure of an aboriginal Aryan golden age, fall, cleansing and renewal, universal to the world of racist paganism. Although a believer in the prehistoric Aryan civilizations of Hyperborea and Atlantis, the primary focus of McVan's historiography is closer to our present age, detailing how the once-glorious Aryan high culture was cast down into the present Wolf Age following the demise of the Norse gods in the previous Ragnarök. In the tradition of Yockey and Christensen, McVan argues that the primary cause of the fall was spiritual. With the advent of Jewish Christianity, there began a dramatic process of degeneration. "If ever there were a birth of tragedy, it was when Aryan man turned his back on the indigenous Gods of his race," McVan writes (1999). "On that day he sacrificed the very roots of his being, ushering in the labyrinth of his own descent." The level of folk consciousness gradually diminished, and the metaphysical race lost knowledge of itself as race. Following a selective reading of Jung, Wotansvolk asserts that the Aryan gods never died but remained dormant through the centuries of Christian dominion, deeply embedded in the Aryan psyche. With the völkisch revival of the late nineteenth century and the rise of the national socialist movement, the archetypical forces again began to manifest. Paraphrasing Jung, Wotansvolk likens Wotan to a long quiescent volcano that at any moment may forcibly resume its activity. With overwhelming power, the suppressed Gods of the Blood will return with a vengeance, Wotansvolk says confidently ("Wotan" n.d.), pointing to the ascendancy of Hitler as an historical example: "Nowhere since Viking times has the direct, singular effect of Wotan consciousness been more evident than in the folkish unity of National Socialist Germany."

Wotansvolk recommends that its followers practice daily meditation as the technique by which "the highest spiritual knowledge is acquired and union with the great gods of our folk is eventually gained." In this field we encounter noticeable Hindu and Buddhist influences, although in the watered-down version prolific in the Western milieu of alternative spirituality. Much like Serrano, McVan envisions Aryan man as a universe with all its worlds, as a microcosmic reflection of Yggdrasil, evolving toward perfection. Along the spine are found seven energy centers, "wheels" or "gateways," each associated with a specific rune. The spiritual ascendancy of individual man begins with meditation using these chakras of the Runic Tree of Man as contemplative focuses. In addition to individual practice, adherents to Wotansvolk philosophy are encouraged to connect with the archetypical gods through communal pagan ceremonies. "The practice of Wotanism ritual and ceremony of the annual festivals is recognized as the most effective way of impressing on our Aryan folk the wisdom, ethics and customs of our ancestors. Celebrating our indigenous traditions is as ancient as our race and is essential to our identity, unity, and survival as a people" (McVan 1997: 142). Wotansvolk performs the generic heathen "blot" ceremonies that celebrate the cycles of nature, but differs from other Norse pagans in the explicitly racial dimension. During a 1998 Midsummer blot conducted at Wotansvolk headquarters, participants hailed the coming "day of resurrection" of Balder, which will "usher in the new age of light for Aryan man after Ragnarök." "The wheel of life keeps turning," a participant recited loudly, his voice quavering dramatically as a kerosene-soaked swastika was set ablaze. "And in nature's cycle spins creation. Blazing like the sun's great disk, emanations of the high god Balder, a time of sanctification, [highlighting] the mystical nature of race and blood, carriers of primordial substances. The wheel of life keeps turning—the wheel of life keeps turning. I greet the summer solstice and the promise of a Golden Age."

Another significant ritual is the initiation ritual by which a prospect is accepted into the *einherjar* fraternity (McVan 2000). *Einherjar* is a Norse term for the brave warriors who died in battle and were brought to Valhalla, the abode of Odin. In Wotansvolk terminology, it denotes the community of racial warriors who are willing to die in the revolutionary war to establish an Aryan homeland. In the outdoors initiation ceremony, participants should preferably dress in Viking-inspired clothing and carry their swords. After setting up the sacred circle, the ritual leader (*gothi*) invites the gods to "open the mighty gates of Valhalla, Hall of Wotan's chosen warriors, Fearless fighting elite, Pride of the Valkyries," and then bring before them those who have died in battle the name of the initiate. Asking the *einherjar* to accept the initiate into their ranks, the *gothi* places a sword flat on top of the initiate's head as the latter kneels down on one knee. The *gothi* turns to the initiate. "Before our gods and chosen warriors, do you pledge by your solemn word that you shall always uphold with honor, dignity and courage the lifelong commitment to Wotan's Einherjar?" Confirming his pledge, the initiate then stands, and the *gothi* places the sword point at the nape of the initiate's neck to symbolize that death is better than dishonoring his commitment. The initiate is then blindfolded and brought before the lords of Valhalla, among which he now enters. Removing the blindfold, the *gothi* with his thumb presses oil on the initiate's head and gives him the blessings of Odin. Proclaiming that the initiate now is a member of Wotan's Einherjar, the *gothi* then places a sword in the outstretched arms of the initiate. "Through this sword, ancestors of a thousand ages fill thy being" the *gothi* says, and the ceremony concludes with all participants repeating in chorus: "Hail Wotan! Victory or Valhalla!"

Wotansvolk runs a prison outreach ministry recognized as an official vendor by the Federal Bureau of Prisons and by a majority of state prison authorities, and the program will remain a top priority to the new Wotansvolk administration of John Post. There are Wotansvolk congregations—"kindreds"—in every state, including the dozen states where Wotanism/Asatrú/Odinism has not yet been permitted full religious recognition. Prisoners incarcerated in those states are encouraged by Wotansvolk to challenge state regulations in court. In Utah, Ohio, and Wisconsin, legal battles are currently being waged for religious rights and the full recognition of Asatrú as a legitimate religion. As of January 30, 2001, Wotansvolk catered to more than 5,000 prisoners. The states with the strongest presence of Wotansvolk prison kindreds were Arizona, California, Texas, Michigan, Florida, Indiana, Missouri, and Pennsylvania, where three to five hundred Wotansvolk prisoners are found in each state.[3] The Wotansvolk prison outreach ministry has grown with remarkable speed. When I first visited Wotansvolk headquarters in the fall of 1996, there were fewer than a hundred prison kindreds. By the year 2000, there were more than three hundred.

Judging from correspondence between hundreds of individual prisoners and the Wotansvolk headquarters, there seems to be a pagan revival among the white prison population, including the conversion of whole prison gangs to the ancestral religion. To some extent, prison authorities have unwittingly facilitated the Wotansvolk effort by breaking up prison kindreds and transferring leading heathens to other prisons previously without an organized pagan presence. The determined Wotansvolk prison outreach program has earned them a reputation in the world of folkish paganism as being primarily a prison organization. According to Katja Lane (interview 1999), this is far from accurate, as prisoners constitute only an estimated 20 percent of Wotansvolkers in the United States. Yet the observation has some validity in the sense that Wotansvolk seems comparatively more successful in its outreach efforts than other Asatrú/Odinist programs, which partly may be explained by the reputation of David Lane and the legendary Brüders Schweigen in the white-power culture. Wotansvolk donate literature, videos, and ceremonial artifacts to assist prison kindreds in holding regular religious service, study circles, and seasonal ceremonies. In addition, Katja Lane corresponds with prison chaplains, sends them complimentary material on request, and assists inmates legally challenge prison authorities if denied full recognition of Asatrú/Odinism as a legitimate religion. In numerous cases, inmates who have been denied receiving Wo-tansvolk literature, books on runes, or wearing heathen symbols have been advised how to proceed legally, as have prisoners whose heathen material has been confiscated by prison guards. Lane's campaigning has contributed to the fact that all states now permit the wearing of a Thór's hammer as a religious medallion.

In March 2002, the new Wotansvolk administrator John Post announced the formation of the National Prison Kindred Alliance, a joint effort of Wo-tansvolk and a number of independent Asatrú/Odinist tribal networks that aims at proving a more efficient prison outreach ministry and coordinates the efforts of gaining increased religious rights and freedoms for the pagan com-munity behind bars. Imprisoned Order member Richard Scutari (2000) pro-vides an illustration from the inside; describing the kindred activities at the federal penitentiary in Lompoc, California, after authorities approved Odinism as a legitimate religion in 1997: "What was presented to the men spoke to their soul and we averaged from 50 to 55 prisoners at each weekly meeting. We were not only teaching the religion of our ancestors, but were also teaching White culture and White history. We even did a periodic segment we called 'Heroes of the Ages' in which we told the stories of different White heroes of the past, such as Horatius, Leonidas, Hermann, Vercingetorix, Adolf Hitler [and] Bob Mathews." Reflecting on the success of the Wotansvolk prison outreach pro-gram, Katja Lane (interview 1997) elaborates: "Most of the males who still have their instinct as warriors, protectors, defenders of their nation, their womenfolk and their children; these men are the ones who find themselves in prison. They're virtually on the front-line of the battle for the preservation of our race and they are the first casualties. And there you'll find some of the most fervent interest in Odinism. Men in prison, not having to take time to make a living for their families, take time to love their wives and deal with daily problems, turn inward and look for their spiritual soul, and, so those two factors have created a very strong Wotanist presence in the prisons. Prisons, as you know, are very racially tense . . . and usually violent. The men need a sense of their own identity and having an expression for it. So, nearly every prison now, both state and federal, has a kindred, and in nearly every case . . . Odinism or Wo-tanism, are now officially recognized" by the prison authorities.

Concluding Discussion

White-racist religions have emerged during many phases, reflecting the per-ceived status of whiteness in the alchemy of race and nation in the United States. Introduced at the height of white world supremacy, British-Israelism celebrated Anglo-Saxon dominion as the fulfillment of God's intention to bring his chosen people to the Promised Land. When constitutional racism was seriously challenged, the time was ripe for recasting British-Israelism into the increasingly more radical and anti-Semitic Christian Identity that, fused with Klan philosophy and fascist elements, sought to protect white birthright privileges and "hundred percent Americanism." Involved with resisting desegregation were also Rockwell Nazis, many of whom turned esoteric when they reflected on the defeat of National Socialist Germany in World War II and their own failure to uphold white supremacy domestically. Hitler was now cast as a living messiah or an avatar of Vishnu, and fanciful speculation localized his whereabouts among Aryan sages inside the hollow earth—esoteric lore that fit into the imagination of New Age–inspired racist seekers. As white racists began to realize that the good old days of white supremacy were gone, the celebration of Americanism characteristic of the Christian knights of the Ku Klux Klan gave way to a process of radicalization that eventually culminated in declaring war against the federal administration.

Parts of Christian Identity evolved into preachers of racial war, provoking a split between a more National Socialist–oriented violence-prone hard core and a less fascistic soft faction that will probably result in two separate religions of Aryan Israel. In the 1970s and early 1980s, activists in the rising white-power scene began to see Christianity as part of the conspiracy to subdue Aryan man under the power of ZOG. Christian Identity, long the dominant religious dimension of white-power philosophy, was now seriously challenged. With iconoclastic satisfaction, Ben Klassen of the Church of the Creator highlighted the inconsistencies of the Bible and ridiculed Identity efforts to make Jews of white men. With the call for a racial holy war evoked by acts in the surging white-power music industry, Creativity took hold among a new generation Aryan activists.

While Creativity was confined to focusing on racial empowerment with religious zeal, other white power activists found its lack of spiritual content dissatisfying. Searching history for roots and a religious alternative, racists came across the pre-Christian pagan traditions of Europe. Ancient Norse culture is well suited to serve as a source for a supposed racial golden age, as it provides believers with ample but incomplete material of an alternative world of old. Paganism therefore allows racist activists to project their ideals back into legendary times when Aryan society was untainted by the ills of modernity and materialism, when there were no presidents or kings, no federal government or capitalist plutocrats, no junk food, environmental destruction, pornography, or Ricky Lake shows—a wonderful pristine world when not a single Jew wandered through the Nordic woodlands. This was a time when Aryan man lived according to his true nature. When men were men and women were women, a glorious time of heroism and adventure, of nobility and honor, a time of campfires and sagas. Paganism thus seems to appeal to a new generation of Aryan activist who may find more satisfaction in reading J.R.R. Tolkien's *Lord of the Rings* than spending hours in tenuous Bible study classes aiming to prove a Jewish identity of Aryan man. Given the importance of Christianity to white American culture, Identity is likely to live on in the white-power milieu but its claim to monopoly has been broken by a new pattern of white religious racism with a plethora of alternative creeds competing for the soul of the white-racist believer—a pattern that is likely to spawn new "controversial" new religions in the near future.

NOTES

1. This essay is based on material published in my book *Gods of the Blood* (Duke University Press, 2003).

2. Most of this section is also published as the entry "White Power" by Gardell 2003b.

3. Records provided by Katja Lane, 2001.

WORKS CITED

Interviews by Author

Baumgardner, John, 1996. Tape recording. MacIntosh, Florida, November 1.
Butler, Richard G. 1996. Tape recording. Aryan Nations, Hayden Lake, Idaho, September 22.
Christensen, Else. 1998. Tape recording. Parksville, BC, Canada, August 7.
Hale, Matt. 1999. Tape recording. Superior, Montana, September 4.
Lane, David. 1996. Tape recording. Florence, Colorado. November 12.
Lane, Katja. 1997. Tape recording. St. Maries, Idaho, May 6.
———. 1999. Notes. St. Maries, Idaho, October 14.
McVan, Ron. 1996. Tape recording. St. Maries, Idaho, September 25.
———. 1999. Notes. St. Maries, Idaho, October 13.
Mohr, Jack. 1997. Tape recording. Little Rock, Arkansas, March 13.
Weiland, Ted R. 1999. Tape recording. ScottBluff, Nebraska, September 23.
Yarbrough, Gay. 1997. Notes. Leavenworth, Kansas, April 15.

Internet

Thomas, Mark. 1996a. "Requiem for a Witch-Doctor." *Watchman, on-line edition,* www2.stormfront.org/watchman/oklahoma.html. Downloaded August 12.
———. 1996b. "The Quaternity of God." *Watchman, on-line edition,* www2.stormfront .org/watchman/cg.html. Downloaded August 12.
———. 1996c. "The Bosnian Serbs." *Watchman, on-line edition.* www2.stormfront .org/watchman/jan96.html. Downloaded August 9.
———. 1996d. "White Supremacy!" *Watchman, on-line edition.* www2.stormfront.org/ watchman/feb96.html. Downloaded August 9.

————. 1996e. *Watchman, on-line edition.* www2.stormfront.org/watchman/index .html#contents. Downloaded August 19.

Turner, Lisa. 1999. "Women's Frontier to the ADL: We Reject Your Feminist Smear!" www.wcotc.com/wcotcwf. Downloaded August 17, 2001.

Printed Sources

American Institute of Theology. 1981. *Correspondence Bible Course.*

"Aryan Freedom." 1983. *The Odinist* no 77.

Barkun, Michael. 1997. *Religion and the Racist Right. The Origins of the Christian Identity Movement.* Chapel Hill: University of North Carolina Press.

Christensen, Else. 1984. "Odinism—Religion of Relevance." *The Odinist* no. 82.

CSA. 1982a. "What Is Identity Really About?" *CSA Journal* no. 9.

CSA. 1982b. "Why Do We Hate the Jews?" *CSA Journal* no. 9.

Devi, Savitri. 1958. *The Lightning and the Sun.* Niagara Falls, N.Y.: Samsidat.

Gardell, Mattias. 1996. *In the Name of Elijah Muhammad: Louis Farrakhan and the Nation of Islam.* Durham: Duke University Press.

————. 2003a. *Gods of the Blood. The Pagan Revival and White Separatism.* Durham: Duke University Press.

————. 2003b. "White Power." *Encyclopedia of Race and Ethnic Studies,* edited by Ellis Cashmore. London: Routledge.

Godwin, Joscelyn. 1996. *Arktos: The Polar Myth in Science, Symbolism and Nazi Survival.* Kempton, Ill.: Adventures Unlimited Press.

Goodrick-Clarke, Nicholas. 1992. *The Occult Roots of Nazism. Secret Aryan Cults and Their Influence on Nazi Ideology.* London: I. B. Taurus.

————. 1998. *Hitler's Priestess: Savitri Devi, the Hindu-Aryan Myth, and Neo-Nazism.* New York: New York University Press.

Hoskins, Richard Kelly. 1990. *Vigilantes of Christendom.* Lynchburg, Va.: Virginia Publishing.

Klassen, Ben. [1973] 1992. *Nature's Eternal Religion.* Milwaukee, Wis.: Milwaukee Church of the Creator.

————. 1981. *The White Man's Bible.* Otto, N.C.: Church of the Creator.

————. 1987. *RaHoWa! This Planet Is All Ours.* Otto, N.C.: Church of the Creator.

Klassen, Ben, and Arnold DeVries. 1982. *Salubrious Living.* Otto, N.C.: Church of the Creator.

Koehl, Matt. 1982. "A Fresh Start." Letter to members declaring the dissolution of NSWPP, effective January 1, 1983.

————. 1985a. "Resurrection." *NS Bulletin,* January-April.

————. 1985b. "Adolf Hitler: Prophet of a New Age." *NS Bulletin,* April.

————. 1985c. "Birth of a Leader." *NS Bulletin,* July-August.

————. 1985d. "A New Religion." *NS Bulletin,* September-December.

————. 1986. "Building a Spiritual Base." *NS Bulletin,* September-December.

Koestler, Arthur. 1976. *The Thirteenth Tribe.* Palmdale, Cal.: Omni Publications.

Lane, David. 1994. *Revolution by the Number 14.* St. Maries, Id.: 14 Word Press.

————. 1999. *Deceived, Damned and Defiant: The Revolutionary Writings of David Lane,* St. Maries, Id.: 14 Word Press.

Madole, James H. 1973–1977. "The New Atlantis: A Blueprint for an Aryan "Garden of Eden" in North America!" Article series, *National Renaissance Bulletin*, May 1973–February 1977.

McVan, Ron. n.d. "Death." Folder. St. Maries, Id.: 14 Word Press.

———. n.d. "Mind." Folder. St. Maries, Id.: 14 Word Press.

———. 1997. *Creed of Iron. Wotansvolk Wisdom*. St. Maries, Id.: 14 Word Press.

———. 1998. "Haminga." Folder, St. Maries, Id.: 14 Word Press.

———. 1999. "Religion: The Good, the Bad, the Ugly." Folder. St. Maries, Id.: 14 Word Press.

———. 2000. *Temple of Wotan. Holy Book of the Aryan Tribes*. St. Maries, Id.: 14 Word Press.

Metzger, Tom. n.d. "White Aryan Resistance Positions." *WAR Declared*. Fallbrook, Cal.: WAR.

Mills, Rud A. 1957. *The Call of Our Ancient Nordic Religion*. Reprinted Union Bay, B.C., Canada: Wodanesdag Press.

"Neo Tribalism." 1979. *The Odinist* no. 43.

O'Brien, Thomas E. n.d. *Verboten*. Hayden Lake, Id.: Church of Jesus Christ, Christian.

"Odinism and Racial Politics." 1985. *The Odinist* no. 91.

"Racial Consciousness." 1984. *The Odinist* no. 83.

Rich, Evelyn. 1988. *Ku Klux Klan Ideology, 1954–1988*, Vol. 1 and 2. Ann Arbor, Mich.: UMI Dissertation Services.

Scutari, Richard. 2000. "Unbroken Spirit." *Focus Fourteen*, January.

Serrano, Miguel. 1978. *El Cordón Dorado: Hitlerismo Esotérico*. Bogota: Editorial Solar.

———. 1984a. *Adolf Hitler, el Último Avatára*. Bogota: Editorial Solar.

———. 1984b. *NOS. Book of the Resurrection*. London: Routledge.

———. 1991. *Manú: "Por el hombre que vendra."* Bogota: Editorial Solar.

Swift, Wesley A. n.d. *God, Man, Nations and the Races*. Reprint. Hayden Lake, Id.: Church of Jesus Christ, Christian/Aryan Nations.

Weisman, Charles A. 1991. *Who is Esau-Edom?* Burnsville, Minn.: Weisman Publications.

"W.O.T.A.N. Will of the Aryan Nation." n.d. Folder. St. Maries, Id.: 14 Word Press.

Yockey, Francis Parker (aka Ulrik Varange). ([1962] 1991). *Imperium*. Costa Mesa, Cal.: Noontide Press.

19

Modern Satanism: Dark Doctrines and Black Flames

Jesper Aagaard Petersen

The disciple of Asmodeus is a lordly, domineering sort who craves unlimited power. He is ruthless in his pursuits and uncaring of any who might get in his way. He uses his power and influence to learn secrets, which in turn gain him more power, manipulate and command others, and enhance his own physical aspect.

—*Book of Vile Darkness* (Cook 2002)

The *Book of Vile Darkness* is an accessory for a role-playing game, which deals with all aspects of evil in the game world. Here the Game Master finds such devilry as the Disciple of Mephisto, the Angelkiller Greatsword and the Rotting Curse of Urfestra spell, as well as information on torture, poison, fetishes, and addictions. The view on evil is straightforward; evil is "the dark force of destruction and death that tempts souls to wrongdoing and perverts wholesomeness and purity at every turn. Evil is vile, corrupt, and irredeemably dark. It is not naughty or ill-tempered or misunderstood. It is black-hearted, selfish, cruel, bloodthirsty, and malevolent" (5). Even though the book provides a relative approach to evil as a variant rule and considers the difficulties of defining evil, the chosen framework is that evil is bad and wrong, good is pure and right. As such, the villain is evil and the hero good through actions as well as essence—something can be called inherently and radically evil because it is *evil*.

This absolute approach is all very well for a role-playing game intent on giving the players well-defined antagonists as a backdrop for their heroic deeds; it is very different in real life, especially in the context of Western pluralism and secularization. Nevertheless, when the issue is Satanism, this same moral framework is invoked. Questions abound: Why Satan—is he not an evil fiend? Why give up morality—wouldn't we just kill each other? What's the fun of being black-hearted, selfish, cruel, bloodthirsty, and malevolent? My point is that behind the modern-day relativism and rationality of Western society, an instinctive morality built on absolute and very Christian elements provoke us into stereotyping Satanism and Satanists as at worst inherently and radically evil or at best shallow and absurd. This popular discourse about Satanism thus propagates specific understandings tied to the underlying Christian frame of reference, with clear-cut boxes delimiting good and evil; it is clear that Satan, Satanists, and Satanism belong to the latter category, whether it is real or just an act.

In fact, most Satanists and Satanic groups I have encountered are not interested in evil, either in essence or action. They doubt that the Christian moral framework that permeates Western society is doing much good; many Satanists actually consider Christianity or even all organized religion the true evil. Most seriously committed modern Satanists are deeply engaged in moral questions, and consider themselves free thinkers probing the boundaries of nature and culture because we, as human beings, can and should indulge in our mental, emotional, and physical abilities. They are also very human. As such, Satanic groups are composed of ordinary people interested in religious and philosophical matters, not evil monsters or ignorant simpletons. It is important to bracket the Christian worldview and rid ourselves of the instinctive categorization that underlies the popular understanding of Satanism if we are to understand the people involved. Consequently, this chapter deals with the movement of related groups and organizations labeled modern Satanism—a somewhat darker manifestation of the aspirations of modernity, to be sure, but not inherently evil.

Modern Satanism is a conglomerate of ideas expressed in distinctive ways by individual groups, and although both the groups and the underlying ideas may be difficult to press into a unified mold, they nonetheless display characteristic philosophical and indeed religious aspirations. As a starting point for discussion, modern Satanism should be generally understood as a product of the meeting between modern rationality and Western esotericism, and as such, a cousin to the New Age and Human Potential movements.[1] In this sense, Satanism is a variant of the Self-spirituality or Self-religion of the twentieth-century West, utilizing a large number of different sources to express a unique vision of the self and the world.[2] The Self-spirituality of the New Age movement is built on "the monistic assumption that the Self itself is sacred," which results in "general agreement that it is essential to shift from our contaminated mode of being—what we are by virtue of socialization—to that realm which constitutes our authentic nature" (Heelas 1996: 2). This resonates with the founder of the Church of Satan declaring that:

Man needs ritual and dogma, but no law states that an externalized
god is necessary in order to engage in ritual and ceremony performed in a god's name! Could it be that when he closes the gap
between himself and his "God" he sees the demon of pride creeping
forth[?] . . . He no longer can view himself in two parts, the carnal
and the spiritual, but sees them merge as one, and then to his abys-
mal horror, discovers that they are only the carnal—AND ALWAYS
WERE! Then he either hates himself to death, day by day—or re-
joices that he is what he is! (LaVey 1969)

Their definitions of "authentic nature" are very different, of course, but modern
Satanism, the New Age movement, and the Human Potential movement share
a distinct orientation toward the realization of that "authentic nature" of the
individual in opposition to the repression of modern society. For Satanists, this
nature is symbolically expressed in the dual nature of Satan as Adversary and
Ruler of Earth—the prototypical nonconformist, hedonist, and individualist;
they do not subscribe to the overarching Christian framework at all. Thus
Satanism is a combination of positive religious and philosophical aspirations
centered on the individual with negative and critical anti-authoritarian convictions.

Some Satanic groups focus on rational issues, using philosophers such as
Friedrich Nietzsche, Niccolo Machiavelli, and Ayn Rand, as well as the modern-
day sciences of biology, psychology, and physics, to formulate a coherent materialistic worldview with morals to match. As human beings composed of flesh
and gifted with conscious as well as unconscious minds, we must embrace our
individuality and devote ourselves to the cultivation of our unique creative
instincts and carnal desires. This is the philosophy of the outsider, the free-
thinker, the rebel, ever aspiring to break free of the bounds of conventionality
and the slave morality embodied in the Christian Church and "liberal" society.
Thus, the Satan of this type of Satanism is both the rebel and the life force or
vitality of the self, interpreted as a symbol that expresses the continuing thread
of defiance against common norms and rigid dogma. Followers could be called
Rational Satanists.

Other groups highlight the spiritual side, drawing upon Eastern and Western traditions with a mystical angle, such as Tantric Hinduism, Chaos Magick,
and the writings of Aleister Crowley and Austin Osman Spare. This complex
of ideas and practices is commonly referred to as the Left Hand Path of ritual
magic, in contrast to the Right Hand Path of "analytic," cerebral magic and
"white-light" witches. It is more mystical and intuitive in scope, focusing on
darker and more "feminine" aspects of reality. The aim of the Left Hand Path,
according to Richard Sutcliffe, is a "liberation of the individual through decon-
ditioning and, ultimately, gnosis." He continues: "I would emphasize, however,
that while there is undoubtedly an antinomian ethos in the Left Hand Path

magick, the transgression of mores and taboos has more to do with the over-coming of one's own inhibitions and limitations, which are seen to be bound up with socialization, than with any ill-conceived anarchism. . . . [I]t is aimed at self-transmutation through the experience of the *totality* of being" (Sutcliffe 1995: 111). Satanists drawing on these traditions utilize Satan as a real or sym-bolic manifestation of our becoming authentic through desensitivization to social norms and values, a mystical project best understood as a part of the Western esoteric tradition. Thus, they could be called Esoteric Satanists.

I shall return to definitional and typological matters below; the preceding comments are, on the one hand, pointers intended to help readers grasp the subject in its totality, and, on the other, a warning that a study of modern Satanism is in many ways a study of Satanisms conjoined not in surface man-ifestations but in a depth structure of individuality, rebellion, and Otherness symbolized in the figure of Satan.[3]

The chapter begins with a short historical outline of the Satanic subculture followed by a presentation of various groups and spokespersons in order to summarize the available source material. Next, a discussion of the connecting themes, beliefs, and practices will be given in an attempt at systematization; included here is an analysis of some common typologies that have to be ad-dressed to establish a general analytical frame of reference. This study concen-trates on the modern groups, not on witchcraft, Devil worship, or Satanic Abuse issues, though these matters are of course interpreted in the construc-tion of tradition undertaken by both the groups themselves and their oppo-nents. Finally, some suggestions for future research are formulated.

Modern Religious Satanism—A Historical and Sociological Portrait

The history of modern Satanisms is a short one, comparable with the history of most new religious movements that mushroomed on the North American continent in the sixties and seventies. The problem, as stated above, is that Satanism lacks organizational and even doctrinal coherence, making it a sub-culture with many faces. I shall try to describe the development of modern Satanism in brief while summarizing the available literature on the subject, and combine that with a sociological profile on some major formations that have significantly affected the development of the movement. But first, modern religious Satanism has to be separated from Satanism as a more general phe-nomenon in history and fiction.

First, most if not all of the alleged historical instances of Satanism point toward Devil worship, that is, inverted Christian rituals based on the theology of the Christian faith, or the misunderstood practices of some pre- or non-Christian religion. But the distinction between Satanism and Devil worship is important. Modern Satanism should, as mentioned above, be understood as a product of the meeting between modernity and Western esotericism, and the Satan of Satanism is therefore more in tune with Man the animal or a cosmic force than the enemy invoked by medieval Inquisitors and modern-day Christian fundamentalists.[4] It is equally important, though, to acknowledge that both modern Satanists and Christians use historical metaphors as mythical realities, to quote Marshall Sahlins.[5] Thus analyses of Satanism should state whether they focus on the Christian scarecrow and his minions—that is, the history of Devil worship in the Christian worldview and the highly mythical function of medieval atrocity stories in the Western world—or the modern Satan of religious Satanism established by LaVey in the late sixties. The latter use the same historical instances in a different sociological context—that of the oppressed minority—and with a different mythological goal, that of legitimation.

Nevertheless, the claims of ancient lineage and constancy are erroneous as historical statements whether they point toward evil anti-Christians lurking in the shadows of Christendom or heroic freethinkers and medieval hedonists dancing in the moonlight. They are constructions, and true as such only in the context of mythical structure. This critical view should be combined with an understanding of the differences between Christian conceptions of the Devil and his alleged worshipers in history, and real groups with real conceptions of their own, including their own take on their history and tradition, where Satan is transformed into something different.

Second, what we have in terms of historical evidence amounts to statements made under torture, uncorroborated testimonies, and highly tendentious sources. Reviewing the various descriptions and analyses of historical Satanism, most fall in the sensational and/or theological group that take the evidence at face value; examples include Montague Summers, Richard Cavendish, and Arthur Lyons.[6] Even the often-cited Chambre Ardente affair in seventeenth-century France and the Hellfire clubs in England in the eighteenth century are more mythical than historical in nature. There might have been small groups of heretical Christians worshiping the Devil somewhere and sometime, but these instances are unrecorded and unimportant for this study, as are the Black Masses put on for show in the decadent cities of late-nineteenth-century Europe. Though it is impossible to prove a negative, we are left with no conclusive proof of any large-scale Satanic activity, conspiratorial or otherwise, before the twentieth century, and organized Satanic groups are quite rare prior to the 1960s.[7]

History

The history of modern religious Satanism can be divided into three phases.[8] In the first phase, from 1966 to 1975, organized Satanism emerged out of the occult subculture with the formation of the Church of Satan (CoS). Thus, the birth of modern Satanism can be traced to the actions of Anton Szandor LaVey (born Howard Stanton Levey in 1930), whose informal "Magic Circle" was transformed into the (in)famous Church of Satan on Walpurgisnacht, April 30, 1966 in San Francisco. Quickly reacting to the enormous amount of media attention, he conducted a Satanic wedding, funeral, and baptism, as well as weekly Satanic rituals and courses on various occult topics, thereby gaining a solid membership. In 1969, LaVey published *The Satanic Bible*, the most influential Satanic manifesto to date, followed by *The Compleat Witch* (1970) and *The Satanic Rituals* (1972). This first phase can be characterized by the carnivalesque showmanship of LaVey and the elitist counterculture of the CoS in the first half (1966–1970), and routinization resulting in mounting internal conflict in the Church in the second half (1970–1975).

The second phase, from 1975 to around 1995, is demarcated on one side by the dramatic schism in 1975 that resulted in the formation of the Temple of Set, and on the other side by the Internet boom of the mid-nineties and the death of Anton LaVey in 1997. In the early seventies, LaVey became dissatisfied with the side show of characters involved in the hierarchy of the Church of Satan, began chartering "grottoes" (local organizations) for independent activities, and commenced a revision of the degree system, from a traditional eso-

FIGURE 19.1. Anton LaVey and Diane Hagerty with their four-month-old grandson Stanton on LaVey's forty-eighth birthday (April 11, 1978). Courtesy of Zeena Schreck.

teric structure of examination and formulaic color coding to a more practical system of merits and functions. Other CoS members were dissatisfied for different reasons: the increasingly atheistic ideology of the CoS and/or LaVey's somewhat fickle administration of titles. Lead by Michael Aquino, a large group eventually split to form the theistic, highly organized Temple of Set (ToS). The seventies and eighties saw the birth and decline of a large number of smaller churches, temples, and orders that emerged in the wake of CoS's initial success, which often simulated some aspects of the church while differing on others.[9] The CoS itself made a turn toward Nazi-chic in the eighties in an attempt to replicate the conflict with Western society's norms and values, but this was discontinued when LaVey resumed active control of the church in the early nineties. The conflict was real enough, though, as a massive moral panic influenced public opinion in the eighties and early nineties; this affected not only self-declared Satanic groups but also innocent victims of the Satanic Ritual Abuse Scare. Here, the goals of anticultism, fundamentalist Christianity, child-saving movements, and psychiatric authorities converged in a highly influential wave of modern anti-Satanism disseminated by the media, social care workers, and law enforcement officers, resulting in allegations, arrests, and convictions of hundreds, although nothing was proven or even plausible.[10]

The third phase, from 1995 to the present, is dominated by the upsurge of activity stimulated by the democratization of the Internet around 1995, which has increased the visibility of and communication between Satanic groups and individuals. Encouraging both creativity and discord, the Internet radically altered the structure of the Satanic subculture, as even small minorities of one could construct an outlet potentially inspiring many. The result was, and is, a huge number of virtual groups. This unstable situation prompted the larger organizations to protect their material and members by asserting their authority.[11] Another important event was the death of Anton Szandor LaVey in 1997, which almost immediately aroused revolt in the Church of Satan. This was short-lived, though, as high-ranking members such as Blanche Barton, Peter H. Gilmore and Peggy Nadramia assumed leadership, with Peter Gilmore as high priest. Again, this has alienated some individuals from the line of the church and has created new groups, mainly online. This third phase could therefore be characterized by increased differentiation of Satanic ideology as a whole and in the power structures of the subculture as information becomes available through virtual platforms, paralleled by an increased rhetoric of legitimation from the larger organizations.

To supplement this short historical presentation of the Satanic movement it is important to examine some central outlets in depth. I have selected the Church of Satan and the Temple of Set, as they constitute the major organizations, and the Satanic Reds, the 600 Club, and the Satanic Media Watch, as three important manifestations of Satanism today.

Anton Szandor LaVey and the Church of Satan

Much has been written on this charismatic high priest and his organization.[12] From its humble beginnings in San Francisco in 1966, the CoS has attracted many interested in magic and the occult and has survived numerous schisms, exposés, and attacks from within and without. The history of the organization has already been outlined. Today the Church of Satan is essentially a decentralized, cell-like structure where first-level (registered) membership is attained by filling out a registration statement and paying a hundred dollars to the central administration. Individual members have as much contact with the organization as needed, and most members have little to do with the church or even local grottoes. Second-level (active) membership and higher levels of involvement (activities such as grotto master and agent, or the degrees of priest/priestess, magister/magistra, and magus/maga) are very rare (see the *Church of Satan Information Pack*—"Affiliation with the Church of Satan"). No exact membership figures are available, as the decentralized structure and one-time registration fee make it impossible to draw the line between active and inactive involvement. Active members probably number in the hundreds, but many more may be registered and nearly one million have purchased *The Satanic Bible* (Baddeley 1999: 72).[13]

The CoS is officially governed by the Council of Nine, of which the high priest, Peter H. Gilmore, the high priestess, Peggy Nadramia, and the Magistra Templi Rex, Blanche Barton, are the most vocal. Practically speaking, the members and grottoes are self-sufficient, and the council concentrates on matters of doctrine, general guidelines, and administration of Dr. LaVey's estate (through the Order of the Trapezoid). As such, the council is engaged in protecting the authority of LaVey's writings and is only concerned with individual members' beliefs and practices when they run counter to the interests of the church (warnings and even excommunication are not unheard of). In that respect the CoS manifests a top-down doctrinal rigidity.[14]

Philosophically, the Church of Satan can be classified as pragmatic egoistic humanism, a Self-religion focused on empowerment and self-realization for the "Alien Elite."[15] The free will of the individual and the emotional and sensual facets of the human existence are lauded as being as important aspects of human nature as the intellect; the teachings are frequently clothed in arguments that are simultaneously materialistic, Darwinistic, and atheistic, while appealing to occult traditions as well. The use of Satan is symbolic and points to the central doctrines of opposition to norms and values, nonconformity, and hedonism in order to realize one's self-interest. Peter H. Gilmore states that "Satanists do not believe in the supernatural, in neither God nor the Devil. To the Satanist, he is his own God. Satan is the symbol of Man living as his prideful, carnal nature dictates. The reality behind Satan is simply the dark evolutionary force that permeates all of nature and provides the drive for survival and propagation inherent in all living things. Satan is not a conscious entity to be worshipped, rather a reservoir of power inside each human to be tapped at will" ("Satanism: The Feared Religion" in *The Church of Satan Information Pack*). This "dark force" is often referred to as the Black Flame. Rituals, called Greater Magic, are "intellectual decompression chambers" used to invoke "change in situations or events in accordance with one's will" (LaVey 1969: 110). A ritual can thus be characterized as a "psychodrama," where heightened emotion is used to alter reality (LaVey 1969: 109–128; 1972: 11–27). Both Greater Magic and manipulation, called Lesser Magic, are used as each individual Satanist sees fit, as they are conceived of as pragmatic techniques that work, not spiritual dogma. The central convictions of the CoS are formulated in short statements and rules found in LaVey's books and articles that are constantly reproduced in articles and communiques from spokespersons of the church: *The Nine Satanic Statements, The Eleven Rules of the Earth, The Nine Satanic Sins*, and the *Pentagonal Revisionism* program.[16]

The source material itself can be categorized into "official" documents and interpretations. The official documents include *The Satanic Bible, The Satanic Rituals*, and *The Satanic Witch* (LaVey 1969, 1972, 1989), as well as the documents mentioned above, all written by Anton Szandor LaVey.[17] It is important to bear in mind that these sources are manifestations of Satanic philosophy, *not* scripture, even though the CoS sometimes treat them as such. They are not transcendental truths but statements of the Satanic worldview and ethos. Semi-official documents include *The Devil's Notebook* and *Satan Speaks!* by Anton LaVey (LaVey 1992, 1998) and Blanche Barton's *The Church of Satan* and *The Secret Life of a Satanist* (Barton 1990a, 1990b).

The interpretations of the party line could be classified as orthodox and unorthodox. Clearly orthodox documents are *The Church of Satan Information Pack* and most of the material found on the official Web site and the Web sites of active members, and in *The Cloven Hoof* and *The Black Flame*. Unorthodox interpretations, such as the Dark Doctrines of Tani Jantsang and Philip Marsh (discussed below), are regularly removed from the CoS-sponsored sites and materials, but since the advent of the Internet they have proven to be increasingly difficult to suppress. Thus many orthodox documents deal with these unorthodox sources (see for example the "Satanic Bunco Sheet" and "Church of Satan Chat Room Policies" in *The Church of Satan Information Pack*, and "Sycophants Unite!" on the official Web site). I shall return to these matters of doctrinal rigidity and legitimation strategies below.

Academic interest in the CoS goes back to the early seventies, when this new group of "black urban witches" caught the eye of anthropologists and sociologists. Based on extensive participant observation, Edward Moody (Moody 1971, 1974) analyzed the socio-psychological effects of the magical worldview and considered magic a pragmatic solution to problems of self-esteem and anxiety. Through the inversion of Christian dogma and practices

Satanists redefine evil, thus asserting the relativity of norms and values in society and the good in evil. This in turn reconditions the magician to express and indulge in personal desires and to be free from repression. The inversion of Christianity is therefore a means to an end, the liberation and empowerment of the individual, not the central tenet of Satanism (Moody 1974: 366).[18]

Marcello Truzzi (Truzzi 1972, 1974a, 1974b) examines the continuum of beliefs and social organization found in the "occult revival," specifically modern witchcraft. After classifying Satanists as Black Witches, he eventually defines the Church of Satan as a specific type of "group-affiliated, non-stereotypical Satanists" (Truzzi 1974a: 639): "Its doctrines are primarily those of a materialistic (anti-mystical and anti-drugs) philosophy of anti-Puritanism and pro-indulgence coupled with a highly Machiavellian set of social ethics emphasizing success and survival by *any* means and a basically elitist political posture. This highly cynical and epicurean world view is coupled with a belief in the efficacy of magic and its ritual. However, magic is largely redefined to make it compatible with science, and nothing is viewed as being truly supernatural" (Truzzi 1974a: 644–645). This could easily be written of the CoS today. He continues: "The name 'Satanism' and its other seeming relations to Christianity are actually somewhat misleading, for these are mainly used in a symbolic sense. . . . Thus, the Church of Satan is not really a sect of Christianity in the same sense as are most present and past Satanic groups" (ibid.: 645). Although I am skeptical about the "past Satanic groups" to which Truzzi refers and not happy to include Christian heretics in the category of "Satanist" at all, I fully endorse the statement of difference between modern Satanism and Christianity.

Randall Alfred disagrees, but on a different level (Alfred 1976). As was the case with Moody's study, Alfred builds his analysis on protracted participant observation in the early phases of the CoS, but the theoretical angle is Weberian, analyzing the complex motivations underlying the Church, its founder, and adherents. Alfred describes six attractions of Satanism for its members: hedonism, magic, diabolism, iconoclasm, millenarianism, and the charisma of LaVey. He elaborates especially on the last factor for the specific dynamics of the church. He argues that the ambivalence of the founder toward play and seriousness, authority and rebellion, is reflected in the church itself (197), and that the Church of Satan might best be described as evolving toward the position of Protestant sect,[19] as the conflict between the individualistic philosophy of hedonism and the discipline and authority needed to perform magic—and indeed be a *Church* of Satan—is resolved "eventually in favor of the long-dominant traditional value systems of post-reformation Western culture" (199). He concludes: "Thus, while retaining Protestantism's worldly interest in the value of work and discipline, Satanism no longer rejects the enjoyment of the mundane fruits of those labors. It is a final ratification of the spirit of capitalism. . . . Satanism provides the religious legitimation for worldly hedonism in place of 'worldly asceticism' " (ibid.). On a sociological level, the Church of Satan is thus deeply embedded in the Christian culture of which it is a part, even though it cannot be said to be "an inversionary sect, a topsy-turvy Christianity" (189). I consider this analysis astute, but somewhat outdated, as the original Church of Satan indeed broke under the weight of these internal conflicts. The modern church is decentralized and individualistic, and has stopped explicit appeals to "long-dominant traditional value systems of post-Reformation Western culture." It is very true, though, that the Church of Satan (and indeed most modern Satanists) repeatedly reorients itself along a scale of respectability and outrage, thus continually emphasizing the nonconformist attitude that is at odds with Western society while basically affirming a secular, scientific, and even capitalist ethos of rationality.

This line of reasoning is picked up and expanded in the work of James R. Lewis (Lewis 2002a, 2002b). He is particularly interested in the complex relations among Anton LaVey's charismatic authority, his rational legitimation strategies, and some followers' appeal to traditional modes of legitimation. First, *The Satanic Bible* "is treated as an authoritative document which effectively *functions* as scripture within the Satanist community. In particular, LaVey's work is quoted to legitimate particular positions as well as to delegitimate the positions of other Satanists. This legitimation strategy appears to have been unconsciously derived from the Judeo-Christian tradition, which locates the source of religious authority in a sacred text" (Lewis 2002b: 2). Although it can be found throughout the Satanic subculture, this strategy is

FIGURE 19.2. The Church of Satan's original ritual chamber. Courtesy of Zeena Schreck.

especially successful within the CoS, both in order to ensure the doctrinal rigidity mentioned above and to manifest the "real" Satanism of the church when confronted with heterodox interpretations from non-CoS Satanists. Thus *The Satanic Bible* functions as traditional authority in Weberian terms. This is at odds with the intentions of the founder, who appealed to personal charisma reinforced by rational claims to authority that are still extant in the non-CoS elements of the Satanic subculture. Lewis writes that

> when LaVey founded the Church of Satan, he grounded Satanism's legitimacy on a view of human nature shaped by a secularist appropriation of modern science. Unlike Christian Science, Scientology and other groups that claimed to model their approach to spirituality after the *methods* of science, LaVey's strategy was to base Satanism's "anti-Theology" in the secularist *world view* derived from natural science. . . . At the same time, LaVey went beyond contemporary secularism by suggesting the reality of mysterious, "occult" forces— forces he claimed was not supernatural, but where, rather, natural forces. (Lewis 2002b: 3–4)

In other words, Satanism is legitimate because it is rational: a reasonable religion built on a sound understanding of human nature and the empirical world.

These two strategies have existed side by side in the Satanic movement, especially since LaVey's death. Many Satanists consider *The Satanic Bible* authoritative in matters of Satanic philosophy and practice, while simultaneously adhering to LaVey's explicit appeal to independent, rational thought. Within the CoS, however, "LaVey's successors have come to place excessive stress on their role as bearers of his legacy, even asserting that only CoS members are 'real' Satanists and characterizing Satanists outside the fold as 'pseudo' Satanists. In terms of Weber's analysis, one would say that CoS's legitimation strategy has narrowed to focus almost exclusively on CoS's claim to traditional authority" (ibid.: 4). In effect, the "routinization of charisma" has created a tradition, "orthodox LaVeyan Satanism," which is contrasted with "unorthodox pseudo-Satanism." This development has been amplified by the Internet, a virtual battleground that has enabled the unorganized network of non-CoS Satanists to voice their constructions of tradition (see Petersen forthcoming).

The Church of Satan has spawned numerous splinter groups in its nearly forty years of existence. From the Church of Satanic Brotherhood (1973) to the Church of Satanic Liberation (1986), the First Church of Satan (1994 or 1998) and the First Satanic Church (1999), the wish to return to the "original premises" of a Satanic church has remained strong. The most successful splinter group is still the Temple of Set.

Michael Aquino and the Temple of Set

As with the CoS, the history of the Temple of Set (ToS) is intimately bound up with the biography of its founder, Michael Aquino. He joined the CoS in 1969 and rose rapidly in the Church's hierarchy. After falling out with Anton LaVey over matters of the structure and direction of the church, he led a group of dissenters to form a serious esoteric organization in 1975. He was affirmed in this decision through a Working of Greater Black Magic where he communicated with the Prince of Darkness in his original form of the Egyptian god Set, who charged Aquino to found a temple and become its high priest.[20]

The Temple of Set is still led by Aquino today.[21] It is a closely knit organization of individual ranks, pylons (local groups), and orders (divisions of interest) topped by the Council of Nine, the executive director, and the high priest. Membership is by application and contact with a priest or priestess, followed by an evaluation period; the focus is on the individual Setian's (first degree member's) development and creativity on the road to becoming a second-degree Adept. As with the CoS, the higher ranks are reserved for administrative offices and are bestowed upon competent individuals.[22] Unlike to the CoS, each member must be affiliated with a Pylon and, later, an Order, even though the practical interaction with the ToS resembles that of the CoS, as the self-realization of the individual is more important than the temple as such (see the Religious Movements Homepage). All in all, ToS resembles an individualistic rendition of the magical orders of nineteenth-century Europe, like masonic lodges, the Ordo Templi Orientis, the Astrum Argentum, and the Golden Dawn.

Membership figures are difficult to come by due to temple policy; estimates range from three hundred (personal communication with James R. Lewis) to five hundred (Bromley and Ainsley 1995, La Fontaine 1999), with about fifty in Britain (Harvey 1995). Zeena Schreck, daughter of Anton LaVey, joined the temple in 1995, but led a schism in 2002; it is likely that this has affected the ToS in terms of membership.

Philosophically, the Temple of Set is an intellectual wing of esoteric Satanism and leans heavily on the writings of Aleister Crowley and elements of Western esotericism in general (ceremonial magic[k], mysticism, and the Left Hand Path). A greater focus is laid on magical Workings and studies that aid the process of "becoming" (*xeper* or "kheffer"), that is, realizing the true nature of the individual Satanist. They are walking the Left Hand Path, which "involves the conscious attempt to preserve and strengthen one's isolate, psyche-centric existence against the objective universe (OU) while apprehending, comprehending, and influencing a varying number of subjective universes (SU)" (Aquino [1975] 2000: 23). Here the basic tenets are laid out: the uniqueness of the individual, the importance of knowledge, and the practice of Greater

Black Magic to strengthen individual existence and influence subjective universes (which in turn affects the objective universe; see ibid.: 88). A short description can be found in Harvey (1995: 288–289). The transcendence of the individual psyche is also proposed—in effect, the ToS believes in the immortality of the true self that *is*, and the xeper is the ability to align your consciousness with that authentic self (Aquino [1975] 2002: 51–56). That is achieved through knowledge understood as a conjunction of intellect and intuition, akin to *gnosis* and described as self-initiation (ibid.: 21–22).

These doctrines are summed up in the figure of Set/Satan and the Black Flame. Set, as the true semblance of the Prince of Darkness, is real—ToS is theistic. But he is neither related to the Judeo-Christian context nor worshiped as a god. He *is* what every adept aspires to become—fully self-conscious, knowledgeable, and true to his inner essence—totally apart. Presumably he is "becoming" as well, but that is unclear. His gift to humanity is that which sets us apart from nature: the questioning intellect identified as the *Black Flame of Set* (described as the Gift of Intellect, Gift of Set, and Gift of Knowledge), "which brought isolate self-consciousness to higher life" (ibid.: 95). This evolutionary leap was thus brought to us by Set and obliges us to "become." As noted above, magic—both Greater and Lesser—is used to aid the magician's "becoming" by staging alterations in consciousness and the world. It is thus a very personal endeavor, deeply rooted in the worldview of the temple's adherents. In practice, however, the example of a Greater Magic Working resembles rituals of the CoS (compare Aquino [1975] 2002: 86ff. with LaVey 1969: 107ff.).

The source material is sparse, as the temple restricts access to documents of central importance and does not permit participation in rituals by noninitiates (Aquino [1975] 2002: 21, 91). It is not that it regards its literature as esoteric secrets as such, but the truth is dangerous to the wrong minds: "There are no penalties for revealing 'esoteric secrets' in the Temple. We exist to *promote* knowledge of truth, not to conceal it. Setians should understand, however, that some of the truths known to the Priesthood of Set can be dangerous to oneself or others if misapplied, just as a loaded gun in the hands of a child is dangerous" (Ibid.: 21). *The Book of Coming Forth by Night* is a "channeling," comparable to Aleister Crowley's *Book of the Law*, and is consequently imparted with much authenticity (Aquino 1975). In it the intelligence of Set speaks directly. The entire *Jeweled Tablets of Set*—of which only the introduction to the first part (the *Crystal Tablet of Set*), called either *Black Magic* or *Black Magick in Theory and Practice*, is in my possession (Aquino [1975] 2002)—is an encyclopedia of knowledge composed of tablets keyed to specific degrees in the temple hierarchy. Finally, I should mention the huge e-book, *The Church of Satan* (Aquino 1999), an analysis of and compilation of documents relating to the CoS.

Academic interest in the temple is meager. The only extended treatments with which I am familiar are Gini Graham Scott's *The Magicians* (Scott 1983) and an article by Graham Harvey (Harvey 1995).

The Internet Boom of the 1990s—Satanic Reds, the 600 Club, and the Satanic Media Watch

As I have said repeatedly, the status of modern Satanism is one of pluralism and fragmentation—it is a decentralized movement. In fact, it always has been; the major factor today is the increased visibility and accessibility of Satanism (and esoteric and occult material in general) on the Internet, which is valuable in terms of information exchange and retrieval, as well as general communication and contact, but detrimental to authority and closer community building. The main point is that as Satanism, organizationally speaking, is set free from the closed circles that have maintained doctrinal integrity, individualism and eclecticism are amplified. This is not all new, as Satanic literature such as *The Satanic Bible* has had an independent life outside the CoS for decades; what is new is that the Satanists who previously worked alone can now participate visibly, freely, even anonymously in the manifestation of modern Satanism by maintaining a home page or even just engaging in debate on Usenet groups or message boards. The paradox is that this increase in personal expression undermines doctrinal coherence, which causes new, local groups to develop, using the Internet to establish contacts. This complex of activity on- and off-line demands demarcation strategies to separate "us" from "them," again increasing fragmentation.[23]

Several studies have addressed the status of modern Satanism on the Internet. Some focus on the new geographical areas made visible (Smoczynski 2003 on Poland, Alisauskienen 2003 on Lithuania), others on legitimation strategies and the doctrinal conflicts magnified by the Net (Petersen forthcoming). James R. Lewis has conducted an Internet survey of modern Satanism (Lewis 2001a) which in many respects portray Satanism and Satanists online.

The larger organizations have a presence on the Net, but they cannot (and often will not) control the information present. That does not mean that they do not care. Assertions of "real" Satanism and allegations of "pseudo" Satanism signal borders in virtual space. To investigate the electronic abyss outside the safe harbors of CoS and ToS, I have selected three interesting manifestations of Satanism in the Internet age: a loose affiliation called Satanic Reds, a message board and online community dubbed The 600 Club, and an online archive entitled Satanic Media Watch and News Exchange.

Satanic Reds was founded in 1997 as an outlet for the prolific writer Tani Jantsang and associates such as Philip Marsh. Tani Jantsang describes herself as a "generational Satanist," born into the Dark Doctrines that are put forward on the Web site and in various articles.[24] As such, her philosophical standpoints and practices apparently preceded her relationship with the Church of Satan through groups such as the Starry Wisdom Sect and the Kishites in the sixties and seventies.[25] Nevertheless, she worked extensively with the CoS in the eighties and nineties, but disagreements after Anton LaVey's death resulted in excommunication from the CoS and the launching of Satanic Reds.

The Web site itself is organized as a huge archive of articles, spells, rituals, links, and a chat room, and is operated by the People's Commissar (Jantsang). People join by filling out a registration form; the membership count is unknown, but is probably less than a hundred. This is less important than the fact that the online articles and especially the printed essays available to order are read and discussed by many Satanists interested in something deeper than *The Satanic Bible*. Apparently anyone can join and feel free to join other groups as well—it is an association of Satanists on the Left Hand Path with left-wing sympathies (a double provocation, one might add).

On the basis of the material, it is clear that Satanic Reds should be classified as highly esoteric Satanism, as it advocates a radically syncretistic and eclectic version of the Left Hand Path religious tradition combined with modern-day political philosophy. The articles describe the unified "dark tradition" or "Dark Doctrines" found around the globe in many cultures, including those of Christianity and Islam. The main influences seem to be Hinduism, especially the Advaita Vedanta and Tantric traditions; Buddhism, again mainly the Abhidharma school; Daoism; and various mystical traditions, such as Jewish Kabbalah. The main principles are the Boundless Darkness and the Flame, and the emanation doctrine of Being and Becoming:

> 1. Satan is the "dark force" that permeates all of nature and motivates all things to act according to their inner nature. The Boundless Darkness Itself is SAT. The ACTION of emanating out of, unfolding out of, springing forth, is TAN. The motivator *and* the act of motivating all things are together: Satan. Satan is that which is the origin of all *and* the unmoved mover, and it is described by both the unfolding and the thing unfolded: Satan. . . . 3. The "big bang" came from a spark within the one Dark Presence and all that results from the "big bang" is permeated by the Dark Force. The universe was emanated by this force going from Chaos-Dark to Cosmos-Light.
> (*The Nine Satanic Postulates*, nos. 1 and 3)

This mystical cosmogenesis reevaluates the figure of Satan and integrates it in a monistic emanation complex. It is a doctrine of Darkness and Light-in-Darkness, stages of being and becoming, and a Dark Flame infused in our universe of matter and energy. Satan is thus both a concept that describes the ceaseless dynamics of the universe and a reality, a Dark Force suffused through all the emanated universe. In reality, all is One with the Dark Presence or Boundless Darkness (that is "none"). The Satanist resonates with this gnosis, a knowledge that is also an intuitive practice, and strives to become what is already his or her inner core through a participation in the unending change of the physical universe: "And all this is the esoteric meaning of 'Do as Thou Wilt' for that truly is the *whole* of the Law, Cosmic Law and SAT-TAN-ic Law. . . . Man is just another animal: Self-inner-truth-Wisdom is knowing what kind of animal a human is" (*The Nine Satanic Postulates*, no. 9).

These doctrines form the backbone of the Left Hand Path, which is both mystical and practical, esoteric and dialectical materialist. Again, the point is unity: "There is no conflict between these paths [Left and Right Hand Paths] if they are True; they are yin/yang and exist together and this embodies real stratification in the sense of people naturally working at their own abilities. I.e., what you are good at, naturally comes easy! Because of this, there is always RHP in LHP, and always LHP in RHP. There is the 'Being' of the receptive LHP and then the 'Becoming' which is the active RHP. There is the Knowledge of the LHP that leads to the deeds of the RHP. Everything is Yin and Yang. Passive Idea; Active Deed. Like Sat-Being and Tan-Becoming" (*Left Hand Path and Right Hand Path: Defined*: 2). In practice, a Satanic Red is doing pretty much what other Satanists are doing: "What They Will." Their rituals are as eclectic as their doctrines, often adopting the fiction of H. P. Lovecraft (the Cthulhu mythos) and other appropriate material to heighten the effect. In this regard they resemble modern Wiccan movements and Chaos Magick,[26] and even the pragmatic explications of the CoS and ToS.

On the issue of distinctness, *Satanic Reds* argues that "Satanic Reds exists as an alternative to the 'Satanism' that is so tied up with Christianity. It is, in fact, a Left Hand Path organization as far as occult doctrines go. The doctrines are wholly outside of the Christian world view. The concepts of becoming (xeper) and Inner Will (thelema) are in these Doctrines, and always were from ancient times. But the wailing angst of people rebelling against their own Christian backgrounds is wholly left out" (*Why Do We Call Ourselves Satanic Reds? FAQ*: 2). This is "true" Satanism, ancient and wholly outside the Christian framework, working with the traditions of Eastern and Western esotericism (note the discreet nods to Egyptian religion and the ToS in the use of *xeper* and to Aleister Crowley with *thelema*) and not the "wailing angst" of the more secular, rational Satanism of the CoS. Even Satan, as noted before, is Satan, Sat, and Tan, and not a Hebrew fiend.

The ToS and the Satanic Reds represent religious Satanisms, that is, groups with an esoteric outlook that goes beyond the atheistic iconoclasm of the CoS and other more secular groups; there is no doubt that they involve religious constructions of tradition and religious rhetoric. The legitimation often seems rational, but now clothed in a discourse of tradition explicitly infusing the dictums of modern science (observation, hypothesis, verification) with esoteric meaning: This is true, because they and the Dark Adepts before them know it to be true.

The 600 Club is a community site launched around 1996–1997 by Rick Rinker. It is affiliated with the First Church of Satan, but has about seven hundred active "members" from all parts of the Satanic subculture. The name is derived from The 700 Club, a part of the Christian Broadcasting Network dedicated to online communication and off-line contact between Christians. The Satanic version has undergone extensive revision in the past couple of years (I mentioned it in my study on Satanism on the Internet, Petersen forthcoming) from a bazaar of every possible interest to the Satanist (soft-porn sites, music, and clothing, as well as links to Satanic sites and a message board) to a more sober community site centered on the message board and archives. In that regard it resembles other Satanic community sites such as British Satanism (www.Satanism-uk.org) and the Danish Satanic Net (www.Satanisknet .dk). Its goals seem to be mainly communicative, and it utilizes the structural aspects of the Internet, namely, visibility, accessibility, and (limited) interaction to reach newcomers and dabblers on the fringe of Satanism as well as old-time contacts to improve doctrinal coherence and virtual community.

Satanic Media Watch and News Exchange was established in 1998 in the wake of the moral panic that gripped the United States, Britain, Norway, and others (including New Zealand) in the eighties and early nineties. Fear of Satanic Ritual Abuse, multiple personality disorder, and Satanic cults coalesced into a "Satanic Panic" of huge proportions. Many Satanists naturally felt threatened by the turn of events (and some were actually accused, such as Michael Aquino). One response was to gather information and distribute it along with some sensible material on "real" Satanists. This has been done from the mid-nineties by Amina Lap, the founder of the site and sole administrator. Today, the site is an archive of articles and documents dealing with many aspects of the Panic. I have included this site as an example of the concrete manifestation of hard-core rational Satanism that attempts to influence public opinion through the use of scientific methods and rational arguments, and as such an expression of rational self-interest.

The Satanic Worldview

As mentioned earlier, a systematic attempt to delineate beliefs and practices is difficult due to the disparities between different groups. The evolution of modern Satanism has been unplanned as a whole, and groups often develop as offshoots from earlier, now obsolete or "wrong" attempts to demarcate Satanism, frequently both starting anew and drawing upon older material at the same time. As stated at the beginning of the chapter, two broad lines of thought are visible: rationalistic, atheistic Satanism, now visible in the writings of Anton LaVey and the Church of Satan; and esoteric, theistic Satanism found in the Temple of Set. Many variations exist, focusing on either the philosophical or the religious side of these lines. Thus, one might find a theist in the Church of Satan, or a more idiosyncratically inclined Setian in the Temple of Set— these are general outlines, not rigid dogma. Nevertheless, both the human-oriented and Satan-oriented Satanists are opposed to the Devil-worshiper, a Christian variety of Satanist which is to be found in Christian myths of Satanic Conspiracies and in small numbers among black metal enthusiasts, young adolescents, and perhaps even a few mentally disturbed criminals. Consequently, a certain amount of consensus is found in the Satanic movement at large pertaining to a core tradition, a few generally accepted rules, a shared iconography, and opposition to the ordinary worldview of the Western world.

Typologies Revisited

Before moving on, it is useful to evaluate previous attempts to classify the bewildering number of groups, offshoots, and single-member organizations subsumed under the common denominator of Satanism. I have chosen four typologies found in the academic literature, although one is polemic in nature: Robert Hicks's "police model of Satanic crime"; Jean La Fontaine's "Christian" and "self-styled" Satanism; Marcello Truzzi's "black and white witches," which is developed into a complex of ideal types; and Massimo Introvigne's simple double scale of "youth and adult groups" coupled with "rational and occult Satanism."

Robert Hicks reviews (and condemns) the "occult-crime model," motivated by fundamentalist Christianity and composed of different levels of involvement: dabblers, self-styled Satanists, organized Satanists, and traditional Satanists (Hicks 1990a, 1990b, 1991a, 1991b). *Dabblers* "are mostly children, teenagers, or very young adults who, in unsophisticated fashion, play with Satanic bits and pieces," such as Dungeons and Dragons and heavy metal lyrics. Self-styled Satanists are mainly mass murderers. Organized Satanists "include public groups, such as the Church of Satan and the Temple of Set." Finally, traditional Satanists "include transgenerational family Satanism, the cult survivor's tales, and day-care-center ritual abuse. Such Satanists comprise an international underground, tightly organized and covert, responsible for upwards of 50,000 human sacrifices a year" (Hicks 1990a: 283).

This typology illustrates a conspiracy-oriented understanding of Satanism and the persons involved, presenting a vicious spiral of entanglement from the first stages of dabbling to the wholly evil network of powerful cultists. It is therefore of little use to a study that is not connected with Christian theology and the worldview of the fundamentalist or at least orthodox Christian. I accept the "dabbler" category as a variant of modern popular cultural Satanism, but purely in its own terms and not connected with a ruse of evil, and I accept the category of public, official organizations as the empirical starting point for discussion. In my opinion, the remaining categories, as well as the overall

system of classification, are irrelevant, as they are rhetorical, defining a problem to be dealt with rather than classifying information.[27]

Jean La Fontaine's contribution to the monumental *Athlone History of
Witchcraft and Magic in Europe* (La Fontaine 1999) distinguishes two distinct
patterns: the Christian myth of the Enemy and his minions and the concrete
sociological reality of modern-day Satanists. As such, she uses a simple typology consisting of Christian Satanism and modern Satanism—in her terms,
alleged (mythical) and self-styled (occultist) Satanists (ibid.: 86–88). I fully endorse this framework, but one must extrapolate from the categories somewhat.
Strictly speaking, the category of alleged Satanists should be separate from that
of modern, religious Satanists, and the second category split up into several
types. As will be shown, I have included the Christian stereotype, as some
groups ostensibly live out the myth, and many groups integrate the fear of the
myth as a shock tactic. It must nevertheless be borne in mind that Christianity
is not the primary frame of reference for the groups covered by this chapter.

Marcello Truzzi's work with modern witchcraft (Truzzi 1972, 1974a, 1974b)
arranges groups along a white-black axis, according to the view held on magic
(the typology is used in Alfred 1976 as well). The various subgroups are then
categorized according to sociological and ideological content: independent, sol-
itary Satanists (comprising traditional Satanists, acid-culture eclectic Satanists,
and psychotic cases) and *group-affiliated Satanists* of two types: one, pure, stereotypical Satanists (traditional Satanists, acid-culture eclectic Satanists, sexual
Satanisms, and heretical, anti-Catholic Satanists), and two, non-stereotypical
Satanists (called Palladists or Luciferianists and comprising Baphometists,
idiosyncratic, charismatic Satanists, and the Church of Satan) (Truzzi 1974a:
639 ff.).[28]

Again, the typology has some limitations. First, I agree that the term
"witch" can be used to demarcate Satanism and position the subculture in
relation to established religious organizations, practices, and orientations. It is
indeed used by Anton LaVey (LaVey 1970, 1989). But I find it counterproductive to reproduce an emic categorization of "black" and "white," used deroga-
torily, when all Satanic groups (except the ToS) disregard the categories. The
ethical framework invoked is not applicable, and potentially confuses readers.
Second, I'm not sure the witchcraft aspect of modern Satanism is as strong
today as it was at the outset. Much has happened since the early seventies. I
would rather associate Satanism with the general growth of the Human Potential movement and New Age groups than with neo-pagans and Wiccan
groups. On the other hand, neo-pagans are usually grouped analytically within
the New Age movement (see for example Hanegraaff [1996] 1998), as I propose to do with Satanism as well. Third, many of the phenomena included in
Truzzi's typology are either cultural interpretations of Satanism, such as the
acid-culture eclectic Satanists and the sexual Satanisms, or manifestations of
Christian stereotypes, namely the heretical, anti-Catholic Satanists and the tra-

ditional Satanists. Again, as with La Fontaine's typology, Christianity is not the primary frame of reference for modern Satanism.

Finally, Massimo Introvigne's typology orients modern Satanism along two axes of religious organization and doctrinal content: Adult groups are organized with doctrine, hierarchy, and so on, whereas while youth Satanism, although it can be loosely organized, is subcultural practice. Rational Satanism is atheistic, along the lines I have drawn above, whereas occult Satanism is filled with interpretations of theistic Satanism (Introvigne 1997a). My only argument is with the last category of theistic Satanism, as Introvigne's definition of Satanism rests on "the adoration of Satan or the Devil from the Bible" (ibid.: 8–9). As I have repeatedly made clear, Christianity is secondary for the groups examined here. I will basically propose similar categories with different nomenclature and content.

I have found that modern Satanism is best described inclusively when viewed as a social and cultural phenomenon, and exclusively when viewed as a religious and philosophical one. Thus, the typology presented below is broad when taken as a whole, but rather limited when dealing with modern Satanic groups as a religious phenomenon.

First, one should separate the popular cultural conceptions of Satanism from more organized and systematic belief systems backed by a group of some sort. The popular understanding of Satanism is rooted in Christian values and concepts, that is, a myth of the enemy or the opposition, and the highly visible individuals and groups "living out" this mythical frame. Whether we consider Satanism *in* popular culture, as when some heavy metal groups, role-playing games, movies, or television series use occult or even overtly Satanic iconography, references, or plotlines to sell material, or Satanism *as* popular culture, found in the adolescent subcultures "dabbling" with forbidden emotions and desires, Satanism is based on society's fears and prohibitions, and is a curious mix of romantic tradition, Christian demonology, and comparative mythology. This stereotype could be called the popular model of Satanism, and it is reinforced by several empirical manifestations:[29]

- the symbolic (and sometimes violent) insurrection targeting everything "Christian," as in the violent subculture found among some Black Metal enthusiasts;
- the "Satanism" of the teenage room, combining *Buffy the Vampire Slayer*, inverted crosses, black lipstick, and copies of books on the occult and witchcraft.

Although these embodiments can be very sincere and are deeply meaningful for the persons involved, they reflect common concerns and anxieties of adolescents, not modern Satanism per se.[30] This is inverted Christianity, Devil worship, and rebellion, rather than a new, coherent belief system with philosophical, mythical, and practical aspects. By "playing evil," a symbolic resistance can be voiced against dominant society, and problems can be negotiated. It is necessary to distinguish between this popular Satanism and the following two types, which are variants of modern, religious Satanism proper, even though an interest in adolescent Satanism could eventually lead to a serious involvement with the established groups outlined below (see Lewis 2001a).

As stated in the introduction, the three main traits I use to define modern Satanism are "Self-religion," that is, the realization of an "authentic nature"; the use of Satan as a positive and negative symbolic expression of this aspiration; and a coherent organization or body of work. Thus I position modern Satanism in the field between modern rationality and Western esotericism far from the Christian framework from which Satan has been drawn. There are two ideal types:

- the more secular and rational, if provocative, groups using Satan as a symbol for nonconformity and the Self. This is an atheistic, egoistic Humanism that views "authentic nature" as the carnal human animal, appeals to Darwinism and materialism, and considers magic a psychological or perhaps supranatural practice;
- and the syncretistic and esoteric groups honoring Satan as a metaphysical force or a personified being, often infused in nature, or humanity, or the intellect. "Authentic nature" is "becoming" an essence. These religions draw heavily on Eastern traditions and Western esotericism.

Although the latter could be incorporated into the study of Western esotericism proper by analyzing the source material with Antoine Faivre's six characteristics of esotericism,[31] the former fits better with the Human Potential movement (Stone 1976). Both, however, are considered modern religious Satanism.

Now let us return to the common ground of tradition, rules, iconography, and worldview of the Satanic movement.

Iconography and Aesthetics

Let me start with the iconography. It seems that the "material" pentagram (five-pointed star; refer to Figure 19.2), often customized with a goat's head, lightning bolts, hammer and scythe, colors, or letters, is in widespread use among Satanic groups.[32] The history of this sign and modern usage do not necessarily correspond, but the community-building aspect, as well as the indication of special significance of the wearer to the larger society, is clear. Thus, the pentagram or Baphomet, as it is commonly called when inscribed with a goat's head and Hebrew letters spelling "Leviathan," demonstrates the philosophical and religious stance to insiders as well as outsiders, and the personal views of the individual Satanist. It is a powerful symbol that stirs feelings of dread, uneasiness or contempt in the average American or European because of the association with black magic, Satanism, and esoteric lore. There is some truth to this, as it is a design with an impressive lineage, associated with Pythagoras and Renaissance Hermeticism and found in German grimoires (see Ellis forthcoming), Eliphas Levi's *The History of Magic* and *The Key to the Mysteries*, and Anton LaVey's *Satanic Bible*.[33]

Today most Wiccans utilize the "spiritual" pentagram, while Satanists use the "material pentagram" to denote carnality and materialism. Some Satanic groups have detailed interpretations:

> the Pentagon in the center of our Pentacle . . . is a house; it is not inverted; it is the correct way and, in the Dark Doctrine, represents YOU. . . . The Five Points of the Pentacle, or rather the "Blazing Angles" that radiate from the House represent things in the Dark Doctrine. Starting from top to right point, going clockwise, and making this very simple: 1. Our Roots in the sense of physical generations. 2. Justice implying natural stratification. 3. The Anima or Vajra Root of our individual Being and our animal nature. 4. Our Inner Wellbeing or Psyche. 5. Nature in us and around us and in which we live. The X that is formed by the crossed lines where the top point of the inner Pentagon (House) is, represents Heart, Feelings, Eros. (*Why Do We Call Ourselves Satanic Reds? FAQ*: 2)

Others just use it as the time-worn emblem for the Adversary, black magic, or the physical aspect (that is, earth, pleasure, carnality). Combined with the goat's head (in itself a symbol of earth), a torch (reason), or lightning bolts (the Black Flame), it is a potent symbol of modern Satanism.

Regarding the penchant for black clothes and gothic style, there are certainly differences between members within and across groups, although a purely impressionistic survey conducted by looking at my contacts in Denmark confirmed an affinity for the unique and striking, often black, in young and old. This might be coincidence, or it might be put in context through the theory put forward in *The Satanic Bible*:

> Learning to effectively utilize the command to LOOK, is an integral part of a witch's or warlock's training. To manipulate a person, you must first be able to attract and hold his attention. The three methods by which the command to look can be accomplished are the utilization of sex, sentiment, or wonder, or any combination of these. . . . Visual imagery utilized for emotional reaction is certainly the most important device incorporated in the practice of lesser

magic. Anyone who is foolish enough to say "looks don't mean a thing" is indeed deluded. Good looks are unnecessary, but "looks" certainly are needed! (LaVey 1969: 111–113)

Bear in mind that *The Satanic Bible* was followed by *The Compleat Witch* (now *The Satanic Witch*), a handbook in lesser magic or manipulative techniques where Erving Goffman meets William Mortensen. This might explain the black garments and sinister appearance.

Finally, a quote from Rafal Smoczynski's paper on "Polish Cyber Satanism" (Smoczynski 2003) might put some things in perspective: "[The] French sociologist [Michel Maffesoli] asserts that while neo-tribal groups have weak powers of discipline, they have strong powers of inclusion and solidarity. Maffesoli states: 'These powers are displayed in a group. As the highest social good, the members of [the] tribe are marked by it wearing particular types of dress, exhibiting group-specific styles of adornment and espousing the shared values and ideals of [the] community.' . . . Aesthetics is a way of feeling in common while the strong ideological position is view[ed] as not so . . . important" (ibid.: 3). This concept of neo-tribalism might explain the various, perhaps instinctual, techniques of community building employed by ultimate individualists working within a group. Even the "Alien elite" needs a common ground.[34]

Tradition, Rules, and Worldview

The common ideological and philosophical core can be summed up by the rough definition I proposed in the introduction: Satanism is a combination of positive religious and philosophical aspirations centered on the individual and negative and critical anti-authoritarian convictions. James R. Lewis's description of *The Satanic Bible* might capture the essence of Satanism in general: "Despite the book's diverse source material and piecemeal assembly, it nevertheless coheres as a succinct—and, apparently, quite attractive—statement of Satanic thought and practice" (Lewis 2002a: 7). The worldview itself is a coherent statement of eclecticism around the multivocal symbol of Satan, with a core of individualism and self-realization and an amorphous periphery of construction and usage of tradition. As such, modern religious Satanism taps into the "cultic milieu" discussed by Colin Campbell (Campbell 1972; see also Hanegraaff [1996] 1998, Hammer 2001, and Hermonen forthcoming), which reinforces the similarities with the New Age movement. It is also a solid statement of secularization; as Peter Berger notes: "inasmuch as secularization is a global trend, there is a global tendency for religious contents to be modified in a secularizing direction. In the extreme cases . . . this may lead to the deliberate excision of all or nearly all 'supernatural' elements from the religious tradition, and a legitimation of the continued existence of the institution that once embodied the tradition in purely secular terms. In other cases it may just mean that the 'supernatural' elements are de-emphasized or pushed into the background, while the institution is 'sold' under the label of values congenial to secularized consciousness" (Berger 1967: 146). The Church of Satan and later the decentralized movement I have been discussing are both a consequence of and a reaction to this secularizing trend.

Anton LaVey used a number of sources for his work: traditional folklore, the romantic idea of the Promethean Satan, Western esotericism (especially Aleister Crowley and Eliphas Levi), and modern philosophies of Ayn Rand, Ragnar Redbeard, Charles Darwin, and Friedrich Nietzsche (Lewis 2002a). This body of "tradition" is augmented by other groups: Eastern traditions of Tantric Hinduism and the Buddhism of Nagarjuna, Egyptian myths and imagery, modern sociology, biology, and physics. All are enmeshed in organizational strategies of legitimation and authority and individual appropriations of material. As illustrated in the section on the Church of Satan above, many Satanists have an ambivalent relationship with *The Satanic Bible*. On one hand it is the primer, the "wake-up call" for beginners, but on the other it represents the doctrinal rigidity of a church. It is clear, though, that Anton LaVey laid the ground rules for a Satanic organization.

Even though the Church of Satan was founded during the psychedelic revolution and in the hippie capital of the world, San Francisco, LaVey deplored the use of drugs and was generally a man of law and order (Alfred 1976). These are still generally accepted as pragmatic rules of survival in a world that has major issues with Satanists—there is no need to provoke needlessly (Lewis 2001a). Members of most organizations uphold the laws of the country and do not engage in illegal acts; if they do, they are thrown out. In addition, members exercise control and are aware of the image they are projecting. This is a doctrine of self-preservation: No Satanist should advocate aberrations such as Nazism or the abuse of children in public, as this image has a detrimental effect on all Satanists. In addition, classical Devil worship is frowned upon as a Christian, dependent behavior unsuited for a true individualist.

Modern religious Satanism adapts to the society of which it is a part; therefore, the specific manifestation of opposition to authority structures varies from country to country. All Satanists have a problem with Western secular Christianity and fundamentalists, but the reactions take different shapes according to time, place, and circumstance (Harvey forthcoming). Whether Satanism is clothed in the garbs of elitism, ritual magic, or hyperrational science, it is both an antirepressive ideology that attacks all perceived hypocrisy and a human-oriented religion of self-realization. Most of all it is a product of and answer to modernity, to secularization, detraditionalization, fragmentation, reflexivity, and individualization.

Suggestions for Further Research

New religious movements are constantly producing groups that manifest interpretations and reevaluations of religious material from the cultic milieu. Academic work on these movements and the New Age have flourished in the nineties, as both detailed monographs and attempts at theoretical explication have been published. It is all the more astounding, then, that the rich subfield of modern religious Satanism has been neglected. This chapter seeks to stimulate interest through a review of primary and secondary sources, but much work remains to be done.

First, studies based on fieldwork are a feasible way to understand varieties of modern Satanism. Edward Moody and Randall Alfred conducted covert participant observation in the Church of Satan in the late sixties (Moody 1971, 1974; Alfred 1976), but since then all studies have focused on textual material. Online "fieldwork" is another way of securing new data; the Internet is a gold mine of groups and material that needs systematization and analysis (see Petersen forthcoming).

Sociological and comparative monographs on the Satanic subculture, clusters within its or even individual groups are desperately needed, as almost no groups except the Church of Satan have been examined thoroughly. Discourse analysis of the individual appropriations of tradition and legitimacy could be an interesting way of understanding the conflicts inherent in a subculture based on individuality and the performance of Otherness (Lewis 2002b, Harvey forthcoming). In addition, theories of syncretism and eclecticism might point out directions for further study close to the source material; analysis of influential documents, such as *The Satanic Bible* (LaVey 1969), *The Satanic Rituals* (LaVey 1972), *The Book of Coming Forth by Night* (Aquino 1975), and various documents by Tani Jantsang and Phil Marsh might reveal the complexities in the different interpretations of Satanic and Occult tradition.

In many ways it would be prudent to integrate the study of modern Satanism with general research into the Human Potential movement and the New Age movement, as they share many traits (see York 1995, Heelas 1996, Hanegraaff [1996] 1998, Hammer 2001).

NOTES

1. The "rationality and esotericism" angle has been utilized by Wouter Hanegraaff, Roelof van den Broek, and Olav Hammer in excellent studies on the New Age movement and esoteric currents in Western Europe (Hanegraaff [1996] 1998, van den Broek & [1996] Hanegraaff 1998, Hammer 2001). Much is owed to Frances A. Yates's and Antoine Faivre's seminal studies on Western esotericism (Yates [1964] 2002, [1972] 2002, Faivre 1994, Faivre and Needleman 1992).

2. See Paul Heelas's *The New Age Movement* (Heelas 1996) and Graham Harvey's "Satanism in Britain Today" (Harvey 1995) and "Satanism: Performing Alterity and Othering" (Harvey, forthcoming).

3. Thus, neither "subculture," "community," nor "movement" is satifying or analytically clear a descriptive term, as it is difficult to characterize a fragmented network of shared outlook and aesthetics with little organization, ideology, or practice in common (see Peter H. Gilmore's critique in "The Myth of the 'Satanic Community' and other Virtual Delusions" at www.churchofSatan.com/pages/mythcommunity.html, accessed July 4, 2002, and Lewis 2002a: n. 2). I am using "subculture" and "movement" throughout this chapter for lack of a better terminology.

4. For a history of the Devil, see Forsyth 1987; Russell 1977, 1981, 1984, 1986, 1991; and Pagels 1996.

5. In *Islands of History* (Sahlins 1985), Marshall Sahlins convincingly argues for the "historization of structure" and "structurization of history" through an analysis of British and Hawaiian interpretations of the same historical events; as such, "[e]vents . . . cannot be understood apart from the values attributed to them" (154). Historical narrative is thus infused with mythical meaning, making history a metaphor for the reality of the myth. This in turn subjects the structure to constant transformation, as "cultural meanings are . . . altered [when b]urdened with the world" (138).

6. See Summers [1926] 1956, Cavendish 1967, and Lyons 1970, 1988.

7. See Stevens 1996, Medway 2001, and Kaplan, forthcoming, for a substantiation of this argument. Solid studies of historical Satanism as a Christian discourse include Stevens 1996, La Fontaine 1999, Medway 2001, and Dyrendal 2003. Unfortunately, Jeffrey Russell's impressive study of the Devil in history is marred by a Christian bias, a strange theory of history, and an unsightly arrogance toward modern religion (see Russell 1977, 1981, 1984, 1986, 1989). For a sound if somewhat idealistic presentation of Satanism in history from an insider (a journalist who is also a priest in the Church of Satan), see Baddeley 1999, part one.

8. Articles and books presenting an overview of the history of modern Satanism include Lyons 1988, Schmidt 1992, Introvigne 1994, 1997, Stevens 1996, Kristiansen 1997, La Fontaine 1999, Baddeley 1999, Bromley and Ainsley 1995, 2000 and Lewis 2001b. See also the Religious Movements Homepage and the Ontario Consultants on Religious Tolerance.

9. See Baddeley 1999: 100ff. and 148ff.; Bromley 2000: 644; and Lewis 2001b: 285ff. for a summary of names and short descriptions; very few have been the subject of a detailed study.

10. See Richardson, Best, and Bromley 1991, Victor 1993, Ellis 2000, and Dyrendal 2003. Many relevant articles on the moral panic are collected in Lewis and Petersen forthcoming.

11. On religion and the Internet, see Dawson and Hennebry 1999, Hadden and Cowan 2000, and Brasher 2001, to name a few. On Satanism and the Internet, see Petersen forthcoming and Smoczynski 2003.

12. Descriptions of or studies on the CoS and LaVey include Moody 1971, 1974; Truzzi 1972, 1974a, 1974b; Alfred 1976; Wright 1991; Taub and Nelson 1993; Harvey 1995; Bromley and Ainsley 1995; Kristiansen 1997, Baddeley 1999; La Fontaine 1999; and Lewis 2002a, 2002b. Internet resources include Ontario Consultants on Reli-

gious Tolerance (OCRT) and the Religious Movements Homepage (see the selected Internet resources list in the reference section). Important sources are LaVey 1969, 1972, 1989, 1992, 1998; and Barton 1990a, 1990b, as well as the critical accounts in Schreck and Schreck 1998 and Aquino 1999. See also the magazines *The Cloven Hoof* (official bulletin of the CoS) and *The Black Flame* (international forum of the CoS), and the huge amounts of material found on the official Web site, Simon Crabtree's site, Vexen Crabtree's site and Matt G. Paradise's site (see the selected internet resources list in the reference section).

13. Marcello Truzzi and Randall Alfred accept the CoS claim of 7,000 registered members in the mid-seventies (see Truzzi 1972: 27 and Alfred 1976: 193). Only a fraction of that constitute active members, as Alfred notes. In addition, the CoS has undergone serious changes since then. The Religious Movements Homepage lists the size of the group at 10,000 members, based on CoS claims in 1997.

14. Two related aspects are important here: the "LaVey Myth" and the purity of the doctrine. For a discussion of the first, see Barton 1990a, 1990b; Wright 1991; Schreck and Schreck 1998; Aquino 1999; and Lewis 2002b. Doctrinal authority is discussed in Lewis 2002a, 2002b, and Petersen forthcoming, as well as below.

15. LaVey 1969, 1972, 1989, 1992, 1998, and Barton 1990a, 1990b discuss elements of the LaVeyan Satanism found in the CoS. The official Web site is a treasure trove of clear and concise articles written by members.

16. See *The Church of Satan Information Pack* for all documents.

17. On the genesis of and sources for *The Satanic Bible*, see Lewis 2002a.

18. This is important, as this redefinition makes it clear that Satanism is not "about" Christianity—it is anti-hegemonic and counter-cultural, but not anti-Christian or left wing.

19. Specifically, he adopts Bryan Wilson's term "manipulationist sect" (Alfred 1976: 199–200).

20. Descriptions of or studies on the ToS include Scott 1983, Harvey 1995, Bromley and Ainsley 1995, Kristiansen 1997, La Fontaine 1999, and Baddeley 1999, as well as the Ontario Consultants on Religious Tolerance (OCRT) and the Religious Movements Homepage. Sources include Aquino 1975, 1999, (1975) 2002, as well as the entire *Jeweled Tablets of Set*, if they can be obtained. See also the magazine *The Scroll of Set*. Interesting Web sites are the official home page and Balanone's Temple of Set Information Site.

21. He was succeeded by Don Webb from 1996 to 2002, but took up the mantle after Webb resigned; see www.balanone.info/baltsfaq.frm6.html#Setians.

22. For more information see Aquino [1975] 2002: 20ff., Harvey 1995: 286.ff., and La Fontaine 1999: 103ff.

23. In many ways this development mirrors that of globalization, which often results in "glocalization"—an accentuation and affirmation of regional awareness and identity, the local, when confronted with the global. See, for example, Tomlinson 1999; the word "glocalization" is Roland Robertson's.

24. See Jantsang 1990a, 1990b, n.d.; Jantsang and Marsh 1990a, 1990b; Jantsang, Marsh, and Gerber 1990; Marsh 1990; Marsh, Hill, and Jantsang 1990, as well as the astonishing amount of material found on the Web site. I have found Jantsang 1990b, Marsh 1990, and Marsh, Hill and Jantsang 1990 to be helpful, along with

introductions such as the FAQ sheet, *The Nine Satanic Postulates*, and Jantsang *Unity of the Dark Tradition and the Roots of Satanic Reds Organization*, as well as *Left Hand Path and Right Hand Path: Defined, Dark Force: Asat, Sat & Tan*, and *The Darkness Was One—A Doctrine of Cosmogenesis* from the Web site. See also Hr. Vad's home page.

25. See *Unity of the Dark Tradition and the Roots of Satanic Reds Organization*.

26. See Sutcliffe 1995.

27. See note 10 for literature on the subject of the "Satanism Scare."

28. Massimo Introvigne has a similar categorization built on ideological content in his early work: *Rationalistic Satanism* (CoS), *Occultistic Satanism* (ToS), *Acid Satanism* (youth oriented), and *Luciferian Satanism* (gnostic) (Introvigne 1991).

29. One could argue that the stereotype should be termed the Christian model of Satanism. I have reserved this term for the concrete Christian framework utilized primarily by conservative Christians, such as Pentecostal movements and traditionalist Catholic groups, and as it is in no way connected with modern Satanism as a new religion, it will not be analyzed in the present study. Further, the term could imply a one-to-one connection between the popular conceptions of Satanism and the folk devils of the historical and recent moral panics, if used to describe both.

30. See Moynihan and Söderlind 1998 and Baddeley 1999 for descriptions of these popular cultural manifestations, and Lowney 1995 and Lewis 2001b for interesting observations on this issue.

31. Correspondences, 2. Living nature, 3. Imagination and Mediations, 4. Experience of Transmutation, 5. Praxis of the Concordance, 6. Transmission; see Faivre and Needleman 1992: xv–xx, Faivre 1994: 10–15, and Sutcliffe 1995: 114ff.

32. The pentagram or pentacle (five-pointed star) with two points up and one point down is usually denoted an "inverted" pentagram, while the one with one point up and two points down is called "normal." I have decided to use the less value-laden terms "material" and "spiritual," as they seem to be accepted by Satanists, Wiccans, and magicians.

33. See Ellis [forthcoming]: chapter 2, www.churchofsatan.com/Pages/BaphometSigil.html and www.geocities.com/satanicreds/baph.html.

34. See also the work of Merja Hermonen (Hermonen 2000; forthcoming).

REFERENCES

Primary Sources

Aquino, Michael. 1975. *The Book of Coming Forth by Night*. San Francisco: Temple of Set.

———. [1975] 2002. *Black Magic*. PDF file obtained by private correspondence. Introductory section of the *Crystal Tablet of Set*, the first volume of the *Jeweled Tablets of Set*.

———. 1999. *The Church of Satan*. 4th ed. E-book (self-published).

Barton, Blanche. 1990a. *The Church of Satan*. New York: Hell's Kitchen.

———. 1990b. *The Secret Life of a Satanist: The Authorized Biography of Anton LaVey*. Los Angeles, Cal.: Feral House.

The Church of Satan Information Pack. Posted at www.churchofSatan.com/pages/cosinfopack.pdf.

Grant, Kenneth. 1994. *Cults of the Shadow*. London: Skoob Books.

Jantsang, Tani. 1990a. *Serpents versus Adamites*. Unpublished document. Received copy from www.geocities.com/satanicreds/dd-ad.html.

———. 1990b. *Package of Doctrines*. Unpublished document. Received copy from www.geocities.com/satanicreds/dd-ad.html.

———. n.d. *Tantra, Vajrayana and Pythagoreanism*. Unpublished document. Received copy from www.geocities.com/satanicreds/dd-ad.html.

———. n.d. *Unity of the Dark Tradition and the Roots of Satanic Reds Organization*. Posted at www.geocities.com/satanicreds/unity-dt.html.

Jantsang, Tani, and Phillip Marsh. 1990a. *Set?*. Unpublished document. Received copy from www.geocities.com/satanicreds/dd-ad.html.

———. 1990b. *Dao. Taoism: The Dark Tradition*. Unpublished document. Received copy from www.geocities.com/satanicreds/dd-ad.html.

Jantsang, Tani, Phillip Marsh, and Jeff Gerber. 1990. *Kaballa: Dark Tradition*. Unpublished document. Received copy from www.geocities.com/satanicreds/dd-ad.html.

LaVey, Anton Szandor. 1969. *The Satanic Bible*. New York: Avon Books.

———. 1970. *The Compleat Witch*. New York: Lancer Books.

———. 1972. *The Satanic Rituals*. New York: Avon Books.

———. 1989. *The Satanic Witch*. Venice, Calif.: Feral House (reprint of LaVey 1970).

———. 1992. *The Devil's Notebook*. Venice, Calif.: Feral House.

———. 1998. *Satan Speaks!* Venice, Calif.: Feral House.

Levi, Éliphas. 1969a [1855–56]. *Transcendental Magic*. Translated by A. E. Waite. London: Rider & Company.

———. 1969b [1860]. *The History of Magic*. Translated by A. E. Waite. London: Rider & Company.

Marsh, Phillip, 1990. *Western Roots, Part One. Pythagoras, Plato and the Hellenes*. Unpublished document. Received copy from www.geocities.com/satanicreds/dd-ad.html.

Marsh, Phillip, Wayne Hill, and Tani Jantsang. 1990. *Western Roots, Part Two*. Unpublished document. Received copy from www.geocities.com/satanicreds/dd-ad.html.

Sycophants Unite! Posted at www.churchofSatan.com/home.html.

Schreck, Zeena LaVey, and Nikolas Schreck. 1998. "Anton LaVey: Legend and Reality." Posted at www.churchofSatan.org/aslv.html.

The Nine Satanic Postulates—Statements of Satano-COMMUNE-ist Reality, Satanic Comm-UNITY.. Written by Comrades in Satanic Reds. Posted at www.geocities.com/satanicreds/9-sat-tan.html.

Why Do We Call Ourselves Satanic Reds? FAQ. No author. Posted at www.geocities.com/satanicreds/faq.html.

Selected Internet Resources

Ascendancy: www.jashan.net/ascendancy.

Balanone's Temple of Set Information Site: www.balanone.info.

CESNUR/Massimo Introvigne: www.cesnur.it.

Church of Satan (Peter Gilmore, Peggy Nadramia, Blanche Barton): www
.churchofSatan.com.
First Church of Satan (Lord Egan/John Allee): www.churchofSatan.org.
The First Satanic Church (Karla LaVey): www.Satanicchurch.com.
Hr. Vad: www.apodion.com/vad.
Matt G. Paradise: www.Satanism101.com/satfaq.
Ontario Consultants on Religious Tolerance (OCRT): www.religioustolerance.org ("Sa-
tanism," "The Church of Satan," "Satanic Ritual Abuse," "Ritual Abuse")
The Prometheus Society: www.geocities.com/prometheus_society.
Religious Movements Homepage: www.religiousmovements.lib.virginia.edu/nrms/
Satanism.
Satanic Media Watch (Amina Lap): http://users.cybercity.dk/ccc44406/smwane/main
.htm.
Satanic Reds (Tani Jantsang, Phil Marsh): www.geocities.com/Satanicreds.
The Satanism Archive: www.necronomi.com/magic/Satanism.
The 600 Club: www.the600club.com.
Temple of Set (Michael Aquino, Nikolas Schreck, Zeena Schreck): www.xeper.org.
Vexen Crabtree: www.djps.co.uk.

Secondary Sources

Alfred, Randall. 1976. "The Church of Satan," in Charles Glock and Robert Bellah,
eds., *The New Religious Consciousness*. Berkeley: University of California Press,
pp. 180–202.
Alisauskiene, Milda. 2003. "Manifestations of Satanism in Catholic Lithuania: The
Case of www.Satan.lt." Paper presented at the CESNUR 2003 international con-
ference "Religion and Democracy: An Exchange of Experiences between East and
West," available at www.cesnur.org/2003/vil2003_alisauskiene.htm. Accessed
June 23, 2003.
Baddeley, Gavin. 1999. *Lucifer Rising: Sin, Devil Worship and Rock 'n' Roll*. London:
Plexus.
Berger, Peter. 1967. *The Sacred Canopy*. New York: Anchor Books.
Brasher, Brenda. 2001. *Give Me That Online Religion*. San Francisco: Jossey-Bass.
Bromley, David G. 2000. "Satanic Bible" and "Satanists," in Wade Clarke Roof, ed.,
Contemporary American Religion. Vol. 2. New York: Macmillan, pp. 643–645.
Bromley, David G., and Susan Ainsley. 1995. "Satanism and Satanic Churches: The
Contemporary Incarnations," in Timothy Miller, ed. *America's Alternative Relig-
ions*. Albany: State University of New York Press, pp. 401–409.
Campbell, Colin. 1972. "The Cult, the Cultic Milieu, and Secularization." *Sociological
Yearbook of Religion in Britain* 5: 119–136.
Cavendish, Richard. 1967. *The Black Arts*. New York: Putnam.
Cook, Monte. 2002. *Book of Vile Darkness*. Dungeons and Dragons Game Accessory.
Renton, Wash.: Wizards of the Coast.
Dawson, Lorne L., and J. Hennebry. 1999. "New Religions and the Internet: Recruit-
ing in a New Public Space." *Journal of Contemporary Religion* 14.1:
17–38.

Dyrendal, Asbjørn. 2003. "True Religion versus Cannibal Others. Rhetorical Constructions of Satanism among American Evangelicals." Ph.d. dissertation, University of Oslo, Faculty of Arts, Department of Cultutral Studies.

Ellis, Bill. 2000. *Raising the Devil: Satanism, New Religions and the Media*. Lexington: University Press of Kentucky.

———. 2004. *Lucifer Ascending: Grassroots Traditions of Occultism*. Lexington: University Press of Kentucky.

Faivre, Antoine. 1994. *Access to Western Esotericism*. Albany: State University of New York Press.

Faivre, Antoine, and Jacob Needleman, eds. 1992. *Modern Esoteric Spirituality*. New York: Crossroad.

Forsyth, Neil. 1987. *The Old Enemy. Satan and the Combat Myth*. Princeton: Princeton University Press.

Hadden, Jeffrey K., and D. E. Cowan, eds. 2000. *Religion on the Internet: Research Prospects and Promises*. Amsterdam: JAI-Elsevier Science.

Hammer, Olav. 2001. *Claiming Knowledge*. Leiden: E. J. Brill.

Hanegraaff, Wouter J. [1996] 1998. *New Age Religion and Western Culture*. Albany: State University of New York Press.

Harvey, Graham. 1995. "Satanism in Britain Today." *Journal of Contemporary Religion* 10.3: 283–296.

———. Forthcoming. "Satanism: Performing Alterity and Othering," in James R. Lewis and Jesper Aagaard Petersen, *The Encyclopedic Sourcebook of Satanism*. Buffalo: Prometheus Books.

Heelas, Paul. 1996. *The New Age Movement*. Oxford: Blackwell.

Hermonen, Merja. 2000. "Aspects of Youth Satanism in Finland," in Jeffrey Kaplan, ed., *Beyond the Mainstream: The Emergence of Religious Pluralism in Finland, Estonia, and Russia*. Helsinki: SKS, pp. 273–288.

———. Forthcoming. "Rationalistic Satanism: Individual as a Member of [a] Countercultural Tribe," in James R. Lewis and Jesper Aagaard Petersen, *The Encyclopedic Sourcebook of Satanism*. Buffalo: Prometheus Books.

Hicks, Robert D. 1990a. "Police Pursuit of Satanic Crime: Part I." *Skeptical Inquirer* 14.3: 276–286.

———. 1990b. "Police Pursuit of Satanic Crime: Part II. The Satanic Conspiracy and Urban Legends." *Skeptical Inquirer* 14.4: 378–389.

———. 1991a. "The Police Model of Satanic Crime," in James Richardson, Joel Best, and David Bromley eds., *The Satanism Scare*. New York: Aldine de Gruyter, pp. 175–191.

———. 1991b. *In Pursuit of Satan. The Police and the Occult*. Buffalo: Prometheus Books.

Introvigne, Massimo. 1991. *Auf den Spuren des Satanismus*. Vienna: Mödling.

———. 1994. *Indagine sul Satanismo. Satanisti e anti-Satanisti dal seicento ai nostri giorni*. Milan: Montadori.

———. 1997a. *Il Satanismo*. Turin: Elle Di Ci.

———. 1997b. "The Gothic Milieu: Black Metal, Satanism, and Vampires." Paper presented at the conference "Rejected and Suppressed Knowledge: The Racist

Right and the Cultic Milieu," Stockholm, February 15–16. Available at www
.cesnur.org/testi/gothic.htm.

Kaplan, Jeffrey. Forthcoming. *Multigenerational Satanism and the Anti-Cult Movement:
The Eternal Conspiracy*, in James R. Lewis and Jesper Aagaard Petersen, eds., *The
Encyclopedic Sourcebook of Satanism*. Buffalo: Prometheus Books.

Kristiansen, Roald E. 1997. "Satan in Cyberspace: A Study of Satanism on the Internet in the 1990's," in Roald E. Kristiansen and Nikolay M. Terebikhin, eds., *Religion, Church, and Education in the Barents Region*. Arkhangelsk, Russia: Pomor
University Publishing House. Updated version on www.love.is/roald/Satanism
.html, accessed August 19, 2003.

La Fontaine, Jean S. 1999. "Satanism and Satanic Mythology," in Bengt Ankerloo and
Stuart Clark, *Witchcraft and Magic in Europe*. Vol. 6, *The Twentieth Century*. London: Athlone Press, pp. 81–140.

Lewis, James R. 2001a. "Who Serves Satan? A Demographic and Ideological Profile."
Marburg Journal of Religion 6.2. Available at www.uni-marburg.de/
religionswissenschaft/journal/mjr/lewis2.html.

———. 2001b. *Satanism Today: An Encyclopedia of Religion, Folklore, and Popular Culture*. Santu Barbara, Calif.: ABC-Clio.

———. 2002a. "The Satanic Bible: Quasi-scripture/Counter-scripture." Paper pre-
sented at the international CESNUR conference "Minority Religions, Social
Change and Freedom of Conscience," Salt Lake City and Provo, June 20–23.
Available at www.cesnur.org/2002/lewis.htm.

———. 2002b. "Diabolical Authority: Modern Satanism, Anton LaVey and *The Satanic Bible*." Available at www.uni-marburg.de/religionswissenschaft/journal/
mjr/lewis3.html.

Lewis, James R., and Jesper Aagaard Petersen, eds. Forthcoming. *The Encyclopedic
Sourcebook of Satanism*. Buffalo: Prometheus Books.

Lowney, Kathleen S. 1995. "Teenage Satanism as Oppositional Youth Subculture."
Journal of Contemporary Ethnography 23: 453–484.

Lyons, Arthur. 1970. *The Second Coming: Satanism in America*. New York: Dodd,
Mead.

———. 1988. *Satan Wants You: The Cult of Devil Worship in America*. New York: Mysterious Press.

Medway, Gareth J. 2001. *Lure of the Sinister: The Unnatural History of Satanism*. New
York: New York University Press.

Moody, Edward J. 1971. "Urban Witches," in James P. Spradley and David W. Mc-
Curdy, eds., *Conformity and Conflict. Readings in Cultural Anthropology*. Boston:
Little, Brown, pp. 280–290. Reprinted in E. Tiryakian, ed., *On the Margins of the
Visible: Sociology, the Esoteric and the Occult*. New York: John Wiley 1974, pp. 223–
234.

———. 1974. "Magical Therapy: An Anthropological Investigation of Contemporary
Satanism," in Irving I. Zaretsky, and Mark P. Leone, eds., *Religious Movements in
Contemporary America*. Princeton: Princeton University Press, pp. 355–382.

Moynihan, Michael, and Didrik Söderlind. 1998. *Lords of Chaos: The Bloody Rise of the
Satanic Metal Underground*. Venice, Calif.: Feral House.

Pagels, Elaine. 1996. *The Origin of Satan*. New York: Vintage Books.

Petersen, Jesper Aagaard. Forthcoming. "Binary Satanism: The Construction of Community in a Digital World," in James R. Lewis and Jesper Aagaard Petersen, eds., *The Encyclopedic Sourcebook of Satanism*. Buffalo: Prometheus Books.

Richardson, James, Joel Best, and David Bromley, eds. 1991. *The Satanism Scare*. New York: Aldine de Gruyter.

Russell, Jeffrey Burton. 1977. *The Devil. Perceptions of Evil from Antiquity to Primitive Christianity*. Ithaca: Cornell University Press.

———. 1981. *Satan. The Early Christian Tradition*. Ithaca: Cornell University Press.

———. 1984. *Lucifer. The Devil in the Middle Ages*. Ithaca: Cornell University Press.

———. 1986. *Mephistopheles. The Devil in the Modern World*. Ithaca: Cornell University Press.

———. 1989. *The Prince of Darkness*. Ithaca: Cornell University Press.

———. 1991. "The Historical Satan," in James Richardson, Joel Best, and David Bromley, eds., *The Satanism Scare*. New York: Aldine de Gruyter, pp. 41–49.

Sahlins, Marshall D. 1985. *Islands of History*. Chicago: University of Chicago Press.

Schmidt, Joachim. 1992. *Satanismus—Mythos und Wirklichkeit*. Marburg: Diagonal Verlag.

Scott, Gini Graham. 1983. *The Magicians*. New York: Irvington.

Smoczynski, Rafal. 2003. "Polish Cyber Satanism: A Group in Statu Nascendi." Paper presented at the CESNUR 2003 international conference "Religion and Democracy: An Exchange of Experiences between East and West." Available at www.cesnur.org/2003/vil2003_smoczynski.htm. Accessed June 23 2003.

Stevens, Phillips. 1996. "Satan and Satanism," in Gordon Stein, ed., *The Encyclopedia of the Paranormal*. Buffalo: Prometheus Books, pp. 657–670.

Stone, Donald. 1976. "The Human Potential Movement," in Charles Glock and Robert Bellah, eds., *The New Religious Consciousness*. Berkeley: University of California Press, pp. 93–115.

Summers, Montague. [1926] 1956. *The History of Witchcraft and Demonology*. London: Routledge and Kegan Paul.

Sutcliffe, Richard. 1995. "Left Hand Path Ritual Magic: A Historical and Philosophical Overview," in Graham Harvey and C. Hardman, eds. 1995. *Paganism Today*. London: HarperCollins, pp. 109–138.

Taub, Diane E. and Lawrence D. Nelson. 1993. "Satanism in Contemporary America: Establishment or Underground?" *Sociological Quarterly* 34.3: 523–541.

Tomlinson, John. 1999. *Globalization and Culture*. Oxford: Polity Press.

Truzzi, Marcello. 1972. "The Occult Revival as Popular Culture. Some Random Observations on the Old and the Nouveau Witch." *Sociological Quarterly* 13 (Winter): 16–36. Abridged as "Witchcraft and Satanism" in E. Tiryakian, ed. *On the Margins of the Visible: Sociology, the Esoteric and the Occult*. New York: John Wiley, 1974, pp. 215–222.

———. 1974a. "Towards a Sociology of the Occult: Notes on Modern Witchcraft," in Irving I. Zaretsky, and Mark P. Leone, eds., *Religious Movements in Contemporary America*. Princeton: Princeton University Press, pp. 628–645.

———. 1974b. "Definitions and Dimensions of the Occult: Towards a Sociological

Perspective," in E. Tiryakian, ed. 1974. *On the Margins of the Visible: Sociology, the Esoteric and the Occult.* New York: John Wiley, pp. 243–255.

van den Broek, Roelof, and Wouter Hanegraaff, eds. 1998. *Gnosis and Hermeticism from Antiquity to Modern Times.* Albany: State University of New York Press.

Victor, Jeffrey S. 1993. *Satanic Panic: The Creation of a Contemporary Legend.* Chicago: Open Court.

Wright, Lawrence. 1991. "Sympathy for the Devil." *Rolling Stone,* September 5.

Yates, Frances A. [1964] 2002. *Giordano Bruno and the Hermetic Tradition.* London: Routledge.

———. [1972] 2002. *The Rosecrucian Enlightenment.* London: Routledge.

York, Michael. 1995. *The Emerging Network: A Sociology of the New Age and Neo-pagan Movements.* Lanham, Md.: Rowman and Littlefield.

Index

Italicized page references denote illustrations.